D1254928

PRENTICE HALL

Social Studies

The quality choice for today's classrooms

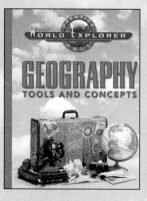 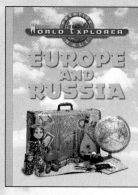 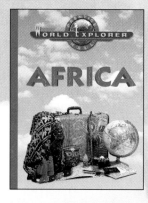 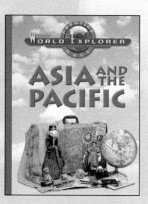

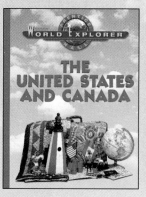 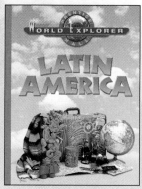 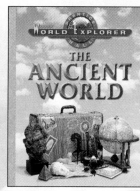 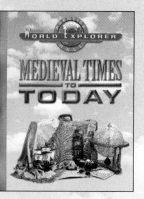

The world studies program that lets you choose.

PRENTICE HALL
Simon & Schuster Education Group
A VIACOM COMPANY

Upper Saddle River, New Jersey
Needham, Massachusetts

Copyright © 1998 by Prentice-Hall, Inc., a Viacom Company, Upper Saddle River, New Jersey 07458. All rights reserved. No part of this book may be reproduced or transmitted in any form or by any means, electronic or mechanical, including photocopying, recording, or by any information storage and retrieval system, without permission in writing from the publisher. Printed in the United States of America.

ISBN 0-13-433697-6

3 4 5 6 7 8 9 10   01 00 99 98

The only middle grades world that can truly provide the right materials to fit your

Prentice Hall World Explorer lets you choose the right balance of history, geography, and cultures for the regions of the world that you cover in your middle grades curriculum. No more being confined to the contents of a single text. No more having to spend valuable time locating additional resources. All this with hands-on activities and skills; interdisciplinary connections; integrated technology; and manageable resources to support your teaching style.

YOU CHOOSE what's right

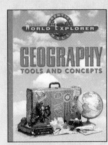

A few of the most popular COURSE CONFIGURATIONS:

	GEOGRAPHY TOOLS AND CONCEPTS	EUROPE AND RUSSIA	AFRICA
Eastern Hemisphere*	GEOGRAPHY TOOLS AND CONCEPTS	EUROPE AND RUSSIA	AFRICA
Western Hemisphere*	GEOGRAPHY TOOLS AND CONCEPTS		
World History			
Western Civilization		EUROPE AND RUSSIA	
Pacific Rim	GEOGRAPHY TOOLS AND CONCEPTS		
World Cultures		EUROPE AND RUSSIA	AFRICA

studies program curriculum.

YOU CHOOSE the right balance of geography, history, and culture.

for your course of study.

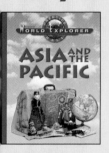   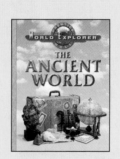 

ASIA AND THE PACIFIC	THE UNITED STATES AND CANADA	LATIN AMERICA	THE ANCIENT WORLD	MEDIEVAL TIMES TO TODAY
ASIA AND THE PACIFIC				
	THE UNITED STATES AND CANADA	LATIN AMERICA		
			THE ANCIENT WORLD	MEDIEVAL TIMES TO TODAY
	THE UNITED STATES AND CANADA		THE ANCIENT WORLD	
ASIA AND THE PACIFIC	THE UNITED STATES AND CANADA	LATIN AMERICA		
ASIA AND THE PACIFIC	THE UNITED STATES AND CANADA	LATIN AMERICA		

*Available in single, hard-bound volume

Only World Explorer provides this many management resources— built right into the program.

Designed from the start to have more time-saving resources for middle grades teachers, the World Explorer program has brand-new ways to help you coordinate your program, scheduling, assessment, team teaching, interdisciplinary connections, and other valuable resources.

- **Managing Time and Instruction**
- **Block Scheduling**
- **Assessment Opportunities**
- **Activities and Projects**
- **Resource Pro™ CD-ROM**
- **FYI**
- **Technology Options**
- **Flexible Planning Guide**

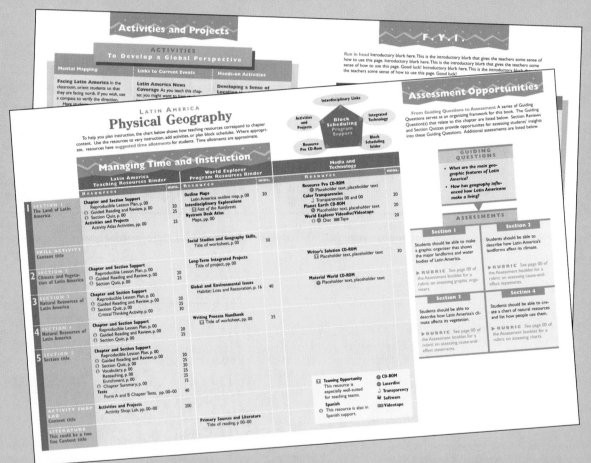

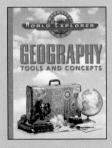

TECHNOLOGY OPTIONS

- Teacher's Edition wraparound with barcodes
- Point-of-use technology references
- Integrated video presentations

Guided Reading Audiotapes *
Computer Test Bank
  (MAC/Windows)
 World Video Explorer
    Videodiscs *
    Videotapes
Resource Pro™ CD-ROM
Material World CD-ROM
Planet Earth CD-ROM
Writer's Solution CD-ROM
available in Spanish

FLEXIBLE PLANNING GUIDE

This key supplement makes it easy to plan, schedule, and coordinate World Explorer's multi-book program.
- Course configurations
- Pacing charts
- Scope and sequence of skills
- Correlations to national standards

RESOURCE PRO™ CD-ROM

- Teaching Resources
- Planning Express™
- Computer Test Bank

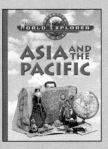
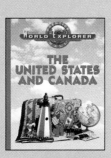

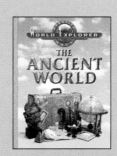

Coverage of all World Explorer program skills is provided in the Student Edition and Teacher's Edition.

Skills Activity
Students learn, practice, and apply core social studies skills through the use of hands-on activities.

MEDIEVAL TIMES TO TODAY SKILLS SCOPE AND SEQUENCE

MAP AND GLOBE SKILLS

SKILL	BOOK	PAGE
Parts of a Map	STUDENT	234
Comparing Maps of Different Scale	STUDENT	235
Understanding Distortions in Map Projections	STUDENT	232–233
Using Political and Physical Maps	STUDENT	236–237
Using Regional Maps	TEACHER	39
Using Isolines	TEACHER	20
Using Distribution Maps	TEACHER	113
Using Route Maps	STUDENT	122–123

CRITICAL THINKING SKILLS

Expressing Problems Clearly	STUDENT	216–217
Identifying Central Issues	TEACHER	149
Distinguishing Fact From Opinion	STUDENT	162–163
Recognizing Bias	TEACHER	177
Recognizing Cause and Effect	STUDENT	76–77
Drawing Conclusions	TEACHER	205

CHART, GRAPH, AND ILLUSTRATION SKILLS

Interpreting Line Graphs	STUDENT	180–181
Using a Time Line	TEACHER	199
Reading Tables	STUDENT	26–27
Understanding Special Geography Maps	TEACHER	213

READING AND WRITING SKILLS

Previewing	TEACHER	83
Reading Actively	TEACHER	45
Assessing Your Understanding	STUDENT	100–101
Using the Writing Process	TEACHER	75
Writing for a Purpose	TEACHER	51

STUDY AND RESEARCH SKILLS

Locating Information	TEACHER	95
Organizing Information	TEACHER	173
Organizing Your Time	STUDENT	54–55

Skills Mini-lessons
These lessons supplement and reinforce core social studies skills that are not formally presented in the student book.

Map and Globe Handbook
Students practice and review basic geography skills that focus on understanding maps and charts.

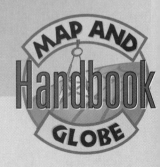

Use this daily pacing chart to help plan a twelve-week course or an eighteen-week course for Medieval Times to Today.

Block Scheduling
Suggested times are for daily class periods between 40 and 50 minutes long. For planning extended blocks or for teachers who wish to vary the pace of instruction, see the "Managing Time and Instruction" charts before each chapter or the Resource Pro™ CD-ROM.

	12-WEEK COURSE	18-WEEK COURSE
ACTIVITY ATLAS	2 DAYS	3 DAYS

CHAPTER 1
THE BYZANTINE AND MUSLIM EMPIRES

	12-WEEK COURSE	18-WEEK COURSE
Section 1 Byzantium: Rome's Eastern Empire	1.5	2
Section 2 The Rise and Spread of Islam	1	2
Section 3 The Religion of Islam	1	2
SKILLS ACTIVITY Reading Tables	1	1.5
Section 4 Islam's Golden Age	1.5	2
CHAPTER 1 REVIEW, ACTIVITIES, AND ASSESSMENT	1.5	1.5

CHAPTER 2
CIVILIZATIONS OF AFRICA

Section 1 The Bantu Migrations	1	1.5
Section 2 Kingdoms of West Africa	1.5	2
Section 3 Trading States of East Africa	1.5	2
SKILLS ACTIVITY Organizing Your Time	1	1.5
CHAPTER 2 REVIEW, ACTIVITIES, AND ASSESSMENT	1.5	1.5

CHAPTER 3
THE ANCIENT AMERICAS

Section 1 Cultures of Middle America	1	2
Section 2 The Incas	1	2
Section 3 Cultures of North America	1.5	2
SKILLS ACTIVITY Recognizing Cause and Effect	1	1.5
CHAPTER 3 REVIEW, ACTIVITIES, AND ASSESSMENT	1.5	1.5
Literature	1	1.5

CHAPTER 4
CIVILIZATIONS OF ASIA

Section 1 Golden Ages in China	1.5	2
Section 2 Feudalism in Japan	1.5	2
Section 3 The Great Mughal Empire in India	1	2
SKILLS ACTIVITY Assessing Your Understanding	1	1.5
CHAPTER 4 REVIEW, ACTIVITIES, AND ASSESSMENT	1	2

CHAPTER 5
EUROPE IN THE MIDDLE AGES

Section 1 Feudalism: A System for Living	1	2
Section 2 The Rise of Cities	1	2

	12-WEEK COURSE	18-WEEK COURSE
Section 3 The Crusades	1	2
SKILLS ACTIVITY Using Route Maps	1	1.5
Section 4 Kings and Popes	1	2
CHAPTER 5 REVIEW, ACTIVITIES, AND ASSESSMENT	1.5	1.5
Literature	1.5	2

CHAPTER 6
A NEW AGE IN EUROPE

Section 1 The Renaissance and Reformation	1.5	2
Section 2 The Age of Exploration	1	1.5
Section 3 The Age of Powerful Kings	1	2
Section 4 Conquests in the Americas and Africa	1.5	2
SKILLS ACTIVITY Distinguishing Fact From Opinion	1	1.5
CHAPTER 6 REVIEW, ACTIVITIES, AND ASSESSMENT	1.5	1.5
ACTIVITY SHOP Lab	1.5	2

CHAPTER 7
CHANGES IN THE WESTERN WORLD

Section 1 Limits on Monarchs	1	2
Section 2 The Enlightenment	1	2
SKILLS ACTIVITY Interpreting Line Graphs	1	1.5
Section 3 The Industrial Revolution	1.5	2
Section 4 Revolution and Imperialism	1	2
CHAPTER 7 REVIEW, ACTIVITIES, AND ASSESSMENT	1.5	1.5

CHAPTER 8
A CENTURY OF TURMOIL

Section 1 World Wars and Revolution	1	2
Section 2 Breaking Colonial Ties	1	2
Section 3 Our Shrinking Globe	1	2
SKILLS ACTIVITY Expressing Problems Clearly	1	1.5
CHAPTER 8 REVIEW, ACTIVITIES, AND ASSESSMENT	1.5	1.5
ACTIVITY SHOP Interdisciplinary	1.5	2
TOTAL NUMBER OF DAYS	60	90

T7

Choose from this wide variety of resources for management, extensions, and assessment.

Components

- Student Editions
- Teacher's Editions

Teaching Resources Binders
- Chapter and Section Support
- Spanish Support
- Activities and Projects
- Tests
- Social Studies and Geography Skills

Program Teaching Resources Binder
- Primary Sources and Literature Readings
- Long-term Integrated Projects
- Outline Maps
- Environmental and Global Issues
- Writing Process Handbook
- Assessment Handbook

Technology in the Classroom
Social Studies Educator's Handbooks
Nystrom Desk Atlas
Posters

- Teacher's Flexible Planning Guide
- Color Transparencies with Overlays

- Guided Reading Audiotapes *
- Computer Test Bank (MAC/Windows)
- World Video Explorer
    Videodiscs *
    Videotapes
- Resource Pro™ CD-ROM
- Material World CD-ROM
- Planet Earth CD-ROM
- Writer's Solution CD-ROM
- Interdisciplinary Explorations

* Available in Spanish

| See us on the Internet | http://www.phschool.com |

Contact your local representative or call **1-800-848-9500.**

PRENTICE HALL
MultiMedia

PRENTICE HALL
Simon & Schuster Education Group
A VIACOM COMPANY

MEDIEVAL TIMES
TO
TODAY

PRENTICE HALL
Needham, Massachusetts
Upper Saddle River, New Jersey

Program Authors

Heidi Hayes Jacobs

Heidi Hayes Jacobs has served as an educational consultant to more than 500 schools across the nation. Dr. Jacobs is an adjunct professor in the Department of Curriculum on Teaching at Teachers College, Columbia University. She completed her undergraduate studies at the University of Utah in her hometown of Salt Lake City. She received an M.A. from the University of Massachusetts, Amherst, and completed her doctoral work at Columbia University's Teachers College in 1981.

The backbone of Dr. Jacobs's experience comes from her years as a teacher of high school, middle school, and elementary school students. As an educational consultant, she works with K–12 schools and districts on curriculum reform and strategic planning.

Brenda Randolph

Brenda Randolph is the former Director of the Outreach Resource Center at the African Studies Program at Howard University, Washington, D.C. She is the Founder and Director of Africa Access, a bibliographic service on Africa for schools. She received her B.A. in history with high honors from North Carolina Central University, Durham, and her M.A. in African studies with honors from Howard University. She completed further graduate studies at the University of Maryland, College Park, where she was awarded a Graduate Fellowship.

Brenda Randolph has published numerous articles in professional journals and bulletins. She currently serves as library media specialist in Montgomery County Public Schools, Maryland.

Michal L. LeVasseur

Michal LeVasseur is an educational consultant in the field of geography. She is an adjunct professor of geography at the University of Alabama, Birmingham, and serves with the Alabama Geographic Alliance. Her undergraduate and graduate work is in the fields of anthropology (B.A.), geography (M.A.), and science education (Ph.D.).

Dr. LeVasseur's specialization has moved increasingly into the area of geography education. In 1996, she served as Director of the National Geographic Society's Summer Geography Workshop. As an educational consultant, she has worked with the National Geographic Society as well as with schools to develop programs and curricula for geography.

Special Program Consultant

Yvonne S. Gentzler, Ph.D.
College of Education
University of Idaho
Moscow, Idaho

Content Consultants for *Medieval Times to Today*

**Barbara Brown, Laurence Michalak,
Ruth Mitchell-Pitts, Leslie Swartz,
Janet Valliant, Robert Young**
Affiliations on page iii.

PRENTICE HALL
Simon & Schuster Education Group
A VIACOM COMPANY

Upper Saddle River, New Jersey
Needham, Massachusetts

Copyright © 1998 by Prentice-Hall, Inc., a Viacom Company, Upper Saddle River, New Jersey 07458. All rights reserved. No part of this book may be reproduced or transmitted in any form or by any means, electronic or mechanical, including photocopying, recording, or by any information storage and retrieval system, without permission in writing from the publisher. Printed in the United States of America.

Student Edition ISBN: 0-13-433697-6
Teacher's Edition ISBN: 0-13-433698-4

4 5 6 7 8 9 10   01 00 99 98

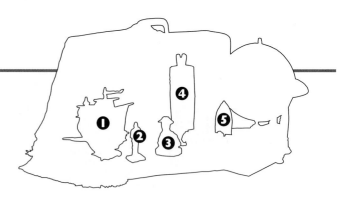

On the Cover

❶ Model of the Pinta

❷ Model of knight in armor

❸ Chinese sculpture based on an animal form

❹ African mask

❺ Griffin gargoyle plaque

Content Consultants for the World Explorer Program

Africa
Barbara Brown
Africa Studies Center
Boston University
Boston, Massachusetts

Ancient World
Maud Gleason
Department of Classics
Stanford University
Stanford, California

East Asia
Leslie Swartz
Harvard University
East Asian Outreach
Program at the
Children's Museum
of Boston
Boston, Massachusetts

Latin America
Daniel Mugan
Center for Latin American
Studies
University of Florida
Gainesville, Florida

Middle East
Elizabeth Barlow
Center for Middle
Eastern and North
African Studies
University of Michigan
Ann Arbor, Michigan

North Africa
Laurence Michalak
Center for Middle East
Studies
University of California
Berkeley, California

Religion
Michael Sells
Department of Religion
Haverford College
Haverford, Pennsylvania

Russia, Eastern Europe, Central Asia
Janet Valliant
Center for Russian,
Eastern European, and
Central Asian Studies
Harvard University
Cambridge,
Massachusetts

South Asia
Robert Young
South Asia Regional
Studies
University of
Pennsylvania
Philadelphia,
Pennsylvania

Western Europe
Ruth Mitchell-Pitts
Center for West European
Studies
University of North
Carolina
Chapel Hill, North
Carolina

Teacher Advisory Board

Jerome Balin
Lincoln Junior High
School
Naperville, Illinois

Linda Boaen
Baird School
Fresno, California

Nikki L. Born
Harllee Middle School
Bradenton, Florida

Carla Bridges
Concord Middle School
Concord, North Carolina

Bruce L. Campbell
Walled Lake Middle
School
Walled Lake, Michigan

**Barbara Coats
Grabowski**
Russell Middle School
Omaha, Nebraska

David Herman
North Carroll Middle
School
Hampstead, Maryland

Fred Hitz
Wilson Middle School
Muncie, Indiana

William B. Johnson
La Mesa Junior High
School
Canyon Country,
California

Kristi Karis
West Ottawa Middle
School
Holland, Michigan

Kristen Koch
Discovery Middle School
Orlando, Florida

Peggy McCarthy
Beulah School
Beulah, Colorado

Deborah J. Miller
Whitney Young Middle
School
Detroit, Michigan

Lawrence Peglow
Greenway Middle School
Pittsburgh, Pennsylvania

Lyn Shiver
Northwestern Middle
School
Alpharetta, Georgia

The World Explorer Team

*The editors, designers, marketer, market researcher, manager, production buyer, and manufacturing buyer
who made up the World Explorer team are listed below.*

Jackie Bedoya, Bruce Bond, Ellen Brown, David Lippman, Catherine Martin-Hetmansky,
Nancy Rogier, Olena Serbyn, Carol Signorino, John Springer, Susan Swan

TABLE OF CONTENTS

MEDIEVAL TIMES TO TODAY
1

ACTIVITY ATLAS | 2

CHAPTER 1 The Byzantine and Muslim Empires | 8
1 Byzantium: Rome's Eastern Empire | 9
2 The Rise and Spread of Islam | 15
3 The Religion of Islam | 21
◈ Skills Activity Reading Tables | 26
4 Islam's Golden Age | 28
Chapter 1 Review and Activities | 34

CHAPTER 2 Civilizations of Africa | 36
1 The Bantu Migrations | 37
2 Kingdoms of West Africa | 43
3 Trading States of East Africa | 49
◈ Skills Activity Organizing Your Time | 54
Chapter 2 Review and Activities | 56

CHAPTER 3 The Ancient Americas | 58
1 Cultures of Middle America | 59
2 The Incas | 65
3 Cultures of North America | 71
◈ Skills Activity Recognizing Cause and Effect | 76
Chapter 3 Review and Activities | 78
◆ Literature From "The Americas in 1492" by Jamake Highwater | 80

CHAPTER 4 Civilizations of Asia | 82
1 Golden Ages in China | 83
2 Feudalism in Japan | 89
3 The Great Mughal Empire in India | 94
◈ Skills Activity Assessing Your Understanding | 100
Chapter 4 Review and Activities | 102

CHAPTER 5   **Europe in the Middle Ages**   **104**

   1   Feudalism: A System for Living   105
   2   The Rise of Cities   111
   3   The Crusades   117
   Skills Activity   Using Route Maps   122
   4   Kings and Popes   124
   Chapter 5   Review and Activities   130
   Literature   "Of Swords and Sorcerers"
     by Margaret Hodges and Margery Evernden   132

CHAPTER 6   **A New Age in Europe**   **136**

   1   The Renaissance and Reformation   137
   2   The Age of Exploration   143
   3   The Age of Powerful Kings   150
   4   Conquests in the Americas and Africa   156
   Skills Activity   Distinguishing Fact From Opinion   162
   Chapter 6   Review and Activities   164
   Activity Shop Lab   Making a Compass   166

CHAPTER 7   **Changes in the Western World**   **168**

   1   Limits on Monarchs   169
   2   The Enlightenment   174
   Skills Activity   Interpreting Line Graphs   180
   3   The Industrial Revolution   182
   4   Revolution and Imperialism   188
   Chapter 7   Review and Activities   194

CHAPTER 8   **A Century of Turmoil**   **196**

   1   World Wars and Revolution   197
   2   Breaking Colonial Ties   204
   3   Our Shrinking Globe   210
   Skills Activity   Expressing Problems Clearly   216
   Chapter 8   Review and Activities   218
   Activity Shop Interdisciplinary   History Quiz Wizards   220

PROJECT POSSIBILITIES   **222**

REFERENCE   **224**

   Map and Globe Handbook   225
   Atlas   242
   World View   256
   Glossary of Geographic Terms   264
   Gazetteer   266
   Biographical Dictionary   268
   Glossary   270
   Index   274
   Acknowledgments   278

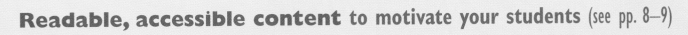

Readable, accessible content to motivate your students (see pp. 8–9)

OF SPECIAL INTEREST

A hands-on, active approach to practicing and applying key social studies skills

Reading Tables   26
Organizing Your Time   54
Recognizing Cause and Effect   76
Assessing Your Understanding   100
Using Route Maps   122
Distinguishing Fact From Opinion   162
Interpreting Line Graphs   180
Expressing Problems Clearly   216

Engaging, step-by-step activities for exploring important topics in medieval times to the present

Lab: Making a Compass   166
Interdisciplinary: History Quiz Wizards 220

High-interest selections written by authors who give us pictures of history

From "The Americas in 1492" by
   Jamake Highwater   80
"Of Swords and Sorcerers" by
   Margaret Hodges and Margery
   Evernden   132

HEROES

Sundiata   46
Toyotomi Hideyoshi   91
Queen Nzingha   160
Toussaint L'Ouverture 190

A Medieval Manor   109
The First Computer   211

My Village   96
Zoo   208

MAPS

World: Physical 2
Human Settlement: 500 and Today 3
The World About 1500 4
The Columbian Exchange 7
Byzantine and Muslim Empires 8
The Arabian Peninsula, A.D. 650s 16
The Spread of Islam 20
The Byzantine and Muslim Empires:
  Place Location 35
West and East African Kingdoms
  and Cities 36
Africa: Natural Vegetation 38
The Bantu Migrations 40
West Africa Trade Routes 44
Africa: Place Location 57
Ancient Civilizations of North and
  South America 58
The Ancient Americas: Place Location 79
Ancient Empires of China 82
The Tang and Song Empires 84
Japan: Physical (About A.D.1000) 90
Tamerlane's Empire and the Delhi
  Sultanate 95
The Mughal Empire Under Babur
  and Akbar 97
Asia: Place Location 103
Kingdoms and States of Europe
  About A.D. 1100 104

Invasions of the Roman Empire 106
Trade Centers in Europe 113
The Crusades 119
The Children's Crusade 123
Europe and the Holy Land: Place
  Location 131
Major Religions in Europe 141
European Voyages of Exploration 146
Spanish and Portuguese Empires in
  the Americas 159
European Empires in the Americas:
  Place Location 165
Napoleon's Power in Europe, 1812 191
European Colonies in Africa 192
The Western World: Place Location 195
Independence Since 1945 206
The World's Leading Exporters 213
Africa and India: Place Location 219
Mercator Projection 232
Equal-Area Projection 233
Robinson Projection 233
Azimuthal Projection 233
West Africa: Population Density 234
Russia: Political 236
Hawaii: Physical 237
North Africa and the Middle East:
  Oil Production 238
Atlas 242

CHARTS, GRAPHS, AND TABLES

Byzantine and Muslim Empires 27
Inventions of Tang and Song Dynasties 88
Plan of a Slave Ship 160
Achievements of the Scientific Revolution 176
Population of Dallas, Texas, 1900–1990 180
United States Work Force, 1890–1990 181

Time Line: Revolution and Wars
  1914–1945 198
The World's Leading Exporters 213
Earth's Revolution and the Seasons 228
Climate Regions 240
Natural Vegetation Regions 241

Active learning approaches to involve and engage students (see pp. 2–7)

Activating Prior Knowledge

Three sets of reading strategies are introduced on pages viii and ix. Before students read the strategies, use questions like these to prompt a discussion about reading:

- Before you read, what do you do to help you read better?

- How do you figure out the meaning of what you read?

- Do you take a different approach to different kinds of reading, such as a paperback novel or your math textbook?

Discussion of their answers will help students become aware of their own reading processes.

Introducing the Strategies

Point out to students that reading is a process. If students are conscious of their process, they can improve their reading. Point out that there are three sets of reading strategies: **Before You Read, While You Read,** and **After You Read.** Explain that these are the behaviors that good readers exhibit. As students practice these strategies, they too will increase their reading fluency and comprehension.

Be sure to reinforce the idea that students might use several of these strategies at the same time, or they might go back and forth among them. There is no set order for applying them.

READ ACTIVELY

How can I get the most out of my social studies book?
How does my reading relate to my world? Answering questions like these means that you are an active reader, an involved reader. As an active reader, you are in charge of the reading situation!

The following strategies tell how to think and read as an active reader. You don't need to use all of these strategies all the time. Feel free to choose the ones that work best in each reading situation. You might use several at a time, or you might go back and forth among them. They can be used in any order.

BEFORE YOU READ

Give yourself a purpose

The sections in this book begin with a list called "Questions to Explore." These questions focus on key ideas presented in the section. They give you a purpose for reading. You can create your own purpose by asking questions like these: How does the topic relate to my life? How might I use what I learn at school or at home?

Preview

To preview a reading selection, first read its title. Then look at the pictures and read the captions. Also read any headings in the selection. Then ask yourself: What is the reading selection about? What do the pictures and headings tell about the selection?

Reach into your background

What do you already know about the topic of the selection? How can you use what you know to help you understand what you are going to read?

WHILE YOU READ

Ask questions

Suppose you are reading about the continent of South America. Some questions you might ask are: Where is South America? What countries are found there? Why are some of the countries large and others small? Asking questions like these can help you gather evidence and gain knowledge.

Predict

As you read, make a prediction about what will happen and why. Or predict how one fact might affect another fact. Suppose you are reading about South America's climate. You might make a prediction about how the climate affects where people live. You can change your mind as you gain new information.

Connect

Connect your reading to your own life. Are the people discussed in the selection like you or someone you know? What would you do in similar situations? Connect your reading to something you have already read. Suppose you have already read about the ancient Greeks. Now you are reading about the ancient Romans. How are they alike? How are they different?

Visualize

What would places, people, and events look like in a movie or a picture? As you read about India, you could visualize the country's heavy rains. What do they look like? How do they sound? As you read about geography, you could visualize a volcanic eruption.

AFTER YOU READ

Respond

Talk about what you have read. What did you think? Share your ideas with your classmates.

Assess yourself

What did you find out? Were your predictions on target? Did you find answers to your questions?

Follow up

Show what you know. Use what you have learned to do a project. When you do projects, you continue to learn.

READ ACTIVELY **ix**

Developing Student Reading

Point out to students that the sections in this book have a Before You Read feature. Each one is enclosed in a yellow box (see page 9 for an example). It includes Reach Into Your Background, which helps students think about what they already know so that they can apply their prior knowledge to what they're reading. Before You Read also includes Questions to Explore, which focus on the main ideas in the section. Each Question to Explore relates to one of the Guiding Questions for the book. See the list of Guiding Questions on the following page.

Students will also find Read Actively margin notes in every section. Encourage them to respond to these prompts to reinforce their active reading process.

Supporting English Language Learners

Preview and predict Suggest that students look at the title, headings, maps, charts, and photos to guess what the section is about.

Ask questions Tell students that every fact an author writes has a purpose. Have them question the purpose of details as they read them. As they find answers and discover meaning, they can formulate new, deeper questions.

Visualize Have students think how the places they read about would affect their senses. What would it smell like there? What would they see and hear and feel?

Assess Have students review their predictions and see how well they did. What helped them make good predictions?

READ ACTIVELY **ix**

Introducing the Guiding Questions

This book was developed around five Guiding Questions about history from the medieval times to today. They appear on the reduced Student Edition page to the right. The Guiding Questions are intended as an organizational focus for the book. All of the chapter content, activities, questions, and assessments relate to the Guiding Questions, which act as a kind of umbrella under which all of the material falls. You may wish to add your own Guiding Questions to the list in order to tailor them to your particular course. Or, as a group activity, you may want to ask your class to develop its own Guiding Questions.

Ask a volunteer to read the Guiding Questions out loud to the class. These questions will guide students as they learn about history from medieval times to today.

Introducing the Project Preview

The projects for this book are designed to provide students with hands-on involvement in the content area. On the reduced Student Edition page to the right, students are introduced to the projects. Complete information about them appears on pages 222–223. You may assign projects as cooperative activities, whole class projects, or individual projects. Each project relates to at least one of the Guiding Questions.

MEDIEVAL TIMES TO TODAY

To understand today's world, we must learn about its past. Ancient civilizations laid strong foundations for modern cultures. The years between ancient and modern times have added greatly to the structure of those cultures. These years have been marked by inventions and revolutions. They have seen civilizations and empires thrive and fade, each leaving its mark on its descendants. In this book, you will learn how the ideas, events, and people of these years have shaped our lives.

Guiding Questions

The readings and activities in this book will help you discover answers to these Guiding Questions.

- ☛ How did physical geography affect the development of societies around the world?

- ☛ How did each society's belief system affect its history, government, and economy?

- ☛ What accomplishments in technology, learning, or artistic expression were found in each society?

- ☛ What was the pattern of day-to-day life in these societies?

- ☛ How did these societies interact with other societies?

Project Preview

You can also discover answers to the Guiding Questions by working on projects. Preview the following projects and choose one that you might like to do. For more details, see page 222.

The Birth of a Nation Prepare the "biography" of a country that interests you. Have a classroom Nation Celebration.

One Job Through the Ages Make and illustrate a time line for an occupation that has existed since the Middle Ages.

Two Tales of One City Compare a historic city's past and present by making a poster and captioned pictures.

Major Migrations Keep a classroom Migrations Map, and mark the movement of people from some areas of the world to others through history.

Resource Directory

Teaching Resources

📁 **Book Projects,** in the Activities and Projects booklet, provides students with directions on how to complete one of the projects described on these two pages. You may wish to assign or have students choose a project at the beginning of the course.

Program Resources

📁 **Long-Term Integrated Projects** booklet, in the Program Resources Binder, provides opportunities for students to make comparisons across regions through a variety of long-term projects. You may wish to assign or have students choose a project at the beginning of the course.

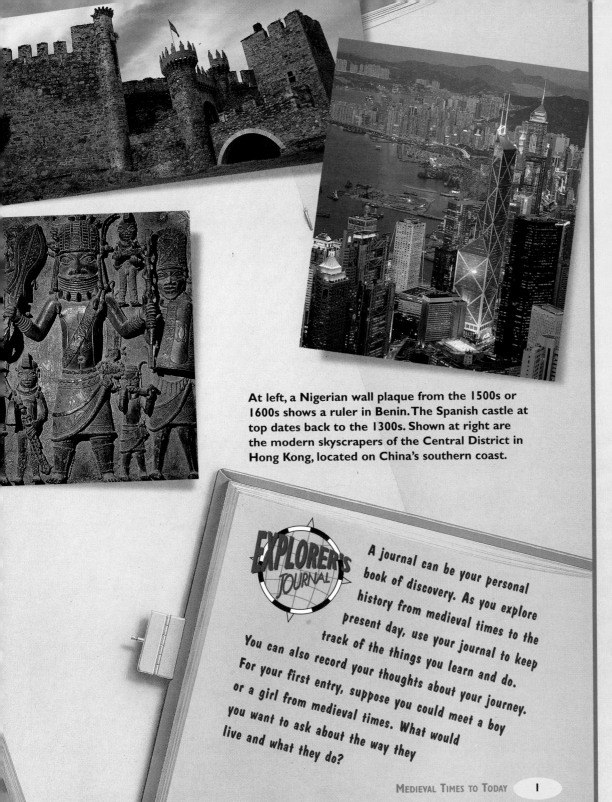

At left, a Nigerian wall plaque from the 1500s or 1600s shows a ruler in Benin. The Spanish castle at top dates back to the 1300s. Shown at right are the modern skyscrapers of the Central District in Hong Kong, located on China's southern coast.

EXPLORER'S JOURNAL

A journal can be your personal book of discovery. As you explore history from medieval times to the present day, use your journal to keep track of the things you learn and do. You can also record your thoughts about your journey. For your first entry, suppose you could meet a boy or a girl from medieval times. What would you want to ask about the way they live and what they do?

Invite students to discuss the three photographs. Use them as a prompt for discussion of what students know about history from medieval times to today. You may want to begin a K-W-L chart on the board with the headings What We **K**now About Medieval Times to Today, What We **W**ant to Know About Medieval Times to Today, and What We **L**earned About Medieval Times to Today. Have students fill in the first column with several things they agree they already know. Then ask them to brainstorm what they would like to know about history from medieval times to today to add to the second column. Students can fill in the third column as they work through the text.

Using the Explorer's Journal

Have students begin their Explorer's Journal as the paragraph on the student book page suggests. If at all possible, encourage students to use a separate small notebook for their Explorer's Journal entries. They can add to this Journal as they learn more about history from medieval times to today.

Teacher's Flexible Planning Guide includes a guide to the Prentice Hall World Explorer program, a skills correlation, and a variety of pacing charts for different course configurations. You may wish to refer to the guide as you plan your instruction.

Resource Pro™ CD-ROM allows you to create customized lesson plans and print all Teaching Resources and Program Resources, plus the Computer Test Bank, directly from the CD-ROM.

Lesson Objectives

1. Describe the relative locations and sizes of the Earth's continents.

2. Explain changes in population distribution from medieval times to today.

3. Identify changes in political boundaries from medieval times to today.

4. Define the Columbian Exchange and explain its effects.

Lesson Plan

1 Engage

Warm-Up Activity

Ask students to define the word *history*. You might ask students to share anecdotes about the history of your community or of their families.

Activating Prior Knowledge

Invite students to tell some ways that history affects the present. For example, a family whose ancestors went to California during the 1849 Gold Rush may live in that state still.

Answers to ...

LOCATION

1. seven; a great deal; Europe and Asia; Australia and Antarctica (entirely south), Europe and North America (entirely north), South America, Africa, and Asia (both sides)

PLACE

2. Atlantic, Pacific, Indian, and Arctic oceans; Atlantic Ocean; Pacific Ocean; All the oceans are connected.

DISCOVERY ACTIVITIES ABOUT

Medieval Times to Today

Learning about history means being an explorer and a geographer. No explorer would start out without first checking some facts. Begin by exploring the maps on the following pages.

LOCATION

1. Look at the Earth's Continents How many continents are there? Use a ruler to compare the size of the continents. Find the smallest one. How much do the continents vary in size? Which two continents share the same landmass? Which continents are completely north or south of the Equator? Which ones lie on both sides of the Equator?

PLACE

2. Look at the Earth's Oceans Use the map below to find the Earth's oceans. Which ones appear on the map? Which ocean separates North America from Europe? Which one separates North America from Asia? Why do you think some people say that there is just one ocean, the "world ocean"?

World: Physical

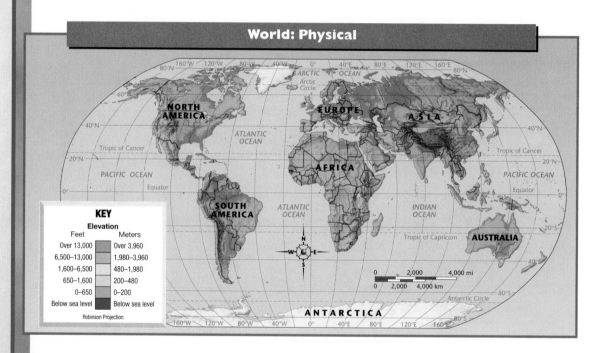

KEY

Elevation

Feet	Meters
Over 13,000	Over 3,960
6,500–13,000	1,980–3,960
1,600–6,500	480–1,980
650–1,600	200–480
0–650	0–200
Below sea level	Below sea level

Robinson Projection

0   2,000   4,000 mi
0   2,000   4,000 km

2   MEDIEVAL TIMES TO TODAY

Resource Directory

Teaching Resources

Activity Atlas in the Activities and Projects booklet, pp. 3–5, provides a structure that helps students complete the activities in the Medieval Times to Today Activity Atlas and encourages discovery learning.

Human Settlement, 500 and Today

KEY

Persons per sq mi	Persons per sq km
520 and over	200 and over
260–519	100–199
130–259	50–99
25–129	10–49
1–24	1–9
Under 1	Under 1

● Major city, A.D. 500

(Selected cities labeled)

Robinson Projection

0 1,000 2,000 mi

0 1,000 2,000 km

▶ These fishing tools are from the 300s or 400s. They were found in the country of Mali in Africa.

MOVEMENT

3. Investigate Human Settlement The map shows the major cities where people lived more than 1,500 years ago. The colors on the map show where people live today. What is the main difference between the two? Why do you think the change has occurred?

INTERACTION

4. Compare Human Settlement to the Location of Physical Features Look at the map on the opposite page. Identify at least three types of places where people have settled. For example, do people tend to settle along the edges of continents, at the coasts, or in the middle of continents? What natural features seem to attract human settlement? What natural features seem to discourage it?

2 Explore

Tell students to carefully study all the material in the Activity Atlas. Pair students as "Medieval Times" and "Today" journalists. Direct pairs to choose two or three facts and trends about their time. Urge them to focus on these issues as they study history since medieval times.

Answers to ...

MOVEMENT

3. Many more people live in the interior of continents today; better transportation, overcrowding at coastal areas

INTERACTION

4. at coasts, near water, at ports, on level lands; at the coasts; water, transportation; mountains

Lesson Plan *continued*

3 Teach

Ask students to create three-column charts with the headings *Medieval Times, Today,* and *Reasons for Change*. Invite students to complete their charts with data from the text. Students' explanations for change should be supported with facts from the section. This activity should take about 25 minutes.

Background

Global Perspectives

As movement around the world has increased, so has the importance of port cities. Many were founded or became more globally significant since medieval times. Some examples include Montreal, Canada; Calcutta, India; Cape Town, South Africa; Salvador, Brazil; and Sydney, Australia. Traders and settlers arrived first in port cities and then slowly ventured into interior lands.

Answers to ...

PLACE

5. The Roman Empire is gone, replaced by many nations. Native American civilizations have been replaced by the United States, Mexico, and Canada.; empires have been replaced by countries; North America; possible answers: colonization of one nation by another; absorption of one nation into another

REGIONS

6. All of Africa is covered by countries. Empires are no longer there; about 50

PLACE

5. Explore Changes in Political Boundaries
Many countries and political boundaries have changed since the 1500s, but some things have stayed much the same. Look at the map on this page and at the World: Political map in the Atlas. What changes do you notice in Europe? In North America? In Africa? In what part of the world have boundaries changed the most? Name two reasons that political boundaries might change.

REGIONS

6. Investigate Boundary Changes in Africa
Again compare the map on this page with the World: Political map in the Atlas. This time look closely at Africa. Africa in about 1500 was a land of kingdoms, empires, and trading states. Now look at the World: Political map, which shows Africa today. Name two differences between the two maps. About how many countries in Africa exist today?

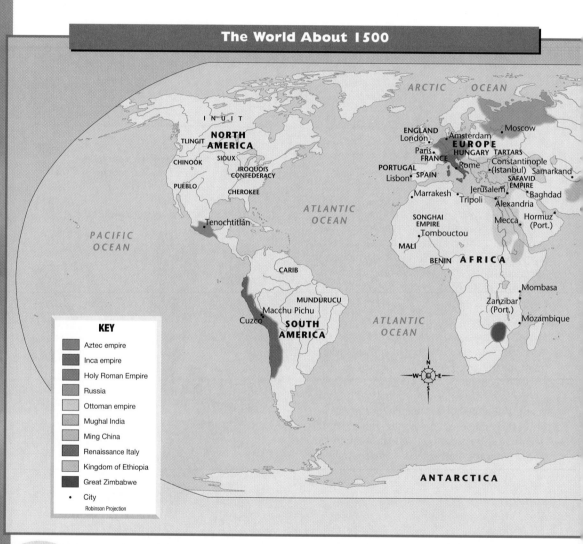

The World About 1500

KEY
- Aztec empire
- Inca empire
- Holy Roman Empire
- Russia
- Ottoman empire
- Mughal India
- Ming China
- Renaissance Italy
- Kingdom of Ethiopia
- Great Zimbabwe
- • City

Robinson Projection

7. Follow Geo Leo Geo Leo is looking back and forth between the map on these two pages and the World: Political map in the Atlas. He has a few things to say about them. Identify which map he means with each question.

"I will describe something on one or both maps, and you tell me which map I mean. Ready? Let's play!"

A. I'll start with an easy one. I see a world of continents and oceans, in which there are countries on nearly every continent. Am I looking at a map of the world in the 1500s, today, or both?

B. Look at this! The map shows the Holy Roman Empire in Europe. Which map do I mean? Am I looking at the map of the world in the 1500s or of today?

C. North America sure looks popular. There are dozens of nations who call this continent home. Each group has a different name, but they don't seem to have firm political borders. Which map am I looking at?

D. Look at North America now! Instead of dozens of different nations, the continent is covered by just three large countries. Is this the map of today or of the 1500s?

ASIA

Beijing

Nanking

Delhi

Canton

Goa

PACIFIC
OCEAN

Malacca
(Port.)

INDIAN
OCEAN

AUSTRALIA

0   1,000   2,000 mi
0 1,000 2,000 km

GEO LEO

BONUS

Which world map shows more countries? Why do you think this is so?

Five Themes of Geography

Place Have students use the map on this page to find Ivan the Great's Russia and Babur's Mughal empire. On which continent are they located? (Asia)

Regions Ask students which region was most densely populated in about 1500 (Europe and the area around the Mediterranean).

Movement Have students choose a continent on the World: Physical map on the first page of the Activity Atlas. Ask students which continents explorers from that continent could reach overland and which could be reached only by crossing water. (Answers will vary, but should reflect world geography accurately.)

Human-Environment Interaction Ask students to name physical features people have overcome in expanding human population from medieval densities to those of today (deserts, oceans, mountains, vast interior lands).

Location Ask students to name a continent which can only be reached by water, no matter where outside that continent the journey begins (Australia).

Answers to . . .

PLACE

7. A. today **B.** The World About 1500 **C.** The World About 1500 **D.** today

BONUS

the map of the world today; because there are many more people and more political divisions

4 Assess

Charts should note continents have remained basically the same since medieval times. Political boundaries and population densities, however, have changed a great deal. For example, population has spread more fully around the globe, and political boundaries have shifted due to colonization. Charts should note exchange of ideas and products between Europe and the Americas.

Activity

Interdisciplinary Connections

Science Ask students to use an atlas or an almanac to locate regions where the resources of the Columbian Exchange are still produced today. Urge students to explore the climatic similarities and differences between these regions and those from which the resources originated. Discuss whether the interaction of cultures begun by the Exchange has lasted.

Answers to ...
MOVEMENT

8. with a list of words linked by arrows; yes, more animals went from Europe to the Americas; about the same number of plants went in each direction; Answers will vary, but should note the common presence of these foods in modern diets.; chickenpox, measles, scarlet fever, malaria, and smallpox

MOVEMENT

8. Investigate the Columbian Exchange

When Christopher Columbus and other explorers sailed from Europe to the Americas and back, they brought many things with them. People now call this movement of plants, animals, and diseases the Columbian Exchange. The map on the next page shows the Columbian Exchange. Study the map carefully. How does the map show you whether things came from Europe to the Americas or from the Americas to Europe?

Did more animals go from Europe to the Americas, or was it the reverse? What about plants? How many of the foods you usually eat first came from Europe? What diseases were transferred to the Americas?

◀ Wild rice is still harvested by Native Americans as it has been for hundreds of years—with canoes and sticks. This picture was taken on the Leech Lake Indian Reservation in Minnesota.

▼ These familiar fruits and vegetables were part of the Columbia Exchange from Europe to the Americas.

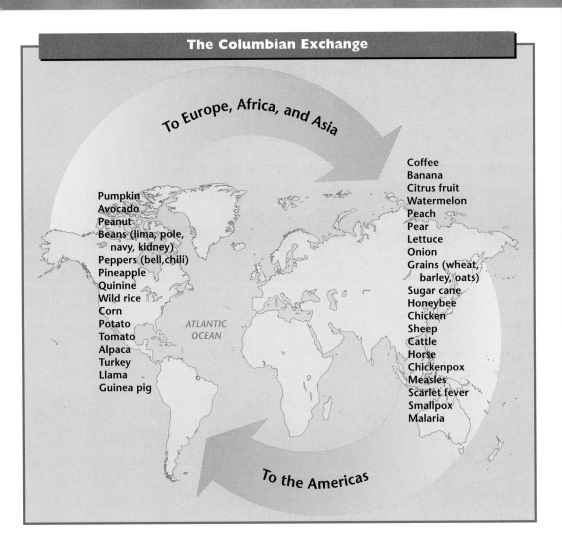

The Columbian Exchange

To Europe, Africa, and Asia

Pumpkin
Avocado
Peanut
Beans (lima, pole,
    navy, kidney)
Peppers (bell, chili)
Pineapple
Quinine
Wild rice
Corn
Potato
Tomato
Alpaca
Turkey
Llama
Guinea pig

ATLANTIC
OCEAN

Coffee
Banana
Citrus fruit
Watermelon
Peach
Pear
Lettuce
Onion
Grains (wheat,
    barley, oats)
Sugar cane
Honeybee
Chicken
Sheep
Cattle
Horse
Chickenpox
Measles
Scarlet fever
Smallpox
Malaria

To the Americas

Activity

Discovery Learning

Country Quiz Pair students to play the following game: One partner identifies a place on any of the Activity Atlas maps. The other partner must then use all the Activity Atlas maps to list as many facts as possible about that place, both in medieval times and today. When both partners have had several turns, have them quiz other teams with their lists. Quizzing teams should offer clues from their lists one at a time as other teams try to locate the specified place with as few clues as possible.

MEDIEVAL TIMES TO TODAY
The Byzantine and Muslim Empires

To help you plan instruction, the chart below shows how teaching resources correspond to chapter content. Use the resources to vary instruction, add activities, or plan block schedules. Where appropriate, resources have **suggested time allotments** for students. Time allotments are approximate.

Managing Time and Instruction

	Medieval Times to Today Teaching Resources Binder		World Explorer Program Resources Binder	
	Resource	**mins.**	**Resource**	**mins.**

1 SECTION 1
Byzantium: Rome's Eastern Empire
	Chapter and Section Support
	Reproducible Lesson Plan, p. 4
	Ⓢ Guided Reading and Review, p. 5
	Ⓢ Section Quiz, p. 6
	Critical Thinking Activity, p. 20
		
		20
		25
		30
			Outline Maps
			  Mediterranean Europe: Political, p. 21
			Nystrom Desk Atlas
			Ⓣ **Primary Sources and Literature**
			  Readings
			Writing Process Handbook
			  Limiting a Topic, p. 15
			Interdisciplinary Explorations
			  The Glory of Ancient Rome
				
				20
				
				40
				
				25

SKILLS ACTIVITY Reading Tables	**Social Studies and Geography Skills,** Reading a Flowchart, p. 57	30		

2 SECTION 2
The Rise and Spread of Islam
	Chapter and Section Support
	Reproducible Lesson Plan, p. 7
	Ⓢ Guided Reading and Review, p. 8
	Ⓢ Section Quiz, p. 9
	Social Studies and Geography Skills,
	  Maps with Accurate Shapes: Conformal
	  Maps, p. 15
		
		20
		25
		
		30
			Outline Maps
			  Saudi Arabia: Political, p. 30
			  North Africa: Political, p. 31
			  South Asia: Physical, p. 36
				
				20
				20
				20

3 SECTION 3 The Religion of Islam	**Chapter and Section Support** Reproducible Lesson Plan, p. 10 Ⓢ Guided Reading and Review, p. 11 Ⓢ Section Quiz, p. 12	 20 25		
4 SECTION 4 Islam's Golden Age	**Chapter and Section Support** Reproducible Lesson Plan, p. 13 Ⓢ Guided Reading and Review, p. 14 Ⓢ Section Quiz, p. 15 Ⓢ Vocabulary, p. 17 Reteaching, p. 18 Enrichment, p. 19 Ⓢ Chapter Summary, p. 16 **Tests** Forms A and B Chapter Tests, pp. 2–7	 20 25 20 25 25 15 40	**Outline Maps** Saudi Arabia: Political, p. 30	 20

Activities and Projects

Block Scheduling Program Support

Interdisciplinary Links

Resource Pro™ CD-ROM

Media and Technology

Assessment Opportunities

From Guiding Questions to Assessment A series of Guiding Questions serves as an organizing framework for this book. The Guiding Questions that relate to this chapter are listed below. Section Reviews and Section Quizzes provide opportunities for assessing students' insights into these Guiding Questions. Additional assessments are listed below.

Media and Technology

Resource	mins.
📹 🖥 🔊 World Video Explorer	20
🖥 Planet Earth CD-ROM	20
▭ Color Transparencies 89, 90	20
🖥 Planet Earth CD-ROM	20
▭ Color Transparency Historical Map Set 3	20
🖥 Planet Earth CD-ROM	20
▭ Color Transparency 92	20
🖥 Planet Earth CD-ROM	20
🖥 Material World CD-ROM	20
▭ Color Transparency 152	20
🎧 🔊 Guided Reading Audiotapes	20
▭ Color Transparency 171	
(Graphic organizer web template)	20
🖥 The Writer's Solution CD-ROM	30
🖴 Computer Test Bank	30

T **Teaming Opportunity** This resource is especially well-suited for teaching teams.	🖥 **CD-ROM**
	🖥 **Laserdisc**
	▭ **Transparency**
	🖴 **Software**
S **Spanish** This resource is also in Spanish support.	📹 **Videotape**
	🎧 **Audiotape**

GUIDING QUESTIONS

- *How did physical geography affect the development of societies around the world?*

- *What accomplishments in technology, learning, or artistic expression were found in each society?*

ASSESSMENTS

Section 1

Students should be able to create a chart showing contributions by the Byzantine empire to world culture.

▶ **RUBRIC** See the Assessment booklet for a rubric on assessing charts.

Section 2

Students should be able to create a map showing the spread of Islam by the year A.D. 1500.

▶ **RUBRIC** See the Assessment booklet for a rubric on assessing a map produced by a student.

Section 3

Students should be able to give an oral presentation on the Five Pillars of Islam.

▶ **RUBRIC** See the Assessment booklet for a rubric on assessing an oral presentation.

Section 4

Students should be able to write a short report outlining some of the intellectual developments during the golden age.

▶ **RUBRIC** See the Assessment booklet for a rubric on assessing a report.

Activities and Projects

Mental Mapping

The Islamic World Distribute outline maps of the world. Ideally, national borders will be shown and countries will be labeled, though this is not essential.

Tell students there are about one billion Muslims in the world. Ask them to identify the countries or areas in which they think at least 50 percent of the population is Islamic. Encourage students to offer suggestions. As necessary, help them recognize that North Africa (above the equator), Southwest and central Asia, Afghanistan, Pakistan, Bangladesh, Indonesia, southern Malaysia, and parts of the Balkan peninsula of Europe all have a predominantly Muslim population.

Links to Current Events

Islamic France Although the Muslims did not conquer France in 732, many Muslims live in France today as the result of the French colonization of North Africa. People from formerly French colonies such as Algeria have immigrated to France. Muslims in France often face prejudice and discrimination, however, as do Muslims in many parts of Europe and the United States. Encourage students to find news articles about the situation of Muslims in France, the United States, or other countries. Have them report on efforts by the Islamic community to sustain their culture through holidays, customs, and styles of dress.

Hands-On Activities

Arabic Numbers Help students see the importance of Arabic numerals to modern science and mathematics by having them do some computations using Roman and Arabic numerals. For example, write 387 (CCCLXXXVII) on the board in Roman numerals. After they decipher the number, ask them to multiply by 3 (III). Chances are, most will find it impossible to do this unless they mentally convert the number to Arabic numerals and perform the operation in their heads.

Discuss the uses of mathematics in modern science and technology. Help students see that none of these fields could have developed without the system of Arabic numerals that allows easy computation.

Mapping Empires Have students locate the Byzantine empire and the Islamic empire on a map of Europe and Asia. Suggest that they use striped or blended colors to show areas where one superseded the other. *Basic*

Byzantine Have students consult a dictionary to find the many definitions of the word "byzantine." Then have them work in small groups to locate pictures to illustrate each definition. Examples of the types of illustrations they might seek include maps showing the location of Byzantium, examples of architecture and painting, an Orthodox church or church official, and a maze. Have them write the

definition they are illustrating on a card to accompany each map or picture. *English Language Learners*

Istanbul Suggest that students read a travel guide to Istanbul. Have them plan an itinerary for a one-week visit to the city. They should list two things to see or do for each of the seven days in the city. Tell them to write their itinerary so that it will interest others in making the trip. *Average*

Modern Islam Suggest that students research the celebration of Ramadan today in different parts of the world. Encourage them to consider parts of the world where there is a significant Muslim minority as well as a majority, and an area where there

is a community of Muslim immigrants within a non-Islamic nation. For example, they might look at the celebration of Ramadan in Saudi Arabia, Indonesia, Senegal, and London. Ask them to create a poster depicting the four celebrations. They should try to find one thing all the celebrations have in common and one way that each reflects the local culture and geography. *Challenging*

F.Y.I.

This page can help you extend your own and students' understanding of the concepts in this chapter. You may want to browse through some of the suggestions in the **Bibliography.** Interdisciplinary Links can connect social studies understandings to areas elsewhere in the curriculum through the use of other Prentice Hall products. **National Geography Standards** reflected specifically in this chapter are listed for your convenience. Some hints about appropriate **Internet Access** are also provided. **School to Careers** provides insights into the practical uses of some of the concepts in this chapter as they might pertain to various careers.

BIBLIOGRAPHY

FOR THE TEACHER

Ayoub, Abderrahman, Jamila Binous, Abderrazak Gragueb, Ali Mtimet, and Hedi Slim. *Umm El Madayan: An Islamic City Through the Ages.* Houghton, 1994.

Fry, Plantagenet Somerset. *The Dorling Kindersley History of the World.* Dorling, 1994.

FOR THE STUDENT

Easy
Macdonald, Fiona. *A Sixteenth-Century Mosque.* Bedrick, 1994.

Morley, Jacqueline. *A Roman Villa.* Bedrick, 1992.

Average
James, Simon. *Ancient Rome.* Viking, 1992.

Moktefi, Mokhtar. *The Arabs in the Golden Age.* Millbrook, 1992.

Challenging
Ancient Rome. Dorling, 1995. DK Pocket series.

Corbishley, Mike. *Rome and the Ancient World.* Facts, 1993.

LITERATURE CONNECTION

Al-Saleh, Khairat. *Fabled Cities, Princes, and Jinn from Arab Myths and Legends.* Bedrick, 1995.

Macaulay, David. *City: A Story of Roman Planning and Construction.* Houghton, 1974.

Sutcliff, Rosemary. *The Eagle of the Ninth. The Silver Branch.* Sunburst, 1993.

INTERDISCIPLINARY LINKS

Subject	Theme: Religion
MATH	Middle Grades Math: Tools for Success *Course 1*, Lesson 1-1, **Making Frequency Tables** *Course 2*, Lesson 1-1, **Reporting Frequency**
SCIENCE	Prentice Hall Science *Ecology: Earth's Natural Resources,* Lesson 2-1, **Land and Soil Resources**
LANGUAGE ARTS	Prentice Hall Literature *Bronze,* **Djuha Borrows a Pot, How the Animals Kept the Lions Away**

NATIONAL GEOGRAPHY STANDARDS

Students explore the 18 National Geography Standards throughout *Medieval Times to Today.* Chapter 1, however, concentrates on investigating the following standards: 3, 4, 6, 9, 10, 11, 12, 13, 15, 16, 17. For a complete list of the standards, see the *Teacher's Flexible Planning Guide.*

SCHOOL TO CAREERS

In Chapter 1, The Byzantine and Muslim Empires, students learn about Byzantium and the religion of Islam. Students also learn about reading tables. Knowing something about the Byzantine and Muslim empires can help students prepare for careers in many fields, such as history, foreign relations, museum administration, and so on. Reading tables is a skill useful for researchers, teachers, accountants, and others. The curriculum presented in this book, as in all eight titles of Prentice Hall's *World Explorer* program, is designed to prepare students not only for careers but also for good citizenship—of the world as well as of this country.

INTERNET ACCESS

Many social studies teachers and students use Internet browsers, or search engines, to investigate particular topics. For the best results, use narrow rather than broad topics. Try these for Chapter 1: Byzantium, Mecca, Islam, Maimonides. Finding age-appropriate sites is an important consideration when using the Internet. For links to age-appropriate sites in world studies and geography, visit the Prentice Hall Home Page at:
http://www.phschool.com

Connecting to the Guiding Questions

As students complete this chapter, they will focus on the history and development of the Byzantine and Muslim empires. Content in this chapter thus corresponds to the following Guiding Questions:

● How did physical geography affect the development of societies around the world?

● What accomplishments in technology, learning, or artistic expression were found in each society?

Using the Map Activities

Locate the boundaries of Europe and Asia before beginning the activities.

• It was located where Europe and Asia meet.

• Students should indicate at least two places.

Heterogeneous Groups

The following Teacher's Edition strategies are suitable for heterogeneous groups.

Cooperative Learning
What's in a Name?   p. 10
Explore the Role
of Women   p. 24

Critical Thinking
Distinguishing Facts
From Opinions   p. 18
Recognizing Cause
and Effect   pp. 19, 29

Interdisciplinary Connections
Mathematics   p. 19
Art   pp. 23, 29

CHAPTER 1
The Byzantine and Muslim Empires

SECTION 1
Byzantium
ROME'S EASTERN EMPIRE

SECTION 2
The Rise and Spread of Islam

SECTION 3
The Religion of Islam

SECTION 4
Islam's Golden Age

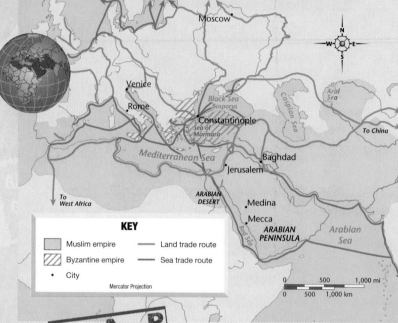

KEY

▨	Muslim empire	—	Land trade route
▨	Byzantine empire	—	Sea trade route
•	City		

Mercator Projection

0   500   1,000 mi
0   500   1,000 km

MAP ACTIVITIES

The Byzantine and Muslim empires covered a vast area stretching from Europe to India. The map shows lands and bodies of water that were important to one or both empires. To understand more about these empires, do the following activities.

Explore a city
Find Constantinople on the map. Study its location. Why do you think it is described as being at a crossroads between Europe and Asia?

By land and by sea
Look closely at the map. Notice that some routes are land trade routes and some are sea trade routes. How many places can you find where a land route and a sea route join to become one continuous route?

Resource Directory

Media and Technology

💿 📼 **From Alexandria to the Information Highway,** from the World Video Explorer, introduces students to the ways that information has been stored from the Muslim empire to the present.

Chapter 2

Byzantium
ROME'S EASTERN EMPIRE

BEFORE YOU READ

Reach Into Your Background

Think of the neighborhood in which you live. What advantages does your neighborhood have because of its location?

Perhaps it is near a shopping mall, a park, or the beach. How important is location to a community?

Questions to Explore

1. How did the Byzantine empire survive for such a long time?
2. What major contributions did the Byzantine empire make to world culture?

Key Terms

strait
icon
patriarch
schism

Key People and Places

Justinian
Moscow
Constantinople
Rome
Venice

Prince Igor (EE gor) of Moscow, in what today is Russia, watched as a large force of his warships sailed across the Black Sea in A.D. 941. The prince was sure that Constantinople, capital of the Byzantine empire, would soon be his.

As his fleet drew closer to the city, the prince's excitement turned to horror. Byzantine ships hurled "Greek fire" at the invaders from Moscow. Anything the "fire" touched burst into flames. Soon, most of Prince Igor's fleet was ablaze.

"Greek fire" was made from a formula so secret that it was never written down. Even today, no one knows exactly how it was made, except that it contained petroleum. But this deadly weapon gave the Byzantines tremendous power throughout the Mediterranean area.

▼ This painting was made about 700 years after "Greek fire" was invented. It shows a scene like the one that shocked Prince Igor. "Greek fire" exploded into flame when it contacted water, making it a deadly weapon in sea battles.

Teaching Resources

📁 **Reproducible Lesson Plan** in the Chapter and Section Support booklet, p. 4, provides a summary of the section lesson.

📁 **Guided Reading and Review** in the Chapter and Section Support booklet, p. 5, provides a structure for mastering key concepts and reviewing key terms in the section. Available in Spanish in the Spanish Support booklet, p. 4.

Program Resources

📁 Material in the **Primary Sources and Literature Readings** booklet extends content with a selection related to the concepts in this chapter.

📁 **Outline Maps** Mediterranean Europe: Political, p. 21

Lesson Objectives

1 Explain the longevity of the Byzantine empire.

2 Identify some major contributions of the Byzantine empire to world culture.

Lesson Plan

1 Engage

Warm–Up Activity

Give each student several tokens or buttons. Next, place a toll collector at the classroom door, then lead students first out and then back into the classroom. Students must pay a toll each time they pass through the door. Have the token collector count and note on the chalkboard the number of tokens paid. Discuss why being a region's token collector might be a profitable role for a nation.

Activating Prior Knowledge

Have students read Reach Into Your Background in the Before You Read box. Have students discuss how easy or difficult it is to get to places where they can engage in their favorite activities.

2 Explore

As students read, suggest that they consider these questions: Where was the Byzantine empire centered? Why was its location so critical to its survival and prosperity? What was Justinian like as a man and as an emperor? Why is he remembered today? How did Roman Catholic and Greek Orthodox views of Christianity differ?

Activity

Cooperative Learning

What's in a Name?
Suggest that students work in groups of four to construct a time line showing the sequence of city names for Constantinople (Byzantium, Constantinople, and Istanbul). Each entry should indicate who ruled the city, who took over the city, the dominant religion of the conquerors, and the meaning of the new name for the city. Group members can choose roles such as researcher, designer, artist, and narrator or presenter. *English Language Learners, Visual*

Answers to ...

A CITY ON TWO CONTINENTS

Constantinople, located on two continents, was accessible by both land and sea.

A City on Two Continents

Today, Constantinople is known as Istanbul. It is the largest city in Turkey. Centuries ago it was a large city, too. In A.D. 1000, it spread across the fringes of Europe and Asia at the Bosporus, and had a population of about one million people. **Critical Thinking** How did Constantinople's location help its development as a trade center?

Constantinople's Geography

From the 600s to the 1400s, the Byzantines used "Greek fire" to defend their capital against attacks by outside groups. All of these groups wanted to control Constantinople. The map at the beginning of this chapter can help you understand why.

Locate Constantinople on the map. Notice that it is located on the Bosporus. The Bosporus is a **strait**, or a narrow passage that links two bodies of water. It connects the Black Sea and the Sea of Marmara, which flows into the Mediterranean Sea. The Bosporus also links two continents, Europe and Asia.

Constantinople's location made it a natural crossroads of trade. The Byzantines grew rich from the trade routes that they controlled—from Moscow to the Mediterranean, and from China all the way to Western Europe. The Byzantines charged duties, or taxes, on all goods that went through the city. They made money off of every item traded.

Building the Byzantine Empire

Constantinople was not always a Byzantine city. First, it was part of Greece. Later, it was part of the Roman Empire. In these times, the city was called Byzantium.

Resource Directory

Program Resources

Nystrom Desk Atlas

Media and Technology

📽 Color Transparencies 89, 90

💿 **Planet Earth** CD-ROM includes satellite images and physical maps of the Mediterranean world which allow students to view the physical geography of the region.

In A.D. 330, Constantine, the first Christian emperor of the Roman Empire, moved his capital from Rome to Byzantium. The city was then renamed Constantinople, which means "City of Constantine." Today, the city belongs to the modern country of Turkey and is called Istanbul.

The Roman Empire Splits into East and West Perhaps you already know something about the great Roman Empire, from which the Byzantine empire emerged. At its height, the Roman Empire reached all the way from Britain to Egypt.

But even the greatest and most powerful empires do not last forever. In your own lifetime, the world has seen the breakup of an empire called the Soviet Union. Hundreds of years ago, the Roman Empire broke apart. It split into eastern and western divisions.

The western half of the Roman Empire was overrun by invaders in A.D. 476. The eastern half survived as the Byzantine empire until 1453. Why did the Byzantine empire last so long? The simple answer is trade. Because Constantinople was a trading crossroads, the empire remained strong.

The Byzantines also had a strong army, the best in the world. Byzantine fighters used not only "Greek fire," but many other weapons, including stone missiles, to drive back their enemies.

A Great Emperor Clever rulers also helped to maintain the empire. Byzantine emperors had much more power than most rulers have today. They thought of themselves as representatives of God on the Earth.

Among the greatest of Byzantine emperors was Justinian, who ruled from 527 to 565. Justinian was not a typical emperor. He was born into a poor family, and he married an actress. He was easygoing and polite with everyone. He never lost his temper, even when provoked. Also, he was ready to listen to the ideas of all his subjects, from the highest noble to the poorest peasant. At the same time, he was very stubborn. His advisers knew that once he had made a decision, there was no point in trying to change his mind.

Justinian ruled long and well. His success was due, in part, to hard work. He had great energy and self-discipline, and rarely gave up on a task until it was completed. Another reason for Justinian's success was his wife, Theodora. As empress, she took an active role in politics. Many of Justinian's most intelligent decisions were made on her advice.

Yeats and Byzantium The great Irish poet William Butler Yeats wrote a poem called "Sailing to Byzantium." In it, Byzantium symbolizes a culture that stresses youth and art. Yeats describes an artificial bird made "of hammered gold and gold enameling." Legends said that birds like this "sang" from trees also made of gold. These legends also said that the goldsmiths who made the singing birds came from Greece.

▼ In this mosaic made in the 500s, the Empress Theodora is shown wearing a crown. Theodora is famous for many things, including the work she did to gain rights for Byzantine women.

Program Resources

Interdisciplinary Explorations
The Glory of Ancient Rome

3 Teach
Have students develop an outline script for a television news magazine report titled "The Long-Lived Byzantine Empire: Causes and Effects." Students may suggest the use of visual images, choosing from section art if they wish. This activity should take about 30 minutes.

4 Assess
See the Answers to the Section Review. You may also assess students' scripts.

Acceptable scripts identify the importance of location and religion.

Commendable scripts use section artwork creatively to demonstrate causes and effects.

Outstanding scripts recognize the lasting impact of the Byzantine empire.

Background

Biography

The Woman Behind the Throne Theodora, wife of Emperor Justinian, proved to be an influential empress. She was involved in diplomacy, urging parties to abide by a peace treaty. She instituted disaster relief, helping the residents of Antioch after an earthquake destroyed their city. Under her auspices, hospitals for the poor were established. Theodora also championed women's rights, prohibiting the traffic of young girls and easing the laws of divorce to give greater benefits to women. Theodora was evidently formidable. Opponents often disappeared without a trace.

Background

Global Perspective

Silk Intrigues Justinian worked diligently to maintain Constantinople's position as a trade center for goods coming from China. When wars with Persia closed part of the Silk Road, Justinian tried to establish alternate routes to China but had little success. However, in the mid 500s, two Persian monks smuggled a load of silkworms out of China. They exchanged the silkworms and their knowledge of the industry for a monetary reward. The booty was used to start a lucrative state-owned silk industry.

Background

Links Across Time

Code of Hammurabi Justinian was not the first ruler to set down a code of specific laws. Hammurabi, was responsible for the Code of Hammurabi, produced 2,300 years earlier. Like Justinian, Hammurabi did not make up the laws. Rather, each of the rulers was instrumental in clarifying the laws, eliminating conflicting laws, and making certain that citizens of the empire knew what the laws were and what punishments would accrue for breaking the laws.

READ ACTIVELY

Ask Questions Think of questions you might ask about the role of religion in the breakup of the Byzantine empire.

Fall of the Byzantine Empire

After Justinian's death in 565, the Byzantine empire began to decline. In 1453, it completely collapsed. This fall was sparked by an argument about politics and religion.

A Religious Dispute Most of the people and all of the rulers in the Byzantine empire were Christians. However, they did not agree on how to worship God. Some people prayed to saints or holy people represented on **icons,** or paintings of these saints or holy people. Others believed that people should pray only to God. The Byzantine empire grew weaker as its people took sides on religious questions.

The religious arguments spread from Constantinople to Rome. The **patriarch,** leader of the Church in Constantinople, and the pope, leader of the Church in Rome, took opposite sides. In 1054, they each took steps to throw the other out of the Church.

Holy Paintings

Byzantine Christians treasured icons like this one of Mary and Jesus. They kept these holy paintings in their churches and their homes, where they worshipped and prayed before them. Artists made icons by applying color in hot wax or egg yolk to a board covered with plaster, glue, and cloth. **Critical Thinking** How did the issue of icons help to cause a split in the Christian Church?

Answers to ...

HOLY PAINTINGS

Some people prayed to saints depicted on icons; others prayed only to God, including the patriarch in Constantinople and the pope in Rome.

In late March, 1453, a force of about 70,000 Ottoman Turks surrounded the city of Constantinople. The defending force, which numbered about 7,000, held out for two months. On May 29, 1453, however, the city fell to the Ottomans. This French painting of the attack shows a key to the Ottoman victory. The Ottomans dragged some of their ships overland and launched them into Constantinople's harbor—practically inside the city. **Critical Thinking** Why do you think so many different groups of people wanted to gain control of Constantinople?

Background

Links Across Time

A New Architecture
Among the most tangible of Justinian's accomplishments is the characteristic great dome architecture of Byzantine churches. Justinian relied on two mathematicians, Anthemius of Tralles and Isidorus of Miletus, to create an entirely new concept for the design of Hagia Sophia, destined to be Constantinople's cathedral. The church design focuses on a huge central dome supported by exterior arches rather than interior pillars and required innovations in engineering as well as architecture. The result is an unusually spacious interior.

These acts by the Church's most powerful leaders led to a **schism,** or split, in the Christian world. Like the Roman Empire, the Church was divided into eastern and western halves. In the Byzantine east, the Church was called Greek Orthodox. In the west, it was called Roman Catholic. The Roman Catholic and Orthodox Churches remain separate today.

The Fall of Constantinople Splitting from the Roman Catholic Church made the Byzantine empire a target for invasion. Encouraged by the Roman Catholic Church, an army from the west attacked Constantinople in 1204. This army captured, but could not hold, the city. Later, the Italian city of Venice took control of Constantinople. Eventually, in 1453, it was captured by the Ottoman Turks, non-Christian enemies of the Byzantines.

What the Byzantines Gave Us

Major achievements of the Byzantines affect our world today. Perhaps the most important is a system of laws.

The Code of Justinian When Justinian became emperor, laws were completely disorganized. Some laws repeated others. Some laws contradicted each other. The greatest minds in the Byzantine empire could not make sense of the law—much less enforce it.

READ ACTIVELY

Connect What happens when you play a game and the rules are not clear and easy to understand?

Answers to ...

THE FALL OF CONSTANTINOPLE

Its location made it a natural crossroads for trade. The people of the city grew rich from the trade routes they controlled.

Section 1 Review

1. (a) narrow passage linking two bodies of water (b) painting of a holy person (c) leader of the Church of Constantinople (d) split

2. (a) important emperor of Byzantium (b) city from which Prince Igor of Russia tried unsuccessfully to invade Byzantium (c) capital of the Byzantine empire (d) capital of the western Roman Empire and the center of the Roman Catholic Church (e) Italian city that controlled Constantinople during its declining years

3. trade

4. Students may note the Code of Justinian, laws that still form part of European legal systems, and the preservation of ancient Greek and Roman achievements for modern use.

5. Possible answer: Religion was important, and a disagreement over such a key issue led people to take sides against one another. With one side centered in Rome, with the pope, and the other in Constantinople, with the patriarch, the schism naturally resulted.

6. Letters should note the strategic location of the city for trade.

▲ Hagia Sophia, the largest church in the Byzantine empire, was the greatest monument of Justinian's reign. It took 10,000 workers five years to build the massive church with its 185-foot (56-m) high dome.

Justinian ordered his lawyers to clean up the mess. They worked long and hard to write a summary, called the Code of Justinian, that clearly spelled out the laws and explained their meanings. The Code became the backbone of the legal systems of many European nations.

Preserving Ancient Knowledge The Byzantines made another great contribution to our world. They recorded and saved the knowledge of ancient Greece and Rome. The period of Byzantine rule in the east was a period of disorder and destruction in Western Europe. If the Byzantines had not copied and cared for ancient books, Greek and Roman advances in science, mathematics, and health care would have been lost.

SECTION 1 REVIEW

1. Define (a) strait, (b) icon, (c) patriarch, (d) schism.

2. Identify (a) Justinian, (b) Moscow, (c) Constantinople, (d) Rome, (e) Venice.

3. On what was the power and strength of the Byzantine empire based?

4. How do Byzantine achievements affect the world today?

Critical Thinking

5. Drawing Conclusions Why do you think the disagreement over icons led to the split in the Christian Church?

Activity

6. Writing to Learn You are a foreign visitor to Constantinople. Write a letter to your country's leaders explaining why they might want to gain control of the city.

Resource Directory

Teaching Resources

📁 **Critical Thinking Activity** in the Chapter and Section Support booklet, p. 20, helps students apply the skill of identifying central issues.

📁 **Section Quiz** in the Chapter and Section Support booklet, p. 6, covers the main ideas and key terms in the section. Available in Spanish in the Spanish Support booklet, p. 5.

The Rise and Spread of Islam

BEFORE YOU READ

Reach Into Your Background

If you spent a lot of time exploring wild and lonely places, what would you think about? In this section, you will read about a holy man who had an important experience while spending time alone.

Questions to Explore

1. How did the geography of the Arabian Peninsula affect Arab culture?
2. How did Muhammad's teachings spread?

Key Terms

nomad
prophet
hijra

Key People and Places

Muhammad
Khadijah
Mecca
Medina

The religion of Islam teaches that in about A.D. 610, a man named Muhammad went into a cave in the desert to pray. Suddenly he heard the voice of an angel cry, "Proclaim!" (To proclaim means to announce or declare something.)

Stunned, Muhammad asked, "What shall I proclaim?" The answer came quickly. He was to proclaim the one true God.

According to Muslim teaching, Muhammad was frightened at first. He was unsure that he was worthy of this mission. But he obeyed. And his acceptance of the command to "proclaim God" brought great changes to the world.

Geography of the Arabian Peninsula

Muhammad lived on the Arabian Peninsula, in the city of Mecca. Locate the peninsula on the map on the next page. Then find Mecca. It lies about 45 miles (72 km) inland from the Red Sea. As the map shows, Mecca sits on the eastern edge of a large desert. The desert takes up most of the Arabian Peninsula.

▼ In Muhammad's time—as today—a huge desert covered much of the Arabian Peninsula.

Teaching Resources

📁 **Reproducible Lesson Plan** in the Chapter and Section Support booklet, p. 7, provides a summary of the section lesson.

📁 **Guided Reading and Review** in the Chapter and Section Support booklet, p. 8, provides a structure for mastering key concepts and reviewing key terms in the section. Available in Spanish in the Spanish Support booklet, p. 6.

Lesson Objectives

1 Explain the impact of geography on Arab culture.

2 Trace the spread of Muhammad's teachings.

Lesson Plan

1 Engage

Warm–Up Activity

Ask students to recall a recent major change such as changing schools or relocating to a new community. Discuss the feelings students have had about these changes, focusing on the idea that change is both exciting and potentially frightening.

Activating Prior Knowledge

Have students read Reach Into Your Background in the Before You Read box. Prompt students to consider times when they explored wild and lonely places with their minds, for example, when lying in bed at night or while reading a book about the wilderness.

2 Explore

Post the following questions for students to consider as they read the section text: What was life like for Bedouins living on the Arabian Peninsula? How did religion play a role in that life? What were some different reactions to Muhammad's teachings? Why did people react as they did, both negatively and positively?

Background

Links Across Time

New Business Methods
From 750 to 1350, Muslims dominated the trade routes along the Silk Road, in West Africa, in East Africa, and in India. They not only found new and exotic goods to trade, they developed new and exotic ways to trade. They bought and sold goods on credit, they set up partnerships, and they established locations for exchanging currency. To avoid carrying large sums of cash across thousands of miles, they developed a way to transfer money from one location to another—a precursor to today's checks. Merchants could deposit funds at one location and, with a letter of credit, withdraw funds at a second location.

Answers to ...

MAP STUDY

Cairo, Jerusalem, and Damascus

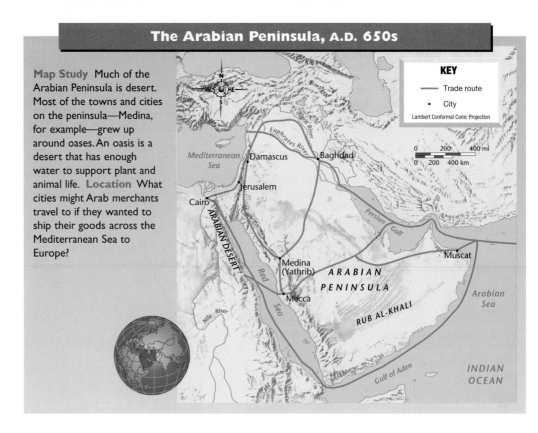

The Arabian Peninsula, A.D. 650s

Map Study Much of the Arabian Peninsula is desert. Most of the towns and cities on the peninsula—Medina, for example—grew up around oases. An oasis is a desert that has enough water to support plant and animal life. **Location** What cities might Arab merchants travel to if they wanted to ship their goods across the Mediterranean Sea to Europe?

KEY
— Trade route
• City
Lambert Conformal Conic Projection

ACROSS THE WORLD

"Hub Cities" Trade hubs like Mecca became great cities all over the world. London, England, grew into a great city because it is a port. Ships from all over the world brought goods to London that were then sent throughout the British empire. St. Louis, Missouri, lies where the Mississippi and Missouri rivers join. These rivers were major shipping routes. St. Louis also was the jumping off place for settlers moving west.

An Avenue of Trade Mecca was a crossroads on a busy avenue of trade when Muhammad was growing up in the late 500s. Long camel trains filed through the city. They carried perfumes, ivory, spices, silk, and precious metals such as gold.

From Mecca, some caravans traveled northwest to markets in what today is Syria. From Syria, goods could be shipped across the Mediterranean Sea to Europe. Other caravans turned northeast after leaving Mecca. They made a dangerous journey across the desert to markets in the area now known as Iraq.

Bedouins and Merchants The desert was home to many groups of Bedouins (BED oo inz), an Arab people. The Bedouins were **nomads,** or people who moved from one area to another. To make a living, they herded sheep, camels, and goats. They followed planned routes, traveling from one water hole to the next. The desert yielded little food for the Bedouins' animals. Mostly they grazed on thorny bushes. Water was also scarce, for people as well as animals. Well water was often so bitter or salty that only the animals could drink it.

In addition to herding animals, the Bedouins acted as guides for trade caravans. Occasionally they would raid one of the caravans, stealing all the trade goods. To avoid being robbed, Meccan traders often

Resource Directory

Teaching Resources

Maps with Accurate Shapes: Conformal Maps in the Social Studies and Geography Skills booklet, p. 15, provides additional skill practice.

Program Resources

Outline Maps Saudi Arabia: Political, p. 30;
North Africa: Political, p. 31;
South Asia: Physical, p. 36

Media and Technology

Color Transparencies Historical Map Set 3

Planet Earth CD-ROM includes World Wonders, Cultural: Hagia Sophia, Turkey.

made agreements with the Bedouins. Muhammad's great-grandfather, a wealthy merchant, helped to make these agreements.

Meccan merchants used religion to seal their alliances with the Bedouins. The merchants invited their Bedouin allies to worship in a holy place called the Kabah (KAH buh). The Kabah was a cube-shaped building in the center of Mecca. It held a rock known as the Black Stone, a meteorite that had fallen to the Earth from space. The Black Stone was sacred to the Meccans. The Kabah also contained many other objects that were sacred to Meccans and Bedouins alike.

Meccans closely guarded the Kabah and all the holy objects that it contained. The Kabah drew worshippers from all over Arabia. The Kabah is shown in the picture below.

Muhammad's Life

Though Muhammad's great-grandfather was a wealthy merchant, Muhammad did not grow up rich. By the time he was born, about 570, the family had fallen on hard times.

In addition to being poor, Muhammad was also an orphan. His parents died before he turned seven years old. An uncle took care of Muhammad until he grew up. Then Muhammad went to work in Mecca's brisk caravan trade. Muhammad's job took him to many other parts of the world. Several times he traveled to Syria, which was then part of the Byzantine empire.

A Place of Worship

Muslims consider the Kabah the holiest site in all of Islam. When Muslims worship at the Kabah, they put on two white sheets with no seams—a sign of innocence. Then they walk around the Kabah seven times. You can see that the people in the picture are moving—they appear blurred. Finally, they touch or kiss the Black Stone embedded in the southeast side of the Kabah.
Critical Thinking Why was the Kabah important to the people of Arabia?

3 Teach

Have students create a flow-chart about the rise and spread of Islam. Charts should include callouts or labels at intervals to identify and explain key events or stages in the flow. Students' conclusions or generalizations should be supported by data from the text. This activity should take about 20 minutes.

Activity

Journal Writing

Early Life Talk with students about Muhammad's early life experiences. Ask students how these experiences might affect a boy's developing character. Then challenge students to write a brief character description of Muhammad in their journals. Suggest that they draw on his life experiences to support their descriptions.

Answers to . . .

A PLACE OF WORSHIP

The Kabah holds a meteorite, the Black Stone, sacred to Meccans, as well as other holy objects sacred to Meccans and Bedouins alike.

4 Assess

See the answers to the Section Review. You may also assess students' flowcharts.

Acceptable flowcharts include at least four accurate facts correctly sequenced.

Commendable flowcharts include some conclusions drawn from section text.

Outstanding flowcharts note the disparity of people's reactions to Muhammad's teachings.

Activity

Critical Thinking

Distinguishing Facts From Opinions *Suitable as a whole class activity.* Have a volunteer read aloud the first two paragraphs under *The Hijra: From Mecca to Medina.* Ask students to identify some facts and opinions in the text. For example, it is a fact that many Meccans disagreed with Muhammad. However, their ideas—that the new religion threatened their old gods and so on—represent opinions. *English Language Learners*

READ ACTIVELY

Ask Questions What do you want to know about Muhammad's work?

When he was 25 years old, Muhammad married a wealthy widow named Khadijah (kha DEE jah). Muhammad had worked for Khadijah before they got married. She had been impressed by his hard work and honesty. After their marriage, Muhammad continued to manage caravans for Khadijah. In his free time, he walked in the hills outside Mecca. Troubled by problems he saw in society, Muhammad liked to be alone to pray and think. It was during one of these trips to the hills that he heard the angel's command to proclaim the message of God.

Muhammad's Mission The angel said that people had abandoned the true faith. Instead of worshipping God alone, they worshipped many idols, or false gods. The angel gave Muhammad a mission. He was to pass on to the people all the messages that he would receive from God. Then the people would submit to, or agree to obey, the one true God. Muhammad would begin with the Arabs, but God's message was for the whole world.

Muhammad did as he was told. People who accepted his teachings came to be known as Muslims, which means "persons who submit." Their faith came to be known as Islam, which means "submission to God."

► ▼ After Mecca and Medina, Jerusalem, in the country of Israel, is the holiest city in Islam. The Shrine of the Rock (right), with its gleaming bronze dome, was built in A.D. 691 over the spot where Muslims believe Muhammad rose into heaven. The entrance to the shrine (below), is decorated with Islamic holy writings.

The Hijra: From Mecca to Medina Few Meccans listened to Muhammad. They thought his teachings about the new religion threatened their old gods. Abandoning the old gods, they thought, would end Mecca's importance as a place for worshippers.

Muhammad also taught that all people were brothers and sisters in a community established by God. This idea, too, angered the Meccans. They shouted insults at Muhammad when he preached. They threw garbage and stones at his followers. As time went on, the attacks became more and more violent. Eventually Muhammad and his followers were forced to flee the city.

People in Yathrib (YATH rub), a city north of Mecca, invited Muhammad to come to their city. They saw him as a wise man who could settle disputes in their city. Many of them also believed that Muhammad was a **prophet,** or a person who carried God's message. Muhammad seized this opportunity. In 622, he and his followers went to Yathrib.

The movement of early Muslims from Mecca to Yathrib is known as the **hijra** (HIJ rah), which means "the migration." The year of the hijra, 622, became year 1 on the Muslim calendar.

After the hijra, the name of Yathrib was changed to *Medina,* which means "city" and is short for "city of the Prophet." Medina quickly became a great Islamic center.

Expansion of Islam

Look at the map on the next page. As it shows, Islam did not remain limited to the city of Medina. In 630, Muhammad returned in triumph to Mecca. By the time of Muhammad's death in 632, Islam had spread across the Arabian Peninsula. Within the next 100 years, Islam surged west to North Africa, Spain, and southern France. It pushed east to the borders of northern India and China.

How did Islam spread so far so fast? One reason was that people did not like the nearby Byzantine and Persian empires. Their rulers were harsh and oppressive. The new religion promised a new way of life that made sense. Also, Muhammad and his people were expert traders. Merchants traveled to many parts of Asia, North Africa, and the Mediterranean Coast. They took their religion with them.

City of the Prophet

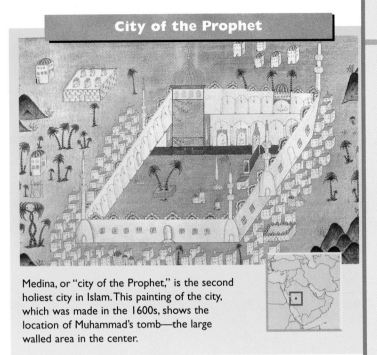

Medina, or "city of the Prophet," is the second holiest city in Islam. This painting of the city, which was made in the 1600s, shows the location of Muhammad's tomb—the large walled area in the center.

Muhammad and the Spider There are many legends about the time of the hijra. One of the most famous tells about a spider's role in saving Muhammad's life. When Muhammad fled from Mecca, he entered a cave to rest. After he had gone into the cave, a spider spun a web across the entrance. Muhammad's pursuers saw the web across the entrance and were convinced that he could not be in the cave. They went on and Muhammad was saved.

Activity

Interdisciplinary Connections

Mathematics Using a Gregorian calendar—which dates time from the birth of Jesus Christ—and information from the text, have students calculate the current year on the Muslim calendar. Then challenge students to calculate the Muslim dates for dates you provide, such as the date of the founding of your community, Columbus' arrival in the Americas, a student's birthday. (all dates are [Gregorian date] − 622 years)

Activity

Critical Thinking

Recognizing Cause and Effect *Suitable as an individual activity.* Tell students to write a brief cause-and-effect paragraph explaining why Islam spread so quickly. Urge students to use a cause-and-effect diagram to outline their thinking before they begin to write. Remind students that some effects have multiple causes. *Visual, English Language Learners*

Resource Directory

Teaching Resources

📁 **Section Quiz** in the Chapter and Section Support booklet, p. 9, covers the main ideas and key terms in the section. Available in Spanish in the Spanish Support booklet, p. 7.

1. (a) person who moves often from one area to another (b) person who carried God's message (c) movement of early Muslims from Mecca to Yathrib

2. (a) prophet who received and spread the messages from God which became the Muslim faith (b) Muhammad's wife (c) crossroads of trade where Muhammad grew up (d) city where Muhammad fled after Meccans rejected his teachings

3. The desert offered so little food and water that Bedouins had to move often to find enough for themselves and their animals. Their nomadic lifestyle enabled them also to become guides for traders passing through the area.

4. Muslim traders brought their religion with them as they traveled to Asia, North Africa, and the Mediterranean Coast. The religion promised a new way of life, a life without harsh and oppressive rulers.

5. People ignored his teachings; people attacked Muhammad when he preached.

6. Speeches should reflect Muhammad's teachings.

Answers to ...
MAP STUDY

632–1500; Muhammad and his people were traders who traveled to many parts of Asia, North Africa, and the Mediterranean Coast taking their religion with them.

The Spread of Islam

Map Study In a little over 100 years after Muhammad's death, Islam had spread from Arabia east into Southwest Asia and west across North Africa into southern Europe. By the 1500s, it had spread into West Africa and Central and South Asia. **Place** Between which years did Islam spread to India? **Movement** What impact might trade have had on the spread of Islam?

ATLANTIC OCEAN
Tours
FRANCE
SPAIN
Cordoba
Rome
Granada
Black Sea
Constantinople
NORTH AFRICA
Mediterranean Sea
Damascus
Baghdad
Alexandria
Jerusalem
Cairo
PERSIA
INDIA
SAHARA
ARABIAN DESERT
EGYPT
Medina
Mecca
ARABIA
Arabian Sea
Bay of Bengal
Caspian Sea
Red Sea

INDIAN OCEAN

KEY
☐ Muslim lands by A.D. 632
☐ Muslim lands by A.D. 661
☐ Muslim lands by A.D. 750
☐ Muslim lands by A.D. 1500
• City
Lambert Azimuthal Equal-Area Projection

0   600   1,200 mi
0   600   1,200 km

Another key reason for the spread of Islam was that Muhammad united the Arabs in his region into one community. Once they were working together, they became a powerful people. Islam respected Jews and Christians. It also recognized Abraham, Moses, Jesus, and others as earlier prophets. Jews and Christians were allowed to practice their own faiths. They did, however, have to pay special taxes.

SECTION 2 REVIEW

1. Define (a) nomad, (b) prophet, (c) hijra.

2. Identify (a) Muhammad, (b) Khadijah, (c) Mecca, (d) Medina.

3. How did the geography in which the Bedouins lived affect their lives?

4. How did Islam spread beyond Arabia?

Critical Thinking

5. Expressing Problems Clearly Briefly state two problems Muhammad faced in Mecca when he began teaching.

Activity

6. Writing to Learn You are a Bedouin herder at the time Muhammad was beginning to preach. Write a speech to deliver to fellow Bedouins. In the speech, tell why you think Muhammad's teachings will help improve your life.

SKILLS MINI LESSON

Using Isolines
To **introduce** the skill, explain that *isoline* means "equal lines." Direct students' attention to the isolines on the Spread of Islam map. Point out that the lines on this map connect places where Islam had spread as of a certain date. Have students **practice** the skill by identifying the different time periods indicated on the map and noting the colors or patterns used to highlight each time period. Then challenge students to **apply** the skill by identifying places where Islam spread during each of the four time periods.

The Religion of Islam

BEFORE YOU READ

Reach Into Your Background

What beliefs do you share with friends or family members? Perhaps you share beliefs about right and wrong or good and bad. In this section, you will learn about the beliefs shared by Muslims.

Questions to Explore

1. What basic beliefs do Muslims share?
2. What beliefs do Muslims share with Christians and Jews?

Key Terms
muezzin
mosque
Ramadan
hajj
Quran

Key People
Shiites
Sunnis

Lesson Objectives

1 Identify basic beliefs shared by Muslims.

2 Describe some beliefs shared by Muslims, Jews, and Christians.

Lesson Plan

1 Engage

Warm–Up Activity

Encourage students to list in their journals how *they* view Muslims. Urge them to draw both on earlier sections in this book and on their own knowledge and experiences. Tell students to keep their lists for comparison and revision as they read Section 3.

Activating Prior Knowledge

Have students read Reach Into Your Background in the Before You Read box. Then invite volunteers to share some of their responses with the class. Note on the chalkboard some commonly held beliefs. Remind all students to be respectful of each other's beliefs.

A **muezzin** (moo EZ in), a man who calls Muslims to prayer, looks out over the city and begins his call to noon prayers. The call rings out in four directions. "There is no god but God, and Muhammad is His prophet."

All over the world, faithful Muslims heed the call. Some kneel in houses of worship called **mosques** (mahsks). Others kneel outside—on the banks of the Indus River, in the Arabian Desert, or along the Mediterranean Sea. No matter where they are, the kneeling Muslims face Mecca. "There is no god but God," the faithful respond, "and Muhammad is His prophet."

Muslim Belief

This scene of prayer has been repeated around the world every day for hundreds of years. No matter where they live, Muslims share beliefs with others in the Islamic world. Their basic beliefs are expressed in what Muslims call the Five Pillars of Islam: faith, prayer, sharing, fasting, and pilgrimage. These five practices are the foundations of Islam.

▼ A muezzin calls Muslims to prayer from the top of this graceful spiral minaret in Samarra, Iraq.

Resource Directory

Teaching Resources

📁 **Reproducible Lesson Plan** in the Chapter and Section Support booklet, p. 10, provides a summary of the section lesson.

📁 **Guided Reading and Review** in the Chapter and Section Support booklet, p. 11, provides a structure for mastering key concepts and reviewing key terms in the section. Available in Spanish in the Spanish Support booklet, p. 8.

2 Explore

As they read, have students try to answer the following questions: How does each of the Five Pillars of Islam work to hold Muslim communities together? How did medieval Muslims view Jews and Christians? Why do you think these relationships changed in other times? How was life different for Muslim men than for Muslim women? What key disagreement separated Shiites and Sunnis?

3 Teach

Have students create a Venn diagram comparing Muslim beliefs with those of Jews and Christians. Tell students to make the circle containing Muslim beliefs larger than that holding information about the ideas of Jews and Christians. Students may add a brief summary of the diagram. This activity should take about 15 minutes.

Background

Global Perspective

Same Stories, Three Books The Quran, the Christian Bible, and the Jewish Torah each mention the same important religious figures, for instance, Moses, Abraham, David, Solomon, Job, and Jonah. In fact, some stories—for example, the story of Noah and the Ark—can be found in all three books.

ACROSS THE WORLD

Common Practices Other major religious groups besides Muslims practice fasting. It may be required or voluntary. Christians, for instance, may fast during the season of Lent, which honors the 40 days that Jesus fasted in the wilderness. Jews fast on several occasions. The most important is Yom Kippur, or the Day of Atonement. Hindus and Buddhists also fast to celebrate certain holy days.

▶ Fasting during Ramadan is one of the five pillars of Muslim faith. These people in Cairo, Egypt, are waiting for the sunset prayer so they can break their daylong fast. In the time of the Muslim empire, people celebrated late into the night during Ramadan. Children carried small lanterns to light their way. Street magicians performed tricks, and storytellers and poets recited tales for the crowds.

The Five Pillars of Islam The first pillar, faith, is based on the words of the call to prayer: "There is no god but God, and Muhammad is His prophet." This call expresses the Muslim statement of faith. The belief in one God is also the basis for the Jewish and Christian religions.

Through the second pillar, prayer, Muslims communicate with God. The muezzin calls Muslims to prayer from the minaret, or tower, of a mosque. Muslims pray five times a day—in the morning, at noon, in the afternoon, at sunset, and in the evening. The muezzin signals the various prayer times.

The third pillar is sharing. Muslims who can do so give a generous share of what they own to Muslims who are poor or sick.

The fourth pillar, fasting, occurs during a special month called **Ramadan** (ram uh DAHN). During Ramadan, Muslims fast from sunrise to sunset every day. They neither eat nor drink. In the evenings, children stay up late and join their parents in breaking the fast with a sweet, such as a few dates, and a cool drink. Then everyone sits down to an "evening breakfast."

Resource Directory

Media and Technology

Color Transparency 92

Planet Earth CD-ROM includes Thematic Maps: World Religions which allows students to explore the influence of Islam in modern times.

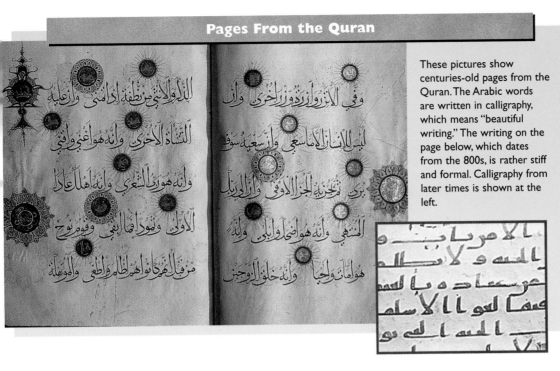

Pages From the Quran

These pictures show centuries-old pages from the Quran. The Arabic words are written in calligraphy, which means "beautiful writing." The writing on the page below, which dates from the 800s, is rather stiff and formal. Calligraphy from later times is shown at the left.

The fifth pillar is the **hajj** (haj), a pilgrimage, or sacred journey, to Mecca. All Muslims who can afford to do so try to make the hajj once in their lives. In Mecca, they meet other Muslims from all over the world.

The Quran   As you read about the Five Pillars, you may have gotten a sense that Islam is a not just a set of beliefs. It is a way of life. Islam is a guide to the way Muslims should live, conduct family life, and deal with others.

The things God revealed to Muhammad included the rules of Islam, which are written in a book called the **Quran** (koo RAHN). Many Muslims know the Quran by heart. Like the Torah, or Jewish holy book, and the Christian Bible, the Quran contains many kinds of writing, including stories, promises, warnings, and instructions.

Relationships Outside and Inside Islam

There is a reason for the similarity of the Quran to Jewish and Christian holy books. Muslims, like Jews and Christians, regard Adam, Noah, Abraham, and Moses as important people in their religious histories. Muhammad saw himself as the last prophet in a long line of prophets that included all of these people.

People of the Book   Muhammad felt respect for Jews and Christians. He called them "people of the Book." Muslims, Jews, and Christians all practice a religion revealed in holy writings. They all believe in one single God.

4 Assess

See the answers to the Section Review. You may also assess students' diagrams.

Acceptable diagrams contain factual entries in each section.

Commendable diagrams list Muslim beliefs in sufficient detail to note differences within the faith.

Outstanding diagrams include a summary recognizing major areas of overlap between the three religions.

Activity

Interdisciplinary Connections

Art   Islam opposed depicting images of living things—people or animals. This forced Islamic artists to find other sources of inspiration. They developed geometric patterning and a scrollwork called arabesque. Copies of the Quran, particularly those made from 700–1000, also relied on calligraphy, the art of beautiful writing. Have students develop designs for borders and small illustrations using either arabesques or calligraphy. Invite volunteers to share their art with the class. *Visual*

Explore the Role of Women Organize students into groups to create written, oral, or pictorial comparisons between the role of women in Islam and the role of women in other cultures and times. Students may be grouped according to chosen cultures/ times or by tasks such as research, writing, or exhibit preparation. Some possible cultures/times for compari-son include Victorian England, the United States about 1900, ancient Rome, modern China, and Orthodox Judaism. *Visual*

Links Across Time

Iran When the Safavid tribe conquered Iran in the 1500s, they secured power in part by joining forces with Shiite religious leaders. Iran became a primarily Shiite Islamic state. Shiite Muslims gathered here, emigrating from Sunni–ruled states. Shiite rulers in Iran exerted strong power within the nation, as both government and citizens respected their position. Religious leaders retain this influence in Iran today.

Answers to ...

A MUSLIM WOMAN

Men were more likely to be involved in life outside the home. Men inherited a greater share of property when a parent died.

Rulers of the Muslim empire saw Jews and Christians as "protected people." As long as they accepted Muslim rule, Jews and Christians were allowed to practice their religions. They were also free to pursue their own business affairs.

Men's and Women's Roles Muhammad insisted that all Muslims were equal in spirit—whether rich or poor, men or women. This equality allowed women to have many rights in early Islamic society that they did not have in other lands. For instance, they had a right to an education and could not be married without their agreement.

Despite this type of equality, men and women had very different roles in Islamic communities. Men were more likely to be involved in life outside the home. They inherited a greater share of property after a parent died. Muslim men were expected to treat their wives kindly and to provide for them.

As Islam moved into other lands, Muslims sometimes adopted the attitudes toward women that they found in the places they conquered. In a few Muslim countries today, women must cover their faces when they go out of the house. Some Muslims find support for this in the Quran, which says that all believers, both men and women, should dress modestly.

Schism: Sunni and Shiite Muslims Earlier you read about a schism that split the Christian Church in two at the time of the Byzantine empire. A schism, or split, also occurred in Islam.

A Muslim Woman

Arabs who settled in Persia and Byzantine lands adopted the practice of secluding women in a separate part of the house. From this section of the home, women planned and oversaw the day-to-day life of the household. This painting, which was made in the late 1500s, shows a Persian woman sitting in her garden and writing. **Critical Thinking** How did the roles of Muslim men and women differ?

◄ These men and boys are worshipping at a mosque in Brunei, a small nation in Southeast Asia. Like most Muslims, they are Sunni. Only about 10 percent of all Muslims are Shiites.

In 656, Uthman (ooth MAHN), the ruler of the Muslim empire, died. His death split the Islamic world in two. The two groups disagreed over who should be the rightful leader of Islam.

The smaller group, the Shiites (SHEE eyets), argued that the ruler should be a direct descendant of Muhammad. They believed that Muhammad's descendants would be inspired by God, just as Muhammad had been. They also thought that this leader should tell Muslims what the Quran means.

The larger group of Muslims, the Sunni (SOON ee), disagreed. They argued that any truly religious Muslim could lead the community. They believed that no one man, not even the leader of Islam, should tell Muslims what the Quran taught. The Sunni argued that a group of Muslim scholars could best say what the holy book means.

SECTION 3 REVIEW

1. **Define** (a) muezzin, (b) mosque, (c) Ramadan, (d) hajj, (e) Quran.

2. **Identify** (a) Shiites, (b) Sunni.

3. What shared beliefs unite Muslims?

4. What do Muslims, Jews, and Christians have in common?

Critical Thinking

5. **Identifying Central Issues** One of Islam's pillars is sharing. How would sharing one's wealth help the community? What do you think would happen if people in the community did not share their wealth with people who were less fortunate?

Activity

6. **Writing to Learn** A friend has asked you to explain the Muslim religion. Write a letter describing the Five Pillars of Islam.

Resource Directory

Teaching Resources

 **Section Quiz** in the Chapter and Section Support booklet, p. 12, covers the main ideas and key terms in the section. Available in Spanish in the Spanish Support booklet, p. 9.

Section 3 Review

1. (a) man who calls Muslims to prayer (b) Muslim house of worship (c) month in Muslim calendar during which fasting occurs (d) pilgrimage to Mecca (e) Muslim sacred book

2. (a) minority of Muslims who believe religious leaders must be direct descendants of Muhammad (b) majority of Muslims who believe any religious Muslim can lead a community

3. Five Pillars of Islam, use of the Quran, and ideas about equality and roles of men and women

4. belief in one God, use of a sacred book, shared prophets, and key figures in religious history

5. Students may note that sharing wealth helps more fragile parts of the community grow stronger and that without sharing, those fragile elements might fail, or break.

6. Letters should accurately name and describe the Five Pillars: faith, prayer, sharing, fasting, and the hajj.

Lesson Objectives

① Explain the elements and function of a table.

② Read a table in context.

Lesson Plan

1 Engage

Warm-Up Activity

To **introduce** the skill, have students read the opening paragraphs of the activity. Draw a workstation table on the chalkboard, writing the word *chores* on its surface. Draw a large slash through the entire picture.

Activating Prior Knowledge

Invite students to come to the chalkboard and draw the kind of table Damon and Angie are discussing.

2 Explore

Direct students' attention to the sample table. Ask a volunteer to read aloud the Get Ready text. Point out and correct any discrepancies between the sample table and those drawn on the chalkboard by students. Then have students read the rest of the Skills Activity.

3 Teach

Allow students to work in small groups or independently to create the table described in Try It Out. As they **practice**, urge students to place data carefully in the correct cells. Ask volunteers to explain their tables to the class.

Reading Tables

"**A**ngie, it's your turn to take out the garbage," said Damon. His sister Angie looked surprised.

"No, it isn't!" she said. "I took it out last week."

"Maya took it out last week," Damon said. "And I took it out the week before. Now it's your turn to take out the garbage, my turn to vacuum, and Maya's turn to do laundry."

Angie shook her head. "Wait a minute, Maya did laundry last week, and you vacuumed, didn't you? You have it all mixed up."

"How are we supposed to figure this out?" said Damon. "It gets too confusing."

"We just need to keep it straight. Why don't we make a table?"

Damon nodded. "You know, that is not a bad idea, Angie! One look at a table of our chores would settle our fights."

Get Ready

Damon and Angie hit upon a good way to organize information. A simple table would keep track of who should do what chores on which days. Tables help you to organize ideas in a visual way. A table can sometimes answer a question better than a written paragraph.

You see tables all the time. Most of your textbooks include tables. You will also find them in newspapers, in magazines, and in computer programs. With tables, people can arrange ideas in a way that is easy to understand at a glance.

Resource Directory

Teaching Resources

Reading a Table in the Social Studies and Geography Skills booklet, p. 62, provides additional skill practice.

Try It Out

Here is your chance to make and use a table of something you are very familiar with—weekly household or classroom chores. Make your table by following the illustration and these three simple steps.

A. Choose a topic for your table. Every table has a topic, or subject. You will make a table called *Chores for a Month.* It will show the classroom or household chores that different people have to do each week.

B. Create the columns for your table. Create the columns for your table. A table is made up of vertical columns and horizontal rows. Your table will have one column for each week of the month. The columns will be labelled *Week 1, Week 2, Week 3,* and *Week 4.*

C. Create the rows for your table. Each row lists one chore, such as emptying the wastebasket or washing the chalkboards.

D. Put the data in your table. In each cell of the table, write the name of the person or group who is to do that chore that week. To begin, put your finger on the label of the first chore, and trace the row until your finger is under *Week 1.* In that cell, write the name of the person or group who must do the first chore during the first week. Follow the same steps for the other chores and other weeks.

Now look at your completed table. You can see how easy it is to keep the chores and weeks straight.

Apply the Skill

The table below is about a much bigger topic—the Byzantine and Muslim empires. This table shows more information, but you can read it in the same way as you read the *Chores for a Month* table. Trace a row and column to their meeting point to find information. For example, if you trace the row *Location* to where it meets the column *Muslim Empire,* you will find the location of the Muslim empire. Study the table carefully to answer the questions that follow.

1. **Determine the purpose of the table.** What empires are being compared? How is the information in the table organized?

2. **Use the table.** When did the Muslim empire begin? What was the major city of the Byzantine empire? Where were the different empires located?

3. **Analyze the information.** How do the two empires differ? What do they have in common? Why do you think they are being compared in this table?

Byzantine and Muslim Empires

	Byzantine Empire	Muslim Empire
Time Period	A.D. 527–1453	A.D. 640–1750
Location	Bordering on the Mediterranean Sea in Southwest Asia, southeastern Europe, and northern Africa	Northern Africa and Southwest Asia
Major City	Constantinople	Mecca
Religion	Christianity	Islam
Source of Wealth	Trade	Trade
Scientific and Mathematical Contributions	Records of Greek and Roman advances in science, mathematics, and health care	Avicenna's medical discoveries, algebra, an improved decimal system, and scientific classification

4 Assess

Have students **apply** the skill by completing the final activity section. To **assess**, display the table where all can view it. Invite students to come up and trace their way to various cells and explain the contents. Evaluate students' ability to locate data and the accuracy of their answers.

Answers to ...

TRY IT OUT

Students' charts should resemble the model chart pictured in the illustration.

APPLY THE SKILL

1. Byzantine and Muslim; by Time Period, Location, Major City, Religion, Source of Wealth, and Scientific and Mathematical Contributions for each empire
2. A.D. 640; Constantinople; Muslim: northern Africa and southwest Asia; Byzantine: surrounding the Mediterranean Sea in Southwest Asia, southeastern Europe, and northern Africa
3. The Muslim empire began later and lasted longer than the Byzantine empire. The Muslim Empire was also smaller and included the practice of Islam rather than Christianity; Both created wealth through trade, both had holdings in Southwest Asia, and made key scientific and mathematical contributions; They are being compared to quickly and easily show similarities and differences between the two empires.

SECTION 4

Islam's Golden Age

Lesson Objectives

1 Explain how the strengths of the Islamic world led to its golden age.

2 Identify key contributions of Islam's golden age to science, mathematics, and literature.

Lesson Plan

1 Engage

Warm–Up Activity

Ask students what modern scientific achievements—home appliances, communication devices, medical advances—most affect their lives. Urge students to consider the circumstances in modern culture that have made these achievements possible.

Activating Prior Knowledge

Have students read Reach Into Your Background in the Before You Read box. Suggest that they generate ideas from the following prompts: a certain grade in school, time on a sports team or with an activity group, a special friendship.

BEFORE YOU READ

Reach Into Your Background

In this section, you will read about the golden, or great, years of the Muslim empire.

Think about your own life. Was there a time that was very special? What made it special?

Questions to Explore

1. What strengths of the Islamic world led to its golden age?

2. What did Islam's golden age contribute to science, mathematics, and literature?

Key Terms

caliph   tolerance
patron

Key People and Places

Omar Khayyám
Harun ar-Rashid
Maimonides
Baghdad

▼ This beautifully decorated cover of an edition of Omar Khayyám's poems has one of his most famous verses printed around the edge.

Omar Khayyám (oh mahr ky YAHM) was a skilled Muslim astronomer and one of the most famous mathematicians in the world. Khayyám was also a great poet. The series of poems he wrote in the Persian language some 900 years ago are still read today. This is one of his poems:

> "When I was a child, I sometimes
> went to a teacher.
> And sometimes I taught myself, but
> eventually I learned
> The limits to all knowledge: we come into
> this world upon
> the waters, we leave it on the wind."

Do you agree with Omar Khayyám? Do you think knowledge is limited? What do you think Omar Khayyám means when he writes, "I learned/The limits to all knowledge: we come into this world upon/the waters, we leave it on the wind"?

Resource Directory

Teaching Resources

📁 **Reproducible Lesson Plan** in the Chapter and Section Support booklet, p. 13, provides a summary of the section lesson.

📁 **Guided Reading and Review** in the Chapter and Section Support booklet, p. 14, provides a structure for mastering key concepts and reviewing key terms in the section. Available in Spanish in the Spanish Support booklet, p. 10.

Program Resources

📁 **Outline Maps** Saudi Arabia: Political, p. 30

A Baghdad Courtyard

In the 760s, the caliph al-Mansur decided to build his capital at Baghdad, a small village on the banks of the Tigris River. By 800, Baghdad was a thriving city with a huge population. Many of Baghdad's people lived in courtyard buildings like the one shown here. The courtyards allowed residents some privacy and blocked out the noise and hustle of the city.

Wise Leadership Promotes a Golden Age

The multitalented Omar Khayyám lived during Islam's golden age. Scholars see this period, from about 800 to 1100, as one of the most brilliant in world history.

Lasting works of literature, like the poetry of Omar Khayyám, were created in the golden age. Medical and mathematical knowledge expanded. Scientific experiments were made.

Why did all this happen during this time? Before a society can afford to give artists and scientists time to do their work, it needs money. And the Islamic world had plenty. The empire had grown rich from the many lands it controlled and from trade.

Find Baghdad on the map at the end of Section 2. Baghdad was the capital of the Muslim empire during Islam's golden age. You can see from the map that Baghdad, like Constantinople, was a natural center for trade.

With a finger, trace a route from India to Baghdad. Now trace a route from the Mediterranean Sea to Baghdad. Traders from all over the world brought their goods to the caliph's court. The **caliph** was the chief ruler of Islam. He was Muhammad's successor, or the person who next had the right to rule.

READ ACTIVELY

Predict Why would Baghdad's location almost guarantee that it would become a wealthy city?

Media and Technology

Color Transparency 152

Planet Earth CD-ROM includes thematic maps of the United States and the world, plus World Wonders, Cultural: The Golden Gate Bridge, San Francisco.

Material World CD-ROM includes a portrait of an American family from Pearland, Texas, plus geographic data on the United States.

2 Explore

After students read the section, have them discuss and answer the following questions: What was life like for artists and scientists during Islam's golden age? How did the leaders of the Muslim empire contribute to these conditions? How did geography and economics influence the golden age?

Activity

Critical Thinking

Recognizing Cause and Effect *Suitable as an individual activity.* Have students write a persuasive letter to a government official or newspaper editor advocating financial support for artists and scientists. Tell students to use the example of Islam's golden age to support their argument. *English Language Learners*

Activity

Interdisciplinary Connections

Art Prompt students to make a poster advertising a traveling exhibit of Islam's golden age. Posters should highlight some of the artifacts and historic details that the exhibit will present. Students may use data from the section text and additional library research. Consider pairing English Language Learners as photo researchers with native English speakers. *Visual, English Language Learners*

3 Teach

Have students create a concept web with "Islam's Golden Age" in the center. Tell them to fill the outer circles with data from the section. Students may create hierarchies of circles if these can be supported by the text. This activity should take about 15 minutes.

4 Assess

See the answers to the Section Review. You may also assess students' webs.

Acceptable webs contain accurate data from each major subsection.

Commendable webs are hierarchically structured in a logical order.

Outstanding webs recognize the cause-and-effect relationship between Islam's flourishing economy and its intellectual achievements.

Harun ar-Rashid: A Powerful Caliph   Harun ar-Rashid (hah ROO nar ash EED) became caliph of Baghdad in 786. His rule was a time of prosperity for the people, and he himself was very wealthy. For 23 years, Harun ruled the world's most glamorous court. He and his favorite subjects ate off of gold plates and drank from goblets studded with jewels.

But Harun did not use the riches of Baghdad just to have fun. He was a great **patron,** or supporter, of the arts. Harun paid many skilled writers, musicians, dancers, and artists to live in Baghdad. He lavishly rewarded those whose works pleased him. One musician is said to have received 100,000 silver pieces for a single song.

Islam's Tolerance Is Rewarded   Tolerance, or acceptance of differences, was one of Islam's major features during the golden age. Jews and Christians who accepted Muslim rule were free to practice their religions. They also had the power to run things within their own communities. They did, however, have to pay more taxes than Muslims. And they could not carry weapons.

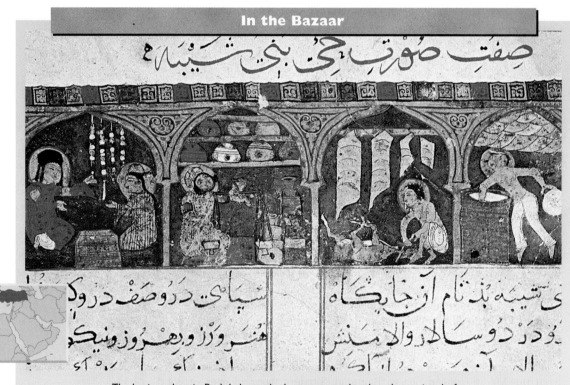

In the Bazaar

The busiest place in Baghdad was the bazaar, or marketplace. It consisted of miles of streets covered by a roof. Merchants at the bazaar sold local goods and products from all over the Muslim empire.

Maimonides was a religious scholar as well as a doctor and philosopher. In 1180, he completed the *Mishneh Torah,* or "Repetition of the Law." In it, Maimonides tried to classify and explain all the laws of Judaism. This picture shows the title page of an edition published in Italy. **Critical Thinking** How did Islamic attitudes toward non-Muslims help Maimonides in his work?

Background

Biography

Ibn an-Nafis and Ibn al-Quff Two Muslim doctors in the 1200s contributed to the important discovery that blood circulates through the human body. Ibn an-Nafis, born in Syria c. 1210, began the discovery. He noted that blood is pumped from the heart to the lungs for purification, back to the heart, and then around the body. Ibn al-Quff, born in 1233, completed the picture by identifying the capillaries through which blood returns from arteries to veins.

Activity

Interdisciplinary Connections

Language Arts Have students read a tale from *The Thousand and One Nights.* Then urge student groups to present a dramatic storytelling or staged play of the tale. Ask the class to identify elements of Muslim history and Islam's golden age in the presentations. *Kinesthetic, Auditory Learners*

Answers to . . .

A BOOK OF LAWS

Because Muslims tolerated both Christians and Jews, Maimonides was able to complete his work on the Torah.

The Muslim empire benefited from this policy of tolerance. Jews and Christians helped to create Islam's golden age. Maimonides (my MAHN uh deez), a Jew who lived in the Muslim empire in the 1100s, is a good example of this. Maimonides was a doctor. He spent time in Spain, North Africa, and Southwest Asia. He was also a great thinker. In his book *Guide for the Perplexed,* Maimonides tried to explain how people could believe in science and religion at the same time. Today, people still study and think about his ideas.

Intellectual Achievements in the Golden Age

Muslim scholars of the golden age made lasting contributions to human understanding of the physical world. Some of these contributions to science, medicine, and mathematics are shown in the chart on the next page.

Have you ever read a book or seen a film about Aladdin and his magic lamp? This is just one of the stories gathered in *The Thousand and One Nights.* This collection of tales is made up of Indian and Persian

LINKS TO MATH

Math Masters How would you multiply large numbers without a number for zero? How could you talk about below-freezing temperatures without negative numbers? Early Muslim mathematicians "borrowed" the idea of zero from Indian mathematicians. Muslims also invented positive and negative numbers. Their work in math enabled later scientists to make great discoveries in astronomy, physics, and chemistry.

Background

Daily Life

Storytelling/Poetry Some Muslim groups took the Quran prohibition against lying to mean that fiction was forbidden. However, poetry and tall tales were considered exceptions. Storytellers and poets would gather around a desert campfire and share their creations long into the night. A favorite subject was bravery in battle.

Background

Biography

al-Ghazali (1058–1111) Sufis were not just poets, they were thinkers. Born of Persian origin, Abu Hamid al-Ghazali was a great Sufi philosopher and seeker. He gave up his teaching job to wander the land, trying to fit together Sufi ideas and Islam. In his work *Restoration of the Sciences of Religion*, al-Ghazali suggests some ways to get closer to God.

Hafiz (1325–1389) Another Sufi poet was Hafiz, also known as Muhammad Shams od-Din. He wrote during the 1300's, usually using the rhyming couplets called ghazals. Hafiz's poems were passionate and often focused on love.

fairy tales, Egyptian romances, and Arab legends and love stories. *The Thousand and One Nights* reached Western Europe in the early 1700s, when a French scholar translated the tales.

Muslim writers also created serious works. Poetry was particularly important in the Islamic world. Poets were treated like stars, much like popular musicians are today. You have already read a poem from one Muslim poet, Omar Khayyám.

Some people used poetry to teach ideas and beliefs. The Sufis (SOOF eez) were one group of Muslims who did this. They taught that the world will reveal its mysteries to the seeker who makes careful observations. Although some Sufis were Islamic scholars, they tried to draw close to God through prayer and a simple life. Many had little respect for religious authority. Some Sufis poked fun at Islamic scholars with whom they disagreed.

Arab Contributions to Mathematics and Science

▶ The great Islamic scientist and philosopher Ibn Sina lived from 980 to 1037. He organized the medical knowledge of the Greeks and Arabs into the *Canon of Medicine.*

▲ Arab scientists were fascinated by water-driven machines. In this drawing, water falling into the cups causes the globe at the top to turn.

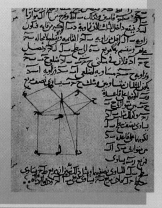

▶ Arab mathematicians invented algebra. They also studied ideas from the past, like the formula shown here. It explains how to find the length of one side of a right triangle when you know the length of the other sides.

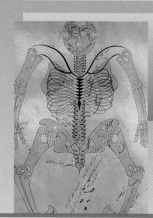

◀ Doctors studied diagrams like this one in the hospital libraries of Baghdad, Cairo, and Damascus.

Resource Directory

Teaching Resources

▢ **Section Quiz** in the Chapter and Section Support booklet, p. 15, covers the main ideas and key terms in the section. Available in Spanish in the Spanish Support booklet, p. 11.

▢ **Vocabulary** in the Chapter and Section Support booklet, p. 17, provides a review of key terms in the chapter. Available in Spanish in the Spanish Support booklet, p. 13.

▢ **Reteaching** in the Chapter and Section Support booklet, p. 18, provides a structure for students who may need additional help in mastering chapter content.

A Sufi Preacher

Here, a group of Muslims listens carefully to the words of a visiting Sufi preacher. Sufis were renowned for their preaching. It was largely through their work as missionary preachers that Islam spread to Central Asia, India, and Africa south of the Sahara. **Critical Thinking** What kind of message do you think the Sufi might be preaching?

The most famous Sufi poet, Jalal ad-Din ar-Rumi (juh LAHL ud DEEN ur ROO mee), founded a religious group called the Whirling Dervishes in the West. They used music and dance to communicate with God. Rumi composed the verses that appear below:

> "**N**ever think the earth [empty] or dead—
> It's a hare, awake with shut eyes:
> It's a saucepan, simmering with broth—
> One clear look, you'll see it's in ferment [motion]."

SECTION 4 REVIEW

1. **Define** (a) caliph, (b) patron, (c) tolerance.

2. **Identify** (a) Omar Khayyám, (b) Harun ar-Rashid, (c) Maimonides, (d) Baghdad.

3. What helped bring about Islam's golden age?

4. What were some achievements in science, mathematics, and literature during the golden age?

Critical Thinking

5. **Recognizing Cause and Effect** How did the economy of the Muslim empire affect the golden age?

Activity

6. **Writing to Learn** Study the two poems you have read in this section. Then try to write a similar poem yourself. Share your poem by reading it aloud or posting it on the bulletin board in your classroom.

📁 **Enrichment** in the Chapter and Section Support booklet, p. 19, extends chapter content and enriches students' understanding.

📁 **Spanish Glossary** in the Spanish Support booklet, pp. 83–91, provides key terms translated from English to Spanish as well as definitions in Spanish.

📁 **Chapter Summary** in the Chapter and Section Support booklet, p. 16, provides a summary of chapter content. Available in Spanish in the Spanish Support booklet, p. 12.

📁 **Cooperative Learning Activity** in the Activities and Projects booklet, pp. 20–23, provides two student handouts, one page of teacher's directions, and a scoring rubric for a cooperative learning activity on writing articles about the art of Istanbul.

Media and Technology

🎧 **Guided Reading Audiotapes** (English and Spanish)

Section 4 Review

1. (a) chief ruler of Islam (b) supporter (c) acceptance of differences

2. (a) Muslim poet, astronomer, and mathematician (b) caliph of Baghdad and great patron of the arts (c) Jewish doctor and philosopher during Islam's golden age; (d) capital of the Muslim empire during Islam's golden age

3. Students should note that prosperity arising from trade enabled Islamic rulers to support intellectual pursuits.

4. Possible answers: Maimonides' writings about science and religion, Ibn an-Nafis and Ibn al-Quff's medical work, scientific classification by Ibn Sina; algebra; *The Thousand and One Nights*, poetry.

5. Economic prosperity enabled leaders to patronize the arts and sciences.

6. Poems should reflect the philosophical nature of the models.

Answers to ...

A SUFI PREACHER

Answers may vary. Students may suggest that the Sufis are preaching about the mysteries of the world.

Reviewing Main Ideas

1. its location as a crossroads of trade

2. the Code of Justinian and the Byzantines' role in recording ancient Greek and Roman accomplishments

3. Mecca was a crossroads of trade. Caravans and traders from many cultures met here.

4. People in these areas did not like the rule of the Byzantine and Persian empires.

5. faith, prayer, sharing, fasting, and pilgrimage

6. They share the belief in one God, in a holy book, and in certain common prophets.

7. It enabled great Jewish and Christian thinkers to contribute to the golden age.

8. Answers will vary, but should reflect accurate facts from Section 4.

Reviewing Key Terms

Sentences will vary, but should reflect an accurate understanding of each key term.

Critical Thinking

1. Possible answer: He enjoyed the experience of viewing, hearing, and reading their works.

2. Both were militarily strong, both were excellent traders, both had gifted leaders.

Review and Activities

Reviewing Main Ideas

1. What enabled the eastern part of the Roman Empire to survive after the western Roman Empire fell?

2. What contributions of the Byzantine empire affect the world today?

3. How did Mecca's location affect the culture that developed there?

4. Why did people in the former Byzantine and Persian empires adopt Muhammad's ideas?

5. What are the Five Pillars of Islam?

6. What beliefs do Muslims, Jews, and Christians share?

7. How did the Muslim empire's policy of tolerance affect the golden age of Islam?

8. Name one scientific, one mathematical, and one literary accomplishment of Islam's golden age.

Reviewing Key Terms

Use each key term below in a sentence that shows the meaning of the term.

1. strait
2. patriarch
3. schism
4. nomad
5. prophet
6. hijra
7. muezzin
8. mosque
9. Ramadan
10. hajj
11. Quran
12. caliph
13. patron
14. tolerance

Critical Thinking

1. **Drawing Conclusions** Why do you think Harun ar-Rashid spent so much money on writers, musicians, dancers, and artists?

2. **Making Comparisons** What strengths were found in both the Byzantine and Muslim empires?

Graphic Organizer

Copy the diagram onto a separate sheet of paper. Then fill in the empty circles to complete the diagram.

Graphic Organizer

Sample answers are shown.

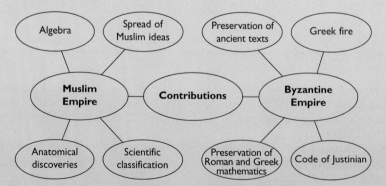

Map Activity

The Byzantine and Muslim Empires
For each place listed below, write the letter from the map that shows its location.

1. Arabian Peninsula
2. Mecca
3. Constantinople
4. Bosporus
5. Mediterranean Sea
6. Black Sea
7. Baghdad

Place Location

Writing Activity

Writing a Monologue
A monologue is a speech by one person, often spoken to oneself. Choose one of the people you have read about in this chapter. Write a monologue that describes an important moment in his or her life.

Internet Activity
Use a search engine to find *Islamic History in Arabia and the Middle East.* Explore the links to learn about Islam. Make a class timeline with pictures and text to show the important events in the rise and spread of Islam.

Skills Review

Turn to the Skills Activity.
Review the four steps for making a table. Then answer the following:
(a) What is the purpose of the columns and rows in the table?
(b) What are some kinds of information you might show on a table?

How Am I Doing?

Answer these questions to help you check your progress.

1. Do I understand why the Byzantine empire survived for many centuries?
2. Can I explain how the Muslim empire expanded?
3. Can I explain the basic beliefs of Islam?
4. What information from this chapter can I use in my book project?

Internet Activity

If students are having difficulty finding this site, you may wish to have them use the following URL, which was accurate at the time this textbook was published:
http://www.islam.org/ mosque/ihame/ hist.htm

You might also guide students to a search engine. Four of the most useful are Infoseek, AltaVista, Lycos, and Yahoo. For additional suggestions on using the Internet, refer to the Prentice Hall Social Studies' Educator's Handbook "Using

the Internet," in the *Prentice Hall World Explorer Program Resources.*

For additional links to world history and culture topics, visit the Prentice Hall Home Page at :
http://www.phschool.com

How Am I Doing?

Point out to students that this checklist is a quick reminder of what they learned in the chapter. If their answer to any of the questions is *no* or if they are unsure, they may need to review the topic.

Map Activity

1. F   4. C   6. D
2. G   5. B   7. E
3. A

Writing Activity

Monologues should clearly and accurately identify the speaker. Facts and characteristics should be consistent with data from the chapter.

Skills Review

(a) The rows and columns help organize the data in the table.
(b) Answers may vary, but should reflect an appreciation for the types of data suitable for a table.

Resource Directory

Teaching Resources

📁 **Chapter Tests** Forms A and B are in the Tests booklet, pp. 2–7.

Program Resources

📁 **Writing Process Handbook** includes Limiting a Topic, p. 15, to help students with the Writing Activity.

Media and Technology

📽 **Color Transparencies** Color Transparency 171 (Graphic organizer web template)

💿 **Prentice Hall Writer's Solution** Writing Lab CD-ROM

💾 **Computer Test Bank**

💿 **Resource Pro™ CD-ROM**

Civilizations of Africa

To help you plan instruction, the chart below shows how teaching resources correspond to chapter content. Use the resources to vary instruction, add activities, or plan block schedules. Where appropriate, resources have suggested time allotments for students. Time allotments are approximate.

Managing Time and Instruction

	Medieval Times to Today Teaching Resources Binder		World Explorer Program Resources Binder	
	Resource	mins.	Resource	mins.
1 SECTION 1 The Bantu Migrations	**Chapter and Section Support** Reproducible Lesson Plan, p. 22		**Outline Maps** North Africa: Political, p. 31	20
	S Guided Reading and Review, p. 23	20	Africa: Political, p. 33	20
	S Section Quiz, p. 24	25	West and Central Africa: Political, p. 34	20
	Social Studies and Geography Skills, Reading a Natural Vegetation Map, p. 25	30	**Nystrom Desk Atlas** T **Primary Sources and Literature Readings**	40
			Writing Process Handbook Writing an Introduction, p. 29	25
SKILLS ACTIVITY Organizing Your Time	**Social Studies and Geography Skills,** Planning Your Time, p. 107	30		
2 SECTION 2 Kingdoms of West Africa	**Chapter and Section Support** Reproducible Lesson Plan, p. 25		**Outline Maps** West and Central Africa: Political, p. 34	20
	S Guided Reading and Review, p. 26	20		
	S Section Quiz, p. 27	25		
	Social Studies and Geography Skills, Reading a Trade Map, p. 39	30		
3 SECTION 3 Trading States of East Africa	**Chapter and Section Support** Reproducible Lesson Plan, p. 28		**Outline Maps** East and Southern Africa: Physical, p. 35	20
	S Guided Reading and Review, p. 29	20		
	S Section Quiz, p. 30	25		
	S Vocabulary, p. 32	20		
	Reteaching, p. 33	25		
	Enrichment, p. 34	25		
	S Chapter Summary, p. 31	15		
	Critical Thinking Activity, p. 35	30		
	Tests Forms A and B Chapter Tests, pp. 8–13	40		

Activities and Projects

Block Scheduling Program Support

Interdisciplinary Links

Resource Pro™ CD-ROM

Media and Technology

Media and Technology

Resource	mins.
◀▶ ⊘ Ⓢ World Video Explorer	20
⊘ Planet Earth CD-ROM	20
▭ Color Transparencies 51, 52, 71, 92, 93	20
⊘ Planet Earth CD-ROM	20
▭ Color Transparency 72	20
⊘ Planet Earth CD-ROM	20
▭ Color Transparencies 73, 51, 52	20
🎧 Ⓢ Guided Reading Audiotapes	20
▭ Color Transparency 171	
(Graphic organizer web template)	20
⊘ The Writer's Solution CD-ROM	30
🖫 Computer Test Bank	30

T **Teaming Opportunity**
This resource is especially well-suited for teaching teams.

Ⓢ **Spanish**
This resource is also in Spanish support.

⊘ **CD-ROM**

⊘ **Laserdisc**

▭ **Transparency**

🖫 **Software**

◀▶ **Videotape**

🎧 **Audiotape**

Assessment Opportunities

From Guiding Questions to Assessment A series of Guiding Questions serves as an organizing framework for this book. The Guiding Questions that relate to this chapter are listed below. Section Reviews and Section Quizzes provide opportunities for assessing students' insights into these Guiding Questions. Additional assessments are listed below.

GUIDING QUESTIONS

- *How did physical geography affect the development of societies around the world?*

- *How did these societies interact with other societies?*

ASSESSMENTS

Section 1

Students should be able to create a natural vegetation map of Africa.

▶ **RUBRIC** See the Assessment booklet for a rubric on assessing a map produced by a student.

Section 2

Students should be able to state the effect of trade on the kingdoms of West Africa.

▶ **RUBRIC** See the Assessment booklet for a rubric on assessing cause-and-effect statements.

Section 3

Students should be able to write a paragraph on the importance of the city-state Kilwa around A.D. 1200.

▶ **RUBRIC** See the Assessment booklet for a rubric on assessing a writing assignment.

Activities and Projects

Mental Mapping

African Geography Ask students what kind of climate and vegetation they think of when they think of Africa. Some may think Africa is primarily jungle; the post-Lion King generation may view it as mostly savanna, however. This is a more accurate picture. Point out too that much of Africa is desert.

Since Africa is one of the easier shapes to recall, give students a few minutes to draw their own maps of Africa. Ask them to try to locate the major deserts of Africa, the savanna, and the rain forest regions. Suggest they try to locate the Nile and the Congo rivers. Then give them a chance to compare their maps with a published map. Have them make any changes or additions necessary.

Links to Current Events

Ethiopian Jews In the late 1980s and early 1990s, tens of thousands of Ethiopian Jews who faced severe persecution were airlifted to Israel. These people were mostly the descendants of Jews who sought refuge in Ethiopia in the 500s B.C. after Babylon overran Israel. Have students trace the route ancient Jews might have traveled from Jerusalem to Ethiopia and then back to Jerusalem in the late 1900s. Suggest that students write paragraphs describing each journey as it might have been experienced by a child about their age.

Hands-On Activities

Salt and Gold Have students compare the per-ounce prices of salt and gold in the United States today. To find the information, they can consult the business section of a daily newspaper and a price label on a box of table salt. Have them figure out how many pounds of salt would be needed to equal the value of an ounce of gold.

Suggest that they use this information in a skit, cartoon, or diagram. Why is the value of salt in the United States today so much less than it was in West Africa during the time of the great empires?

Migration and Trade On an outline map of Africa and Asia, have students show routes of the Bantu migration, trade routes in West Africa, trade routes between East Africa and the Arab world as well as India, and trade routes leading to Zimbabwe. Direct students to use different colors and types of lines to differentiate these routes. *Average*

Iron Working Suggest that students research traditional Bantu iron-working techniques. They can create a flowchart, diagram, or series of cartoon panels to show the steps involved in creating metal tools in ancient Africa. *Challenging*

Mansa Musa Have students put themselves in the place of an inhabitant of Cairo or Mecca who sees the arrival of Mansa Musa's caravan. They can write a one- or two-paragraph letter describing the spectacle to a relative who did not witness the event. *Basic*

Zimbabwe Have students review the variety of goods that were traded at ancient Zimbabwe. Suggest that they make a simple illustrated "catalog" of goods that could be bought, sold, and traded at Zimbabwe. It should be designed so that people who spoke different languages could communicate and trade. *English Language Learners*

F.Y.I.

This page can help you extend your own and students' understanding of the concepts in this chapter. You may want to browse through some of the suggestions in the **Bibliography. Interdisciplinary Links** can connect social studies understandings to areas elsewhere in the curriculum through the use of other Prentice Hall products. **National Geography Standards** reflected specifically in this chapter are listed for your convenience. Some hints about appropriate **Internet Access** are also provided. **School to Careers** provides insights into the practical uses of some of the concepts in this chapter as they might pertain to various careers.

BIBLIOGRAPHY

FOR THE TEACHER

Gish, Steven. *Ethiopia.* Cavendish, 1996.

Haskins, Jim, and Joann Biondi. *From Afar to Zulu: A Dictionary of African Cultures.* Walker, 1995.

Mann, Kenny. *Ghana, Mali, Songhay: The Western Sudan.* Dillon, 1996.

Minks, Louise. *Traditional Africa.* Lucent, 1995.

FOR THE STUDENT

Easy
Wisniewski, David. *Sundiata: Lion King of Mali.* Clarion, 1992.

Average
Koslow, Philip. *Ancient Ghana: The Land of Gold. Mali: Crossroads of Africa. Songhay: Empire Builders.* Chelsea, 1995.

Challenging
Koslow, Philip. *Asante: The Gold Coast.* Chelsea, 1996.

Kummer, Patricia K. *Cote D'Ivoire (Ivory Coast).* Children's Press, 1996.

LITERATURE CONNECTION

Aardema, Verna. *Misoso: Once Upon a Time Tales from Africa.* Apple Soup, 1994.

Lottridge, Celia Barker. *The Name of the Tree: A Bantu Folktale.* McElderry, 1989.

McKissack, Patricia, and Frederick McKissack. *The Royal Kingdoms of Ghana, Mali, and Songhay: Life in Medieval Africa.* Holt, 1994.

Price, Leontyne. *Aïda.* Gulliver, 1990.

INTERDISCIPLINARY LINKS

Subject	Theme: Movement
MATH	Middle Grades Math: Tools for Success *Course 1*, Lesson 1-2, **Make a Table** *Course 2*, Lesson 1-2, **Using a Computer to Graph Data**
SCIENCE	Prentice Hall Science *Ecology: Earth's Natural Resources,* Gazette, **Keeping the White Rhino Alive** *Ecology: Earth's Living Resources,* Gazette, **What Became of Africa's Animals?**
LANGUAGE ARTS	Choices in Literature *Deciding What's Right,* **The Judgment of the Wind, Children of Wax** Prentice Hall Literature *Copper,* **Osebo's Drum, The Cow-Tail Switch**

NATIONAL GEOGRAPHY STANDARDS

Students explore the 18 National Geography Standards throughout *Medieval Times to Today.* Chapter 2, however, concentrates on investigating the following standards: 3, 4, 5, 6, 9, 10, 11, 12, 13, 14, 15, 16, 18. For a complete list of the standards, see the *Teacher's Flexible Planning Guide.*

SCHOOL TO CAREERS

In Chapter 2, Civilizations of Africa, students study selected civilizations of the region. Additionally, they address the skill of organizing your time. Knowing something about the civilizations of Africa can help students prepare for careers in archaeology, diplomacy, and education. Organizing your time is a useful skill for people in all careers. The curriculum presented in this book, as in all eight titles of Prentice Hall's *World Explorer* program, is designed to prepare students not only for careers but also for good citizenship—of the world as well as of this country.

INTERNET ACCESS

Many social studies teachers and students use Internet browsers, or search engines, to investigate particular topics. For the best results, use narrow rather than broad topics. Try these for Chapter 2: Bantu, Mansa Musa, Aksum, Ethiopia. Finding age-appropriate sites is an important consideration when using the Internet. For links to age-appropriate sites in world studies and geography, visit the Prentice Hall Home Page at:
http://www.phschool.com

Connecting to the Guiding Questions

As students complete this chapter, they will focus on the geography and the cultures of the Bantu-speaking people, the West African kingdoms, and the trading states of East Africa. The content of this chapter corresponds to these Guiding Questions:

- ● How did physical geography affect the development of societies around the world?

- ● How did these societies interact with other societies?

Using the Map Activities

Have students identify some of the physical features in the regions of the old kingdoms. Discuss what role geography might have played in these ancient kingdoms.

- • western: Mali, Ghana, Songhai; eastern: Aksum, Kilwa, Ethiopia, Zimbabwe

- • Ghana, Mali, Ethiopia, Zimbabwe

Heterogeneous Groups

The following Teacher's Edition strategies are suitable for heterogeneous groups.

Cooperative Learning
African Wildlife   p. 38
Critical Thinking
Drawing Conclusions   p. 41
Interdisciplinary
Connections
Art   p. 50

CHAPTER **2**

Civilizations of Africa

SECTION 1
The Bantu Migrations

SECTION 2
Kingdoms of West Africa

SECTION 3
Trading States of East Africa

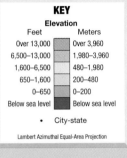

KEY
Elevation

Feet		Meters
Over 13,000		Over 3,960
6,500–13,000		1,980–3,960
1,600–6,500		480–1,980
650–1,600		200–480
0–650		0–200
Below sea level		Below sea level

• City-state

Lambert Azimuthal Equal-Area Projection

0   400   800 mi
0 400 800 km

Africa was home to two of the world's earliest civilizations, Egypt and Nubia. As these glorious cultures declined, new ones were arising throughout the continent. The map shows some of the powerful kingdoms and cities of the period from 900 B.C. to A.D. 1500. To help you get to know them, do the following activities.

Study the map
Read the names of the different kingdoms on the map. Which were in the western part of Africa? Which were in the eastern part?

Recognizing names that lived on
Compare the map on this page with the political map of Africa in the Atlas at the back of this book. Which modern countries carry the names of ancient kingdoms?

Resource Directory

Media and Technology

Geography: The Bantu Migration, from the World Video Explorer, enhances students' understanding of the significance of the Bantu migration.

The Bantu Migrations

BEFORE YOU READ

Reach Into Your Background

Many American families move from one part of the United States to another. If you and your family were to move to another state, what would you take with you? What might be the same in your new home? What might be different?

Questions to Explore

1. What are some of Africa's major physical features?
2. What were the Bantu migrations, and how did they affect African cultures?

Key Terms

savanna
oasis
migration
clan

Key Place

Sahara

Historians know quite a lot about the history of North Africa. But of the history of Africa south of the Sahara, historians have only a sketchy knowledge. For more than 2,000 years, the Sahara cut off the larger part of Africa from Europe and European historians.

Today, scientists and historians are working to piece together the history and cultural traditions of the area south of the Sahara. The task is a slow and difficult one. In many ways, it is like working to solve a puzzle. For thousands of years, the Africans seldom used materials that lasted, such as stone. The wood and clay they used to build and to keep records often disintegrated.

Even the iron tools and weapons the Africans used did not last. Iron corrodes, or rusts, fairly quickly. Since some African cultures did not have a Bronze Age during which they worked with more lasting metals, often little is left for scientists to find.

In the 1900s, scientists began to use modern techniques in their study of Africa. Some gathered stories told by traditional storytellers. These spoken histories led the scientists to new areas of exploration. Modern forms of travel also helped. Africa's physical geography was no longer the challenge it had been in the past.

▼ A modern-day griot, or storyteller, from Mali carries out his job of remembering and telling his people's history. He illustrates his story by drawing diagrams in the earth.

Lesson Objectives

1. Describe the physical features of Africa.
2. Trace the migration of the Bantu-speaking people.
3. Identify the contributions made by the Bantu-speaking people to other African cultures.

Lesson Plan

1 Engage

Warm-Up Activity

Ask students to list some of the major geographic features of North America (such as mountains, deserts, plains, and so on). Point out that many groups of people migrated north to south and east to west in North America. Ask students what changes in ways of life a group might make when it moves from the forests in the east to the mountains in the west. What customs might the people bring with them? What new ways might they adopt?

Activating Prior Knowledge

Have students read Reach Into Your Background in the Before You Read box. Ask students to imagine moving to an area of the country where people speak with a different accent—in the deep South, for example, or in the Northeast. Ask them to speculate about how their own language might change.

Teaching Resources

📁 **Reproducible Lesson Plan** in the Chapter and Section Support booklet, p. 22, provides a summary of the section lesson.

📁 **Guided Reading and Review** in the Chapter and Section Support booklet, p. 23, provides a structure for mastering key concepts and reviewing key terms in the section. Available in Spanish in the Spanish Support booklet, p. 15.

Program Resources

📁 Material in the **Primary Sources and Literature Readings** booklet extends content with a selection related to the concepts in this chapter.

📁 **Outline Maps** North Africa: Political, p. 31;
Africa: Political, p. 33;
West and Central Africa: Political, p. 34

2 Explore

Have students read the section and explore the following questions: What are some of Africa's main physical features? Why did the Bantu-speaking peoples migrate to other regions? What were some of the life ways of the Bantu-speakers? What did other cultures learn from the Bantu-speakers?

Activity

Cooperative Learning

African Wildlife Have students work in small groups to create trading cards showing the wildlife of various regions of Africa. Each card should include the following items: a picture of the physical geography of each region, a written description of each location, a picture of the animals found in that region, and the name and description of each animal. Encourage groups to divide the tasks among the group members: one member may be assigned to research and copy pictures, another might write the text, while another may compile the information on the cards. Display completed cards around the classroom.
Visual, Verbal, English Language Learners

Answers to ...

MAP STUDY

Regions Tropical savanna, desert scrub, and tropical rain forest; along the Mediterannean coast and at the southern tip of Africa

The Physical Geography of Africa

Look at the map below. Notice that Africa's rain forests are located on either side of the Equator. Farther from the Equator, bands of grasslands curve around the rain forests. To the north and south of the grasslands are dry areas.

Africa's tropical rain forests are areas of thick vegetation. These areas receive plenty of rainfall all year. The heat and moisture support a rich environment of trees, plants, and animals.

Much of Africa to the north and south of the rain forests is tropical **savanna.** This is an area of gently rolling land covered by grasses, occasional trees, and thorny bushes. In some places, the grass is lush and tall. In others, it is short and sparse. Most of Africa's farming takes place in the savanna.

Beyond the savanna lies the desert. The Sahara—the largest desert in the world—stretches across most of North Africa. It is so big that nearly all of the United States could fit within its borders. It is a place of pale yellow to deep red sands, rocky mountains, and salt flats. There are some oases too. An **oasis** is an area of vegetation fed by springs and underground water. Oases are surrounded by desert.

READ ACTIVELY

Visualize Visualize Africa's tropical savanna. What might it look and sound like?

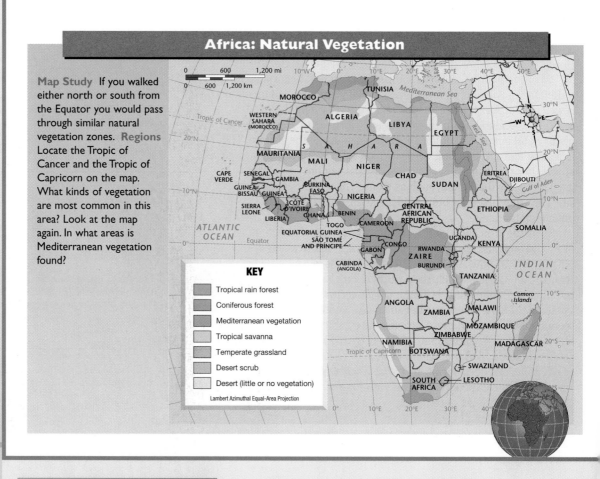

Africa: Natural Vegetation

Map Study If you walked either north or south from the Equator you would pass through similar natural vegetation zones. **Regions** Locate the Tropic of Cancer and the Tropic of Capricorn on the map. What kinds of vegetation are most common in this area? Look at the map again. In what areas is Mediterranean vegetation found?

KEY
- Tropical rain forest
- Coniferous forest
- Mediterranean vegetation
- Tropical savanna
- Temperate grassland
- Desert scrub
- Desert (little or no vegetation)

Lambert Azimuthal Equal-Area Projection

Resource Directory

Teaching Resources

Reading a Natural Vegetation Map in the Social Studies and Geography Skills booklet, p. 25, provides additional skill practice.

Program Resources

Nystrom Desk Atlas

Media and Technology

Color Transparencies 51, 52, 71, 92, 93

Planet Earth CD-ROM includes satellite images and physical maps of Africa which allow students to view the physical geography of the regions in which the Bantu migrations took place.

Africa's physical geography offers some dramatic sights. Giraffes graze on the plains below Kenya's 19,340-foot (5,895-m) Mount Kilimanjaro (left). Victoria Falls (right), on the Zambezi River, plunge 343 feet (105 m) and give off clouds of spray. Africans call the falls "The Smoke That Thunders."

Most of Africa is a huge plateau, edged by narrow coastal plains. In East Africa, a steep cliff marks the point where the plateau and the coastal plains meet. Rivers create great waterfalls over cliffs of the plateau. This eastern half of the continent also has huge freshwater lakes and high mountains.

The Bantu Migrations

The physical barriers formed by forests, mountains, and rushing rivers did not halt great **migrations,** or movements, of people. During these migrations, groups of Africans moved from West Africa toward the south. Look at the map on the next page and, with your finger, trace the routes of the migrations.

Among the largest population movements in human history, the Bantu (BAN too) migrations began about 2,000 years ago and went on for about 1,000 years. Bantu was the name of the family of languages that these people spoke. For this reason, we today call them Bantu-speakers. Historians have been able to figure out where the Bantu migrations started and ended by looking at where Bantu-speakers live today.

No one knows exactly why the Bantu-speaking peoples began to move from their homeland in West Africa. However, it probably had to do with population growth. The population grew so large that there was not enough land for everyone. When the land became scarce in a particular area, small groups left in search of land elsewhere.

Iron Age Farmers The practice of farming spread from Egypt to West Africa thousands of years ago. Around 400 B.C., these early African farming cultures began making iron tools. The earliest of these Iron Age settlements in West Africa is known as the Nok culture. The Nok lived in what is today northern Nigeria. Historians believe that the Nok were the first people living south of the Sahara to use iron tools.

3 Teach

Have students develop an "African booklet" that describes the major physical features of Africa, the history of the Bantu-speaking people and their migrations, and the changes made and brought by Bantu-speakers as they migrated to other regions. This activity should take about 30 minutes.

Background

Global Perspectives

North American Migrations   The migration and spread of people from their place of origin was a common occurrence in prehistoric times. In North America, a group of people who shared a common Algonquian language came to be known as the Cree Indians. In prehistoric times, they inhabited the forests around Hudson Bay in what is now Canada. As their population grew, they spread west and south, sometimes driving out other tribes who stood in their way. Eventually, bands of Cree spread as far west as the northern plains. Today, the Cree are spread out over the north, from eastern Canada to as far west as the state of Montana in the United States.

SKILLS MINI LESSON

Using Regional Maps
To **introduce** the skill, tell students that a regional map shows a large piece of land within a larger area; a regional map usually shows an area that has common characteristics within it. Direct students' attention to the Africa: Natural Vegetation map. Point out that this map is a regional map—it indicates regions of desert, forest, grassland, and so on. Have students **practice** the skill by identifying which color is used to represent desert scrub. Then have them indicate what type(s) of vegetation occur in Zaire. To **apply** the skill, have student pairs develop three true or false questions based on information on the map. Have pairs exchange and answer one another's questions.

See the answers to the Section Review. You may also use students' completed booklets as an assessment.

Acceptable booklets include descriptions of at least one geographic feature, one way of life element, and one change made or brought by Bantu-speakers.

Commendable booklets include descriptions of several geographic features, two or more facts about Bantu way of life, or changes made or brought by Bantu-speakers.

Outstanding booklets include a full description of geographic features, a clear explanation of the life ways of Bantu-speaking people, and the changes they brought to other African peoples through their migrations.

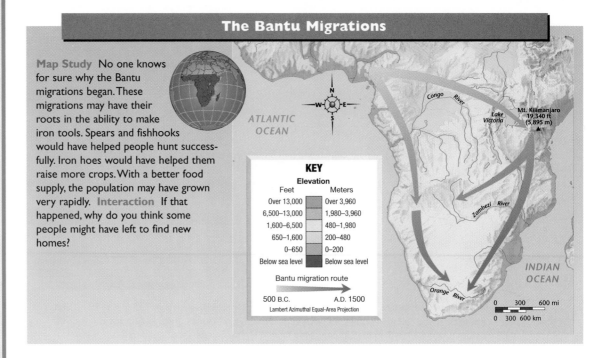

The Bantu Migrations

Map Study No one knows for sure why the Bantu migrations began. These migrations may have their roots in the ability to make iron tools. Spears and fishhooks would have helped people hunt successfully. Iron hoes would have helped them raise more crops. With a better food supply, the population may have grown very rapidly. **Interaction** If that happened, why do you think some people might have left to find new homes?

KEY
Elevation

Feet	Meters
Over 13,000	Over 3,960
6,500–13,000	1,980–3,960
1,600–6,500	480–1,980
650–1,600	200–480
0–650	0–200
Below sea level	Below sea level

Bantu migration route

500 B.C. ➞ A.D. 1500
Lambert Azimuthal Equal-Area Projection

Predict What kinds of changes did the Bantu-speakers make as they migrated through Africa?

Africa had always been a place where groups of people moved from region to region. Hunters and gatherers moved in search of game and other foods. Herders moved to provide their animals with fresh grazing lands. The Bantu-speakers were part of a long line of peoples to follow this tradition. It is the size of the Bantu migrations that made them so amazing.

In early times, most Bantu-speaking people were fishers, farmers, and herders. They lived in villages made up of families from the same **clan,** or group of families who trace their roots to the same ancestor. Many of these clans traced their ancestry through the mother rather than the father. For this reason, belongings and positions of power were passed on through the mother's side of the family.

The Bantu-speaking peoples moved slowly from their traditional homelands. Each generation moved a fairly short distance in the search for better farmland and more grazing lands. As they spread out from their homelands, the technology and culture of the Bantu-speakers also spread to new areas.

Bantu-Speakers Move South Often, Bantu-speakers moved into areas where other people already lived. When this happened, the Bantu-speakers sometimes joined the groups already living there. Often, they married people from the cultures they found in their new homes. Because of this, the older cultures of the area often adapted to the cultures of the Bantu-speaking peoples. At other times, the Bantu-speakers drove out the people they found in a new area. As these new areas

Answers to ...

MAP STUDY

There might not have been enough land for each family to farm as their own. There might have been little land available for grazing animals.

40 CHAPTER 2

also became crowded, some groups moved on. This process was repeated from one generation to the next for hundreds of years. In time, Bantu-speakers settled throughout Central and Southern Africa.

Learning and Teaching   As the Bantu-speaking peoples migrated, they entered different environments. Often, they had to change the way they lived. For instance, they learned new ways of farming and caring for livestock.

But the people already living in these areas also learned from the Bantu-speakers. In each area they crossed, the Bantu-speaking people passed on what they had learned. They introduced new crops, such as

Cattle Herders in East Africa

Many Bantu-speakers settled in the East African highlands, where the climate was ideal for raising cattle. Today, descendants of those settlers—like these Maasai herders—still raise cattle in East Africa.

Background

Biography

Shaka Zulu (c. 1787– 1828)   Shaka is considered the greatest military leader of the Zulus, a Bantu-speaking people living in southern Africa. As a young man, Shaka became a trusted military commander for the Zulu leader Dingiswayo. When Dingiswayo was murdered, Shaka took his place as chief. Shaka proceeded to shape the Zulu army into an extraordinary force that brought terror to other southern African kingdoms. Under Shaka's leadership, Zulu warriors became some of the finest soldiers in the world. In just four years, his forces conquered southern African Bantu-speaking kingdoms in a region as large as the country of France. He then united them into one great Zulu nation.

Activity

Critical Thinking

Drawing Conclusions
Suitable as a whole class or an individual activity. Have students work in pairs to investigate the differences between Stone Age and Iron Age tools. Then have the class discuss how Iron Age tools were superior to Stone Age tools. Ask students to draw conclusions about how iron tools made life easier for people.

1. (a) gently rolling land covered by grasses, occasional trees, and thorny bushes (b) vegetation fed by underground water, surrounded by desert (c) movement of people from one place to another (d) group of families who trace their roots to the same ancestor

2. The largest desert in the world, it stretches across most of North Africa.

3. Most of Africa is a huge plateau, edged by narrow coastal plains.

4. The Bantu-speakers married people from other cultures, who adapted to their culture; Bantu-speakers sometimes drove out people from their homes; Bantu-speakers brought new technology to other peoples.

5. The Bantu-speakers taught others to use iron for making tools and weapons, which changed the way people lived. Bantu-speakers brought their languages to new areas, and today millions of Africans speak a Bantu language.

6. Responses will vary. Possible responses may include: new languages, use of iron, new kinds of foods.

Answers to ...

IRON TOOLS

They introduced new crops and their languages.

Iron Tools

Iron tools gave the Bantu-speaking peoples more control over their environment. With strong axes, they could cut trees and clear the land. Their sharp, iron-headed spears and arrows were powerful weapons for hunting and defense. This arrowhead was made by the Hadza people of Tanzania using metalworking techniques that are centuries old. **Critical Thinking** What things, other than metalworking, did Bantu-speakers introduce to the lands they settled?

yams and bananas, to parts of Africa. They also taught people what was probably their most valuable skill—metalworking. Knowing how to make iron weapons and tools changed the way people lived throughout Africa.

As they moved through Africa, the Bantu-speakers left behind something else: their languages. Today, about 180 million Africans still speak Bantu languages. About 200 of the languages spoken in Africa south of the Sahara are related to the Bantu language family.

SECTION 1 REVIEW

1. **Define** (a) savanna, (b) oasis, (c) migration, (d) clan.
2. **Identify** Sahara.
3. Briefly describe Africa's physical geography.
4. How did the Bantu-speaking peoples change the lives of other African peoples?

Critical Thinking
5. **Identifying Central Issues** People have made important discoveries and developed new ways of doing things throughout history. Name two important contributions made by Bantu-speakers. Tell why these contributions are important.

Activity
6. **Writing to Learn** You are living in the Africa of a thousand years ago. Some Bantu-speaking people have moved into an area near your village. You have made friends with a Bantu-speaker your own age. Write a journal entry describing what your new friend has taught you about his or her people.

Resource Directory

Teaching Resources

📁 **Section Quiz** in the Chapter and Section Support booklet, p. 24, covers the main ideas and key terms in the section. Available in Spanish in the Spanish Support booklet, p. 16.

Kingdoms of West Africa

BEFORE YOU READ

Reach Into Your Background

How does trade affect your life? Consider the everyday things around you—the clothes you wear, the electrical appliances you use, and so on—as you think of your answer.

Questions to Explore

1. Why were gold and salt equally valuable to West African merchants?
2. How did the religion of Islam influence the empire of Mali?

Key Terms

silent barter
province

Key People and Places

Mansa Musa
Sundiata
Mali
Ghana
Tombouctou
Songhai

Lesson Objectives

1. Identify the role that gold and salt played in West African trade.

2. Describe the successive trade empires that arose in West Africa.

3. Explain how Islam influenced the West African empire of Mali.

Lesson Plan

1 Engage

Warm-Up Activity

Ask student volunteers to discuss occasions when they traded things with one other. For example, they may have traded one kind of candy or other food to a friend for a kind they liked better; they may have exchanged jewelry or baseball cards; or they may have traded a prized possession for something else that they wanted badly. Explain that this kind of trade, or barter, was the basis for ancient trading empires.

Activating Prior Knowledge

Have students read Reach Into Your Background in the Before You Read box. Ask students to generate a list of food items that come from other countries or other parts of this country. Ask students to discuss how their lives would be different without these things.

Five hundred slaves each carried a staff made of gold. Soldiers, with swords hanging from gold chains, rode horses decorated with gold. Hundreds of doctors, teachers, government officials, and musicians marched along. The procession included more than 60,000 people in all—and 80 camels, each loaded with 300 pounds (136 kg) of gold. This was the sight that greeted the astonished people of the city of Cairo, Egypt, one day in July 1324. It was the caravan of Mansa Musa (MAHN sah moo SAH), emperor of Mali. A hundred years later, people in the Egyptian city of Cairo still talked about Mansa Musa's amazing visit—and about the gifts of gold he handed out.

▼ Mansa Musa's fame spread well beyond Africa. This likeness of him was included on a map made in Europe in the 1300s.

Empires Built on Trade

Mali, the kingdom ruled by Mansa Musa, was just one of the rich trading empires that arose in West Africa between A.D. 800 and 1600. These empires controlled important trade routes across the Sahara, the desert that lies between North Africa and the West African coast. Merchants traveling through these empires had to pay taxes on all the trade goods they carried with them. This made the rulers of these empires rich. In return, the rulers kept peace and order throughout the land. This meant that the merchants could travel safely.

Teaching Resources

📁 **Reproducible Lesson Plan** in the Chapter and Section Support booklet, p. 25, provides a summary of the section lesson.

📁 **Guided Reading and Review** in the Chapter and Section Support booklet, p. 26, provides a structure for mastering key concepts and reviewing key terms in the section. Available in Spanish in the Spanish Support booklet, p. 17.

2 Explore

Have students read the section and explore the following questions: How did gold and salt contribute to the rise of great trading empires? Why was Ghana's location ideal for trade? How did Mansa Musa help build Mali into a great empire? How did West African empires expand their borders?

Background

Links Across Time

Salt Mines Much of the salt traded for gold came from the heart of the western Sahara, from salt deposits left behind by the inland sea, which disappeared thousands of years ago. The region was harsh. There was no vegetation, and water had to be shipped in to the miners. The deposits were great enough to allow the salt to be mined and removed in huge slabs. Some slabs were large enough to be used for building homes. Mining salt was extremely difficult and dismal work assigned to slaves.

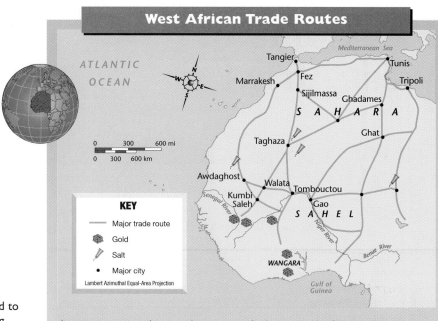

West African Trade Routes

KEY
— Major trade route
▨ Gold
⬎ Salt
• Major city
Lambert Azimuthal Equal-Area Projection

As you can see on the map, the sources of salt were in the Sahara, while the sources of gold lay far to the south in West Africa. **Location** Why were Tombouctou, Gao, and Kumbi Saleh good locations for trading cities?

▼ Arab traders traveled to the West African trading kingdoms by camel caravan. Camels were ideally suited to survive weeks of travel across the Sahara with little or no water.

Gold for Salt Gold and salt were the heart of trade in West Africa. Most of the gold came from a forested region in southern West Africa called Wangara. Most of the salt came from mines in the central Sahara.

Salt was very valuable. People needed it to flavor food and to preserve meat. Their bodies needed salt to stay healthy. In some parts of West Africa, salt was scarce, but gold was not. Therefore, salt became the chief product for which West Africans traded their gold.

Silent Barter The merchants and the Wangaran gold miners worked out a way to trade without words. It is known as **silent barter,** or trading without speaking. To *barter* means "to trade without using money." In the 900s, the Arab geographer al Masudi (al mas oo DEE) described the process of silent bartering. It began when the miners traced a boundary to mark a place to trade. The description continued:

Resource Directory

Teaching Resources

📁 **Reading a Trade Map** in the Social Studies and Geography Skills booklet, p. 39, provides additional skill practice.

Program Resources

📁 **Outline Maps** West and Central Africa: Political, p. 34

Media and Technology

▨ **Color Transparency** 72

💿 **Planet Earth** CD-ROM includes satellite images and physical maps of West Africa.

Answers to . . .
MAP STUDY

Sample answer: They were located midway between the salt supply and the gold supply.

"When the merchants reach this boundary they place their wares and cloth on the ground and then depart; and . . . the people . . . come bearing gold which they leave beside the merchandise and then depart. The owners of the merchandise then return and, if they are satisfied with what they have found, they take [the gold]. If not they go away again and the people . . . return and add to the price until the bargain is concluded."

READ ACTIVELY

Visualize Visualize two groups carrying on a trade using the system of silent barter.

Ghana's Trade Empire

The first West African trade empire founded on the gold-salt trade was Ghana. In about A.D. 300, the people of Ghana began to conquer neighboring peoples and to take control of trade routes across the Sahara.

Ghana's location was ideal. It was just north of the rich goldfields. Land routes south from the Sahara went through Ghana. Trade soon made Ghana rich. By about A.D. 800, Ghana was a major trading kingdom. Salt, cloth, and horses were exchanged for kola nuts, gold, and fine woods.

▼ Gold has long been a symbol of wealth to the people of West Africa. These elephant charms (below) and this decorated umbrella knob (left) were made in the 1800s by craftworkers from the West African kingdom of Asante.

3 Teach

Have students develop a chart with the column headings *Ghana, Mali,* and *Songhai* and the row headings *Time Span, Major Trade Goods,* and *Important Facts.* Have students fill in the boxes with facts from this section. This activity should take about 20 minutes.

Background

Links Across Time

Ghana The kingdom of Ghana disappeared as a major trading empire in the 1200s. In contrast, the modern nation of Ghana emerged in the 1900s. The Portuguese arrived in what is now Ghana in 1471, and named the area the "Gold Coast," because of the quantities of gold found there. The British later made the Gold Coast one of its colonies. In 1957, the Gold Coast achieved independence and renamed itself Ghana. Today, Ghana still trades in gold, and also in cacao seeds used to make chocolate, in fine hardwoods, and in other raw materials.

SKILLS MINI LESSON

Reading Actively
To **introduce** the skill, tell students that reading actively means being involved before, during, and after reading. For example, during reading, active readers ask questions and predict what might happen, visualize the events, and think about the characters and what readers might do in the same situation. Have students **practice** the skill by reading the Read Actively—Visualize feature on this page. Have them discuss the pictures they see in their mind and compare their visualizations to the information in the text. Have students **apply** the skill by using the Read Actively features throughout the chapter actively.

4 Assess

See the answers to the Section Review. You may also use students' completed charts as an assessment.

Acceptable charts include most of the important facts in the section.

Commendable charts include one or more facts in each box and include several entries under *Important Facts*.

Outstanding charts include accurate and significant facts in each box and demonstrate a clear understanding of the main ideas in the section.

Background

Links Across Time

Trading Partners Many of the raw materials and manufactured goods produced in Africa find their way to the United States. For example, 65 percent of Angola's exports come to the United States. Other key African trading partners with the United States include Comoros, Congo, Gabon, Guinea, Liberia, and Ethiopia. Products and materials include coffee, bananas, diamonds, oil, gold, vanilla, perfume, palm oil, tobacco, cocoa, wool, sugar, peanuts, tires, textiles, plastics, motors, and steel.

The picture shows market day outside the Great Mosque in Djenné (jeh NAY), a city in the modern country of Mali. During the 1300s, Djenné was an important city and center of Muslim learning in the kingdom of Mali. **Critical Thinking** What do you think was the major economic activity in Djenné?

HEROES

Overcoming Obstacles Sundiata had to overcome many difficulties in his life. As a boy, he was captured in a battle. Though his life was spared, his father, the king, was killed. Throughout his boyhood, Sundiata was lame and could barely stand, let alone walk. But he was determined to succeed in retaking his kingdom. In time, he led a revolt and took back his father's throne. Then he went on to conquer other neighboring peoples.

The kingdom's capital, Kumbi Saleh, was divided into two cities. One was the center of trade. The other was the royal city, where the king had his court and handed down his decisions.

Around A.D. 1000, the power of Ghana began to fade. Invaders from the north overran Ghana's cities. Many Ghanaians fled the area. By the 1200s, Ghana had broken into small independent states. Soon, most of the trade in the area was controlled by a powerful new kingdom, Mali.

The Empire of Mali

Mali, located in the Upper Niger Valley, was founded in about 1000. Under the leadership of Sundiata (sun JAHT ah), who came to power in 1230, Mali took control of the gold-salt trade across the Sahara. Sundiata put his people to work clearing and planting land and herding cattle. By the time he died in 1255, Mali had grown rich from trade and agriculture. It was the most powerful kingdom in West Africa.

The Rule of Mansa Musa In 1312, Mansa Musa became ruler of Mali. During his 25-year rule, he greatly expanded the empire. He also adopted Islam and made it the official religion of Mali.

A faithful Muslim, Mansa Musa went on a hajj, a journey to the holy city of Mecca. His journey brought new ties with the Muslim peoples of North Africa and Southwest Asia. It was during this pilgrimage that he made the spectacular visit to Cairo.

Answers to ...

A CENTER OF TRADE AND WORSHIP

trade

Mansa Musa used his new ties to make Mali a center of learning as well as of wealth. Muslim merchants who came to Mali built mosques and brought in religious leaders and scholars. The scholars taught students to read the Quran, the holy book of Islam. They also taught such subjects as arithmetic, medicine, and Islamic law.

With the help of a Muslim architect, Mansa Musa built several magnificent mosques in the city of Tombouctou (tohn book TOO). Muslim teachers and writers settled in the city, and students flocked here by the thousands. It became the leading center of learning that Mansa Musa had wanted it to be. Some merchants even grew rich buying and selling books and manuscripts.

Mali Grows Weak While Mansa Musa ruled, Mali had many peaceful and prosperous years. But in the late 1300s, about 50 years after he died, Mali's power began to fade. Raiders attacked from the north, and fighting broke out within the empire. Many **provinces,** or small regions of the country, became independent.

LINKS TO LANGUAGE ARTS

Most Valued: Books! In the early 1500s, a traveler named Leo Africanus wrote about Tombouctou. It was, he said, a city of power and culture. Its king supported "countless infantry, . . . many [judges], [educated] doctors and men of religion." He continued, "[In Tombouctou] more profit is made from the sale of books than from any other merchandise."

◄ Tombouctou, pictured here, is no longer a great and powerful city. However, it still plays an important part in the West African salt trade.

Background

Daily Life

Life in Mali In Mali's countryside, people followed traditional ways, living in clan groups. Each clan was divided into castes, with each caste representing a particular trade, such as artisan, farmer, or hunter. When a boy reached 12 years old, he was apprenticed to the caste of his uncles. If a boy was very talented in his craft, he might be sent to Tombouctou to be apprenticed to a master craftsman of his trade. Young girls were ready for marriage as soon as they were able to bear children.

Background

Links Across Place

Tombouctou The name Tombouctou, also spelled *Timbuktu,* has entered the English language vocabulary as a word expressing the idea of a destination that is very distant as well as difficult to reach. Someone might say, for example, "He packed so many things for his trip that you would think he were traveling to Timbuktu."

1. (a) trading without speaking (b) small regions of a country

2. (a) Mali ruler who greatly expanded the empire (b) military leader who founded Mali (c) empire located in the Upper Niger Valley (d) first West African gold-for-salt trade empire (e) city built by Mansa Musa; center of learning and trade (f) province that broke away from Mali and became the leading state in West Africa

3. Salt was scarce in some parts of West Africa, and West Africans traded their gold for it.

4. Mansa Musa made Islam the official religion and used his ties with the Muslim world to make Mali a center of learning.

5. Gold and salt were the two main trade goods that brought wealth to West Africa, leading to the development of kingdoms.

6. Responses will vary. Possible responses may include mention of the wealth of the empire, the architecture, the prevalence of books and learning, and the practice of Islam.

Bronze Sculpture From Benin

Ghana, Mali, and Songhai developed in West Africa's grassland region. At the same time, other kingdoms arose in the forest lands to the south. One such kingdom was Benin (beh NEEN), which was located around the mouth of the Niger River in what today is Nigeria. The people of Benin were famous for their bronze artwork. This sculpture, which dates from the 1600s, shows the head of a Beninese princess.

Songhai

One of the provinces that broke away from Mali was Songhai (SAWNG hy). By the end of the 1400s, Songhai was the leading state in West Africa. Like the rulers of Ghana and Mali, Songhai's leaders expanded the borders of their country by conquest. With each conquest, Songhai gained control over more trade routes and sources of gold and salt.

In less than 100 years, Songhai, too, lost its power. In the late 1500s, the people of Songhai began fighting among themselves. The empire was weakened and fell easily to the guns and cannons of an army from what is now Morocco, in North Africa. The era of great trading empires in West Africa came to an end.

SECTION 2 REVIEW

1. Define (a) silent barter, (b) province.

2. Identify (a) Mansa Musa, (b) Sundiata, (c) Mali, (d) Ghana, (e) Tombouctou, (f) Songhai.

3. Why was salt so important in West Africa?

4. What important change did Mansa Musa bring to Mali?

Critical Thinking

5. Identifying Central Issues What did gold and salt have to do with the development of the kingdoms of West Africa?

Activity

6. Writing to Learn You are a foreign student at the university in Mansa Musa's Tombouctou. Write a letter to friends telling them about Mali.

Resource Directory

Teaching Resources

📁 **Section Quiz** in the Chapter and Section Support booklet, p. 27, covers the main ideas and key terms in the section. Available in Spanish in the Spanish Support booklet, p. 18.

Trading States of East Africa

Section 3

Lesson Objectives

① Explain what cultures influenced the ancient kingdoms of Aksum and Ethiopia.

② Describe the role of trade in the ancient city-states of East Africa.

③ Identify the role that Great Zimbabwe played in East African trade.

BEFORE YOU READ

Reach Into Your Background

Trade is as important today as it was when the ancient African trading kingdoms were all-powerful. Consider things

you use every day. Where were they made? How might your life be different if there were no trade among the countries of the world?

Questions to Explore

1. What cultures influenced Aksum and Ethiopia?
2. Why did so many city-states develop along the coast of East Africa?

Key Terms

city-state
Swahili

Key Places

Aksum
Ethiopia
Kilwa
Great Zimbabwe

Lesson Plan

1 Engage

Warm-Up Activity

Ask students to imagine a world without any means of modern transportation or communication, a world in which the only way to learn about another place is to visit it personally or hear the accounts of other travelers. Ask students to discuss what it would be like in such a world to receive trade goods from other regions, or to hear the stories of traders and travelers about far distant places.

Activating Prior Knowledge

Have students read Reach Into Your Background in the Before You Read box. Ask students to look at the labels on their clothes, shoes, handbags, or bookbags to see where the items originated. Then have the class generate a list of items that the United States might trade with these other countries whose clothes and shoes we import.

Solomon, king of Israel, wanted to build a great temple. He sent messages to the merchants of the world saying that he would pay in gold and silver for building materials. Legends state that a merchant from the East African kingdom of Sheba took goods to Solomon and was impressed by the magnificent capital of Israel, Jerusalem. When he returned home, the merchant told his queen about the city.

The queen of Sheba wanted to see Jerusalem and Solomon for herself. She gathered a group of servants and packed gifts of gold and other precious things. Then she made the long journey to Jerusalem.

Solomon entertained the queen of Sheba and her people lavishly. Soon the queen fell in love with Jerusalem and with Solomon. She remained in Jerusalem for some time. According to legend, the child of Solomon and the queen of Sheba eventually became ruler of Sheba.

Aksum and Ethiopia

This story, told in the Bible, is one of the first references made to the kingdom of Sheba. Some historians believe that Sheba was the land we know today as Aksum. This wealthy trading state in East Africa thrived thousands of years ago.

▼ This modern painting shows the queen of Sheba meeting Solomon in Jerusalem. The emperors of Ethiopia claimed to be descendants of Solomon and Sheba.

Teaching Resources

📁 **Reproducible Lesson Plan** in the Chapter and Section Support booklet, p. 28, provides a summary of the section lesson.

📁 **Guided Reading and Review** in the Chapter and Section Support booklet, p. 29, provides a structure for mastering key concepts and reviewing key terms in the section. Available in Spanish in the Spanish Support booklet, p. 19.

Program Resources

📁 **Outline Maps** East and Southern Africa: Political, p. 35

2 Explore

Have students read the section and explore the following questions: How did Christianity come to Aksum? What happened to the people of Aksum when they were driven out by the Muslims? How did Kilwa become a wealthy city-state? What did Great Zimbabwe supply to East African trade?

3 Teach

Have students develop a table with the following entries: *Aksum, Ethiopia, Kilwa*, and *Great Zimbabwe*. Next to each entry, have students write at least two sentences about the topic. This activity should take about 20 minutes.

Activity

Interdisciplinary Connections

Art Dhows are small ships that were the workhorses of East African trade. In fact, dhows of the same basic design travel both on inland waterways and on the open sea today. Dhows are attractive vessels, notable for their single, large lateen (triangular) sail. Organize the class into groups to learn more about these important vessels. Students in each group can assign roles to group members: researcher, planner, model maker, and presenter. Students should present their findings, along with a model dhow, to the class. *Kinesthetic, Visual*

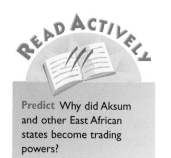

Predict Why did Aksum and other East African states become trading powers?

▶ Two important items traded at Aksum were myrrh (left) and frankincense (right). Myrrh was used in perfumes and as a medicine. Frankincense was used as a medicine and in religious services.

Wealth Through Trade Around 1000 B.C., people from Arabia sailed across the Red Sea and settled along the coast of northeastern Africa. One of the trading posts they set up along the coast was called Aksum. In 586 B.C., many Jews from Israel found refuge in Aksum when their homeland was overrun by a neighboring kingdom. In time, they mixed with the farmers already living in the area.

As the number of people in Aksum grew, so did its strength. Aksum sat on the trade route between Asia and the Mediterranean Sea. Foreign merchants came seeking such African goods as gold, ivory, and spices.

Along with their trade goods, these foreign merchants brought their ideas and beliefs to Aksum. Christianity was one such belief.

During the A.D. 300s, Aksum's king became a Christian. He soon made Christianity the official religion. This strengthened Aksum's ties with neighboring Christian traders. Over time, Christians came to Aksum from North Africa and Europe. They encouraged the people of Aksum to adopt some of the new and different forms of art, education, and literature they had brought with them.

For several hundred years, Aksum kept its control of the major trade routes linking Africa with Europe and Asia. Then, Muslim traders fought with the rulers of Aksum for control of the trade routes. They also quarreled over religion. Eventually, the people of Aksum were driven southward, away from the coast.

Resource Directory

Media and Technology

Color Transparencies 51, 52, 73

Planet Earth CD-ROM includes satellite images and physical maps of East Africa.

Churches of Solid Rock

In the 1100s, an Ethiopian ruler named Lalibela ordered his people to build a number of churches out of solid rock. Over time, 11 such churches were carved into the red stone of northern Ethiopia. The church of St. George, shown here, is 40 feet tall and shaped like a cross. **Critical Thinking** Compare the methods used to build Lalibela's churches with regular building methods.

Ethiopia Forced into the mountains of the interior, the rulers of Aksum set up the Christian kingdom of Ethiopia. Surrounded by Muslim areas, Ethiopia was cut off from most of the rest of the Christian world. As a result, the Ethiopians developed their own very distinctive type of Christianity.

East Africa

Other trade centers developed south of Aksum, along the east coast of Africa. These trading centers were port cities. Each was a **city-state,** a city that has its own government and often controls much of the surrounding land. All thrived on trade, especially with China, India, and Southwest Asia. By 1200, there were about 30 of these city-states along the coast from what is now Somalia to Mozambique.

The City-State of Kilwa One of the most important of the city-states was Kilwa, which was located on the coast of what is now the country of Tanzania. Kilwa was a Muslim city with orchards and fruit gardens watered by beautiful streams. The ruler of Kilwa charged duties, or taxes, on all goods that entered the port. Kilwa grew rich from these taxes and from trade.

L·I·N·K·S ACROSS TIME

Prester John, the Priestly King For years, people in Europe had heard stories about a fabulously rich Christian kingdom in Africa. However, no one knew where it was. According to these stories, the kingdom was ruled by a man named Prester, or "Priest," John. By the 1400s, Portuguese ships were exploring Africa's coast. One of their tasks was to find Prester John and his kingdom. However, their search proved fruitless. Today, many people believe that Prester John's kingdom was actually Ethiopia.

4 Assess

See the answers to the Section Review. You may also use students' completed tables as an assessment.

Acceptable tables include two accurate statements about each topic.

Commendable tables include at least two significant facts for each topic.

Outstanding tables include the main ideas of the section related to each topic.

Background

Global Perspectives

Italian City-States About the same time that city-states were developing along the coast of East Africa, they were also developing in Italy. Cities such as Florence, Milan, Pisa, and Venice developed their own self-government, independent of emperors or nobles outside their domain. While important city-states such as Florence became important centers of the arts, they often waged war against one another. Eventually, war among the city-states so weakened them that they fell to foreign invaders.

Answers to ...

CHURCHES OF SOLID ROCK

Answers may vary, but students' responses should indicate that most churches are built by placing stones or wood to enclose an open space. In contrast, Lalibela's churches were solid rock or stone with a space hollowed out of the center.

SKILLS MINI LESSON

Writing for a Purpose To **introduce** the skill, tell students that in school, much of their writing will be to present information. They will need to make sure that the facts are accurate and arranged in a logical order, and that all important facts are included. Students will also need to consider their audience. Who will read their writing? Will they need to define or explain special terms for their readers? Have students **practice** the skill by having the class choose one topic from this section on which to write several paragraphs presenting information. Ask what details they would include, and then list them on the chalkboard. Next have the class decide on how to order the details. Ask them who their audience will be and whether they need to define terms or give their readers any additional information. Have students **apply** the skill by using the above steps to write a paragraph presenting information about Kilwa.

Journal Writing

Traveling to Kilwa Tell students they are traders traveling to Kilwa. Suggest that they compose a journal entry describing the sights and sounds they see upon entering the city. Encourage students to describe who they are, how long they plan to stay, and what kind of trades they hope to make. If students are keeping an Explorer's Journal, as described in the opening two pages of this book, you may wish to do this writing activity as part of that journal.

Background

Daily Life

Kiswahili Most people call the language Swahili, but in this tongue, the language of the Swahili people is called *Kiswahili*. Students may be interested to count from one to ten in Kiswahili: moja, mbili, tatu, nne, tano, sita, saba, nane, tisa, kumi.

▶The ruins of Kilwa's great mosque give a hint of the splendor of this wealthy seaport. Ibn Battuta (IHB uhn bat TOO tah), a Muslim traveler from North Africa, visited Kilwa in the 1330s. He wrote that it was "one of the most beautiful and best constructed towns in the world."

READ ACTIVELY

Ask Questions Think of some questions you might ask about the history of the Swahili people.

The merchants of Kilwa traded with foreigners for many items. These included jewelry and cotton from India; porcelain and silk from China; and honey, wheat, rice, and other foods from Europe and Southwest Asia. For these items, the Kilwans traded gold, ivory, and iron. They also sold slaves they had captured in Africa's interior.

A New Language and Culture The people of Kilwa and the other city-states on Africa's east coast were descendants of Arabs and Bantu-speaking people. Their culture and language were called **Swahili** (swah HEE lee), which means "of the coast." Swahili is a Bantu language with borrowed Arabic words.

Beginning in the 1500s, armies from the European country of Portugal captured and looted Kilwa and other Swahili cities. Then they built forts up and down the coast and took over the trade routes on the Indian Ocean.

But the influence of Swahili culture remained. Swahili people still live along the east coast of Africa. Swahili is the official language of the modern African nations of Kenya and Tanzania, and most East Africans use it for business. Many East African cities and islands still have Swahili names.

Resource Directory

Teaching Resources

📁 **Section Quiz** in the Chapter and Section Support booklet, p. 30, covers the main ideas and key terms in the section. Available in Spanish in the Spanish Support booklet, p. 20.

📁 **Vocabulary** in the Chapter and Section Support booklet, p. 32, provides a review of key terms in the chapter. Available in Spanish in the Spanish Support booklet, p. 22.

📁 **Reteaching** in the Chapter and Section Support booklet, p. 33, provides a structure for students who may need additional help in mastering chapter content.

📁 **Enrichment** in the Chapter and Section Support booklet, p. 34, extends chapter content and enriches students' understanding.

Today, stone ruins mark the site of a once-grand city called Great Zimbabwe, or "stone house." The city included nearly 20 separate neighborhoods, set off by stone walls, and the Great Enclosure, shown here. The walls of the egg-shaped Great Enclosure are 30 feet (9 m) high and 20 feet (6 m) thick. Builders made the walls without using mortar or cement. **Critical Thinking** Why do you think the people of Great Zimbabwe built such strong walls?

Great Zimbabwe

The gold that the merchants of Kilwa and other Swahili city-states traded came from Africa's interior. Most of it was mined in the area surrounding Great Zimbabwe, a kingdom in the highlands between the Zambezi and Limpopo rivers. Great Zimbabwe was founded about A.D. 1100 by a group of Bantu-speaking people called the Shona (SHOHN uh). Most of the people were farmers and herders.

After a time, Great Zimbabwe weakened and lost power. Hundreds of years later, Europeans arrived and seized the lands where the Shona had lived. But the glory of Great Zimbabwe was not lost. Its stone ruins still stand, and its name lives on in the present-day nation of Zimbabwe.

SECTION 3 REVIEW

1. **Define** (a) city-state, (b) Swahili.

2. **Identify** (a) Aksum, (b) Ethiopia, (c) Kilwa, (d) Great Zimbabwe.

3. What cultures influenced the peoples of Aksum and Ethiopia?

4. With whom did the city-states of East Africa trade?

Critical Thinking

5. **Making Comparisons** Compare and contrast Kilwa and Zimbabwe. How were they alike? How were they different?

Activity

6. **Writing to Learn** You are a traveler visiting one of the kingdoms or city-states mentioned in this section. Write a short letter home describing some of the things you see.

Teaching Resources

📁 **Spanish Glossary** in the Spanish Support booklet, pp. 83–91, provides key terms translated from English to Spanish as well as definitions in Spanish.

📁 **Chapter Summary** in the Chapter and Section Support booklet, p. 31, provides a summary of chapter content. Available in Spanish in the Spanish Support booklet, p. 21.

📁 **Cooperative Learning Activity** in the Activities and Projects booklet, pp. 24–27, provides two student handouts,

one page of teacher's directions, and a scoring rubric for a cooperative learning activity on simulation: trading items with silent barter.

📁 **Critical Thinking Activity** in the Chapter and Section Support booklet, p. 35, helps students apply the skill of recognizing bias.

Media and Technology

🎧 **Guided Reading Audiotapes** (English and Spanish)

Section 3 Review

1. (a) city that has its own government and often controls much of the surrounding land (b) "of the coast," and refers to the culture and languages of a Bantu-speaking people

2. (a) kingdom on the coast of northeastern Africa (b) Christian kingdom founded in the mountains by the leaders of Aksum (c) city-state located on an island off the coast of what is now Tanzania (d) kingdom in the highlands between the Zambezi and Limpopo rivers

3. Jews from Israel and Christians from North Africa and Europe influenced the peoples of Aksum and Ethiopia.

4. The city-states of East Africa traded with China, India, and Southwest Asia.

5. Alike: Both were inhabited by Bantu-speaking people; the remnants of both cultures live on today. Different: Kilwa was on an island; Great Zimbabwe was inland. Kilwa was a city-state; Great Zimbabwe was not. Kilwa was important for its trade, Great Zimbabwe for mining gold.

6. Responses will vary. Possible responses may include mention of trade and trade goods, types of people in the kingdom (Jewish, Christian, Muslim), the wealth of the kingdoms, and a description of the land.

Answers to ...

GREAT ZIMBABWE

The kingdom was near where gold was mined, so it might want protection from those who wanted to steal the gold.

Lesson Objectives

1. Identify the necessary steps to organizing time for school assignments.

2. Organize the time needed for a hypothetical school assignment.

Lesson Plan

1 Engage

Warm-Up Activity

To **introduce** the skill, read aloud the opening paragraphs. Then draw a series of steps on the chalkboard.

Activating Prior Knowledge

Invite volunteers to tell how they organize time. Urge other students to write down their methods. Discuss some of the common methods, asking students which work best.

2 Explore

Read the Get Ready text with students, polling the class on the time-organizing strategies. Discuss what some other steps might be, culling ideas from students' earlier suggestions. Then direct students to finish reading the Skills Activity.

SKILLS ACTIVITY

Organizing Your Time

Have you ever fallen behind in your work at school? Have you wondered whether you would ever catch up? Join the club. At one time or another, most students feel this way—even the ones who seem to have no trouble. It can be hard to juggle homework, chores, after-school activities, and free time.

If you organize your time carefully, however, you can keep up with your work and activities more easily. You can learn to do this just as you learn any other skill. Organizing your time is the key to keeping up in school, keeping a good attitude, and keeping your head above water!

Get Ready

Learning to organize your time is mostly common sense. When you get a homework assignment, for example, the method below is a good one to follow.

- Find out when the assignment is due.
- Identify the steps in the assignment and how long each step will take.
- Start the assignment as early as possible.
- Arrange your time so that you have enough time to complete each step in the assignment.

Resource Directory

Teaching Resources

Planning Your Time in the Social Studies and Geography Skills booklet, p. 107, provides additional skill practice.

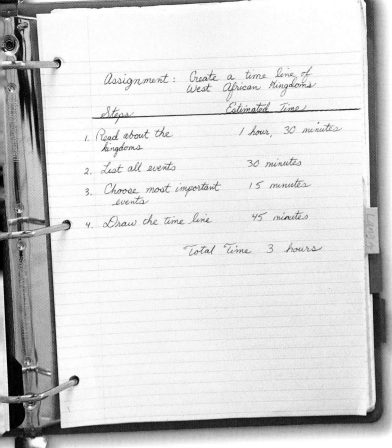

Assignment: Create a time line of
West African Kingdoms

Steps	Estimated Time
1. Read about the kingdoms	1 hour, 30 minutes
2. List all events	30 minutes
3. Choose most important events	15 minutes
4. Draw the time line	45 minutes

Total Time   3 hours

◀ Here is one girl's plan for completing a homework assignment. Your plan might look different, but be sure to include the steps involved and the time you think each one will take.

Try It Out

In order to organize your time well, you must start by knowing what you have to do. For example, you need to be able to identify the different tasks that make up a homework assignment. You must also have a good sense of how long it takes to do each task. Then you can set aside the right amount of time for each part of a homework assignment. Make a plan for completing a homework assignment by following the steps below.

A. Choose a homework assignment you now have. Pick one that includes reading and writing and that is not too different from your other assignments.

B. Identify the steps of the assignment. Divide the assignment into logical parts such as reading a chapter, taking notes, and answering questions. If the assignment is to write a paper, divide the writing into the steps of the writing process.

C. Estimate how much time the assignment will take. Write down estimated times for each step and for the whole assignment. Base your estimate on your experience.

Apply the Skill

Now test your plan. Do the assignment. As you work, time yourself. Write down the actual time it takes to complete each step and compare it to your estimated time. How close was your estimate? How can this exercise help you organize your time for your next homework assignment?

3 Teach

Have students **practice** the skill by completing the Try It Out activity. Ask students to exchange plans with a partner who will comment on the thoroughness of the steps and accuracy of the time estimates.

4 Assess

Have students **apply** the skill by completing the final activity section. When students finish, ask them how long each step actually took them and whether they had omitted any steps in their planning. Then **assess** by evaluating the accuracy of students' time estimates and the logic of their organization.

Answers to . . .

TRY IT OUT

Students' answers should reflect a logical progression of tasks from beginning to completion of assignment.

APPLY THE SKILL

Answers will vary, but should reflect students' understanding that schedules may need to be revised.

Reviewing Main Ideas

1. The three main vegetation zones of Africa are rain forest, savanna, and desert.

2. The migrations were a movement of Bantu-speaking people from West Africa toward the south that began about 2,000 years ago and went on for more than 1,000 years.

3. Gold was abundant in West Africa, but salt was scarce. Empires were built on the trade of these two main trade items. West Africa was in a key location on the trade routes.

4. Muslims came and built mosques and attracted scholars and religious leaders; Mali became a center of learning.

5. Jews from Israel and Christians from North Africa came to Aksum. When the people of Aksum were driven out by Muslims, Christians from Aksum built the kingdom of Ethiopia.

6. They were port cities located along the coast. They had access to gold from the interior of Africa, and they thrived on trade with China, India, and Southwest Asia.

Reviewing Key Terms

1.	true	**4.**	Swahili
2.	true	**5.**	clan
3.	true	**6.**	silent barter

Critical Thinking

1. Trade brought wealth, which helped build kingdoms. Cultures of West and East Africa, exposed to new ideas from foreign traders, adopted new ways of doing things.

2. Alike: Both grew wealthy from trade and were influenced by new ideas brought by foreign traders. Different: West African empires controlled overland trade routes, trading mainly with Muslims from the north; East African city-states were port cities and traded mainly with India, China, and Southwest Asia. West African empires stretched over a large region; East African city-states were smaller. East African city-states were peopled mainly by Bantu-speaking peoples.

Review and Activities

Reviewing Main Ideas

1. What are the three main vegetation zones of Africa?

2. What were the Bantu migrations?

3. Why did trading empires develop in West Africa?

4. What impact did Islam have on Mali?

5. Describe the cultures that influenced the development of Aksum and Ethiopia.

6. What factors helped the ancient city-states on the coast of East Africa to thrive?

Reviewing Key Terms

Decide whether each statement is true or false. If it is true, write "true." If it is false, change the underlined term to make the statement true.

1. The vast grasslands of Africa are called <u>savannas.</u>

2. An <u>oasis</u> is a vital watering spot for desert travelers.

3. Bantu-speaking people moved south in what are known as <u>migrations.</u>

4. <u>Islam</u> refers to the language and culture of some East African people.

5. A <u>city-state</u> is a group of people with the same ancestor.

6. A <u>clan</u> is a way to trade without words.

Critical Thinking

1. Understanding Cause and Effect How did trade help to change cultures in West and East Africa?

2. Making Comparisons What did the trading empires of West Africa and the city-states of East Africa have in common? In what ways were they different?

Graphic Organizer

Copy the chart onto a separate sheet of paper. Then, in each empty oval, write an important fact about trade in early Africa.

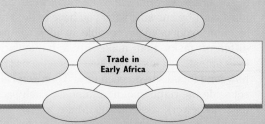

Graphic Organizer

Sample answer shown, other answers are possible.

Map Activity

Africa

For each place listed below, write the letter from the map that shows its location.

1. Great Zimbabwe
2. Sahara
3. Tombouctou
4. Mali
5. Ethiopia
6. Ghana
7. Kilwa

Place Location

Writing Activity

Writing a Report

You are a Portuguese explorer who has visited Kilwa and several of the other port cities of Africa. Write a report to your rulers giving reasons why they may want to gain control of these cities.

Internet Activity

Use a search engine to find *African Travel Gateway*. Scroll down and click on **African Focus**. Then click on **Zimbabwe Focus**. Choose **Great Zimbabwe South & East**. Read the two pages about the ruins of Great Zimbabwe. Write down three facts about who built Great Zimbabwe and how.

Skills Review

Turn to the Skills Activity.

Review how to organize your time. Then answer the following questions: (a) When you applied the plan to your homework, was your time estimate high, low, or just right? (b) How can this skill help you at home, at school, and at play?

How Am I Doing?

Answer these questions to help you check your progress.

1. Can I describe the physical geography of the continent of Africa?
2. Do I understand how ancient cultures in East Africa compare to cultures in West Africa?
3. Can I identify some historic events or achievements that have shaped the modern cultures of Africa?
4. What information from this chapter can I use in my book project?

Internet Activity

If students are having difficulty finding this site, you may wish to have them use the following URL, which was accurate at the time this textbook was published:

http://cy.co.za/atg/home. html

You might also guide students to a search engine. Four of the most useful are Infoseek, AltaVista, Lycos, and Yahoo. For additional suggestions on using the Internet, refer to the Prentice Hall Social Studies' Educator's Handbook "Using the Internet," in the *Prentice Hall World Explorer Program Resources*.

For additional links to world history and culture topics, visit the Prentice Hall Home Page at:
http://www.phschool.com

How Am I Doing?

Point out to students that this checklist is a quick reminder of what they learned in the chapter. If their answer to any of the questions is *no* or if they are unsure, they may need to review the topic.

Map Activity

1. G   4. B   6. A
2. D   5. E   7. F
3. C

Writing Activity

Responses will vary. Possible responses may include the following reasons: great wealth of cities; situated on established trade routes; gold from the interior can be easily acquired.

Skills Review

(a) Answers may vary but should accurately reflect the accuracy of students' estimates.
(b) Accept any reasonable responses.

Resource Directory

Teaching Resources

Chapter Tests Forms A and B are in the Tests booklet, pp. 8–13.

Program Resources

Writing Process Handbook includes Writing an Introduction, p. 29, to help students with the Writing Activity.

Media and Technology

Color Transparencies
Color Transparency 171
(Graphic organizer web template)

Prentice Hall Writer's Solution Writing Lab CD-ROM

Computer Test Bank

**Resource Pro™ CD-ROM**

The Ancient Americas

To help you plan instruction, the chart below shows how teaching resources correspond to chapter content. Use the resources to vary instruction, add activities, or plan block schedules. Where appropriate, resources have suggested time allotments for students. Time allotments are approximate.

Managing Time and Instruction

	Medieval Times to Today Teaching Resources Binder		World Explorer Program Resources Binder	
	Resource	**mins.**	**Resource**	**mins.**
I. SECTION I **Cultures of Middle America**	**Chapter and Section Support** Reproducible Lesson Plan, p. 37 Ⓢ Guided Reading and Review, p. 38 Ⓢ Section Quiz, p. 39 **Social Studies and Geography Skills,** Drawing Conclusions, p. 52	 20 25 30	**Outline Maps** Central America and the Caribbean: Political, p. 9 **Nystrom Desk Atlas** Ⓣ Primary Sources and Literature Readings **Writing Process Handbook** Writing Effective Paragraphs, pp. 27–28	 20 40 25
SKILLS ACTIVITY **Recognizing Cause and Effect**	**Social Studies and Geography Skills,** Recognizing Cause and Effect, p. 49	30		
2 SECTION 2 **The Incas**	**Chapter and Section Support** Reproducible Lesson Plan, p. 40 Ⓢ Guided Reading and Review, p. 41 Ⓢ Section Quiz, p. 42 Critical Thinking Activity, p. 50	 20 25 30	**Outline Maps** Latin America: Physical, p. 6 Latin America: Political, p. 7	 20 20
3 SECTION 3 **The Cultures of North America**	**Chapter and Section Support** Reproducible Lesson Plan, p. 43 Ⓢ Guided Reading and Review, p. 44 Ⓢ Section Quiz, p. 45 Ⓢ Vocabulary, p. 47 Reteaching, p. 48 Enrichment, p. 49 Ⓢ Chapter Summary, p. 46 **Tests** Forms A and B Chapter Tests, pp. 14–19	 20 25 20 25 25 15 40	**Outline Maps** The United States and Canada: Physical, p. 12 The United States and Canada: Political, p, 13	 20 20
LITERATURE *The Americas in 1492* by Jamake Highwater			Ⓣ Primary Sources and Literature Readings	40

Block Scheduling
Program Support

- Block Scheduling Folder
  PROGRAM TEACHING RESOURCES
- Activities and Projects
- Interdisciplinary Links
- Resource Pro™ CD-ROM
- Media and Technology

Media and Technology

Resource	mins.
(VIDEO) (CD) (S) World Video Explorer	20
(CD) Planet Earth CD-ROM	20
(T) Color Transparencies 66, 85	20
(T) Color Transparencies 64, 86	20
(CD) Planet Earth CD-ROM	20
(T) Color Transparency 78	20
(A) (S) Guided Reading Audiotapes	20
(T) Color Transparency 171 (Graphic organizer web template)	20
(CD) The Writer's Solution CD-ROM	30
(SW) Computer Test Bank	30

T Teaming Opportunity
This resource is especially well-suited for teaching teams.

S Spanish
This resource is also in Spanish support.

CD-ROM

Laserdisc

Transparency

Software

Videotape

Audiotape

Assessment Opportunities

From Guiding Questions to Assessment A series of Guiding Questions serves as an organizing framework for this book. The Guiding Questions that relate to this chapter are listed below. Section Reviews and Section Quizzes provide opportunities for assessing students' insights into these Guiding Questions. Additional assessments are listed below.

GUIDING QUESTIONS

- *How did physical geography affect the development of societies around the world?*
- *What accomplishments in technology, learning, or artistic expression were found in each society?*

ASSESSMENTS

Section 1

Students should be able to create a chart listing the achievements of the Mayan and Aztec civilizations.

▶ **RUBRIC** See the Assessment booklet for a rubric on assessing charts.

Section 2

Students should be able to create a clay model of the terraces used by the Incas for farming.

▶ **RUBRIC** See the Assessment booklet for a rubric on assessing student performance on a project.

Section 3

Students should be able to simulate a Pueblo rain dance.

▶ **RUBRIC** See the Assessment booklet for a rubric on assessing a simulation.

Activities and Projects

Mental Mapping

Ancient Civilizations Ask students to name some civilizations of the Ancient Americas. List them on the chalkboard. Be sure all of these are included: Aztec, Maya, Inca, Mound Builders, Anasazi. Ask students to locate each of these civilizations on a physical map of North, South, and Central America. Allow students to work together to locate these civilizations in Mexico and Guatemala, Peru, the Mississippi valley and southeastern United States, and the southwestern United States.

Invite students to offer what information they know about the geography and climate of each these regions. They may know, for example, that Peru is extremely mountainous and that large parts of Mexico and Guatemala are hot and humid with thick vegetation.

Links to Current Events

Native Americans Today Have students look for references to native peoples of Central America, South America, or North America in the news today. Students might work in small groups to find current information about specific peoples such as the Incas of Peru, the Mayas of Guatemala and Mexico, Pueblo Indians of the American Southwest, or other Native Americans of the United States. Encourage students to find out why the groups are in the news, how and where they live today, and how their heritage affects their culture today.

Hands-On Activities

Do Knot Talk Knotted ropes were used to keep records and communicate in the Incan empire. Native Americans of the southwestern United States also used knots to communicate among groups who spoke different languages. Have students work in pairs of small groups to devise a code based on knots. They might devise a "language" of a dozen words or concepts that could be expressed with knots. Then provide nylon cord or another type of string or cord that is easily tied and untied and have them take turns trying to create and decipher knot messages. Give them a chance to report on their successes and difficulties.

Aztec Landfill Suggest that students try building models of the "floating gardens" of Tenochtitlán. They might use pans of water and real dirt and plants to create the rafts or islands of land surrounded by canals on which they planted corn. They can also choose to use clay, flour and salt, or any other materials to make their models. *English Language Learners*

Pros and Cons Students can probably find much to admire and much to criticize in Incan society. Encourage them to sort through their impressions and reactions by having them list the things they admire in Incan society. Then have them list

the things they would want to change. Ask students to think about ways their perspective might be different had they lived in the time and place of the Incan empire. For example, they would not necessarily expect the kinds of political freedoms found in a democracy. On the other hand, they might still resent being forced to work. *Average*

Plan an Exhibit Students who are intrigued by the Mound Builders might want to research some mounds and prepare a fact file on mounds. They could collect data such as the longest mound, tallest mound, oldest mound, and most mysterious mound. Have them arrange this

information on a poster or bulletin board. Encourage them to find pictures of as many mounds as they can and to locate the mounds on a map of the United States. *Challenging*

F.Y.I.

This page can help you extend your own and students' understanding of the concepts in this chapter. You may want to browse through some of the suggestions in the **Bibliography. Interdisciplinary Links** can connect social studies understandings to areas elsewhere in the curriculum through the use of other Prentice Hall products. **National Geography Standards** reflected specifically in this chapter are listed for your convenience. Some hints about appropriate **Internet Access** are also provided. **School to Careers** provides insights into the practical uses of some of the concepts in this chapter as they might pertain to various careers.

BIBLIOGRAPHY

FOR THE TEACHER

Arnold, Caroline. *City of the Gods: Mexico's Ancient City of Teotihuacan.* Clarion, 1994.

Baquedano, Elizabeth. *Aztec, Inca, and Maya.* Dorling, 1993.

Hill, Emily. *The Visual Dictionary of Ancient Civilizations.* Dorling, 1994.

FOR THE STUDENT

Easy
DeFrates, Joanna. *What Do We Know About the Aztecs?* Bedrick, 1995.

Shemie, Bonnie. *Houses of Adobe: Native Dwellings: The Southwest.* Tundra, 1995.

Average
Garcia, Guy. *Spirit of the Maya: A Boy Explores His People's Mysterious Past.* Walker, 1995.

Wood, Tim. *The Aztecs.* Viking, 1992.

Challenging
Heily, Mathilde, and Remy Courgeon. *Montezuma and the Aztecs.* Holt, 1996.

Meyer, Carolyn, and Charles Gallenkamp. *The Mystery of the Ancient Maya.* McElderry, 1995. (New ed.)

LITERATURE CONNECTION

Trimble, Stephen. *The Village of Blue Stone.* Macmillan, 1990.

Wisniewski, David. *The Rain Player.* Clarion, 1991.

INTERDISCIPLINARY LINKS

Subject	Theme: Culture
MATH	Middle Grades Math: Tools for Success *Course 1*, Lesson 8-6, **Draw a Diagram** *Course 2*, Lesson 1-3, **Making Data Displays**
LANGUAGE ARTS	Choices in Literature *Communication Explosion*, **The Secret Among the Stones** Prentice Hall Literature *Bronze*, **Popocatepetl and Ixtlaccihuatl, Coyote and Little Turtle**

NATIONAL GEOGRAPHY STANDARDS

Students explore the 18 National Geography Standards throughout *Medieval Times to Today*. Chapter 3, however, concentrates on investigating the following standards: 1, 2, 3, 4, 5, 7, 8, 9, 10, 11, 14, 15, 16, 17. For a complete list of the standards, see the *Teacher's Flexible Planning Guide*.

SCHOOL TO CAREERS

In Chapter 3, The Ancient Americas, students learn about the Incas and the cultures of Middle and North America. Additionally, they address the skill of recognizing cause and effect. Understanding the cultures of the early Americas can help students prepare for careers in many fields, such as history, philosophy, sociology, and so on.

Recognizing cause and effect is a skill useful for customer service agents, farmers, weather forecasters, and so on. The curriculum presented in this book, as in all eight titles of Prentice Hall's *World Explorer* program, is designed to prepare students not only for careers but also for good citizenship—of the world as well as of this country.

INTERNET ACCESS

Many social studies teachers and students use Internet browsers, or search engines, to investigate particular topics. For the best results, use narrow rather than broad topics. Try these for Chapter 3: hieroglyph, aqueduct, Tenochtitlán, Cuzco, pueblo. Finding age-appropriate sites is an important consideration when using the Internet. For links to age-appropriate sites in world studies and geography, visit the Prentice Hall Home Page at:
http://www.phschool.com

The Ancient Americas

Connecting to the Guiding Questions

In this chapter, students will read about the ancient cultures of Middle, South, and North America. Content in this chapter thus corresponds to the following Guiding Questions:

● How did physical geography affect the development of societies around the world?

● What accomplishments in technology, learning, or artistic expression were found in each society?

Using the Map Activities

Have students read the names of the civilizations and cultures on the map. Then have student pairs find the names of the present-day countries in which these cultures are located.

• Mayas, Aztecs, Incas, Mound Builders, Anasazi

• Guatemala, Costa Rica; Mexico; Peru, Bolivia, Chile, Argentina; the United States

Heterogeneous Groups

The following Teacher's Edition strategies are suitable for heterogeneous groups.

Critical Thinking
Recognizing Cause and Effect   p. 61

Interdisciplinary Connections
Math   p. 66

Cooperative Learning
Planning a Tour   p. 74

SECTION 1
Cultures of Middle America

SECTION 2
The Incas

SECTION 3
Cultures of North America

KEY

Mayas A.D. 300–900
Aztecs A.D. 1200s–1521
Incas A.D. 1400s–1535
Mound Builders 700 B.C.–A.D. 1700
Anasazi A.D. 100–1200
— Pueblo 1200–Present
Lambert Azimuthal Equal-Area Projection

NORTH AMERICA — SOUTHWEST — Cahokia — EASTERN WOODLANDS — Mississippi River — ATLANTIC OCEAN — Gulf of Mexico — Tenochtitlán — Caribbean Sea — MIDDLE AMERICA — PACIFIC OCEAN — Amazon River — ANDES MOUNTAINS — SOUTH AMERICA — Cuzco

MAP ACTIVITIES

In ancient times, several different civilizations and cultures developed in North and South America. To help you to get to know the names and locations of these civilizations and cultures, do the following activities.

Locate a civilization
Find the areas labeled North America, Middle America, and South America. Which civilizations and cultures developed in each area?

What country is it today?
Find the locations of these civilizations and cultures on the maps in the Atlas in the back of your book. In what present-day countries were these cultures located?

Resource Directory

Media and Technology

 A Trip To: Machu Picchu, from the World Video Explorer, enhances students' understanding of Incan civilization.

Chapter 4

Cultures of Middle America

Reach Into Your Background

Think about your own culture. How have your grandparents contributed to your way of life? What about your parents? What can you pass on to the next generation?

Questions to Explore

1. What did the Mayas accomplish?
2. What made the Aztecs powerful?

Key Terms

maize
slash-and-burn agriculture
hieroglyph
causeway
aqueduct
artisan

Key Places

Tenochtitlán
Lake Texcoco

In about A.D. 1325, the Aztec people of central Mexico began looking for a place to build a new capital city. Legend says that they asked Huitzilopochtli (hwits il uh PAWCH lee), their god of war, where they should build. He told them to build the city at the place where they saw an eagle perched on a cactus and holding a snake in its beak.

When the Aztecs found the sign their god had described, they were dismayed. It was such an unlikely setting for a city. The eagle was perched on a cactus growing on a rocky outcrop in a swamp. But their god had given them this sign. Therefore, they built Tenochtitlán (tay nawch tee TLAHN), the world's finest city of the time, on a swampy island at the center of Lake Texcoco.

▼ This carving shows the sign that told the Aztecs where to build their capital. Legend says that they were told to build where they saw an eagle perched on a cactus and holding a snake in its beak.

The Geographic Setting

The Aztecs were not the first civilization or culture to develop in the Americas. Many Native American peoples had lived here for thousands of years. These various peoples developed ways of life that fit their geographic setting.

The land in the Americas has great variety. Rugged mountains and highland plateaus stretch from the icy north of North America all the way down the spine of South America to the tip of the continent. Other parts of the two continents are covered by vast plains or deserts.

Lesson Objectives

1. Relate Mayan civilization to its physical geographic setting.
2. Summarize the accomplishments of Mayan and Aztec civilizations.
3. Compare the Mayan and Aztec empires.

Lesson Plan

1 Engage

Warm-Up Activity

Have students read Reach Into Your Background in the Before You Read Box. Ask students what studying other cultures and civilizations can teach us. Define *civilization* as a society in which there are cities, social classes, and an organized economic system and government.

Activating Prior Knowledge

Have student partners create K-W-L charts about the Mayas and the Aztecs. Work with the students as they fill in information in the What We Know and What We Want to Know columns. Encourage them to add to the final column, What We Learned, as they read the section.

Teaching Resources

Reproducible Lesson Plan in the Chapter and Section Support booklet, p. 37, provides a summary of the section lesson.

Guided Reading and Review in the Chapter and Section Support booklet, p. 38, provides a structure for mastering key concepts and reviewing key terms in the section. Available in Spanish in the Spanish Support booklet, p. 24.

Program Resources

Material in the **Primary Sources and Literature Readings** booklet extends content with a selection related to the concepts in this chapter.

Outline Maps Central America and the Caribbean: Political, p. 9

2 Explore

After students read the section, have them contribute to a chart describing the Mayan and Aztec civilizations. Discuss and record the political and economic organizations, religions, cities, and social classes in these two societies. Discuss why there are social classes with specific tasks in an advanced society. Remind students that in an advanced society, farmers raise enough food to support everyone. This frees some people to become artisans, warriors, priests, and leaders.

3 Teach

Student partners will use the information from the chart and discussion to make a Venn diagram that compares and contrasts the civilizations of the Mayas and the Aztecs. This activity should take about 15 minutes.

4 Assess

See the answers to the Section Review. You may also use the students' diagrams for assessment.

Acceptable diagrams list at least two similarities and one difference.

Commendable diagrams show three similarities and two differences.

Outstanding diagrams show a complete understanding of the similarities and differences between the two cultures.

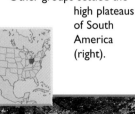

▼ ▶ The first people who settled the Americas lived in many different natural settings. Some groups made their homes in dense woodlands (below). Other groups settled the high plateaus of South America (right).

LINKS ACROSS TIME

Play Ball! The Mayas were enthusiastic ballplayers. On a court about the size of a football field, they played a game rather like soccer and basketball put together. The ball was a hard piece of rubber. The players could hit the ball with their elbows, wrists, shoulders, and hips but not with their hands or feet. And the ball could not touch the ground. To score, a player had to pass the ball through one of two stone hoops set high on walls.

The Americas also have many different climates. North American climates range from extreme cold in the far north to hot, almost tropical, in the south. Middle and South American climates also vary, but the most common climate is tropical.

The Mayas

It was in the tropical climate of southern Mexico and Central America that one important civilization, the Mayas, developed. The Mayan way of life, which was based on farming, flourished from about A.D. 300 to 900. Today, descendants of the early Mayas still live in Mexico and Central America. Many still practice some of their ancient traditions.

A Farming Culture Mayan farmers grew many different crops, such as beans, squash, peppers, avocados, and papayas. But maize, or corn, was their most important crop. They held maize in such high regard that they worshipped a god of corn.

To plant their corn, the Mayas first had to clear the land. They cut down the trees. Then they burned the tree stumps, later using the ash as fertilizer. Finally, they planted seeds. After a few years, the soil was worn out. The Mayas then chose a new area to clear and plant. This technique is called **slash-and-burn agriculture.**

Resource Directory

Program Resources

Nystrom Desk Atlas

Media and Technology

Color Transparencies 66, 85

Planet Earth CD-ROM includes satellite images and physical maps of Latin America, plus World Wonders, Cultural: Chichen Itza, Mexico.

Religion and Cities   Crops need the sun and the rain to grow. It is not surprising then, that the Mayas worshipped the forces of nature as well as a corn god. To honor their gods, the Mayas held great festivals.

The Mayas conducted the most important of these festivals in large temples. The temples stood atop soaring pyramids in the centers of Mayan cities. Each Mayan city had one ruler, who governed the city and the area around it. Priests and nobles assisted him. These people of power and high position lived in large houses that surrounded the temples. The ordinary people lived on the outskirts of the city. Beyond the city limits lay the farms.

Mayan Achievements   Mayan priests created a calendar to plan when to hold important religious festivals. The Mayas also developed a system of writing using signs and symbols called hieroglyphs.

About A.D. 900, the Mayas suddenly left their cities. No one knows why. Crop failures, war, disease, drought, or famine may have killed many Mayas. Or perhaps people rebelled against their leaders. When the Mayas left their cities, their civilization declined.

LINKS TO SCIENCE

An Accurate Calendar
The Mayas were great astronomers. They watched the skies and plotted the movements of the sun, moon, and stars. Using their observations, they designed a calendar of 365 days. It had 18 "months," each of which was 20 days long. The extra five days fell at the end of the year. These were considered bad luck days.

Activity

Critical Thinking

Recognizing Cause and Effect   Have students identify which of the following statements are causes and which are effects. Ask students to explain their choices.

- The Mayas wanted to grow corn.
- The Mayas cut and burned the trees on the land.
- The soil was quickly washed away.

Verbal, Auditory

Background

Global Perspectives

Hieroglyphics   The ancient civilizations of Egypt and Sumer in Mesopotamia also developed *hieroglyphics* in which signs and symbols stand for ideas, things, or sounds. In contrast, the signs and symbols of Mayan hieroglyphics stood for sounds, ideas, or individual words.

Mayan Wall Paintings

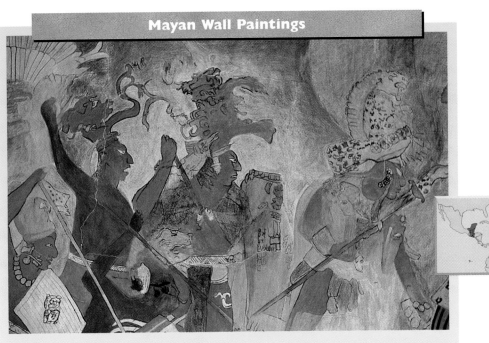

This picture shows one of the murals, or wall paintings, found in a Mayan temple in Bonampak, Mexico. The murals were painted in the late A.D. 700s, probably to celebrate the birth of a prince. This mural portrays a battle scene. The figure on the right is wearing a jaguar headdress. The jaguar was one of the Mayan gods of war. **Critical Thinking** Why do you think the Mayas included battle scenes among pictures celebrating the birth of a prince?

Answers to . . .

MAYAN WALL PAINTINGS

Answers may vary. Students might suggest that the Mayas hoped the new prince would be successful in battle.

Links Across Time

Waterworks Like the Aztecs, ancient Romans built aqueducts, primarily to bring water to the cities throughout the empire. In contrast, many modern aqueducts are designed to bring irrigation water to dry desert regions. One of the most extensive aqueduct systems in the world is located in California. The goal of the system is to move water from northern California, which accounts for 70 percent of the supply, to southern California, which accounts for 77 percent of the demand. One portion of the system stretches for 242 miles (387 km) and provides one billion gallons of water per day.

READ ACTIVELY

Visualize Picture the city of Tenochtitlán. How would this city built in a lake look unusual?

The Aztecs

Another ancient civilization of Middle America was that of the Aztecs. They arrived in the Valley of Mexico in the A.D. 1100s. Within 100 years, they controlled all the land in central Mexico between the Gulf of Mexico and the Pacific Ocean. In the center of their empire was Tenochtitlán, the capital they had built on Lake Texcoco.

Tenochtitlán: City in the Lake You have already read about how the Aztecs chose a spot for their capital. In spite of its swampy location, Tenochtitlán was a magnificent city. At the center was a huge square. All around it stood pyramid-temples, palaces, and large stone houses. Canals crisscrossed the city. People used the canals to transport goods and to move about the city. **Causeways,** or raised streets of hard earth, connected the city to the mainland.

As the city grew, the Aztecs realized that they needed more farmland. Their answer to the problem was to build "floating gardens." These were islands the size of football fields. The Aztecs made them by piling rich earth from the bottom of Lake Texcoco onto rafts made of wood. After a while, the roots of plants and trees grew down to the lake bottom, anchoring the rafts.

In addition, the Aztecs built **aqueducts,** pipes or channels designed to carry water from distant sources. These carried fresh springwater from the mainland to storage areas in the city.

Floating Gardens

The Aztecs began building a floating garden by driving a wooden frame into the lake bed. Next, they placed a raft of reeds or wood inside the frame. Then, they piled layers of weeds, mud from the lake bottom, and earth on the raft. They planted trees to root the raft to the lake bed and to provide shade for the garden. Over time, mud and earth fell through the raft filling the space underneath. **Critical Thinking** Why did the Aztecs need to build floating gardens?

Labels: Trees, Crops, Weeds, mud, and earth, Flowers, Frame

Answers to ...

FLOATING GARDENS

As the city in the lake grew, they needed more farmland.

This modern painting of a battle between the Tlaxcaltecs and Aztecs illustrates an almost constant part of Aztec life—war. Most Aztec men were expected to serve as soldiers. They were well trained and well equipped. They had armor of quilted cotton, swords, and bows and arrows. After military training, young men's heads were shaved, except for a strand of hair at the nape of their necks. Only after a soldier took a captive in war could the strand be cut. **Critical Thinking** How did the Aztecs treat the people they defeated in war?

Background

Biography

Moctezuma (c. 1480–1520) As emperor, he ruled the Aztecs from 1502 to 1520. Under his direction, the empire spread to the region of Honduras. Moctezuma believed that Hernan Cortés, the Spanish invader, was Quetzalcoatl, the legendary white god who had sailed away and promised to return. Therefore, Moctezuma at first welcomed the Spanish and did not realize their intentions until it was too late. The Spanish conquered his capital city and seized him. Moctezuma appealed to his subjects, but they attacked the palace and stoned him to death.

A Warlike Way of Life Although Tenochtitlán was a peaceful place, the Aztecs themselves were a warlike people. In the 1400s, Aztec warriors began conquering the other people in the region. Soon, the Aztecs controlled a huge empire. One ruler, the emperor, ruled over all the Aztec lands.

The Aztecs forced the people they conquered to pay tributes, or taxes, in the form of food, gold, or slaves. They also took thousands of prisoners of war to serve as human sacrifices. The Aztecs believed that they had to sacrifice humans so that the sun would have enough strength to rise every day. Human blood was what gave the sun strength. If the sun did not rise, crops could not grow, and the people would starve. Priests made the offerings daily. In very bad times, members of noble Aztec families were sometimes sacrificed to please the sun god.

Because of their respect for war, it is not surprising that the upper class of Aztec society was made up of military leaders as well as members of the royal family, priests, and nobles. The next class of

Resource Directory

Teaching Resources

Drawing Conclusions in the Social Studies and Geography Skills booklet, p. 52, provides additional skill practice.

Answers to . . .
THE AZTEC WAY OF WAR

The Aztecs forced the people they defeated to pay a tribute in the form of food, gold, or slaves. Sometimes they used prisoners of war as human sacrifices.

1. (a) corn (b) process in which trees are felled and stumps burned to make farmland (c) signs and symbols used as writing (d) raised street (e) pipes or channels designed to carry water from distant sources (f) skilled worker who practices a trade or creates jewelry, clothing, pottery, sculptures, or other goods

2. (a) capital city of the Aztecs (b) lake in central Mexico with an island on which the Aztecs built Tenochtitlán

3. The Mayas built cities and located temples atop pyramids. They developed a calendar and a system of hieroglyphic writing.

4. Aztec society was well organized. The Aztecs were very skilled engineers, creating canals, causeways, and aqueducts for their city.

5. Both civilizations were based on farming and had cities, temples, and pyramids. Their political organizations consisted of a ruler, priests, nobles, warriors, and the social classes beneath them, which were made up of artisans, farmers, and slaves. Both societies had strong religions. Both groups had a system of writing.

6. Answers will vary. Accept any reasonable answer.

Answers to ...

THE ROLE OF AZTEC WOMEN

Possible answer: Men were expected to fight in wars. Women were expected to raise and train their daughters, prepare food, and weave cloth.

The Role of Aztec Women

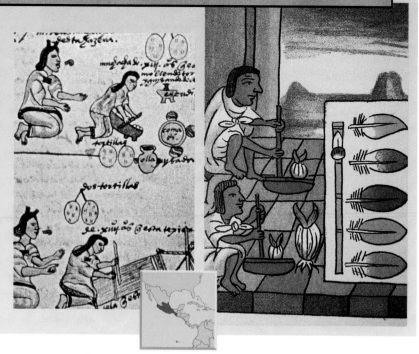

In these paintings, made during the 1500s, Aztec mothers teach their daughters to grind corn into flour (right and far right) and to weave cloth (right). In Aztec society, girls of 13 were expected to grind flour, make tortillas, and cook meals. By the time they became adults, they had to be skilled at weaving. Some of the cloth they wove was made into capes and used for trade. Some was used to decorate temples. The finest cloth went to make clothes for the nobles to wear.
Critical Thinking How did the skills required of Aztec men and Aztec women differ?

society was made up of warriors. Below them came artisans and traders. **Artisans,** or skilled workers who practice a trade, created jewelry, garments, pottery, sculptures, and other goods. Most people, however, were farmers. Slaves—most of whom were prisoners captured in battle—were at the bottom of Aztec society.

Aztecs spent much of their time in religious practices. Like the Mayas, they worshipped hundreds of gods and held many religious ceremonies. The main purpose of these ceremonies was to win the favor of the gods and bring about good crops or a victory in war.

SECTION 1 REVIEW

I. Define (a) maize, (b) slash-and-burn agriculture, (c) hieroglyph, (d) causeway, (e) aqueduct, (f) artisan.

2. Identify (a) Tenochtitlán, (b) Lake Texcoco.

3. What were some of the achievements of the Mayas?

4. What do you think made the Aztec empire strong?

Critical Thinking
5. Making Comparisons In what ways were the Mayan and Aztec empires alike?

Activity
6. Writing to Learn List the three features you found most interesting about Mayan or Aztec life. Use these to write a poem about either the Mayas or the Aztecs.

Resource Directory

Teaching Resources

Section Quiz in the Chapter and Section Support booklet, p. 39, covers the main ideas and key terms in the section. Available in Spanish in the Spanish Support booklet, p. 25.

The Incas

BEFORE YOU READ

Reach Into Your Background

Throughout history, rulers have tried to promote the unity, or oneness, of their empire and their people.

Suggest two ways in which you might help bring about unity among your classmates. Name two things you could do to encourage unity in your neighborhood.

Questions to Explore

1. How did Incan rulers establish a system for effectively ruling their vast empire?

2. What were some accomplishments of the Incas?

Key Terms

quipu
terrace

Key Place

Cuzco

Lesson Objectives

1. Determine how the Incas ruled a vast empire.

2. Trace how the needs of the empire resulted in advances in building and farming.

3. Evaluate the unification methods used by the Incan rulers.

Lesson Plan

1 Engage

Warm-Up Activity

Have students read Reach Into Your Background in the Before You Read box. Discuss what kinds of things unify a group of people.

Activating Prior Knowledge

Make a concept web on the chalkboard with *Incan Empire* in the center. Draw other circles or ovals around the center and label them *Political Organization, Economic Organization, Religion, Farming*, and *Cities*. Ask students to add what they know about the Incas to the web. As they read and discuss this section, they will add more information.

High in the mountains, a young boy races along a narrow stone highway. He breathes heavily, relieved that he has almost reached his goal. He lifts a conch-shell trumpet and blows. It is the signal telling the next runner to get ready.

The boy is a relay runner, chosen for his speed and endurance. The Incas depended on runners to carry messages to and from the capital at Cuzco. Like every other royal messenger, the boy knows his stretch of royal highway so well that he could run it on the darkest night.

As the runner reaches the end of his stretch of road, he passes the message to the next runner. He recites the message he memorized at the start of his run.

▼ An Incan relay runner announces his arrival by blowing a conch-shell trumpet.

Securing the Empire

Incan relay runners covered a lot of territory, for the Incan empire was huge. It stretched some 2,500 miles (4,023 km) along the Andes Mountains from what is now the country of Ecuador through the

Teaching Resources

📁 **Reproducible Lesson Plan** in the Chapter and Section Support booklet, p. 40, provides a summary of the section lesson.

📁 **Guided Reading and Review** in the Chapter and Section Support booklet, p. 41, provides a structure for mastering key concepts and reviewing key terms in the section. Available in Spanish in the Spanish Support booklet, p. 26.

2 Explore

After students read the section, have them contribute to the web on the chalkboard that describes Incan civilization. Discuss how the Incan leaders created an effective system for ruling places that were far away. How did the need to communicate with far-away parts of the empire lead to great achievements in building and engineering?

Activity

Interdisciplinary Connections

Math Invite interested students to find out more about the quipus created by the Incas and how they were used. Students can present the information to the class in an oral report accompanied by a demonstration of how to keep count on a quipu.

▶ The Incas believed that gold was the sweat of the sun god and that the gleaming metal reflected the sun god's glory. All the gold belonged to the emperor. It was used only for ceremonial objects, like these decorated knives.

LINKS TO MATH

An Official Census High government officials made sure that the Incan empire ran smoothly. They decided where people would live and what kind of work they would do. They used a census, or official count of the people, to keep track of everyone in the land. Such records helped officials make sure that the people paid taxes and registered to work on public projects.

countries of Peru, Bolivia, Chile, and Argentina. But this great empire had small beginnings. In about the year 1200, the Incas settled in Cuzco (KOOS koh), a small village high in the Andes. Through wars and conquests they extended their control practically the length of this mountain range, about 2,500 miles (4,023 km). Many different peoples lived within the borders of this huge empire.

The Rule of the Incas The Incas developed their own system of government to rule their empire. At its head was a ruler called "Sapa Inca," or "the emperor." People believed that he was descended from the sun god. He, and only he, owned the land and divided it among the people.

Incan rulers used interesting methods to unify the huge empire and its people. One ruler, for example, made the Incan language, Quechua (KECH wah), the official language of the empire. He sent people into newly conquered lands to teach Incan customs and laws and to set up schools that taught Incan religion and history.

All people were expected to pay taxes to the empire. Men had to work on public projects. They might farm land, mine gold, or build roads. Women wove cloth for government officials. Farmers and their families gave the government parts of the crops they raised. In return, the government took care of the poor, the sick, and the elderly.

Resource Directory

Program Resources

 Outline Maps Latin America: Physical, p. 6; Latin America: Political, p. 7

Media and Technology

Color Transparencies 64, 86

Although the Incas did not have a written language, they did create an unusual system for keeping detailed records. Government officials noted information about births, deaths, taxes, and harvests on knotted strings called **quipus** (KEE poos). Every quipu had a main cord with several colored strings attached. Each color represented a different item. Knots of varying sizes stood for numbers.

A System of Roads and Bridges To control the empire, the emperor and his officials had to know what was going on. To accomplish this, they needed a communication system—the runners. But these messengers needed roads to travel on. The Incas, therefore, built a large system of highways and bridges.

The roads served another purpose besides communication. In times of trouble, they allowed the army to travel quickly. As the soldiers traveled, they picked up supplies at stations along the way. Thus, the emperor could keep control of every part of the empire.

READ ACTIVELY

Connect Think of some ways in which you might communicate and keep records if your society had no written language.

Bridges From the Past

This rope bridge, strung across a gorge in the Andes, is similar to those used by the Incas. Incan bridges were made with strong cords of braided vines and reeds. The bridges were part of the huge road network that linked every part of the empire. Only soldiers and government officials were allowed to use this system of roads and bridges. **Critical Thinking** Why were bridges important in controlling the Incan empire?

3 Teach

Have student partners evaluate how the Incas ruled their empire by making a chart similar to this chart.

Way of Unifying the Empire	Advantage	Disadvantage
(one language)	(Everyone can communicate)	(Some groups might resent using the Incan language.)

Next to each means of unifying the empire, have students list advantages and disadvantages of the idea. This activity should take about 20–25 minutes.

Background

Links Across Time

All Roads Lead to Rome
The Roman Empire (31 B.C.–A.D. 476) was composed of far-flung provinces with foreign cultures. The Romans unified their empire physically with roads and bridges. They used the Latin language to unify the disparate cultures. They also set up schools to teach Roman customs, religion, and history. Roman law was the law of the entire empire. Centuries later, the Incas used similar methods to unify their empire.

Answers to ...

BRIDGES FROM THE PAST

Along with roads, bridges made possible quick communication and the timely dispatch of armies if trouble arose.

4 Assess

See the answers to the Section Review. You may also use students' charts for assessment.

Acceptable charts list at least three items in column one and logical evaluations.

Commendable charts show a more complete list of items and a deeper understanding of how the Incas united their empire.

Outstanding charts show original thinking about advantages and disadvantages of these attempts to unify the empire.

Background

Global Perspectives

Stonework The Incas transported stones from quarries in the mountains across great distances using human power exclusively. They had no horses or wheeled vehicles to drag loads and no levers to lift heavy stones. Even so, their monumental stone buildings can be compared to the pyramids of ancient Egypt. Researchers know that the Egyptians used sleds and wooden rollers to move huge blocks of stone that they had brought by barge across the Nile from the quarries in the western desert. Workers dragged and pushed these stone blocks up ramps to add them to the pyramid. At present, archaeologists are not sure how the Incas lifted the huge stones used in their buildings.

A Perfect Fit

These finely fitted granite stones are part of a building that still stands in the old Incan capital of Cuzco. Using hammers and chisels, skilled Incan stoneworkers carved 12 corners in the large stone. Then they fitted other stones around it to make a sturdy wall. If the stones of this wall were rocked by earthquakes, they simply moved, then settled back into place.

Incan Achievements

A network of roads was not the only Incan achievement. Incan engineering feats still amaze people today. For example, they changed the direction of rivers. And they were master builders.

Building With Stone Without any of our modern power tools, Incas built magnificent bridges and huge cities. They built fortresses on mountaintops. Much of what they built is still standing.

The Incas built these fortresses and cities mainly with stone. Sometimes they chose huge stones and used them just as they came from the mountains. Other times they broke the stones into smaller blocks. To break up the stone, they cut a long groove in the surface of the rock. Then they drove stone or wooden wedges into the groove until the rock split.

When the Incas made a wall, they made sure its large, many-sided stones fit together almost perfectly. After a wall was finished, the fit was so tight that not even a very thin knife blade could be slipped between two stones. They did all this with only hammers of stone and chisels of bronze.

Many examples of Incan stonework can still be seen in the Peruvian city of Cuzco, once the capital of the Incan empire. Its ancient stone walls and buildings have withstood major storms and earthquakes for centuries.

READ ACTIVELY

Ask Questions Think of three questions you might ask about Incan building methods and achievements.

Machu Picchu (MAHCH oo PEEK choo), too, is a great example of Incan building and engineering. The Incas built this city on a high and narrow ridge between two peaks in the Andes Mountains. Using huge stone blocks from the mountaintops, they created acres and acres of buildings, walls, and plazas. They carved stairs into the face of the mountain to connect city buildings. They also cut roads into the bare rock. More than 500 years later, people still use these roads. In fact, the workers who built Machu Picchu did more than build a city. They changed the shape of the mountain landscape.

◀ ▼ The ancient city of Machu Picchu (below) is located high in the Andes about 54 miles (87 km) from Cuzco. It was home for several thousand people. It also served as a religious center. Some of the buildings located on higher ground (left) housed stones that the Incas considered holy.

Background

Daily Life

Incan Food The Incan farmers grew hundreds of types of potatoes, the staple food of their diet. These potatoes had a variety of shapes, colors, and flavors. Potatoes were so important that the Incas developed a way of freeze-drying them so that they could be stored for years. First, the potatoes were left out overnight to freeze. The next day, people stepped on piles of potatoes to stamp out the moisture and to take off the peel. Again, the potatoes were left out in the cold mountain air to freeze for several nights. Finally, they were put in the sun to dry and then stored in a dark, cool place.

Teaching Resources

📁 **Critical Thinking Activity** in the Chapter and Section Support booklet, p. 50, helps students apply the skill of drawing conclusions.

1. (a) knotted string used to keep records in business, farming, and government (b) steplike ledge cut into a mountainside and used as a field for crops

2. capital city of the Incan empire

3. Students should mention that the Incan government was headed by "Sapa Inca," or "the emperor," who owned the land and divided it among the people, and that everyone paid taxes and did work for the government in return for the government's support of the poor, sick, and elderly.

4. to establish a communication system for soldiers and government officials so that they might more easily control the empire

5. The Incas built impressive stone buildings and fortresses that have withstood earthquakes. They changed the direction of rivers, built bridges, and created terraces to increase farmland.

6. Students' answers should mention that unity in their empire would keep conquered peoples from rebelling and would encourage the cooperation necessary to keep the political and economic systems working.

7. Students' descriptions should include items mentioned in the text as they would be seen by an explorer or outsider of Incan culture.

Answers to ...

TERRACE FARMING

Terraces allowed the Incas to use the sloped land on mountains for farming.

Terrace Farming

The Incas built their terraces using stone walls. The area behind the wall was leveled out and lined with a layer of gravel to help with drainage. Then, earth was piled over the gravel. Finally, stone-lined channels were built to carry water to the terraces. These terraces in the mountains near Cuzco are still in use today. **Critical Thinking** How did the building of terraces help Incan farmers?

More Land for Farms Because they lived among steep, dry, and rugged mountains, the Incas had little natural farmland. They did two things to increase the amount of land available for farming.

First, they built a system of canals and aqueducts. The water that flowed through this system turned dry land into fertile fields.

To make use of the land on the slopes of the mountains, the Incas built **terraces**. These steplike ledges cut into the mountainside could then be used as fields for crops. The terraces also stopped soil from being washed away by rain. Incan farming techniques such as terracing are still used in the Andes today.

SECTION 2 REVIEW

1. Define (a) quipu, (b) terrace.

2. Identify Cuzco.

3. What were the main features of the Incan system of government?

4. Why did the Incas build a system of roads and bridges?

5. What advances did the Incas make in building and farming?

Critical Thinking

6. Recognizing Cause and Effect Why do you think that unity was an important goal of Incan rulers?

Activity

7. Writing to Learn You are an explorer seeing an Incan city for the first time. Write a description of what you see. In your description, include building methods and materials, farming techniques, and other interesting points of information.

Resource Directory

Teaching Resources

📁 **Section Quiz** in the Chapter and Section Support booklet, p. 42, covers the main ideas and key terms in the section. Available in Spanish in the Spanish Support booklet, p. 27.

Cultures of North America

Reach Into Your Background

In what kinds of homes do people in your part of the country live? What do these homes tell you about the environment and cultures of your area?

Questions to Explore
1. What was the role of mounds in the cultures of the Mound Builders of North America?

2. How did the environment affect the way of life of the people of the Southwest?

Key Term
pueblo

Key Place
Cahokia

Looking out of the airplane window, you see a huge earthen snake. It twists and turns across the landscape. You realize that the shape of the snake was created with mounds of dirt. What could those mounds be? It is obvious that they were formed centuries ago. Who could have made them? And why would anyone make such an effort to form a shape that could only be seen from above?

For years after they were discovered, these ancient mounds baffled scientists. Archaeologists found different kinds of mounds in other parts of the country. But nobody knew what they were or who had built them. Only now are scientists beginning to solve this ancient mystery.

▼ Monk's Mound, the largest mound in Cahokia, Illinois, measures about 1,000 feet (300 m) by 800 feet (240 m) at its base. It rises to a height of about 100 feet (30 m).

Lesson Objectives

1. Learn about the uses of the mounds built by native North Americans.

2. Relate the ways of life of the people of the Southwest to their environment.

3. Describe the relationship between the Anasazi and Pueblo cultures.

Lesson Plan

1 Engage

Warm-Up Activity

Have students preview this section by reading the first two paragraphs and looking at the photographs on this page. Invite them to speculate on what these structures might have been built for and why the pictured mound has the shape of a snake.

Activating Prior Knowledge

Have students read Reach Into Your Background in the Before You Read box. Ask students how the weather, the building materials available, and landforms influence what the buildings are made of and look like.

Teaching Resources

📁 **Reproducible Lesson Plan** in the Chapter and Section Support booklet, p. 43, provides a summary of the section lesson.

📁 **Guided Reading and Review** in the Chapter and Section Support booklet, p. 44, provides a structure for mastering key concepts and reviewing key terms in the section. Available in Spanish in the Spanish Support booklet, p. 28.

Program Resources

📁 **Outline Maps** The United States and Canada: Physical, p. 12; The United States and Canada: Political, p. 13

2 Explore

After students read the section, discuss the following questions: What were the two different uses of the mounds? How were the mounds in Cahokia similar to Aztec pyramids? (There were temples on top where ceremonies were held.) How did the desert environment affect the way of life of the Anasazi in the Southwest? How did the Pueblos use the mesas that surrounded them? Why did they perform rain dances?

3 Teach

Have students work in groups of four to make up a quiz that covers the information in the section. When the quizzes are completed, have them exchange and answer one another's quizzes. Then suggest that groups evaluate their quizzes by comparing them to the Section Review. This activity should take about 30 minutes.

Answers to . . .

THE GREAT SERPENT MOUND

It was a cemetery.

The Great Serpent Mound

Built between 1,300 and 3,000 years ago, the Great Serpent Mound in Ohio is the largest image of a snake in the world. The "uncoiled" length of the serpent is about 1,300 feet (396 m). **Critical Thinking** For what purpose was the Great Serpent Mound built?

READ ACTIVELY

Predict Why did Native American peoples build mounds?

The Mound Builders

Separate groups of Native American peoples built different kinds of mounds. The groups were known by different names and lived at various times from about 1000 B.C. to the A.D. 1600s. Today, all of these people are known as Mound Builders.

The Mound Builders were just some of the Native Americans who lived in the region called the Eastern Woodlands. This region lies between southern Canada and the state of Tennessee, and between the Mississippi River and the Atlantic Ocean.

Resource Directory

Media and Technology

Color Transparency 78

Planet Earth CD-ROM includes satellite images and physical maps of North America.

The Mounds of Cahokia The once-great city of Cahokia (kuh HOH kee uh) in what is now Illinois offers an example of one type of mound found in the Eastern Woodlands. Cahokia was a large city. Many of the buildings in the city were built on mounds. Some of these mounds were shaped like flat-topped pyramids. Temples for worshipping gods and buildings used for ceremonies once stood on top of these mounds. The largest mound in Cahokia has a base bigger than that of the Great Pyramid in Egypt.

Cahokia's mounds are not natural. Thousands of workers built them by moving basketfuls of dirt by hand. They accomplished all this with simple tools of wood, stone, and shell.

The Great Serpent Mound The serpent mound in Ohio served a very different purpose from that of Cahokia's pyramid mounds. This twisting, snakelike structure was a cemetery. Called the Great Serpent Mound, it is just one of many similar mounds in Ohio. When you look at these mounds from above, they are shaped like animals. Some served as graves for as many as 1,000 people.

The mounds also hold some of the precious belongings of the Mound Builders. Researchers probing the serpent mounds have found jewelry made of shell and copper, clay statues, and other works of art. Some of these items are made from materials that are not from Ohio. Researchers, therefore, believe that the Mound Builders must have been involved in extensive trading.

People of the Southwest

The mounds of the Eastern Woodlands are truly amazing. However, they are just a small part of the fascinating story of Native Americans in North America. Other Native American groups made their homes in the rocky deserts and forested mountains of the Southwest. Today, this region includes the states of New Mexico, Arizona, Utah, and Colorado. Here, too, environment affected the Native American way of life. One present-day Pueblo elder explained it like this:

❝The story of my people and the story of this place are one single story. No man can think of us without thinking of this place. We are always joined together.❞

▼ Native Americans of the Southwest made their pottery by hand. To make the black dye used in decorating the pottery, they boiled the roots of various plants.

4 Assess

See the answers to the Section Review. You may also use students' quizzes for assessment.

Acceptable quizzes cover the main facts of the section.

Commendable quizzes ask questions that require critical thinking.

Outstanding quizzes show originality and present thought-provoking questions on this material.

Background

Global Perspectives

Burial Mounds and Pyramid Tombs In the Great Serpent Mound near Hillsboro, Ohio, built by the Adena peoples, important persons were buried in coffins made from hollowed-out logs. They were buried with gifts to their spirits, such as jewelry, pottery, tools, and tobacco pipes made of intricately carved clay or stone. The practice of burying people with gifts or supplies for the afterlife dates back to prehistoric times. For example, Egyptian nobles and pharaohs were buried with lavish luxuries. In China, an ancient ruler was buried with an entire army of life-size terra-cotta soldiers, each with a unique face.

Teaching Resources

🗀 **Section Quiz** in the Chapter and Section Support booklet, p. 45, covers the main ideas and key terms in the section. Available in Spanish in the Spanish Support booklet, p. 29.

🗀 **Vocabulary** in the Chapter and Section Support booklet, p. 47, provides a review of key terms in the chapter. Available in Spanish in the Spanish Support booklet, p. 31.

🗀 **Reteaching** in the Chapter and Section Support booklet, p. 48, provides a structure for students who may need additional help in mastering chapter content.

Activity

Cooperative Learning

Planning a Tour Propose that groups of four students each decide on a tour of places in North, South, or Middle America. The purpose of the tour would be to visit the remains of the civilizations covered in this chapter. Each group should plan an itinerary for a trip covering three weeks. Groups should also decide what they want to see, and find out how they would get from one place to another. Students can use library, Internet, and travel agency sources to help plan their tour. Groups can present tour plans to the class in the form of illustrated brochures.

L·I·N·K·S ACROSS TIME

Acequias Today's New Mexicans use an irrigation system invented by the ancient Pueblos. The region only receives between 8 and 13 inches of rain a year, but it does have rivers. People dig *acequias* (uh SAYK yuhz), or narrow, shallow ditches, from a river to the fields. Some of the water soaks the soil. The main acequia finally empties the remaining water back into the river.

▼ Modern Hopi corn dancers perform a ceremonial rain dance at a tribal gathering in the town of Gallup, New Mexico.

The Anasazi: The Ancient Ones The Anasazi (an uh SAH zee) were among the first cultures to develop in the Southwest. The word *Anasazi* means "ancient ones." These people lived long ago and came from outside the region. Centuries ago, the Anasazi moved into the Southwest from the far north. At first, they wandered the Colorado Plateau and other nearby areas. In time, they settled and began growing corn, beans, squash, and other vegetables. They built complicated systems of canals to bring water to dry lands where they had settled. They also grew cotton and wove it into cloth, and made pottery and baskets.

By A.D. 100, permanent Anasazi villages dotted the landscape. At first, the people lived in pit houses, circular houses built partly underground. However, they found that such dwellings were not easy to protect against enemy attack. Therefore, they built some of their villages into the sides of steep cliffs. And sometimes they built villages on top of mesas, or high, flat-topped hills. These villages, called **pueblos,** were a lot like our high-rise apartment buildings. As many as 1,200 people might live in one village.

The Pueblo Peoples Anasazi customs lived on among later groups we call the Pueblo people. The Pueblos used the same apartment-type villages built into cliffs. And, like the Anasazi, they were

📁 **Enrichment** in the Chapter and Section Support booklet, p. 49, extends chapter content and enriches students' understanding.

📁 **Spanish Glossary** in the Spanish Support booklet, pp. 83–91, provides key terms translated from English to Spanish as well as definitions in Spanish.

📁 **Chapter Summary** in the Chapter and Section Support booklet, p. 46, provides a summary of chapter content. Available in Spanish in the Spanish Support booklet, p. 30.

📁 **Cooperative Learning Activity** in the Activities and Projects booklet, pp. 28–31, provides two student handouts, one page of teacher's directions, and a scoring rubric for a cooperative learning activity on writing a message using your own hieroglyphics.

Media and Technology

🎧 **Guided Reading Audiotapes** (English and Spanish)

Mesa Verde Pueblo

During the 1100s, Native Americans in southwestern Colorado built these cliff dwellings at Mesa Verde (left). Families stored goods in rooms at the back of the cliff and lived in rooms near the front. They used the circular underground rooms, or *kivas*, in the foreground of the picture for religious ceremonies. People used ladders to go from level to level (below).

farmers. Their crafts included weaving, basket making, and pottery making.

The Pueblos believed in many spirits. They wanted to please these spirits, who controlled the rain that watered their plots of corn, beans, and squash. Many times during the year, men gathered in an underground room called a *kiva* to ask the spirits to send rain. They appealed to *kachinas,* or cloud spirits, by performing special rain dances.

SECTION 3 REVIEW

1. **Define** pueblo.

2. **Identify** Cahokia.

3. Why did the Native Americans of the Eastern Woodlands build mounds?

4. How did the Anasazi and Pueblo peoples use the land?

Critical Thinking
5. **Drawing Conclusions** It took a lot of time and hard work to build the mounds. What might this effort tell you about the values and beliefs of the cultures that built the mounds?

Activity
6. **Writing to Learn** Write two paragraphs telling what your life might be like if you were a teenager living in a pueblo.

Using the Writing Process

You may **introduce** the skill by reviewing the steps of the writing process: *prewriting*, in which students write down their ideas on the topic and begin to organize them; *writing a first draft; revising;* and *publishing* or *sharing the final copy*. Have students **practice and apply** the skill by writing a story about life in a Pueblo "apart-

ment house." As prewriting, students can generate ideas about characters and plots. Then they can write a first draft as a homework assignment, and go over the draft with a writing partner. Using the suggestions from this peer conference, they can revise their story, again as homework, and then bring in a final copy to share with their classmates. Publish these stories in a class book for your classroom library.

Activity

Journal Writing

Visit to a Mound Tell students to describe a mound they have read about as if they were visiting the site. Then have them describe the feelings they have looking at the mound from the air or the ground. If students are keeping an Explorer's Journal, as described in the opening pages of their books, you may wish to do this writing activity as part of that journal.

Section 3 Review

1. village built on top of high hills, they were like high-rise apartment buildings

2. large city of the Mound Builders in present-day Illinois

3. Some of the mounds were for burials, and others were flat-topped pyramids with ceremonial buildings or chief's dwellings on top.

4. The Anasazi and Pueblo people used the land to grow corn, beans, squash, other vegetables, and cotton, and they built irrigation canals to bring water to dry areas. They both used the mesas for their dwellings.

5. Student answers should show an awareness of the fact that the burial of their people was extremely important to the Mound Builders and that the building of temples meant that they had a strong religion. They might also mention that the people were cooperative and organized enough to undertake large building projects.

6. Students' answers will vary, but should mention what it is like to live in a multi-family dwelling.

Recognizing Cause and Effect

Lesson Objectives

1. Define the terms *cause* and *effect*.

2. Recognize cause and effect signal words.

3. Identify causes and effects in context.

Lesson Plan

1 Engage

Warm-Up Activity

To **introduce** the skill, ask students the questions from the opening scenario. Then read aloud the remaining text in the opening paragraph. Write the terms *cause* and *effect* on the chalkboard.

Activating Prior Knowledge

Challenge students to give examples of cause-and-effect relationships. Write some of these on the chalkboard. Have students note, on the chalkboard or a sheet of paper, definitions for each term.

2 Explore

Have students read the Get Ready text. Then invite a volunteer to record examples from the text on the chalkboard, next to students' own examples. Ask another student to record the definitions for *cause* (something that makes an event or situation happen) and *effect* (a result of a cause) on the chalkboard. Together, compare both the definitions and examples with those students identified earlier. Tell students to finish reading the Skills Activity.

Wondering why things happen is something every human being does. Why is the sky blue? Why does the sun rise in the east? This curiosity is one reason some people become scientists or historians. Curiosity has driven us to learn how history has shaped our world. When we ask "why" about something, we are actually trying to figure out causes and effects.

Get Ready

A cause is something that makes an event or situation happen. For example, lack of sleep causes you to be tired. An effect is a result of a cause. Being tired is the effect of not getting enough sleep.

Causes and effects may be short term, such as not going to bed early enough making you tired the next morning. However, causes and effects can also be long term. For example, a war is generally the effect of many causes over a period of time.

Try It Out

To figure out causes and effects in something you are reading, it can help to look for certain words that are clues. *Because, so,* and *since* are words that can signal a cause. *Therefore* and *as a result* are some words that signal an effect.

▼ Doing a good job at school is one result of getting enough sleep every night.

Resource Directory

Teaching Resources

Recognizing Cause and Effect in the Social Studies and Geography Skills booklet, p. 49, provides additional skill practice.

Sometimes effects become causes of other effects. For example, the effect of not getting enough sleep is being tired. And being tired could cause you to not do well on a test.

You can help yourself understand cause-effect relationships by making a cause-effect diagram like this one.

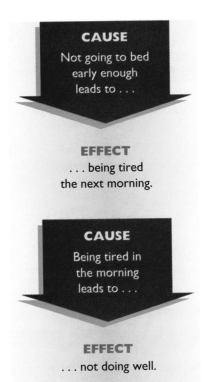

CAUSE
Not going to bed early enough leads to . . .

EFFECT
. . . being tired the next morning.

CAUSE
Being tired in the morning leads to . . .

EFFECT
. . . not doing well.

Apply the Skill

Read the paragraph at top right. Look for causes and effects. Make a cause-effect diagram if you need to. Then list the cause-effect relationships that you find in the paragraph. Remember that sometimes an effect becomes a cause of another effect.

The Need for Land

As Tenochtitlán grew, the Aztecs realized that they needed more land. They especially needed more farmland on which to grow food for the increasing number of people who lived in the city. However, Tenochtitlán was built on Lake Texcoco, and land was in short supply. The Aztecs, therefore, had to create new land. Their answer to the problem was to build "floating gardens." Using mud from the lake bottom, they built small islands about the size of football fields. After a while, the roots of plants and trees grew down to the lake bottom, anchoring the islands. The Aztecs used the islands to grow tomatoes, squash, chili peppers, and other food crops. These crops increased the food supply by a considerable amount. As a result, there was enough food to support an even larger population in Tenochtitlán.

▲ The floating gardens built by the Aztecs still exist. They are in Mexico City.

3 Teach

Have students **practice** the skill by completing the cause-and-effect diagram described in Try It Out. Model how to use the signal words to link causes and effects into statements. Explain that this is one way to verify the causal relationship. Invite students to share their diagrams and statements with the class.

For additional reinforcement, ask students to write three cause-and-effect statements about a topic of their choosing.

4 Assess

Direct students to **apply** the skill to the boxed paragraph. To **assess**, evaluate their skill as students work together to identify causes and effects in the paragraph. Invite individual students to point out signal words such as *therefore* and *as a result*.

Answers to. . .

APPLY THE SKILL

Answers will vary. Sample answers are shown.

C: Tenochtitlán was built on a lake.
↓
E&C: Land was in short supply.
↓
E&C: The Aztecs needed new land.
↓
E: They built floating gardens.

C: The Aztecs grew food on their new islands.
↓
E&C: The food supply was increased.
↓
E&C: There was enough food for the growing population.
↓
E: The population grew.

Chapter Review 3

Reviewing Main Ideas

1. The Mayas made advances in mathematics and astronomy, created a calendar, and built cities with temples and tall pyramids.

2. The Aztecs were skilled warriors. They became rich through taxes paid by the groups they conquered. They had a well-organized government run by a royal family, nobles, priests, and military leaders.

3. The roads linked the capital and seat of government, Cuzco, to all parts of the Incan empire. The Incas could send an army on these roads to quell a rebellion. They used the roads for a system of communication, in which runners carried messages to all parts of the empire.

4. The Incas built stone fortresses and buildings so strong that they have survived until the present in spite of storms and earthquakes. They cut terraces into the mountains to make more farmland to feed the large population.

5. Some of the mounds built by the Mound Builders were used as cemeteries, others were bases for temples.

6. (a) The Pueblos wanted to please the spirits so that they would send rain. (b) To please the spirits, they did rain dances dressed like cloud spirits, or *kachinas*.

Reviewing Key Terms

Sentences should show the correct meanings of words through context.

Critical Thinking

1. Students' answers should show an awareness of the fact that a calendar is necessary for farming in order to know when to plant and when to harvest. The calendar also was needed for their religious festivals.

2. Students' answers should stress the fact that the environment dictates the way of life of a people. The dry environment meant that the people were anxious about rain, which influenced their religious beliefs. They also had to irrigate the land in order to farm, so they developed a system of bringing water from rivers.

CHAPTER 3 Review and Activities

Reviewing Main Ideas

1. What were the major achievements of the Mayas?
2. How did the Aztecs become powerful?
3. How did a system of roads and bridges help the Incas keep their empire together?
4. (a) Name two Incan achievements, one in building and one in farming. (b) Tell why each was important.
5. What purposes did the mounds built by the Mound Builders serve?
6. (a) Why did the Pueblos want to please the spirits? (b) What did they do to please them?

Reviewing Key Terms

Use each key term below in a sentence that shows the meaning of the term.

1. maize
2. slash-and-burn agriculture
3. hieroglyph
4. causeway
5. aqueduct
6. artisan
7. quipu
8. terrace
9. pueblo

Critical Thinking

1. **Drawing Conclusions** Why might it have been important for the Mayas to have a good calendar?

2. **Identifying Central Ideas** Explain the meaning of this quotation: "No man can think of us without thinking of this place. We are always joined together." Give an example from one of the cultures of the Southwest that supports this statement.

Graphic Organizer

Copy the chart onto a separate sheet of paper. Then fill in the empty boxes to complete the chart.

	Where They Lived	What They Were Like	Major Achievement
Mayas			
Aztecs			
Incas			
Mound Builders			
Anasazi			
Pueblo			

Graphic Organizer

	Where They Lived	What They Were Like	Major Achievement
Mayas	southern Mexico, Central America	farming culture	calendar hieroglyphs
Aztecs	central Mexico	warlike	floating gardens
Incas	within the Andes mountains	warlike, farming culture	roads and bridges, stonework, terraced farming
Mound Builders	Eastern Woodlands	woodland culture	mounds
Anasazi	American southwest	farming culture	built cities into sides of cliffs
Pueblo	American southwest	farming culture	built cities into sides of cliffs

Map Activity

The Ancient Americas
For each place listed below, write the letter from the map that shows its location.

1. Tenochtitlán

2. Cahokia

3. Middle America

4. Andes Mountains

5. Cuzco

Place Location

Writing Activity

Writing a Letter to the Editor
Assume that the government of a state wants to build an airport across land on which the Mound Builders once built a mound. Do you think the government should be allowed to destroy the mound? Why or why not? Write a letter to the editor of a newspaper explaining your reasons.

Internet Activity

Use a search engine to find **NOVA Online/Ice Mummies of the Inca/Site Map.** Choose **The Expedition** to join the discovery of the ice mummy Sarita. Explore the links under **Lost Worlds.** What do the artifacts found with Sarita tell about the Incas? Make a book of Sarita artifacts. Print out or make your own pictures and explain the significance of each artifact.

Skills Review

Turn to the Skills Activity.

Review the ways you can recognize cause and effect. Then complete the following: (a) What question does cause and effect answer? (b) Explain two different kinds of causes.

How Am I Doing?

Answer these questions to help you check your progress.

1. Can I describe the geographic setting of the Americas' early cultures?

2. Do I understand how cultures in the Americas compare to one another?

3. Can I identify ways in which the environment affected the lives of the early peoples who lived in the Americas?

4. What information from this chapter can I use in my book project?

Internet Activity

If students are having difficulty finding this site, you may wish to have them use the following URL, which was accurate at the time this textbook was published:
http://www2.pbs.org/ wgbh/pages/ nova/peru/table.html

You might also guide students to a search engine. Four of the most useful are Infoseek, AltaVista, Lycos, and Yahoo. For additional suggestions on using the Internet, refer to the Prentice Hall Social Studies' Educator's Handbook "Using the Internet," in the *Prentice Hall World Explorer Program Resources*.

For additional links to world history and culture topics, visit the Prentice Hall Home Page at:
http://www.phschool.com

How Am I Doing?

Point out to students that this checklist is a quick reminder of what they learned in the chapter. If their answer to any of the questions is *no* or if they are unsure, they may need to review the topic.

Map Activity

1. B	3. C	5. E
2. A	4. D	

Skill Review

(a) Cause and effect answers the question, "Why?" (b) Causes can be either long term or short term.

Writing Activity

Letters should be well organized and express a clear opinion with reasons to back it up. The letter form should be correct.

Resource Directory

Teaching Resources

📁 **Chapter Tests** Forms A and B are in the Tests booklet, pp. 14–19.

Program Resources

📁 **Writing Process Handbook** includes Editing for Writing Effective Paragraphs, pp. 27–28, to help students with the Writing Activity.

Media and Technology

🖨 **Color Transparencies** Color Transparency 171 (Graphic organizer web template)

💿 **Prentice Hall Writer's Solution** Writing Lab CD-ROM

💾 **Computer Test Bank**

💿 **Resource Pro™ CD-ROM**

1 Compare community portraits in a historical narrative.

2 Relate a literary work to information about its historical and geographic context.

Lesson Plan

1 Engage

Building Vocabulary

Point out that notes in the margin can help students understand certain words and can give helpful hints as students read. Vocabulary respelled in the margin include: *tlaxcalli*, *copalxocotl*, *itacatl*, and *calmecac*.

Ask how the pronunciations of these words differ from English pronunciations of the same letter combinations.

Activating Prior Knowledge

Have students read Reach Into Your Background in the Before You Read box. Help students identify some ways that Mexican civilizations have influenced American culture today, for example, food, language, or dress.

2 Develop Student Reading

Direct students to read the selection. Suggest that they look for interesting details of daily life, comparing these to modern equivalents.

FROM

The Americas in 1492

BY JAMAKE HIGHWATER

BEFORE YOU READ

Reach Into Your Background

What do you know about the year 1492? You probably know that in this year, Christopher Columbus first landed in the Americas. In this year, the colonization of the Americas began. At that time, the Europeans referred to the Americas as the New World.

The Americas may have been new to the Europeans, but the people who lived here did not think of it as new. They had entire kingdoms, languages, and religions very different from those of the Europeans.

In Mexico in 1492, the Aztecs had a great empire, ruled by the powerful Moctezuma, also known as Montezuma.

Questions to Explore

1. How does this selection help you understand life in Mexico before colonization?
2. What were some different parts of Aztec society?

---

tlaxcalli (tlaks KAL ee)
copalxocotl (koh puhlks un KAH tuhl)

The Aztec day began when the priests at the top of the great pyramids beat wooden gongs and sounded trumpets made of conch seashells. It was still dawn as the people awakened in all the houses, great and humble. Most of the homes were made of sunbaked bricks and consisted of one large family room, with the kitchen located in a separate building in the courtyard. In the first light of the day, the women fanned the coals of their cooking fires until they burst into flame. In the gardens turkeys began to strut and gobble, while in the houses there was the rumble of corn grinders. Soon there was also the rhythmic sound of the women slapping lumps of dough between their hands to make the pancake-like bread called *tlaxcalli* (or tortillas). Now all the families came together to have breakfast, a simple meal of bread and a beer-like drink called *octli*. Then, after a bath in fresh water, using a soap made from the root of the *copalxocotl* tree, they put on their sandals and tied their cloth cloaks over their shoulders and were ready for work.

Outside the city, most people worked in the fields from dawn to dusk. For their long day they packed a picnic lunch, which

---

Resource Directory

Program Resources

Material in the **Primary Sources and Literature Readings** booklet provides additional literature selections on the region under study.

they called *itacatl,* and then they went into the fields owned by their town or village. They grew corn, vegetables, and flowers, for which the Aztecs had a great affection. All Mexicans shared this love of gardens. The people grew flowers everywhere—in their courtyards, in broad fields along the lakes, and even on their rooftops. . . .

The common people of Mexico were born, they worked, and then they died. They had little opportunity for education or advancement. During the first years of their lives, boys were taught to carry wood and water. By the age of six, girls learned how to spin cloth and to cook. At the age of fifteen, young people who showed signs of intelligence and talent were allowed to enter the *calmecac*—a temple school where their education was entrusted to priests.

For the Aztec people of wealth and power, life was very different from the existence of the farmers and their families. They had lavish food and educational opportunities. They lived in the great city among the splendid temples and pyramids, and they wandered among the magnificent buildings and gardens as free people.

In the main plaza at the heart of the royal city of Tenochtitlán, there was a great sea of human bodies and human baggage. Then, quite suddenly, the tangle of the crowd opened into the vast empty space at the entrance of the palace. Only men of power and rank were allowed to walk in this expansive entranceway. One by one they came to the Council Chamber of Montezuma to plead for favors or to beg forgiveness for an offense. He was more than a ruler. He was very nearly a god—so great and so holy that no one was allowed to look upon his face. He was elected from the most royal of Aztec lineages by a council of nobles, warriors, and high priests. But once he ascended to the throne, he was utterly out of reach even to those who had elected him, so vast was his power. . . .

▲ This is one artist's idea of daily life along a canal in the Aztec empire.

itacatl (it uh KAH tuhl)
calmecac (KAL muhk ak)

Connect How did Aztec education differ from your own?

EXPLORING YOUR READING

Look Back
1. How did the Aztec day begin? How is this similar to the way your day begins?

Think It Over
2. How did the common Aztec people live differently from the wealthy?

3. Why do you think the Aztecs honored Moctezuma in the ways that they did?

Go Beyond
4. Compare the life of Moctezuma to that of a United States president. How were the two lives similar or different?

Ideas for Writing: A Short Story
5. Write a story about a young person living in Tenochtitlán who receives a rare opportunity to see Moctezuma. What are the circumstances of the meeting? What are the young person's impressions of the great leader?

3 Assess
Work through the Exploring Your Reading questions with students.

1. With the sound of gongs and trumpets. Answers will vary.
2. Common people lived simple lives focused on farming and survival. Most had no education. Wealthy people lived in the city among elaborate temples and pyramids. They had plenty of food and could get an education.
3. They believed he was holy and had limitless power.
4. Both are elected and held in high esteem. Moctezuma, unlike a United States President, had total power and was treated like a god.
5. Stories should contain circumstances as well as characters consistent with factual information in the text.

Background

About the Author
Jamake Highwater, a Native American of Blackfoot and Cherokee parentage, recalls a childhood of "vivid teachings [about] the Indian world." Many of Highwater's writings have focused on Native American culture.

About the Selection
"The Americas in 1492" appears as part of a collection titled *The World in 1492,* edited by Jean Fritz and published by Henry Holt & Co. in 1992.

Civilizations of Asia

To help you plan instruction, the chart below shows how teaching resources correspond to chapter content. Use the resources to vary instruction, add activities, or plan block schedules. Where appropriate, resources have **suggested time allotments** for students. Time allotments are approximate.

Managing Time and Instruction

	Medieval Times to Today Teaching Resources Binder		World Explorer Program Resources Binder	
	Resource	**mins.**	**Resource**	**mins.**
1 SECTION 1 Golden Ages in China	**Chapter and Section Support** Reproducible Lesson Plan, p. 52		**Outline Maps** China and Neighboring Countries: Political, p. 41	20
	Ⓢ Guided Reading and Review, p. 53	20		
	Ⓢ Section Quiz, p. 54	25	**Nystrom Desk Atlas**	
	Social Studies and Geography Skills, Identifying the Main Idea, p. 41	30	Ⓣ **Primary Sources and Literature** Readings	40
			Writing Process Handbook Using Transitions, p. 30	25
SKILLS ACTIVITY Assessing Your Understanding	**Social Studies and Geography Skills,** Determining If You Understood What You Read, p. 74	30		
2 SECTION 2 Feudalism in Japan	**Chapter and Section Support** Reproducible Lesson Plan, p. 55		**Outline Maps** Japan and the Koreas: Political, p. 42	20
	Ⓢ Guided Reading and Review, p. 56	20		
	Ⓢ Section Quiz, p. 57	25		
3 SECTION 3 The Great Mughal Empire in India	**Chapter and Section Support** Reproducible Lesson Plan, p. 58		**Outline Maps** India: Political, p. 38	20
	Ⓢ Guided Reading and Review, p. 59	20	**Interdisciplinary Explorations**	
	Ⓢ Section Quiz, p. 60	25	*India: Beyond the Golden Age*	
	Ⓢ Vocabulary, p. 62	20		
	Reteaching, p. 63	25		
	Enrichment, p. 64	25		
	Ⓢ Chapter Summary, p. 61	15		
	Critical Thinking Activity, p. 65	30		
	Tests Forms A and B Chapter Tests, pp. 20–25	40		

Block Scheduling Folder
PROGRAM TEACHING RESOURCES

Activities and Projects

Block Scheduling Program Support

Interdisciplinary Links

Resource Pro™ CD-ROM

Media and Technology

Assessment Opportunities

From Guiding Questions to Assessment A series of Guiding Questions serves as an organizing framework for this book. The Guiding Questions that relate to this chapter are listed below. Section Reviews and Section Quizzes provide opportunities for assessing students' insights into these Guiding Questions. Additional assessments are listed below.

Media and Technology

Resource	mins.
🔊 📀 🅢 **World Video Explorer**	20
📀 **Planet Earth CD-ROM**	20
⌷ **Color Transparencies 95, 137, 150**	20
📀 **Planet Earth CD-ROM**	20
⌷ **Color Transparencies 76, 96, 145**	20
📀 **Planet Earth CD-ROM**	20
⌷ **Color Transparencies 53, 169**	20
🎧 🅢 **Guided Reading Audiotapes**	20
⌷ **Color Transparency 171**	20
(Graphic organizer web template)	
📀 **The Writer's Solution CD-ROM**	30
💾 **Computer Test Bank**	30

T	**Teaming Opportunity** This resource is especially well-suited for teaching teams.	📀	**CD-ROM**
		📀	**Laserdisc**
		⌷	**Transparency**
🅢	**Spanish** This resource is also in Spanish support.	💾	**Software**
		🔊	**Videotape**
		🎧	**Audiotape**

GUIDING QUESTIONS

- *How did each society's belief system affect its history, government, and economy?*
- *What accomplishments in technology, learning, or artistic expression were found in each society?*

ASSESSMENTS

Section 1

Students should be able to state the effect of printing during the golden ages of China.

▶ **RUBRIC** See the Assessment booklet for a rubric on assessing cause-and-effect statements.

Section 2

Students should be able to give an oral presentation that describes the development of feudalism in Japan.

▶ **RUBRIC** See the Assessment booklet for a rubric on assessing an oral presentation.

Section 3

Students should be able to write a paragraph about the achievements of the Mughal emperor Akbar.

▶ **RUBRIC** See the Assessment booklet for a rubric on assessing a writing assignment.

Activities and Projects

Mental Mapping

Ancient Civilizations Have students locate China, Japan, and India on outline maps that show Europe, Asia, and Africa. Based on the locations of these countries, ask them what physical features they think might have been important in the history of these civilizations.

Students might mention such attributes as the vast size of China, the fact that Japan is a collection of islands surrounded by ocean, and the barrier formed by the Himalaya Mountains that cut off India from much of Asia along with the proximity of the subcontinent to Africa.

Links to Current Events

The China Trade Europeans were eager to trade with China to obtain silk, tea, china, and other goods during the golden ages in China. Today, the United States is still eager to trade with China. Ask students to compare and contrast the trade with China of five or six hundred years ago with the "China trade" of today. What does China offer U.S. companies? Why is trade with China still a challenge? Physical barriers like mountains and deserts are no longer a problem — what barriers do the United States and European countries have to overcome to trade with China today? Students might mention such barriers as cultural differences or the power of the Chinese government to limit the import of foreign goods, among other responses.

Hands-On Activities

Invasions This book describes the invasion of China, Japan, and India by Mongols. Have students locate the Mongols in relation to China, Japan, and India. Taking into account physical barriers like oceans, mountains, and deserts, have students use a globe or wall map to suggest routes the Mongol invaders might have taken to penetrate each region.

Ask students whether any of these kingdoms could have or should have erected defenses against the Mongols. Allow them to suggest ideas.

Glossary Have students create an illustrated glossary of words having to do with feudal Japan. They should include the key terms for Section 2, such as *samurai, bushido,* and *shogun.* Each entry should include a definition and an illustration drawn or photocopied by the student. Encourage students to add additional words from the text or other sources to their glossaries. *English Language Learners*

Taj Mahal Ask students to put together facts about the Taj Mahal. Have them write each fact on a 3 x 5 index card. Then have them arrange their cards around an illustration of the Taj Mahal on a wall or bulletin board. *Basic*

Ancient Inventions Paper was invented in ancient China, as were many other items. Have students research some inventions of ancient China. How was each one made and used in China? How long did each one take for the invention to spread to other parts of the world? Did people in other parts of the world change the way they made or used the item? If so, how and why? *Average*

Biography Ask students to think about the qualities of a great leader. Invite them to choose one of the emperors described in this chapter. Encourage them to write a short biography of this person, emphasizing the qualities that made him a great leader. Then ask them to think about whether a person like this would be a successful leader in today's world. Why or why not? Ask them to write several paragraphs discussing either changes in the requirements for leadership today or the ways in which the qualities needed are the same. *Challenging*

F.Y.I.

This page can help you extend your own and students' understanding of the concepts in this chapter. You may want to browse through some of the suggestions in the **Bibliography**. **Interdisciplinary Links** can connect social studies understandings to areas elsewhere in the curriculum through the use of other Prentice Hall products. **National Geography Standards** reflected specifically in this chapter are listed for your convenience. Some hints about appropriate **Internet Access** are also provided. **School to Careers** provides insights into the practical uses of some of the concepts in this chapter as they might pertain to various careers.

BIBLIOGRAPHY

FOR THE TEACHER

Mason, Antony. *The Children's Atlas of Civilizations*. Millbrook, 1994.

Platt, Richard. *The Smithsonian Visual Timeline of Inventions*. Dorling, 1994.

Reid, Straun. *The Silk and Spice Routes: Inventions and Trade*. New Discovery, 1994.

FOR THE STUDENT

Easy
Macdonald, Fiona. *A Samurai Castle*. Bedrick, 1995.

Major, John S. *The Silk Route: Seven Thousand Miles of History*. HarperCollins, 1995.

Average
Doran, Clare. *The Japanese*. Thomson, 1995. Look into the Past series.

Hinds, Kathryn. *India's Gupta Dynasty*. Benchmark, 1996.

Millar, Heather. *China's Tang Dynasty*. Benchmark, 1996.

Challenging
Yue, Charlotte, and David Yue. *Armor*. Houghton, 1994.

LITERATURE CONNECTION

Alexander, Lloyd. *The Remarkable Journey of Prince Jen*. Dutton, 1991.

Barry, David. *The Rajah's Rice: A Mathematical Folktale from India*. Scientific American, 1994.

Haugaard, Erik Christian. *The Boy and the Samurai*. Houghton, 1991.

INTERDISCIPLINARY LINKS

Subject	Theme: Civilization
MATH	Middle Grades Math: Tools for Success *Course 1*, Lesson 5-5, **Look for a Pattern** *Course 2*, Lesson 3-4, **Too Much or Too Little Information**
LANGUAGE ARTS	Prentice Hall Literature *Copper*, **Breaker's Bridge, The Horse Snake, The Wise Old Woman**

NATIONAL GEOGRAPHY STANDARDS

Students explore the 18 National Geography Standards throughout *Medieval Times to Today*. Chapter 4, however, concentrates on investigating the following standards: 3, 5, 6, 11, 13, 16. For a complete list of the standards, see the *Teacher's Flexible Planning Guide*.

SCHOOL TO CAREERS

In Chapter 4, Civilizations of Asia, students learn about China, Japan, and India. Additionally, they learn how to assess their understanding of what they read. Knowing more about the civilizations of Asia can help students prepare for careers in many fields, such as international trade, diplomacy, government, the arts, and so on.

Assessing your understanding is particularly useful for representatives, editors, reporters, attorneys, and others. The curriculum presented in this book, as in all eight titles of Prentice Hall's *World Explorer* program, is designed to prepare students not only for careers but also for good citizenship—of the world as well as of this country.

INTERNET ACCESS

Many social studies teachers and students use Internet browsers, or search engines, to investigate particular topics. For the best results, use narrow rather than broad topics. Try these for Chapter 4: Silk Road, Tang Taizong, shogun, Taj Mahal. Finding age-appropriate sites is an important consideration when using the Internet. For links to age-appropriate sites in world studies and geography, visit the Prentice Hall Home Page at:
http://www.phschool.com

Connecting to the Guiding Questions

In this chapter, students will read about the great civilizations of medieval Asia in China, Japan, and India. Content in this chapter thus corresponds to two Guiding Questions:

● How did each society's belief system affect its history, government, and economy?

● What accomplishments in technology, learning, or artistic expression were found in each society?

Using the Map Activities

Have students compare maps of China in medieval and contemporary times. Discuss what parts of modern China were separate countries in the Middle Ages.

● smaller

● Students should recognize that the major cities tended to be located on rivers or along a coastline.

Heterogeneous Groups

The following Teacher's Edition strategies are suitable for heterogeneous groups.

Critical Thinking
Recognizing Cause
and Effect   p. 89
Identifying Central
Issues   p. 97
**Interdisciplinary
Connections**
Language Arts   p. 92
Cooperative Learning
Art and
Architecture   p. 98

CHAPTER 4

Civilizations of Asia

SECTION 1
Golden Ages in China

SECTION 2
Feudalism in Japan

SECTION 3
The Great Mughal Empire in India

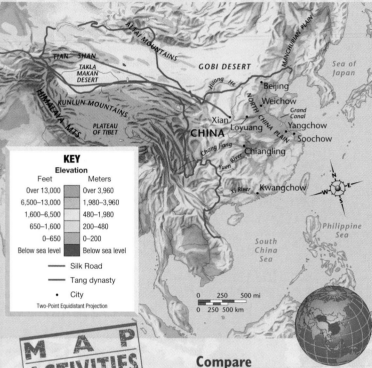

KEY
Elevation

Feet	Meters
Over 13,000	Over 3,960
6,500–13,000	1,980–3,960
1,600–6,500	480–1,980
650–1,600	200–480
0–650	0–200
Below sea level	Below sea level

—— Silk Road
—— Tang dynasty
● City

Two-Point Equidistant Projection

0   250   500 mi
0 250 500 km

MAP ACTIVITIES

Between the A.D. *600s and 900s, several great empires arose in Asia. One of the most advanced began in China. At this time, the boundaries of China were very different from what they are today. To become familiar with the Chinese empire of this time, do the following activities.*

Compare boundaries
Compare the former boundaries of China during the Tang dynasty with its boundaries today. Find the present-day boundaries of China by looking at the Asia: Political map in the Atlas in the back of this book. Was China formerly larger or smaller?

Study key locations
Describe the landforms and the locations of major rivers on the map of China on this page. Where were the main cities located?

Resource Directory

Media and Technology

Culture: Invention of China's Golden Age, from the World Video Explorer, enhances students' understanding of the many contributions of Chinese civilization to world culture.

Chapter 5

Golden Ages in China

BEFORE YOU READ

Reach Into Your Background

Suppose that future historians describe the 1900s as the "golden age" of the United States. Think about life as you know it. What do you think are the best features of the American way of life? What accomplishments of the United States do you think people in the future will remember?

Questions to Explore

1. How did the ideas of Confucius influence Chinese society during the Tang and Song dynasties?

2. Why are the years of the Tang and Song dynasties called the golden ages of China?

Key Terms

dynasty   porcelain
merit system   movable type

Key People and Places

Tang Taizong   Silk Road
Confucius   Grand Canal

Lesson Objectives

1. Analyze the importance and value of the ideas of Confucius in China.

2. Identify the achievements of the Song and Tang dynasties in the golden ages of China.

Lesson Plan

1 Engage

Warm-Up Activity

Have students preview the section. Use the Skills Mini-Lesson on previewing to help students get the most from previewing the section.

Activating Prior Knowledge

Have students read Reach Into Your Background in the Before You Read box. Students' responses will vary. Lead students in a discussion of what makes a "golden age," such as a time of peace and prosperity or technological and artistic achievement.

T ang Taizong (tang ty zung), who ruled China from A.D. 626 to 649, fought in many battles. From the age of 16, he had been in the military. Now, late in his reign, Taizong was tired of war. He read and reread the works of Confucius (kun FYOO shus), an ancient Chinese teacher. Confucius taught that if a ruler set a good example, no one would commit crimes.

According to legend, Taizong visited a prison and saw 290 men who had been sentenced to die. It was then a Chinese custom to kill all the condemned on the same day each year. Taizong took pity on the men. He said he would allow them to go home to visit their families if they promised to return the next day. All 290 men returned. Taizong was so moved that he set them all free.

▼ This painting, which dates from the 1700s, shows Tang Taizong with his pet hawk.

A Glorious Heritage

The Chinese often tell this story to show what a good ruler Taizong was. He tried to put into practice the teachings of Confucius, who taught about relationships among family members and among members of society. Confucius wanted to bring peace and stability to China. He believed that if all people treated each other with respect, society

SKILLS MINI LESSON

Previewing

To **introduce** the skill, point out to students that previewing a section of a text is a bit like viewing the coming attractions at the movies. A preview gives an overview of the topics covered, helps remind them about what they already know concerning the topic, and points to what they want to learn. Have students **practice** the skill by looking at the titles, major headings, and illustrations in each section of the chapter. Then ask them which two cultures seem most alike and why. In what ways does the remaining culture seem different? Next, have students **apply** the skill by asking them to preview Section 1. Tell them to skim the first two paragraphs, look at the text headings, and read the captions to the illustrations. Suggest that they form two questions they hope to answer by reading the first section.

2 Explore

Have students read Section 1. Then invite them to contribute to a chart describing China during its golden ages. Write the following list on the chalkboard: *government, trade, technology, important ideas.* Have students discuss how the merit system gave China a good government, why China was sought after in world trade, what its chief technological inventions were and how they changed the world, and why the ideas of Confucius were valuable.

Background

Biography

Wu Hou (625–705) One of the most remarkable members of the Tang dynasty was empress Wu Hou. Once a low-ranking concubine of the emperor T'ai-tsung, Wu used her position, personality, and ruthlessness to secure her position as empress. In spite of her dubious path to power, Wu Hou instituted policies that reformed Chinese society. She chose her associates without regard to their social standing, replacing the military and political aristocracy with a more scholarly bureaucracy drawn from the gentry. The overall effect was to establish a more unified empire capable of enacting necessary social changes.

Answers to ...
MAP STUDY
the Song dynasty

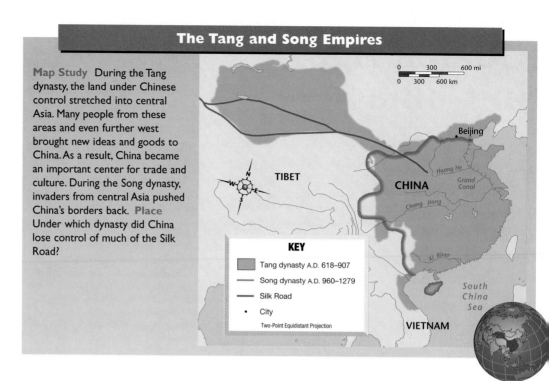

The Tang and Song Empires

Map Study During the Tang dynasty, the land under Chinese control stretched into central Asia. Many people from these areas and even further west brought new ideas and goods to China. As a result, China became an important center for trade and culture. During the Song dynasty, invaders from central Asia pushed China's borders back. **Place** Under which dynasty did China lose control of much of the Silk Road?

KEY

▨ Tang dynasty A.D. 618–907

— Song dynasty A.D. 960–1279

— Silk Road

• City

Two-Point Equidistant Projection

LINKS TO LANGUAGE ARTS

Poems—and Legends Li Bo probably was the greatest poet of the Tang dynasty. He had an adventurous life—once he was even accused of treason. His poems, however, dealt with quieter subjects, such as nature and friendship. At the age of 61, while visiting relatives, he died. Soon a legend about his death spread across the country. It said that Li Bo was in a boat at night. The moon's reflection was so beautiful that he reached out to seize it, fell overboard, and drowned.

would be healthy. After Taizong's reign, many of Confucius' ideas took root in Chinese government.

Tang Taizong was the greatest ruler of the Tang dynasty. A **dynasty** is a series of rulers from one family. The Chinese give their family names first. Tang is the family name of Tang Taizong. The Tang dynasty lasted about 300 years, from A.D. 618 to 907.

The Tang dynasty united the Chinese in a large empire that reached from the Pacific Ocean to Persia. Fighting among different groups of people within the empire ended the Tang dynasty. Order was restored by the Song dynasty. The Song ruled from 960 to 1279. The map above shows the boundaries of the two dynasties.

During the Tang and Song dynasties, China entered a golden age, a time of great political and cultural achievement. The golden age of the Tang and Song dynasties happened for several reasons. One reason was the introduction of the **merit system** in hiring government officials. Under the merit system, officials had to pass tests and prove their ability to do the work. Before the Tang dynasty, officials came from rich and powerful families. They were allowed to keep their positions for life even if they did not do a very good job. Hiring people based on their ability to do the job, rather than on their wealth or social position, improved the government.

The Tang and Song rulers also encouraged music, art, and fine writing. In addition, the Chinese introduced a number of key inventions during this period. During its golden ages, China became one of the most advanced and powerful empires in the world.

Resource Directory

Teaching Resources

📁 **Reproducible Lesson Plan** in the Chapter and Section Support booklet, p. 52, provides a summary of the section lesson.

📁 **Guided Reading and Review** in the Chapter and Section Support booklet, p. 53, provides a structure for mastering key concepts and reviewing key terms in the section. Available in Spanish in the Spanish Support booklet, p. 33.

Program Resources

📁 Material in the **Primary Sources and Literature Readings** booklet extends content with a selection related to the concepts in this chapter.

📁 **Outline Maps** China and Neighboring Countries: Political, p. 41

A Golden Age in Trade

Another reason China flourished during the Tang and Song dynasties was its trade. China produced goods that were highly prized in Southwest Asia and Europe. And its system of roads and canals helped to make travel and trade easier.

Trade Goods: Silk, Porcelain, and Tea   One of the most prized trade goods produced by China was silk. Because of its natural beauty, silk is often called "the queen of fibers." Silk comes from the cocoons of caterpillars called silkworms. For a long time, only the Chinese knew how to make silk. Even after others discovered the Chinese secret, Chinese silk was of the best quality. People in Southwest Asia and Europe were willing to pay high prices for Chinese silk.

Another prized Chinese product was **porcelain,** a strong and beautiful type of ceramic. Because it was first made in China, porcelain is often called "china." The Chinese developed the process for making porcelain during the Tang dynasty. They made beautiful vases, plates, cups, bowls, and figurines. For hundreds of years, the Chinese produced the best porcelain in the world.

READ ACTIVELY

Predict What products do you think China traded during its golden ages?

Tang Treasures

Europeans and South Asians paid dearly for Chinese trade goods, such as luxurious silk robes like the one worn by the woman in this illustration (left). Porcelain was another popular Chinese trade item. This man on horseback (right) shows the Tang love of green, brown, and yellow colors in ceramics. The vessel (below) shows the fine detail many Chinese porcelain-makers used. The vessel is designed to look like a well with a water jar.

Program Resources

Nystrom Desk Atlas

Media and Technology

Color Transparencies 95, 137, 150

Planet Earth CD-ROM includes satellite images and physical maps of China and East Asia, plus World Wonders, Cultural: The Great Wall, China.

3 Teach

Direct student partners to plan a traveling museum exhibition titled "China's Golden Ages." Suggest that they list which of China's accomplishments or inventions they would include as part of the exhibit. Have them prepare an exhibition catalog in which they identify each exhibition entry, tell what the entry represents, indicate why it was important to China, and describe what effect it had on the world outside China. This activity should take about 25 minutes.

Activity

Journal Writing

Trader's Log   Tell students they are traders on their way to China to trade for some of China's most popular goods. Suggest they write a journal entry that describes the sights along the way, the bustle of the trading centers, and the actual trades. Entries should list goods brought from Europe to trade and identify goods the trader will take home. If students are keeping an Explorer's Journal, as described in the Book Opener, you may wish to do this writing activity as part of that journal.

4 Assess

See the answers to the Section Review. You may also use students' exhibition catalogs and discussions for assessment.

Acceptable catalogs list at least three exhibition entries.

Commendable catalogs indicate an understanding of what part exhibition entries played in China's history.

Outstanding catalogs show an understanding of how China's advances affected the world outside of China.

Background

Global Perspectives

Tea Tea drinking has been a part of Chinese culture since at least A.D. 350. The custom spread to Japan, where tea became the focus of an elaborate ceremony still practiced in that country today. Other Asian countries adopted this drink, and tea began to be imported by Europeans around 1600. Tea quickly gained popularity in Europe, especially in England, and was sent from here to the colonies in North America. The colonists' desire for tea—and the British crown's desire to tax tea—contributed to the colonies' fight for independence.

Art and Meditation

Traditionally, most Chinese paintings are landscapes painted on silk. Often the painter includes water, rocks, and plants. Usually, there are few signs of human life. The Chinese believed that such scenes, painted well, helped the painter and the viewer meditate, or focus, on important forces in the natural world. These forces—light and darkness, wind and water—were believed to hold the natural world together.

▼ Most goods carried along the Silk Road were small, costly items. These included tea, pepper, jade, ivory, and porcelain—like the goose shown below.

The Chinese also discovered the use of tea. At first, tea was used as a medicine. Later, during the Tang dynasty, it became the custom to drink tea as a beverage. The custom spread from China to Japan and other countries. Soon tea became a major crop. Every year, much of it was shipped out of the country for sale.

Trade Routes: The Silk Road and the Grand Canal
Chinese silk, porcelain, tea, and other products traveled across roads and waterways to other countries in Asia and Europe. One important trade route was the Silk Road, which stretched all the way from China to the Mediterranean Sea. Camels, horses, and donkeys carried goods along the 4,000-mile (6,436-km) Silk Road. The Silk Road was not one long road. It was really many roads that connected with one another. Long stretches of the route crossed mountains and deserts. Travel was often difficult and dangerous, even though rest stations were built along the road. A Chinese historian described a trip through the huge Gobi Desert:

❝You see nothing in any direction but the sky and the sands, without the slightest trace of a road; and travelers find nothing to guide them but the bones of men and beasts.❞

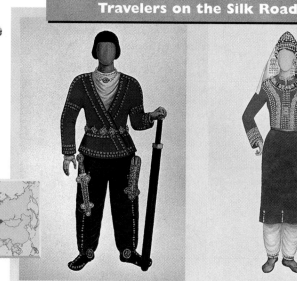

Travelers on the Silk Road

What might travelers on the Silk Road have worn? These paintings are reconstructions of clothing found in graves along the Silk Road in Central Asia. The outfits are of fine cloth decorated with gold.

Large amounts of grain and manufactured goods were also moved along a great network of rivers and canals in China. The Grand Canal connected the Huang He (HWAHNG huh) and Chang Jiang (chahng jee AHNG). Work on the canal began in the 500s B.C. and continued for hundreds of years. The canal helped join northern and southern China. Stretching for more than 1,000 miles, the Grand Canal is still the longest canal ever built.

Printing Spreads Knowledge

During the golden ages, the Chinese developed trade products and trade routes that helped make their country rich. Chinese inventions of the period also had a great impact on their culture. The most important invention was a method of printing.

Before the invention of printing, all books were copied by hand. As a result, the number of books available was very small. The Chinese began printing in the A.D. 500s. They used blocks of wood on which they carved the characters of an entire page. Then they brushed ink over the wooden page. Finally, they laid a piece of paper over the block to make a print. Carving the pages of a book took a long time. But after the woodblocks were made, printers could make many copies of the book.

Around 1045, a Chinese printer named Bi Sheng (bee shehng) developed another method of printing using **movable type.** In this kind of printing, each character or piece of type is a separate piece. The pieces can be moved and reused. Bi Sheng made many separate characters out of clay. Then he put together the characters he needed to make the pages of a book. But the Chinese language has thousands of different characters. Most printers found woodblock printing easier and faster than the use of movable type.

The World's Oldest Book

This illustration is found in the *Diamond Sutra,* the world's oldest surviving book. It was printed in A.D. 868 from six carved wooden blocks. The book discusses various features of the Buddhist religion.
Critical Thinking What impact did the development of printing have on life in China?

READ ACTIVELY

Visualize Visualize yourself copying a whole book by hand. How long do you think it would take you?

Background

Global Perspectives

Types of Type The Chinese used wood, tin, and porcelain to form their type. In contrast, Johannes Gutenberg molded his movable type from a mixture of lead, tin, and antimony. Each letter was a single piece of type which could be combined with other letters and used several times. The lead letters proved to outlast letters made of other materials. Gutenberg's printing press was adapted from a machine used to press grapes or cheese. This press could print about 300 sheets of paper a day. Gutenberg developed his movable type in about 1440, and he produced his famous printed Bible in 1456. By 1500, several million books were being produced in about a thousand print shops in Europe.

Resource Directory

Teaching Resources

Identifying the Main Idea in the Social Studies and Geography Skills booklet, p. 41, provides additional skill practice.

Answers to . . .

THE WORLD'S OLDEST BOOK
The invention of printing spread knowledge throughout China. Books were readily available, and many people learned how to read and write.

1. (a) series of rulers from one family (b) system which requires individuals to pass an examination before they can become government officials (c) strong and beautiful type of ceramic that is also known as "china" (d) method of printing in which each individual character is a separate piece of type

2. (a) great emperor of the Tang dynasty (b) influential Chinese philosopher (c) overland trade route from China to Europe on which silk was brought for trading (d) canal connecting the Huang He and the Chang Jiang

3. Answers may vary. Students' descriptions should mention the influence of Confucian ideas on family life, government, and all social relationships and that these ideas contributed to China's golden age.

4. Answers may vary. Sample answer: In each dynasty, peace and stability came to China. The ideas of Confucius took root in government. There were great achievements in music, art, and fine writing. Chinese trade in silk, porcelain, and tea flourished. The Chinese invented printing and movable type and built the Grand Canal, the longest canal in the world.

5. Possible similarities include the following: the peace and stability of both societies, the strong economy due to trade, the technological inventions that each spread to the rest of the world, and the achievements in the arts.

6. Answers may vary. Accept all reasonable responses.

Inventions of the Tang and Song Dynasties

The Tang and Song dynasties were a golden age for science and technology. Some developments took hundreds of years to spread to other parts of the world. The use of gunpowder and fireworks (below), for example, did not reach Europe until the late 1300s.

Invention	Date	Description
Block Printing	750	Printers carved words onto a large wooden block. They inked the block, then pressed paper onto it to transfer the print. Many copies of the same page could be made quickly.
Gunpowder	850	The Chinese first used gunpowder to make fireworks. By about 1,000, however, they were making explosives to be used in warfare.
Smallpox Vaccine	900s	To stop the spread of smallpox, healthy people were given tiny doses of the disease. This helped them build an immunity to smallpox.
Compass	990	Sailors used the magnetic compass to navigate.
Movable Type	1030	Printers carved individual characters on small blocks. They combined the blocks to form a page. The same blocks could be reused to produce different pieces of writing.

The invention of printing helped spread knowledge throughout China. Books were sold in marketplaces. Many people learned how to read and write. One Song emperor wrote a poem telling about the importance of books:

> **"T**o enrich your family, no need to buy good land: Books hold a thousand measures of grain. For an easy life, no need to build a mansion: In books are found houses of gold.**"**

SECTION 1 REVIEW

1. Define (a) dynasty, (b) merit system, (c) porcelain, (d) movable type.

2. Identify (a) Tang Taizong, (b) Confucius, (c) Silk Road, (d) Grand Canal.

3. What impact did the ideas of Confucius have on society during China's golden ages?

4. Identify the important accomplishments of the Tang and Song dynasties.

Critical Thinking

5. Making Comparisons In what ways were China's golden ages like the present times in the United States?

Activity

6. Writing to Learn The invention of printing made books available to many people. What would your life be like without books? Write a journal entry expressing your thoughts.

Resource Directory

Teaching Resources

Section Quiz in the Chapter and Section Support booklet, p. 54, covers the main ideas and key terms in the section. Available in Spanish in the Spanish Support booklet, p. 34.

Feudalism in Japan

SECTION 2

BEFORE YOU READ

Reach Into Your Background

Children often play at being soldiers. You might have played such games when you were younger. But for many people, military life is not a game. It is a career. What are your impressions of the life of a soldier? Does a soldier's life interest you? Why or why not?

Questions to Explore

1. How did feudalism develop in Japan?
2. Why did the Tokugawa shoguns shut off Japan from the rest of the world?

Key Terms

samurai
daimyo
bushido
feudal system
shogun

Key People

Minamoto Yoritomo
Tokugawa Ieyasu

About 900 years ago, warriors called the **samurai** (sam uh ry) rose to fame and power in Japan. The word *samurai* means "those who serve." Samurai swore an oath to serve their leaders. They followed a code of rules. And they obeyed these rules without question. Honor meant more to a samurai than did wealth or life. A samurai would rather die than shame himself. Consider these guidelines for a samurai:

> "The way of the warrior is something you must [think about] in every detail, day and night, on the assumption that you may not be able to live through the day. You may win or lose, depending on the circumstances. But you can't shame yourself. . . . An accomplished warrior doesn't think whether he's going to win or lose, but dashes into the place of death with single-minded determination.
>
> A samurai must be careful about everything and try not to show any weakness.
>
> Surrendering is something a samurai never does, be it for deceiving the enemy or for the emperor."

▼ Samurai warriors wore heavy armor made of small iron scales tied with silk and leather. Their face masks were designed to frighten enemies and to withstand spear thrusts.

Teaching Resources

📁 **Reproducible Lesson Plan** in the Chapter and Section Support booklet, p. 55, provides a summary of the section lesson.

📁 **Guided Reading and Review** in the Chapter and Section Support booklet, p. 56, provides a structure for mastering key concepts and reviewing key terms in the section. Available in Spanish in the Spanish Support booklet, p. 35.

Lesson Objectives

1. Relate the geographic setting of Japan to its culture and history.

2. Trace Japanese history from the medieval period to the 1600s.

3. List the reasons for Japanese isolation from the 1600s to the 1850s.

Lesson Plan

1 Engage

Warm-Up Activity

Have students look at a map of Japan and discuss how its geographic setting influenced life here. Ask: *What advantages does a nation have if it is surrounded by the ocean? How does living on an island influence the way of life for people on the island?*

Activating Prior Knowledge

Have students read Reach Into Your Background in the Before You Read box. Hold a class discussion about the questions. Remind students not to judge one another's choices.

Activity

Critical Thinking

Recognizing Cause and Effect *Suitable as an individual or a whole class activity.* When students read the first paragraphs of the section, ask: *How did this code of rules for samurai create outstanding soldiers?* Suggest that they place their answers in a cause-and-effect chart. *Verbal, Visual*

2 Explore

Have students read Section 2. Then ask them to work with a partner to make a pyramid showing the social class structure of medieval Japan. (Emperor at top followed by shogun, then daimyo, samurai, and peasants at the base of the pyramid) Next, ask them to describe either the importance of the samurai in Japanese culture or way of life and in the government of medieval Japan.

Background

Global Perspectives

The Code of Chivalry The knights of Europe were similar in some ways to the samurai. They were part of a feudal system and swore loyalty to a lord who they served. However, their code of behavior, the code of chivalry, differed greatly from bushido. Chivalry was based on Christian ideals. Knights were to use their strength to protect the weak and to fight against injustice. Knights valued courage in battle as highly as the samurai. A cowardly knight was dishonored by having his sword and spurs broken.

Answers to . . .

MAP STUDY
countries closest to Japan, across the Sea of Japan—North and South Korea and China

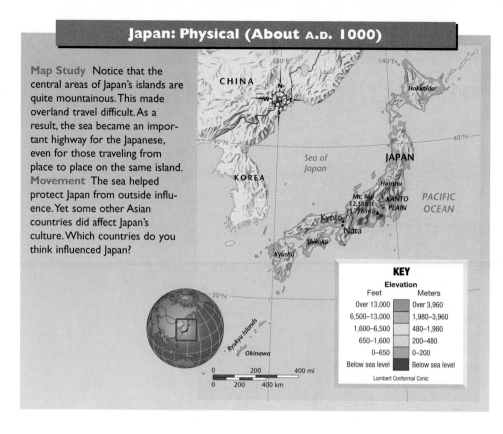

Japan: Physical (About A.D. 1000)

Map Study Notice that the central areas of Japan's islands are quite mountainous. This made overland travel difficult. As a result, the sea became an important highway for the Japanese, even for those traveling from place to place on the same island. **Movement** The sea helped protect Japan from outside influence. Yet some other Asian countries did affect Japan's culture. Which countries do you think influenced Japan?

KEY
Elevation

Feet	Meters
Over 13,000	Over 3,960
6,500–13,000	1,980–3,960
1,600–6,500	480–1,980
650–1,600	200–480
0–650	0–200
Below sea level	Below sea level

Lambert Conformal Conic

0   200   400 mi
0   200   400 km

Predict What do you think a samurai's responsibilities were?

A Country of Islands

Today the way of life of the samurai seems strange to most people outside Japan. But life in Japan 900 years ago was unusual in many ways. One reason Japan was so different is its unusual geography.

Study the map of Japan on this page. Japan is a group of mountainous islands in the Pacific Ocean about 100 miles (160 km) across the water from Korea. It is about 500 miles (800 km) from China. For centuries, the sea protected Japan from invaders. But the sea also served as a highway for the Japanese. It served as a link between their own islands. In this geographic setting, the Japanese developed a distinctive way of life.

The Rise of the Samurai

Why were warriors so important in Japan if the sea kept the country safe from invaders? Against whom were the Japanese fighting? The answer is that they fought with each other as different groups tried to gain power.

Feudalism Develops in Japan To understand the Japanese system of government, you have to go far back in history. For centuries, emperors ruled Japan from the city that is now called Kyoto. Over time,

Resource Directory

Program Resources

Outline Maps Japan and the Koreas: Political, p. 42

Media and Technology

Color Transparencies 76, 96, 145

Planet Earth CD-ROM includes satellite images and physical maps of East Asia and Japan, plus World Wonders, Natural: Mt. Fuji, Japan.

wealthy families created large private estates in the country and gained much power. Between 1000 and 1200, the emperor lost more and more power. Estate owners, called **daimyo** (dy myoh), became more independent. They hired bands of samurai to protect them and the peasants who farmed their land from rival daimyo.

As the daimyo gained power, a new political and military system developed in Japan. Under this system, the daimyo and the samurai were closely connected. The samurai promised to obey and to be loyal to their daimyo. They followed a set of rules for warriors called **bushido** (boo shee doh). These rules stressed honor, discipline, bravery, and simple living. A samurai's loyalty to his daimyo was stronger than his loyalty to his own family. He was expected to gladly give his life for his lord.

This system of government, in which less powerful people promise loyalty to more powerful people, is called a **feudal system.** Think of a feudal system as a kind of pyramid. At the bottom of the pyramid were many poor and powerless people, the peasants. Then came more powerful people. In Japan, these were the samurai. Next came local lords—the daimyo. Then came the most powerful lord in Japan, the **shogun** (shoh gun), or great general.

CITIZEN HEROES

To Be a Leader Toyotomi Hideyoshi (toh yoh toh mee hih day yoh shee) started life as a peasant. Through hard work, he became a fine warrior. Because of his great military skills, he became a chief lieutenant in the army of a powerful daimyo. Then, in 1582, the daimyo was assassinated. Hideyoshi took his place. A skillful leader, he went on to unite Japan. Hideyoshi had risen far from poor beginnings. The people of Japan idolized Hideyoshi.

Waiting to See the Shogun

The shogun expected loyalty from the daimyo. In return, the shogun did not interfere in the way the daimyo ruled their own lands. Here, a group of daimyo wait to see the shogun. **Critical Thinking** Why was it important for the shogun to have the loyalty of the daimyo?

3 Teach

Student partners can make a time line of the events in Japanese history covered in this section. When they have completed their time lines, have students discuss how the feudal system worked in Japan and how the shoguns came to rule. Ask: *Why did the Tokugawa shoguns decide to shut Japan off from the rest of the world?* This activity should take about 20 minutes.

4 Assess

See the answers to the Section Review. You may also use students' time lines and discussion for assessment.

Acceptable time lines list at least three separate events between the rise of the daimyo and the end of shogun rule in 1867.

Commendable time lines list more than three events and several time spans.

Outstanding time lines and discussions show an understanding of the cause-and-effect relationship between certain events.

Answers to . . .

WAITING TO SEE THE SHOGUN
Daimyo or estate owners employed samurais or warriors to protect their interests. Without the daimyo's support, shoguns risked petty battles and wars.

Global Perspectives

Japanese Trade and Christian Missionaries In the early 1500s, armed conflicts between China and Japan virtually stopped trade between the two countries. However, the Japanese still wanted Chinese gold and silk, and the Chinese wanted Japanese silver. The Portuguese became the intermediaries between the two nations. From the port of Macao, China, granted to the Portuguese by the Chinese for trading purposes, a huge ship sailed to Japan with a cargo of valuable silks to be exchanged for Japanese silver. The Portuguese traders were joined by Catholic Jesuit priests who enjoyed favor with both the rulers of China and of Japan.

Activity

Interdisciplinary Connections

Language Arts After students have read about the isolation of Japan, have them discuss whether they feel this was a good way to protect Japan from foreign invasion. Suggest that students work in groups of four to develop a pro and con chart for isolation. Encourage students to consider questions such as What was gained by isolating Japan? What was lost? Once student groups complete their discussion, have them prepare a Point-Counterpoint television editorial expressing their group's view on Japan's isolation. *Auditory, English Language Learners*

LINKS TO LANGUAGE ARTS

Lady Murasaki's Novel In the early 1000s, Lady Murasaki Shikibu wrote *The Tale of Genji*, the first novel ever written. It begins with the life and loves of Prince Genji (gehn jee). Then it tells about his children and grandchildren. Lady Murasaki describes court life in great detail. Her characters are complex and true to life. Some people consider *The Tale of Genji* as the best Japanese novel ever written.

Shoguns Gain Control The first shogun did not take power in Japan until 1192. All through the 1100s, Japan was torn by war as samurai armies battled one another. Two powerful families—the Minamoto (mee nah moh toh) and the Taira (ty rah)—fought for control of the country. In 1185, the Minamoto family won. Yoritomo (yor ee toh moh), the head of the Minamoto family, made himself the ruler of the country.

In 1192, the emperor of Japan named Yoritomo shogun. Shoguns ruled Japan in the emperor's name until 1868. The emperor held a position of honor but had no real power. Japan's period of military rule lasted almost 700 years.

Some of Japan's shoguns had problems uniting the country's many daimyo and their samurai bands. During the rule of weak shoguns, local samurai bands were always at war.

Isolation for Japan

Within a century after shogun rule started, Japan was threatened by an attack from the Mongols. The Mongols came from a country called Mongolia, north of China. Under their fierce and brilliant leader, Kublai Khan (KOO bluh kahn), the Mongols had already conquered China. Kublai Khan twice tried to take over Japan. He failed both times.

Kublai Khan

This picture is of the great Chinese leader, Kublai Khan. He ruled a huge empire, but he wanted more. In the late 1200s, he decided to invade Japan. In 1274, his invasion fleet got only as far as the island of Kyushu. A violent storm frightened the sailors back to China. When Kublai Khan tried again in 1281, another violent storm destroyed his ships. The Japanese called this storm *kamikaze* (kah muh kah zee) or "divine wind."

The Arrival of Europeans For nearly 300 years after the Mongols were beaten, few foreigners came to Japan. Then, in 1543, some Portuguese sailors were blown off course and landed in Japan. The Japanese showed great interest in the guns that the Portuguese carried. In the years that followed, many European traders and Christian missionaries arrived. A lively trade developed, and thousands of Japanese became Christians.

The Tokugawas Cut Off Japan
The European influence in Japan did not last long. In 1603, Tokugawa Ieyasu (toh kug oh wah eye yaw soo) became shogun. Ieyasu was determined to bring order to the country. He wanted to end the fighting among warring samurai bands. Ieyasu divided Japan into about 250 regions, each headed by a daimyo. The daimyos promised to serve the shogun and swore loyalty to him.

Ieyasu feared that Europeans might try to conquer Japan. He and the Tokugawa rulers who followed him isolated Japan from Westerners. The shoguns outlawed Christianity and forced Europeans to leave the country. They banned most foreign travel and trade. They closed Japanese ports to outsiders. They stopped the building of large ships that could travel great distances.

In effect, they closed Japan to the outside world. Shut off from others, the Japanese continued their own distinctive culture. Their isolation lasted for 250 years, until 1853.

▼One distinctive feature of Japanese culture is a form of theater called *no*. In this drama, dancers in colorful robes tell folk stories, moving to the slow music of chants, flutes, and drums.

SECTION 2 REVIEW

1. **Define** (a) samurai, (b) daimyo, (c) bushido, (d) feudal system, (e) shogun.

2. **Identify** (a) Minamoto Yoritomo, (b) Tokugawa Ieyasu.

3. Describe the feudal system in Japan.

4. What measures did the Tokugawas take to close Japan off to other countries?

Critical Thinking

5. **Recognizing Cause and Effect** The warrior class in feudal Japan included about 5 of every 100 Japanese. How does this help explain why warfare was so common?

Activity

6. **Writing to Learn** What if you could interview a samurai from feudal Japan? Write five interview questions that you would ask about his life or about bushido.

Resource Directory

Teaching Resources

📁 **Section Quiz** in the Chapter and Section Support booklet, p. 57, covers the main ideas and key terms in the section. Available in Spanish in the Spanish Support booklet, p. 36.

1. (a) warrior class of Japan (b) feudal lords who owned land and employed samurai to defend them (c) set of rules which governed the samurai (d) system of government in which less powerful people promise loyalty to more powerful people (e) military ruler

2. (a) first shogun in 1192 (b) shogun who united Japan and closed it to foreign contact

3. Answers may vary. Sample answer: The feudal system is like a pyramid, with the emperor at the top, then the shogun, who ruled in the emperor's name, the daimyo, and the samurai. Peasants were at the bottom and supported all the other classes.

4. The shoguns outlawed Christianity and forced Europeans to leave the country. Foreign travel and trade were forbidden, and Japanese ports were closed to outsiders.

5. Answers will vary. Students should mention that the daimyo competed for land and power and needed many samurai for their armies.

6. Answers will vary. Accept all reasonable responses.

Lesson Objectives

① Describe the importance of Hinduism in India and the impact of Muslim rulers.

② Determine why Akbar was a wise and great ruler.

③ Summarize the reasons for the downfall of the Mughal empire.

Lesson Plan

1 Engage

Warm-Up Activity

Have students study the map of India. Ask them to describe India's physical geography. Then have them discuss how India's geography may have helped or hindered its rulers.

Activating Prior Knowledge

Have students read Reach Into Your Background in the Before You Read box. Discuss what makes a great leader. List qualities that students suggest on the chalkboard, for example: *courage, a sense of fairness, intelligence.*

SECTION 3

The Great Mughal Empire in India

BEFORE YOU READ

Reach Into Your Background

What qualities do you respect in a leader? Think about

American presidents. Which ones do you think were great leaders? Why?

Questions to Explore

1. What impact did Mughal rule have on India?
2. Why is Akbar considered one of the world's great rulers?

Key Terms

Hinduism   sultan
caste system

Key People and Places

Tamerlane   Shah Jahan
Babur   Delhi
Akbar   Taj Mahal

Even before he invaded India, people had heard of the Mongol conqueror Tamerlane (TAM ur layn). Throughout Asia and the Middle East, he had destroyed entire cities and killed all the people.

Tamerlane's campaign into India was no different. In 1398, he invaded the country and destroyed fields and crops as well as towns. At the city of Delhi, Tamerlane quickly defeated the Indian army. Then he left the city a mass of ruins. His troops took everything of any value. They killed most of the people. Those they did not kill they took as slaves. After the destruction, it was reported that "not a bird on the wing moved for two months."

▼ The people of Asia feared Tamerlane because of his ferocity in battle.

The Muslim Invasion of India

The Mongols were not the first to invade India. Long before the Mongols came, India's great wealth had tempted many groups.

Seeking India's Wealth India had always been called a land of riches. In northern India, a great civilization flowered during the Gupta (GOOP tuh) dynasty, from 320 to about 540. The Gupta dynasty built beautiful cities and traded in jewels and spices. The people in the Gupta empire practiced **Hinduism,** a religion and a way of life that developed in India over a long period of time.

Resource Directory

Teaching Resources

📁 **Reproducible Lesson Plan** in the Chapter and Section Support booklet, p. 58, provides a summary of the section lesson.

📁 **Guided Reading and Review** in the Chapter and Section Support booklet, p. 59, provides a structure for mastering key concepts and reviewing key terms in the section. Available in Spanish in the Spanish Support booklet, p. 37.

Program Resources

📁 **Outline Maps** India: Political, p. 38

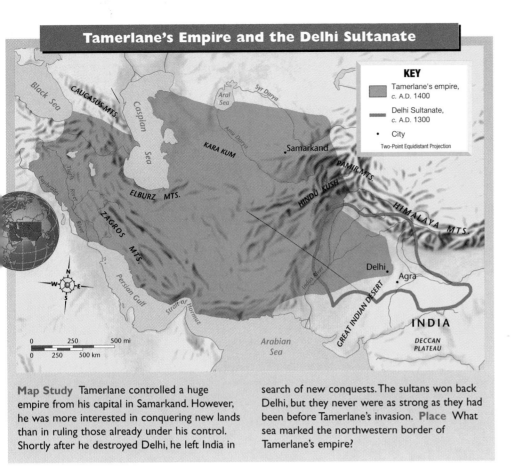

Tamerlane's Empire and the Delhi Sultanate

KEY

Tamerlane's empire, c. A.D. 1400

Delhi Sultanate, c. A.D. 1300

• City

Two-Point Equidistant Projection

Map Study Tamerlane controlled a huge empire from his capital in Samarkand. However, he was more interested in conquering new lands than in ruling those already under his control. Shortly after he destroyed Delhi, he left India in search of new conquests. The sultans won back Delhi, but they never were as strong as they had been before Tamerlane's invasion. **Place** What sea marked the northwestern border of Tamerlane's empire?

Hindus accepted many gods, but believed that all these gods were just different aspects of one supreme being. They also believed that each person must search for his or her own religious truth. And Hindus believed that social classes were part of the natural order of the universe.

The Hindu **caste system,** a strict system of social classes, controlled every part of everyday life. Caste determined people's jobs. At the top of the caste system were the priests, teachers, and judges. Next came the warriors. Then came a social group made up of farmers and merchants. The fourth class was made up of craftworkers and laborers. Finally there was a group of poor and powerless people called the "Untouchables." Though this unequal system was hard on the lower classes, it brought India stability. During the Gupta dynasty, India entered a golden age.

But India's golden age came to an end as different groups attacked the empire. Muslim invaders poured into India. From 1206 to 1526, the Muslims controlled an empire that covered much of what is now India, Bangladesh, and Pakistan. A **sultan,** or Muslim king, ruled the empire. Because its capital was at Delhi, the empire was called the Delhi Sultanate.

LINKS TO LANGUAGE ARTS

Common Ground The Hindu sacred books were written in a language called Sanskrit. It may be one of the world's oldest languages. Sanskrit influenced many other languages in the world, such as ancient Greek and Latin. Today, words with ancient Sanskrit roots exist in most modern European languages. *Mother* and *father,* for example, have Sanskrit roots.

2 Explore

Direct students to read Section 3. Then ask volunteers to create a class chart on the chalkboard. Next have students create a pyramid of the caste system on the chalkboard. Discuss what Hinduism contributed to the culture of India, citing the influence of the religion on everyday life and the caste system.

Background

Daily Life

Hindu Worship Worship is part of the daily life of devout Hindu families. Each home has an altar for the special god that the family chooses to worship. In Hinduism, each of the many gods represents an aspect of the Divine. Individuals and families are free to choose which aspect they will worship. Worship varies according to the caste of the family, the god, and the region in which they live. On the family altar is a small idol, a picture, or a sacred object. The wife prepares food, flowers, incense, and fire for offerings to the god. Pious families perform morning, midday, and evening worship. The husband usually leads the worship service.

Answers to . . .

MAP STUDY
the Black Sea

SKILLS MINI LESSON

Locating Information You may **introduce** the skill by asking students to generate a list of sources of information on the Mughal empire in India. Ask students for entry names or terms they would look up in indexes to encyclopedias and other references. List these names on the chalkboard. Guide students as they **practice** the skill by looking up these entries in an encyclopedia index to determine whether they yield sufficient information on the topic. The goal of this activity is to increase students' ability to use an index to find information. Students can **apply** this skill as they research a specific topic about Mughal India, such as achievements of a specific ruler, Muslim beliefs, art, literature, why the empire collapsed, and so on. Suggest that each member of the group find two facts on the topic and tell briefly how the information was found.

3 Teach

Students will individually write short essays answering these two questions: 1) What did Hinduism contribute to India? and 2) Why was Akbar a great ruler? Invite volunteers to read their answers aloud. This activity should take about 20 minutes.

4 Assess

See the answers to the Section Review. You may also use students' essays for assessment.

Acceptable essays describe the Hindu religion and caste system and give one or two main reasons for Akbar's greatness.

Commendable essays expand on the importance of Hinduism and of Akbar to India.

Outstanding essays show an understanding of how religious tolerance helped Akbar unite and strengthen his empire.

My Village

Paramita Hazra
age 11
India

In this painting, the artist shows a scene from everyday life in her village. In many rural areas in India, people follow ways of life similar to those followed by people in the 1500s and 1600s. **Critical Thinking** What in the painting illustrates traditional ways?

Unlike earlier conquerors, the Muslims did not become a part of Hindu society. Muslim culture was based on ideas that were very different from those of Hindu culture. These differences caused conflicts between Hindus and Muslims. Religious differences still divide Hindus and Muslims in India today.

The Invasion of the Mongols   It was the Delhi Sultanate that Tamerlane, who was also a Muslim, invaded. But Tamerlane cared little about ruling India. He mainly wanted the country's riches. From Delhi, his soldiers carried off more pearls, rubies, diamonds, and golden dishes than they could count. They also took hundreds of slaves. Shortly after Tamerlane's troops left, the sultan regained Delhi. But the empire split apart into smaller kingdoms.

A descendant of Tamerlane, a Turkish prince named Babur (BAH boor), later took advantage of the disorder in northern India. In 1526, he attacked the sultan's army. Babur's troops were outnumbered almost 10 to 1. And while the sultan's forces had 100 elephants, Babur's troops had none. But Babur's troops were better fighters, and they had cannons. They defeated the sultan, and Babur went on to conquer most of northern India. He founded the brilliant Mughal (MOO gul) empire, which lasted into the 1700s.

Answers to . . .

MY VILLAGE
Answers may vary. Sample answer: The woman is using a traditional stove to cook, the man is working the fields by hand.

Resource Directory

Program Resources

Interdisciplinary Explorations
India: Beyond the Golden Age

Media and Technology

Color Transparencies 53, 169

Planet Earth CD-ROM includes satellite images and physical maps of India and South Asia, plus World Wonders, Cultural: Taj Mahal.

The Mughal Empire

Mughal is another word for "Mongol." Like Babur, the Mughal emperors were Muslims. But the people they ruled were mostly Hindus. Under earlier Muslim rulers, Indian society had remained divided by religion. But Babur's grandson, Akbar (AK bar), persuaded Hindus and Muslims to live more peacefully together.

Akbar, the Greatest Mughal Emperor Akbar was only 13 years old when he came to power. As he grew up, he became a talented soldier and greatly expanded the empire. He also ruled well. Akbar realized that the best way to make the empire peaceful was to be fair to people of different religions. Unlike earlier Muslim rulers, he allowed Hindus to practice their religion freely.

Akbar divided the empire into provinces. He gave government jobs to qualified people, whatever their religion. Hindu warriors served as generals, governors, administrators, and clerks. Akbar also ended unfair taxes on non-Muslims. And he regularly brought together scholars of different religions for discussion. Akbar searched for religious truth and listened to differing viewpoints.

LINKS ACROSS TIME

The Games We Play
Parcheesi, a popular board game, originated in India. Akbar loved the game. He had workers cut the design of the board into the pavement of one of his courtyards. Then he would play the game—using servants from the palace as the playing pieces!

The Mughal Empire Under Babur and Akbar

KEY

— Mughal empire under Babur: A.D. 1526–1530

☐ Mughal empire under Akbar: A.D. 1556–1605

• City

Two-Point Equidistant Projection

Peshawar.

Indus River

Lahore.

Delhi.

Agra.

Ganges River

INDIA

Arabian Sea

Bombay.

Bay of Bengal

0   200   400 mi
0   200   400 km

.Goa

Map Study By the end of his reign, Babur had seized most of the lands that had been controlled by the Delhi sultans. Through conquest, treaties, and marriage agreements, Akbar greatly increased the Mughal empire. In 1605, when Akbar died, the Mughals controlled most of northern India. **Place** The mouths of which two important rivers came under Mughal control during Akbar's reign?

Activity

Critical Thinking

Identifying Central Issues
Suitable as either an individual or a whole class activity.
Ask students to choose which of the following sentences best describes the central issue of Akbar's reign. Have students explain their choice.
(a) Religious tolerance helped Akbar to unite his empire.
(b) Religious tolerance stopped the conflicts between Hindus and Muslims and brought peace to India.
(c) Akbar gave government jobs to Hindus as well as Muslims.

Answers to . . .

MAP STUDY
Ganges and Indus

In this painting, made around 1600, Akbar (sitting in right center) receives visitors to the splendid palace. Akbar loved the arts, and the artists who worked at his court made beautiful miniature paintings like this one. The paintings showed court celebrations, battles, gardens, and often Akbar himself. **Critical Thinking** What does this painting tell you about the artist's attitudes toward nature?

Activity

Cooperative Learning

Art and Architecture
Organize the class into three groups, according to interest, to do research on Chinese art objects made of porcelain and jade, Japanese painting, or the architecture of Mughal India. Once research is complete, groups should present their research to the class in the form of an exhibit of pictures, with either an audiotape explaining the various pictures or an oral report. Group members should choose roles, such as researcher, artist, scriptwriter, or narrator. *Visual, English Language Learners*

Visualize Suppose that you wanted to build a monument in honor of someone you love. Visualize what the monument would look like.

The emperor also supported the arts. He set up studios for painters at his court. He supported poets, even though he himself never learned to read and write.

Akbar ruled for 49 years. During that time, his way of governing became firmly established in India. This allowed the empire to develop and expand for 100 more years under less-talented emperors. Because of his wise rule, Akbar is known as the Mughal's greatest leader.

Decline of the Mughals

More than 100 years after Akbar's death, the Mughal empire began to fall apart. Rulers began to spend too much money on wars and on expensive building projects.

Reign of Shah Jahan The grandson of Akbar, Shah Jahan (shah juh HAHN), became emperor in 1628. Of all the Mughal emperors, Jahan spent the most money on extravagant buildings. The most famous of his buildings is the Taj Mahal (tahzh muh HAHL). This "dream in marble," as one observer called it, is a tomb for Mamtaz (mahm TAHZ)

Answers to . . .

AKBAR HOLDS COURT
Answers may vary. Sample answer: The artist emphasized the beauty of trees, flowers, birds, and animals, showing the Mughal interest in nature.

Resource Directory

Teaching Resources

Section Quiz in the Chapter and Section Support booklet, p. 60, covers the main ideas and key terms in the section. Available in Spanish in the Spanish Support booklet, p. 38.

Vocabulary in the Chapter and Section Support booklet, p. 62, provides a review of key terms in the chapter. Available in Spanish in the Spanish Support booklet, p. 40.

Reteaching in the Chapter and Section Support booklet, p. 63, provides a structure for students who may need additional help in mastering chapter content.

Critical Thinking Activity in the Chapter and Section Support booklet, p. 65, helps students apply the skill of distinguishing fact from opinion.

Mahal, the emperor's wife. When she died at age 39, Shah Jahan was overcome with grief. The two had been constant companions. She even went on his military campaigns. He had asked her opinion on many issues. After she died, Jahan set out to build her a tomb "as beautiful as she was beautiful."

To build the Taj Mahal, Jahan called together 20,000 craftworkers and laborers from all over India, Asia, and Europe. Working for 22 years, they built this stunning monument in Agra in northern India.

The Empire Declines The cost of Shah Jahan's building projects was enormous. Added to the cost of his wars, they drained the empire of money. Shah Jahan's son, Aurangzeb (OR ung zeb), spent still more money in expensive wars. He also reversed Akbar's policies toward Hindus. Aurangzeb tried to force Hindus to convert to Islam, and he began to tax them again. Many Hindus rebelled.

Fighting the rebels cost still more money. After Aurangzeb's death in 1707, the empire split into many small kingdoms.

▲ Many people feel the Taj Mahal in Agra, India, is the grandest example of the Mughal architecture.

SECTION 3 REVIEW

1. **Define** (a) Hinduism, (b) caste system, (c) sultan.

2. **Identify** (a) Tamerlane, (b) Babur, (c) Akbar, (d) Shah Jahan, (e) Delhi, (f) Taj Mahal.

3. What did the Mughal rulers achieve in India?

4. In what ways did Akbar prove himself a wise ruler?

Critical Thinking

5. **Expressing Problems Clearly** Summarize some of the reasons for the downfall of the Mughal empire.

Activity

6. **Writing to Learn** Suppose Akbar is a leader under a system of government like the United States government. He is running for reelection. You are his campaign manager. Write a short speech stating why voters should reelect him.

📁 **Enrichment** in the Chapter and Section Support booklet, p. 64, extends chapter content and enriches students' understanding.

📁 **Spanish Glossary** in the Spanish Support booklet, pp. 83–91, provides key terms translated from English to Spanish as well as definitions in Spanish.

📁 **Chapter Summary** in the Chapter and Section Support booklet, p. 61, provides a summary of chapter content. Available in Spanish in the Spanish Support booklet, p. 39.

📁 **Cooperative Learning Activity** in the Activities and Projects booklet, pp. 32–35, provides two student handouts, one page of teacher's directions, and a scoring rubric for a cooperative learning activity on creating a museum exhibit about feudalism in Japan.

Media and Technology

🎧 **Guided Reading Audiotapes** (English and Spanish)

Section 3 Review

1. (a) ancient religion and way of life in India (b) a division of people into social classes (c) Muslim king

2. (a) Mongol who invaded India in 1398 (b) founder of the Mughal empire (c) great and wise Mughal emperor (d) emperor who built the Taj Mahal (e) capital of the Mughal empire in India (f) tomb built for his wife by Shah Jahan

3. The Mughal rulers united India and expanded the empire. Under Akbar, there was peace and religious tolerance. He supported the arts and literature. Mughal emperors built beautiful buildings, such as the Taj Mahal.

4. Akbar was wise to tolerate other religions, especially Hinduism, because it allowed the people to live in peace and harmony. He gained the loyalty of Hindus by allowing them to work for the government.

5. The downfall of the Mughals came about because of the money they spent on wars and on monuments. The emperor Aurangzeb was intolerant of Hindus. He tried to convert them to Islam and taxed them unfairly, which caused them to rebel.

6. Students' speeches should show how Akbar's wisdom and tolerance would help unite Americans and result in policies that would benefit all citizens. Students might mention that he would give all groups a voice in government and would support the arts and literature.

Assessing Your Understanding

Lesson Objectives

1 Identify key strategies used in assessing understanding.

2 Practice assessing understanding in context.

Lesson Plan

1 Engage

Warm-Up Activity

Write the question, *Did you get the point?* on the chalkboard. Then **introduce** the skill by reading aloud the opening paragraphs.

Activating Prior Knowledge

Ask students what they think assessing understanding means. Prompt them with the posted question, asking how they might determine whether they "got the point."

2 Explore

Have students read the text under Get Ready. Ask students to name some other times in their studies when it might be appropriate to stop and assess understanding (after a lecture, during the research process, when given directions for a test). Post some of these replies on the chalkboard. Then have students read the rest of the Skills Activity.

What does a good grade mean? Among other things, it means that your teacher believes that you understand an assignment. For example, you get a good grade on a test when you understand the subject well enough to answer most of the questions correctly. You get a good grade on a paper when you understand your topic well enough to write about it clearly and completely.

How do you know whether you understand something or not? Sometimes you might think you understand an assignment but later find out that you have made some mistakes. Assessing, or measuring, how well you understand something is a skill itself.

Get Ready

Suppose you have an assigned reading in a textbook. When you finish a section, you should stop to assess your understanding of the text. If you find that you understand it perfectly, then you can move on. However, if you realize that there is something you do not understand, then stop. Think about how you can begin to figure out what you have missed.

Why was I given this assignment?

What are the main ideas of the assignment?

Resource Directory

Teaching Resources

Determining if You Understood What You Read in the Social Studies and Geography Skills booklet, p. 74, provides additional skill practice.

Try It Out

How do you measure your understanding? Take a self-survey. Choose one reading assignment you completed recently. Review the selection, and then think about it as you read and answer each question below.

A. Why were you given this assignment?

B. What are the main ideas of the assignment?

C. How does this assignment relate to what you already know?

D. How could you use the information from the assignment in the future?

If you answered all four questions with confidence, then you probably understood the reading well. If you are not so sure about any of your answers, review the assignment with the questions in mind.

Apply the Skill

Practice assessing your understanding with the short reading assignment in the box. Read the assignment, then complete the activities that follow.

Answer the following questions.

1 Why were you given this assignment?

2 What is the main point of the selection?

3 How does knowing about Sui Wendi relate to what you already know about Chinese history?

4 How can you use the information in the selection as you learn more about China?

Think of ways to improve your understanding. List at least three things you can do to better understand the reading assignment.

Sui Wendi

From A.D. 581 to 604, a man named Sui Wendi (originally named Yang Chien) ruled China as emperor. Sui Wendi unified China after it had been divided for about 300 years. Long after his death, China has remained united and powerful. The people of China, who are about one fifth of the world's population, have probably suffered fewer wars than many other peoples.

Yang Chien was born in 541 to a powerful family in northern China. He worked for the emperor of the northern Chou dynasty. He quickly became a valued official. He helped the emperor gain control of most of northern China. Shortly after the emperor's death, Yang Chien became emperor himself. He took the new name Sui Wendi.

As emperor, Sui Wendi wanted to rule more than northern China, so he invaded southern China. In 589, he became ruler of all of China. He built a new capital city for his empire. He also began reconstruction of the Grand Canal. This canal now connects the Chang Jiang and the Huang He, which are the two greatest rivers in China.

Sui Wendi also reformed the ways in which government officials were chosen. His civil service tests and other new rules helped to create a talented and skilled group of officials. Unlike officers in earlier times, these came from all social classes.

This cautious but strong leader ruled until his death in 604. His political and military actions had long-lasting effects in Chinese history.

3 Teach

Direct students to use the Try It Out activity to **practice** the skill. You might offer a selection of assignments and allow students choosing the same assignment to work together. Invite students or groups to share their answers with the class.

For additional reinforcement, pair students who want review with those feeling confident. Have pairs reread the assignment aloud together, discussing each question as appropriate.

4 Assess

Have students **apply** the skill by completing the final activity. Initiate a class discussion of the follow-up questions. You may **assess** students' skill levels by evaluating their contributions to the discussion.

Answers to ...

TRY IT OUT

Students' answers will vary, but should reflect a general understanding of a previous assignment.

APPLY THE SKILL

1. to practice assessing understanding
2. The political and military actions of Sui Wendi had long-lasting effects on China's history.
3. Possible answer: Sui Wendi preceded the Tang dynasty; he used Confucian ideas in choosing government employees.
4. Possible answers: to trace the impact of Sui Wendi's actions in later times; to compare Sui Wendi's rule with other Chinese emperors

Possible answers: take notes, discuss the assignment with a friend, create an outline, highlight main ideas.

Review and Activities

Reviewing Main Ideas

1. How were Confucian ideas put into practice during the Tang and Song dynasties?
2. Describe the achievements of the Tang and Song dynasties.
3. How did feudalism work in Japan?
4. Why did the Tokugawa shoguns refuse to let Japan stay in touch with the rest of the world?
5. How were the Mughal rulers different from earlier Muslim rulers of India?
6. Describe how Akbar ruled India.

Reviewing Key Terms

Match the definitions in Column I with the key terms in Column II.

Column I

1. class of warriors in feudal Japan
2. set of rules for Japanese warriors that stressed honor, discipline, bravery, and simple living
3. series of rulers from one family
4. strict system of social classes among Hindus
5. government system in which less powerful people promise to be loyal to more powerful people

Column II

a. dynasty
b. samurai
c. bushido
d. feudal system
e. caste system

Critical Thinking

1. **Making Comparisons** In which ways were Tang Taizong of China and Akbar of India alike as rulers?
2. **Drawing Conclusions** Europeans took over the land that eventually became the United States. Considering this, do you think the Tokugawa shoguns were right in thinking that Europeans might try to take over Japan? Explain your answer.

Graphic Organizer

Copy the chart onto a separate sheet of paper. Complete the chart by describing important characteristics or accomplishments of each civilization.

Civilization	Description
Tang and Song Dynasties	
Feudal Japan	
Mughal Empire	

Reviewing Main Ideas

1. The Tang and Song dynasties put into practice Confucian ideas such as the leader setting a moral example, people treating each other with respect, strong families, and a merit system for government employment.

2. The Tang and Song rulers brought peace to China. They encouraged music, art, and fine writing. Trade in silk, porcelain, and tea flourished, making the economy strong. Printing was invented, and many people learned to read and write. The Grand Canal, linking China's two most important rivers, was built.

3. The emperor was the head of the feudal system, but the ruling power was held by the shogun. He controlled the daimyo, or feudal lords, who employed samurai to protect their lands and to wage war. The peasants supported these upper classes.

4. The Tokugawa shoguns thought that Europeans would try to gain control of their country, so they expelled all foreigners and refused to trade with the outside world.

5. Earlier Muslim rulers had discriminated against the Hindus, the majority in India, by not letting them participate in government. The Mughal rulers practiced religious tolerance and involved the Hindus in government.

6. Akbar ruled India wisely. He practiced religious tolerance, which united Hindus and Muslims. He supported the arts and literature. He set up a strong government.

Reviewing Key Terms

1. b
2. c
3. a
4. e
5. d

Critical Thinking

1. They were both wise rulers who brought peace and unity to their countries. They both supported the arts and literature.

2. Students' answers will vary. Many will probably say that the shoguns were right to protect their country against the Europeans, but some may present reasons why it was not necessary to isolate the country to do so.

Graphic Organizer

Students' chart entries may vary. Sample chart shown.

Civilization	Description
Tang and Song Dynasties	China's golden age saw the beginning of a merit system for government employment. Rulers encouraged music, art, fine writing. Inventions included block printing, gunpowder, compass, movable type.
Feudal Japan	Government was similar to a pyramid: Shogun, or great general, at the top; then came local lords called daimyo; beneath them were samurai; and the system was supported by the peasants, the people at the bottom of the pyramid.
Mughal Empire	Muslim rulers ruled Hindu people. Akbar, the greatest emperor, gave government jobs to qualified people without regard to religion. Akbar supported the arts. Shah Jahan, one of the last Mughal emperors, was responsible for the construction of the Taj Mahal.

Map Activity

Asia
For each place listed, write the letter from the map that shows its location.

1. China during the Tang dynasty

2. Silk Road

3. Grand Canal

4. Japan

5. Mughal empire

6. Delhi

Place Location

Writing Activity

Writing a Story
Bushido required that samurai show complete loyalty to their daimyo. A samurai's family took second place behind his daimyo. Write a brief story that illustrates a samurai's loyalty to his daimyo.

Internet Activity

Use a search engine to find **ChinaPage.** Choose **China Room.** Explore the links **History, Chinese Poetry, Chinese Painting,** and **Portrait Galleries.** Choose an emperor, a writer, or an artist and write a brief biography of his or her life and works. Include a portrait and an example of his or her work in your biography.

Skills Review

Turn to the Skills Activity. Review the four questions for assessing how well you understand something you have read. Explain what steps you might take if you could not answer all the questions.

How Am I Doing?

Answer these questions to check your progress.

1. Can I describe the accomplishments of the Tang and Song dynasties?

2. Do I understand how feudalism developed in Japan and why the shoguns cut off Japan from the world?

3. Can I tell how Mughal rule affected India and why Akbar was a great ruler?

4. What information from this chapter can I use in my book project?

Internet Activity

If students are having difficulty finding this site, you may wish to have them use the following URL, which was accurate at the time this textbook was published:

http://www.chinapage.com/china.html

You might also guide students to a search engine. Four of the most useful are Infoseek, AltaVista, Lycos, and Yahoo. For additional suggestions on using the Internet, refer to the Prentice Hall Social Studies' Educator's Handbook "Using the Internet," in the *Prentice Hall World Explorer Program Resources.*

For additional links to world history and culture topics, visit the Prentice Hall Home Page at:
http://www.phschool.com

How Am I Doing?

Point out to students that this checklist is a quick reminder of what they learned in the chapter. If their answer to any of the questions is *no* or if they are unsure, they may need to review the topic.

Map Activity

1. D   3. E   5. B
2. A   4. F   6. C

Writing Activity

Students' stories should show the importance of loyalty, honor, and bravery to a samurai.

Skills Review

Students' proposed steps should indicate ways to increase their understanding of the reading.

Resource Directory

Teaching Resources

📁 **Chapter Tests** Forms A and B are in the Tests booklet, pp. 20–25.

Program Resources

📁 **Writing Process Handbook** includes Using Transitions, p. 30, to help students with the Writing Activity.

Media and Technology

🖨 **Color Transparencies**
Color Transparency 171
(Graphic organizer web template)

💿 **Prentice Hall Writer's Solution**
Writing Lab CD-ROM

💾 **Computer Test Bank**

💿 **Resource Pro™ CD-ROM**

Europe in the Middle Ages

To help you plan instruction, the chart below shows how teaching resources correspond to chapter content. Use the resources to vary instruction, add activities, or plan block schedules. Where appropriate, resources have **suggested time allotments** for students. Time allotments are approximate.

Managing Time and Instruction

		Medieval Times to Today Teaching Resources Binder		World Explorer Program Resources Binder	
		Resource	**mins.**	**Resource**	**mins.**
1	**SECTION 1** **Feudalism: A System for Living**	**Chapter and Section Support** Reproducible Lesson Plan, p. 67 Ⓢ Guided Reading and Review, p. 68 Ⓢ Section Quiz, p. 69	20 25	**Outline Maps** Western Europe: Physical, p. 17 Mediterranean Europe: Political, p. 21 **Nystrom Desk Atlas** Ⓣ Primary Sources and Literature Readings **Writing Process Handbook** Proofreading, p. 37 **Environmental and Global Issues** Human Rights, pp. 25–30	20 20 40 25 30
	SKILLS ACTIVITY **Using Route Maps**	**Social Studies and Geography Skills,** Understanding Road Maps, p. 35 Reading a Road Map, p. 36	30 30		
2	**SECTION 2** **The Rise of Cities**	**Chapter and Section Support** Reproducible Lesson Plan, p. 70 Ⓢ Guided Reading and Review, p. 71 Critical Thinking Activity, p. 83 Ⓢ Section Quiz, p. 72 **Social Studies and Geography Skills,** Analyzing Art, p. 59	20 30 25 30	**Outline Maps** Western Europe: Physical, p. 17 Central Europe: Political, p. 20 Mediterranean Europe: Political, 21 **Environmental and Global Issues** Waste Disposal and Recycling, pp. 31–36	20 20 20 30
3	**SECTION 3** **The Crusades**	**Chapter and Section Support** Reproducible Lesson Plan, p. 73 Ⓢ Guided Reading and Review, p. 74 Ⓢ Section Quiz, p. 75 **Social Studies and Geography Skills,** Identifying Central Issues, p. 42	20 25 30	**Outline Maps** Mediterranean Europe: Political, p. 21	20
4	**SECTION 4** **Kings and Popes**	**Chapter and Section Support** Reproducible Lesson Plan, p. 76 Ⓢ Guided Reading and Review, p. 77 Ⓢ Section Quiz, p. 78 Ⓢ Vocabulary, p. 80 Reteaching, p. 81 Enrichment, p. 82 Ⓢ Chapter Summary, p. 79 **Tests** Forms A and B Chapter Tests, pp. 26–31	20 25 20 25 25 15 40	**Outline Maps** Western Europe: Physical, p. 17 Central Europe: Political, p. 20 Eastern Europe: Physical, p. 22 **Environmental and Global Issues** Topic: Conflict, pp. 37–42	20 20 20 30
	LITERATURE *Of Swords and Sorcerers* by Margaret Hodges and Margery Evernden			Ⓣ Primary Sources and Literature Readings	40

Block Scheduling Folder
PROGRAM TEACHING RESOURCES

- Activities and Projects
- Interdisciplinary Links
- **Block Scheduling Program Support**
- Resource Pro™ CD-ROM
- Media and Technology

From Guiding Questions to Assessment   A series of Guiding Questions serves as an organizing framework for this book. The Guiding Questions that relate to this chapter are listed below. Section Reviews and Section Quizzes provide opportunities for assessing students' insights into these Guiding Questions. Additional assessments are listed below.

Media and Technology

Resource	mins.
(◧) 🖋 Ⓢ World Video Explorer	20
⊐ Color Transparency 89	20
⊐ Color Transparencies 89, 90, 133, 134	20
🖋 Planet Earth CD-ROM	20
⊐ Color Transparency 136	20
⊐ Color Transparency 89	20
🎧 Ⓢ Guided Reading Audiotapes	20
⊐ Color Transparency 171	
(Graphic organizer web template)	20
🖋 The Writer's Solution CD-ROM	30
⊟ Computer Test Bank	30

- Ⓣ **Teaming Opportunity**
  This resource is especially well-suited for teaching teams.
- Ⓢ **Spanish**
  This resource is also in Spanish support.
- 🖋 **CD-ROM**
- 🖋 **Laserdisc**
- ⊐ **Transparency**
- ⊟ **Software**
- (◧) **Videotape**
- 🎧 **Audiotape**

GUIDING QUESTIONS

- *How did each society's belief system affect its history, government, and economy?*
- *What was the pattern of day-to-day life in these societies?*

ASSESSMENTS

Section 1

Students should be able to enact a feudal ceremony between a lord and his vassal.

▶ **RUBRIC**   See the Assessment booklet for a rubric on assessing a role-playing activity.

Section 2

Students should be able to write a short report about life in medieval towns and cities around 1400.

▶ **RUBRIC**   See the Assessment booklet for a rubric on assessing a report.

Section 3

Students should be able to create a time line of the various crusades for the Holy Land.

▶ **RUBRIC**   See the Assessment booklet for a rubric on assessing a time line.

Section 4

Students should be able to state the effect of the Magna Carta on England.

▶ **RUBRIC**   See the Assessment booklet for a rubric on assessing cause-and-effect statements.

Activities and Projects

Mental Mapping

Europe in the Middle Ages
Have students locate Europe on a map. Ask them to identify countries of Europe such as Spain, Germany, Poland, and Hungary.

Point out that many of these countries have existed for a relatively short time. Many have had borders that changed during the 1900s. You may wish to point out that the borders of Germany and the Czech Republic have changed in the last decade. Remind students, however, that there are many buildings in Europe that predate these countries. Ask students what kinds of old buildings they might expect to find on a trip to Europe. They should mention castles and cathedrals. Tell them that in this chapter they will learn why so many castles and cathedrals were built during the Middle Ages and what their role was in European society.

Links to Current Events

Church and State
Explain that although the United States was founded on the principle of separation of church and state, many European countries have official state churches. Although most European countries today tolerate the practice of different religions by their citizens, that has not always been the case. In addition, the official church of a country usually receives many benefits from the government.

Suggest that students locate articles regarding controversial church/state issues in the United States. Ask them to think about the advantages and disadvantages of separating church and state.

Hands-On Activities

Role-Play
Give students a chance to role-play some of the push/pull factors that led people to move from manors to towns. Manors provided protection and stability, yet physical comforts were few and there were few chances for social mobility. Manors became overcrowded, and town life attracted people with skills and trades, as well as others who just wanted a better chance. Still, cities were crowded, dangerous, and dirty. Role-play could show one peasant trying to decide whether to stay on the manor or take a chance and move to a town. Other students could play four types of roles: a) people on the manor urging the peasant to stay, b) people on the manor urging the peasant to go, c) townspeople who urge the peasant to move to town, and d) townspeople cautioning the peasant to stay on the manor.

Two Feudal Systems Direct students to make a graphic organizer comparing and contrasting feudal Japan and feudal Europe. They should include such things as the dates when the systems were the major form of government, the social groups involved, the advantages and disadvantages for people living under the system, and the causes of the demise of the system. *Average*

Crusades Have students make a story map showing the routes traveled by Crusaders traveling from Europe to the Holy Land. Ask them to label and date the routes of two or more crusade journeys. They may locate specific events in place and time on the map. *Basic*

Write an Epic Suggest that students write a mock epic, using some elements of the literature of the Middle Ages. They can describe either a personal experience, such as a trip or a personal achievement, or a current event. Encourage students to have fun with this form. *Challenging*

Medieval Manor Encourage students to create a bird's eye view or map of a medieval manor. Suggest they use the drawing of the medieval manor in the student text as a starting point and a model, but urge them to add additional information or make any changes they would make if they were lord or lady of the manor. *English Language Learners*

F.Y.I.

This page can help you extend your own and students' understanding of the concepts in this chapter. You may want to browse through some of the suggestions in the **Bibliography. Interdisciplinary Links** can connect social studies understandings to areas elsewhere in the curriculum through the use of other Prentice Hall products. **National Geography Standards** reflected specifically in this chapter are listed for your convenience. Some hints about appropriate **Internet Access** are also provided. **School to Careers** provides insights into the practical uses of some of the concepts in this chapter as they might pertain to various careers.

BIBLIOGRAPHY

FOR THE TEACHER

Fritz, Jean, Katherine Paterson, Patricia and Frederick McKissack, Margaret Mahy, and Jamake Highwater. *The World in 1492.* Holt, 1992.

Langley, Andrew. *Medieval Life.* Knopf, 1996.

Morpurgo, Michael. *Arthur, High King of Britain.* Harcourt, 1995.

Rice, Chris, and Melanie Rice. *How Children Lived.* Dorling, 1995.

FOR THE STUDENT

Easy
Ancona, George. *Cutters, Carbers, and the Cathedral.* Lothrop, 1995.

Howe, John. *Knights.* Orchard, 1995.

Average
Gravett, Christopher. *Knight.* Knopf, 1993.

Howarth, Sarah. *The Middle Ages.* Viking, 1993.

Steele, Philip. *Castles.* Kingfisher, 1995.

Challenging
Corrain, Lucia. *Giotto and Medieval Art: The Lives and Works of the Medieval Artists.* Bedrick, 1995.

LITERATURE CONNECTION

Brooks, Polly Schoyer. *Beyond the Myth: The Story of Joan of Arc.* Lippincott, 1990.

Talbott, Hudson. *King Arthur: The Sword in the Stone.* Morrow, 1991.

Yolen, Jane, ed. *Camelot.* Philomel, 1995.

INTERDISCIPLINARY LINKS

Subject	Theme: Growth
MATH	Middle Grades Math: Tools for Success *Course 1,* Lesson 6-7, **Exploring Surface Area** *Course 2,* Lesson 4-7, **Make a Table**
LANGUAGE ARTS	Choices in Literature *Communication Explosion,* **The Bayeux Tapestry** *Deciding What's Right,* **The Boy Who Drew Sheep** *Where Paths Meet,* **Our English Language: One From All** Prentice Hall Literature *Copper,* **Dragon, Dragon; Iduna and the Magic Apples**

NATIONAL GEOGRAPHY STANDARDS

Students explore the 18 National Geography Standards throughout *Medieval Times to Today.* Chapter 5, however, concentrates on investigating the following standards: 2, 3, 4, 5, 6, 10, 11, 12, 13, 14, 16. For a complete list of the standards, see the *Teacher's Flexible Planning Guide.*

SCHOOL TO CAREERS

In Chapter 5, Europe in the Middle Ages, students learn about feudalism, the rise of cities, and the Crusades. Additionally, they address the skill of using route maps. Understanding medieval Europe can help students prepare for careers in many fields, such as education, the arts, philosophy, and so on. Using route maps is a skill useful for geographers, forest rangers, truck drivers, and others. The curriculum presented in this book, as in all eight titles of Prentice Hall's *World Explorer* program, is designed to prepare students not only for careers but also for good citizenship—of the world as well as of this country.

INTERNET ACCESS

Many social studies teachers and students use Internet browsers, or search engines, to investigate particular topics. For the best results, use narrow rather than broad topics. Try these for Chapter 5: middle ages, feudalism, chivalry, Crusades, Joan of Arc. Finding age-appropriate sites is an important consideration when using the Internet. For links to age-appropriate sites in world studies and geography, visit the Prentice Hall Home Page at: **http://www.phschool.com**

Connecting to the Guiding Questions

In this chapter, students will read about Europe in the Middle Ages: feudalism, the rise of cities, the Crusades, and the conflicts between kings and popes. Content in this chapter thus corresponds to the following Guiding Questions:

● How did each society's belief system affect its history, government, and economy?

● What was the pattern of day-to-day life in these societies?

Using the Map Activities

Have students study the map of Europe of 800 years ago. Ask them to share what they know of the kingdoms and states they see on the map.

- Sample answer: Portugal, France, Hungary

- Holy Roman Empire, Kingdom of France, Kingdom of Aragon; Adriatic Sea, Mediterranean Sea

Heterogeneous Groups

The following Teacher's Edition strategies are suitable for heterogeneous groups.

Cooperative Learning
Feudalism in Japan and
Europe   p. 108
Medieval Fair   p. 128
Interdisciplinary
Connections
Language Arts   p. 114
Critical Thinking
Recognizing Cause
and Effect   p. 125

CHAPTER 5 Europe in the Middle Ages

SECTION 1
Feudalism: A System for Living

SECTION 2
The Rise of Cities

SECTION 3
The Crusades

SECTION 4
Kings and Popes

MAP ACTIVITIES

About 800 years ago, Europe was made up of many separate kingdoms and states. These are labeled on the map above. To begin your exploration of Europe during this time, do the following activities.

Study the map
Read the names of the different kingdoms shown on the map. Which names are familiar? Which names are not familiar?

Plan a trade route
Trace the route that a merchant ship might have taken between Venice and Barcelona. Which kingdoms would it pass? Through which bodies of water would it sail?

Resource Directory

Media and Technology

 A Trip To: Europe's Castles, from the World Video Explorer, enhances students' understanding of the significance of castles in medieval Europe.

Chapter 6

Feudalism: A System for Living

Lesson Objectives

1. Trace the origins of feudalism and understand how it worked.

2. Evaluate the positive and negative aspects of feudalism as a political and an economic system.

BEFORE YOU READ

Reach Into Your Background

Have you ever ridden a local bus? Have you used public parks? If so, you have used services provided by your local government. Do you think your community does a good job providing services that people need? Why or why not?

Questions to Explore

1. How did feudalism protect people during the dangerous times of the early Middle Ages?

2. What was life like on a medieval manor?

Key Terms
Middle Ages
medieval
feudalism
vassal
manor
self-sufficient
serf

Key People and Places
Charlemagne
Gaul

As darkness fell, a young man prepared for a special ceremony. The next day he would stop being a squire, or knight-in-training, and become a real knight. It was a big step up in life.

The squire put on a white tunic and red and black cloaks. Then he walked to the church, where he spent the night alone, praying. The next morning he entered the castle courtyard, where knights and ladies had gathered. His lord presented him with his sword, spurs, and shield. The squire knelt. Then he felt the lord's sword lightly tap him on each shoulder. "In the name of God, Saint Michael, and Saint George, I call you a knight," declared the lord. "Be loyal, brave, and true."

The young man had become a knight, an important person in European society. Before all else, a knight was expected to be loyal and true to the lord who knighted him. His lord, in turn, was loyal to a more powerful lord. That lord might be loyal to a king. A thousand years ago, governments in Europe depended on each person's loyalty to those who had more land and wealth. Each knight and lord was also supposed to watch over the people in his care, who were less powerful.

▼ This picture shows a squire being knighted. He receives his broadsword and other weapons from his lord.

Lesson Plan

1 Engage

Warm-Up Activity

Give students two minutes to list on a sheet of paper what they know about the Middle Ages in Europe. Write these words on the board as memory prompts: *feudalism, knights, chivalry, lord and lady of the manor, serfs.* Ask students to add information to each of these words or phrases.

Activating Prior Knowledge

Have students read Reach Into Your Background in the Before You Read box. Discuss how the government knows what the people need. Ask students to list what services people receive from the government and what they give the government back (taxes, serve on juries and as soldiers in wartime, work for the government, and so on).

Teaching Resources

📁 **Reproducible Lesson Plan** in the Chapter and Section Support booklet, p. 67, provides a summary of the section lesson.

📁 **Guided Reading and Review** in the Chapter and Section Support booklet, p. 68, provides a structure for mastering key concepts and reviewing key terms in the section. Available in Spanish in the Spanish Support booklet, p. 42.

Program Resources

📁 Material in the **Primary Sources and Literature Readings** booklet extends content with a selection related to the concepts in this chapter.

📁 **Outline Maps** Western Europe: Physical, p. 17; Mediterranean Europe: Political, p. 21

2 Explore

After students read Section 1, have them contribute to a semantic map that addresses the following questions: How did feudalism develop? Why did it develop? What were the primary roles and responsibilities of lords of the manor? Vassals? What role did peasants and serfs play in the manor organization?

3 Teach

Let students debate the positive and negative aspects of feudalism. Make a chart on the chalkboard labeled *Positive* and *Negative*, and ask students to contribute statements to both sides. Ask students if they think feudalism was basically a useful system for protecting people and society, considering the historical period in which it developed. Allow students to debate this question. This activity should take about 20 minutes.

Medieval Times

This kind of government came about because it filled the needs of communities for protection during the Middle Ages. What are the Middle Ages? Historians usually say that ancient times lasted until about A.D. 500. They say that modern times actually started about A.D. 1500. The years in the middle, between ancient times and modern times, are called the **Middle Ages.** This part of history is sometimes called **medieval** (mee dee EE vul) times. *Medieval* means "from the Middle Ages."

The Collapse of the Roman Empire   In ancient times, the Roman Empire protected much of Western Europe. When it no longer had an army strong enough to defend its borders, the empire became weaker. In wave after wave, invaders claimed parts of the empire. They destroyed towns and cut off trade routes. They kept their own languages and laws. By doing this, the invaders broke the bonds that

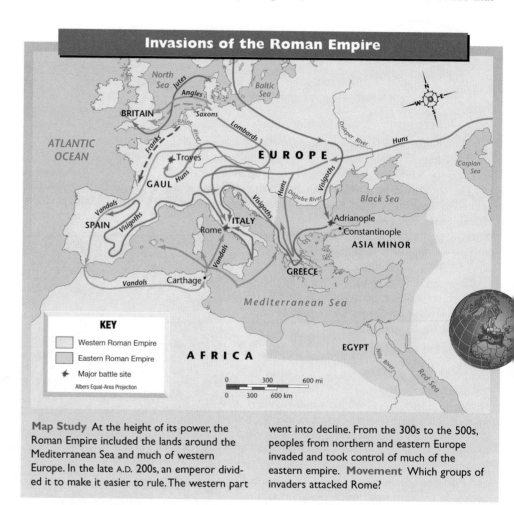

Map Study At the height of its power, the Roman Empire included the lands around the Mediterranean Sea and much of western Europe. In the late A.D. 200s, an emperor divided it to make it easier to rule. The western part went into decline. From the 300s to the 500s, peoples from northern and eastern Europe invaded and took control of much of the eastern empire. **Movement** Which groups of invaders attacked Rome?

Resource Directory

Program Resources

Nystrom Desk Atlas

Media and Technology

Color Transparency 89

Answers to ...
MAP STUDY

Vandals, Visigoths, Lombards

The Crowning of Charlemagne

Charlemagne brought the rule of law back to a large area of what had been the western Roman Empire. He also supported the Catholic Church. In return for this support, Pope Leo III crowned Charlemagne emperor on Christmas Day in 800.

4 Assess

See the answers to the Section Review. You may also use students' charts and discussion for assessment.

Acceptable charts indicate how feudalism met the needs of the people of that time.

Commendable charts indicate some of the drawbacks of the system, such as severe economic and political inequality.

Outstanding charts indicate that today, elements such as lack of freedom and self-determination would be rejected.

had held the Roman Empire together. Even reading and writing were in danger of vanishing, because many invading groups could not do either.

Charlemagne's Empire As time went on, the invading groups set up small kingdoms throughout Europe. One group, the Franks, claimed the area called Gaul, which is now the country of France. In 768, a skilled military leader named Charlemagne (SHAR luh mayn) became king of the Franks. He soon expanded his kingdom into an empire by conquering much of Western Europe.

During his rule of more than 45 years, Charlemagne worked to keep Western Europe united. He also established schools to promote learning and culture. The rulers who came after Charlemagne were weak. They could not defend his empire against new waves of invasions. By the end of the 800s, Charlemagne's empire had fallen apart.

Feudalism: A Basis for Government

Perhaps the fiercest attacks against Charlemagne's empire were made by the Vikings. These tough warriors came from northern Europe, where Denmark, Sweden, and Norway are now. Their attacks began around 800 and continued for about 300 years. Relying on

▲ Some people believe this gold crown set with jewels was worn by Charlemagne.

Background

Biography

Carolus Magnus
Charlemagne (742–814), also known as Charles the Great and Carolus Magnus, moved aggressively to unite nearly all the Christian lands of Western Europe. At the center of Charlemagne's rule was a desire to raise the cultural level of the court as well as the empire in general. Charlemagne was the first Frankish king to establish a permanent residence (at Aachen). With the help of noted scholars, he established a court library, which housed the works of Church Fathers as well as those of ancient authors. Charlemagne then extended his efforts to raise the level of morality, religious observance, and the process of justice throughout the empire. This movement was called the Carolingian Renaissance.

Activity

Cooperative Learning

Feudalism in Japan and Europe Invite groups of students to compare feudalism in Europe and in Japan. Suggest that they address the following questions in their comparison: How were they similar? Why did a system like feudalism develop in both places? What conditions influenced the creation of both of these systems of social organization? Students can present their comparisons in a three-minute television news magazine report. Encourage students to assign roles to group members such as researcher, artist, scriptwriter, and announcer. *Auditory, English Language Learners*

Vikings in America Vikings looked beyond Europe for conquest. They went into North Africa. They traveled westward to Greenland and beyond. *The Tales of the Greenlanders*, a Norwegian saga, describes a journey to lands west of Greenland. The storyteller gives clues about the location of Vinland, a settlement founded in this new land. Historians who have worked with these clues think that Vinland was probably somewhere in what is now New England, the northeast region of the United States.

▼ Knights carried colorful coats of arms into battle. They knew the coats of arms so well, they could identify each other at a glance.

surprise, the Vikings looted towns and murdered the people living in them. The people of Europe had to find a way to defend themselves against the Vikings. Slowly they worked out a new system of government that could protect small towns and entire kingdoms.

Creating Order The medieval power system was constructed like a pyramid. The people at the top of the system had the most power. They were kings and queens. Next in power were nobles, then knights, and finally peasants. This system is called **feudalism.**

In medieval Europe, power belonged to those who controlled the land. A landowner gave a share of land, called a *fief* (feef), to another man who promised to be loyal to the landowner, to follow his laws, and to fight for him. In this system, the landowner was called a lord, and the man who promised to be loyal to him was his **vassal.** A vassal could also be a lord. However, he had much less power than the great lord to whom he swore loyalty.

The agreement between lord and vassal was begun in a solemn ceremony. Like a new knight, the vassal knelt before the lord and swore to be loyal. The lord, in turn, promised to treat the vassal with honor. Then the lord gave the vassal a handful of dirt or some other symbol of the fief he was to receive.

Feudal Duties A lord's chief duty was to protect his vassals and their lands. If a vassal with young children died, the lord became the children's protector. The lord also asked his vassals' advice before making laws or going to war.

Vassals had other duties besides serving in the lord's army. When the lord called them, they had to appear at a special gathering called the lord's court. They also had to make special payments of money or goods to the lord when his oldest daughter married or when his oldest son became a knight.

Women of noble class also played an important part in feudal society. Like the men in her family, a noblewoman was often sent to friends or relatives for training. After her training was finished, she took her place as lady of the household. She managed the household, performed necessary medical tasks, and supervised servants. When her husband or father was off fighting, she often served as "lord of the manor."

Peasants and Manors

A lord might rule over one manor or many. A **manor** was a large estate that often included a village as well as farmlands inhabited by peasants. The manor was very important in the feudal system, since a lord depended on the wealth his manor provided.

A Medieval Manor

The most important building on a manor was the lord's house, or the manor house. It was surrounded by a fence or wall for protection. Beyond the lord's house lay the village. It consisted of a church, peasants' homes, a blacksmith's shop, a mill for grinding grain into flour, and other workplaces. The fields outside the village where crops were grown were part of the manor, too. **Critical Thinking** Why could a manor be called self-sufficient?

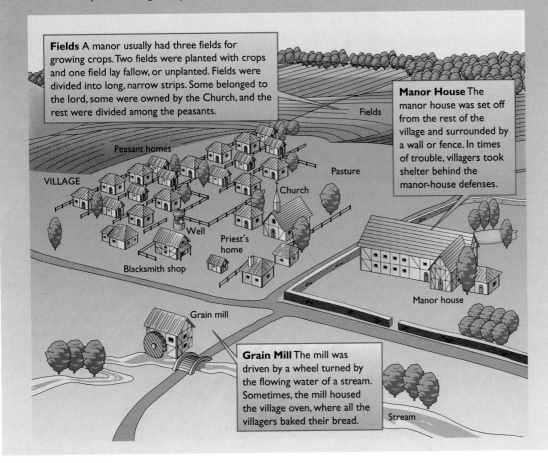

Fields A manor usually had three fields for growing crops. Two fields were planted with crops and one field lay fallow, or unplanted. Fields were divided into long, narrow strips. Some belonged to the lord, some were owned by the Church, and the rest were divided among the peasants.

Fields

Manor House The manor house was set off from the rest of the village and surrounded by a wall or fence. In times of trouble, villagers took shelter behind the manor-house defenses.

Peasant homes

VILLAGE

Pasture

Church

Well

Priest's home

Blacksmith shop

Manor house

Grain mill

Grain Mill The mill was driven by a wheel turned by the flowing water of a stream. Sometimes, the mill housed the village oven, where all the villagers baked their bread.

Stream

A Complete Community The illustration above shows the plan of a typical manor. The manor was governed by the lord. He made the rules and acted as judge. He also chose officials to manage the farming and other daily work. Since the manor was often far from towns and villages, its residents had to be **self-sufficient,** or able to supply their own needs, including food, shelter, and clothing. While most peasants were farm laborers, the manor would also have a carpenter, a shoemaker, a metalworker called a smith, and other skilled workers.

Exploring Technology

A Medieval Manor The manor's efforts to be self-sufficient meant using the land and the people in the most efficient way possible. Many, although not all, manors practiced some form of crop rotation. One scheme allowed for division of the farmland into three parts. One part was planted in rye or wheat in autumn, another in oats or barley in spring. The third field would lie fallow. Livestock were allowed to graze in the fallow field as well as in an uncultivated area called the "commons."

Decisions concerning which crops to plant, when, and in which fields were generally made by the entire community. While stewards and other powerful people might lobby for one decision over another, once the decision was made the plan was implemented and enforced by the entire community.

The manor tended to be self-sufficient in metal items as well. The manor's smith made shoes for oxen as well as horses. Further, the smith was responsible for knife blades, pots, kettles, cauldrons, and cups. The smith also provided tools for woodworking and carpentry including billhooks, saws, nails and other fasteners.

Answers to ...

A MEDIEVAL MANOR

People on the manor could grow and process their own food, manufacture their own tools and clothing, and provide for their religious needs.

1. (a) period between A.D. 500 and 1500 (b) from the Middle Ages (c) economic and political system of the Middle Ages (d) person who swore allegiance to a lord (e) medieval self-sufficient community ruled by a lord (f) able to provide for all of one's needs (g) peasant who belonged to the land owned by the lord of the manor

2. (a) king of the Franks who came to power in 768 (b) area now called France

3. Students' answers may vary, but should reflect the following points: (a) Feudalism benefited the wealthy and powerful by having people bound to support them through agriculture and crafts and the payment of money or goods. (b) The poor gained protection from invaders, but lost their freedom to own land and had to give a major part of what they produced to their lord. Serfs lost the freedom to leave the manor and seek a better life.

4. The peasant had to work in the lord's fields, but he could farm a small strip for himself. He had to give a part of this harvest to the lord as well. Peasants generally lived in one-room huts.

5. Students' answers will vary, but should be supported by reasons. Students should show awareness that the poor of that historical period had few options beyond seeking the protection of warriors against invaders and that the rights of common people were not recognized at that time.

6. Students' answers will vary. Accept all reasonable responses.

▶ This illustration, made in France during the 1400s, shows the kinds of work peasants had to do on a manor. These tasks included plowing, sowing seeds, pruning trees, and tending sheep.

READ ACTIVELY

Visualize Picture in your mind the inside of a peasant's hut.

The Lives of the Peasants and Serfs   The peasants did all the labor on the manor. They farmed the lord's fields to raise food for his household. In return, each peasant family could farm a small strip of land for itself. However, the family still owed the lord a part of the fall harvest.

Peasants lived in one-room huts with just a single window. For heat and cooking, they built a fire on the dirt floor. Without a chimney, smoke filled the dark, cramped interior before drifting out of a hole in the roof.

In most cases, peasants were **serfs.** This means that they belonged to the land. They were considered part of the manor on which they lived. When a noble was given a manor, its serfs became his. They could not marry or leave the manor without his agreement.

Although serfs were property, they were not quite slaves. A serf who saved enough money to buy a plot of land could become a free peasant. A serf who escaped to a city and managed to live there for a year and a day without being caught also became free. As you will soon read, this custom had a big effect on medieval Europe.

SECTION 1 REVIEW

1. Define (a) Middle Ages, (b) medieval, (c) feudalism, (d) vassal, (e) manor, (f) self-sufficient, (g) serf.

2. Identify (a) Charlemagne, (b) Gaul.

3. (a) How did feudalism benefit the wealthy and powerful? (b) How did it affect the poor?

4. Describe the life of a peasant on a medieval manor.

Critical Thinking

5. Identifying Central Issues Was feudalism the best way of providing protection for the poor? Give reasons for your answer.

Activity

6. Writing to Learn You are a medieval lord. List the various tasks you might perform in this position. Which tasks do you think you would like? Which do you think you would dislike? Explain your answers.

Resource Directory

Teaching Resources

Section Quiz in the Chapter and Section Support booklet, p. 69, covers the main ideas and key terms in the section. Available in Spanish in the Spanish Support booklet, p. 43.

Program Resources

Environmental and Global Issues Topic: Human Rights, pp. 25–30

The Rise of Cities

BEFORE YOU READ

Reach Into Your Background

Think about the jobs the people in your community do.

How did they train for these jobs? Keep your answers in mind as you read this section.

Questions to Explore

1. How did the Roman Catholic Church influence life in the Middle Ages?
2. How did the growth of trade affect life in the Middle Ages?

Key Terms

clergy
excommunicate
guild
apprentice
chivalry
troubadour

A city's buildings tell a lot about what the city's people value and believe in. In modern times, for example, skyscrapers make a statement about the importance of big business in today's society.

Medieval cities also had buildings that soared above the rest. These buildings, however, had nothing to do with business. The grandest building in any medieval city was almost always a cathedral—an especially large church. It made a statement about the importance of religion.

The word *religion* in Europe in the early Middle Ages usually referred to the largest and most powerful religious organization of the time, the Roman Catholic Church. It had so much more influence than other religions that it was usually called simply "the Church."

The Church in the Middle Ages

Why was the Church so powerful? During the Middle Ages, life was short and hard for many people. They were comforted by the Roman Catholic belief that they could enjoy the rewards of heaven after death if they lived good lives. The **clergy**, the men who performed the services of the Church, helped people follow Church rules about how to live. The clergy performed marriages and funerals. They blessed the sick

▼ The cathedral in Aachen, Germany—the burial place of Charlemagne—was built in the late 700s. The large section on the right was added in the 1300s.

Teaching Resources

📁 **Reproducible Lesson Plan** in the Chapter and Section Support booklet, p. 70, provides a summary of the section lesson.

📁 **Guided Reading and Review** in the Chapter and Section Support booklet, p. 71, provides a structure for mastering key concepts and reviewing key terms in the section. Available in Spanish in the Spanish Support booklet, p. 44.

Lesson Objectives

1. Describe the role of the Church in medieval society.

2. Trace the growth of cities and the rise of a middle class and how they changed medieval life.

3. Assess the impact of the growth of trade in the later Middle Ages.

4. Summarize the cultural achievements in learning and the arts.

Lesson Plan

1 Engage

Warm-Up Activity

Show students pictures of some of the great cathedrals built in the Middle Ages in Europe, such as Chartres, Reims, and Notre Dame in France, and Canterbury, Salisbury, and St. Paul's in England. You might also have on hand David Macaulay's book *Cathedral* for students interested in learning how a great cathedral was built.

Activating Prior Knowledge

Have students read Reach Into Your Background in the Before You Read box. Discuss how government and economic leaders are trained in contemporary universities. Point out that these universities can be supported by state, private, and church or other religious group funds.

2 Explore

After students read Section 2, ask them to discuss how the Roman Catholic Church influenced life in the Middle Ages. Have them list the jobs done by the Church that are now done by governments. Then ask students how international trade again became active in the later Middle Ages. How did this change the society of that time?

Background

Links Across Time

Stained-Glass Windows
Early churches had rather small windows (without glass) that could be covered by shutters or perhaps oiled linen in bad weather. Glaziers during the Middle Ages were not able to make large sheets of glass. Therefore, as windows in churches and cathedrals grew larger, glaziers worked to piece together small shapes of glass to form larger windows, eventually adding color to the glass shapes to create magnificent stained-glass windows.

Answers to ...

A CHURCH SERVICE

They gave comfort to people during hard and trying times.

A Church Service

In this painting, made in Spain in the 1200s, a priest (on the left, holding a jug) performs a baptism. This ceremony symbolically washed away the man's sins and signaled the start of his new life in the Church. The clergy were deeply involved in people's lives, from birth to death. **Critical Thinking** How did services like baptisms and funerals help add to the Church's influence?

L I N K S
TO
ART

Glass for the Glory of God The grandeur of cathedrals was increased by the use of stained glass in windows. Richly colored pieces of glass were pieced together by craftworkers to show scenes from the Bible. The windows took many years to create and were very expensive. Rich nobles and merchants gave money to the Church to pay for these windows. Their gifts to the Church were meant to show that they were good Christians and that they deserved to go to heaven.

and the dying. The clergy also listened when believers came to church to confess their wrongdoings. In the name of God, the clergy then forgave the believers for the wrongs to which they had confessed.

The Church in Everyday Life The Church was also powerful because it took on many of the jobs government does today. In the United States, leaders have always been careful to keep government and religious organizations separate. For example, the government is not allowed to adopt a national religion or to support the activities of any religion. Nor are religious organizations allowed to run the government.

In the Middle Ages, the Church made laws and set up courts to enforce them. It gained great wealth by collecting taxes. It also took fiefs from lords in exchange for services performed by clergy. These Church lands were farmed by men and women who dedicated their lives to serving the Church. The men were called monks, and the women, nuns. These monks and nuns developed better ways of growing crops and tending livestock. In this way, the Church helped to improve the economy of the Middle Ages, which was based on farming.

The Church as Peacekeeper High Church officials also exercised great political power as advisors to kings. The Church helped limit warfare among feudal lords. When a lord rebelled, the Church could threaten to **excommunicate** him, or prevent him from taking part in Church life. A lord seldom ignored this threat, because if he were excommunicated, no one would associate with him.

Resource Directory

Teaching Resources

Analyzing Art in the Social Studies and Geography Skills booklet, p. 59, provides additional skill practice.

Program Resources

Outline Maps Western Europe: Physical, p. 17;
Central Europe: Political, p. 20;
Mediterranean Europe: Political, p. 21

Media and Technology

Color Transparencies 89, 90, 133, 134

Towns Grow as Trade Revives

By about A.D. 1000, the strong governments created by the Church and powerful lords had restored some order in Europe. This order meant that populations could grow. Many manors became crowded. Providing food and clothing for everyone who lived on the manor became difficult. Many lords gladly allowed peasants to buy their freedom. These farmers and craftworkers set up small communities outside the manor. As more people moved to them, these communities grew into towns.

The Rise of a Middle Class Many peasants who left the manor to work in towns saw their lives improve. They made enough money to pay for more than their basic needs. Some even became members of the middle class, a group between nobles and peasants. The middle class included merchants, traders, and craftspeople. Serfs still bound to the manor heard these success stories and longed to move to the towns. Some saved their money and bought their freedom. Others simply ran away.

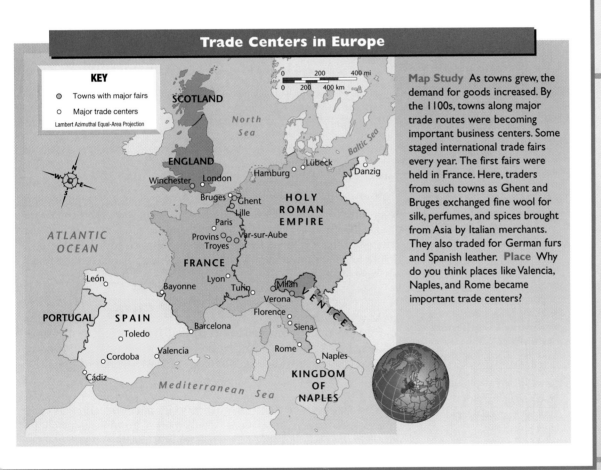

Trade Centers in Europe

KEY
- ◎ Towns with major fairs
- ○ Major trade centers

Lambert Azimuthal Equal-Area Projection

Map Study As towns grew, the demand for goods increased. By the 1100s, towns along major trade routes were becoming important business centers. Some staged international trade fairs every year. The first fairs were held in France. Here, traders from such towns as Ghent and Bruges exchanged fine wool for silk, perfumes, and spices brought from Asia by Italian merchants. They also traded for German furs and Spanish leather. **Place** Why do you think places like Valencia, Naples, and Rome became important trade centers?

3 Teach

Have student partners make two charts to summarize important information in this section. You might suggest that the charts be similar to the following:

Church		
Spiritual Importance to People	Jobs Done by Church	Achievements

Cities			
Who Lived There	Importance to Economy	Guilds	Culture and Learning

Give students about 20 minutes to fill in both charts.

Background

Daily Life

Monasteries and Convents Daily life in a monastery or convent was dedicated to prayer, meditation, study of religion, manual labor, and active service to the community, such as teaching, preaching, or nursing. Monasteries and convents followed a "rule," or set of regulations, that governed every aspect of their daily lives. Monasteries preserved classical literature and the writings of the early Church fathers by copying books by hand and illustrating them with beautiful drawings. Convents were often the only hospitals available to help the sick.

SKILLS MINI LESSON

Using Distribution Maps

You can **introduce** distribution maps by indicating that they help give a picture of the relative location or density of an event or item. Direct students' attention to the Trade Centers in Europe map. Ask students to explain the key, scale, and compass rose. Then have them **practice** the skill by using the map to answer the following questions: Near what geographic or human-made features were most major trade centers located? Why? Which areas had the greatest concentration of markets and fairs? Have students suggest reasons why these locations were chosen. To **apply** the skill, suggest that student pairs use the map to develop three True or False questions. Have student pairs exchange and answer one another's questions.

Answers to . . .

MAP STUDY

because of their location on the Mediterranean, a major transportation route

4 Assess

See the answers to the Section Review. You may also use students' charts for assessment.

Acceptable charts list the main facts given in the text.

Commendable charts show an understanding of the importance of these two social institutions.

Outstanding charts demonstrate original thinking backed by reasons and examples.

Activity

Interdisciplinary Connections

Language Arts Invite students to find tales of knights and chivalry, or other aspects of medieval life, to read and write about. List King Arthur of Britain, Roland of France, and El Cid of Spain as possible subjects. Books such as *The Midwife's Apprentice* and *Catherine, Called Birdy,* both by Karen Cushman (published by HarperCollins), provide tales of everyday medieval life. Suggest that students respond to their reading by writing about a hero or heroine, writing a tale or poem of their own, reading a tale aloud or on audiotape, or dramatizing a tale. *English Language Learners*

Answers to . . .
A MEDIEVAL MARKET

People could shop for food, clothing, housewares, and other goods in one location. But people had fewer choices; food was not kept cool or protected; there is no sign of advertising.

LINKS ACROSS THE WORLD

Angkor Wat: An Asian Capital When London and Paris were growing into cities, Angkor Wat (AN kor waht) was already the capital of a huge empire in Asia. The Hindu rulers of the Khmer empire founded Angkor Wat in A.D. 802. For more than 300 years, the city grew. Each ruler built more magnificent temples than the ruler before him. Then, in about 1431, the Khmer capital was abandoned and a new capital was built. The ruins of Angkor Wat are in what is today the country of Cambodia. Visitors have described its temples as "grander than anything in Greece or Rome."

A Medieval Market

Most medieval towns had a market where local and foreign goods were sold. This scene shows grocers at work. Carpenters, barbers, butchers, bakers, and other tradespeople also might have stalls at the market. **Critical Thinking** How are medieval markets similar to the places you shop? How are they different?

Towns Grow Along Trade Routes The increased law and order in Europe also meant that trade routes and waterways came into use again. Merchants traveled to Africa and Asia to buy valued goods. They gathered at river crossings and along highways to sell their goods. Before long, towns sprang up in these locations. The map on the previous page shows where these trading cities arose.

Life in Towns and Cities

By 1400, some towns had as many as 10,000 people. Town life was not at all like manor life. Townspeople were not self-sufficient. Instead, like our society today, town life was based on the exchange of money for goods and services.

The Growth of Guilds In every city and town, merchants and craftworkers formed associations called guilds. A **guild** included all the people in town who practiced a certain trade. Thus there was a guild of weavers; another of grocers; and another of masons, or people who worked with stone. Each guild made rules to help its members earn good wages. The guilds set prices and prevented outsiders from selling goods in town. They also set standards for the quality of goods. Those who belonged to guilds paid dues. This money was used to help needy members, or to support the families of members who had died.

Women also worked actively in the guilds. Girls became apprentices in guilds for weaving, papermaking, surgery, and so on. An **apprentice** is an unpaid worker being trained in a craft. Women often joined the same guild as their fathers or husbands. Because they were familiar with the family craft, they often kept the shops in which finished goods were sold.

Between the ages of 8 and 14, a boy who wanted to learn a certain craft became an apprentice. He lived and worked in the home of a guild master. After seven years, the boy became a journeyman. He traveled from town to town, working with different masters. In time, guild officials examined the journeyman's work. If it met their standards, he could join the guild.

Overcrowding and Disease Organizing guilds helped medieval people improve their lives. Yet there was much they did not know about making healthy cities. Cities often had walls for protection,

READ ACTIVELY

Connect How is your education different from that of a guild apprentice?

A Master and His Apprentice

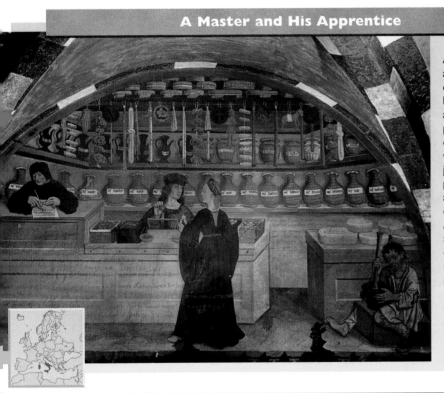

At the left of this picture, an apothecary, or maker of medicines, checks his books. In the center, his apprentice weighs out a prescription for a customer. On the right, a worker, possibly a journeyman, grinds powders with a mortar and pestle. Journeymen often were not well paid. Also, it might take them several years before they could win acceptance into a guild and become masters themselves. **Critical Thinking** Why do you think the guild system was set up?

Background

Links Across Time

Sanitation Medieval European cities were filthy and disease-ridden. Most medieval Europeans feared that bathing would lead to chills and death. They avoided baths except in the summer months. It was not unusual for poorer Europeans to be ridden with lice.

Background

Global Perspectives

Higher Learning Arabs formed the first universities, schools where many subjects were taught. Among the oldest is the University of Al-Azhar, founded in Cairo, Egypt, in 970. The oldest European university is in Bologna, Italy. Its law school was founded in 890, but it did not become a university until the late 1000s. An important right claimed by medieval universities was freedom to explore all subjects without interference from the government or the Church. However, the Church often tried to suppress ideas contrary to its teachings.

Answers to ...
A MASTER AND HIS APPRENTICE

Answers will vary. Most students will mention points such as: craftworkers wanted to protect their jobs; craftworkers wanted to ensure the quality of the goods they produced; craftworkers wanted to make sure there would be people to carry on the craft.

1. (a) men who performed the services of the Roman Catholic Church (b) prevent a person from taking part in Church life (c) organization of people who practiced a certain trade (d) young person who was an unpaid worker learning a craft (e) qualities of a knight (f) traveling performer who sang about the deeds of knights

2. Students' answers should include that the Church helped people deal with their hard lives by providing spiritual comfort and help. It also performed a lot of the functions usually done by governments. The Church made and enforced laws, collected taxes, improved the economy, and kept the peace between warring lords.

3. As trade became more important, towns grew larger as more peasants who had bought their freedom moved there; trade routes and waterways were used more; and cities developed from towns situated near rivers and highways.

4. (a) A serf who stayed in a town for a year and a day without being caught became free. In the town, the former serf had a chance to learn a trade and improve his economic condition. (b) Serfs would lose their ability to return to the manor. They might be separated from their families, and they would lose the security of manor life.

5. Answers will vary, but should be backed up by well thought-out reasons.

so space in them was limited. Houses were crowded together, streets were filthy with waste thrown from windows, and sicknesses spread quickly.

One disease, the Black Death, wiped out a third of Europe's population—that's one out of every three people—in just four years. The Black Death was another name for bubonic plague, a disease spread by fleas on rats. By the time victims noticed the swellings and black bruises that were symptoms of the disease, it was too late. Death usually followed quickly. As one French clergyman wrote, "He who was well one day was dead the next." At its height, the Black Death claimed 800 people each day in the city of Paris. It would take centuries for people in Europe to begin to make their cities clean, healthy places to live.

▼ This 1300s painting shows the people of Tournai, a city in what today is Belgium, burying victims of the Black Death. About 40 million Europeans were killed by the bubonic plague.

Medieval Culture and Learning

Despite the hardships, medieval life was not all a struggle for survival. The growing cities attracted traveling scholars, and young men flocked to cathedral schools to hear their lectures. By 1200, many cathedral schools had become universities with full-time scholars. Students studied subjects such as grammar, reasoning, and mathematics. Some even went on to higher studies in philosophy, law, or medicine.

Writing about chivalry blossomed in the Middle Ages. **Chivalry** was the name for the noble qualities knights were supposed to have. A knight was supposed to be brave and loyal and do heroic deeds to win the love of a worthy woman. Traveling performers called **troubadours** (TROO buh dorz) wandered from place to place singing about the chivalrous deeds of knights for their ladies.

SECTION 2 REVIEW

1. Define (a) clergy, (b) excommunicate, (c) guild, (d) apprentice, (e) chivalry, (f) troubadour.

2. Why was the Church so important to people during the Middle Ages?

3. What major changes took place in medieval society as trade became more important?

Critical Thinking

4. Drawing Conclusions (a) What might a serf gain by escaping to town? (b) What would the serf lose?

Activity

5. Writing to Learn Do you think a young person should be expected to start learning a trade between the ages of 8 and 14? Write a paragraph expressing your views. Give reasons for your answer.

Resource Directory

Teaching Resources

📁 **Critical Thinking Activity** in the Chapter and Section Support booklet, p. 83, helps students apply the skill of making comparisons.

📁 **Section Quiz** in the Chapter and Section Support booklet, p. 72, covers the main ideas and key terms in the section. Available in Spanish in the Spanish Support booklet, p. 45.

Program Resources

📁 **Environmental and Global Issues** Topic: Waste Disposal and Recycling, pp. 31–36

The Crusades

Reach Into Your Background

In this section, you are going to read about wars fought over religion and resources.

Think of other reasons why people go to war. Do you accept these reasons? Why or why not?

Questions to Explore

1. Why did the Crusades take place?
2. How did the Crusades cause lasting changes in Europe?

Key Term
Crusades

Key People and Places
Pope Urban II
Peter the Hermit
Saladin
Holy Land
Jerusalem

Lesson Objectives

1. Determine the religious and economic reasons for the Crusades.
2. Summarize the events of the First Crusade.
3. Explain how the Crusades changed medieval society.
4. Evaluate the actions of crusaders.

Lesson Plan

1 Engage
Warm-Up Activity

Invite students to preview this section by reading the first three paragraphs and then skimming the headings and looking at the maps and illustrations. Discuss the location of the Holy Land on the map and where the crusaders came from. Ask students to write down two questions they want to answer as they read this section.

Activating Prior Knowledge

Have students read Reach Into Your Background in the Before You Read box. Give students time to think about their position on this subject. Then have the class debate whether wars are ever justified.

O n November 18, 1095, a crowd gathered in the French town of Clermont to hear an urgent message from Pope Urban II:

"Y ou common people who have been miserable sinners, become soldiers of Christ! You nobles, do not [quarrel] with one another. Use your arms in a just war! Labor for everlasting reward."

▼ This picture shows Pope Urban II calling for a crusade to the Holy Land.

The war to which Pope Urban II called the people of Europe was in Palestine, a small region on the eastern shore of the Mediterranean Sea. Jews, Christians, and Muslims called this place the "Holy Land." To all three religions it was sacred. Now, said the Pope, the Holy Land had fallen to an enemy. Christians must win it back.

Causes of the Crusades

Over the next 200 years, the Church launched four bloody wars to capture Palestine. These wars are called the **Crusades.** The word comes from *crux,* the Latin word for "cross." Crusaders, from knights to peasants, carried the Christian cross into battle against the enemy, the Seljuk (SEL jook) Turks.

Teaching Resources

📁 **Reproducible Lesson Plan** in the Chapter and Section Support booklet, p. 73, provides a summary of the section lesson.

📁 **Guided Reading and Review** in the Chapter and Section Support booklet, p. 74, provides a structure for mastering key concepts and reviewing key terms in the section. Available in Spanish in the Spanish Support booklet, p. 46.

2 Explore

After students read Section 3, have them discuss the reasons for the Crusades and their results. How did the Crusades change European life? Ask students to debate whether or not the Crusades were justified and to evaluate how they were conducted. Which actions should have been avoided?

Background

Links Across Time

Jerusalem Modern "pilgrims" travel to Jerusalem, now the capital of the state of Israel, to visit the holy places of Judaism, Christianity, and Islam. Jews visit the site of King Solomon's Temple, of which only the Western Wall remains. On the Temple Mount is the Dome of the Rock, a Muslim mosque built between 685 and 691. Muslims believe that here Muhammad was carried to heaven by the angel Gabriel. Near the Temple Mount is the Via Dolorosa ("Street of Sorrows"), where it is believed that that Jesus walked on his way to Calvary. At the sites of the crucifixion and burial, and where Christians believe that Jesus was resurrected, is the Church of the Holy Sepulcher. Part of the church was built by the crusaders in the 1100s.

▲ Huge armies of crusader knights sailed to Palestine hoping to drive the Muslim Turks from the Holy Land.

▼ This container, called "The Right Arm of Saint Louis," held the remains of Louis IX of France. He led a crusade to the Holy Land in 1248.

The Rise of the Turks The Seljuks, a Turkish ethnic group, came from Central Asia. They moved into Southwest Asia, where they became Muslims. By 1071, the Turks had invaded and captured much of the Byzantine empire. Then they took the sacred city of Jerusalem from the Byzantines.

The Byzantine emperor in Constantinople asked Pope Urban II to send knights to fight the invaders. The pope agreed.

Attacks on Pilgrims Since about A.D. 300, European Christians had been traveling to Jerusalem. These people were pilgrims—people who journey to a sacred place. When the Turks took over Palestine, they turned the pilgrims away. Some were attacked and murdered. The violence occurred even though Islamic teaching states that Jews and Christians are fellow believers in God. The Turks' attacks gave the pope a religious reason to call Christians to action.

Land, Trade, and Wealth The Church had other reasons for launching the Crusades. Europeans wanted not only Palestine's holy sites, but control of its key trade routes between Africa, Asia, and Europe as well. The map on the next page shows Palestine's ideal location lying close to three continents.

The Church also had its eye on the rich empire of the Byzantines. Although Pope Urban II had agreed to help the Byzantine emperor, the two were rivals. The pope hoped to weaken the Byzantine empire and control its wealthy trade routes. This possibility encouraged European merchants to join the crusaders.

A Series of Crusades

Urban II's best hope for reopening the Holy Land rested with the lords and their trained, experienced knights. But before the lords could assemble armies, a band of common people set out to fight the Muslims.

Resource Directory

Teaching Resources

📁 **Identifying Central Issues** in the Social Studies and Geography Skills booklet, p. 42, provides additional skill practice.

Program Resources

📁 **Outline Maps** Mediterranean Europe: Political, p. 21

Media and Technology

🖳 **Color Transparency** 136

💿 **Planet Earth** CD-ROM includes World Wonders, Cultural: Jerusalem which enhances the importance of Jerusalem at the time of the Crusades.

Peter the Hermit and the People's Crusade   In 1096, before the First Crusade, Peter the Hermit, a small, ordinary-looking man who wore monk's robes, gathered an army of common people. In some cases, whole villages packed up and followed him.

Peter, however, had no experience in organizing such a large group. As more people joined, food became scarce. Crusaders broke away to loot towns. Many died when local troops fought back. Others were taken prisoner.

Peter and the rest of his army went on to Constantinople. The Byzantine emperor advised him to wait for help from an army of knights. Peter agreed, but his army rebelled. His soldiers attacked the Turks, who easily defeated them. Only a small part of his army survived.

READ ACTIVELY

Visualize Visualize a day's march as you follow Peter.

3 Teach

Assign student partners the task of filling in the following graphic on the Crusades. This activity should take about 20 minutes.

When — Why — Who
Crusades
What Happened
Result — Result — Result

4 Assess

See the answers to the Section Review. You may also use students' charts for assessment.

Acceptable charts list at least two reasons under *Why* and two results, and cover the main events in the text.

Commendable charts are more detailed and complete.

Outstanding charts contain evaluations of actions of the crusaders.

The Crusades

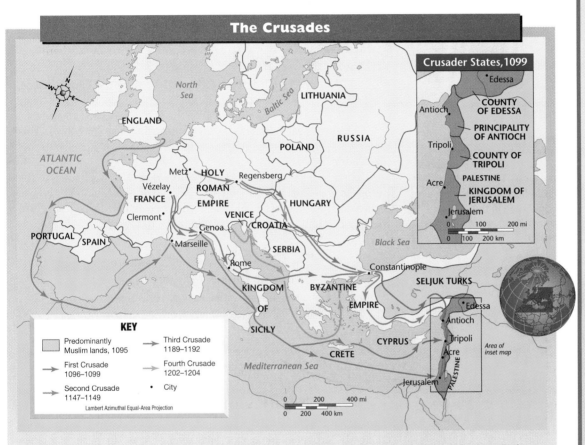

Crusader States, 1099

• Edessa
COUNTY OF EDESSA
Antioch
PRINCIPALITY OF ANTIOCH
Tripoli
COUNTY OF TRIPOLI
Acre
PALESTINE
KINGDOM OF JERUSALEM
Jerusalem
0   100   200 mi
0   100   200 km

KEY

Predominantly Muslim lands, 1095

→ First Crusade 1096–1099

→ Second Crusade 1147–1149

→ Third Crusade 1189–1192

→ Fourth Crusade 1202–1204

• City

Lambert Azimuthal Equal-Area Projection

0   200   400 mi
0   200   400 km

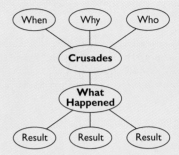

Area of inset map

Map Study In 1099, after the First Crusade, the crusaders set up four separate states in the Holy Land. These states are shown in detail on the inset map. Later crusades—including several not shown on the map— were launched to protect the crusader states. Even so, by the late 1200s, Muslim forces had retaken all of the Holy Land. **Movement** In which crusade did crusaders travel to the Holy Land mostly by sea? Which crusade did not reach the Holy Land? Where did it end?

Answers to . . .

MAP STUDY

the Third Crusade; the Fourth Crusade; Constantinople

Journal Writing

Crusader Ask students to consider what life as a knight or a knight's servant might have been like during one of the Crusades. Have students compose a journal entry that reflects their feelings as they set out on the Crusade. Suggest that they include descriptions of some of the places they pass through on their way to the Holy Land. If students are keeping an Explorer's Journal, as described in the Book Opener, you may wish to do this writing activity as part of that journal.

▲ The city of Jerusalem was very important to Christians. In fact, many considered Jerusalem to be the center of the world. This world map, taken from an English prayer book made in the 1200s, shows Jerusalem in the center.

Predict What changes do you think the Crusades made in European life?

At last, armies of knights arrived in Constantinople. They treated the Byzantines badly, killing and looting. The Byzantines regretted asking for their help.

Joined by the last of Peter's army, the knights captured Jerusalem in 1099. While taking control of the city, the crusaders killed 10,000 of its Muslim and Jewish inhabitants. This was the First Crusade.

Later Crusades After the First Crusade, Christians set up four kingdoms in Palestine. They are shown on the map on the previous page. The Muslims made repeated attacks to try to destroy these kingdoms. This forced the Christians to launch three more Crusades to keep control of the region.

Then a strong Muslim leader rose to power. He was known to the Europeans as Saladin (SAL uh din). By 1187, Saladin had retaken Jerusalem. King Richard I of England tried to persuade Saladin to return the holy city to the Christians. Saladin refused, saying:

                        "To us Jerusalem is as precious . . . as it is to you,
                       because it is the place from where our Prophet
                   [Muhammad] made his journey by night to heaven. . . .
                   Do not dream that we will give it up to you.**"**

Even so, Saladin had great respect for King Richard. So he agreed to reopen the city to Christian pilgrims.

Results of the Crusades

Though Christians never recaptured the Holy Land, the Crusades changed Europe in important and lasting ways. In particular, they increased trade and made the use of money more common.

For much of the Middle Ages, most people tended not to use money. Instead they exchanged services for land or protection. But crusading nobles needed to buy armor and supplies. They raised money by letting individuals, and also whole towns that were built on their lands, buy

The Beginnings of Banking

As the use of money grew, so did the banking industry. The earliest European banks were set up in the great Italian trade cities, such as Florence, Siena, and Venice. This picture shows Italian bankers taking deposits and issuing loans. **Critical Thinking** How did the Crusades contribute to the growth of banking?

ACROSS THE WORLD

An Expanded World
During the Crusades, European Christians learned much about the world outside Europe. They came into contact with new people, places, and ideas. They came to understand that millions of people lived in regions they had not even known existed. Some Europeans traveled to far-off places. Most of these travelers were either traders or priests hoping to convert people to Christianity. Francesco Pegolottia (frahn CHAY scoh pay goh LAWT tee uh), a merchant from Florence, Italy, was one of these travelers. His book, *Merchant's Handbook,* was a valuable manual about trading with Asia.

their freedom. In this way, feudalism grew weaker, towns became more important, and money came into widespread use.

During the Crusades, European ships carried armies and supplies across the Mediterranean Sea. These ships returned from the Holy Land with rugs, jewelry, glass, and spices. Soon, these goods were in great demand. Thus, the Crusades helped trade grow during the later Middle Ages.

SECTION 3 REVIEW

1. Define Crusades.

2. Identify (a) Pope Urban II, (b) Peter the Hermit, (c) Saladin, (d) Holy Land, (e) Jerusalem.

3. (a) Why did Pope Urban II launch the Crusades? (b) What were some other reasons for the Crusades?

4. How did the Crusades lead to economic changes in Europe?

Critical Thinking

5. Recognizing Cause and Effect What problems led the crusaders to fail?

Activity

6. Writing to Learn Were Peter the Hermit and his peasant crusaders determined and brave, or just foolish? Write a newspaper editorial on this question. Give reasons for your opinion.

Resource Directory

Teaching Resources

Section Quiz in the Chapter and Section Support booklet, p. 75, covers the main ideas and key terms in the section. Available in Spanish in the Spanish Support booklet, p. 47.

Section 3 Review

1. series of attempts by Europeans to gain control of the Holy Land

2. (a) pope who called on Europeans to come to the aid of the Byzantine emperor (b) leader of ordinary people on the First Crusade (c) Muslim leader (d) Palestine (e) city sacred to Jews, Christians, and Muslims

3. (a) to protect Christian churches and pilgrims and to help restore Byzantine rule to the Holy Land (b) to conquer new territory and gain greater wealth; to open trade routes to Asia to Europeans

4. Sample answer: The Crusades resulted in an increase of trade among Europe, the Middle East, and Asia. Money came into greater use, and the banking industry grew. Nobles raised money for armies by letting people buy their freedom. Towns grew and feudalism weakened.

5. Students' answers should include disorganized armies, military strength of the people of Palestine and their desire to repel the invaders, bad treatment of Byzantine people by the crusaders.

6. Accept all reasonable answers supported by examples and written in newspaper editorial form.

Answers to . . .

THE BEGINNINGS OF BANKING

People participating in a Crusade often had to purchase supplies along the route of the Crusade. Merchants, eager to break into new markets, needed a safe and convenient way to handle money.

SKILLS ACTIVITY

Using Route Maps

Lesson Objectives

1 Identify the elements and purpose of a route map.

2 Read a route map in context.

Lesson Plan

1 Engage

Warm-Up Activity

To **introduce** the skill, invite three students to read aloud the opening paragraphs in character. As students listen, post a political or physical map of Europe on a bulletin board or wall.

Activating Prior Knowledge

Ask students to describe a route map, if possible. Then invite volunteers to identify and model elements needed to make the posted map into a route map. List these on the chalkboard or trace them onto the posted map.

2 Explore

With students, read the Get Ready text. Highlight any route map elements from the text which students failed to identify earlier. Have volunteers add these to the posted list or tracing. Then tell students to read the rest of the Skills Activity.

Michaela sat at the dining room table with her schoolbooks. Her grandmother looked up and said, "What have you got there?"

"Gram, have you ever heard of the Children's Crusade?" Michaela asked.

"Oh, yes," Gram answered. "They were the French and German children who made a pilgrimage to Jerusalem in the Middle Ages."

"They never made it across the Mediterranean Sea," Michaela said. "But they traveled all the way from France and Germany. I wonder if they had to cross the Alps!"

"Do you have a map of the route they took?" asked Gram.

"No, just a map of Europe. Isn't that enough?"

Get Ready

When people move from one place to another, they follow a certain route. Many journeys have played important roles in history, and historical route maps show the paths of such journeys. A route map shows exactly where people went and how they got there.

A route map can show many of the same things you find on other maps, such as political borders, major landforms, and bodies of water. It also includes common map features such as a title, key, scale, compass rose, and labels. On every route map, a line shows the path of the journey.

Try It Out

To understand how to use route maps, make one of your own. You will need a sheet of paper, colored pencils, a map of your community, and a ruler.

Resource Directory

Teaching Resources

Understanding Road Maps in the Social Studies and Geography Skills booklet, p. 35, provides additional skill practice.

Reading a Road Map in the Social Studies and Geography Skills booklet, p. 36, provides additional skill practice.

A. Make a map. Draw a simple map of the area that includes your school and your home.

B. Add symbols. Mark the location of your school and your home with appropriate symbols. Identify the symbols in a map key.

C. Add routes. Using a colored pencil, draw a line to show the route you take from home to school. Use a different color to draw a line that shows another route, such as your path to visit a friend. In the map key, indicate the meanings of different colored lines.

Apply the Skill

Now that you have practiced with a modern route map of an area close to home, you have the skills you need to read a route map of a long-ago journey.

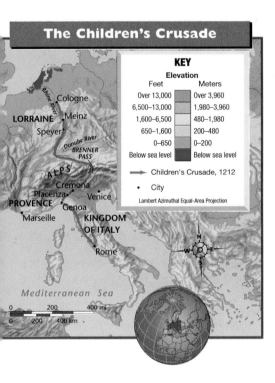

The Children's Crusade

KEY

Elevation

Feet	Meters
Over 13,000	Over 3,960
6,500–13,000	1,980–3,960
1,600–6,500	480–1,980
650–1,600	200–480
0–650	0–200
Below sea level	Below sea level

→ Children's Crusade, 1212

• City

Lambert Azimuthal Equal-Area Projection

The route map below shows the path of the Children's Crusade. For background on the Crusade, read the selection in the box. Then use the information and the map to complete the activities.

The Children's Crusade

In the year A.D. 1212, thousands of young people from Germany and France began a journey to Jerusalem. The crusaders, aged 10 to 18, believed that because they were poor and faithful, God would help them capture the holy city. The children also believed that God would part the Mediterranean Sea, letting them cross to Jerusalem.

The long march took its toll on the children. Many starved to death. Others froze. When they reached the sea at Genoa and the miracle parting did not happen, many turned back. Others managed to find places on ships but were lost in storms or captured when they landed. Some almost made it as far as Rome.

❶ Become familiar with the map. What is the map's title? Where did the Children's Crusade take place? What does the map key show?

❷ Understand the routes shown. How is the route of the crusaders shown? Where did the crusaders begin their journey? What was their goal? Did their route take them across rivers? Across mountains? How can you tell? Where did their journey actually end?

❸ Draw conclusions. How do you think the journeys might have affected the children? What difficulties may they have faced?

3 Teach
Confirm that students have the necessary materials to **practice** the skill with the Try It Out activity. Assist students in translating the physical experience of traveling to school into visual terms on the route map. Suggest that students travel the route in their minds, noting milestones on paper as these are reached mentally.

4 Assess
Prompt students to **apply** the skill by reading the map of the Children's Crusade. To **assess**, evaluate students' responses to the follow-up questions. Students should be able to use the map scale and key accurately, and should draw logical conclusions.

Answers to . . .
APPLY THE SKILL

1. The Children's Crusade; Europe; the route of the Children's Crusade in 1212, cities, and elevation
2. a line with an arrow; Cologne, Germany; Jerusalem (not shown on map); yes; yes; the route shown crosses rivers and mountains; Rome
3. Sample answer: Children would probably be tired, frightened, lonely, hungry, perhaps cold, as well as excited on the outbound journey, and sad on the return trip. Difficulties may have included poor weather, lack of supplies, dangers from unfriendly people or wild animals.

Section 4

Lesson Objectives

1. Describe the importance of the Magna Carta.

2. Identify the reasons for the development of nations in Europe.

3. Determine the reasons for the conflicts between kings and popes in the later Middle Ages.

Lesson Plan

1 Engage

Warm-Up Activity

Invite students to imagine that they are advisors to a king. The king wants to unite the many lords in his kingdom under his leadership. What should he offer to these lords to get them to pledge loyalty to him as their king? Tell students that money is not the issue. List ideas students think of on the chalkboard.

Activating Prior Knowledge

Have students read Reach Into Your Background in the Before You Read box. Discuss what makes Americans feel like one nation. List on the chalkboard what we have in common as students suggest ideas.

Kings and Popes

BEFORE YOU READ

Reach Into Your Background

Nations came into being in Europe as the Middle Ages came to an end. The people of the United States come from many different backgrounds.

Sometimes we feel divided by our differences. Still, as citizens of the United States we have much in common. What makes us feel like one nation?

Questions to Explore

1. Why did kings and popes come into conflict in the Middle Ages?

2. What events made nations out of the kingdoms of Europe in the late Middle Ages?

Key Terms
nation
the Magna Carta
Parliament

Key People and Places
Pope Gregory VII
King Henry IV
King John
Joan of Arc
Runnymede
Orléans

▼ King Henry IV kneels before Pope Gregory VII and asks for his forgiveness. Countess Mathilde, shown on the right, arranged for the two men to meet.

The king regretted disobeying the pope. For three days, he waited outside the gates of the castle where Pope Gregory VII was staying. Barefoot in the winter cold, the king begged forgiveness for the mistake he had made. Would the pope forgive Henry IV of Germany?

In the Middle Ages, kings and popes often quarreled over who should pick Church officials called *bishops*. Since bishops were part of the Church, popes claimed the right to choose them. Kings also wanted this right because bishops often controlled large areas of their kingdoms.

This was the power struggle that caused Henry IV to beg for the pope's forgiveness. King Henry had been choosing bishops even though Pope Gregory VII had ordered him not to. In response, Gregory excommunicated the king and declared that his people no longer had to obey him.

Henry traveled to Gregory to beg for forgiveness. After three long days, the pope gave in. He allowed Henry to rejoin the Church.

Resource Directory

Teaching Resources

📁 **Reproducible Lesson Plan** in the Chapter and Section Support booklet, p. 76, provides a summary of the section lesson.

📁 **Guided Reading and Review** in the Chapter and Section Support booklet, p. 77, provides a structure for mastering key concepts and reviewing key terms in the section. Available in Spanish in the Spanish Support booklet, p. 48.

Program Resources

📁 **Outline Maps** Western Europe: Physical, p. 17;
Central Europe: Political, p. 20;
Eastern Europe: Physical, p. 22

◀ During the Middle Ages, many wealthy nobles lived in luxury. At dinner time, they might be waited on by 10 or more servants. These nobles were so rich and powerful that they rivaled kings. With the decline of feudalism, however, kings gained more power.

2 Explore

After students read Section 4, have them discuss why kings and popes were in conflict. How did kings gain power? How did the Crusades make the nobles weaker? What part did the Magna Carta play in helping to unite England as a nation?

3 Teach

Assign student partners the task of writing a letter to a king in the late Middle Ages, telling him how to unite the nobles in his kingdom under his leadership. Tell them to use the information in the text and the graphics for suggestions. This activity should take about 20 minutes.

Activity

Critical Thinking

Recognizing Cause and Effect Ask students to make a cause-and-effect chart or graphic that presents at least three reasons why feudalism declined in the later Middle Ages.

Nation Building Begins

Pope Gregory made a great mistake in treating King Henry IV in this way. In 1081, Henry invaded Italy, where the pope lived. By 1084, Henry had replaced Gregory with a new pope. Gregory was sent into exile and died far from his home. Henry IV's success in overthrowing Pope Gregory VII was a hint of things to come. As kings gained power, they dared to put their own wishes before those of the Church.

The Decline of Feudalism When the 1200s began, Europe was still a feudal society. For most people, the only important authority was the local lord. He protected them from invaders and made the laws, just as our government does today.

While there were kings who reigned over kingdoms, their power was far from complete. The wealthiest lords also had great influence. Many of them saw themselves as nearly the king's equal. In fact, it was not unusual for a noble to have more land, vassals, and knights than his king.

Media and Technology

 Color Transparency 89

Lesson Plan continued

4 Assess

See the answers to the Section Review. You may also use students' letters for assessment.

Acceptable letters show that students understand why the king had the power to unite the nobles and at least one thing he had to offer in exchange for their loyalty.

Commendable letters show two or more things the king could offer the nobles and an understanding of why the king had greater power than the nobles.

Outstanding letters contain all of the above and show a clear understanding of the balance of power that had to be maintained between king and nobles, as exemplified by the Magna Carta and Parliament.

In time, kings gained power as different forces weakened feudalism. The Crusades, for example, did much to weaken nobles. Many gave up land to raise money to join the Crusades. Other families lost their land when kings claimed the estates of nobles who died in the Crusades. Kings also began to support the new towns in exchange for money. They agreed to protect towns and made laws to help towns grow rich. Then, with the money paid by townspeople, kings hired armies and used them to attack troublesome nobles.

In these ways, kings became the main authority in their kingdoms. Gradually their kingdoms began to be real nations. A **nation** is a community that shares a government. A common language and culture are other things that sometimes unite the people of a nation.

England Becomes More United

On June 15, 1215, about 2,000 English nobles gathered at Runnymede, a meadow along the Thames River in England. Dressed in armor and carrying banners, they had marched from London, a short distance away. Now they prepared to meet with King John.

This was an unusual meeting. The king had not called it. The nobles were the ones who had demanded the meeting. King John, who once had had enormous power, had been forced to attend.

READ ACTIVELY

Predict What could have caused King John to attend the meeting at Runnymede?

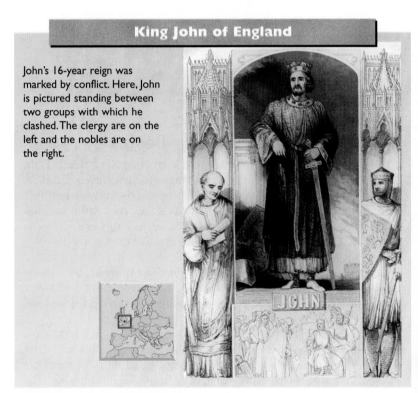

King John of England

John's 16-year reign was marked by conflict. Here, John is pictured standing between two groups with which he clashed. The clergy are on the left and the nobles are on the right.

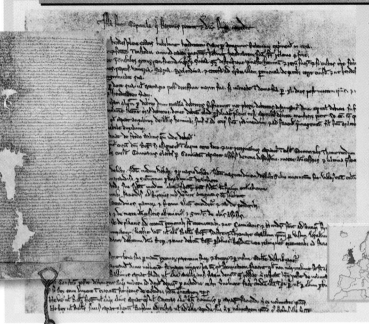

This shows a copy of the Magna Carta made many years after King John's reign. The original document, with John's seal attached, is shown in the inset. On the surface, the Magna Carta is simply a list of the nobles' grievances against King John. Underlying this list, however, is the principle that the government may not interfere with the rights of individuals. **Critical Thinking** How did the Magna Carta limit the power of English monarchs?

Background

Links Across Time

Trial by Jury The Magna Carta was the first step in the development of constitutional government in England. This document guaranteed nobles the right to advise the king and give their consent to all laws and taxes that the king proposed. This was a feudal right that previous kings had generally accepted, but that King John had violated. This right was used throughout English history as the justification for a parliament. In the 1600s, the Magna Carta was used to curb the power of tyrannical English kings. One article in the charter said that no freeman could be imprisoned, have property taken, be exiled or executed, except by lawful judgment of his peers (equals) or by law. This provision led to trial by jury.

King John Gets Into Trouble When John had become king of England in 1199, he quickly moved to increase his wealth and power. He taxed people heavily. He jailed his enemies unjustly and without trial. Even the most powerful nobles were hurt by John's unfair actions.

John also clashed with the pope by objecting when a man he did not like was made bishop. He seized Church property. The pope struck back by excommunicating John and declaring that he was no longer king.

The Magna Carta John was now at the mercy of the nobles and clergy he had angered with his earlier actions. Now that he was in trouble with the pope, the nobles and clergy struck back. With the bishops' help, the nobles made a list of demands and called John to Runnymede. There he put his royal mark on their document, which was called the **Magna Carta** (MAG nuh KAR tuh), or the "Great Charter." Once John's mark was on the paper, it became law.

The Magna Carta limited a king's power over the nobles. The king could no longer jail nobles without just cause, nor could he tax them without their agreement. The Magna Carta also paved the way for the first **Parliament,** a council that would advise the English king in government matters.

In some ways, the Magna Carta made King John and the kings who followed him more powerful. Because nobles had a say in government, England became more united behind its royal ruler. It became a true nation instead of a quarreling collection of feudal fiefs.

LINKS ACROSS THE WORLD

The Declaration of Independence More than 500 years after King John signed the Magna Carta, another group demanded their rights. British colonists in North America thought that they were being treated unfairly. They complained about unfair taxation. When Parliament and the king refused to listen to their demands, the colonies declared their independence from Britain. The ideas in the Declaration of Independence are largely based on the laws and ideas that grew out of the Magna Carta.

Answers to ...

THE MAGNA CARTA

The king could no longer jail nobles without just cause. The king could no longer tax nobles without their agreement.

Medieval Fair Students can summarize their study of medieval Europe by presenting a medieval fair to the class and perhaps to the school. Have students volunteer for one of the following areas: making a medieval costumes exhibit, building a model of a castle, presenting steps in the building of a cathedral, using cellophane to model a stained-glass window, and so on. Students who choose the same topic should also decide which task they will complete: research, art direction, construction, gathering materials, scriptwriting, or narration. *Kinesthetic, Auditory*

The Hundred Years' War

The idea of nationhood was taking hold all over Europe in the late Middle Ages. In Spain, for example, a royal marriage united the king and queen of the two largest kingdoms. In Russia, Moscow's rulers were expanding their territory and their power over other princes. The new nations did, however, have many growing pains.

England and France at War One of the difficulties these young nations had was conflict with one another. In particular, England and France often clashed. One conflict between them led to the Hundred Years' War, which lasted from 1338 to 1453.

The English king owned and controlled a large amount of land in France. In 1328, the French king died and Edward III, who was king of England, decided he should become the new king of France. The French nobles did not agree. Determined to get his way, Edward III invaded France. Many bloody battles were fought, but nothing was settled. England won most of the battles, but the French continued to fight. The war dragged on, fought by one king after another.

Joan of Arc's Victory England continued to gain ground in the war until 1429. Then a 17-year-old peasant girl named Joan of Arc joined the French army. Deeply religious, Joan believed that God had called her to lead the French forces at the battle of Orléans (OR lay ahn). She met with the young French king and convinced him that she should

An English Victory

This battle of the Hundred Years' War took place in 1346 at Crécy (kray SEE), France. Archers armed with longbows enabled the English, at the left, to defeat a bigger French force, at the right. An English archer using a longbow could hit a target 300 yards (274 m) away. He also could fire five arrows in the time it took a French archer, who was armed with a crossbow, to shoot just one. In the Battle of Crécy, English archers killed half the French force, including about 1,000 knights.

Resource Directory

Teaching Resources

📁 **Section Quiz** in the Chapter and Section Support booklet, p. 78, covers the main ideas and key terms in the section. Available in Spanish in the Spanish Support booklet, p. 49.

📁 **Vocabulary** in the Chapter and Section Support booklet, p. 80, provides a review of key terms in the chapter. Available in Spanish in the Spanish Support booklet, p. 51.

📁 **Reteaching** in the Chapter and Section Support booklet, p. 81, provides a structure for students who may need additional help in mastering chapter content.

Program Resources

📁 **Environmental and Global Issues** Topic: Conflict, pp. 37–42

◄ This picture, dating from the 1400s, shows Joan of Arc's first meeting with the French king. In several battles in 1429, Joan defeated the English army and broke its spirit. To this day, the French consider Joan of Arc a heroine.

command his army. Then she went on to Orléans. There the French greeted her with hope and curiosity. One person who was there said:

> "People could not weary of seeing her, and it seemed to all a great marvel that she could sit on her horse with such ease and grace. And in truth she bore herself as highly in all ways as a man-at-arms who had followed the wars from his youth."

Under Joan's command, the French defeated the English at Orléans. She then led her forces to victory in four other battles. In 1430, Joan was taken prisoner by the English, tried as a witch, and burned at the stake. Her death came too late to help England's cause. It did not help England recover from its string of losses. By 1453, France had reclaimed all but a small portion of its lands. With the English troops in retreat, the French were on their way to becoming a strong and united nation.

SECTION 4 REVIEW

1. **Define** (a) nation, (b) the Magna Carta, (c) Parliament.
2. **Identify** (a) Pope Gregory VII, (b) Henry IV, (c) King John, (d) Joan of Arc, (e) Runnymede, (f) Orléans.
3. What caused struggles between kings and popes in the Middle Ages?
4. Describe some events that helped European kingdoms become nations in the late Middle Ages.

Critical Thinking
5. **Understanding Cause and Effect** Explain how the actions taken by England's King John led to the creation of the Magna Carta.

Activity
6. **Writing to Learn** Suppose that you are a French soldier preparing for the battle of Orléans. Describe your reaction to the news that a young peasant girl, Joan of Arc, is your new commander.

📁 **Enrichment** in the Chapter and Section Support booklet, p. 82, extends chapter content and enriches students' understanding.

📁 **Spanish Glossary** in the Spanish Support booklet, pp. 83–91, provides key terms translated from English to Spanish as well as definitions in Spanish.

📁 **Chapter Summary** in the Chapter and Section Support booklet, p. 79, provides a summary of chapter content. Available in Spanish in the Spanish Support booklet, p. 50.

📁 **Cooperative Learning Activity** in the Activities and Projects booklet, pp. 36–39, provides two student handouts, one page of teacher's directions, and a scoring rubric for a cooperative learning activity on writing a documentary.

Media and Technology

🎧 **Guided Reading Audiotapes** (English and Spanish)

Section 4 Review

1. (a) community that shares a government and often has a common language and culture (b) agreement between King John and the English nobles (c) governing body of England

2. (a) pope who excommunicated King Henry IV (b) king who sought to replace the pope (c) king who signed the Magna Carta (d) woman who led the French troops to victory against England in the Hundred Years' War (e) field where the Magna Carta was signed (f) site of the battle in which Joan of Arc led the French forces to victory

3. The kings and popes fought over the power to appoint bishops, who were church officials who controlled large areas of land.

4. Answers may vary, but should indicate that the kings gained power over the Church and nobles. Nobles raised money for the Crusades by selling land and letting towns buy freedom. The towns grew and gained in power. The kings began to support and protect the towns in exchange for money. With this money, the kings raised armies to gain more control over the nobles. The Magna Carta helped unify the nobles of England under the king while giving them power to approve laws and taxes and protecting their rights.

5. King John had taxed people heavily and without the nobles' consent. He jailed his enemies unfairly and without trial. He seized Church property and clashed with the pope, who excommunicated him.

6. Students' answers will vary. Most students will probably mention the hope that the arrival of Joan gave to the French soldiers. Accept all reasonable responses.

Reviewing Main Ideas

1. (a) because there was no central government after the end of the Roman Empire. (b) The feudal lords protected the peasants, who farmed the land. Because of their military power, the lords could offer this protection.

2. The peasants farmed the land, gave most of their harvest to the lord, and kept some to support their families. There were craftsmen, blacksmiths, people who made clothes and shoes, and other workers needed to make the manor self-sufficient. The knights learned the arts of war to protect the manor.

3. Clergy provided spiritual comfort, made peace between warring nobles, established schools, and helped the sick and the needy. The clergy and nuns lived in monasteries and convents. They tilled the Church's lands and improved agricultural methods.

4. (a) Towns were places where goods were traded. As trade grew, craftspeople and peasants bought their freedom from and settled in towns. (b) A guild included all people in a town who practiced a certain trade. The guild set prices and standards of quality and used dues to help needy members.

5. (a) The Church wanted to protect pilgrims and win back the Holy Land. (b) Merchants wanted trade routes to Asia to be opened up to Europeans.

6. The feudal lords sold land and let peasants buy their freedom in order to raise money to go on the Crusades. This led to a weakening of their power and to the growth of towns, which came under the protection of the kings. The kings gained land and money, which they used to raise armies to increase their power.

7. Both kings and popes wanted the power to appoint Church officials, called bishops, because they controlled large tracts of land.

8. Kings gained power as the feudal system weakened. Government became centralized under kings and queens, and nations became stronger.

Reviewing Key Terms

Sentences should show the meaning of each term through the context.

Review and Activities

Reviewing Main Ideas

1. (a) Why did the people of the Middle Ages need protection? (b) How did the feudal system provide this protection?

2. How was work divided among the people who lived on a medieval manor so that they could meet their own needs?

3. Describe what the clergy did during the Middle Ages.

4. (a) What caused towns to spring up during the Middle Ages? (b) What role did guilds play in a town?

5. (a) Why did the Church call for people to fight in the Crusades? (b) Why were merchants interested in the Crusades?

6. How did the Crusades lead to the weakening of feudalism?

7. Why did kings quarrel with popes over the appointment of Church officials?

8. How did the growing importance of kings help nations become stronger in Europe in the Middle Ages?

Reviewing Key Terms

Use each key term below in a sentence that shows the meaning of the term.

1. Middle Ages
2. feudalism
3. vassal
4. manor
5. self-sufficient
6. serf
7. clergy
8. excommunicate
9. guild
10. apprentice
11. chivalry
12. nation
13. Parliament

Critical Thinking

1. **Recognizing Cause and Effect** Provide evidence to support this statement: "As order was restored in Europe, the feudal system grew weaker."

2. **Making Comparisons** Compare a manor peasant to a guild master's apprentice. How were their lives similar? How were they different?

Graphic Organizer

Copy the chart onto a sheet of paper, then fill in the empty boxes to complete the chart.

	Place in Medieval Society	Role in Crusades	Role in Rise of Cities
Church			
Kings			
Nobles			
Peasants			
Merchants			

Graphic Organizer

Students' answers may vary. Sample chart entries are shown.

	Place in Medieval Society	Role in Crusades	Role in Rise of Cities
Church	Church comforted people and helped keep peace.	Church launched the Crusades to protect holy places.	
Kings	Kings ruled limited regions and extracted loyalty from nobles and lords.		Kings supported towns and cities in exchange for money. Made laws favoring cities.
Nobles	Nobles pledged allegiance to other nobles or king. They also pledged to protect peasants.	Nobles sold land and allowed peasants to buy their freedom to raise money for Crusades.	As nobles' power declined, cities' power increased.
Peasants	Peasants worked in manor fields to produce farm goods to support themselves and nobles.		As peasants purchased their freedom, they moved to cities to find work.
Merchants		Merchants desired access to Asian trade routes.	Towns and cities were located where merchants sold their goods.

Map Activity

Place Location

Europe and the Holy Land
For each place listed below, write the letter from the map that shows its location.

1. England
2. France
3. Jerusalem
4. Mediterranean Sea
5. Rome
6. Constantinople

Writing Activity

Write a Letter
In this chapter, you have met medieval people from all walks of life. Suppose that you could interview one of these people, famous or unknown, to find out more about his or her life.

Write a letter in which you introduce yourself to this person and ask for an interview. Be sure to explain why the person's life interests you, and what you want to learn by interviewing him or her.

Internet Activity
Use a search engine to find *The Crusades (Text and Archives)*. Read several first-person accounts of the Crusades. Then write your own first-person account as if you had taken part in one of the Crusades.

Skills Review

Turn to the Skills Activity.
Review how to use route maps. Then answer the following questions: (a) How does a route map differ from other maps? (b) Why is the map key important?

How Am I Doing?

Answer these questions to help you check your progress.

1. Can I describe the feudal pyramid and the manor system of medieval Europe?
2. Can I explain why medieval cities developed and describe what they were like?
3. Do I understand the causes and effects of the Crusades?
4. Do I know how medieval kingdoms grew into strong nations?
5. What information from this chapter can I use in my book project?

Critical Thinking

1. Students' responses should offer appropriate information to support the statement.

2. Students' responses should identify ways, and provide specific examples to show how, the lives were similar and different.

Map Activity

1. A	3. F	5. C
2. B	4. D	6. E

Writing Activity

Students' letters should contain a self introduction, an explanation of why the student wants to interview that person, and what the student hopes to learn from the interview. Correct letter form should be used.

Skills Review

(a) Students' answers will vary, but should suggest that route maps indicate the direction, or possible direction, of travel from one place to another. (b) The key can tell who traveled along a route or can distinguish an earlier route from a later one.

Resource Directory

Teaching Resources

📁 **Chapter Tests** Forms A and B are in the Tests booklet, pp. 26–31.

Program Resources

📁 **Writing Process Handbook** includes Proofreading, p. 37, to help students with the Writing Activity.

Media and Technology

🖥 **Color Transparencies**
Color Transparency 171
(Graphic organizer web template)

💿 **Prentice Hall Writer's Solution** Writing Lab CD-ROM

💾 **Computer Test Bank**

💿 **Resource Pro™ CD-ROM**

Internet Activity

If students are having difficulty finding this site, you may wish to have them use the following URL, which was accurate at the time this textbook was published:

http://history.hanover.edu/ medieval/crusades.html

You might also guide students to a search engine. Four of the most useful are Infoseek, AltaVista, Lycos, and Yahoo. For additional suggestions on using the Internet, refer to the Prentice Hall Social Studies' Educator's Handbook "Using the Internet," in the *Prentice Hall World Explorer Program Resources*.

For additional links to world history and culture topics, visit the Prentice Hall Home Page at:
http://www.phschool.com

How Am I Doing?

Point out to students that this checklist is just a quick reminder for them of what they learned in the chapter. If their answer to any of the questions is *no* or if they are unsure, they may need to review the topic.

Lesson Objectives

❶ Interpret and dramatize a historical legend.

❷ Relate a literary work to information about its historical context.

Lesson Plan

1 Engage

Building Vocabulary

Point out that notes in the margin can help students understand certain words and can give helpful hints as students read. Vocabulary defined in the margin include: *fealty, gimlet,* and *scabbard.*

Using a dictionary, urge students to learn the history of each vocabulary word and to note any additional meanings for each word.

Activating Prior Knowledge

Have students read Reach Into Your Background in the Before You Read box. Then discuss why some historical figures become legends. Ask students to explain their feelings for a much-admired real or fictional figure.

2 Develop Student Reading

Direct students to read the selection. Urge them to visualize each scene as if they were watching Arthur's battle or standing at the edge of the lake. Tell them to think about what they would see, hear, or smell in these locations.

Of Swords and Sorcerers

FROM *THE ADVENTURES OF KING ARTHUR AND HIS KNIGHTS*
BY MARGARET HODGES AND MARGERY EVERNDEN

BEFORE YOU READ

Reach Into Your Background

How should a good and just ruler behave? What traits should a king or queen have? What do you admire in people who lead others?

People have read and enjoyed the stories of King Arthur for hundreds of years. To many, he symbolizes the virtue and justice of a good ruler. According to legend, he was loved and respected by all of his people.

Legends about King Arthur exist in many forms, and stories about him have been written and rewritten in several languages. The following selection is one tale of Arthur's meeting his friend Pellinore and finding his sword named Excalibur.

Questions to Explore

1. Why did King Arthur's subjects consider him such a good king?
2. Who is Merlin? What role does he play in this story?

petty *adj.*: unimportant; of low rank

fealty *n.*: loyalty to a feudal lord

gimlet *adj.*: having a piercing quality

malice *n.*: mean wish to damage or hurt someone

No king before Arthur had been able to unite the realm and rule it. This Arthur did. Lightnings and thunders surrounded him as he fought. In twelve great battles he defeated petty kings who had been constantly at war, laying waste all the land. The last to surrender was Arthur's own brother-in-law, King Lot of Orkney. When Lot laid down his arms and swore fealty to Arthur, he sent his sons to become knights at Camelot.

One son was Gawain, handsome and strong, whom Arthur called Gawain the Courteous. Another was Mordred, whose foxy smile and gimlet eyes concealed malice and a thirst for power. Gawain took the vows of knighthood in good faith, but Mordred's vows were insincere, and he soon began listening at the castle doors in hope of ferreting out secrets that might damage the court and someday play into his own hands. He saw that the time to strike

Resource Directory

Program Resources

📁 Material in the **Primary Sources and Literature Readings** booklet provides additional literature selections on the region under study.

◄ The Round Table of King Arthur and his knights.

had not yet come. The powers of heaven and earth all seemed to be on Arthur's side. The people loved him, and Camelot was in its glory.

Now there came a day when Arthur rode with Merlin seeking adventure, and in a forest they found a knight named Pellinore, seated in a chair, blocking their path.

"Sir, will you let us pass?" said Arthur.

"Not without a fight," replied Pellinore. "Such is my custom."

"I will change your custom," said Arthur.

"I will defend it," said Pellinore. He mounted his horse and took his shield on his arm. Then the two knights rode against each other, and each splintered his spear on the other's shield.

"I have no more spears," said Arthur. "Let us fight with swords."

"Not so," said Pellinore. "I have enough spears. I will lend you one."

Then a squire brought two good spears, and the two knights rode against each other again until those spears were broken.

"You are as good a fighter as ever I met," said Pellinore. "Let us try again."

Two great spears were brought, and this time Pellinore struck Arthur's shield so hard that the king and his horse fell to the earth.

Then Arthur pulled out his sword and said, "I have lost the battle on horseback. Let me try you on foot."

READ ACTIVELY

Predict Who will win the fight?

Background

About the Author

Margaret Hodges has been writing and sharing stories since early childhood. Hodges believes that myths and legends are important in our modern world. She hopes to retell more myths, "so that the young can respond to them."

Margery Evernden has penned several books for children. Margaret and Margery first told a cycle of Arthurian tales at the Carnegie Library of Pittsburgh.

About the Selection

The selection is an excerpt from a chapter in the book by Margaret Hodges and Margery Evernden, *Of Swords and Sorcerers: The Adventures of King Arthur and His Knights,* published in 1993 by Simon and Schuster Children's Books.

3 Assess

Work through the Exploring Your Reading questions with students.

I. to pass through the forest; to teach Pellinore not to fight without good cause

2. Excalibur, a special sword, and its scabbard

3. first on horseback, with spears, then on foot, with swords and hands

4. Possible answers: Pellinore would have killed Arthur because he had Arthur pinned down and was about to cut off his head.

5. They love and admire him. His knights think it is wonderful to be led by such a brave man who risks his life just as they do.

6. Possible answers: He is brave; he is willing to take the same risks as his men; he notes others' strengths. He would be a good leader today because he would choose advisers carefully.

7. Poems should show originality in choice of tool and special powers. Language should reflect vivid sensory words and poetic rhythm.

Activity

Journal Writing

Character Study Suggest that students write a journal entry indicating which of the characters is their favorite and why. Have them tell which character they would like to be most like.

▶ Several suits of armor perhaps similar to those of the knights of the Round Table.

Ask Questions What more would you like to know about King Arthur?

wrath *n.:* great anger or rage
hermit *n.:* person who lives alone and away from others
salve *n.:* an oily substance used as medicine on the skin

Pellinore thought it unfair to attack from his horse, so he dismounted and came toward Arthur with his sword drawn. Then began such a battle that both were covered with blood. After a while they sat down to rest and fought again until both fell to the ground. Again they fought, and the fight was even. But at last Pellinore struck such a blow that Arthur's sword broke into two pieces. Thereupon the king leaped at Pellinore. He threw him down and pulled off his helmet. But Pellinore was a very big man and strong enough to wrestle Arthur under him and pull off the king's helmet. All this time Merlin had watched, silent, but when he saw that Pellinore was about to cut off Arthur's head, he interfered.

"Do not kill this man," he said to Pellinore. "You do not know who he is."

"Why, who is he?" said the knight.

"It is King Arthur," said Merlin.

When he heard this, Pellinore trembled with fear of the royal wrath, for he would not knowingly have fought against the king. Then Merlin cast a spell of sleep on Pellinore so that he fell to the earth as if dead.

"Alas," said Arthur, "you have killed the best knight I ever fought."

"Have no fear," said Merlin. "He will awake in three hours as well as ever he was."

Then he mounted Pellinore's horse and led Arthur to a hermit, who bound up the king's wounds and healed them with good salves, so that he might ride again and go on his way.

But Arthur said, "I have no sword."

"Never fear," said Merlin. "Not far away is a sword that can be yours." So they rode on until they came to a broad lake of clear water. Far out in the middle of the lake Arthur saw an arm clothed in shining white and holding a noble sword, its golden hilt richly set with jewels.

"Lo," said Merlin, "yonder is the sword Excalibur."

Then they saw a lady floating toward them as if she walked on the water. Her garments were like a mist around her.

"That is the Lady of the Lake," said Merlin. "Within the lake is a rock, and within the rock is a palace, and within the palace lives this lady with many other ladies who serve her. She is called Vivien. Speak to her as a friend, and she will give you that sword."

So, when she had come close, Arthur said to her, "Lady, I wish that sword were mine, for I have no sword."

"It shall be yours," said the lady, and she showed Arthur a little boat lying at the edge of the lake. "Row out to the sword," she said. "Take it with its scabbard." Then she disappeared. Arthur and Merlin rowed out into the lake, and Arthur took the sword from the hand that held it. And the arm and the hand vanished under the water.

Arthur and Merlin rowed to shore and went on their way, and whenever Arthur looked on the sword, he liked it well.

"Which do you like better?" asked Merlin. "The sword or the scabbard?"

"I like the sword better," said Arthur.

"The scabbard is worth ten such swords," said Merlin, "for while you wear the scabbard, you will never lose blood, no matter how sorely you are wounded."

So they rode back to Arthur's court, and all his knights marveled when they heard that the king risked his life in single combat as his poor knights did. They said it was merry to be under such a chieftain.

READ ACTIVELY

Visualize Picture the Lady of the Lake as she floats across the water.

scabbard *n.*: a case or cover for a sword or dagger
chieftain *n.*: the head of a clan; leader of many people

EXPLORING YOUR READING

Look Back

1. Why did Arthur fight Pellinore?
2. What gift does Arthur receive at the end of the story?

Think It Over

3. Describe how Arthur and Pellinore fight.

4. How do you think the fight would have ended if Merlin had not interfered? Why do you think so?
5. How do Arthur's subjects feel about him? What did his knights think when they heard about his fight with Pellinore?

Go Beyond

6. What qualities does Arthur have that make him a good ruler? What kind of a ruler do you think he would be in today's world? Why?

Ideas for Writing: Poem

7. Many characters in myths and legends have tools or weapons that protect them or give them special powers. Write a poem about a character who receives one such tool. What are its powers? How does it help your character?

Activity

Cooperative Learning

Drama Suggest students work in groups of four to draft a dramatic version of the selection. Tell them to set the scene and include stage directions for all characters' movements. Encourage students to assign roles—scriptwriter, director, set designer, and scenery artist—to group members. Invite students to present their plays to the rest of the class. *Kinesthetic, Auditory*

Activity

Critical Thinking

Identifying Central Issues *Suitable as an individual activity.* Prompt students to write a short biography of King Arthur based on information from the selection. In it, students should note both narrative information about Arthur's life and descriptive data about his characteristics. Biographies should respond to the question: Why has King Arthur become such a legend?

MEDIEVAL TIMES TO TODAY
A New Age in Europe

To help you plan instruction, the chart below shows how teaching resources correspond to chapter content. Use the resources to vary instruction, add activities, or plan block schedules. Where appropriate, resources have suggested time allotments for students. Time allotments are approximate.

Managing Time and Instruction

	Medieval Times to Today Teaching Resources Binder		World Explorer Program Resources Binder	
	Resource	**mins.**	**Resource**	**mins.**
SECTION 1 **The Renaissance and Reformation**	**Chapter and Section Support** Reproducible Lesson Plan, p. 85 Ⓢ Guided Reading and Review, p. 86 Ⓢ Section Quiz, p. 87	 20 25	**Outline Maps** Central Europe: Political, p. 20 Mediterranean Europe: Political, p. 21 **Nystrom Desk Atlas** Ⓣ **Primary Sources and Literature** **Readings** **Writing Process Handbook** Locating Information, pp. 17–18	 20 20 40 25
SKILLS ACTIVITY **Distinguishing Fact From Opinion**	**Social Studies and Geography Skills,** Distinguishing Fact From Opinion, p. 43	30		
SECTION 2 **The Age of Exploration**	**Chapter and Section Support** Reproducible Lesson Plan, p. 88 Ⓢ Guided Reading and Review, p. 89 Critical Thinking Activity, p. 101 Ⓢ Section Quiz, p. 90 **Social Studies and Geography Skills,** Visualizing What Things Look Like, p. 73	 20 30 25 30	**Outline Maps** The World: Physical, p. 2	 20
SECTION 3 **The Age of Powerful Kings**	**Chapter and Section Support** Reproducible Lesson Plan, p. 91 Ⓢ Guided Reading and Review, p. 92 Ⓢ Section Quiz, p. 93 **Social Studies and Geography Skills,** Analyzing Art, p. 59	 20 25 30	**Outline Maps** Western Europe: Political, p. 18	 20
SECTION 4 **Conquests in the Americas and Africa**	**Chapter and Section Support** Reproducible Lesson Plan, p. 94 Ⓢ Guided Reading and Review, p. 95 Ⓢ Section Quiz, p. 96 Ⓢ Vocabulary, p. 98 Reteaching, p. 99 Enrichment, p. 100 Ⓢ Chapter Summary, p. 97 **Tests** Forms A and B Chapter Tests, pp. 32–37	 20 25 20 25 25 15 40	**Outline Maps** Latin America: Political, p. 7 West and Central Africa: Political, p. 34 **Environmental and Global Issues** Topic: Human Rights, pp. 25–30	 20 20 30
ACTIVITY SHOP: LAB **Making a Compass**	Activity Shop: Lab, p. 6	30		

Block Scheduling Folder
PROGRAM TEACHING RESOURCES

Activities and Projects

Block Scheduling Program Support

Interdisciplinary Links

Resource Pro™ CD-ROM

Media and Technology

From Guiding Questions to Assessment A series of Guiding Questions serves as an organizing framework for this book. The Guiding Questions that relate to this chapter are listed below. Section Reviews and Section Quizzes provide opportunities for assessing students' insights into these Guiding Questions. Additional assessments are listed below.

Media and Technology

Resource	mins.
▣ ⊘ ⑤ World Video Explorer	20
▱ Color Transparencies 132, 138, 139, 140	20
▱ Color Transparencies 1, 2, Historical Map Set 4	20
▱ Color Transparencies 135, 141, 143, Historical Map Set 5	20
☊ ⑤ Guided Reading Audiotapes	20
▱ Color Transparency 171 (Graphic organizer web template)	20
⊘ The Writer's Solution CD-ROM	30
▤ Computer Test Bank	30

GUIDING QUESTIONS

- *How did each society's belief systems affect its history, government, and economy?*
- *How did these societies interact with other societies?*

ASSESSMENTS

Section 1

Students should be able to create a glossary of the key terms in the section.

▶ **RUBRIC** See the Assessment booklet for a rubric on assessing a glossary.

Section 2

Students should be able to create a web of the advances made by Portuguese sailors.

▶ **RUBRIC** See the Assessment booklet for a rubric on assessing graphic organizers.

Section 3

Students should be able to write a paragraph on the power of kings after the middle ages.

▶ **RUBRIC** See the Assessment booklet for a rubric on assessing a writing assignment.

Section 4

Students should be able to create a map showing the reach of Spain's empire in North and South America in the 1540s.

▶ **RUBRIC** See the Assessment booklet for a rubric on assessing a map produced by a student.

Ⓣ **Teaming Opportunity** This resource is especially well-suited for teaching teams.	⊘ **CD-ROM**
	⊛ **Laserdisc**
	▱ **Transparency**
Ⓢ **Spanish** This resource is also in Spanish support.	▤ **Software**
	▣ **Videotape**
	☊ **Audiotape**

Activities and Projects

Mental Mapping

The Renaissance and Age of Exploration in Europe
Distribute unlabeled physical maps of Europe. Give students a few minutes to locate and label northern Italy, Germany, England, Scotland, Portugal, Spain, and France. Explain that the emphasis is on general location rather than on exact borders, since the borders of many of the places they are locating have changed.

Then list the following names on the chalkboard: Leonardo da Vinci, Martin Luther, Ferdinand Magellan, Christopher Columbus, and Louis XIV. Ask students to write each name on the country or countries most closely associated with that person. Not every country will have a name to go with it. Give students a chance to discuss their choices.

Links to Current Events

Exploration Ask students to think about the ways the space programs of different countries compare to the efforts by European countries to explore the oceans and the Americas. Have students find out which countries have launched space vehicles. Have them compare the number of countries involved in space exploration and the goals of space exploration with efforts to explore the oceans and the Americas. What are some arguments for and against space exploration? Could similar arguments have been made about voyages of exploration in the 1400s? What is the role of technology in both efforts? Ask them to compare the use of space vehicles with the ships used by Columbus and Magellan.

Hands-On Activities

Building Empires Ask students to think about what is needed to build an empire. Distribute 3 x 5 index cards. Have students work in small groups to list the composition of an empire. Empires may include such factors as technology, wealth, strong leaders, land, and so on. Have them write their ingredients on cards. Then give each group a chance to go to a wall or bulletin board to assemble their empires and explain why they chose the ingredients they did.

Renaissance Art Invite students to find out about the many ways that art changed during the Renaissance. For example, new types of paint were invented, perspective was introduced, and art became associated with individuals. Suggest that they find one or more paintings or works of art that exemplify the attitudes and approaches to art that developed in the Renaissance. *Challenging*

Explorers Have students make a story map showing the routes taken by Columbus or Magellan and his crew. Have them locate and label specific events in place and time on the map. *Basic*

A Night to Remember Have students write a letter describing a party at the court of Versailles during the reign of Louis XIV. Encourage them to look at pictures or do additional research so they can describe the way people were dressed, the food and the way it was served, the king, the rooms and furniture, and the entertainment or activities. *Average*

Pictograms Suggest that students look at some Aztec pictograms or carvings to familiarize themselves with the Aztec style. Then ask them to try to depict one of the events described in this chapter—such as the arrival of Cortés, the destruction of Tenochtitlán, or any of the related events—in a picture or series of pictures drawn and colored in this style. *English Language Learners*

F.Y.I.

This page can help you extend your own and students' understanding of the concepts in this chapter. You may want to browse through some of the suggestions in the **Bibliography. Interdisciplinary Links** can connect social studies understandings to areas elsewhere in the curriculum through the use of other Prentice Hall products. **National Geography Standards** reflected specifically in this chapter are listed for your convenience. Some hints about appropriate **Internet Access** are also provided. **School to Careers** provides insights into the practical uses of some of the concepts in this chapter as they might pertain to various careers.

BIBLIOGRAPHY

FOR THE TEACHER
Flowers, Sarah. *The Reformation.* Lucent, 1995.

Saari, Peggy, and Daniel B. Baker. *Explorers and Discoverers: From Alexander the Great to Sally Ride.* UXL, 1995.

Ventura, Piero. *1492: The Year of the New World.* Putnam, 1992.

FOR THE STUDENT
Easy
Alper, Ann Fitzpatrick. *Forgotten Voyager: The Story of Amerigo Vespucci.* Carolrhoda, 1991.

Maestro, Betsy, and Giulio Maestro. *The Discovery of the Americas.* Lothrop, 1991.

Average
Richmond, Robin. *Introduce Michelangelo.* Little, 1992.

Wood, Tim. *The Renaissance.* Viking, 1993.

Challenging
Fritz, Jean. *Around the World in a Hundred Years: From Henry the Navigator to Magellan.* Putnam, 1994.

Marrin, Albert. *The Sea King: Sir Francis Drake and His Times.* Atheneum, 1995.

LITERATURE CONNECTION
Fisher, Leonard Everett. *Prince Henry the Navigator.* Macmillan, 1990.

Llorente, Pilar Molina. *The Apprentice.* Sunburst/Farrar, 1994.

Romei, Francesca. *Leonardo da Vinci: Artist, Inventor, and Scientist of the Renaissance.* Bedrick, 1995.

INTERDISCIPLINARY LINKS

Subject	Theme: Reawakening
MATH	Middle Grades Math: Tools for Success *Course 1*, Lesson 9-6, **Scale Drawings**
SCIENCE	Prentice Hall Science *The Nature of Science*, Lesson 2-2, **Measurement Tools**
LANGUAGE ARTS	Choices in Literature *The Me You See*, **The Captive Outfielder**

NATIONAL GEOGRAPHY STANDARDS

Students explore the 18 National Geography Standards throughout *Medieval Times to Today*. Chapter 6, however, concentrates on investigating the following standards: 2, 3, 4, 5, 6, 7, 9, 10, 12, 13, 15, 16. For a complete list of the standards, see the *Teacher's Flexible Planning Guide*.

SCHOOL TO CAREERS

In Chapter 6, A New Age in Europe, students learn more about this region. Additionally, they address the skill of distinguishing fact from opinion. Knowing about this region can help students prepare for careers in many fields, such as history, international relations, diplomacy, and so on. Distinguishing fact from opinion is a skill used in many careers, including journalism, business, law enforcement, and so on. The curriculum presented in this book, as in all eight titles of Prentice Hall's *World Explorer* program, is designed to prepare students not only for careers but also for good citizenship—of the world as well as of this country.

INTERNET ACCESS

Many social studies teachers and students use Internet browsers, or search engines, to investigate particular topics. For the best results, use narrow rather than broad topics. Try these for Chapter 6: Renaissance, Martin Luther, divine right, Louis XIV. Finding age-appropriate sites is an important consideration when using the Internet. For links to age-appropriate sites in world studies and geography, visit the Prentice Hall Home Page at: **http://www.phschool.com**

Connecting to the Guiding Questions

In this chapter, students will focus on the changes in Europe that began in the late 1400s. They will also focus on the ways that these changes affected other societies in the world. Content in this chapter thus corresponds to the following Guiding Questions:

● How did each society's belief systems affect its history, government, and economy?

● How did these societies interact with other societies?

Using the Picture Activities

Have students look at the picture on this page. Ask them what they think travel on this kind of ship would be like.

• Sample answer: It has large sails and the hull appears very sturdy. It probably can hold many supplies.

• Responses will vary.

Heterogeneous Groups

The following Teacher's Edition strategies are suitable for heterogeneous groups.

Interdisciplinary Connections
Art   pp. 140, 145, 151
Language Arts   pp. 148, 157
Math   p. 148

Cooperative Learning
Navigational Tools   p. 144
Other Explorers   p. 147

Critical Thinking
Recognizing Cause and Effect   p. 159

CHAPTER 6

SECTION 1
The Renaissance and Reformation

SECTION 2
The Age of Exploration

SECTION 3
The Age of Powerful Kings

SECTION 4
Conquests in the Americas and Africa

A New Age in Europe

PICTURE ACTIVITIES

The late 1400s began an age of great change in Europe. One aspect of this change was a new sense of curiosity about other lands. The picture above shows a replica, or exact copy, of one of the ships commanded by Christopher Columbus when he crossed the Atlantic Ocean to the Americas in 1492. To learn more about exploration and other changes of this period, do the following activities.

Study the picture
What do you notice about the design of the ship that might make it suitable for undertaking long ocean voyages? What kind of storage areas do you think the ship has?

Make connections
What do you think might cause people to set out on a voyage into the unknown? Would you make such a trip? Why or why not?

Resource Directory

Media and Technology

Spotlight On: The Renaissance, from the World Video Explorer, enhances students' understanding of the significance of the Renaissance in Europe.

Chapter 7

The Renaissance and Reformation

BEFORE YOU READ

Reach Into Your Background

What do you do when you think of or hear about an interesting new idea? You probably share it. Maybe you share it by telling someone else about it. During the Renaissance and Reformation, many people in Europe had new ideas they wanted to share.

Questions to Explore

1. Why did the Renaissance begin in northern Italy rather than in northern Europe?
2. Why did many northern European leaders want to adopt Protestant religions?

Key Terms

Renaissance
perspective
Reformation
indulgence
Protestant

Key People and Places

Leonardo da Vinci
Michelangelo
Martin Luther
Florence

Have you ever wanted to fly like a bird? Leonardo da Vinci (lee uh NAR doh duh VIN chee) did. This brilliant artist and scientist who lived about 500 years ago thought that people could learn to fly. He studied birds and bats, as well as winged toys and seeds, to learn about flying.

Leonardo never built a working airplane. But, as you can see from his drawings, he drew plans for one. He also made drawings of what looked like early examples of a parachute and a helicopter.

Leonardo was just one of many gifted Europeans who lived between 1300 and about 1600. This was the time of the **Renaissance** (REN uh sahns), or rebirth of learning in Europe. Toward the end of the Middle Ages, people again became deeply interested in art,

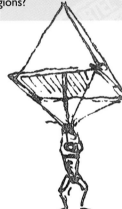

▼ Leonardo's drawing of a parachute (left) looks very much like the real thing. He used what he had learned about bat wings in this idea for a flying machine (below).

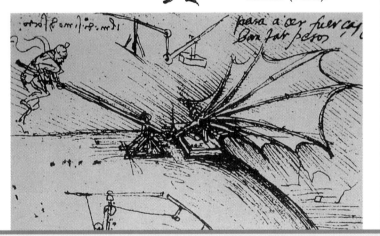

Teaching Resources

📁 **Reproducible Lesson Plan** in the Chapter and Section Support booklet, p. 85, provides a summary of the section lesson.

📁 **Guided Reading and Review** in the Chapter and Section Support booklet, p. 86, provides a structure for mastering key concepts and reviewing key terms in the section. Available in Spanish in the Spanish Support booklet, p. 53.

Program Resources

📁 Material in the **Primary Sources and Literature Readings** booklet extends content with a selection related to the concepts in this chapter.

📁 **Outline Maps** Central Europe: Political, p. 20; Mediterranean Europe: Political, p. 21

Lesson Objectives

1 Explain why the Renaissance began in northern Italy rather than in northern Europe.

2 Identify the reasons why northern European leaders wanted to adopt Protestant religions.

Lesson Plan

1 Engage

Warm-Up Activity

Write the terms *Renaissance man* and *Renaissance woman* on the chalkboard. Call on volunteers to explain what they think the terms mean. Point out to students that the terms come from the time known as the Renaissance, a period in history that they are about to study.

Activating Prior Knowledge

Have students read Reach Into Your Background in the Before You Read box. Ask students to think of interesting ideas that they have read or heard about. Call on volunteers to share their ideas with the class.

2 Explore

Have students skim through the text and illustrations in Section 1. Have them find answers to the following questions: What was life like in the northern Italian city-states? How did art change during the Renaissance? Who were some important artists of the Renaissance? What was the Reformation?

Background

Links Across Time

Inside the Human Body
Leonardo Da Vinci's human figure drawings show that he had rather advanced and complete knowledge of the human anatomy. Leonardo developed this knowledge himself, without the help of X-rays or other technological advances, by studying cadavers to gain insight into the skeletal and muscular architecture of the human body. Leonardo kept detailed drawings of his study of anatomy. These drawings, together with his art, helped usher in an age of realism in painting and sculpture.

▲ The city-state of Florence on the Arno River was an important center of the Renaissance in Italy. Its artists and poets were supported by the city's wealthy merchants and bankers.

ACROSS THE WORLD

Building on the Past
People during the Renaissance did not work in isolation. Often, they built upon ideas and methods brought to Europe from other parts of the world. The learning that was carried to Spain by the Muslims of North Africa was an important part of this exchange. For example, the Muslims reintroduced the works of Aristotle and other Greek thinkers and scientists to Europe.

literature, science, and many other subjects. People changed the way they saw themselves and their world. The Renaissance began in northern Italy and spread to the rest of Europe.

The World That Made Leonardo

Italy, where Leonardo lived, was an unusual place. During the Middle Ages, life in Italy was easier than in much of the rest of Western Europe. People in northern Europe were threatened by war and disease. They depended on the protection of the clergy and local lords, who were controlled by popes and kings.

But in northern Italy people lived in city-states, or cities that had self-rule. The lives of these people were not as closely controlled by popes and kings. Instead, power was held by wealthy merchants. These merchants controlled European trade with Asia. Muslim traders brought precious goods like silk and spices from the East to the Mediterranean. From here, Italian merchants transported the goods throughout Europe, reselling them at top prices.

Because of their wealth from trade, some northern Italians had more time to think, to read, and to create and enjoy art. In the world of Renaissance Italy, artists competed for fame and money like athletes of today. Wealthy and powerful families sponsored artists and art schools. Because they were proud of their cities and their families, the wealthy built fine homes. Many were religious people who expressed their love of God by spending money to build and decorate churches. Others hoped that offerings of beautiful works of art would lead God to forgive their sins. Some popes sponsored the arts because they hoped to inspire loyalty to the Church.

Resource Directory

Program Resources

Nystrom Desk Atlas

Media and Technology

 Color Transparencies 132, 138, 139, 140

The Renaissance Artist

From its birthplace in northern Italy, the Renaissance spread to other European lands. After all, Italian artists had much to teach other Europeans. They had studied and copied the classical art of ancient Greece and Rome. Like the artists of these two civilizations, they wanted to show things as they really were.

Techniques Used by Artists   To better understand how to draw and paint people, Italian artists studied the bones, muscles, and organs of the body. They used **perspective** in their paintings. This is the technique of showing objects as they appear to the eye. One of the ways they did this was to make distant objects smaller in relation to closer objects. This made scenes in their paintings look as they appeared to the human eye. In addition, they used light and shadow to make the things they painted look solid.

Michelangelo and the Sistine Chapel   Michelangelo (my kul AN juh loh) was one of these artists. Sponsored by Lorenzo de Medici (loh RENT soh duh MED uh chee), a wealthy citizen of Florence, and others, Michelangelo began his career as a sculptor. He carved marble so that it looked like flowing cloth, rippling muscle, and twisting hair. But his most famous work is a painting, not a sculpture. Actually, it is many paintings. Together these paintings cover the ceiling and walls

▼ This statue of the Virgin Mary holding the body of her son, Jesus, in her arms, still brings an emotional response from visitors to St. Peter's Church in Rome. Michelangelo created it in 1499, when he was in his early 20s.

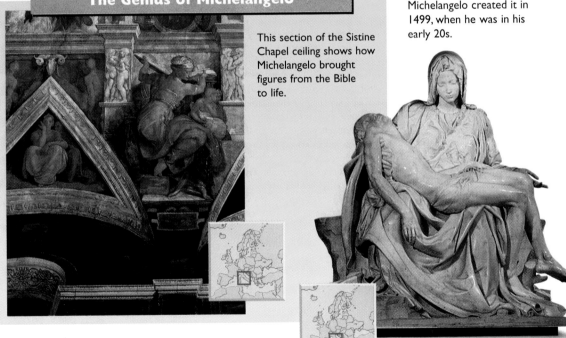

The Genius of Michelangelo

This section of the Sistine Chapel ceiling shows how Michelangelo brought figures from the Bible to life.

3 Teach

Have students create three web diagrams based on the information in this section. The hub of each diagram should include one of the three main headings of the section: *The World That Made Leonardo, The Renaissance Artist,* or *The Reformation.* The extensions from each hub should provide supporting details for each main heading. This activity should take about 30 minutes.

4 Assess

See the answers to the Section Review. You may also use students' web diagrams as an assessment.

Acceptable diagrams include two to three facts for each heading.

Commendable diagrams include at least four facts for each heading.

Outstanding diagrams include cause-and-effect relationships for events.

Activity

Journal Writing

Renaissance Sights   Invite students to imagine that they are traveling through northern Italy during the Renaissance. Have them record the sights and sounds they observe. If students are keeping an Explorer's Journal, as described in the opening pages of their books, you may wish to do this writing activity as part of that journal.

Activity

Interdisciplinary Connections

Art   Help students appreciate the difficulties faced by Michelangelo as he painted the ceiling of the Sistine Chapel. Suggest that each student draw a picture sitting at a table or desk. Next, have students tape their papers to the bottoms of chairs or desks. Direct them to try to draw the same picture while lying on their backs. Ask students to compare their two drawings. *Visual, Kinesthetic*

Background

Global Perspectives

The Dome   In addition to the Sistine Chapel, Michelangelo designed the dome for Saint Peter's Basilica in Vatican City. Michelangelo's dome became the model for later domes all around the world, including the Capitol in Washington, D.C., and many state capital buildings in the United States.

Visualize Visualize Michelangelo working on the Sistine Chapel paintings. How do you think he would feel after a day's work?

of the Sistine Chapel in the Vatican in Rome, Italy. Michelangelo did these paintings for Pope Julius II. See the picture on the previous page for a view of the Sistine Chapel ceiling.

It took Michelangelo about four years to finish painting the Sistine Chapel. He worked on scaffolding, or a framework, 80 feet (24 m) above the ground. Much of the time he painted lying on his back. Sometimes he stood for hours with his arm up in the air and his neck bent backward.

The pope was angry because the work took so long. Once he even hit Michelangelo with his cane and threatened to push him from the scaffolding. But Michelangelo kept working. When he finished, viewers were amazed. Michelangelo had used his artist's understanding of bone and muscle to bring scenes from the Bible to life in paint.

The Reformation

Michelangelo's work showed the great power of the Roman Catholic Church in his time. But not everyone was happy with the Church. In 1517, five years after Michelangelo finished painting the Sistine Chapel, a German monk named Martin Luther sharply criticized the Church. Luther nailed a list of his complaints on the door of a church in Wittenberg, Germany. This act changed the religion of his times. The change he caused was called the Reformation because it was meant to reform, or improve, religious customs.

Martin Luther Speaks Out

Martin Luther was a professor of Bible studies at the University in Wittenberg, Germany. This modern stained-glass window shows him nailing up a list of complaints against the Roman Catholic Church. Below Luther's right hand is a symbol of Christianity. It is made up of the first two Greek letters in the word *Christ*. Other symbols on the window include an ink pot with a quill pen, a desk, and books. **Critical Thinking** Why do you think the artist might have used these symbols?

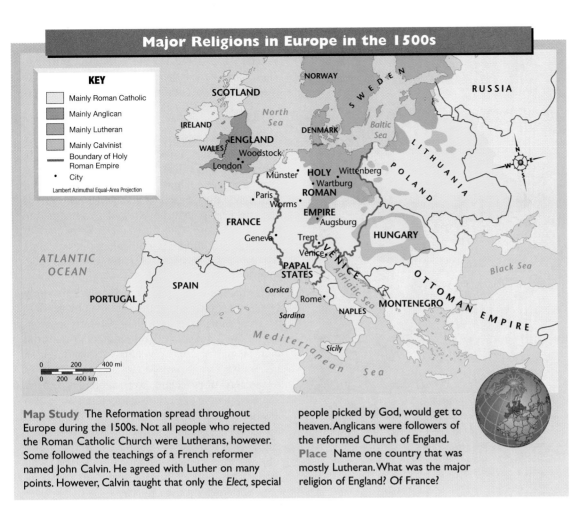

Major Religions in Europe in the 1500s

KEY
- Mainly Roman Catholic
- Mainly Anglican
- Mainly Lutheran
- Mainly Calvinist
- ——— Boundary of Holy Roman Empire
- • City

Lambert Azimuthal Equal-Area Projection

0   200   400 mi
0   200   400 km

Map Study The Reformation spread throughout Europe during the 1500s. Not all people who rejected the Roman Catholic Church were Lutherans, however. Some followed the teachings of a French reformer named John Calvin. He agreed with Luther on many points. However, Calvin taught that only the *Elect,* special people picked by God, would get to heaven. Anglicans were followers of the reformed Church of England. **Place** Name one country that was mostly Lutheran. What was the major religion of England? Of France?

Background

Links Across Place

Other Reformers
Luther's call for reform spread to other parts of Europe. In Geneva, Switzerland, John Calvin started a new religion that eventually included strict codes of behavior. Calvinism spread to other countries and resulted in other Protestant religions. In Scotland, John Knox adapted Calvinist ideas to a religion that became known as Presbyterianism. In England, King Henry VIII, upset because the Roman Catholic Church would not grant him an annulment from his first wife, broke away from the Church and established the Anglican church.

The Protestant Reformation   Luther's beliefs were very different from those of the pope. According to Luther, people did not need bishops and popes to tell them what God wanted them to do. Belief in God, not obedience to the Church, was the key to getting into heaven.

Luther especially disliked the way the Church raised money by selling **indulgences,** official pardons given by the pope. If people committed a sin, they could pay money to the Church for an indulgence and be forgiven. Luther believed that the Church did not have the power to do this.

In Germany, princes and nobles who disliked the power of the pope quickly accepted Luther's ideas. These rulers wanted to collect their own taxes and make their own laws. They wanted the same powers enjoyed by the leaders of Italy's city-states. By the time Luther died, most of what is now northern Germany was Lutheran. That is, people there believed in Luther's ideas about how to be a Christian, not in the ideas of the Roman Catholic Church.

Answers to ...

MAP STUDY

Norway, Sweden, or Denmark; Anglican; Roman Catholic

1. (a) rebirth of learning in Europe toward the end of the Middle Ages (b) technique of showing objects as they appear to the eye (c) change in religion intended to reform religious customs (d) official pardons given by the pope in exchange for money (e) a person who protested against Roman Catholicism, forming a new religion

2. (a) Italian artist and scientist of the Renaissance (b) Italian artist of the Renaissance who painted the Sistine Chapel (c) monk who caused the Reformation (d) Italian city-state and home to Michaelangelo

3. Northern Italy was composed of city-states, which were controlled by wealthy merchants. The merchants controlled European trade with Asia. Because of their wealth from trade, some northern Italians had time to pursue activities such as reading and art. This increased interest in subjects such as art, literature, and science resulted in the Renaissance.

4. Sample answer: The kings and nobles were envious of the pope's power. They wanted the power to collect their own taxes and make their own laws.

5. Students might indicate that people were astonished because the figures were so true to life, and they knew how difficult it must have been to paint a ceiling.

6. Students' letters should explain the changes that are needed.

Ignatius Loyola

The words in the book held by Ignatius Loyola are the Latin for "To the greater glory of God." To achieve this aim, Loyola gave up his life as a noble in Spain to become a priest.

People with views similar to Luther's spread protests against the Roman Catholic Church to other parts of northern Europe. These people were called **Protestants** because their religions grew out of protest against Roman Catholicism.

The Catholic Reformation Many Roman Catholics agreed with some of the criticisms made by Protestants. But they did not turn away from the Church. Instead, they worked from inside the Church to change it. Pope Paul III was the first pope who worked to change the Church during the Catholic Reformation. Working with other Church leaders, he was able to solve many problems in the Church. Even though the Catholic reformers brought about many changes, they continued to preach that only the clergy could explain the Bible to people.

This effort to improve the Church inspired people. St. Vincent de Paul worked to help the poor people of Paris. Ignatius Loyola founded the Society of Jesus. Jesuits, as members of the society were called, were among the best-educated people of Europe at this time. They also became well known for their work as teachers. In more than 500 schools in Catholic countries, they taught children about religion as well as other subjects. Many Jesuits became missionaries who traveled throughout Europe trying to win back those who had left the Church.

SECTION 1 REVIEW

1. Define (a) Renaissance, (b) perspective, (c) Reformation, (d) indulgence, (e) Protestant.

2. Identify (a) Leonardo da Vinci, (b) Michelangelo, (c) Martin Luther, (d) Florence.

3. What conditions in northern Italy led to the Renaissance?

4. Why did kings and nobles in northern Europe want to break away from the Roman Catholic Church?

Critical Thinking

5. Identifying Central Issues Why do you think people were so astonished by Michelangelo's work in the Sistine Chapel?

Activity

6. Writing to Learn You are a Catholic who thinks that your Church needs to reform. Write a letter to a friend explaining why changes are needed.

Resource Directory

Teaching Resources

Section Quiz in the Chapter and Section Support booklet, p. 87, covers the main ideas and key terms in the section. Available in Spanish in the Spanish Support booklet, p. 54.

The Age of Exploration

Reach Into Your Background

Think about a time when you traveled to a new place, alone or with your family. Perhaps you asked directions before you went. Maybe someone looked at a map. Did you get lost? Did you see things that surprised you?

Questions to Explore

1. How did Portugal lead the way in European exploration of the world outside Europe?
2. How did other explorers help Europeans learn about new lands?

Key Terms

navigator
caravel
astrolabe
circumnavigate

Key People and Places

Henry the Navigator
Ferdinand Magellan
Cape Bojador
Strait of Magellan

Look at the map on this page. It was drawn in the 1470s by an Italian mapmaker. Europe, Asia, and Africa cover the whole map. The Americas are nowhere to be seen.

At this time, Europeans had done little exploring beyond their own shores. In fact, the vast majority of Europeans never left their own town or village. They had very little knowledge of, or interest in, other lands. With the new spirit of curiosity of the Renaissance, however, their attitudes began to change.

Europe Expands Its Horizons

By the early 1400s, people in many European countries had grown tired of paying high prices to Italian merchants for Asian goods. They wanted to gain control of the rich trade with the East themselves. They realized that to do this they would have to find a new trade route to Asia.

▼ This map is from one of the world's oldest printed atlases.

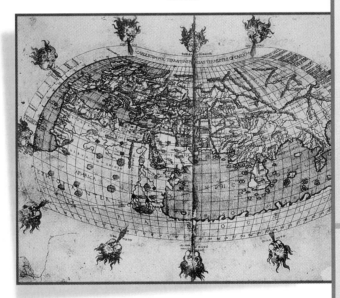

Teaching Resources

📁 **Reproducible Lesson Plan** in the Chapter and Section Support booklet, p. 88, provides a summary of the section lesson.

📁 **Guided Reading and Review** in the Chapter and Section Support booklet, p. 89, provides a structure for mastering key concepts and reviewing key terms in the section. Available in Spanish in the Spanish Support booklet, p. 55.

Lesson Objectives

1. Explain how Portugal led the way in European exploration of the world outside Europe.

2. Describe the ways that other explorers helped Europeans learn about new lands.

Lesson Plan

1 Engage

Warm-Up Activity

Refer students to the title of Section 2. Discuss what reasons people might have for exploring. If necessary, prompt students by asking them how this term could be applied to modern times.

Activating Prior Knowledge

Have students read Reach Into Your Background in the Before You Read box. Ask students to give examples of the kinds of tools they might use when traveling.

Background

Global Perspectives

Spices Of all the goods brought to Europe, spices were the most desirable. Europeans used spices to enhance the flavor of foods as well as to preserve foods. In the 1400s, Venice monopolized the spice trade, enabling it to demand high prices. This spurred adventurers in both Portugal and Spain to look for their own routes to Asia. Many early explorations gained financial backing from merchants in the spice trade.

2 Explore

As students read Section 2, suggest that they look for answers to the following questions: Why was Prince Henry of Portugal important to Portuguese explorations? How did Columbus plan to reach Asia? What did Ferdinand Magellan explore?

Activity

Cooperative Learning

Navigational Tools
Organize the class into groups of four. Each group can create an advertisement for one of the advancements in navigation that made the Age of Exploration possible. For example, groups might develop a magazine advertisement, a billboard poster, or a radio or television commercial to advertise advancements such as the compass, the quadrant, the astrolabe, and the caravel. Have students use information in this section and research additional information in other reference books. Encourage students to divide the following roles among group members: researcher, illustrator, writer, editor, and actors (if appropriate). Call on each group to present its advertisement to the class.
Kinesthetic, Visual, Auditory

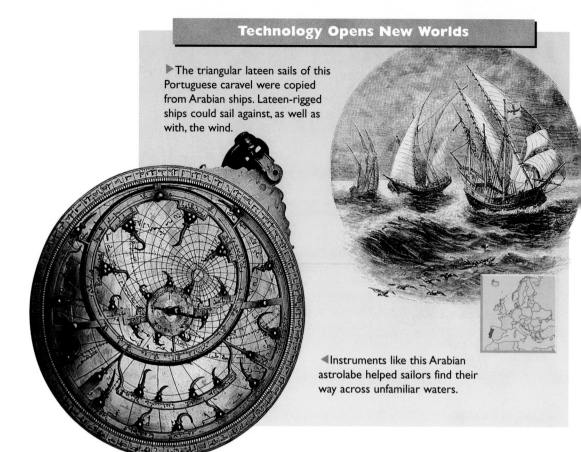

Technology Opens New Worlds

▶The triangular lateen sails of this Portuguese caravel were copied from Arabian ships. Lateen-rigged ships could sail against, as well as with, the wind.

◀Instruments like this Arabian astrolabe helped sailors find their way across unfamiliar waters.

Portugal Takes the Lead Find the political map of Europe in the Atlas at the back of your book. Notice that Portugal is located where the southwestern tip of the continent juts out into the Atlantic Ocean. Would it surprise you to learn that a country with this location has had a long history of seafaring? Portuguese sailors used their great experience on the seas to lead the way in the search for the new trade route.

The success of the Portuguese was due, in large part, to Prince Henry, the son of Portugal's king. In 1419, he opened a school. He invited mapmakers, shipbuilders, and **navigators,** or expert sailors, from all over the country to attend. Although Prince Henry himself did not go exploring, his work won him the title of Henry the Navigator.

Under Prince Henry's leadership, the Portuguese made many advances. His shipbuilders designed a ship called a **caravel.** It was larger, stronger, easier to steer, and much faster than other types of ships. Portuguese sailors also became expert at navigation. They used the compass to find out which direction they were traveling. They measured their latitude, or distance north or south of the Equator, with an **astrolabe** (AS troh layb). They gathered all the information they could from other sailors to make new, more detailed charts and maps of the Atlantic.

Resource Directory

Program Resources

📁 **Outline Maps** The World: Physical, p. 2

Media and Technology

📽 **Color Transparencies** 1, 2, Historical Map Set 4

Prince Henry thought that his sailors might find a route to Asia if they sailed south along the western coast of Africa. While they searched, they could build trading ties with the Africans they met. They could also convert these people to Christianity.

His sailors, however, were unwilling to sail beyond Cape Bojador (BAHJ uh dor). They feared what they might find beyond this small bulge in the coastline of what today is known as the western Sahara. Perhaps they would be attacked by great sea monsters. Or they might be lost forever in what Arab sailors called the "Green Sea of Darkness." Finally, one brave sailor, Gil Eanes (gil YAH neesh), did lead his crew beyond the cape. When he returned safe and sound, the others realized that their fears were unfounded.

Portuguese ships then pushed farther south along Africa's west coast. As they sailed, Portuguese sea captains gathered information on winds, currents, and coastlines. They set up trading posts, bringing such goods as gold and ivory back to Portugal. Finally, in 1497, a Portuguese captain named Vasco da Gama (VAS koh duh GAH muh) rounded the southernmost tip of Africa. From here, he sailed along the eastern coast of Africa and then across the Indian Ocean to India. He returned with a cargo of spices and precious stones. The Portuguese had set up their trade route to Asia.

READ ACTIVELY

Connect The early explorers helped people expand their understanding of the world. What kinds of explorations are people making today to help expand our understanding?

Christopher Columbus

On his first voyage across the Atlantic, Christopher Columbus commanded a fleet of three ships and a crew of about 90 sailors. The journey from Spain to the Americas took more than eight weeks to complete. Below is a copy of the first page of a letter Columbus wrote to King Ferdinand describing the voyage.

Teaching Resources

Visualizing What Things Look Like in the Social Studies and Geography Skills booklet, p. 73, provides additional skill practice.

3 Teach

Have students write biographical sketches about the people discussed in Section 2. Students should include Prince Henry of Portugal, Gil Eanes, Vasco da Gama, Christopher Columbus, and Ferdinand Magellan in their sketches. Sketches should contain information about the country each person represented and the contribution each person made to further knowledge about the new lands. This activity should take about 30 minutes.

Activity

Interdisciplinary Connections

Art Review with students why some sailors were unwilling to sail beyond Cape Bojador. Then ask students to draw cartoons that illustrate the fears that European sailors had about venturing into unknown waters. Display completed cartoons around the classroom. *Kinesthetic, Visual*

Background

Daily Life

Sailing with Da Gama Life for the sailors on Vasco da Gama's expedition was not glamorous. The diary of a crew member indicates that they lived in cramped, narrow quarters during long and boring days. During part of the trip, daily rations were limited to about one pound of beef or half a pound of pork, a pound and a half of biscuits, one and a quarter pints of wine, and two and a half pints of water.

4 Assess

See the answers to the Section Review. You may also use students' biographical sketches as an assessment.

Acceptable biographical sketches include information about the accomplishments of each individual.

Commendable sketches include the country each person represented as well as information about the individual's accomplishments.

Outstanding sketches indicate an understanding of how each person's accomplishments contributed to knowledge about the new lands.

Background

Links Across Place

Amerigo Vespucci A native of Florence, Italy, Amerigo Vespucci claimed that his 1497–1498 voyage made him the first explorer to reach the North American continent. Most scholars discredit his claim to this voyage, but do agree that on a 1499–1500 expedition, Vespucci explored part of the northern coast of South America. Martin Waldseemüller, a German mapmaker who translated a narrative of Vespucci's explorations, suggested the name *America* for this southern continent. The name was applied to both continents after it appeared on a world map published by Waldseemüller in 1507.

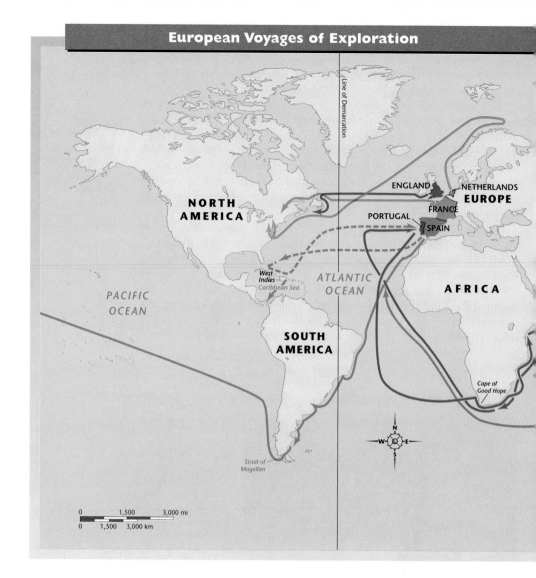

European Voyages of Exploration

Spain's Contribution The Portuguese sailed east to find their route to Asia. An Italian sea captain named Christopher Columbus was convinced that he could reach India by sailing west, across the Atlantic.

Columbus, like many others of his time, accepted that the world was a sphere. Therefore, it made sense to him that a ship sailing west would eventually reach Asia. It made sense to Queen Isabella and King Ferdinand of Spain, too. The thought of the great riches to be gained convinced them to support Columbus's voyage.

What Columbus did not know was that two huge continents lay between Europe and Asia. Thus Columbus reached the Americas, not Asia. Soon, both Spain and Portugal would begin to carve empires out of these continents. In time, other European countries would join them.

Resource Directory

Teaching Resources

Critical Thinking Activity in the Chapter and Section Support booklet, p. 101, helps students apply the skill of drawing conclusions.

A S I A

Line of Demarcation

PACIFIC
OCEAN

Philippine
Islands

East Indies

INDIAN
OCEAN

AUSTRALIA

KEY

Explorers for Portugal
—— Da Gama, 1497–1499

Explorers for Spain
- - - Columbus, 1492–1493
—— Magellan, 1519–1522

Explorers for England
—— Cabot, 1497

Explorers for France
—— Cartier, 1534–1535

Explorers for Netherlands
—— Hudson, 1609

Miller Projection

Map Study This map shows the routes taken by some of the most important European explorers of the late 1400s and 1500s. These sailors often sailed for nations other than their own. In 1497, for example, the Italian Giovanni Caboto made a voyage supported by the English. They called him John Cabot. He hoped to reach Asia by taking a more northerly route than that followed by Columbus. Cabot reached North America and claimed the lands he explored for England. Henry Hudson, an Englishman, sailed for the Netherlands. He explored the river that now bears his name. **Movement** Why do you think Hudson sailed so far north before turning toward the Americas?

Magellan Sails Around the World

Even after Columbus reached the Americas, Europeans did not understand how large the Earth was. They believed that Japan, which they called Cipango (sib PANG goh), was separated from the Americas by only a narrow channel of water. The Portuguese sailor Ferdinand Magellan (FUR din and muh JEL un) was eager to cross that channel.

Magellan Sets Out Magellan was an officer in the Portuguese navy. However, the Portuguese king would not support his journey. Magellan then convinced the Spanish king to back him. Like Columbus, Magellan was mistaken about how far he would have to go.

Activity

Cooperative Learning

Other Explorers Organize students into groups of four. Ask students in each group to find information about the explorations of other explorers of the late 1400s and the 1500s (for example, Bartolomeu Dias, Sir Francis Drake, John Cabot, and Pedro Cabral). Students should find out where the explorer was born, the year of birth and death, which country sponsored the exploration, and what specific achievement resulted from the exploration. Students might present the information in the form of illustrated mobiles. Groups can assign the following tasks to their members: researching, writing, illustrating the mobile, and designing and constructing the mobile. Hang completed mobiles around the classroom. *English Language Learners, Kinesthetic*

Answers to . . .

MAP STUDY

Like Cabot, Hudson was trying to find a more northerly route to Asia.

Activity

Interdisciplinary Connections

Math   Tell students that the Strait of Magellan is 350 miles (560 km) long. Have them use this information and the information in the text to find Magellan's average speed through the Strait. Have students compare their results with an average person's walking speed, then draw a conclusion about the difficulty of the trip. (350 miles ÷ 38 days = 9.2 miles/day, or 0.4 miles/hour. Most students could walk half a mile in less than an hour; the sailing must have been very difficult.)

Activity

Interdisciplinary Connections

Language Arts   Have students work in groups of four to create an in-depth interview with Vasco da Gama, Christopher Columbus, and Ferdinand Magellan. Students should develop a list of questions to ask the explorers as well as the explorers' responses. Invite groups to present their interviews to the class. *Verbal*

Answers to ...
FERDINAND MAGELLAN

The information Magellan had made it possible for him to make plans should emergencies arise, and his experience would help him decide how to manage the long voyage.

Magellan set sail in 1519 with five ships and a crew of about 250 men. Shortly after reaching the coast of South America, the crews of three of the ships refused to sail on. They were afraid that they would never see home again unless they returned the way they had come. Magellan was convinced that he could not make the trip unless all five ships sailed. He needed every sailor and every ship in order to survive, so he used force as well as skill to persuade the crews to go on.

After much searching, the sailors located the passage now called the Strait of Magellan. Ships must pass through these narrow, twisting passages near the tip of South America to get from the Atlantic Ocean to the Pacific Ocean. It took Magellan 38 days to sail through. Strong currents and fierce winds made the journey difficult. Sometimes Magellan thought he was moving rapidly forward when, in fact, his ships were almost at a standstill. The winds in the sails made the ships look like they were making progress while the currents were actually holding them back.

The Voyage Continues   But even before they sailed through the straits, Magellan's crews made a terrible discovery. They had only a third as much food and water as they had thought. Their suppliers had cheated them. They were also unaware that they would soon be facing an ocean far bigger than any they had ever seen.

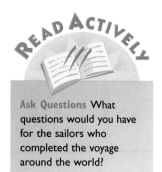

READ ACTIVELY

Ask Questions What questions would you have for the sailors who completed the voyage around the world?

Ferdinand Magellan

Magellan was a knowledgeable and skillful navigator. In the years before 1519, he had gained valuable experience on Portuguese expeditions to India, Africa, and Southeast Asia. Also, as a Portuguese naval officer, he had access to the information about currents, winds, and routes that other Portuguese sailors had collected. **Critical Thinking** How do you think such experience and knowledge helped Magellan to make the difficult voyage around South America?

Resource Directory

Teaching Resources

Section Quiz in the Chapter and Section Support booklet, p. 90, covers the main ideas and key terms in the section. Available in Spanish in the Spanish Support booklet, p. 56.

◄Here, Magellan's ships round the southern tip of South America. Magellan named the area *Tierra del Fuego* (tee EHR uh del FWAY goh), or "Land of Fires," because his sailors saw many fires on land.

With one third of the food they had thought they needed, they continued on a journey that would be much longer than they had expected. The crews had to live on short rations. Some men starved to death or died of disease. Those who lived ate biscuits full of worms. They soaked and cooked the ox hides they had used to cover equipment on the ship. Some even ate sawdust.

Magellan's skill as a sailor took them across the Pacific Ocean. But Magellan did not live to return to Spain. He unwisely became involved in local politics in the Philippines, islands off the coast of Asia. In the spring of 1521, Magellan was killed in battle by a Philippine ruler. More than three years after leaving home, one ship returned to Spain. Of the roughly 250 sailors who had set sail with Magellan, only 18 returned. They were the first people to **circumnavigate,** or sail around, the world.

SECTION 2 REVIEW

1. **Define** (a) navigator, (b) caravel, (c) astrolabe, (d) circumnavigate.

2. **Identify** (a) Henry the Navigator, (b) Ferdinand Magellan, (c) Cape Bojador, (d) Strait of Magellan.

3. What did Henry the Navigator do to make Portugal a leader in exploration?

4. (a) Name two explorers who sailed for the monarch of Spain. (b) Explain what they accomplished.

Critical Thinking

5. **Identifying Central Issues** What special characteristics do you think an explorer needs? Explain your answer.

Activity

6. **Writing to Learn** You are a member of Ferdinand Magellan's crew. Write a journal entry about sailing across the Pacific Ocean for the first time.

Section 2 Review

1. (a) expert sailor (b) kind of ship designed by Portuguese shipbuilders (c) instrument that measured latitude (d) to sail around

2. (a) Prince of Portugal, under whose leadership the Portuguese made many advances in navigation and exploration (b) Portuguese sailor whose crews were the first to sail around the world (c) the part of present-day western Sahara past which sailors in the 1400s were unwilling to sail (d) strait near the tip of South America

3. He opened a school to which he invited mapmakers, shipbuilders, and navigators from all over the world.

4. (a) Christopher Columbus and Ferdinand Magellan (b) Columbus reached the Americas in an attempt to sail west to Asia. Magellan's crews were the first to sail around the world.

5. Answers will vary, but students might mention that explorers need to be courageous, daring, and curious.

6. Students' journal entries should include details about their experience in sailing across the Pacific Ocean for the first time.

SKILLS MINI LESSON

Identifying Central Issues

To **introduce** the skill, stress to students that as they read any material, they should focus on the central issue that the text is addressing. Help students **practice** the skill by giving them the following tips: Identify the topic of the text you are reading. Focus on statements in the text that summarize the content of the particular passage. Identify the central issue. To **apply** the skill, have students read *The Voyage Continues,* and then identify the central issue(s). (Magellan's crews overestimated the amount of food and water they had for the voyage; they also underestimated the length of the voyage.)

SECTION 3

The Age of Powerful Kings

Lesson Objectives

1. Explain how the idea of divine right helped make kings more powerful.

2. Describe the actions that rulers of Europe took to increase their power after the Middle Ages.

Lesson Plan

1 Engage

Warm-Up Activity

Ask students what they think of when they hear the words *monarch, king,* or *queen.* Ask them what countries today have monarchs. Have students explain whether they think kings and queens today have a great deal of power.

Activating Prior Knowledge

Have students read Reach Into Your Background in the Before You Read box. Ask students what powers government leaders of the United States have today. Ask them from where these leaders get their power to govern.

BEFORE YOU READ

Reach Into Your Background

There was a time when kings and queens had the power to tell everyone else what to do. Have you ever dreamed of having such power? Have you ever wondered what it would be like to have all your commands obeyed? To have your wishes fulfilled?

Questions to Explore

1. How did the idea of divine right help make kings more powerful?

2. What actions did the rulers of Europe take to increase their power after the Middle Ages?

Key Terms
democracy
divine right
absolute monarch

Key People and Places
Louis XIV
Cardinal Richelieu
Peter the Great
Versailles

▼ This picture shows Louis XIV and his dinner guests surrounded by servants.

Louis XIV, king of France, was ready for his dinner. He would be eating alone this night. That did not mean he would be by himself. It only meant that he would be the only one eating. Although the meal had just begun, a crowd of servants already surrounded him. It was time for his meat to be brought from the kitchen. Two guards entered first. They were followed by ushers, gentlemen-in-waiting, the keeper of the king's china, and more guards. Somewhere in the crowd were the officers of the food department who actually carried the meat. In all, it required 15 people to bring the meat to Louis.

Louis asked for a drink. "Drink for the King!" cried the gentleman cupbearer. Then he turned to the chief cupbearer, who handed him a gold tray with a glass and drinks. The gentleman cupbearer, the chief cupbearer, and the chief cupbearer's attendant walked to the table. They bowed to the king, and presented the tray. The king helped himself. The gentleman cupbearer bowed to Louis and returned the tray to the chief cupbearer, who took it away. Before the king finished his meal, some 500 people would have helped to prepare and serve it.

Resource Directory

Teaching Resources

📁 **Reproducible Lesson Plan** in the Chapter and Section Support booklet, p. 91, provides a summary of the section lesson.

📁 **Guided Reading and Review** in the Chapter and Section Support booklet, p. 92, provides a structure for mastering key concepts and reviewing key terms in the section. Available in Spanish in the Spanish Support booklet, p. 57.

Louis XIV was shorter than average. To make himself look taller and more powerful, he wore high-heeled shoes and tall wigs. The rich robe that he wears in this portrait is embroidered with golden fleur-de-lis (flur duh LEE) symbols. This flower-like design was the mark of French royalty. This sun symbol (below) was specially designed for Louis.
Critical Thinking What qualities of Louis' character do you think are shown by his clothes and his specially-designed sun symbol?

The Age of Absolute Rule

Why did Louis XIV have so many people waiting on him? What right did he have to all this service? Was it just because he was the leader of France? Stop and think for a minute. What gives our government the right to lead us? We, the people, give our government that job—because we live in a democracy. In a **democracy,** the people elect representatives to govern. They choose the government. Yet not all governments are democracies.

The Divine Right of Kings   France was not a democracy in the 1600s. The people did not choose their king. They believed that God chose the king, and that the king was God's representative. The king's right to rule was divine—that is, it was thought to come directly from God. This idea is called the **divine right** of kings, and many Europeans believed in it 400 years ago.

The Growth of Absolute Monarchy   King Louis XIV was an **absolute monarch.** He had absolute, or complete, power over every part of life in his kingdom. Absolute monarchs did not share power with nobles or parliaments or the people. Louis was so powerful that he became known as the "Sun King." Just as the sun was the center of the solar system, Louis was the center of the French nation.

Program Resources

☐ **Outline Maps** Western Europe: Political, p. 18

---

2 Explore

Ask students to read Section 3, noting the answers to the following questions: From where did French monarchs in the 1600s claim they received their right to rule? How did Louis XIV expand his power? How did the rulers of Spain and Russia expand their power?

Activity

Interdisciplinary Connections

Art   Discuss the lifestyle and power of Louis XIV of France. Then ask students to work in pairs to create a family crest that symbolizes the rule of Louis XIV. Encourage students to think of symbols that would be appropriate to describe the king's character and his kind of leadership. Suggest that students use these symbols in their crests. Display completed crests around the classroom, and encourage a class discussion to evaluate the effectiveness of the symbols used in the crests.
Kinesthetic

Answers to . . .
LOUIS XIV, FRANCE'S SUN KING

The clothes and sun symbol indicate that Louis XIV was very vain.

Have students write a script for a segment of a "You Are There" television news show set in the 1600s. Their news segment should provide details to support the following statement: "Since the Middle Ages ended, European rulers have taken action to increase their power." Students should use the information in the section for their scripts. This activity should take about 20 minutes.

4 Assess

See the answers to the Section Review. You may also use students' completed scripts as assessment.

Acceptable scripts include information about the ways that power was increased in one or two European countries after the Middle Ages.

Commendable scripts include details about the ways that power was increased in several European countries.

Outstanding scripts show an understanding of the causes and effects that worked together to increase the power of monarchs.

Court Dress Nobles at Versailles dressed as though they were always on stage. Gentlemen wore richly embroidered jackets that reached to their knees. Wide sleeves showed that they had money to spend on costly fabrics. Ladies wore dresses with trains that might be 40 feet (12 m) long. The most important item was the wig. Men wore fancy, oversized wigs. Women's wigs were piled high, and trimmed with lace, ribbons, and even real birds' nests.

It is amazing to think of one person being so powerful. It took a long time for the French kings to gain absolute power. King Louis was as powerful as he was because other kings had gradually taken power away from the nobles. This process had been going on for 150 years.

Absolute Rule in France

Before Louis became king, Cardinal Richelieu (RISH loo) had served as chief minister to Louis' father, Louis XIII. For 18 years, Richelieu worked to increase the power of France and the French king. To do this, he had to destroy the power of the nobles. He allowed wealthy merchants to buy titles of nobility. Then he stripped the old nobles of some of their rights. He also started businesses for the French government. These businesses earned a great deal of money for the crown. Altogether these changes made the nobles weaker and the king wealthier and more powerful.

Louis XIV came to the French throne in 1643, a year after Richelieu's death. As Louis was only four years old, another French Church official, Cardinal Mazarin (maz uh RAN), ruled for him. When Mazarin died in 1661, Louis was glad to be rid of him. He wanted power all to himself. He took steps to further weaken the nobles. He also reduced the power of the Church. "I am the state," he declared.

Life at the Sun King's Court One way in which Louis showed his power was with his lifestyle. He lived in incredible luxury at Versailles (vur SY), his huge palace outside Paris.

The Architect of Absolute Monarchy

This painting shows Cardinal Richelieu from three different angles. Richelieu was the real ruler of France during the 18 years he advised Louis XIII. While in office, Richelieu greatly increased the power of the French monarchy. His aim, he said, was "to make the King absolute in his kingdom in order to establish order therein." **Critical Thinking** How did Richelieu achieve his goal of making the king's power absolute?

Answers to ...

THE ARCHITECT OF ABSOLUTE MONARCHY

First he decreased the power of the nobles by allowing wealthy merchants to purchase titles of nobility. He also started successful businesses for the crown.

Resource Directory

Teaching Resources

Analyzing Art in the Social Studies and Geography Skills booklet, p. 59, provides additional skill practice.

Some 30,000 laborers worked 40 years to complete his magnificent estate. Many nobles lived at Versailles with Louis. Having the nobles at Versailles made it easier for Louis to keep an eye on them. If he had left them on their estates, they might have been a threat to his power. To keep them satisfied, Louis gave huge parties with lots of entertainment. He treated them well and, for the most part, left them free from paying taxes. This made the nobles forget that they were little more than the king's prisoners.

All of this luxury and entertainment cost a great deal of money. As you have just read, the nobles rarely were taxed. Most merchants and craftspeople also managed to avoid taxes. That meant that the poorest and weakest people—the peasants—in France paid for the luxury of Louis XIV's court.

France at War Louis' aim was to make France the greatest nation in Europe. To do this, he encouraged the growth of industry. He also supported efforts to build an empire in Asia and the Americas. He went to war to gain new territories. From 1667 until 1713, France was almost constantly at war with other European countries.

All of these wars took their toll. They cost huge sums of money. They won France little in the way of more land or power. By the time Louis died in 1715, France had huge debts. Even the silverware collection at Versailles had been sold to help pay for France's wars.

▼ Today, the Palace of Versailles and its gardens still attract countless tourists. This sculptured candleholder (shown in oval) is one example of the magnificent decorations found inside the palace.

Background

Global Perspectives

Modern Absolute Rulers In modern times, absolute rulers are usually dictators. Whereas the European monarchs after the Middle Ages claimed to rule by divine right, many of today's dictators came to power by taking control of their country's ruling political party. Dictators in the 1900s include Adolf Hitler (Germany), Joseph Stalin (Soviet Union), Mao Zedong (People's Republic of China), Kim Il Sung (North Korea), Hafez al-Assad (Syria), and Saddam Hussein (Iraq).

Background

Links Across Place

The Wars in North America While France was fighting wars in Europe in 1702, it was also fighting a war, known as Queen Anne's War, in North America. This war was one of a group of conflicts known as the Seven Years' War. The conflicts involved the French (with their Native American allies) and the British (with their colonial allies). Just as in Europe, the wars in North America were fought to establish claims to land.

Daily Life

Changes Under Peter the Great Peter the Great's attempt to modernize Russia also involved the clothing styles of Russian men. After traveling to Western Europe, Peter ordered Russian men to replace their traditional long robes with the short coats that men in Western Europe wore. All men, except peasants and clergy, were also required to shave their beards. Peter ordered that models of the new style be displayed at town gates, so that all Russian men could see it and copy it.

European Monarchs Gain Power

Louis XIV was not the only powerful ruler in Europe. There were also King Ferdinand and Queen Isabella of Spain. When they married, they joined their separate kingdoms into one. It then became a major European nation. Like Louis, they worked to limit the power of the nobles. In addition, they built up Spain's army. With this powerful force, they drove the Moors from Spain. The Moors were North African Muslims who had occupied parts of Spain since the A.D. 700s. Ferdinand and Isabella also supported voyages of exploration. These voyages resulted in the building of a huge empire in the Americas.

Peter the Great became czar of Russia in 1682, when he was 10 years old. However, he did not actually rule Russia until he reached the age of 17. For the next 36 years, he modernized the Russian army and navy and improved Russian farming and industry. He expanded Russia's territory, adding land with ports so Russia could trade by sea.

Like Louis XIV, Peter the Great limited the power of the nobles to strengthen his own position. And, also like Louis, Peter the Great lived in a magnificent palace that he built to show the rest of the world his wealth and power.

▼ When they married, Ferdinand of Aragon and Isabella of Castile united their two Spanish kingdoms. Castile means "country of castles." Isabella's favorite castle was this one, Alcazar, in the city of Segovia.

St. Petersburg

In 1703, Peter the Great of Russia founded the city of St. Petersburg. He called the city his "window to the West." He wanted to make Russia more like Western Europe. The Winter Palace, shown here, was not completed until after his death. However, as Peter hoped, it echoed the splendor of Louis XIV's palace at Versailles. The Winter Palace is now a museum housing world-famous paintings and sculptures. **Critical Thinking** Why do you think Peter the Great wanted to build a splendid palace like Versailles?

In England, kings and queens had to share power. Although English monarchs like Henry VII and Elizabeth I did strengthen the power of monarchs, the nobles of England held power through Parliament. This power had been given to them by the Magna Carta. When Charles I came to power, he claimed that he could ignore Parliament because he ruled by divine right. Parliament did not agree. War broke out, and Charles I was executed in 1649. Future English monarchs found that they could rule only if they accepted limitations on their power.

SECTION 3 REVIEW

1. Define (a) democracy, (b) divine right, (c) absolute monarch.

2. Identify (a) Louis XIV, (b) Cardinal Richelieu, (c) Peter the Great, (d) Versailles.

3. What do you think Louis XIV meant when he said "I am the state"?

4. Which groups did European monarchs weaken to make themselves more powerful?

Critical Thinking
5. Distinguishing Fact From Opinion Is the following sentence fact or opinion? "Louis XIV made France the greatest nation in Europe." Explain your answer.

Activity
6. Writing to Learn Write a description of a day at Versailles as it might appear to a noble. Then write a description of how the day might look to a peasant.

Resource Directory

Teaching Resources

Section Quiz in the Chapter and Section Support booklet, p. 93, covers the main ideas and key terms in the section. Available in Spanish in the Spanish Support booklet, p. 58.

Section 3 Review

1. (a) form of government in which people elect representatives to govern (b) idea that a monarch's right to rule comes directly from God (c) monarch who had complete power over every part of life in the kingdom

2. (a) absolute monarch of France, known as the "Sun King" (b) chief minister of King Louis XIII (c) powerful ruler of Russia in the 1700s (d) luxurious palace of Louis XIV

3. He meant that all power rested in him.

4. European monarchs weakened the nobles and the Church.

5. It's an opinion. It states what someone thinks or believes about France.

6. Students' entries should contrast the two viewpoints.

Answers to . . .
St. Petersburg

to show that he was as rich and powerful as the French king

Conquests in the Americas and Africa

Lesson Objectives

1 Explain how Spain built an empire in the Americas.

2 Analyze the ways that the Atlantic slave trade affected Africa.

Lesson Plan

1 Engage

Warm-Up Activity

Ask students what images come to mind when they hear the word *civilization*. Call on volunteers for their responses. Then ask students to identify civilizations that they have studied in the past. Discuss the kinds of situations that could destroy a civilization.

Activating Prior Knowledge

Have students read Reach Into Your Background in the Before You Read box. Ask them what places in their community, if any, reflect a Spanish influence. If there are no Spanish influences, ask students to identify other ethnic influences in their community.

Background

Daily Life

Religion in Aztec Life
Several gods ruled daily life in the Aztec empire. Quetzalcoatl was considered the inventor of writing and was associated with death and resurrection. Other important gods included the war and sun god, Huitzilopochtli, and Tlaloc, the rain god.

BEFORE YOU READ

Reach Into Your Background

Los Angeles, California; Santa Fe, New Mexico; El Paso, Texas—you have heard the names of these American cities before. Maybe you have visited one. Or perhaps you live in one. These cities have Spanish names. Some of the old buildings in these cities look like buildings in Spain. The first Europeans to explore and settle California, New Mexico, and Texas were from Spain. They left their mark on the language and culture of the people who live there today.

Questions to Explore

1. How did Spain build an empire in the Americas?

2. How did the Atlantic slave trade affect Africa?

Key Terms
encomienda
conquistador

Key People and Places
Moctezuma
Hernan Cortés
Malinche
Francisco Pizarro
Tenochtitlán

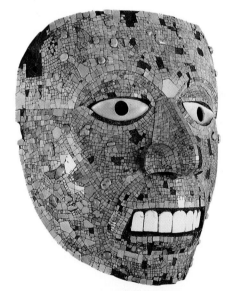

▼ This mask of Quetzalcoatl was made with many small pieces of stone.

About a hundred years before Louis XIV ruled France, another king had sat down to a splendid dinner. Moctezuma (mahk the ZOOM uh) was the ruler of the powerful Aztec empire in the Valley of Mexico. Like Louis, Moctezuma was usually the only one who ate at his dinners. Also like Louis, he was not alone. More than 400 people brought him his food. After his servants had put down the food, Moctezuma looked over the huge selection and chose the foods he wanted. Then servants drew a wooden screen around him to protect him from onlookers. His food was served by his personal servants.

Moctezuma was powerful. But he and other Aztecs believed that the gods were still more powerful. An ancient Aztec legend said that long ago the Aztecs had disobeyed the gods. It said that someday the white-skinned god Quetzalcoatl (ket sahl koh AHTL) would come from the east to punish them.

In 1519, it seemed to happen. Moctezuma and the Aztecs heard about a group of pale-skinned men who had landed on the coast. The Aztecs wondered if these men could be Quetzalcoatl and his followers.

Resource Directory

Teaching Resources

📁 **Reproducible Lesson Plan** in the Chapter and Section Support booklet, p. 94, provides a summary of the section lesson.

📁 **Guided Reading and Review** in the Chapter and Section Support booklet, p. 95, provides a structure for mastering key concepts and reviewing key terms in the section. Available in Spanish in the Spanish Support booklet, p. 59.

Program Resources

📁 **Outline Maps** Latin America: Political, p. 7; West and Central Africa: Political, p. 34

The Aztecs' Magnificent Capital

This painting of the Aztec capital, Tenochtitlán, was made by the Mexican artist Diego Rivera in the 1940s. It is one of a series of murals, or wall paintings, on Mexican history that Rivera painted in the National Palace in Mexico City.

The Conquest of the Aztec Empire

The leader of the pale-skinned men was the Spaniard Hernan Cortés (hur NAN kor TEZ). Soon after landing in present-day Mexico, he met a Native American woman named Malinche (mah LIHN chay). She told him stories about the wealth of the Aztecs. Cortés, who was searching for gold, was intrigued. When Malinche told him about the hatred many of the native peoples had for the Aztecs, Cortés began to plan.

He asked other Native American peoples to help him against the Aztecs. At first he had little success. But Malinche, who could speak several native languages, helped to persuade these Native Americans to join with Cortés against the Aztecs.

The Conquest Begins When Cortés arrived in Tenochtitlán (tay nawch tee TLAHN), the Aztec capital, Moctezuma welcomed him. The Aztecs were afraid that Cortés might be the returning Quetzalcoatl, so they treated him and his men as honored guests. But the Spaniards knew that they were surrounded by danger.

LINKS TO ART

City of Dreams: Tenochtitlán "When we saw the many cities and villages built both on the water and on dry land . . . we could not resist our admiration. . . because of the high towers [pyramids], and other buildings of masonry. . . ." This is how Bernal Diaz, a soldier with Cortés, described the Aztec capital. At the time of the Spaniards' arrival, Tenochtitlán was 10 times larger than the largest city in Spain. Within a few years it was gone, totally destroyed by the Spanish conquerors.

2 Explore

Have students read Section 4 and examine the visuals. Then have them find answers to the following questions: Why did Moctezuma welcome Hernan Cortés and his men? How did Cortés conquer Tenochtitlán? How did the Spanish claim lands in Central and South America? Why was there a market for slaves in the Americas? How did the slave trade affect Africa?

Activity

Interdisciplinary Connections

Language Arts Many accounts of Cortés's conquest of the Aztec empire are available. Encourage students to use the library to find these accounts and to read them. Ask them to prepare oral reports that summarize the information that they have found. Have students present their reports to the class. *Auditory*

Media and Technology

 Color Transparencies 135, 141, 143, Historical Map Set 5

3 Teach

Ask students to use the information in this section to create a captioned mural titled "Conquests in the Americas and Africa." The mural should provide facts and visuals that answer the Questions to Explore and should focus on the conquests of the Aztecs and the Incas and the slave trade in Africa. Display and discuss completed murals. This activity should take about 30 minutes.

Background

Biography

Defender of the Native Americans The Native Americans' treatment by the Spanish under the encomienda was opposed by Bartolomé De Las Casas, a Spanish missionary and historian. De Las Casas was born in Seville, Spain, in 1474. In 1512, he was given an encomienda as a reward for serving in several expeditions. Having witnessed the abuses that the Native Americans suffered, he worked to improve the conditions of the Native Americans. He was instrumental in Spain's passage of the New Laws in 1542, which brought about some improvements in the lives of Native Americans in the Spanish colonies. De Las Casas died in Madrid in July 1566.

Answers to ...

CORTÉS THE CONQUISTADOR

They believed they could find great wealth in the Americas.

Cortés tried to convince Moctezuma to surrender to Spain. After several months, Moctezuma agreed. The peace was a short one, however. Spanish soldiers killed several Aztecs. Then the Aztecs began to fight the Spaniards. The battle was fierce and bloody. Moctezuma was killed. Cortés and his army barely escaped.

With the help of Native American allies, Cortés surrounded and attacked Tenochtitlán. In 1521, the Aztecs finally surrendered. By then, about 240,000 Aztecs had died, and 30,000 of Cortés's allies had been killed. Tenochtitlán and the Aztec empire lay in ruins.

After the Conquest Cortés then took control of the land, which he called New Spain. He built his new capital, Mexico City, on the site of Tenochtitlán.

Like most Europeans, Cortés tried to make life in New Spain like that in his home country. He imported European plants and farm animals such as sugar cane, barley, wheat, cattle, pigs, and chickens. He also introduced a new economic system, the **encomienda** (en KOH mee en duh), to Mexico. In this system, the Spanish king gave settlers large areas of land. Along with each piece of land, the new Spanish landlord received the labor of the Native Americans who lived on it. In return, the landlords were supposed to protect the Native Americans. They were also expected to persuade the Native Americans to adopt the Roman Catholic faith. The landlords also were supposed to allow the Native Americans to work their own plots of land to grow food. The encomienda

Cortés the Conquistador

Hernan Cortés, pictured here, was the first of the Spanish conquistadors (kon KEES ta dorz), or conquerors. The Spanish king gave conquistadors the right to hunt for treasure in the Americas. Not content with conquering the Aztec empire, Cortés led an expedition to Central America. However, he found no treasure there. **Critical Thinking** The conquistadors had to pay for their own expeditions. Why do you think they were willing to risk losing everything on expeditions to the Americas?

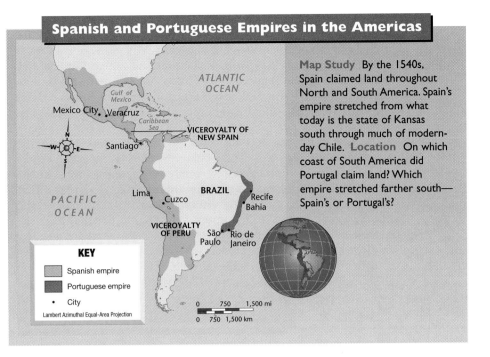

Spanish and Portuguese Empires in the Americas

ATLANTIC OCEAN

Gulf of Mexico

Mexico City • Veracruz

Caribbean Sea

VICEROYALTY OF NEW SPAIN

Santiago •

PACIFIC OCEAN

Lima • • Cuzco

BRAZIL

Recife
Bahia

VICEROYALTY OF PERU

São Paulo • • Rio de Janeiro

KEY

Spanish empire

Portuguese empire

• City

Lambert Azimuthal Equal-Area Projection

0   750   1,500 mi
0   750 1,500 km

Map Study By the 1540s, Spain claimed land throughout North and South America. Spain's empire stretched from what today is the state of Kansas south through much of modern-day Chile. **Location** On which coast of South America did Portugal claim land? Which empire stretched farther south— Spain's or Portugal's?

---

system was meant to be like the medieval manor system. In reality, it became a kind of slavery. Many Native Americans were worked to death.

In the years after the fall of the Aztecs, Cortés and other Spanish **conquistadors** (kon KEES ta dors), or conquerors, traveled throughout Central and South America and parts of the Caribbean. They claimed the land and the people who lived on it for Spain and the Roman Catholic Church. Francisco Pizarro, for example, conquered the Incan empire in 1533.

Amazingly, Pizarro managed to take control of an empire of some 12 million people with an army of about 200 soldiers. How was this possible? First, a war was raging in the empire. Some of the people rebelling against Incan rule sided with Pizarro. Further, European diseases like smallpox had killed thousands of people in the region. Many of those who had survived the disease were too sick to fight.

Europeans and Africans Clash

Europeans were looking for riches in other lands as well. Once the Portuguese had opened up the coast of West Africa to trade, sailors from other European countries followed. British, French, and Dutch ships visited Africa to trade for gold, ivory, and pepper. Occasionally, they traded for enslaved people as well. One British ship brought five enslaved Africans to England in the 1540s. No one would buy them, so they were taken back to Africa. Europe did not offer a big market for slavery. At this time, Europe had enough cheap labor. It did not need more workers.

LINKS TO SCIENCE

Disease in the Americas
Many of America's native peoples were killed by Europeans without ever going into battle. The Europeans brought new diseases to the Americas— diseases against which the Native Americans had no built-up immunity. Smallpox and measles killed thousands. The Aztec and Incan empires were greatly weakened by diseases that swept through their populations. The same thing happened in North America.

4 Assess

See the answers to the Section Review. You may also use students' completed murals as assessment.

Acceptable murals indicate and illustrate at least one fact that answers each of the Questions to Explore.

Commendable murals include illustrations as well as at least two facts that answer each of the Questions to Explore.

Outstanding murals include illustrations and captions that show an understanding of how the Spanish began to build an empire in the Americas and how the slave trade affected Africa.

Activity

Critical Thinking

Recognizing Cause and Effect *Suitable as an individual or a group activity.* Ask students to create two graphic organizers showing the effects of the conquests of Cortés and Pizarro on the Native Americans. The top box for one graphic organizer might include the following cause: *Cortés attacks the Aztecs.* The top box for the other might include *Pizarro attacks the Incas.* Students should extend lines from each of the two boxes and include on these lines the effects on the Native Americans.

Answers to . . .
MAP STUDY

east; Spain's

The Kingdom of Benin
With the arrival of the Europeans, the slave trade in the African kingdom of Benin expanded drastically. The suppression of the slave trade, as well as constant fighting for the acquisition of more territory, led to the decline of the kingdom of Benin. The kingdom of Benin (located in present-day southern Nigeria), however, was once a thriving commercial center. Its capital city, also called Benin, was an important cultural and trade center in West Africa. Although the people of Benin did not have a written language, a record of their civilization remains on bronze plaques, which the Benin ruler commissioned to decorate the pillars of his palace. In addition, European explorers recorded descriptions of daily life in Benin in their journals.

HEROES

To Be a Leader Queen Nzingha (ehn ZIHNG ah) united many of the people of Southern Africa to fight the Portuguese. Nzingha was a true military leader. She often led her troops in raids against the Portuguese invaders. Often, she and her soldiers were able to free enslaved Africans who were being sent to the Americas. For a time, she was even able to close off all the slave-trade routes through her lands.

Slavery Comes to the Americas There was a market for slaves in the Americas, however. Spanish and Portuguese settlers in the Americas wanted workers for their plantations and mines. At first they had enslaved Native Americans. But many Native Americans became sick and died from diseases or the brutal working conditions. Others ran away. To replace them, the Europeans began importing enslaved Africans.

No one is sure just how many enslaved Africans were taken to the Americas. Some historians put the number at about 12 million. An equal number or more may have died before or on the journey to the Americas. Some were cut down by disease before they even left Africa. Others got sick and died on the crowded slave ships that crossed the Atlantic. People were sometimes packed in so tightly that they had to lie on their sides, cupped together like spoons, for the entire journey. The air in the holds where they traveled was so poor that there was often not enough oxygen to keep a candle burning. "The shrieks of the women, and the groans of the dying, rendered the whole a scene of horror," one survivor later recalled.

Plan of a Slave Ship

This diagram made by an English artist in 1790 shows how enslaved Africans were carried on a "loose-pack" slave ship. On such a ship, people could lie on their backs. On a "tight-pack" ship, people had to lie on their sides. This meant that more slaves could be crammed onto the ship. It is no wonder that so many enslaved Africans died on these ships. **Critical Thinking** Why did slave traders want to cram so many slaves aboard their ships?

Answers to . . .
PLAN OF A SLAVE SHIP

More slaves per trip meant more money per trip.

Resource Directory

Teaching Resources

Section Quiz in the Chapter and Section Support booklet, p. 96, covers the main ideas and key terms in the section. Available in Spanish in the Spanish Support booklet, p. 60.

Vocabulary in the Chapter and Section Support booklet, p. 98, provides a review of key terms in the chapter. Available in Spanish in the Spanish Support booklet, p. 62.

Reteaching in the Chapter and Section Support booklet, p. 99, provides a structure for students who may need additional help in mastering chapter content.

Program Resources

Environmental and Global Issues Topic: Human Rights, pp. 25–30

The Slave Trade

A European slave trader pays an African for some enslaved men on the coast of West Africa in the early 1800s. **Critical Thinking** What impact do you think the slave trade had on Africa?

ACROSS THE WORLD

A Global Exchange The movement of peoples from Africa and Europe to the Americas opened up a global exchange of goods and ideas. Europeans introduced cattle, goats, pigs, and chickens to the Americas. From Africa and Asia came such plants as bananas, coffee, and sugar cane. All became major foods in the Americas. Food crops such as corn, potatoes, and beans from the Americas had a huge impact. The introduction of these crops to Europe, Asia, and Africa made it easier to feed more and more people.

Effects of Slavery   The slave trade created a disaster for Africa. European slavers lured Africans into wars against their neighbors. They even provided them with guns and other deadly weapons. Then the slavers bought men, women, and children captured in the wars. These wars guaranteed the slavers a steady supply of people to buy.

Europeans wanted the youngest and healthiest Africans to provide free labor for the Americas. But the loss of so many of its best people and other problems created by the wars caused Africans to suffer for centuries. Even after the slave trade ended in the late 1800s, its effects continued to be felt.

SECTION 4 REVIEW

1. Define   (a) encomienda, (b) conquistador.

2. Identify   (a) Moctezuma, (b) Hernan Cortés, (c) Malinche, (d) Francisco Pizarro, (e) Tenochtitlán.

3. How were Cortés and Pizarro able to conquer great empires with only small numbers of Spanish soldiers?

4. What impact did the slave trade have on Africa?

Critical Thinking

5. Recognizing Cause and Effect   How did the arrival of the Europeans affect the Aztec and Incan empires?

Activity

6. Writing to Learn   Write two paragraphs, one from the viewpoint of an Aztec soldier defending Tenochtitlán, the other from the viewpoint of one of Cortés's soldiers.

Teaching Resources

📁 **Enrichment** in the Chapter and Section Support booklet, p. 100, extends chapter content and enriches students' understanding.

📁 **Spanish Glossary** in the Spanish Support booklet, pp. 83–91, provides key terms translated from English to Spanish as well as definitions in Spanish.

📁 **Chapter Summary** in the Chapter and Section Support booklet, p. 97, provides a summary of chapter content. Available in Spanish in the Spanish Support booklet, p. 61.

📁 **Cooperative Learning Activity** in the Activities and Projects booklet, pp. 40–43, provides two student handouts, one page of teacher's directions, and a scoring rubric for a cooperative learning activity on simulation: keeping a ship's log.

Media and Technology

🎧 **Guided Reading Audiotapes** (English and Spanish)

Section 4 Review

1. (a) economic system in which the Spanish king awarded settlers large areas of land along with the forced labor of the Native Americans who lived on it (b) Spanish conqueror

2. (a) the ruler of the Aztec empire (b) conquistador who defeated the Aztec empire (c) Native American woman who told Cortés about the wealth of the Aztecs (d) conquistador who defeated the Incas (e) Aztec capital

3. They received help from the native people, who hated the Aztec and Incan rulers; also, European diseases had killed thousands of people in the region.

4. The slave trade was a disaster for Africa because the region lost its best people to slavery. The slave trade also caused wars within Africa.

5. It destroyed the empires.

6. Paragraphs should provide contrasting viewpoints.

Answers to ...

THE SLAVE TRADE

The slave trade caused wars and took from Africa some of the youngest, healthiest, and most capable workers.

SKILLS ACTIVITY

Distinguishing Fact From Opinion

Lesson Objectives

1 Define the terms *fact* and *opinion*.

2 Distinguish facts from opinions in context.

Lesson Plan

1 Engage

Warm-Up Activity

Write the terms *fact* and *opinion* on the chalkboard. Ask a volunteer to read the opening text aloud to **introduce** the skill.

Activating Prior Knowledge

Tell students to make a two-column chart like the one shown.

Fact	Opinion

Ask them to give examples of facts and opinions. Tell students to list their examples, with a definition of each term, under the correct heading on their chart.

2 Explore

Have students read the Get Ready text. Invite volunteers to write the definitions for *fact* (information that can be proved true) and *opinion* (information which cannot be proved true, is a belief, and which evaluates) on the posted chart. Discuss how these compare with the examples and definitions students noted earlier. Then have students read the rest of the Skills Activity.

You have probably heard people say things like these:

"The fact of the matter is...."

"Let's look at the facts."

"That's just your opinion."

"Well, in my opinion...."

Just what is the difference between a fact and an opinion? Distinguishing between them can help you better understand what you read and hear. Knowing the difference can help you make good decisions.

Get Ready

How do facts and opinions differ? Facts are statements that can be proved true. Opinions are personal beliefs. For example, it is a fact that the Earth is round. This has been proved by people who have traveled all the way around the Earth. The shape has been seen by astronauts looking at the Earth from outer space. It is an opinion that the Earth is beautiful. People may believe that, but no one can prove that it is true.

You will often need to make judgments or decisions based on facts, and you must be able to recognize them. How can you tell facts and opinions apart? It's as simple as 1-2-3!

1 Facts can be proved true.

2 Opinions usually cannot be proved true.

3 Opinions often include words and phrases such as "I think," "I believe," or "should," and adjectives such as "great" or "terrible."

Try It Out

Learn to distinguish facts from opinions by playing a simple game. You will need note cards, two pens, and a partner.

Front

Potatoes grow under ground.

Back

Fact

Resource Directory

Teaching Resources

Distinguishing Fact From Opinion in the Social Studies and Geography Skills booklet, p. 43, provides additional skill practice.

A. Make game cards. Give 10 note cards to your partner and keep 10 for yourself. Each of you should then write one fact or one opinion on each of your note cards. For example, "It snowed last week" would be a fact. "We had wonderful weather last week" would be an opinion. Make sure that all of your facts can be proved. On the back of each card, identify your statement as a fact or an opinion. Do not let your partner see these answers!

B. Play the game. Shuffle your cards and give them to your partner face up. Challenge him or her to identify each sentence as a fact or opinion. Award one point for each correct answer. Give a bonus point if your partner can explain how the statement could be proved true if it is a fact or how your partner knew it was an opinion.

C. Switch the cards. Now try your hand at identifying your partner's facts and opinions. Compare scores. Who won?

Apply the Skill

Now look at some facts and opinions about explorers. Read the 10 statements in the box. Use the three qualities of facts and opinions explained in Get Ready. Identify each statement as a fact or an opinion. If it is a fact, explain how it could be proved true. If it is an opinion, tell how you know it is an opinion.

Statements About Explorers

1. Columbus was the greatest explorer in history.

2. It would have been better if European explorers never came to the Americas at all.

3. Vasco da Gama sailed around the Cape of Good Hope to India.

4. Vasco Balboa sighted the Pacific Ocean.

5. Ponce de León was foolish to search for the Fountain of Youth.

6. America is named for the explorer Amerigo Vespucci.

7. Francisco Pizarro came from Spain.

8. John Cabot was a very handsome man.

9. Hernando de Soto and his army traveled through what is today Georgia, South Carolina, North Carolina, Tennessee, Alabama, Mississippi, Arkansas, and Louisiana.

10. Explorers have changed the world more than any other group of people.

Back

Opinion

Front

Potatoes are delicious with sour cream and butter.

3 Teach

In pairs, have students **practice** the skill by playing the Try It Out game. Monitor the choices students make, resolving any disputes. Invite pairs to test the class with their trickiest facts and opinions.

For additional reinforcement, ask students to locate three facts and opinions in a recent magazine or newspaper.

4 Assess

Students may **apply** the skill by completing the final activity. To **assess**, poll the class on each numbered statement. Ask students to explain their fact or opinion votes for each statement. Evaluate the accuracy of students' votes and the logic of their reasoning.

Answers to ...
APPLY THE SKILL

Statements 3, 4, 6, 7, and 9 are facts. They can be proved true by reading historical records. The remaining sentences—1, 2, 5, and 8—are opinions. Each contains opinion words such as *greatest, better, foolish, very, handsome,* and *more than.*

Reviewing Main Ideas

1. They were proud of their cities and homes and wanted works of art to decorate their homes and churches. They hoped that offerings of beautiful works of art would lead God to forgive their sins.

2. Many German princes disliked the power of the pope and wanted the power to collect their own taxes and make their own laws.

3. The instruments helped them to know where they were located and where they were going.

4. They wanted to find new routes to Asia to avoid paying high prices to Italian merchants for Asian goods.

5. They believed that God chose the king to rule them.

6. They destroyed the power of the nobles.

7. They destroyed the empires that existed there.

8. The slave trade caused wars and took from the region some of its youngest and healthiest people.

Reviewing Key Terms

1. i	**4.** f	**7.** d
2. a	**5.** g	**8.** e
3. h	**6.** c	

Critical Thinking

1. The European settlers in the Americas wanted workers for their plantations and mines. To obtain these workers, the Europeans began importing enslaved Africans.

2. He wanted Russia to be able to trade by sea.

CHAPTER 6 Review and Activities

Reviewing Main Ideas

1. List reasons why Italian merchants supported the work of artists during the Renaissance.

2. Why did many princes in Germany adopt the ideas of Martin Luther?

3. Why were instruments like the compass and astrolabe so important to European explorers?

4. Why did European nations support voyages of exploration?

5. Why did the people of France feel that they could not challenge the demands of King Louis XIV?

6. What did European monarchs do to take more power for themselves?

7. How did the Spanish go about building an empire in the Americas?

8. Why was the slave trade a disaster for Africa?

Reviewing Key Terms

Match the definitions in Column I with the key terms in Column II

Column I

1. a ruler who has total power over every aspect of life in a country

2. the rebirth of learning in Europe

3. the belief that a king rules by the will of God

4. a type of ship developed in the 1400s that was stronger and easier to sail than other ships

5. a system in which people govern themselves, choosing their own government

6. the painting technique that makes objects in the distance look smaller relative to objects in the foreground

7. a new, great change in religion intended to reform religious customs

8. an instrument for measuring latitude

Column II

a. Renaissance

b. city-state

c. perspective

d. Reformation

e. astrolabe

f. caravel

g. democracy

h. divine right

i. absolute monarch

Critical Thinking

1. Recognizing Cause and Effect How did the development of empires in the Americas affect trade between European countries and Africa?

2. Expressing Problems Clearly Why did Peter the Great want seaports for his country?

Graphic Organizer

Copy the chart onto a separate sheet of paper. Under each heading, list the names of two people connected with the change given.

Renaissance	Reformation	Exploration	Absolute Monarchy	Conquest of the Americas

Graphic Organizer

Answers may vary. Sample answers shown.

Renaissance	Reformation	Exploration	Absolute Monarchy	Conquest of the Americas
Leonardo da Vinci	Martin Luther	Prince Henry the Navigator	Louis XIV	Hernan Cortés
Michelangelo	St. Vincent de Paul	Magellan	King Ferdinand and Queen Isabella	Francisco Pizarro

Map Activity

European Empires in the Americas

For each place listed below, write the letter from the map that shows its location.

1. Atlantic Ocean
2. North America
3. Pacific Ocean
4. Portuguese empire
5. South America
6. Spanish empire

Place Location

Writing Activity

Writing a Tour Plan

Your school's history club is planning a summer study tour of Europe. Choose four to six places you think should be included on the tour. Discuss what might be seen in these places and explain why they are important to understanding the history of the period covered by this chapter.

Internet Activity

Use a search engine to find **Renaissance and Reformation (Europe/Russia/Eastern Europe).** Choose **Renaissance/Reformation.** Explore the various links. Write a brief essay about science, music or an expression of creativity during this time that interests you most. Give examples to support your essay.

Skills Review

Turn to the Skills Activity.

Review how you can distinguish fact from opinion. Then answer the following questions: (a) What are some fact and opinion language clues? (b) In making a decision, would you base it on facts or opinions? Why?

How Am I Doing?

Answer these questions to help you check your progres.

1. Can I name some changes that the Renaissance and the Reformation brought to Europe?

2. Do I understand the importance of European exploration and how it affected the lives of people in Europe, Africa, and the Americas?

3. Can I explain how absolute monarchs gained power in Europe?

4. What information from this chapter can I use in my book project?

Internet Activity

If students are having difficulty finding this site, you may wish to have them use the following URL, which was accurate at the time this textbook was published:

http://www.execpc.com/~dboals/europe.html

You might also guide students to a search engine. Four of the most useful are Infoseek, AltaVista, Lycos, and Yahoo. For additional suggestions on using the Internet, refer to the Prentice Hall Social Studies' Educator's Handbook "Using the Internet," in the *Prentice Hall World Explorer Program Resources.*

For additional links to world history and culture topics, visit the Prentice Hall Home Page at:
http://www.phschool.com

How Am I Doing?

Point out to students that this checklist is a quick reminder of what they learned in the chapter. If their answer to any of the questions is *no* or if they are unsure, they may need to review the topic.

Map Activity

| 1. B | 3. D | 5. E |
| 2. A | 4. F | 6. C |

Writing Activity

Students should identify places on the tour and should indicate why these places are important to an understanding of the period of history covered in this chapter.

Skills Review

(a) Students' responses will vary but may include clue words, such as I think, I believe, great, best, terrible, which indicate opinions. (b) Answers may vary. Students should support their choice with logical arguments.

Resource Directory

Teaching Resources

Chapter Tests Forms A and B are in the Tests booklet, pp. 32–37.

Program Resources

Writing Process Handbook includes Locating Information, pp. 17–18, to help students with the Writing Activity.

Media and Technology

Color Transparencies
Color Transparency 171 (Graphic organizer web template)

Prentice Hall Writer's Solution Writing Lab CD-ROM

Computer Test Bank

Resource Pro™ CD-ROM

Making a Compass

Lesson Objectives

1 Explain the purpose of a magnetic compass.

2 Describe how magnetic compasses work to locate north.

Lesson Plan

1 Engage

Warm-Up Activity

Ask students to locate north relative to your school. Give students an opportunity to explain their thinking, especially if different answers are offered. Point out that locating directions relative to somewhere else can be tricky—climate or geography can obscure the view, geographic elements can shift, left can become right as perspectives differ. Explain that a compass resolves all these problems by locating north magnetically.

Activating Prior Knowledge

Invite volunteers to read aloud the steps of the Activity Lab. Let students share their thinking about the questions in Step Three. Have students record their predictions on a sheet of paper. Then have students put their predictions on your desk.

2 Explore

Direct students to gather all the Activity Shop materials before beginning to build their compasses.

For centuries, the magnetic compass has helped people find their way. The needle of a compass always points north. If you know where north is, you can always find south, east, and west.

The compass once looked quite different than it does today. Often, people simply used a piece of magnetized iron attached to a piece of cork floating in a bowl of water. Although such compasses were simple, they worked well.

▲ An antique pocket compass.

Purpose

In this activity, you will create your own compass. By observing how the compass acts, you can learn something about the forces that make it work.

Materials

- a small bowl
- enough water to fill the bowl
- a small flat cork disk, $\frac{1}{2}$ to $\frac{3}{4}$ inches across
- a sewing needle
- a bar magnet about 3 inches long

Procedure

In order to understand how a compass works, you must first know that the Earth has its own magnetic field. This magnetic field has two poles. That means it pulls in two opposite directions. The Earth's magnetic poles are very close to the Earth's North Pole and South Pole.

Bar magnets also have north and south magnetic poles. If allowed to move freely, any bar magnet will be drawn by the currents of the strongest nearby magnetic field. It will move so that its poles match the poles of that magnetic field. Before you begin making your own compass, read the steps on the next page.

Resource Directory

Teaching Resources

📁 **Activity Shop: Lab** in the Activities and Projects booklet, p. 6, provides a structure that helps students complete the lab activity.

STEP ONE

Prepare your materials. Fill the bowl with water. Dunk the cork disk in the bowl of water, wetting it completely. Then let it float in the center of the bowl.

STEP TWO

Build your compass. Rub the needle several times across the magnet, from one end to the other. When you do this, the needle itself becomes a weak magnet. Immediately lay the needle flat in the center of the cork disk. You might need to nudge the cork so that it stays near the center of the bowl. Then watch carefully. What happens?

You may need to repeat rubbing the needle, especially if the needle accidentally gets wet. Dry it off, then rub it on the magnet again.

STEP THREE

Test your compass. Turn the cork about one quarter turn and let go. What happens? Next, slowly and carefully rotate the bowl of water. What does the cork do?

Observations

1. What happened when you placed the needle on the cork disk?

2. Did the needle move immediately to one position, or did it seem to sway and hesitate?

3. What happened to the needle when you changed its position or the position of the bowl?

ANALYSIS AND CONCLUSION

1. Why do you think the needle always points in one direction?

2. Why is it necessary for a compass needle to float and move freely?

3 Teach

Have students work in groups or independently to make their compasses. Assist students as necessary in magnetizing their needles. Urge students to treat the compasses very gently or they may not function.

Discuss any discrepancies between the compasses. For example, there may be magnetic influences in your classroom that interfere with some compasses' functioning.

4 Assess

Call on volunteers to read a peer's compass predictions aloud. Then, as a class, write revised answers to the Step Three questions. Evaluate students' contributions to the revised answers for comprehension and accuracy.

Answers to ...

OBSERVATIONS

1. The cork and needle turned until the needle was along a north-south line.
2. The needle hesitated a bit.
3. It turned so that it would be along a north-south line.

ANALYSIS AND CONCLUSION

1. Because the Earth's magnetic field is always in the same direction.
2. Because the magnetic field is not very strong, the needle needs to move easily.

Changes in the Western World

To help you plan instruction, the chart below shows how teaching resources correspond to chapter content. Use the resources to vary instruction, add activities, or plan block schedules. Where appropriate, resources have suggested time allotments for students. Time allotments are approximate.

Managing Time and Instruction

	Medieval Times to Today Teaching Resources Binder		World Explorer Program Resources Binder	
	Resource	**mins.**	**Resource**	**mins.**
1 SECTION 1 Limits on Monarchs	**Chapter and Section Support** Reproducible Lesson Plan, p. 103		**Outline Maps** Western Europe: Political, p. 18	20
	S Guided Reading and Review, p. 104	20	**Nystrom Desk Atlas**	
	S Section Quiz, p. 105	25	T **Primary Sources and Literature Readings**	40
	Critical Thinking Activity, p. 119	30	**Writing Process Handbook** Organizing Material in a Logical Sequence, pp. 23–24	25
SKILLS ACTIVITY Interpreting Line Graphs	**Social Studies and Geography Skills,** Reading a Line Graph, p. 54	30		
2 SECTION 2 The Enlightenment	**Chapter and Section Support** Reproducible Lesson Plan, p. 106			
	S Guided Reading and Review, p. 107	20		
	S Section Quiz, p. 108	25		
	Social Studies and Geography Skills, Learning More About a Topic, p. 76	30		
3 SECTION 3 The Industrial Revolution	**Chapter and Section Support** Reproducible Lesson Plan, p. 109		**Environmental and Global Issues** Topic: Urbanization, pp. 54–58	30
	S Guided Reading and Review, p. 110	20	Topic: Energy and Resources, pp. 2–7	30
	S Section Quiz, p. 111	25		
4 SECTION 4 Revolution and Imperialism	**Chapter and Section Support** Reproducible Lesson Plan, p. 112		**Outline Maps** Western Europe: Political, p. 18	20
	S Guided Reading and Review, p. 113	20	North Africa: Political, p. 31	20
	S Section Quiz, p. 114	25	Africa: Political, p. 33	30
	S Vocabulary, p. 116	20	**Environmental and Global Issues** Topic: Conflict, pp. 37–42	30
	Reteaching, p. 117	25		
	Enrichment, p. 118	25		
	S Chapter Summary, p. 115	15		
	Social Studies and Geography Skills, Identifying Alternatives, p. 51	30		
	Tests Forms A and B Chapter Tests, pp. 38–43	40		

Block Scheduling Folder
PROGRAM TEACHING RESOURCES

Activities and Projects

Interdisciplinary Links

Block Scheduling Program Support

Resource Pro™ CD-ROM

Media and Technology

Media and Technology

Resource	mins.
World Video Explorer	20
Planet Earth CD-ROM	20
Color Transparencies 144, 147, Historical Map Set 8	20
Color Transparency 142	20
Guided Reading Audiotapes	20
Color Transparency 171 (Graphic organizer web template)	20
The Writer's Solution CD-ROM	30
Computer Test Bank	30

T **Teaming Opportunity**
This resource is especially well-suited for teaching teams.

S **Spanish**
This resource is also in Spanish support.

CD-ROM

Laserdisc

Transparency

Software

Videotape

Audiotape

Assessment Opportunities

From Guiding Questions to Assessment A series of Guiding Questions serves as an organizing framework for this book. The Guiding Questions that relate to this chapter are listed below. Section Reviews and Section Quizzes provide opportunities for assessing students' insights into these Guiding Questions. Additional assessments are listed below.

GUIDING QUESTIONS

- *What accomplishments in technology, learning, or artistic expression were found in each society?*
- *How did each society's belief system affect its history, government, and economy?*

ASSESSMENTS

Section 1

Students should be able to create a flowchart of the events that led to the English civil war.

▶ **RUBRIC** See the Assessment booklet for a rubric on assessing graphic organizers.

Section 2

Students should be able to create a table that lists some of the achievements of the scientific revolution.

▶ **RUBRIC** See the Assessment booklet for a rubric on assessing charts.

Section 3

Students should be able to give an oral presentation on the problems of the Industrial Revolution.

▶ **RUBRIC** See the Assessment booklet for a rubric on assessing an oral presentation.

Section 4

Students should be able to write a paragraph about the rise and fall of Napoleon.

▶ **RUBRIC** See the Assessment booklet for a rubric on assessing a writing assignment.

Activities and Projects

Mental Mapping	Links to Current Events	Hands-On Activities

The Industrial Revolution Suggest that students make maps of an imaginary community before and after industrialization. Throughout the world, towns and villages in some countries are currently changing from an agricultural economy to a manufacturing economy.

Ask students how industrialization changes the way people live. They should realize that industrialization encourages centralization as people move to larger towns or cities so they can work in factories. Explain that while in the United States, people who have farms usually live on their farms, in many parts of South Asia and Southeast Asia, people live in tiny villages and farm together on the outskirts of their village. Thus houses might be clustered together.

Encourage students to think about the positive and negative effects of more centralized patterns of living.

Scientific Method Ask students to think about the many ways their daily lives are affected by the results of the use of the scientific method. They may immediately think about modern medicine, but encourage them to think further—foods that are available due to plant breeding; synthetic materials like plastic and nylon, and rain-resistant fabrics such as Gore-Tex; computer chips running microwaves, telephones, and CD players; recording technologies that allow them to view movies with realistic sound and color, and so on.

Have students list the things they think of. Next to each item on their list, ask them to write what filled the function of that material or object before 1750. You might extend this activity by giving students a chance to discuss the positive and negative points of items in each column.

The Solar System Give students a chance to discuss the difference between Galileo's view that the Earth revolves around the sun and the view previously held that the sun revolves around the Earth. Have students demonstrate each of these views of the relationship between the sun and the Earth. Invite students to discuss reasons why some people might have objected so strongly to Galileo's views.

Galileo and Darwin Just as Galileo challenged many beliefs about the place of the Earth in space, Charles Darwin challenged many beliefs about the age of the Earth and the origins of human beings a few centuries later. Ask students to research and write a short paper about the way the ideas of these two men were received and how the men themselves were treated. They may wish to devote part of their essay to a discussion of the difference between the way these men are regarded today and the way they were treated by their contemporaries. *Challenging*

Time Line Direct students to make a time line of events leading up to and resulting from the American Revolution. Suggest that they include events from British history, the publication of ideas of John Locke, and the formation of a new type of government in the aftermath of the war. *Basic*

Obituary Ask students to choose a figure from this chapter, such as Elizabeth I or Napoleon. Invite them to write an obituary that summarizes the achievements, characteristics, and mistakes of that person. *Average*

Flags of Nations One way people express nationalism is through symbols like flags. Today, the flag of France, Great Britain, or Germany represents the entire country and all its citizens. A few hundred years ago, however, flags stood for the ruler or the royal family of a country or region. Invite students to create flashcards with the flags of countries of Europe on the front and the name of the country on the back. Encourage students to challenge each other to recognize the flags. *English Language Learners*

F.Y.I.

This page can help you extend your own and students' understanding of the concepts in this chapter. You may want to browse through some of the suggestions in the **Bibliography. Interdisciplinary Links** can connect social studies understandings to areas elsewhere in the curriculum through the use of other Prentice Hall products. **National Geography Standards** reflected specifically in this chapter are listed for your convenience. Some hints about appropriate **Internet Access** are also provided. **School to Careers** provides insights into the practical uses of some of the concepts in this chapter as they might pertain to various careers.

BIBLIOGRAPHY

FOR THE TEACHER
Blumberg, Rhoda. *Full Steam Ahead: The Race to Build a Transcontinental Railroad*. National, 1996.

Marrin, Albert. *Napoleon and the Napoleonic Wars*. Viking, 1991.

Meltzer, Milton. *Thomas Jefferson: The Revolutionary Aristocrat*. Watts, 1991.

FOR THE STUDENT
Easy
Langley, Andrew. *The Industrial Revolution*. Viking, 1994.

Sis, Peter. *Starry Messenger: Galileo Galilei*. Farrar, 1996.

Average
Parker, Steve. *Galileo and the Universe*. Chelsea, 1995.

Stanley, Jerry. *Big Annie of Calumet: A True Story of the Industrial Revolution*. Crown, 1996.

Challenging
Dash, Joan. *We Shall Not Be Moved: The Women's Factory Strike of 1909*. Scholastic, 1996.

LITERATURE CONNECTION
Freedman, Russell. *The Wright Brothers: How They Invented the Airplane*. Holiday, 1991.

Paterson, Katherine. *Lyddie*. Lodestar, 1991.

Stanley, Diane, and Peter Vennema. *Bard of Avon: The Story of William Shakespeare*. Morrow, 1992.

INTERDISCIPLINARY LINKS

Subject	Theme: Change
MATH	Middle Grades Math: Tools for Success *Course 1*, Lesson 5-2, **Napier's Rods,** Lesson 9-4, **Guess and Test** *Course 2*, Lesson 1-6, **Logical Reasoning**
SCIENCE	Prentice Hall Science *The Nature of Science*, Lesson 1-2, **The Scientific Method—A Way of Problem Solving** *Cells: Building Blocks of Life*, **Connections: A Heated Experiment** *Parade of Life: Monerans, Protists, Fungi, and Plants*, Lesson 1-1, **History of Classification**
LANGUAGE ARTS	Prentice Hall Literature *Copper*, **Between the Devil and the Sea** *Bronze*, **The Highwayman**

NATIONAL GEOGRAPHY STANDARDS

Students explore the 18 National Geography Standards throughout *Medieval Times to Today*. Chapter 7, however, concentrates on investigating the following standards: 4, 5, 6, 9, 10, 11, 12, 13, 14, 15, 16, 17. For a complete list of the standards, see the *Teacher's Flexible Planning Guide*.

SCHOOL TO CAREERS

In Chapter 7, Changes in the Western World, students learn about the development of western civilizations. Additionally, they address the skill of interpreting line graphs. Understanding the changes and development of the West can help students prepare for careers in many fields, such as international trade, philosophy, politics, and so on. Interpreting line graphs is a skill used in many careers, including economics, politics, marketing, demography, and others. The curriculum presented in this book, as in all eight titles of Prentice Hall's *World Explorer* program, is designed to prepare students not only for careers but also for good citizenship—of the world as well as of this country.

INTERNET ACCESS

Many social studies teachers and students use Internet browsers, or search engines, to investigate particular topics. For the best results, use narrow rather than broad topics. Try these for Chapter 7: Elizabeth I, Thomas Jefferson, Enlightenment, Industrial Revolution. Finding age-appropriate sites is an important consideration when using the Internet. For links to age-appropriate sites in world studies and geography, visit the Prentice Hall Home Page at: **http://www.phschool.com**

CHAPTER 7

Changes in the Western World

Connecting to the Guiding Questions

In this chapter, students will focus on political, scientific, industrial, and philosophical trends in the Western world between the late 1700s and 1900. Content in this chapter corresponds to the following Guiding Questions:

● What accomplishments in technology, learning, or artistic expression were found in each society?

● How did each society's belief system affect its history, government, and economy?

Using the Picture Activities

Have students describe the scene in the picture.

• Encourage students to use vivid language.

• Students' captions should describe the action.

Heterogeneous Groups

The following Teacher's Edition strategies are suitable for heterogeneous groups.

Critical Thinking

Expressing Problems
Clearly   p. 172
Identifying Central
Issues   p. 178
Drawing Conclusions pp. 185,
                            191
Recognizing Cause
and Effect   p. 192

Cooperative Learning

Gravity's Heroes   p. 177
Science Invention Fair   p. 185

Interdisciplinary Connections

Language Arts   pp. 178, 184
Mathematics   p. 190

SECTION 1
Limits on Monarchs

SECTION 2
The Enlightenment

SECTION 3
The Industrial Revolution

SECTION 4
Revolution and Imperialism

PICTURE ACTIVITIES

The picture above shows a group of French citizens storming the Bastille (bas TEEL), a prison in Paris, France. This event, which took place on July 14, 1789, was the first violent act in the revolt that brought down the French monarchy. The period from the late 1700s to 1900 saw many such changes in the Western world. To begin your study of this period, do the following activities.

Study the picture
Look at the Bastille, the large building in the left background of the picture. Write a sentence describing the building.

Describe the action
Write a caption for this picture that describes the action. Which is the group of French citizens? Which is the group of soldiers?

Resource Directory

Media and Technology

Spotlight On: The Industrial Revolution, from the World Video Explorer, enhances students' understanding of the Industrial Revolution and its lasting effects.

Limits on Monarchs

BEFORE YOU READ

Reach Into Your Background

Have you ever heard people talk about having a right to do something? Think about the rights people in the United States have. Which rights do you think are important? How did people get these rights?

Questions to Explore

1. Why was the Elizabethan Age a glorious time for England?
2. How did England turn away from absolute monarchy in the 1600s?

Key Terms

civil war
revolution
bill of rights
constitutional monarchy

Key People

Henry VIII
Elizabeth I
William and Mary

Most kings wanted sons to rule after them. They felt that their kingdoms would be more secure with a male on the throne. That is one reason why King Henry VIII of England married six times. He kept hoping for a son who would be king after him.

Each of Henry's six marriages was made to strengthen his ties to a powerful family. When Henry's first wife, Catherine of Aragon, did not produce a son, Henry decided to divorce her. The Roman Catholic Church did not allow divorce. Nor would the pope give Henry special permission to end his marriage. Henry, therefore, broke away from the Church and started a new Protestant church, the Church of England. He named himself head of the new church. Then he ended his marriage to Catherine.

Henry finally did have a son, Edward, who became king but died at age 16. What happened after Edward's death would probably have amazed Henry. One of Henry's daughters, Elizabeth, became the most powerful and successful ruler England had ever known.

▼ King Henry VIII was ambitious and sometimes cruel. He hated to be refused anything he wanted.

Elizabethan England

When Elizabeth I became queen in 1558, she suddenly found herself in a position of great power. Her grandfather, Henry VII, had ended the battling among

---

Lesson Objectives

1 Describe key features of England's Elizabethan Age and explain why this was a glorious time for England.

2 Identify some important changes that occurred in English government during the 1600s.

Lesson Plan

1 Engage

Warm-Up Activity

Ask students to identify some female leaders, whether local, state, or national. Then ask students whether any country has ever been ruled by a woman. Invite volunteers to tell how they would feel about a female President of the United States.

Activating Prior Knowledge

Have students read Reach Into Your Background in the Before You Read box. Then prompt their thinking with questions such as: Can you say whatever you want in the United States? Are you free to live wherever you choose? Can the government of the United States tell citizens what religion to practice?

Teaching Resources

📁 **Reproducible Lesson Plan** in the Chapter and Section Support booklet, p. 103, provides a summary of the section lesson.

📁 **Guided Reading and Review** in the Chapter and Section Support booklet, p. 104, provides a structure for mastering key concepts and reviewing key terms in the section. Available in Spanish in the Spanish Support booklet, p. 64.

📁 **Critical Thinking Activity** in the Chapter and Section Support booklet,

p. 119, helps students apply the skill of expressing problems clearly.

Program Resources

📁 Material in the **Primary Sources and Literature Readings** booklet extends content with a selection related to the concepts in this chapter.

📁 **Outline Maps** Western Europe: Political, p. 18

2 Explore

As students read, urge them to answer the following questions: Why was the Church of England founded? What were some results of this action? What was Elizabeth I like? How was she different than people had expected her to be? What were the subjects of disagreement between English monarchs and Parliament?

3 Teach

Have students create a series of cause-and-effect cards about the section material. Each card should contain a cause on one side and an effect on the other. Students should note clues on both sides, either in writing or with illustrations. Prompt students to quiz each other with the cards, in groups or individually. This activity should take about 30 minutes.

Answers to ...

ELIZABETH I OF ENGLAND

They would not have children to rule after them and keep their dynasties in power.

READ ACTIVELY

Connect Think of some leaders you admire. What qualities do you admire in them?

the armies of local lords. He had made sure that England's monarch would be more powerful than any of the nobles. Her father's break with the Roman Catholic Church also gave the monarch greater power.

The Young Elizabeth   Like her father, Elizabeth was determined and intelligent. As a young woman, she enjoyed music. She loved horseback riding and other sports. Elizabeth also knew several foreign languages. She spoke French and Italian. She read Greek and Latin. Unlike Henry, however, Elizabeth was fair, and she was grateful to those who helped her. Also unlike her father, who married so often, Elizabeth never married. She knew that if she married she would lose her power to her husband.

Elizabeth was also wise enough to get the support of the English people. After she became queen, she traveled throughout the English countryside. She let her people get to know her, and she got to know them. Her plan to win support from the people was a success. The English people came to love and admire their queen.

Elizabeth ruled for 45 years. Those years made up one of the most glorious periods of England's history.

Elizabeth's Monarchy   Elizabeth continued the work of strengthening England. She did this in two ways. First, she prevented war at home. She cleverly found ways to prevent religious wars between Catholics and Protestants in England. The second thing she did to

Elizabeth I of England

With her red hair, Elizabeth I reminded her people of her father. But she turned out to be a far wiser and stronger ruler than Henry VIII. She cleverly used the possibility of marriage to keep the peace. Her Catholic subjects were loyal because they thought she might marry one of their faith. For the same reason, Catholic rulers in Europe were unwilling to go to war with England. At the same time, her Protestant subjects hoped she would marry a Protestant. **Critical Thinking** Why might it be a disadvantage for rulers not to marry?

Resource Directory

Program Resources

Nystrom Desk Atlas

William Shakespeare and the Globe Theater

Did you know that when you say "catch cold" or "fair play," you are quoting the famous playwright William Shakespeare? During the reign of Elizabeth I, Shakespeare (below) wrote and acted in many plays. His group of actors performed the plays at the Globe, an outdoor theater on the south side of the Thames River in London. In the mid-1990s, a replica of the Globe was built on its original site (left).

strengthen England was to go to war with Spain, a rival European power. When Catholic Spain sent a huge fleet to invade Protestant England, Elizabeth sent out her ships to fight off the Spaniards. After the battle, most of the Spanish ships were destroyed in a terrible storm. England was then left with the most powerful navy in the world.

This strong navy allowed England to become a leader in exploration. Sir Francis Drake, a famous English sea captain, sailed around the world. He also delighted Elizabeth by leading pirate attacks on Spanish ships carrying treasure from the Americas. Another Englishman, Sir Walter Raleigh, set up the first English settlement in North America.

Drake and Raleigh were two among many who added to the glory of the Elizabethan Age. It was a golden age for science, art, and writing. Perhaps the greatest writer in the English language, William Shakespeare, began his career during Elizabeth's rule. His works include such plays as *Hamlet, King Lear, Romeo and Juliet,* and *A Midsummer Night's Dream.*

Conflict Between Monarch and Parliament

Even as Elizabeth worked to increase the strength of England, she understood that her power was not absolute. The Magna Carta had put limits on the powers of English rulers. Shortly before she died, Elizabeth told Parliament, a council that advised the monarch: "Though

The Globe Shakespeare's theater in London was called the Globe. It was 3 stories high and had 20 sides, so it was almost round. Inside, the stage was against one wall. Seats for playgoers ran along the other walls. People also stood in the area in front of the stage. Wealthy young people often paid extra to sit on the stage so everyone could see them. The Globe has been rebuilt on its original site in London so people can experience Shakespeare's plays in their original setting.

4 Assess

See the answers to the Section Review. You may also use students' cause-and-effect cards and quiz performance for assessment.

Acceptable efforts show students' ability to accurately link causes and effects, both in creating cards and answering quiz questions.

Commendable efforts show originality in students' clues.

Outstanding efforts reflect students' understanding of multiple causes and effects.

Background

Links Across Time

Women Leaders   Since the time of Elizabeth I, several women have risen to lead nations. Recent female leaders include Indira Gandhi, prime minister of India (1966–1977 and 1980–1984); Golda Meir, prime minister of Israel (1969–1974); Margaret Thatcher, prime minister of Great Britain (1979–1990); Corazon Aquino, President of the Philippines (1986–1992); and Benazir Bhutto, prime minister of Pakistan (1988–1990 and 1993–1996).

Divine Rulers Some rulers of ancient cultures laid claim to more than divine right. In societies such as ancient Egypt and in the Incan culture, rulers were regarded as divine—they were identified with a particular god or thought of as the actual god. In other cultures, such as Mesopotamia and China, the king was considered a principal agent of the divine and occupied a mediating position between the gods and man. The king was thought to have been enthroned by God for the purpose of carrying out God's will.

Activity

Critical Thinking

Expressing Problems Clearly *Suitable as a whole class activity.* The chain of power in England during the 1600s can be confusing. Help students create a family tree of England's rulers on the chalkboard. Begin with Elizabeth I, inviting students to add branches. Where gaps exist, invite interested students to research the succession. *Visual*

Answers to . . .

A KING CONDEMNED TO DEATH

He had ruled for 11 years without Parliment and thought he ruled by divine right.

Predict What do you think happened in England after Queen Elizabeth's death?

God hath raised me high, yet this I account the glory of any crown, that I have reigned with your loves." Elizabeth knew that she ruled with the approval of Parliament and the people.

Elizabeth died in 1603 without heirs. Her closest living relative was James Stuart, king of Scotland, England's northern neighbor. He was offered the crown and became James I of England. Eventually, England and Scotland were joined as the nation we now call Great Britain.

Civil War Breaks Out James believed that he was king by divine right. That is, his power to rule came from God. He also believed that his power was absolute. For long periods of time, he governed without Parliament. His son, Charles I, continued this practice, ruling without Parliament for 11 years.

When Parliament did meet again, it passed laws to limit Charles's power. Angered by this, Charles tried to arrest Parliament's leaders. As a result, war broke out between the king and Parliament. This was a **civil war,** a battle for power between two groups within one country. The English civil war eventually led to the death of Charles I. He was beheaded in 1649. The war actually was a **revolution,** or a sudden change in the way people think or in the way they are ruled.

A King Condemned to Death

During the English civil war, Charles I was supported by the nobility, upper classes, and the clergy. Against him were Parliament, merchants, and the Puritans—Protestants who wanted to make religion simpler. Here, Charles is shown after being found guilty of treason. Below is Charles's death warrant signed by members of Parliament. **Critical Thinking** Why do you think Charles chose to fight rather than share power with Parliament?

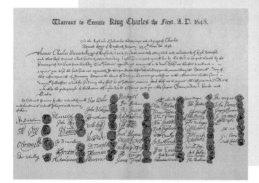

Resource Directory

Teaching Resources

Section Quiz in the Chapter and Section Support booklet, p. 105, covers the main ideas and key terms in the section. Available in Spanish in the Spanish Support booklet, p. 65.

The Monarchy Is Restored

For the next 11 years, Britain was ruled by the people. Then, in 1660, the English brought back the government of kings. The next two monarchs, Charles II and James II, both had disagreements with Parliament. James II also tried to make Britain a Catholic country once again.

Several English leaders looked for a new ruler. They believed that the king had to be Protestant and that he had to respect Parliament. In 1688, they invited the Dutch prince William of Orange "to rescue the nation and the religion." William seemed the obvious choice because his wife was Mary, the daughter of James II. Unlike her father, Mary was a Protestant.

William and Mary's armies quickly drove James out of the country. In what is now called the Glorious Revolution, Parliament officially offered the throne to these new rulers. There was, however, one condition. They had to accept a statement called the Declaration of Rights, which later became the British Bill of Rights. A **bill of rights** is a summary of all the rights held by a people under their government.

Under the English Bill of Rights, all laws had to be approved by Parliament. William and Mary agreed, making Britain a **constitutional monarchy,** a government in which the monarch's power is limited by a set of laws. To this day, Britain remains a constitutional monarchy.

Ruler But Not King

Oliver Cromwell was a leader of Parliament's forces during the civil war. After the war, some of his advisers urged him to take the throne. He refused. Instead, he worked to build a government in which Parliament was supreme. He was a very religious man who believed that everything he did was guided by God. **Critical Thinking** What did Charles I and Cromwell have in common?

SECTION 1 REVIEW

1. Define (a) civil war, (b) revolution, (c) bill of rights, (d) constitutional monarchy.

2. Identify (a) Henry VIII, (b) Elizabeth I, (c) William and Mary.

3. List two accomplishments of Elizabeth I's rule.

4. What brought about the English civil war?

Critical Thinking

5. Identifying Central Issues Why did Parliament insist that William and Mary agree to the Declaration of Rights before allowing them to take the throne?

Activity

6. Writing to Learn Make a list of the rights that you think prevent one person from gaining too much power in the United States.

SKILLS MINI LESSON

Organizing Information

To **introduce** the skill, ask students how they would record information from the section if they were going to write a report on the reign of Elizabeth I. Then draw a circle on the chalkboard with *Elizabeth I* in the center. Explain that a concept map is one way for students to organize information related to a subject, in this case Elizabeth I. To **practice** the skill, invite volunteers to add a ring of secondary circles to the chalkboard map. Each outside circle should contain an important idea or fact about Elizabeth I. Have students **apply** the skill by working in pairs to develop a concept map for England's civil war.

Section 1 Review

1. (a) battle between two groups within one country (b) sudden change in the way people think or are ruled (c) summary of the rights held by a people under their government (d) government in which monarch's power is limited by law

2. (a) king of England who established Church of England (b) powerful and beloved queen of England (c) joint monarchs of England; They ruled under the newly written Bill of Rights, which limited their powers.

3. Possible answers include the prevention of wars between Catholics and Protestants, defeat of Spain, exploration of unknown lands, and patronage of Shakespeare and the arts.

4. Parliament and the monarchy disagreed about how much power each should have.

5. It wanted to be sure that once on the throne, William and Mary did not refuse to accept parliamentary power.

6. Students may note that the United States has no kings, that laws are passed by Congress, and that each branch of government has limited powers.

Answers to ...

RULER BUT NOT KING

Both believed that their actions were the will of God.

Lesson Objectives

1 Trace the origin of changing views about science.

2 Explain the impact of important new ideas on people's views of government.

Lesson Plan

1 Engage

Warm-Up Activity

Tell students that until the 1600s, people based their information of the world on their religious beliefs rather than on scientific evidence. For instance, people might have argued about the number of teeth in a horse's mouth. It was only in the 1600s that people actually thought to open a horse's mouth and count its teeth!

Activating Prior Knowledge

Have students read Reach Into Your Background in the Before You Read box. Then encourage students to share their own experiment experiences. You might also invite a school science teacher to talk about the scientific method.

Activity

Journal Writing

Answering the Church
Have students write a journal entry from Galileo's point of view. Entries should explore his conflict over whether or not to oppose the Church or suppress his beliefs. What might have been Galileo's thoughts and feelings?

The Enlightenment

BEFORE YOU READ

Reach Into Your Background
How do you conduct experiments in science class? You probably try things out, observe what happens, and then note your observations. In this section, you'll learn when and how this way of studying science developed.

Questions to Explore
1. How did new ways of thinking change how people approached science?
2. How did new ways of thinking change how people looked at their governments?

Key Terms
Enlightenment
scientific method
natural law
colony

Key People
Galileo Galilei
Isaac Newton
John Locke
Thomas Jefferson

▼ The Italian scientist Galileo was the first person to study the sky through a telescope.

The whole room was silent. Members of the court leaned forward, waiting for Galileo Galilei (gal uh LAY oh gal uh LAY ee) to respond to the question. Did the great Italian scientist really believe that the Earth moved around the sun?

This was an important question in 1633. The Roman Catholic Church taught that God had made the Earth the center of the universe. If that was true, everything—sun, planets, and stars—moved around the Earth. In the 1500s, a Polish astronomer, Nicolaus Copernicus (koh PUR nuh kuhs), had claimed that this was wrong. He had said that the Earth moved around the sun.

Galileo had quietly supported the ideas of Copernicus. Now the Church court was asking Galileo what he really believed. He knew that he could be put to death if he disagreed with the Church. So he told the court that, in fact, the Earth did not move. He did not say what he truly believed.

As Galileo was being led away, he is said to have muttered something to himself about the Earth. "Nevertheless, it does move," he said.

The Age of Reason

The **Enlightenment** was a period of revolution, a time that saw a major shift in the way people thought. People of the Enlightenment had great confidence in the power of reason. They used reason to shine a new "light" on traditional ideas and

Resource Directory

Teaching Resources

📁 **Reproducible Lesson Plan** in the Chapter and Section Support booklet, p. 106, provides a summary of the section lesson.

📁 **Guided Reading and Review** in the Chapter and Section Support booklet, p. 107, provides a structure for mastering key concepts and reviewing key terms in the section. Available in Spanish in the Spanish Support booklet, p. 66.

redefined their society. The Enlightenment affected politics, art, literature, science, and religion. Many of the new ways of thinking can be traced to the Scientific Revolution of the 1500s and 1600s.

The Scientific Revolution   For hundreds of years, people made their ideas about science fit their religious beliefs. During the Renaissance this began to change. Scientists like Copernicus and Galileo began to look at how the universe really worked. They observed things first, and then drew conclusions based on what they had seen. They used reason to explain the physical world around them.

Galileo's observations led him to new thoughts about objects and the speed at which they fall. You might think that heavier objects fall faster than lighter ones. However, that is not true. Galileo proved that objects fall at the same speed. According to legend, he dropped a light object and a heavy object from a tower at the same time. They landed in the same instant. His observations led him to realize that the old ideas about falling objects were wrong.

He also used a new scientific tool, the telescope, to examine planets. He eventually proved that the Earth was not the center of the universe. For him, observation was more important than old ideas that fit with traditional beliefs.

READ ACTIVELY

Visualize Visualize someone dropping a tennis ball and a bowling ball from the top of a tower, both at the same time. Will the two objects land at the same time? Why or why not?

A New View of the Universe

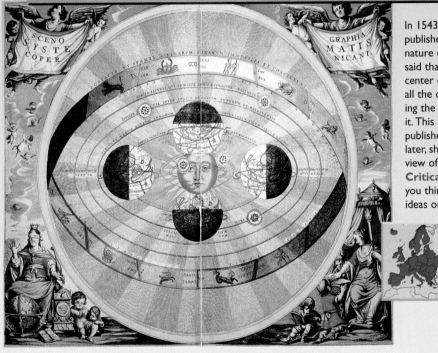

In 1543, Copernicus published his ideas on the nature of the universe. He said that the sun was the center of the universe and all the other planets, including the Earth, moved around it. This map, which was published nearly 120 years later, shows the Copernican view of the universe.
Critical Thinking Why do you think that Copernicus' ideas on the universe were referred to as the Copernican Revolution?

2 Explore

Prompt students to consider the following questions as they read: How did people view science before the Renaissance? How did these views change during the Enlightenment? What kinds of discoveries were made by scientists during the Enlightenment? How did the American colonies test John Locke's ideas? What was England's response?

Background

Biography

Earth Mover   Galileo Galilei (1564–1642) was the first human to study the skies with a telescope. He was the first person to observe that the surface of the moon was irregular, that the Milky Way was a collection of stars, and that Jupiter was surrounded by several moons. His continued efforts to support the sun-centered model of the universe led to censure by the Church and house arrest. During the last years of his life, blind and under house arrest, he continued to work. One of his last accomplishments was to determine how to use a pendulum to regulate the motion of a clock.

Answers to . . .

A NEW VIEW OF THE UNIVERSE

Copernicus' ideas were revolutionary, that is, they represented a major shift in thinking.

3 Teach

Have students complete a three-column chart similar to the following:

Before the Enlightenment	After the Enlightenment	Examples

Students should record important ideas about science and government, as well as specific examples of both new and old ideas, as they read the section. Students may highlight examples they think are important if they can support their choices. This activity should take about 15 minutes.

4 Assess

See the answers to the Section Review. You may also use students' charts for assessment.

Acceptable charts contain at least two accurate definitions and examples in each column.

Commendable charts support examples with persuasive arguments.

Outstanding charts recognize the tremendous importance of the new ideas generated during the Enlightenment.

Answers to ...
CHART STUDY

that the scientific advancements made by one person help the next person make even further advancements

---

Achievements of the Scientific Revolution

Chart Study Many of the scientists listed here met with opposition when they first published their new ideas. Copernicus, for example, was accused of destroying "the whole art of astronomy." Later scientists, however, understood the importance of these contributions. Isaac Newton commented: "If I have seen farther than others, it is because I have stood on the shoulders of giants." **Critical Thinking** What do you think Newton meant by this statement?

Discipline	Date	Contributions
Medicine	1543	Andreas Vesalius published *On the Structure of the Human Body.* His book gave the world the first accurate descriptions of the human body.
	1628	William Harvey described how blood circulates through the body. He was the first physician to use medical experiments.
Chemistry	mid- to late 1600s	Robert Boyle described the basic makeup of all matter. For centuries, people had believed that matter was made up of earth, water, air, and fire.
Astronomy	1543	Nicolaus Copernicus shocked Europe by saying that the Earth and other planets moved around the sun. Until that time, people had believed that the sun, stars, and planets circled the Earth.
Scientific Thought	early 1600s	Philosophers offered new ways to study the world. Francis Bacon stressed the importance of experiment and observation. René Descartes believed that human reasoning leads to understanding.

The Scientific Method   Galileo and other scientists of the Renaissance were developing a new way of learning about the world. Today, it is called the scientific method. In this approach, scientists perform experiments under conditions they control. Then, the scientists record what they have seen. Next, they examine their results. Finally, they decide what the facts are, based on what they have seen. If an experiment is done well, other scientists will be able to do it and get the same results.

New Political Ideas

The ideas of the English scientist Isaac Newton led other thinkers to apply reason to the laws governing society. In the late 1600s, Newton began to ask bold new questions. What, he asked, caused the planets to circle the sun? Studying such questions led Newton to realize that there are natural laws, or forces that rule the behavior of the universe. Newton's observations led him to develop laws of motion and of gravity. He was able to describe these laws using mathematics.

Another Englishman, John Locke, questioned the way society and government worked. Locke looked at human society and tried to figure out its natural laws. In other words, he applied Newton's ideas to society.

A New View of Government Locke and other thinkers came to believe that there are, indeed, natural laws that govern human behavior. Government, they said, should be based on these natural laws. Locke argued that nature had meant human beings to be free. In other words, people had the right to be free. They also had the right to live and the right to own property. If a government took these rights away, it was not acting properly.

Locke went even further. He said that government was based on an agreement between rulers and the people. Rulers should rule only as long as they have the support of the people. If a ruler were to break the agreement by taking away people's rights, people had a right to change the government.

The Impact of Locke's Ideas These were startling ideas. Locke was saying that rulers like those of France, Spain, and Russia should not have absolute, or total, power. Instead, he suggested, rulers had responsibilities toward those they ruled. This was shocking to people who thought that kings ruled by divine right.

People in many countries read books, pamphlets, and newspapers about the new ideas. They began to wonder whether their governments were acting as they should.

READ ACTIVELY

Predict How do you think John Locke's ideas affected the history of the United States?

A Coffee-House Speech

Coffee came to Europe from Southwest Asia in the 1500s. By the mid-1600s, coffee houses had grown up all over London. Over a cup of coffee, customers picked up the news of the day or made business deals. They also took part in lively discussions on politics and new ideas. In this picture of a London coffee house, the central figure is giving a speech to his fellow customers. **Critical Thinking** How would you describe the reactions of the speaker's audience?

Activity

Cooperative Learning

Gravity's Heroes Suggest that students work in groups of four to explore how the work of Isaac Newton and Johannes Kepler affected our present-day view of the solar system. Encourage students to find out what discoveries these scientists made and which universal scientific principles apply to their work. Have students present their findings as a mobile model of the solar system. Encourage students to assign group members roles such as researcher, artist, model maker, and writer/narrator. *Visual, Kinesthetic*

SKILLS MINI LESSON

Recognizing Bias
To **introduce** the skill, ask students whether they think scientists prior to the Enlightenment studied all evidence equally. Then write the term *bias* on the board with its definition: *to lean to a particular point of view.* Have students **practice** the skill by noting on paper the beliefs of Galileo and the Roman Catholic Church about the structure of the universe. Help students see that the Church left out, or would not consider, any evidence about the Earth's placement in that structure that opposed its own view of the universe. Its bias, or attitude, toward other evidence was to suppress it. Students may **apply** the skill by writing a brief paragraph explaining how bias could adversely affect scientific experiments.

Answers to . . .
A COFFEE-HOUSE SPEECH

Some seem interested, others seem preoccupied.

Activity

Critical Thinking

Identifying Central Issues
Suitable as a whole class activity. Organize students into teams to debate the issue of taxation without representation. Urge teams to present their views through the eyes of either the taxed colonists or members of Britain's Parliament.
Auditory

Activity

Interdisciplinary Connections

Language Arts Tell students that there were many speakers and writers who helped forge American ideas about independence. Urge students to find and read writings by one of the following: Samuel Adams, Thomas Paine, or Patrick Henry. In character, have students present a speech or read an essay. Together, identify language that is especially inspiring, and discuss the power of language to persuade people to act. *Auditory, English Language Learners*

▼ Thomas Jefferson (top) wrote the Declaration of Independence (bottom). In the Declaration, he stated that all people had certain rights— "life, liberty, and the pursuit of happiness"—that no government could take away.

Natural Rights in the American Colonies

People in Great Britain's colonies in North America were especially worried about government. A **colony** is a territory ruled by another nation, usually one far away. By the 1750s, these settlements were thriving communities that stretched from Georgia to New Hampshire. The British were finding that it was very expensive to protect their faraway colonies. To help pay for the defense of the colonies, the British wanted to collect taxes from the American colonists.

No Taxation Without Representation Under British law, people could not be taxed unless their representatives had voted for the tax in Parliament. The colonists had no representatives in Parliament. How could it be fair, they asked, to make them pay taxes when they had no way of voting for or against a tax? Did this not mean that the British government was taking away their rights?

As American colonists protested, people in Britain grew worried. They felt that they were losing control of the colonies. They approved more taxes and stricter laws. Americans grew angrier. Leaders like Thomas Jefferson and Benjamin Franklin, who admired the ideas of John Locke, began to think about rebelling. The colonists began to gather weapons and ammunition.

On April 19, 1775, British soldiers marched into Lexington and Concord, towns outside Boston, Massachusetts. Their job was to take weapons and ammunition away from the Americans. The Americans, however, fought back.

The Colonies Declare Their Independence The American Revolution began at Lexington and Concord. In 1776, during the course of the revolt, the Americans declared their independence from Britain.

Thomas Jefferson wrote a document called the Declaration of Independence to explain why the American colonists had rebelled. Jefferson based many of his ideas on those of John Locke. According to Jefferson, governments had power only because the people agreed that they did. He claimed that if a government starts taking away people's rights, the people have a right to change

Resource Directory

Teaching Resources

📁 **Learning More About a Topic** in the Social Studies and Geography Skills booklet, p. 76, provides additional skill practice.

Washington at Yorktown

Here, General George Washington lights a cannon to fire the first shot at the Battle of Yorktown. The American victory at Yorktown marked the end of the Revolutionary War. Washington led the colonial army from 1775 until the end of the war. He was elected the first President of the United States in 1789. **Critical Thinking** Why do you think people elect successful generals to important political offices?

the government or put an end to it. Thus, he said, the colonies had the right to rebel against Great Britain. Putting Jefferson's ideas into effect, however, took a long time.

The colonies had to fight Britain for their freedom. At first, it seemed that they would never win. Then, in 1778, the French came to the aid of the colonists. The colonial army, along with the French army and navy, forced the British to surrender at Yorktown, Virginia, in 1781. The United States of America had won its freedom.

SECTION 2 REVIEW

1. **Define** (a) Enlightenment, (b) scientific method, (c) natural law, (d) colony.

2. **Identify** (a) Galileo Galilei, (b) Isaac Newton, (c) John Locke, (d) Thomas Jefferson.

3. What did Galileo discover about falling objects and about the planets?

4. According to John Locke, when do people have the right to rebel against their government?

Critical Thinking

5. **Making Comparisons** How were the ideas of Isaac Newton and John Locke similar?

Activity

6. **Writing to Learn** Write a declaration in which you list what you think are the basic rights of all people.

Teaching Resources

📁 **Section Quiz** in the Chapter and Section Support booklet, p. 108, covers the main ideas and key terms in the section. Available in Spanish in the Spanish Support booklet, p. 67.

Section 2 Review

1. (a) period of revolution in thought (b) experimentation under controlled conditions with conclusions based on recorded observations (c) patterns in the behavior of the universe (d) territory ruled by another nation

2. (a) Italian scientist who declared that the Earth moved around the sun (b) English scientist who described natural laws using mathematics (c) English thinker who argued that humans have certain basic rights (d) American colonist who used John Locke's ideas to argue for independence from Britain

3. He discovered that objects fall at the same rate, no matter what their weight, and that the planets, including the Earth, move around the sun.

4. Locke believed that government may exist only with the consent of the governed. If the government breaks the agreement, the people have the right to change the government.

5. Both believed that behavior followed natural laws.

6. Declarations should be logically organized and clearly explain each basic right.

Answers to ...

WASHINGTON AT YORKTOWN

because they want a strong leader in case they are involved in a war and because they thought that a person who could wage wars successfully could also govern successfully

SKILLS ACTIVITY

Interpreting Line Graphs

1 Engage

Warm-Up Activity

To **introduce** the skill, have students read the opening paragraphs silently. Ask students if they have ever faced a problem like Steve's and what solutions they could offer to him. Write the term *graph* on the chalkboard.

Activating Prior Knowledge

Invite students to name different kinds of graphs. Then ask them to describe a line graph, noting as many of its elements as possible. You may want to have a volunteer draw a line graph on the chalkboard.

2 Explore

Direct students to read the paragraph under Get Ready. Then ask them to compare the text description of a line graph (a graph using lines to show amounts and how they change over time) with their earlier descriptions and drawings. Direct students to read the rest of the Skills Activity.

Steve had worked hard on his report about Dallas, Texas. He had almost finished writing, and he had two days to hand it in. But the paragraph about the population growth of Dallas still worried him. Each time he tried to write about the number of people living in Dallas at different times in the city's history, it sounded too confusing. One number followed the other in a jumble. He thought about ways to show the population growth in a graph or a diagram.

"I could provide a population map of the city for each decade, but that's too many different maps," Steve thought. "I could make a table showing the population every 10 years, but that wouldn't show the changes at a glance. I need a good graph that will show growth over time."

Get Ready

Graphs are extremely helpful because they show a large amount of information in a simple, easy-to-read way. One of the most common types of graph is the line graph. Line graphs use lines to show amounts. Line graphs are the best graphs to use to show changes in amounts over time.

Try It Out

The graph below is a line graph. You can read, or interpret, it by following these simple steps.

A. Read the title. The title tells you what the line graph is about.

B. Read the labels on the axes. A line graph has two axes. The vertical axis runs up and down. What does this one show? How is it divided? The horizontal axis runs across. This one shows time in years.

C. Read the line. The line on the line graph shows how the amounts given on the vertical axis change over time. What trend, or general change, is shown by the line?

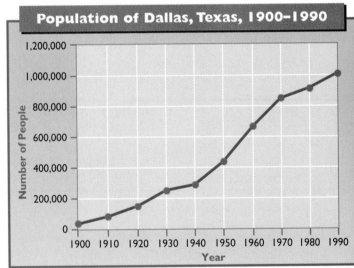

Population of Dallas, Texas, 1900–1990

Teaching Resources

📁 **Reading a Line Graph** in the Social Studies and Geography Skills booklet, p. 54, provides additional skill practice.

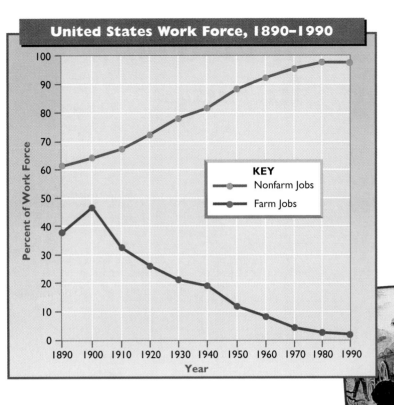

United States Work Force, 1890–1990

KEY
— Nonfarm Jobs
— Farm Jobs

Apply the Skill

The line graph above has two lines instead of one. But it works the same way, and you can apply the same steps to read it.

1 Read the title. What is this line graph about?

2 Read the labels on the axes. What does the vertical axis show? What does the horizontal axis show? How many years are covered by the graph?

3 Read the lines. What does the green line stand for? What does the purple line stand for? What percentage of the work force had farm jobs in 1890? What percentage of the work force had nonfarm jobs in this same year? What percentage of workers had farm jobs in 1990? What percentage of workers had nonfarm jobs in 1990?

4 Summarize the data. Writing a summary is a good way to show that you understand a graph. Write two or three sentences that summarize the changes in the work force between 1890 and 1990.

3 Teach

To **practice** the skill, have students read the Try It Out directions and answer the questions. Monitor students' progress, inviting volunteers to address any points of confusion to the class for clarification.

For additional reinforcement, ask students to add a second line to the graph. You may provide or have students locate the data about population growth in another United States city.

4 Assess

Ask students to **apply** the skill by reading the line graph in the final activity section. To **assess**, pair students with peer evaluators who will note correct and incorrect answers to the activity questions. You might also read students' summaries for evidence of accuracy and comprehension.

Answers to . . .

TRY IT OUT

A. Population of Dallas, Texas, 1900–1990
B. number of people; into equal parts, each representing 200,000 people
C. Since 1940 the population of Dallas, Texas, has steadily increased.

APPLY THE SKILL

1. United States Work Force 1890–1990
2. percent of work force; the time in ten-year intervals; 100
3. The top line stands for nonfarm jobs, the bottom line stands for farm jobs.; about 38 percent; about 62 percent; about 2 percent; about 98 percent

SECTION
3

The Industrial Revolution

Lesson Objectives

1. Describe how the Industrial Revolution changed the way people earned a living.

2. Identify some problems that resulted from the Industrial Revolution.

Lesson Plan

1 Engage

Warm-Up Activity

Show students a hand-knit sweater or scarf. Then offer a machine-knit garment for comparison. Urge students to examine each garment and describe the differences.

Activating Prior Knowledge

Have students read Reach Into Your Background in the Before You Read box. Then suggest that they note each time they use a machine (for example, a school bus, a microwave oven, or a computer) during the school day. Urge students to estimate the amount of time each task took using a machine and how long it might have taken to complete by hand. Have students note which tasks they could not have accomplished without the aid of a machine.

BEFORE YOU READ

Reach Into Your Background
You are surrounded by machines—cars, computers, telephones, television sets, and more. How do these machines influence your life? What would your life be like without them?

Questions to Explore
1. How did the Industrial Revolution change the way people earned a living?
2. What problems arose as a result of the Industrial Revolution?

Key Terms
Industrial Revolution
textile
labor union

Key People
Alexander Graham Bell
Thomas Edison

▼ Fountains of sparks stream from a modern steel furnace. The Industrial Revolution of the 1700s changed forever the way goods are produced.

"The thunder of the blast deafens you," wrote a visitor to an American factory around 1900. "The ever-brightening flame, flashing up finally as high as fifty feet, blinds you; sparks fall everywhere." Another described "the rumbling growl of rollers, the howls of horrible saws . . . the crashing thunder of falling iron plate, the hoarse coughing of great engines, and the hissing of steam."

What an awful place to work! But it was also an exciting place because a revolution was going on in factories all across Europe and North America. This revolution continues today.

A New Kind of Revolution

The thunder and flames of the factories were all part of the **Industrial Revolution**. This was a period of time during which the production of goods shifted from simple hand tools to complex machines. People's lives changed a great deal. This change started in the 1760s, when industry began to grow rapidly.

Several factors made this possible. Trade from Britain's growing empire helped the economy grow rapidly. The British government supported this economic growth by building a

Resource Directory

Teaching Resources

📁 **Reproducible Lesson Plan** in the Chapter and Section Support booklet, p. 109, provides a summary of the section lesson.

📁 **Guided Reading and Review** in the Chapter and Section Support booklet, p. 110, provides a structure for mastering key concepts and reviewing key terms in the section. Available in Spanish in the Spanish Support booklet, p. 68.

strong navy to protect the empire and overseas trade. Businesspeople became wealthy from trade. Therefore, they had money to spend on new ventures such as factories. To support trade, people thought of new ways to make goods quickly and cheaply using machines. They also invented new ways to provide power for all the added machines. The Industrial Revolution changed the ways in which people today work, shop, and spend their free time.

The Industrial Revolution Begins The Industrial Revolution began in Great Britain in the 1760s. The textile, or cloth, business was one of the first to move into factories. Before the 1760s, cloth was made mostly by people working in their homes. People sheared wool from sheep, spun yarn, and wove cloth on a part-time basis. In some ways, this was good. Workers could be with their families and care for their children. It did, however, take a long time to make each piece of cloth. Textiles were expensive. Only the very wealthy had more than one change of clothes. Curtains, tablecloths, and other household items made of cloth were luxuries.

The invention of several machines made it possible to make cloth more cheaply. For example, people had spun fibers into thread using a wheel on a frame. A new invention, the spinning jenny, let each worker spin several bunches of thread at the same time. One worker using a spinning jenny could do the work of eight people using spinning wheels.

The Spindle How did people make thread before there were spinning wheels? People in ancient Egypt, India, and South America used spindles that were long smooth sticks weighted on one end. The spinner started with a mass of short fibers, such as wool. Next, the spinner pulled fibers out and twisted them together. The spinner attached one end of the twisted fibers to the spindle, and twirled the spindle like a top to twist the thread. Finally, the spinner attached the thread to a notch in the spindle and started over.

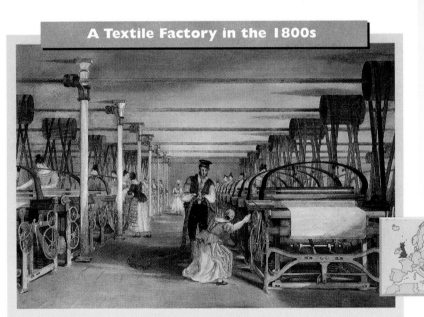

A Textile Factory in the 1800s

Many of the workers in textile factories were women, like the weavers shown here. Factory owners often preferred women, because they could pay women lower wages for doing the same work as men. **Critical Thinking** What kind of job do you think the man in the center of the picture holds? Explain your answer.

Media and Technology

Color Transparencies 144, 147, Historical Map Set 8

2 Explore
Suggest that students keep the following questions in mind as they read: What was life like for most people before the Industrial Revolution? How did the Industrial Revolution change workers' lives? How do you think people felt about the changes in their lives? What were some ways people responded to the changes?

3 Teach
Have students develop a mock slide show about the Industrial Revolution. In the absence of actual slides, students may use photocopied artwork from the text or create their own artwork. Students should write explanatory text to accompany the visual elements. This activity should take about 30 minutes.

4 Assess
See the answers to the Section Review. You may also use students' slide shows for assessment.

Acceptable slide shows include at least five images that represent key section concepts.

Commendable slide shows should include text that recognizes both positive and negative effects of the Industrial Revolution.

Outstanding slide shows reflect creativity and originality in both visual and written elements.

Answers to ...
A TEXTILE FACTORY IN THE 1800S

He is probably a "boss" or manager, since men held such positions of power.

Activity

Interdisciplinary Connections

Language Arts Encourage students to investigate the work of inventors such as Jan E. Matzeliger, Cyrus H. McCormick, Lewis H. Latimer, Elijah McCoy, Norbert Rillieux, Alexander Graham Bell, Granville T. Woods, Henry Ford, or another inventor of their choosing. Have students prepare a one-minute advertisement for the invention. Advertisements should tell what the invention does and what improvements it offers over previous devices.
Kinesthetic, Auditory

Background

Global Perspective

Cotton Production By 1800, England's textile mills were producing 100,000 bales of cotton textiles a year. They needed raw materials badly. The 1793 invention of the cotton gin allowed plantations in the southern United States to rise to the challenge. By 1859, English mill production was up to 4.5 million bales of cotton textiles a year. Meanwhile, United States production of cotton skyrocketed from 3,000 bales in 1790 to 3.8 million bales in 1860.

Answers to ...

THE WIZARD OF MENLO PARK

enormous; Students might also suggest that if Edison had not invented the items, someone else would have.

Connect Think of some ways in which the Industrial Revolution has made your life easier.

The new textile machines, which spun thread and wove cloth, were so big and so fast that they needed more power than a human could supply. People came up with ways to use flowing water to supply power. They dammed rivers and built mills using water wheels. Later, steam engines were used to supply power. The machines had to be housed in one large building, a factory. This meant that people who wanted to work had to leave their homes and families and go to the factories.

The Industrial Revolution Grows Spinning and weaving machines powered by water were among the first inventions of the Industrial Revolution. Steam engines also provided power for textile machines. Soon other industrial inventions took advantage of the new power supply. Mighty steam-driven hammers forged iron parts. Drills and cutters made screws, rods, and other metal parts for farm machines, guns, railroad cars, and engines.

The new inventions made other developments possible. Steel girders could support taller buildings. Trains traveling on steel rails moved people and goods more quickly and cheaply.

New inventions also made the daily life of the average person easier. Inventors like Alexander Graham Bell and Thomas Edison used the power of electricity to create machines that revolutionized everyday life. Bell invented the telephone. Edison invented the phonograph, an early type of sound system. Later, he patented the electric lightbulb and developed a system to provide whole communities with electricity.

The Wizard of Menlo Park

In the 1870s, Thomas Edison set up a laboratory in Menlo Park, New Jersey. There, he and a team of scientists produced dozens of inventions, such as the electric lightbulb, the motion-picture camera, the microphone, and the phonographs shown above. People were so amazed with Edison's work that they called him "the wizard of Menlo Park."
Critical Thinking What impact do you think Edison's inventions had on everyday life?

A London Department Store

The new department stores that opened in the late 1800s changed the way people shopped. Now, people could buy many different kinds of goods, from children's toys to furniture, under one roof. These stores also provided new job opportunities for store managers and shop clerks. This picture shows the busy food section of a London department store.

The Industrial Revolution also created new jobs. Managers were needed to run the factories. Merchants were needed to sell the goods made in the factories. The new jobs presented opportunities that allowed more people to move into the middle class of society—the group of people between the poor and the rich. More people than ever before were able to have comfortable lives.

The Problems of the Industrial Revolution

But not everyone had a better life. Many poor people's lives became harder during the Industrial Revolution. Farmworkers lost jobs to powerful machinery. Many farmers lost their land because they could not compete with wealthier farmers who were able to buy these expensive new machines. In Europe, many people left their homes hoping to make better lives for themselves across the ocean. Some went to the United States. They often found work in American factories. Others went to Canada, South America, Australia, or New Zealand.

Activity

Cooperative Learning

Science Invention Fair
Organize students into teams of three to develop exhibits for an invention fair. Each team should focus on an invention—successful or not—of the Industrial Revolution. Exhibits may include illustrations or working models of inventions. Within each team, students should divide tasks such as research, material gathering, and planning. Have teams send a representative to join an oversight committee responsible for planning the fair's structure and schedule. Open the fair to the school and community if possible. *Visual, Kinesthetic, English Language Learners*

Activity

Critical Thinking

Drawing Conclusions
Suitable as a whole class activity. Show students a physical map of Europe. Then invite volunteers in turn to suggest possible locations for early factories, using the information in the section as a clue. (They were near rivers, such as the Ruhr in Germany.) *Kinesthetic, Visual*

Biography

Jacob Riis In 1870, Jacob Riis came to the United States from his native Denmark. Once homeless and sleeping in barns and alleys, Riis eventually secured work as a reporter for the New York *Tribune* and *Evening Sun*. Contrary to the norm of the day, Riis did not merely rewrite police reports, he investigated his articles. Horrified by the conditions in industrial cities, Riis became a social reformer, writing books and taking arresting photographs about urban poverty. He used flashbulbs—just invented—to capture the dark insides of tenement buildings and bring the enormity of human suffering out into the light. Born in 1849, Jacob Riis died in 1914.

LINKS ACROSS TIME

Industrialization and Cities When Europe became industrialized, masses of people moved to the cities. From 1820 to 1900, London's population grew by more than 6 million. Paris's population grew by about 4.5 million between 1850 and 1930. Today, developing countries like Brazil are becoming industrialized. Again people are on the move. In 1991, the population of São Paulo, Brazil, was 9.6 million. By 2015, population experts say the population will be about 21 million.

A Factory Worker's Life As more and more goods were made in factories, people had to move to cities to earn a living. They were no longer able to work at home at their own pace. Instead, many had to work 12 or more hours a day in the factory. They had few, if any, breaks.

Factories were noisy and dirty. Machines were often dangerous, and people were sometimes injured or killed. Factory workers were poorly paid. Often parents had to put their children to work so that the family could earn enough money to live. For many, life was nothing but endless work.

Workers lived in small, cramped quarters. Soot from smokestacks and trains covered everything, even indoors. The soot made it hard to keep anything clean. Often people in many different houses or apartments shared a single bathroom. Or they had no indoor plumbing at all. Many had to carry water in buckets from the nearest well or stream.

Garbage piled up in the streets. This attracted rats and packs of dogs. Dyes and dust from textile mills poisoned the air and water. Diseases swept easily through such cities. Many people died of cholera and typhus. Even minor diseases could be fatal under such conditions.

A London Street Scene

This drawing of a street in London's East End district was made in 1872. It shows the problems most working people faced in their everyday lives—poor housing, overcrowding, and pollution.

Resource Directory

Program Resources

📁 **Environmental and Global Issues**
Topic: Urbanization, pp. 54–58

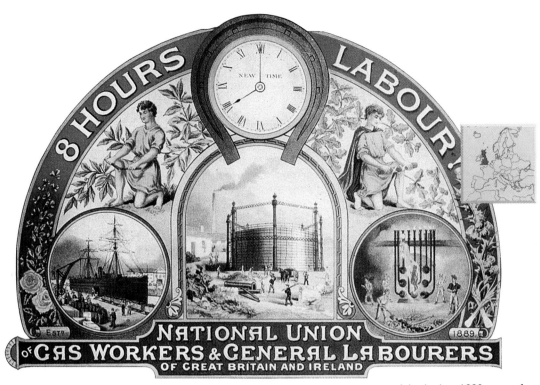

Workers Fight Back   As the Industrial Revolution went on, some workers formed **labor unions.** These were organizations that helped workers improve their pay and working conditions. At first, governments passed laws to keep the unions from becoming powerful. Over time, however, labor unions were accepted. Unions won shorter hours, better pay, and safer working conditions for their members and for other workers.

▲ In the late 1880s, one of the major campaigns of labor unions was for an eight-hour working day, as this British union membership card shows. Most workers did not achieve this goal until the early 1900s.

SECTION 3 REVIEW

1. **Define** (a) Industrial Revolution, (b) textile, (c) labor union.

2. **Identify** (a) Alexander Graham Bell, (b) Thomas Edison.

3. Why did so many people move from the country to cities during the Industrial Revolution?

4. Why did workers join together to form labor unions?

Critical Thinking

5. **Identifying Central Issues** Do you agree or disagree with the following statement: "The Industrial Revolution has improved human life"? Explain your answer.

Activity

6. **Writing to Learn** You are working in a textile mill during the late 1700s. Write a journal entry describing your work day.

Section 3 Review

1. (a) period of time in which production of goods changed from simple hand tools to complex machines (b) cloth (c) organization that helped workers improve pay and conditions

2. (a) inventor of the telephone (b) invented the phonograph; patented the electric light bulb and developed electric systems

3. Students' responses will vary, but should indicate that they moved to take advantage of factory jobs and because machines had replaced them in agricultural work.

4. They wanted to improve both working conditions and pay rates.

5. Students agreeing may cite easier living through labor-saving devices and new jobs. Those disagreeing may cite pollution and other urban problems and job or land loss. Opinions should be clearly stated and well supported.

6. Entries should use vivid language to capture the sights, sounds, smells, and other experiences of a textile mill. Both the challenge and the danger should be reflected.

Teaching Resources

📁 **Section Quiz** in the Chapter and Section Support booklet, p. 111, covers the main ideas and key terms in the section. Available in Spanish in the Spanish Support booklet, p. 69.

Section 4

Lesson Objectives

① Explain some ways that Napoleon changed France.

② Trace efforts by European powers to build empires in the late 1800s.

Lesson Plan

1 Engage

Warm-Up Activity

Ask students to tell what they think are the best qualities of the United States government and way of life. Then ask students what they think are weaknesses of the United States government and way of life. Challenge students to think about ways they can preserve the qualities they admire or change those they consider weaknesses.

Activating Prior Knowledge

Have students read Reach Into Your Background in the Before You Read box. Note friends, older relatives, coaches, or teachers as possible subjects. Then suggest that students explore their feelings in a journal entry.

SECTION 4
Revolution and Imperialism

BEFORE YOU READ

Reach Into Your Background
Have you ever admired someone so much that you thought he or she could do no wrong? How did you feel when you realized that the person had faults, just like other people?

Questions to Explore
1. What changes did Napoleon bring to France?
2. Where and why did European powers seek to build empires in the late 1800s?

Key Terms
Reign of Terror
Napoleonic Code
nationalism
imperialism

Key People and Places
Maximilien Robespierre
Napoleon Bonaparte
Waterloo

▼ Women played an important role in the French Revolution. These poor women of Paris marched to the king's palace at Versailles to demand bread for their hungry children.

Famine gripped Paris in 1789. Thousands of people suffered because there was not enough food. Angry mobs gathered in the streets to protest. On October 5 of that year, thousands of women marched the 12 miles (19 km) from Paris to Versailles. Even though it was raining heavily, they were determined to see the king. They wanted him to come back to Paris so that he could no longer ignore the people's suffering.

The military was eventually able to control the large crowd. Still, the women would not leave without the king. Eventually, King Louis XVI agreed to return to Paris with the crowd. The royal family moved back to Paris. For the next three years, Louis and his family were practically prisoners in their palace in France's capital.

The French Revolution

What had brought the people of France to this situation? What factors led to the French Revolution?

King Louis XVI of France had helped the American colonists win their freedom from the British. Yet he was no great friend of liberty. He had helped because he wanted to reduce the power of the British. The Americans appreciated the help. The French people did not. They had to pay heavy taxes to support the army.

Resource Directory

Teaching Resources

📁 **Reproducible Lesson Plan** in the Chapter and Section Support booklet, p. 112, provides a summary of the section lesson.

📁 **Guided Reading and Review** in the Chapter and Section Support booklet, p. 113, provides a structure for mastering key concepts and reviewing key terms in the section. Available in Spanish in the Spanish Support booklet, p. 70.

Program Resources

📁 **Outline Maps** Western Europe: Political, p. 18; North Africa: Political, p. 31; Africa: Political, p. 33

📁 **Environmental and Global Issues** Topic: Conflict, pp. 37–42

France's Problems France had always had tax problems. Under the French political system, only the working people paid taxes. The nobles and clergy, or church officials, paid nothing. The most successful merchants also found ways to avoid taxes. Thus it was the poorest people who carried the heaviest burden.

As France's money problems grew worse, taxes rose. Louis XVI was unable to solve these problems. The French began to demand that Louis share power. They used the arguments of Enlightenment thinkers to support their demands.

Then came the winter of 1788–1789. It was the worst winter in nearly 100 years. Crops were destroyed. Eighteen million people were starving. Riots broke out. Finally, in May 1789, the king called a meeting of representatives of the three estates, or divisions, of French society—the nobles, the clergy, and the middle class. These representatives formed a National Assembly that wrote a constitution, a plan for a government. France, like England, became a limited monarchy. This marked the beginning of the French Revolution.

When Terror Ruled The king of France had relatives in Austria and Prussia, a state in what is now Germany. They were absolute monarchs. They were afraid that if Louis' power was destroyed, theirs might be too. They sent armies to invade France to help the king. The French Assembly declared war on these foreign powers. When the war began to go badly for France, crowds of French citizens began to riot.

READ ACTIVELY

Ask Questions What questions about the French Revolution would you like to have answered?

The Tennis Court Oath

Louis XVI tried to prevent the National Assembly from writing a new constitution by locking them out of their meeting rooms. However, they gathered in an indoor tennis court. There, they took an oath not to disband until they had written the constitution. This painting of the Tennis Court Oath is by Jacques-Louis David, the most famous French artist of the revolutionary years.

2 Explore

Work with students to answer the following questions: What was life like for the French people under the rule of Louis XVI? How did they feel about their situation, and what actions did they take to change or preserve it? What were some of Napoleon's goals as emperor? How did other nations respond to his efforts? Why might imperialism lead to conflicts or war?

3 Teach

Have students create an annotated time line of section events. Annotations should link events and explain their relationship to key section concepts. Students may draw conclusions if these are supported by facts from the text. This activity should take about 20 minutes.

4 Assess

See the answers to the Section Review. You may also use students' time lines for assessment.

Acceptable time lines include at least six entries in correct sequence with accurate explanations.

Commendable time lines include students' conclusions supported by section facts.

Outstanding time lines recognize that great leaders effect both positive and negative changes.

Teaching Resources

Identifying Alternatives in the Social Studies and Geography Skills booklet, p. 51, provides additional skill practice.

Media and Technology

Color Transparency 142

Background

Biography

Marie-Antoinette Austria had another reason to help the French king. Louis XVI had married Marie-Antoinette, daughter of Francis I, the Holy Roman Emperor and Emperor of Austria. Indeed, Louis XVI married Marie-Antoinette to ensure strong relations with Austria. The marriage was not a happy one, however, and Marie-Antoinette hid her sorrow by indulging in parties and expensive ways. The people, who were suffering terribly, hated her. Late in the Revolution, Marie secretly tried to get more help from Austria. Her efforts failed, and she was executed in 1793.

Activity

Interdisciplinary Connections

Mathematics Ask students to calculate approximately how many French people were executed during the year-long Reign of Terror. Some students may also wish to locate historical population figures for France and calculate the percentage executed.

Answers to ...

NAPOLEON CROSSING THE ALPS

to show Napoleon as a powerful military leader and hero

To Be a Leader When news of the French Revolution reached the French island colony of Saint-Domingue (san duh MANG) in the Caribbean, enslaved Africans decided that they would fight for freedom, too. This revolt was led by a nearly 50-year-old former slave, Toussaint L'Ouverture (too SAN loo vur TOOR). He died in the struggle in 1803. His example, however, inspired the people of Saint-Domingue to keep fighting. Eventually they won out, founding the independent country of Haiti in 1804.

They stormed the palace and captured the king. A few months later, Louis XVI was executed.

A few men who called themselves the Committee of Public Safety seized power. They declared that the new constitution was no longer in effect. Maximilien Robespierre (ROHBZ pyair) led the committee in carrying out what became known as the **Reign of Terror.** For nearly a year, perhaps as many as 70 to 80 people were executed every day. No one was safe. Women and children were killed as well as men. Those who had helped to create the constitution were killed as well as those who had fought against it. Finally, Robespierre himself was executed, and the Reign of Terror ended.

The Age of Napoleon

France was still at war, however. The monarchs of Britain, Holland, and Spain had joined those of Austria and Prussia to defend the rights of kings. A young officer in the French army, Napoleon Bonaparte, won one remarkable victory after another against these foreign armies. In a little over a year, he rose from captain to general. Napoleon continued to astonish the world with his leadership. He took control of the French government in 1799.

Napoleon's Accomplishments Claiming that he was defending the ideals of the revolution, Napoleon brought many reforms

Napoleon Crossing the Alps

In 1797, Napoleon led French forces across the Alps into Austria. When he threatened the Austrian capital, Vienna, the Austrians decided to make peace. As a result, the French hailed Napoleon as a hero. This painting of Napoleon crossing the Alps, like that of the Tennis Court Oath, is by Jacques-Louis David. **Critical Thinking** What do you think David's purpose was in this painting?

Napoleon's Power in Europe, 1812

KEY

- French territory
- States ruled by Napoleon's family
- States under French influence
- French allies, 1812
- ★ Battle sites, 1800–1815
- → Route of Napoleon's invasion of Russia
- • City

Lambert Azimuthal Equal-Area Projection

Map Study By 1812, Napoleon controlled much of Europe. Greedy for more land and glory, Napoleon decided to invade Russia. His plan ended in disaster. In September, 1812, he reached the Russian capital, Moscow. However, he realized he would never be able to hold the city. He decided to return to France. During the journey, the bitter winter weather and constant attacks by Russian soldiers nearly destroyed his army. **Location** Where in Russia did Napoleon fight battles?

Activity

Critical Thinking

Drawing Conclusions
Suitable as a whole class activity. Tell students that one of the main goals of the Napoleonic Code was to protect property, especially the property of the middle class. Challenge students to list some possible laws that might affect this goal. Urge them to use common sense and personal experience as a guide. If students wish, they may locate and read the Napoleonic Code in order to verify their conclusions.

to France. During the revolution, the government had taken control of the Catholic Church. Napoleon, however, knew that religion was important to many French people. He let the Catholic Church operate freely again. He also allowed other religions to have their freedom.

Perhaps Napoleon's most important accomplishment was to reform the laws. He had a team of lawyers study all the laws of France. Many of the laws were poorly written and confusing. The lawyers rewrote the laws so that they were clear and easy to understand. These new laws were called the **Napoleonic Code.**

Napoleon's Downfall In time, Napoleon convinced the French parliament to make him emperor. He received this honor at a grand ceremony in Paris.

As emperor, Napoleon kept many of the reforms of the revolution. For instance, he made sure that the laws applied to everyone, whether rich or poor.

Answers to . . .

MAP STUDY

Smolensk and Borodino

Recognizing Cause and Effect *Suitable as an individual activity.* Tell students to choose a location from the map European Colonies in Africa, 1914. Using the Atlas at the back of the book, have students identify the modern nation in that location. Then suggest that they use the information in World View to determine the main languages spoken there. Help students note the cause-and-effect relationship between nineteenth century colonial powers and the current culture of farmer colonies. *Visual*

However, Napoleon was no perfect hero. Like many people who have power, he hungered for more. He set out to conquer Europe—and practically succeeded. Yet his victories were short-lived. His constant wars also took many lives. He was finally defeated at Waterloo, Belgium, at the hands of the British.

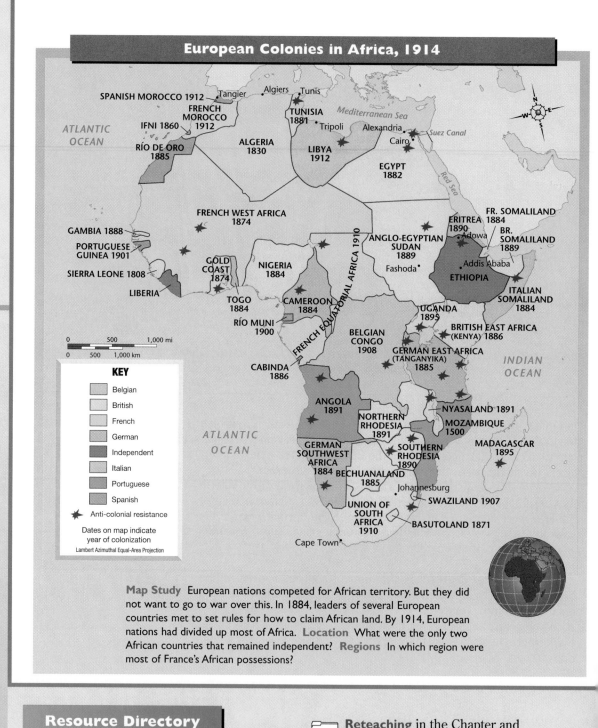

European Colonies in Africa, 1914

KEY
- Belgian
- British
- French
- German
- Independent
- Italian
- Portuguese
- Spanish
- ★ Anti-colonial resistance

Dates on map indicate year of colonization

Lambert Azimuthal Equal-Area Projection

Map Study European nations competed for African territory. But they did not want to go to war over this. In 1884, leaders of several European countries met to set rules for how to claim African land. By 1914, European nations had divided up most of Africa. **Location** What were the only two African countries that remained independent? **Regions** In which region were most of France's African possessions?

Teaching Resources

📁 **Section Quiz** in the Chapter and Section Support booklet, p. 114, covers the main ideas and key terms in the section. Available in Spanish in the Spanish Support booklet, p. 71.

📁 **Vocabulary** in the Chapter and Section Support booklet, p. 116, provides a review of key terms in the chapter. Available in Spanish in the Spanish Support booklet, p. 73.

📁 **Reteaching** in the Chapter and Section Support booklet, p. 117, provides a structure for students who may need additional help in mastering chapter content.

Answers to ...
MAP STUDY

Location Liberia and Ethiopia

Regions northwest Africa

Nations and Empires

As Napoleon and his armies moved through Europe, they carried the ideas and the spirit of the French Revolution with them. The French Revolution told people that they had the right to rule themselves. It also taught them to appreciate their own nation. This desire for independence and pride in one's country is called **nationalism.**

Napoleon's wars gave some the chance to act on these ideals. While the European powers were busy fighting among themselves, some of their colonies took the chance to win their freedom.

Yet, as people in some parts of the world broke away from their foreign rulers, others came under foreign rule. By the 1800s, Europe was strong economically and politically. Confident of their power, European countries began to expand aggressively. There were several reasons for this. First, factories all over Europe needed more raw materials—more cotton, metal, coal, and rubber. Second, the goods the factories made had to be sold somewhere so factory owners could make money. The major countries of Europe set up colonies in Africa and Asia to get raw materials and sell goods. Nations also established colonies to protect trade routes. This effort to create an empire of colonies is called **imperialism.** The map on the previous page illustrates how imperialism affected Africa.

Closely linked to the economic reasons for imperialism were political and military interests. When one country established a colony, others did the same. No one country wanted to see its neighbors gain more power or greater wealth than it had.

France, Germany, Italy, the Netherlands, Portugal, and Belgium were all imperialists. The United States, too, claimed Puerto Rico and the Philippines. The greatest imperialist power of all, however, was Britain. By 1914, the British empire covered about one quarter of the Earth's land surface and included one quarter of the world's population.

▲ In this cartoon from the late 1800s, the Chinese watch helplessly as the colonial powers of Britain, Germany, Russia, France, and Japan claim "slices" of China.

SECTION 4 REVIEW

1. Define (a) Reign of Terror, (b) Napoleonic Code, (c) nationalism, (d) imperialism.

2. Identify (a) Maximilien Robespierre, (b) Napoleon Bonaparte, (c) Waterloo.

3. What did Napoleon do to improve life for the average person in France?

4. (a) Why did European nations create empires? (b) Where did they build their colonies?

Critical Thinking
5. Making Comparisons Compare the rule of King Louis XVI with that of Napoleon.

Activity
6. Writing to Learn Write a journal entry showing how one of the people discussed in this chapter was both a positive influence and a negative influence. List the ways in which this person was a positive influence. Then list the ways in which he or she was a negative influence.

Section 4 Review

1. (a) execution of French people by the Committee of Public Safety (b) clarified laws written under Napoleon (c) desire for independence and pride in one's country (d) effort to create an empire of colonies

2. (a) leader of the French Committee of Public Safety (b) French military leader and emperor (c) battle in which the British army defeated Napoleon

3. He made the laws clearer and applicable to rich and poor alike and allowed religious freedom.

4. (a) to gain access to raw materials and to create markets for industrial goods (b) mostly in Africa and Asia

5. Louis XVI treated the common people poorly. Napoleon improved life for the common people.

6. Entries should accurately link the subject with his or her actions. Commendable entries should explain why influences are negative or positive.

Teaching Resources

📁 **Enrichment** in the Chapter and Section Support booklet, p. 118, extends chapter content and enriches students' understanding.

📁 **Spanish Glossary** in the Spanish Support booklet, pp. 83–91, provides key terms translated from English to Spanish as well as definitions in Spanish.

📁 **Chapter Summary** in the Chapter and Section Support booklet, p. 115, provides a summary of chapter content. Available in Spanish in the Spanish Support booklet, p. 72.

📁 **Cooperative Learning Activity** in the Activities and Projects booklet, pp. 44–47, provides two student handouts, one page of teacher's directions, and a scoring rubric for a cooperative learning activity on creating a bulletin board display about the Industrial Revolution.

Media and Technology

🎧 **Guided Reading Audiotapes** (English and Spanish)

Reviewing Main Ideas

1. Sample answers: peace between English Catholics and Protestants, defeat of Spanish and superiority of British navy, leadership in global exploration, support of the arts and science

2. Parliament, which had grown more powerful during the British civil war, made William and Mary accept the English Bill of Rights, which stated that all laws had to be approved by Parliament.

3. They caused people to question the Earth's place in the universe and begin to look at natural laws, or patterns, of behavior in the universe.

4. They had the right to change the government.

5. They wanted to get factory jobs and to escape job loss resulting from farm work being taken over by machines.

6. In factories, people worked long hours with few breaks. Conditions were dirty and noisy; machines were dangerous. Workers lived in crowded and dirty homes without indoor plumbing. Pollution and garbage caused disease, and many people fell ill or died.

7. He had them rewritten to be clearer and to apply equally to rich and poor.

8. (a) Africa and Asia (b) to access raw materials for industry and to create markets for industrial products

Reviewing Key Terms

Sentences will vary, but should clearly define the listed term.

Critical Thinking

1. It showed French revolutionaries that success was possible and that liberty and a role in government was attainable.

2. Both events included a change in government and an increase in people's power.

CHAPTER 7 Review and Activities

Reviewing Main Ideas

1. Name two things that made the Elizabethan Age a glorious time for England.

2. How did England become a constitutional monarchy?

3. How did Copernicus and Newton change the way people thought about the universe?

4. According to John Locke, what could people do if their government took away their right to freedom?

5. Why did so many people move away from farms during the Industrial Revolution?

6. Describe the working and living conditions of factory workers in the 1800s.

7. How did Napoleon reform the laws of France?

8. (a) In what parts of the world did European powers start colonies in the late 1800s? (b) Why did they do so?

Reviewing Key Terms

Use each key term below in a sentence that shows the meaning of the term.

1. civil war
2. bill of rights
3. revolution
4. constitutional monarchy
5. Enlightenment
6. scientific method
7. natural law
8. colony
9. textile
10. labor union
11. Napoleonic Code
12. nationalism
13. imperialism

Critical Thinking

1. Recognizing Cause and Effect In what ways did the American Revolution influence the French Revolution?

2. Making Comparisons Review the Glorious Revolution and the French Revolution. How were these two events similar? How were they different?

Graphic Organizer

Copy this chart on a separate sheet of paper. Then write the names of four events that grew out of the Enlightenment.

Enlightenment

Graphic Organizer

Students' charts may vary. Sample answers shown.

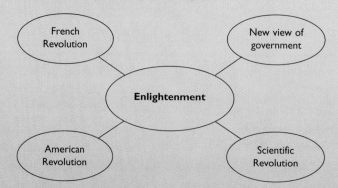

French Revolution — New view of government — Enlightenment — American Revolution — Scientific Revolution

Map Activity

The Western World
For each place listed below, write the letter from the map that shows its location.

1. Versailles
2. Africa
3. France
4. Waterloo
5. Paris

Place Location

Writing Activity

Writing a Tribute
Choose a person from this chapter about whom you would like others to know more. Write a short essay about this person, describing his or her accomplishments.

Internet Activity

Use a search engine to find **The Industrial Revolution II.** Compare "The Hannover Principles" for the design of cities, buildings, and products with the ideas about production during the Industrial Revolution. What are three things people have learned since then?

Skills Review

Turn to the Skills Activity.
Review the three steps for reading a line graph. Then answer the following questions: (a) What is an axis? (b) How can line graphs be helpful in presenting information?

How Am I Doing?

Answer these questions to help you check your progress.

1. Can I discuss the ways in which the Enlightenment affected science and politics in Europe?

2. Do I understand how the Industrial Revolution changed the way people in Europe lived?

3. Can I explain how revolutions changed the governments of France and England?

4. What information from this chapter can I use in my book project?

Internet Activity

If students are having difficulty finding this site, you may wish to have them use the following URL, which was accurate at the time this textbook was published:

http://www.isdesignet.com/ May'95/Cover.html

You might also guide students to a search engine. Four of the most useful are Infoseek, AltaVista, Lycos, and Yahoo. For additional suggestions on using the Internet, refer to the Prentice Hall Social Studies' Educator's Handbook "Using the Internet," in the *Prentice Hall World Explorer Program Resources.*

For additional links to world history and culture topics, visit the Prentice Hall Home Page at:
http://www.phschool.com

How Am I Doing?

Point out to students that this checklist is a quick reminder of what they learned in the chapter. If their answer to any of the questions is *no* or if they are unsure, they may need to review the topic.

Map Activity

1. A   3. B   5. C
2. E   4. D

Writing Activity

Tributes should clearly identify the subject, accurately list his or her accomplishments, and persuasively explain why these are important.

Skills Review

(a) An axis is the graph's vertical or horizontal line, divided into increments. (b) A line graph shows changes in amounts over time and can show things like growth over time at a glance.

Resource Directory

Teaching Resources

Chapter Tests Forms A and B are in the Tests booklet, pp. 38–43.

Program Resources

Writing Process Handbook includes Organizing Material in a Logical Sequence, pp. 23–24, to help students with the Writing Activity.

Media and Technology

Color Transparencies
Color Transparency 171
(Graphic organizer web template)
Prentice Hall Writer's Solution Writing Lab CD-ROM
Computer Test Bank
Resource Pro™ CD-ROM

MEDIEVAL TIMES TO TODAY
A Century of Turmoil

To help you plan instruction, the chart below shows how teaching resources correspond to chapter content. Use the resources to vary instruction, add activities, or plan block schedules. Where appropriate, resources have **suggested time allotments** for students. Time allotments are approximate.

Managing Time and Instruction

	Medieval Times to Today Teaching Resources Binder		World Explorer Program Resources Binder	
	Resource	**mins.**	**Resource**	**mins.**
SECTION 1 **World Wars and Revolution**	**Chapter and Section Support** Reproducible Lesson Plan, p. 121 Ⓢ Guided Reading and Review, p. 122 Ⓢ Section Quiz, p. 123 **Social Studies and Geography Skills,** Analyzing a Photograph, p. 58	20 25 30	**Outline Maps** The World: Political, p. 3 **Nystrom Desk Atlas** Ⓣ Primary Sources and Literature Readings **Writing Process Handbook** Outlining Your Material, p. 25 **Environmental and Global Issues** Topic: Conflict, pp. 37–42 Topic: Human Rights, pp. 25–32	20 40 25 30 30
SKILLS ACTIVITY **Expressing Problems Clearly**	**Social Studies and Geography Skills,** Expressing Problems Clearly, p. 40	30		
2 **SECTION 2** **Breaking Colonial Ties**	**Chapter and Section Support** Reproducible Lesson Plan, p. 124 Ⓢ Guided Reading and Review, p. 125 Ⓢ Section Quiz, p. 126 **Social Studies and Geography Skills,** Recognizing Ideologies, p. 48	20 25 30	**Outline Maps** The World: Political, p. 3	20
3 **SECTION 3** **Our Shrinking Globe**	**Chapter and Section Support** Reproducible Lesson Plan, p. 127 Ⓢ Guided Reading and Review, p. 128 Ⓢ Section Quiz, p. 129 Critical Thinking Activity, p. 134 Ⓢ Vocabulary, p. 131 Reteaching, p. 132 Enrichment, p. 133 Ⓢ Chapter Summary, p. 130 **Social Studies and Geography Skills,** Predicting Consequences, p. 50 **Tests** Forms A and B Chapter Tests, pp. 44–49 Forms A and B Final Exams, pp. 50–55	20 25 30 20 25 25 15 30 40 40	**Outline Maps** The World: Political, p. 3 **Environmental and Global Issues** Topic: Environmental Destruction, pp. 14–19	20 30
ACTIVITY SHOP: INTERDISCIPLINARY **History Quiz Wizards**	Ⓣ Activity Shop: Interdisciplinary, p. 6	30		

Block Scheduling Folder
PROGRAM TEACHING RESOURCES

Activities and Projects

Interdisciplinary Links

Block Scheduling Program Support

Resource Pro™ CD-ROM

Media and Technology

Media and Technology

Resource	mins.
◖◗ ✎ Ⓢ World Video Explorer	20
▱ Color Transparencies 1, 2, 146, 148, 149	20
▱ Color Transparencies 170, Historical Map Set 5	20
✎ Planet Earth CD-ROM	20
▱ Color Transparencies 15, 18, Historical Map Sets 6 and 7	20
⌒ Ⓢ Guided Reading Audiotapes	20
▱ Color Transparency 174 (Graphic organizer table template)	20
✎ The Writer's Solution CD-ROM	30
▯ Computer Test Bank	30

T **Teaming Opportunity**
This resource is especially well-suited for teaching teams.

Ⓢ **Spanish**
This resource is also in Spanish support.

✎ **CD-ROM**

✎ **Laserdisc**

▱ **Transparency**

▯ **Software**

◖◗ **Videotape**

⌒ **Audiotape**

Assessment Opportunities

From Guiding Questions to Assessment   A series of Guiding Questions serves as an organizing framework for this book. The Guiding Questions that relate to this chapter are listed below. Section Reviews and Section Quizzes provide opportunities for assessing students' insights into these Guiding Questions. Additional assessments are listed below.

GUIDING QUESTIONS

- *How did each society's belief system affect its history, government, and economy?*
- *What was the pattern of day-to-day life in these societies?*
- *How did these societies interact with other societies?*

ASSESSMENTS

Section 1

Students should be able to create a time line of selected major military events in the first half of the 1900s.

▶ **RUBRIC**
See the Assessment booklet for a rubric on assessing a time line.

Section 2

Students should be able to create a glossary of the key terms in the section.

▶ **RUBRIC**
See the Assessment booklet for a rubric on assessing a glossary.

Section 3

Students should be able to write a letter to the editor stating how and why countries of the world are trying to protect the environment.

▶ **RUBRIC**
See the Assessment booklet for a rubric on assessing a letter to the editor.

ACTIVITIES
To Develop a Global Perspective

Mental Mapping

The World At War Distribute outline maps of the world and ask students to shade or color the countries that were involved in World War I. Students may not be aware that many countries outside Europe were also involved in the war. Their maps should include Austria, Germany, Hungary, Turkey (Ottoman Empire), Bulgaria, Belgium, British Empire, France, Japan, Montenegro, Russia, Serbia, Italy, San Marino, Portugal, Romania, Brazil, China, Cuba, Greece, Liberia, Thailand (Siam), United States, Costa Rica, Guatemala, Honduras, and Nicaragua.

Ask students why so many countries outside the European continent got involved in the war. They should understand that trade relationships, colonies, and other links often draw countries into wars that would not seem to threaten them directly.

Links to Current Events

NATO Tell students that NATO, the North Atlantic Treaty Organization, was formed after World War II. It included the countries that had fought on the side of the Allies and other countries that allied themselves with those countries for protection against the nations of the Warsaw Pact, the countries of Eastern Europe, and the Soviet Union. Today, the Warsaw Pact does not exist, since the Soviet Union and several other countries that created it no longer exist. NATO does, however. Invite students to find articles about NATO after 1990. What does it do? Who belongs to it? What controversies surround it?

Hands-On Activities

A New Nation Divide students into small groups and ask them to imagine that they are the leaders of a nation that has just achieved its independence. Have them make a list of ten tasks they face in getting their country started. Their list might include items such as creating a constitution and holding elections, as well as setting up a postal system, creating postage stamps, and so on.

Have each group report to the whole class. Create a master list of tasks on the chalkboard. If time allows, give students a chance to discuss the relative importance or necessity of different items on the list.

PROJECTS
To Develop a Global Perspective

After the Cold War Give students two outline maps of Europe and Asia. Have them find a map of Europe and Asia after 1947 and before 1988. Have them identify the borders of the Soviet Union and locate republics within the Soviet Union. Have them identify countries of Eastern Europe. On the second map, ask them to locate and label countries using a map published in 1995 or later. Then ask them to make a chart with two columns. Have them list all the countries that existed before 1988 that were no longer there after 1995. In the second column, have them list countries that are on the map after 1995 that weren't there before 1988. *Average*

Saving the Earth Have students research an environmental issue they think is important. Issues may include global warming, habitat destruction, pollution of air or water resources, or another topic. Ask them to locate an organization that is working on this issue and report on it to the rest of the class, including in their report three actions that students themselves can take to address the problem. *Basic*

Time Line Have students work together to make a large time line. They can use butcher or poster paper and do the time line as a mural. Encourage them to show major events of the 1900s. *English Language Learners*

The Legacy of Gandhi Gandhi's ideas about the use of nonviolent resistance allowed the people of India to win independence from the more powerful Great Britain. Gandhi's ideas influenced the Rev. Martin Luther King, Jr., Cesar Chavez, Lech Walesa, Petra Kelly (founder of the German Green Party), Bishop Desmond Tutu of South Africa, Aung San Suu Kyi (Burmese human rights activist), and numerous others. Ask students to report on the use of Gandhi's ideas and tactics in other movements for independence, equality, or justice of the 1900s. *Challenging*

F.Y.I.

This page can help you extend your own and students' understanding of the concepts in this chapter. You may want to browse through some of the suggestions in the **Bibliography**. **Interdisciplinary Links** can connect social studies understandings to areas elsewhere in the curriculum through the use of other Prentice Hall products. **National Geography Standards** reflected specifically in this chapter are listed for your convenience. Some hints about appropriate **Internet Access** are also provided. **School to Careers** provides insights into the practical uses of some of the concepts in this chapter as they might pertain to various careers.

BIBLIOGRAPHY

FOR THE TEACHER

Bachrach, Susan D. *Tell Them We Remember: The Story of the Holocaust.* Little, 1994.

Kort, Michael G. *China Under Communism.* Millbrook, 1995.

Miller, Christina G., and Louise A. Berry. *Air Alert: Rescuing the Earth's Atmosphere.* Atheneum, 1996.

FOR THE STUDENT

Easy

Fisher, Leonard Everett. *Gandhi.* Atheneum, 1995.

Rand, Gloria. *Prince William.* Holt, 1992.

Average

Clare, John D., ed. *First World War.* Gulliver, 1995.

Pringle, Laurence. *Taking Care of the Earth: Kids in Action.* Boyds, 1996.

Challenging

Hoose, Phillip. *It's Our World, Too! Stories of Young People Who Are Making a Difference.* Joy Street, 1993.

Langone, John. *Our Endangered Earth: What We Can Do to Save It.* Little, 1992.

Symynkywicz, Jeffrey B. *1989: The Year the World Changed.* Dillon, 1995.

LITERATURE CONNECTION

Durell, Ann, Jean Craighead George, and Katherine Paterson, eds. *The Big Book for Our Planet.* Dutton, 1993.

Hamanaka, Sheila, ed. *On the Wings of Peace.* Clarion, 1995.

Yep, Laurence. *Hiroshima: A Novella.* Scholastic, 1995.

INTERDISCIPLINARY LINKS

Subject	Theme: Conflict and Change
MATH	Middle Grades Math: Tools for Success *Course 1*, Lesson 10-8, **Making Predictions** *Course 2*, Lesson 1-8, **Representative Samples and Surveys**
SCIENCE	Prentice Hall Science *Ecology: Earth's Natural Resources*, Gazette, **Prisoners Under Plastic** *Exploring the Universe*, Gazette, **Looking for Life Beyond Earth**
LANGUAGE ARTS	Choices in Literature *Conflict and Resolution*, **Baseball Saved Us, Justice at Last** *Where Paths Meet*, **An Education, Suzy and Leah, Barrio Boy, Achieving the American Dream**

NATIONAL GEOGRAPHY STANDARDS

Students explore the 18 National Geography Standards throughout *Medieval Times to Today*. Chapter 8, however, concentrates on investigating the following standards: 5, 6, 9, 10, 12, 13, 14, 16, 17, 18. For a complete list of the standards, see the *Teacher's Flexible Planning Guide*.

SCHOOL TO CAREERS

In Chapter 8, A Century of Turmoil, students learn about revolution and wars throughout the world. Additionally, they address the skill of expressing problems clearly. Understanding world conflict can help students prepare for careers in many fields, such as travel planning, news commentary, history, government, and so on. Expressing problems clearly is a skill useful in economics, politics, administration, and others. The curriculum presented in this book, as in all eight titles of Prentice Hall's *World Explorer* program, is designed to prepare students not only for careers but also for good citizenship—of the world as well as of this country.

INTERNET ACCESS

Many social studies teachers and students use Internet browsers, or search engines, to investigate particular topics. For the best results, use narrow rather than broad topics. Try these for Chapter 8: Holocaust, racism, Nelson Mandela, Cold War. Finding age-appropriate sites is an important consideration when using the Internet. For links to age-appropriate sites in world studies and geography, visit the Prentice Hall Home Page at:
http://www.phschool.com

A Century of Turmoil

Connecting to the Guiding Questions

In this chapter, students will investigate the major developments of the twentieth century. Content in this chapter thus corresponds to the following Guiding Questions:

- How did each society's belief system affect its history, government, and economy?

- What was the pattern of day-to-day life in these societies?

- How did these societies interact with other societies?

Using the Picture Activities

Invite the class to generate a list of adjectives to describe the mood of the people in the picture.

- Students' captions should indicate that the people seem joyful.

- Answers will vary.

Heterogeneous Groups

The following Teacher's Edition strategies are suitable for heterogeneous groups.

Critical Thinking
Recognizing Cause and Effect   p. 199

Interdisciplinary Connections
Language Arts   pp. 201, 206, 213
Art   p. 214

Cooperative Learning
Economic Systems   p. 211

SECTION 1
World Wars and Revolution

SECTION 2
Breaking Colonial Ties

SECTION 3
Our Shrinking Globe

PICTURE ACTIVITIES

The picture above shows a momentous event in twentieth-century history—the fall of the Berlin Wall in 1989. For nearly 30 years, this mass of concrete and barbed wire separated parents from children and friend from friend. It also served as a symbol for the separation of two world views. Its fall, too, was also a symbol—of hope for a new, more peaceful world. To begin a study of twentieth-century history, do the following activities.

Study the picture
Look closely at the people in the picture. How would you describe their mood?

Write a caption
You are a newspaper editor. Write a 25-word caption describing what is happening in the picture.

Resource Directory

Media and Technology

Spotlight On: Dachau, from the World Video Explorer, enhances students' understanding of the Holocaust.

Chapter 9

World Wars and Revolution

BEFORE YOU READ

Reach Into Your Background

Have you ever promised to help a friend if he or she gets

into trouble? What would you do if your friend asked you to fulfill that promise?

Questions to Explore

1. Why was Russia struck by revolution?
2. Why was the world torn by major wars twice in the 1900s?

Key Terms

czar	armistice
serf	genocide
communism	Holocaust
alliance	atomic bomb

Key People and Places

Vladimir Lenin
Adolf Hitler
Hiroshima
Nagasaki

Nicholas II and Alexandra, rulers of Russia, were very proud of their family. They had four daughters and a son, Alexis. A family friend described Alexis as "one of the handsomest babies one could imagine."

But Alexis was not as healthy as he looked. He had a disease that made it difficult for his blood to clot, or stop flowing. Even the tiniest cut or bruise could kill him. He could not play like other boys. He had to be careful not to get hurt. Everywhere he went, two guards followed him. They were there to try to catch him if he fell.

Alexis was next in line to become the **czar** (zar), or the Russian emperor. But Nicholas's advisors feared that Alexis might not survive long enough to come to the throne.

The Russian Revolution

Like Alexis, the monarchy of Russia was not as healthy as it seemed. Long before Alexis could grow up, the Russian people decided to end the rule of the czars. Nicholas and his family were forced to give up their power.

Why a Revolution? Russia had been ruled by czars for hundreds of years. The czars were absolute rulers. They controlled almost every part of their people's lives. Most people were **serfs,** poor peasant workers who were considered the

▼ This photograph of Czar Nicholas II and his family was taken in 1916. Alexis is seated at his mother's feet.

Teaching Resources

📁 **Reproducible Lesson Plan** in the Chapter and Section Support booklet, p. 121, provides a summary of the section lesson.

📁 **Guided Reading and Review** in the Chapter and Section Support booklet, p. 122, provides a structure for mastering key concepts and reviewing key terms in the section. Available in Spanish in the Spanish Support booklet, p. 75.

Program Resources

📁 Material in the **Primary Sources and Literature Readings** booklet extends content with a selection related to the concepts in this chapter.

📁 **Outline Maps** The World: Political, p. 3

Lesson Objectives

1. Describe the causes and consequences of the Russian Revolution.

2. Identify the basic reasons for World Wars I and II and the effects they had.

Lesson Plan

1 Engage

Warm-Up Activity

Remind students of the chapter title *(A Century of Turmoil)* and point out the section title *(World Wars and Revolution)*. Ask students what conclusions they can draw about the course of events in the twentieth century based on the titles alone.

Activating Prior Knowledge

Have students read Reach Into Your Background in the Before You Read box. Invite volunteers to share some hypothetical consequences of friendships, especially when helping a friend might be harmful to someone else.

2 Explore

As students read the section, ask them to find answers to the following questions: Why was there a revolution in Russia? How did Russia change as a result of the revolution? How did nationalism and alliances lead to World War I? How did the aftermath of World War I help lead to World War II? What was the Holocaust? What impact did the atomic bomb have on the course of the war?

Background

Daily Life

Two Ways of Life In the years leading up to the revolution, the daily lives of Russia's poor and Russia's elite were astoundingly different. The royal family and other upper-class people lived in almost unbelievable extravagance. They lived in palaces, traveled in luxury, and had every need and whim fulfilled by armies of servants. In stark contrast, the poor often were faced with meals of dark bread and a watery cabbage soup. Some peasants could go a year or more without having milk or meat in their diet.

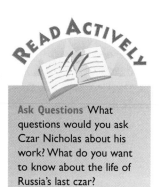

READ ACTIVELY

Ask Questions What questions would you ask Czar Nicholas about his work? What do you want to know about the life of Russia's last czar?

property of wealthy nobles. Serfs had to work the noble's land and also pay him part of the crops they grew for themselves. In exchange, they were allowed to live on the land.

The system of serfdom finally was ended in 1861. But the serfs remained poor. Freedom did not improve their day-to-day lives. The poor people in the cities, too, struggled to have a good life. Even those in the middle class felt that things could be better. Russians grew more and more unhappy with their government.

At the beginning of the 1900s, some Russians began to organize to remove the czar from power. They were willing to fight to create a better government. They were sure that ending the rule of the czars would mean a better life for everyone.

Revolution and War A terrible war that started in Europe in 1914 helped to turn more Russians against the czar. This conflict was called World War I. When Russia entered the war, the people at home suffered greatly. Much of the country's food, fuel, and supplies were used for the war effort. This meant that the people at home had to do without basic needs. Support grew for the people who were calling for change. In 1917, Czar Nicholas was forced to give up the throne. Later, he and his family were executed.

Soon after Nicholas gave up power, rebels led by Vladimir Lenin took control of the government. These rebels wanted a communist government. **Communism** (KAHM yoo nizum) is a theory of government that says that all the people should own the farms and factories. Everyone should share the work equally. And everyone should receive an equal share of the rewards. The Communists withdrew Russia from the world

▼ The first half of the 1900s was a period of great upheaval.

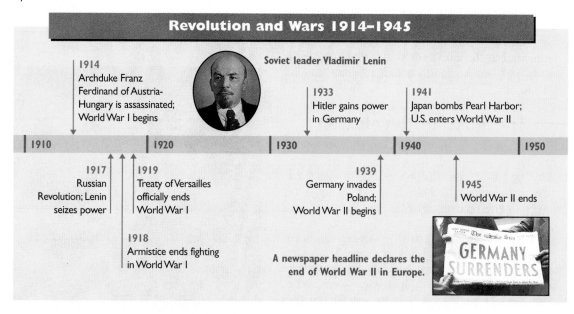

Revolution and Wars 1914–1945

Soviet leader Vladimir Lenin

1914
Archduke Franz Ferdinand of Austria-Hungary is assassinated; World War I begins

1933
Hitler gains power in Germany

1941
Japan bombs Pearl Harbor; U.S. enters World War II

1910 | 1920 | 1930 | 1940 | 1950

1917
Russian Revolution; Lenin seizes power

1919
Treaty of Versailles officially ends World War I

1918
Armistice ends fighting in World War I

1939
Germany invades Poland; World War II begins

1945
World War II ends

A newspaper headline declares the end of World War II in Europe.

GERMANY SURRENDERS

Resource Directory

Program Resources

Nystrom Desk Atlas
📁 **Environmental and Global Issues**
Topic: Conflict, pp. 37–42

Media and Technology

🖨 **Color Transparencies** 1, 2, 146, 148, 149

The Beginning of the Revolution

In March of 1917, angry Russian workers came face to face with the czar's troops in the city of Petrograd (St. Petersburg). The soldiers refused to follow orders to shoot the workers. Instead, they joined the rebellion. Here, soldiers patrol the streets carrying rifles with red flags—the symbol of the revolution. **Critical Thinking** Why do you think the soldiers turned against the czar and refused to obey orders?

war. But the fighting went on in Russia. The Communists fought forces loyal to the czar to hold on to power. They succeeded, creating a new communist nation called the Soviet Union.

Two World Wars

Even after Russia withdrew from World War I, the fighting in Europe continued for another year. World War I was one of the most terrible wars in human history. Never before had so many countries become involved in a single war. And never had the killing been so great.

The Spread of Nationalism For almost 100 years before World War I, Europe had seen only small wars. Two things made a large conflict like World War I possible. One was the growth of nationalism, feelings of loyalty to one's country. Among other things, nationalism encouraged countries to build big armies and to use force to reach their national goals. Feelings of nationalism also helped small conflicts blow up into big ones.

Countries Seek Allies The other main cause of World War I was the development of **alliances**, or agreements that nations make with one another. Usually these alliances include promises to protect each other in case of attack. Nations that have made an alliance are called allies. By teaming up before World War I, nations had hoped to discourage enemy attacks.

LINKS TO ART

Russian Ballet Both before and after the Russian Revolution, ballet was an important form of entertainment in Russia. The school of the Kirov Ballet in St. Petersburg was world famous. Dancers who trained at the school were known for the beauty of their movement. The school continued to train dancers even after the Revolution. Graduates of the Kirov Ballet include Rudolf Nureyev and Mikhail Baryshnikov, two of the greatest dancers of the 1900s.

SKILLS MINI LESSON

Using a Time Line
To **introduce** this skill, indicate to students that a time line is a diagram that shows how dates and events are related to one another. Tell students that they can read a time line in much the same way they read text, from left to right. Events at the left side of the diagram happened before events shown at the right of the diagram. Using time is a way to make sense of the dates and events. Students can **practice** the skill using the Revolution and Wars 1914–1945 time line. Help them determine what years the time line covers (1914–1945). Ask them to describe how specific dates are indicated. Have student partners **apply** the skill by developing five before or after questions based on the information in the time line.

3 Teach

To help students learn and remember the chronological order of the important events discussed in this section, assign partners or small groups the task of creating time lines of the section material. This activity should take about 30 minutes.

Activity

Critical Thinking

Recognizing Cause and Effect *Suitable as an individual or a whole class activity.* Ask students, *What caused World War I?* List their responses on the chalkboard. Lead a discussion of the different causes, helping students to see which causes were long-standing. Ask a volunteer to identify any "long-term" causes on the list. Ask another volunteer to identify any "short-term" causes and explain why they are considered short term. Prompt students by identifying nationalism and the development of alliances as long-term causes and the assassination of the archduke as a short-term cause.
English Language Learners

Answers to . . .

THE BEGINNING OF THE REVOLUTION

They identified with the workers and agreed with goals of the rebellion.

4 Assess

See the answers to the Section Review. You may also use students' time lines as assessment.

Acceptable time lines show in chronological order at least three important events discussed in the section.

Commendable time lines place several events discussed in the section in correct chronological order and indicate an understanding of events that take place over a span of time.

Outstanding time lines indicate an understanding of cause-and-effect relationships between some events.

Background

Links Across Time

The Great War   The earliest names given to the 1914–1918 war include the "War to End All Wars" and the "Great War." These names reflected the belief that the conflict would be the last of the endless stream of small-scale wars that had plagued Europe in recent decades. It was only when Great Britain and France came to Poland's aid in 1939 that the world realized that a second world war was under-way, and that the War to End All Wars did not.

LINKS ACROSS TIME

The Armenian Genocide A spirit of nationalism caused tensions in the empire of the Ottoman Turks during the 1890s. These tensions led to the genocide, or mass killing, of the Armenians, a minority group that lived in the eastern part of the empire. The Muslim Turks accused the Christian Armenians of plotting with the Russians against the Ottoman empire. Turkish leaders ordered a campaign of violence against the Armenians. Over the next 25 years, more than one million Armenian citizens of the Ottoman empire were killed.

Trench Warfare

Shortly after World War I began, both armies in France dug a huge system of defensive trenches. Between the two trench lines lay "No Man's Land," an empty area strewn with barbed wire and pitted with bomb craters. Regularly, soldiers received the order to go "over the top." This meant that they had to leave their trenches and race across "No Man's Land" to attack the enemy lines. Here, French soldiers prepare for an inspection before going into battle.

But alliances also helped nations become unfriendly toward others. Each country knew that its allies would give their support. Because of alliances, many nations were soon drawn into wars against countries with whom they had no real argument.

World War I   The spark that brought European alliances to war was the murder of Archduke Franz Ferdinand of Austria-Hungary. The leaders of Austria-Hungary declared war on Serbia. They suspected the Serbians of organizing the killing. Russia sided with its ally, Serbia. Immediately, Germany joined forces with Austria-Hungary. Then, Britain and France entered the war on the side of Russia. Most other European nations soon chose sides. Eventually, more than 20 nations joined the conflict, including the United States.

Tanks, fighter planes, submarines, machine guns, and poison gas were all used for the first time in World War I. These terrible new weapons led to more deaths than had occurred in any earlier war. Almost 10 million soldiers died. No one knows how many nonsoldiers were killed. The war left large areas of Europe in ruins.

In 1918, the warring nations agreed to an **armistice,** or cease-fire. The winning nations—Britain, France, and their allies—forced a harsh peace agreement on Germany and Austria-Hungary.

World War II   The peace agreement that ended World War I left many nations unhappy. Germany, especially, felt it had been unfairly punished for its part in the war. A political leader named Adolf Hitler took advantage of the discontent among Germans. He formed an organization called the Nazi (NAHT see) party and seized power, promising to make Germany great again. He built up the armed forces. Then, using threats and military force, he began to take control of lands that bordered Germany.

Hitler's desire to build a German empire helped bring about World War II. This Second World War was even more terrible than the first. Germany, Italy, and Japan, or the Axis Powers, fought against Britain, France, the United States, and others, or the Allied Powers.

The immediate cause of World War II was Germany's invasion of Poland. The invasion was made possible by Hitler's agreement with the Soviet Union that the two countries would not fight one another. A secret part of this Nazi-Soviet agreement was that the two countries would divide up Poland and other Eastern European countries between them. Germany invaded Poland in September 1939, a month after the deal with the Soviets was signed. Two days after the invasion, Great Britain and France honored their treaties with Poland and declared war on Germany.

Japan quickly sided with Germany, attacking British and French colonies in Southeast Asia. The Japanese attack on Pearl Harbor, Hawaii, on December 7, 1941, drew the United States into the war. The German invasion of the Soviet Union, also in 1941, led Soviet forces to side with the Allied Powers.

World War II was fought all over the world. But most of the fighting took place in Europe, North Africa, Asia, and the Pacific. Almost all the nations of Europe

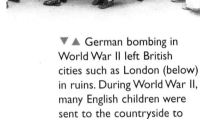

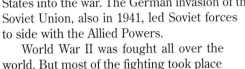

▼▲ German bombing in World War II left British cities such as London (below) in ruins. During World War II, many English children were sent to the countryside to escape the bombing (above).

SECTION 1   201

Activity

Interdisciplinary Connections

Language Arts   Suggest that students work in groups of four to develop a series of news bulletins titled "Hitler on the Move." Each bulletin should detail Hitler's invasion or annexation of Austria, Sudetenland, Czechoslovakia, Lithuania, or Poland. Bulletins should describe Hitler's actions as well as British and French reactions. Encourage students to assign roles—researcher, map-maker, scriptwriter, and narrator—to group members. *English Language Learners*

Survivors' Testimonies
More than 25,000 eyewitness testimonies of Holocaust survivors have been recorded for the Survivors of the Shoah Visual History Foundation. Each testimony includes accounts of life experiences before, during, and after World War II. The testimonies have been recorded to refute allegations that the Holocaust never occurred and to instill racial, ethnic, and cultural tolerance in future generations.

and North Africa were involved. China, several Southeast Asian nations, and Australia took part in the fighting in Asia and the Pacific.

The Nazis committed some of the worst horrors of World War II. Hitler said that Germans were a "superior race." He began a campaign to destroy entire ethnic groups, particularly Jews. This planned killing of entire groups of people is called genocide.

The Nazis sent Jews and other "enemies of the people" to prison camps. In the camps, they were forced to work. Often they were worked to death. Others were tortured or simply killed. More than six million Jews and millions of other Europeans died in the camps. This genocide is now called the Holocaust.

The Holocaust

In Germany and in the countries that they conquered, the Nazis rounded up Jewish men, women, and children and sent them to prison camps. The roundup below took place in 1940 in the Polish city of Warsaw. These men at right managed to survive the horrors of Buchenwald (boo kuhn wahld), a prison camp in central Germany.

Resource Directory

Program Resources

Environmental and Global Issues
Topic: Human Rights, pp. 25–32

▼◀ A mushroom cloud rises above the Japanese city of Hiroshima on August 6, 1945 (below). The explosion destroyed practically every building in the city (left).

World War II also saw the use of a terrible new weapon, the **atomic bomb.** The United States developed this powerful bomb that could destroy whole cities. In 1945, United States President Harry S. Truman decided that an invasion of Japan would cost the lives of many Americans. He made the decision to use the atomic bomb to help end the war quickly. The United States dropped atomic bombs on the Japanese cities of Hiroshima (hir uh SHEE muh) and Nagasaki (nahg uh SAHK ee). The two bombs combined killed about 100,000 people instantly. Thousands of others died later from illnesses caused by radiation poisoning.

The war ended in Europe on May 8, 1945. It ended in Asia on September 2, 1945, shortly after the atomic bombs were dropped on Japan. The United States and its allies had won the war. Yet Europe was once again in ruins, as was much of Japan.

SECTION 1 REVIEW

1. **Define** (a) czar, (b) serf, (c) communism, (d) alliance, (e) armistice, (f) genocide, (g) Holocaust, (h), atomic bomb.

2. **Identify** (a) Vladimir Lenin, (b) Adolf Hitler, (c) Hiroshima, (d) Nagasaki.

3. What were the causes of the Russian Revolution?

4. What were some of the main causes of the two World Wars?

Critical Thinking

5. **Expressing Problems Clearly** How might alliances designed to protect nations draw those nations into war?

Activity

6. **Writing to Learn** Write down five words that describe one of the World Wars. Write a poem describing your feelings about the war. Be sure to include the words you wrote down.

Teaching Resources

▭ **Analyzing a Photograph** in the Social Studies and Geography Skills booklet, p. 58, provides additional skill practice.

▭ **Section Quiz** in the Chapter and Section Support booklet, p. 123, covers the main ideas and key terms in the section. Available in Spanish in the Spanish Support booklet, p. 76.

Section I Review

1. (a) Russian emperor (b) peasant who was considered property of wealthy nobles (c) theory of government that says that all the people should own the farms and factories, share the work equally, and receive an equal share of the rewards (d) agreement that nations make with one another (e) cease-fire (f) systematic killing of entire groups of people (g) the killing of six million Jews during World War II (h) powerful bomb that can destroy several square miles

2. (a) leader of the Russian Revolution (b) Nazi leader of Germany (c and d) Japanese cities on which the United States dropped atomic bombs

3. possible answers: dissatisfaction with the Russian government by the poor and the middle class and the greater hardships brought on by Russia's participation in World War I

4. Possible answer: Main causes of World War I include the growth of nationalism, the development of alliances, and the assassination of Archduke Franz Ferdinand of Austria-Hungary. Main causes of World War II include discontent with the peace treaty that ended World War I, severe economic problems in the 1930s, and Germany's invasion of Poland.

5. Answers will vary, but should demonstrate an understanding of how a country might be forced to enter a war on the side of a country with which it had an alliance.

6. Poems will vary. Reward earnest attempts.

Lesson Objectives

1. Explain why and how colonies won independence in the years after World War II.

2. Discuss the challenges these newly independent nations faced.

Lesson Plan

1 Engage

Warm-Up Activity

Ask students why their country, the United States, is no longer a colony of Great Britain. Explain that many countries in the world today still seek the independence that Americans won, and that many more only achieved this independence in the very recent past.

Activating Prior Knowledge

Have students read Reach Into Your Background in the Before You Read box. Indicate that many nations were told what to do in the years after World War II.

Breaking Colonial Ties

BEFORE YOU READ

Reach Into Your Background
Do you like to make your own decisions? How do you react when people make your decisions for you and tell you what to do?

Questions to Explore
1. How did colonies win independence in the time after World War II?
2. What challenges did the newly independent nations face?

Key Terms
civil disobedience
racism
developing nation
developed nation

Key People and Places
Mohandas K. Gandhi
Nelson Mandela
Ghana
Algeria
South Africa

▼ The newly independent nation of Ghana adopted a flag with a black star symbolizing African freedom.

I t was a great day in world history. A new country was about to be born. More than 70 other countries sent representatives to witness the event.

For many years, the West African region known as the Gold Coast had been a British colony. On this day in 1957, it was breaking its colonial links. The Gold Coast had been ruled by the Portuguese, the Dutch, and then the British. Finally it would be governed by Africans. It would also leave its European name behind and take one that had belonged to an ancient African kingdom—Ghana (GAH nuh).

"We must set an example to all Africa," Ghana's new leader, Kwame Nkrumah (KWAH mee uhn KROO muh), said that day. He was right. After Ghana showed the way, the rest of Africa gradually won its independence from the colonial powers.

Fighting Colonialism

Africa was not the only region to free itself from the bonds of colonial powers. Newly independent nations sprang up in Asia and the Caribbean as well.

During the late 1800s and early 1900s, European countries claimed many areas of the world as their colonies. They sent officials to live in and govern these places. The colonies became a source of wealth for the European countries.

Resource Directory

Teaching Resources

📁 **Reproducible Lesson Plan** in the Chapter and Section Support booklet, p. 124, provides a summary of the section lesson.

📁 **Guided Reading and Review** in the Chapter and Section Support booklet, p. 125, provides a structure for mastering key concepts and reviewing key terms in the section. Available in Spanish in the Spanish Support booklet, p. 77.

When Europeans colonized an area, they brought their cultures and religions with them. Sometimes, the colonial powers also brought useful new ideas to their colonies. But too often, Europeans expected the people already living in the colonies to start doing things their way.

The Europeans also took power away from the people who lived in the colonies. Often they destroyed the economies of the colonies. People who lived in the colonies were forced to grow crops that could be sold instead of crops they could use to feed themselves. People from colonized areas soon became tired of this treatment and wanted to end European rule.

The Colonies and the World Wars During the World Wars, the colonies were expected to side with their colonial rulers. The former French colony of Algeria is a good example. In World War II, Algeria at first sided with France. However, when France was invaded by Germany in 1940, Algeria came under German rule. Then, because Algeria was ruled by Germany, Britain, an ally of France, invaded it. Algerians believed that they had been unfairly caught in a war that was not theirs.

After the war, a number of colonies demanded their independence. Colonies that had helped Britain win the war wanted to be rewarded. And the United States and other nations had promised that all people of the world would be able to choose their own governments after the war.

African demands for self-government quickly gained ground. Africans were tired of being ruled by other countries. And Europeans, weakened by war, found it hard to deny these demands.

READ ACTIVELY

Connect Using what you know about American history, how do you think African colonies reacted to European rule?

Independence in Algeria

Both those who wanted Algeria to remain part of France and those who wanted independence used terror to aid their cause. This picture (left) shows a street in Algiers on March 5, 1962, after more than 100 bomb explosions. The French government called for an end to the violence. This poster (above right) says, "For our children: Peace in Algeria."

2 Explore

As students read the section, ask them to find answers to the following questions: Who controlled most colonies? How did they tend to treat the people in the colonies? How did the two World Wars affect the colonies? What led to the global movement for independence? How was independence achieved? What challenges faced the newly independent nations?

Background

Daily Life

Colonial Legacies Despite independence, the legacy of colonialism lives on in many parts of the world. For example, English is the official language of Botswana, Ghana, Nigeria, Uganda, Zambia, and Zimbabwe. The sole official language of Benin, Congo, Côte d'Ivoire, Gabon, Guinea, Mali, Niger, Senegal, and Zaire is French. There are physical legacies, too: airstrips and roads in Mozambique; a railroad linking Kenya to the coast: and diamond, copper, and gold mines in Botswana and South Africa.

SKILLS MINI LESSON

Drawing Conclusions To **introduce** the skill, point out to students that drawing conclusions involves combining what you know about a place or an event with information you read about that place or event. Have students **practice** the skill by asking them to draw a conclusion from the following statement: Europeans sent officials to live in and govern countries they claimed as colonies. Ask students, *What clues about the Europeans are included in this statement? What do you already know about colonies the Europeans established in North America? What conclusions can you draw about the colonies in Africa and Asia?* Encourage students to **apply** the skill as they read the sections *The Colonies and the World Wars* and *From Self-Government to Independence.*

3 Teach

Have students, individually or in small groups, create three-column charts similar to the chart shown.

From Colonies to Nations		
Before	During	After

To complete the charts, students should answers these questions: What were typical conditions in colonial areas *before* independence? What types of events occurred in these areas *during* the struggle for independence? What challenges did the new nations face *after* they achieved independence? This activity should take about 40 minutes.

Interdisciplinary Connections

Language Arts Historians and political scientists hold varying views on the effects of colonialism. Have students participate in a Point-Counterpoint round-table discussion about colonialism. Encourage students to address the following questions: Is colonialism always an evil practice? Can nations actually benefit from being colonized? *Auditory, English Language Learners*

Answers to ...

MAP STUDY

Africa; the 1960s

Independence Since 1945

Map Study Every nation shown in color on this map was controlled by another country in 1945. The map key indicates the different decades, or ten-year periods, during which each of these nations gained its freedom. Most of the countries in Africa and South and Southeast Asia were colonies of European countries. The countries shown in Eastern Europe came under the control of the Soviet Union after World War II. Most of the countries of central Asia were part of the Russian empire and came under Soviet rule after the 1917 Revolution. **Regions** In 1945, which continent—not counting Australia—had the smallest number of independent nations? During which decade did the greatest number of countries on this continent gain independence?

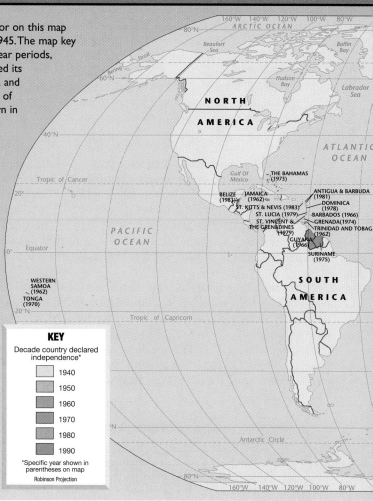

KEY

Decade country declared independence*

- 1940
- 1950
- 1960
- 1970
- 1980
- 1990

*Specific year shown in parentheses on map

Robinson Projection

From Self-Government to Independence Despite the growing world support for African independence, European nations were slow to give up their colonies. They tried to keep them by allowing Africans to have more power in colonial governments. But most Africans thought that this limited self-government was not enough. They wanted full independence.

In some countries, the change to independence was peaceful. Ghana is an example. In other places, like Algeria, it was violent. But whether peaceful or not, the changes were enormous. In 1950, only four African countries were independent of Europe. By 1990, all of Africa except Western Sahara was independent. More than 50 countries had gained their independence.

Resource Directory

Program Resources

📁 **Outline Maps** The World: Political, p. 3

Media and Technology

🖥 **Color Transparencies** 170, Historical Map Set 5

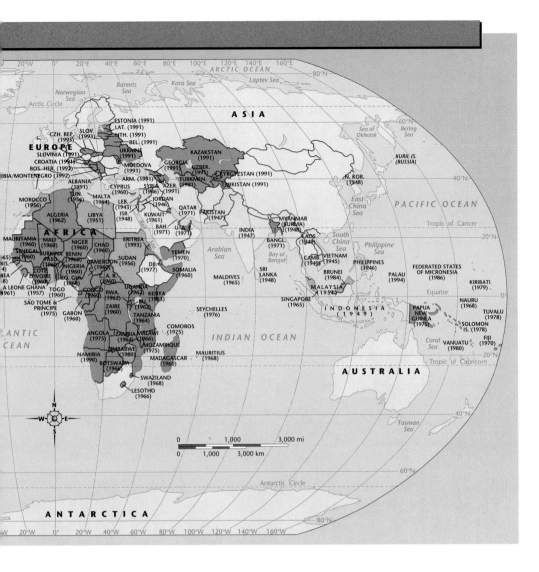

4 Assess

See the answers to the Section Review. You may also use students' charts as assessment.

Acceptable charts contain two accurate facts in each column.

Commendable charts reflect an understanding of the cause-and-effect relationship between conditions before and after independence.

Outstanding charts follow the development of particular conditions or challenges through the process of independence.

Background

Global Perspectives

Nonviolent Protest In the 1950s, Gandhi's philosophy of nonviolence spread far from India. Dr. Martin Luther King, Jr., was introduced to Gandhi's ideas while he studied at Crozer Theological Seminary. By the end of the decade, King had become convinced that nonviolent protest, or civil disobedience, in the form of sit-ins and protest marches, was perhaps the strongest weapon available to people struggling for freedom.

A Global Movement

Independence movements also gained strength in other parts of the world. Great movements and great leaders appeared wherever people wanted self-rule. India's Mohandas K. Gandhi (GAHN dee) was one such leader. He led the movement for India's independence.

Gandhi used **civil disobedience**—breaking a law on purpose in order to protest it—in his movement. He urged people to protest without using force, or to be nonviolent. He organized strikes, fasts, and marches. And he helped Indians find ways to provide for their own needs so they did not have to depend on Great Britain.

After Britain granted India its independence in 1947, the country was split into two new nations. India became a country with a Hindu

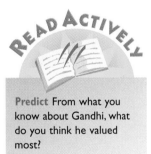

Predict From what you know about Gandhi, what do you think he valued most?

Nelson Mandela (1918–)
Perhaps more than any other figure, Nelson Mandela is celebrated as a symbol of the struggle against the racism that was a chief feature of European colonialism in Africa. In the 1950s, after a series of peaceful efforts, the African National Congress (ANC) failed to achieve equality for blacks in South Africa. Mandela, who had trained as a lawyer, became the leader of the ANC's militant wing. The government jailed Mandela in 1964, accusing him of conspiring to overthrow the government. He remained imprisoned for more than a quarter of a century, becoming the symbolic leader of the struggle for justice in South Africa. When he was released in 1990, he was named head of the ANC and continued his work. In 1993, he was awarded the Nobel Peace Prize. In 1994, Mandela was elected President of South Africa.

Predict What do you think happened when people who did not get along were forced to become part of the same country?

majority. Pakistan became a country with a Muslim majority. The two religious groups began a war with one another. This saddened Gandhi, who all along had struggled for a united India. To protest the fighting, he fasted—that is, he stopped eating. A peace agreement was signed on January 18, 1948. But 12 days later, Gandhi was shot and killed.

Challenges for the New Nations

Violence in India and Pakistan is one example of the problems new nations faced after independence. Often, their leaders were not prepared for the challenges of running a country. Some of the new nations had been shaped by Europeans. People of different ethnic groups who did not get along suddenly found themselves part of the same country. Sometimes this led to civil wars. In some of these countries, the army took control of the government.

Zoo

Nayeem Hassein
age 11
Bangladesh

Bangladesh (bahn gluh DESH), the home of this artist, was once the eastern part of Pakistan. In 1971, it broke away from Pakistan and became an independent nation. The painting shows a zoo in a Bangladeshi city.

Countries such as South Africa, Zimbabwe, and Namibia were free from colonialism. But they had another problem—**racism,** or the belief that one race is better than another. Like other countries around the world, some new African nations made laws that gave power to one group at the cost of another. In South Africa, for example, whites ruled the country for many years after independence. This was so despite the fact there were many more blacks than whites in the country.

Poverty was another problem faced by the new nations. Often their economies were troubled. Most of the world's poorer nations today are former colonies. Many are among the world's developing nations, countries with few industries. Most of the former rulers of colonies are developed nations, having strong economies and many industries.

The problems of the developing nations are slowly being solved. Government by soldiers is giving way to democracy in many countries. In 1994, South Africa's system of official racism ended for good when a black president, Nelson Mandela (man DEL uh), was elected. And nations have been working to improve their economies. The twenty-first century may be a time of success for the developing nations of the world.

▼ Nelson Mandela was a leader of the movement that resisted South Africa's harsh racist laws. For his activities, Mandela was sentenced to life in jail. He was finally released in 1990 to help South Africa move from white rule to majority rule.

SECTION 2 REVIEW

1. **Define** (a) civil disobedience, (b) racism, (c) developing nation, (d) developed nation.

2. **Identify** (a) Mohandas K. Gandhi, (b) Nelson Mandela, (c) Ghana, (d) Algeria, (e) South Africa.

3. Why did colonies want to become independent after World War II?

4. What challenges did colonies face when they became independent nations?

Critical Thinking

5. **Understanding Cause and Effect** How might fighting in World War II have led Africans to demand their independence?

Activity

6. **Writing to Learn** You are an Indian living in the time of British colonial rule. Write a letter to the editor of a newspaper stating your support for the independence movement. Before you begin, make a list of ideas you would include in such a letter.

Resource Directory

Program Resources

📁 **Recognizing Ideologies** in the Social Studies and Geography Skills booklet, p. 48, provides additional skill practice.

📁 **Section Quiz** in the Chapter and Section Support booklet, p. 126, covers the main ideas and key terms in the section. Available in Spanish in the Spanish Support booklet, p. 78.

Section 2 Review

1. (a) breaking a law in order to protest it (b) belief that one race is better than another (c) country with few industries (d) country with many industries

2. (a) Indian leader who worked for independence using civil disobedience (b) black President of South Africa (c) African nation that peacefully won its independence from Europe (d) African nation that won its independence from Europe through warfare (e) country with a history of an official system of racism

3. Answers will vary, but should include that colonies wanted to be rewarded for helping to win the war, and that the United States and other nations had promised countries that they would be able to choose their own governments after the war.

4. Answers will vary, but may include a lack of preparation for independence, different ethnic groups who did not get along having to live together, civil wars, poverty, and a history of racism.

5. Answers will vary, but should refer to the fact that colonies contributed to the war effort and in so doing had gained the right to independence.

6. Letters will vary. Reward letters that demonstrate an understanding of the reasons behind the fight for independence.

Lesson Objectives

1. Explain the origins, course, and ending of the Cold War.

2. Discuss the major economic and environmental challenges facing the world today.

Lesson Plan

1 Engage

Warm-Up Activity

Ask students to generate a list of the greatest challenges their generation faces. Guide students on reaching a consensus on the top two or three challenges.

Activating Prior Knowledge

Have students read Reach Into Your Background in the Before You Read box. Allow volunteers to share appropriate stories. Explain that as students confront today's challenges, they sharpen the skills they will need to meet future challenges.

2 Explore

As students read the section, ask them to find answers to the following questions: What was the Cold War? How did it begin? What were some of the key events of the Cold War? How did it end? What does *interdependent* mean? What economic challenges do the people of the world face? What environmental challenges do they face?

SECTION 3

Our Shrinking Globe

BEFORE YOU READ

Reach Into Your Background
What personal challenges have you faced recently? What did you do to meet these challenges?

Questions to Explore
1. What was the Cold War and how did it end?
2. How are the countries of the world trying to protect their environments?

Key Terms
reunification
capitalist country
Cold War
arms race
interdependent

A young East German man was sitting in a West German restaurant in 1990. He turned to a friend and said, "I wonder what the waitress would say if I told her I was eating chocolate ice cream for the first time." He went on to explain that in East Germany "we have brown ice cream, but there is no chocolate in it."

After World War II, Germany had been divided. East Germany became a communist country. West Germany became a democratic country. Because life was so much better in West Germany, East Germans kept trying to escape to the West. In the early 1960s, the East German government tried to stop these attempts. In the divided city of Berlin, the East Germans built a big, ugly wall to stop people from escaping to the West.

In early November 1989, the East German government suddenly announced that its citizens were free to cross into West Germany. The next day, Germans in Berlin began to tear down the wall. Soon, the two Germanys were reunited.

Reunification, or the rejoining of the two parts of Germany, changed the lives of East Germans. Now they could do all sorts of things they had never done before. As one East German said, "I will live to be 101! The hope is so strong right now. Every day is wonderful!"

▼ The city of Dresden, in the former communist country of East Germany, now has many private businesses, such as this sidewalk café.

Resource Directory

Teaching Resources

📁 **Reproducible Lesson Plan** in the Chapter and Section Support booklet, p. 127, provides a summary of the section lesson.

📁 **Guided Reading and Review** in the Chapter and Section Support booklet, p. 128, provides a structure for mastering key concepts and reviewing key terms in the section. Available in Spanish in the Spanish Support booklet, p. 79.

Program Resources

📁 **Outline Maps** The World: Political, p. 3

Built in 1946, the ENIAC, or Electronic Numerical Integrator and Calculator, was the first general-purpose computer ever made. It was so big that it filled a 1,500 square-foot (140 sq-m) room. It used 18,000 parts called vacuum tubes (inset, bottom left). Today, a laptop computer has more power and memory than the old room-filler. These modern computers use tiny silicon chips (inset, top right) instead of bulky vacuum tubes.

Even though ENIAC filled a room and weighed more than 30 tons, it could not store programs or remember more than 20 ten-figure numbers. However, it could perform 5,000 additions per second. Also, it took 20 seconds to make calculations that took mathematicians 3 days to complete.

A silicon chip no bigger than a penny can store thousands of pieces of information and can perform additions a million times faster than ENIAC.

Each of the 18,000 vacuum tubes acted like a small switch and stood for a particular number or piece of information.

The Cold War

Today, it seems strange that Germany was ever divided. It happened because the Soviet Union and the United States fought on the same side in World War II. But they did not have a friendly relationship. The two countries had very different social and economic systems. The United States and its Western allies were capitalist countries. The Soviet Union was communist. One important difference between the two systems is that **capitalist countries** allow individuals to own property and businesses. In a communist system, the government usually owns and controls these things.

READ ACTIVELY

Ask Questions What questions would you want to ask government leaders during the Cold War about taking part in the arms race?

Media and Technology

Color Transparencies 15, 18, Historical Map Sets 6 and 7

Planet Earth CD-ROM includes interactive political and thematic maps which allow students to investigate and compare modern countries around the world.

Exploring Technology

The First Computer "How much is $\sqrt[16]{2589}$?" That was the lead line in the United States Army's 1946 advertisement for the ENIAC computer. People were astounded at the speed with which ENIAC could complete complex mathematical calculations. The Army was proud of its participation in creating the electronic marvel.

Since that time, computers have been completely transformed. The thousands of vacuum tubes have been replaced by dozens of silicon chips containing hundreds of integrated circuits. Thirty tons of computing ability is now available in a 3-pound laptop computer.

Of the many breakthroughs in computer development, one of the most important may have been the development of the stored program. ENIAC was wired to complete one type of calculation. If another type of calculation was needed, the equipment needed to be rewired by hand. UNIVAC (Universal Automatic Computer), the second generation of computers, made this manual rewiring unnecessary. Engineers and mathematicians had developed a way to store various programs inside the memory of the computer. A computer operator could direct a machine to move from one program to the next with just the flip of a switch. These stored programs were the ancestors of today's computer "software" programs.

3 Teach

To focus students' learning on the Cold War, suggest that students work in pairs to create web diagrams that would satisfactorily explain the Cold War to someone who has never heard of it. This activity should take about 30 minutes.

4 Assess

See the answers to the Section Review. You may also use students' completed web diagrams as assessment.

Acceptable diagrams include five events from the Cold War.

Commendable diagrams link several related events.

Outstanding diagrams link several events showing either their cause-and-effect or sequential relationship.

Activity

Cooperative Learning

Economic Systems
Organize students into groups of four. Suggest that students chose an economic system—either capitalism or communism—as their topic. Have students research the topic and present their findings in a poster, a flyer, or a handbill designed to persuade people that theirs is the better economic system.
Kinesthetic, English Language Learners

▲ In the 1950s, fear of nuclear war was real. People in the United States built bomb shelters and stocked them with food and water. The woman in this shelter is using a device to measure radiation.

▼ During the 1960s and 1970s, Americans organized protests against United States involvement in the Vietnam War.

Resource Directory

Teaching Resources

📁 **Predicting Consequences** in the Social Studies and Geography Skills booklet, p. 50, provides additional skill practice.

📁 **Critical Thinking Activity** in the Chapter and Section Support booklet, p. 134, helps students apply the skill of recognizing cause and effect.

How Tensions Grew   After World War II, the Soviet Union took control of several Eastern European nations and made them into communist countries. These countries—Poland, Czechoslovakia, Hungary, Romania, East Germany, and Bulgaria—were completely under the control of the Soviet Union.

In 1949, Communists also came to power in China. At about the same time, Korea split into communist and capitalist sections, like Germany. It seemed that the entire world was taking sides. One superpower, the United States, led the capitalist world. The other superpower, the Soviet Union, led the communist world. Each side accused the other of trying to take over the world. Each side believed its system was best. A period of distrust and a greatly increased risk of war followed. This period, from 1945 to 1991, is called the **Cold War.**

People call it the Cold War because the superpowers did not actually fight each other. Still, they created a great deal of tension. Each built more and more weapons. Each was afraid that other was stronger. In this **arms race,** or attempt by both sides to assemble the biggest arsenal of weapons, the United States and the Soviet Union built many nuclear bombs. It was a frightening time because both countries had enough nuclear bombs to destroy the whole world.

Wars Break Out   The Cold War also resulted in some "hot" wars. In 1950, communist North Korea invaded South Korea. During the Korean War, the United States and other Western nations sent troops to support the South. China supported the North.

Another war happened after Vietnam split into two countries, a communist north and a noncommunist south. Some Americans believed that if one country in a region became a communist country, others would follow, one after another. To prevent this from happening, the United States sent hundreds of thousands of troops to fight the Communists in Vietnam. However, deaths soon started to increase in the Vietnam War. The United States withdrew its troops in the early 1970s. In 1975, North Vietnam defeated South Vietnam. The whole country became communist.

The Cold War Ends   The Cold War ended in the early 1990s, when communist rule collapsed in Eastern Europe and the Soviet Union. Communism had failed to provide its citizens with personal rights and freedoms. It had also failed to provide them with basic needs such as food, shelter, and clothing. In 1991, the Communists in the Soviet Union lost control of the government. The Soviet Union broke up into many smaller nations.

The leaders of the United States and Russia, the major power of the former Soviet Union, finally declared that they did not consider each other enemies. The 46-year-long Cold War came to an end.

Economic Development and the Environment

With the end of the Cold War, the world became more united. Now, more than ever, the nations of the world are **interdependent.** That means that they need one another. Developed nations need the resources of developing nations so that they can make goods.

Predict What do you think happened when the Cold War ended? How do you think the nations of the world acted toward one another?

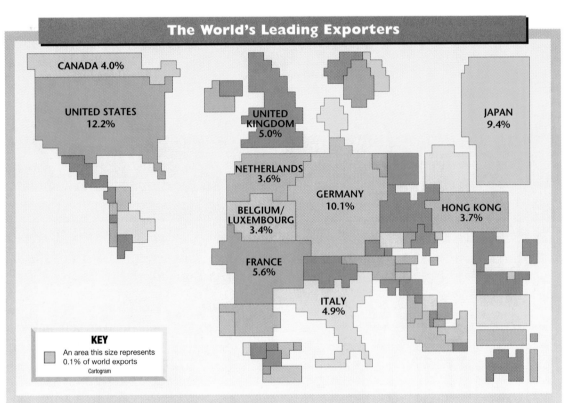

The World's Leading Exporters

CANADA 4.0%

UNITED STATES 12.2%

UNITED KINGDOM 5.0%

JAPAN 9.4%

NETHERLANDS 3.6%

GERMANY 10.1%

BELGIUM/ LUXEMBOURG 3.4%

HONG KONG 3.7%

FRANCE 5.6%

ITALY 4.9%

KEY
An area this size represents 0.1% of world exports
Cartogram

Map Study The map above is a cartogram. On other maps in this book, the size of each country is in proportion to its real area. On a cartogram, the size of a country reflects some other factor. This cartogram shows each country's share of the world's exports. Notice, for example, that the small country of Japan is fairly large on this map. That is because Japan produces a large share of the world's exports. **Movement** Which three countries account for almost one third of the world's exports?

Activity

Interdisciplinary Connections

Language Arts Tell students that one of the most-used weapons of the Cold War was propaganda, spreading ideas to promote a cause or to damage an opposing cause. Propaganda usually presents only one side of an issue; often that presentation relies on emotional reaction rather than logical thought. Have students locate examples of Cold War propaganda—political cartoons, posters, magazine covers. For each example, students should identify the point of view being represented and identify characteristics that make it propaganda. *Visual, English Language Learners*

SKILLS MINI LESSON

Understanding Special Geography Maps
As you **introduce** the skill, point out to students that a cartogram is a special purpose map. Cartograms present and compare statistics. On a cartogram, the size of a location is determined by the statistical feature, such as population or energy consumption associated with that location. Help students **practice** the skill by asking them what statistical feature is represented on the map titled World's Leading Exporters (percent of world exports). Which countries account for most of the world's exports? (the United States and Germany) Suggest that students **apply** the skill by working with a partner to develop two true-or-false questions that can be answered using the map. Have students exchange and answer one another's questions.

Answers to ...

MAP STUDY

The United States, Germany, and Japan

Activity

Interdisciplinary Connections

Art Encourage students to create posters or other artwork that encourages some solution to one of the challenges facing the world today. For example, students might address environmental problems by making posters that discourage littering or encourage recycling. Other students may choose to create artwork that dramatizes some problem, or that illustrates people of different nations working together to solve some problem. *Kinesthetic, Visual*

Activity

Journal Writing

Volunteer Vacation Tell students they have volunteered to help clean up an oil spill similar to the spill from the *Exxon Valdez*. Have students write about their experiences during the cleanup program. Suggest that they describe the wildlife and environment. Encourage them to make suggestions about how similar disasters can be avoided. If students are keeping an Explorer's Journal, as described in the opening pages of their books, you may wish to do this writing activity as part of that journal.

Connect How have people reacted to the challenge of world pollution? Connect the global effort to what is happening in your community.

▼ In 1989, the *Exxon Valdez*, a huge oil tanker, ran aground along the southern coast of Alaska. The damaged ship spilled almost 11 million gallons (42 million liters) of oil into the sea. In this picture, workers clean up after the spill. Many were volunteers.

Developing nations need the tools and know-how of developed nations to become more developed.

Interdependence also means that if one nation has a problem, every nation has a problem. War in one country might make people move to another country, causing hunger or joblessness in the second country. If pollution occurs in one nation, it may spread to another.

Saving the Environment Controlling pollution has become one of the major challenges of today's world. The problem of pollution has been growing since the beginning of the Industrial Revolution in the 1800s. Factories pollute the water and the air. Pesticides—chemicals made to kill insects—pollute the soil. The taking of natural resources, including coal, oil, gold, and timber, has destroyed much of the environment where those resources lie. The wealthy nations have been eager to make use of their resources in spite of the dangers to the environment. And the developing nations have needed the money they can get by selling their resources.

Working Together Some nations have been working together to face environmental challenges. These nations have agreed to search for ways to balance the need for economic growth with the need to protect the environment.

Resource Directory

Teaching Resources

📁 **Section Quiz** in the Chapter and Section Support booklet, p. 129, covers the main ideas and key terms in the section. Available in Spanish in the Spanish Support booklet, p. 80.

📁 **Vocabulary** in the Chapter and Section Support booklet, p. 131, provides a review of key terms in the chapter. Available in Spanish in the Spanish Support booklet, p. 82.

📁 **Reteaching** in the Chapter and Section Support booklet, p. 132, provides a structure for students who may need additional help in mastering chapter content.

Program Resources

📁 **Environmental and Global Issues** Topic: Environmental Destruction, pp. 14–19

Earth Day

Two girls put the finishing touches on a large globe for an Earth Day celebration. The purpose of Earth Day is to make people aware of environmental issues that affect everyone's health and well-being.

LINKS TO SCIENCE

The Recycling Effort

People around the world have come to understand that many of the Earth's resources cannot be replaced. Once these resources have been used, they are gone forever. People have learned that they must be more careful in their use of such resources. Today, many people are recycling goods. They realize that it is economical to reuse as many materials as possible. Paper, metals, and plastics are being reused in many different forms.

Some progress has been made. Ways have been found to clean certain kinds of pollution caused by smoke released from factories. Cars burn gasoline without giving off poisonous lead. Many materials can be recycled. Nations have joined in passing laws to protect endangered animals. People everywhere have become more aware of the importance of protecting the natural world for the health of all. The key to long-term success will be working together.

SECTION 3 REVIEW

1. **Define** (a) reunification, (b) capitalist country, (c) Cold War, (d) arms race, (e) interdependent.

2. How did the Cold War begin, and how did it end?

3. How have nations begun cleaning up the environment?

Critical Thinking

4. **Cause and Effect** Can you think of some ways in which the Cold War might have made environmental problems worse?

Activity

5. **Writing to Learn** Suppose you want to start an environmental club at your school. Make a pamphlet describing the kinds of activities the club will organize. Invite other students to join.

📁 **Enrichment** in the Chapter and Section Support booklet, p. 133, extends chapter content and enriches students' understanding.

📁 **Spanish Glossary** in the Spanish Support booklet, pp. 83–91, provides key terms translated from English to Spanish as well as definitions in Spanish.

📁 **Chapter Summary** in the Chapter and Section Support booklet, p. 130, provides a summary of chapter content. Available in Spanish in the Spanish Support booklet, p. 81.

📁 **Cooperative Learning Activity** in the Activities and Projects booklet, pp. 44–47, provides two student handouts, one page of teacher's directions, and a scoring rubric for a cooperative learning activity on designing World War II posters.

Media and Technology

🎧 **Guided Reading Audiotapes** (English and Spanish)

Section 3 Review

1. (a) rejoining of the two parts of a country (b) country that allows people to own property and businesses (c) period from 1945 to 1991 marked by the rivalry between the United States and the Soviet Union (d) attempt by two sides to assemble the larger arsenal of weapons (e) dependent on one another

2. Answers will vary, but should refer to the Soviet Union's taking control of several Eastern European countries after World War II, the Communists coming to power in China, the development of distrust and suspicion between communist and capitalistic countries at the beginning of the Cold War, and the collapse of communist rule in the Soviet Union at the end of the Cold War.

3. Answers will vary, but may include preventing pollution caused by factory smoke, developing cars that do not give off poisonous lead, and recycling.

4. Answers will vary. Possibilities include that environmental concerns were secondary to concerns about military strength, and that more factories were necessary in order to become economically strong.

5. Proposals will vary. Guide students to form clubs that can accomplish reasonable goals.

SKILLS ACTIVITY

Expressing Problems Clearly

You belong to a very special generation. Your generation will enter a new century as young adults.

As the human race begins a new chapter in history, you will begin a new chapter in your life. This is a good time for looking at the world around you and reflecting upon what you see. What do you like about the world today? What would you like to see changed?

There are a number of situations in the world that need changing, and there always have been. To make a change, you must first know what it is you would like to fix. You have to be able to identify problems and express them clearly.

Get Ready

Expressing problems clearly means stating problems in a direct, complete, and accurate way. The statements should contain facts, not opinions. The facts should be directly related to the problem. By stating problems clearly, you can search for solutions in a more appropriate way. In other words, you will have pinpointed the problem.

Try It Out

Read about the situation that follows and try to clearly express Ben's problem.

Ben had had a rough day. He had run into math class just as Ms. Brown was passing out the tests, and he was too flustered to answer the questions correctly. At soccer practice, he found everyone already playing when got there. He had to wait until the second half to play. When he got home for dinner, his family had practically finished eating, and his chicken was cold. He sat at the table with his meal while his brother and sister started on their homework. He felt so tired.

Lesson Objectives

1. Explain strategies for expressing problems clearly.

2. Practice expressing problems clearly in context.

Lesson Plan

1 Engage

Warm-Up Activity

Invite a volunteer to read aloud the opening paragraphs of the Skills Activity. Then **introduce** the skill by writing the final two sentences of the opening text on the chalkboard.

Activating Prior Knowledge

Have students write a sentence or two explaining what they think "expressing problems clearly" means. Invite volunteers to give examples of times they have used this skill.

2 Explore

Tell students to read the Get Ready text. Help them highlight the skill definition. (Expressing problems clearly means stating problems in a direct, complete, and accurate way.) Note on the chalkboard the two supporting criteria (facts, not opinions; facts directly related to the problem). Recall the student experiences discussed earlier. Did students apply the skill strategies and criteria successfully to their problem? Let students respond. Then have them read the rest of the Skills Activity.

Resource Directory

Teaching Resources

Expressing Problems Clearly in the Social Studies and Geography Skills booklet, p. 40, provides additional skill practice.

A. Identify the parts of the problem.
What is Ben's problem at the moment? What has made his day so rough?

B. Think about the problem. Think about the events of his day. What do they have in common?

C. Express the problem. In one short sentence, describe the problem with Ben's whole day.

Apply the Skill

You can apply those three steps to larger problems. Read the selection in the box. Then complete the steps that follow.

❶ Identify the parts of the problem. What problems are discussed in the selection?

❷ Think about the problem. What do all of these problems have in common? What is the single major cause of the different problems?

❸ Express the problem. Express the main problem discussed in the selection by writing a short, clear sentence. Then write a few sentences explaining how pinpointing the problem is necessary in order to find a solution to it.

> The world's forests have been shrinking for hundreds of years. People have cut them down to make room for living and farming. Many of the woodlands in Europe, North America, and Asia have suffered great losses. Today, tropical rain forests face destruction as well.
>
> The clearing of a rain forest often leaves behind eroded soil that is no good for farming. Trees disappear, and many other plant and animal species become extinct. About two thirds of the world's species live in tropical rain forests. Some people say that thousands of these species are dying out each year. Entire communities of people live in each of the major rain forest regions, and their homes are being destroyed with the rain forests.

▼ An aerial view of one part of the destruction of a rain forest in Brazil.

3 Teach

Have students **practice** the skill by working in pairs to complete the Try It Out activity. Urge students to imagine they are recounting Ben's experiences in an informal setting. How would they convey the heart of his problem? Have pairs share their final sentences with the class, posting some common responses on the chalkboard.

4 Assess

Have students **apply** the skill by completing the final activity. To **assess,** evaluate students' comments in a class discussion of the selection. Have a volunteer read the selection aloud, or display it where all can read it. Discuss the numbered steps and questions together, letting students note the class responses on the chalkboard.

Answers to . . .

TRY IT OUT

Sample answers: **A.** Ben is tired. He has rushed all day long. **B.** He was late for every event of the day. **C.** Because Ben was always late, he had problems in school and at home.

APPLY THE SKILL

1. soil erosion and infertility, plant and animal extinction, destruction of native habitats
2. They are all related to shrinking forests.; deforestation
3. Deforestation is causing many problems for people, animals, and habitats around the world. Possible answer: Pinpointing the problem makes developing specific responses possible. For example, knowing that deforestation causes soil erosion helps scientists decide how to replace harvested trees.

Reviewing Main Ideas

1. The fall of the monarchy in Russia was brought about by dissatisfaction with the Russian government by the poor and the middle class and the greater hardships brought on by Russia's participation in World War I.

2. Main causes of World War I include the growth of nationalism, the development of alliances, and the assassination of Archduke Franz Ferdinand of Austria-Hungary. Effects of the war include widespread death and destruction and the unhappiness of many nations with the peace treaty that ended the war. Main causes of World War II include discontent with the peace treaty that ended World War I, severe economic problems in the 1930s, and Germany's invasion of Poland. Effects of the war include widespread destruction in Europe and Japan.

3. Answers will vary, but should include that colonies wanted to become independent after World War II because they had been mistreated by colonial powers; they wanted to be rewarded for helping to win the war; and they had been promised that, when the war was over, countries would be able to choose their own governments.

4. Answers will vary, but should refer to the social and economic challenges that the new nations faced.

5. (a) The Cold War was the period from 1945 to 1991 marked by the rivalry between the United States, the capitalist superpower, and the Soviet Union, the communist superpower. (b) The Cold War ended because the communist rule in the Soviet Union collapsed.

6. Answers will vary, but may include water, air, and land pollution and the destruction of the environment resulting from the pursuit of natural resources.

Reviewing Key Terms

Sentences will vary, but should reflect the correct meaning of the term.

CHAPTER 8 Review and Activities

Reviewing Main Ideas

1. What brought about the fall of the monarchy in Russia?

2. What were some of the causes and effects of the two World Wars?

3. Why did African nations fight to gain their independence after World War II?

4. What happened to the nations of Africa and Asia after they won their independence?

5. (a) What was the Cold War? (b) Why did the Cold War end?

6. What environmental challenges does the world face today?

Reviewing Key Terms

Use each key term below in a sentence that shows the meaning of the term.

1. czar
2. serf
3. alliance
4. genocide
5. Holocaust
6. atomic bomb
7. civil disobedience
8. racism
9. developing nation
10. developed nation
11. reunification
12. Cold War

Critical Thinking

1. Making Comparisons Compare and contrast the fight for independence by different colonized countries such as India, Ghana, and Algeria.

2. Recognizing Cause and Effect How did the Cold War lead to several "hot" wars?

Graphic Organizer

Copy this chart onto a separate sheet of paper. Then fill in the empty boxes with examples to complete the chart.

Challenges of the 1900s			
Wars			
Differences in Economic Systems			
Environmental Problems			
Colonialism			
Differences in Wealth			

Graphic Organizer

Students' answers may vary. Sample answers shown below.

Challenges of the 1900s			
Wars	avoid World War III	create dialogues to stop civil wars	
Differences in Economic Systems	Capitalist countries allow individuals to own property and businesses.	In communist countries, government owns and controls property and businesses.	
Environmental Problems	controlling pollution	balancing economic growth with environmental protection	protecting endangered animals
Colonialism	During wars, colonies were expected to side with their colonial rulers.	The end of colonialism left some countries ill-prepared to govern themselves.	Government by soldiers is giving way to democracy.
Differences in Wealth	Developing nations need tools and know-how of developed nations.	Developed nations need the resources of developing nations.	

Map Activity

Africa and India
For each place listed below, write the letter from the map that shows its location. Use information in this chapter and the Atlas in the back of your book to complete this activity.

1. India

2. Ghana

3. Algeria

4. South Africa

5. Zimbabwe

Place Location

Writing Activity

Write an Outline
Outline the history of the 1900s. Use facts from this chapter to complete your outline.

Internet Activity

Use a search engine to find **North America/Canada - World War II**. Click on **World War II "54 Years Ago," Navajo Code Talkers**, and **Oral History Archives.** Learn how to write the Navajo Code. Then link to **Navajo Language** to hear it spoken. Write a secret message to a friend.

Skills Review

Turn to the Skills Activity.
Review the three steps for expressing a problem clearly. Then answer the following questions: (a) What questions could you ask in step two? (b) How does expressing a problem clearly make finding the solution easier?

How Am I Doing?

Answer these questions to help you check your progress.

1. Can I explain why world conflicts developed in the 1900s?

2. Do I understand when and how colonies gained their independence?

3. Can I explain how the nations of the world are interdependent?

4. Can I give examples of ways in which nations are responding to environmental challenges?

5. What information from this chapter can I use in my book project?

Internet Activity

If students are having difficulty finding this site, you may wish to have them use the following URL, which was accurate at the time this textbook was published:

http://www.execpc.com/ ~dboals/a-part1a.html

You might also guide students to a search engine. Four of the most useful are Infoseek, AltaVista, Lycos, and Yahoo. For additional suggestions on using the Internet, refer to the Prentice Hall Social Studies' Educator's Handbook "Using the Internet," in the *Prentice Hall World Explorer Program Resources.*

For additional links to world history and culture topics, visit the Prentice Hall Home Page at:
http://www.phschool.com

How Am I Doing?

Point out to students that this checklist is a quick reminder of what they learned in the chapter. If their answer to any of the questions is *no* or if they are unsure, they may need to review the topic.

Critical Thinking

1. Answers will vary, but should demonstrate the basic idea that the path to independence taken by some countries, such as Ghana and India, was relatively peaceful, while the path taken by others, such as Algeria, was violent.

2. Answers will vary. Students should explain that the "hot" wars were eruptions caused by the rivalry and tensions between the two sides in the Cold War.

Map Activity

1. C   **3.** B   **5.** E
2. A   **4.** D

Writing Activity

Outlines will vary. Encourage students to organize their outlines chronologically, either by decades or by major events.

Skills Review

Answers may vary. Sample answers follow. (a) What do these problems or events have in common? How are they alike? (b) Expressing the problem clearly narrows the choices for solutions by automatically eliminating some possibilities.

Resource Directory

Teaching Resources

Chapter Tests Forms A and B are in the Tests booklet, pp. 44–49.

Final Exams Forms A and B are in the Tests booklet, pp. 50–55.

Program Resources

Writing Process Handbook includes Outlining Your Material, p. 25, to help students with the Writing Activity.

Media and Technology

Color Transparencies
Color Transparency 174
(Graphic organizer table template)

**Prentice Hall Writer's Solution** Writing Lab CD-ROM

Computer Test Bank

**Resource Pro™ CD-ROM**

History Quiz Wizards

INTERDISCIPLINARY
ACTIVITY SHOP

Lesson Objectives

1 Locate interesting facts about history from medieval times to today.

2 Develop and write questions about historical facts.

3 Use interdisciplinary skills to answer questions in a history quiz game.

Lesson Plan

1 Engage

Warm-Up Activity

Ask students if they have ever played one of the many popular geography or other trivia quiz games. Urge students to share their experiences, including both board and electronic versions of these games. Invite students to tell what they like best and least about geography and trivia quiz games.

Activating Prior Knowledge

Have students name their favorite chapter or section of their textbook. Invite them to list two or three facts they found especially interesting.

2 Explore

Direct students to carefully read the Activity Shop materials. Then work together to locate data for a sample question in each subject area. Have volunteers draft the sample questions on the chalkboard.

Who figured out the law of gravity? How much has the United States grown since 1776? What was *The Tale of Genji?* If you know the right answers, you win three points!

A history quiz game can give you the chance to sharpen your memory and show what you know. And when you write some of the questions yourself, you will have to hunt through history for interesting facts.

Purpose

In this activity, you will create a game to help you and your classmates learn and remember many of the things you have read in this book.

Players will answer questions from all periods of history from medieval times to today. With a group of your classmates, you will write the questions for the quiz.

Take no more than one hour to look through this book and write questions about the history you find. Be sure to write answers as well. Look for information about the topics described on the next page.

Which ocean did Columbus cross on his journeys?

Resource Directory

Teaching Resources

Activity Shop: Interdisciplinary in the Activities and Projects booklet, p. 7, provides a structure that helps students complete the interdisciplinary activity.

Maps and Globes

Find in this book descriptions of how geography has influenced history. For example, you will read that Christopher Columbus crossed the Atlantic Ocean. Thus you might write the question "Which ocean did Columbus cross on his journeys?" Geography questions will often be answered with the names of countries, cities, landforms, or bodies of water.

Wonderful Words

These questions have to do with language or literature. You can ask for definitions of special words in the text. You can also ask questions about the literature or language of a region. For example, ask, "Why do many Africans speak French?"

How the Earth Works

Questions in this category have to do with science. You might ask about inventors or important scientific discoveries, for example, "What scientist of the Muslim empire made important medical discoveries?"

History Counts

Challenge players to solve a math problem. Use numbers that have to do with historical facts. For example, "The Silk Road was about 3,400 miles long. If a caravan traveled at an average speed of 3 miles per hour, how long would it take to complete the journey?"

Wild Card

Write questions about health, art, music, or any other subject you come across as you read this book. Call this the "wild card" category.

Links to Other Subjects

Maps and Globes .... **Geography**

Wonderful Words .... **Language Arts**

How the Earth Works .... **Science**

History Counts .... **Math**

Wild Card .... **Music, Art, Health**

Prepare Question Cards

Develop at least five questions for each of the categories. Write each question on a note card. Write the answer on the back of the card. Color-code your note cards for the five different question categories.

Play

Choose a scorekeeper. This person will ask the questions and keep track of players' right and wrong answers.

To begin, have the first player select one of the five question categories. The scorekeeper should then choose a card from that category and ask the question written on the card. If the player answers correctly, he or she gets a point for that category. Then the next player takes a turn. A player wins the game by correctly answering three questions in each category.

ANALYSIS AND CONCLUSION

1. Was it easier for you to come up with questions for some categories than for others? Why do you think this was so?

2. What did you learn about history by making this game?

3. What did you learn about history by playing this game?

3 Teach

You might allow students to work in teams, according to the subjects which interest them most or with a student representing each subject area. The game may be played repeatedly, with students organized in different teams. Be sure to rotate scorekeepers into player positions.

4 Assess

Review all students' questions cards before the game is played. Evaluate questions for originality, interest, and pertinence. Evaluate answers for accuracy. You may also assess students' game performance, evaluating their answers for accuracy and their behavior for sportsmanship.

Answers to ...

ANALYSIS AND CONCLUSION

1. Answers will vary. Accept all well-thought-out responses.
2. Students should name one or two facts that they did not previously know.
3. Answers will vary. Accept all reasonable responses.

Lesson Objectives

1 Display knowledge of history from medieval times to today in biographies, time lines, posters, maps, or other projects.

2 Apply understanding from the text to creative presentations.

Lesson Plan

1 Engage

Warm-Up Activity

Invite volunteers to read aloud a Guiding Question from the beginning of this page. Ask what students think the questions mean, urging them to give examples in each case. Then have students read the opening text of the Project Menu. Explain that they will choose one of the projects to work on, while studying history since medieval times.

Activating Prior Knowledge

Challenge students to identify their own project experience strengths and weaknesses. Perhaps they are uncomfortable drawing but enjoy library research. Share and discuss some common experiences.

MEDIEVAL TIMES TO TODAY

PROJECT POSSIBILITIES

As you study history from medieval times to today, you will be reading and thinking about these important questions.

☛ **How did physical geography affect the development of societies around the world?**

☛ **How did each society's belief system affect its history, government, and economy?**

☛ **What accomplishments in technology, learning, or artistic expression were found in each society?**

☛ **What was the pattern of the day-to-day life in these societies?**

☛ **How did these societies interact with other societies?**

It's time to show what you know about medieval times to today.

GEO LEO

Project Menu

The chapters in this book have some answers to these questions. Now you can find your own answers by doing projects alone or with a group. Here are some ways to make your own discoveries about history from medieval times to today.

One Job Through the Ages There were no airplane pilots 500 years ago, but there were doctors, carpenters, and teachers.

Learn about the history of a job that has been around at least since the Middle Ages. Find out how different cultures have practiced and changed this job over the course of history. For example, how has medicine been affected by doctors from the Muslim empire, medieval China, and Europe in the 1800s?

Put what you learn in a time line. Write brief descriptions of the important contributions of different cultures. Add them to your time line, along with illustrations and a title.

Resource Directory

Teaching Resources

📁 **Book Projects** in the Activities and Projects booklet, pp. 8–19, provide a guide to completing the projects described on these two pages. Each project is supported by three pages of structured guidance.

From Questions to Careers
JOBS IN HISTORY MUSEUMS

History museums preserve bits of the past for the enjoyment and education of the people of the present. Some specialize in local history. Others teach about the history of whole nations. Still others are dedicated to specific historical events, like wars or migrations.

Each is also a fascinating place to work. Since most history museums are open to the public, tour guides perform an important job. They show visitors through the museum, explaining exhibits and answering questions. Historians and designers create these exhibits.

Many museums have libraries for historical research. These are usually managed by professional librarians.

Most of these jobs require a college degree. Other jobs, however, do not. There are assistants in many history museums. Jobs in gift shops and information booths are also available for those without a degree. Today, many museums offer on-the-job training.

▶ A tour guide leads a group in the Air and Space Museum.

Two Tales of One City

Since medieval times, the great cities of the world have changed dramatically. Five hundred years ago, few cities existed in the Americas. African cities that are now home to millions were tiny villages.

As you read this book, pick a city that has existed for at least 300 years. Choose a year in that city's past, and compare life in that city then to life in that city today. How big was it? What did it look like? What jobs did the people have? Find the answers to these and other questions. Answer the same questions for today.

Make a poster that compares your city's past with its present. Draw pictures of the city then and now. Write captions describing city life in both times.

The Birth of a Nation

Today there are about 200 nations in the world. Each was formed sometime in the past and became a nation over the years. Choose one nation and learn how it came into being.

Conduct research to learn about the nation's history. What country or empire was it once a part of? How did it achieve its independence? Find the answers to these and other important questions. Identify the most important steps the nation took in arriving at the borders, government, and culture it has today.

Then write a short history of the nation. Discuss its birth and growth. Describe what it is like today. Present your work as part of a "Nation Celebration" in your classroom.

Major Migrations

One of the biggest stories in modern history is the vast movement, or migration, of people from some areas of the Earth to others.

As you read in this book about each major human migration, mark it on a world "Migrations Map" in your classroom. Label each migration with its name and date.

Answer these questions about each one: Who migrated? When? From where did they migrate? Where did they go? How did they travel? Why did they migrate? What were the effects of the migration?

2 Explore

Have students read the Project Menu thoroughly. Discuss the many museum career options. Invite students who have visited museums to share memories of the workers there. If possible, ask a curator from a local museum to visit the class. Then explore each project possibility in class discussion. List essential steps and materials. Discuss useful research avenues.

3 Teach

Allow students to select a project from the menu or develop a project of their own. You may wish to assign projects to students. With students, estimate the necessary time for each project element. Post schedules for all to use, including interim progress report dates. Students may work in pairs on any of the projects, each focusing on different chronological periods.

4 Assess

Display student projects for all to enjoy.

Acceptable projects follow the stated guidelines and include accurate data about the topic.

Commendable projects include data stemming from thorough research and a clear understanding of history from medieval times.

Outstanding projects show evidence of creative and in-depth research, original presentation methods, and critical responses to the guiding questions.

Reference

TABLE OF CONTENTS

Map and Globe Handbook 225

How do you find your way around the world? The Map and Globe Handbook features the skills every geographer needs.

Atlas 242

Where in the world is it? The Atlas provides physical and political maps of the world and its continents.

The World: Political	242
The World: Physical	244
North and South America: Political	246
North and South America: Physical	247
Europe: Political	248
Europe: Physical	249
Africa: Political	250
Africa: Physical	251
Asia: Political	252
Asia: Physical	253
Australia, New Zealand, and the Pacific Islands: Physical-Political	254
The Arctic and Antarctica	255

World View 256

What's your favorite country? World View lists information about every country in the world!

Glossary of Geographic Terms 264
Gazetteer 266
Biographical Dictionary 268
Glossary 270
Index 274
Acknowledgments 278

MAP AND Handbook GLOBE

This Map and Globe Handbook is designed to help you develop some of the skills you need to be a world explorer. These can help you whether you explore from the top of an elephant in India or from a computer at school.

You can use the information in this handbook to improve your map and globe skills. But the best way to sharpen your skills is to practice. The more you practice the better you'll get.

GEO CLEO and GEO LEO

Table of Contents

Five Themes of Geography   226

Understanding Movements of the Earth   228

Maps and Globes Represent the Earth   229

Locating Places on a Map or a Globe   230

Map Projections   232

Parts of a Map   234

Comparing Maps of Different Scale   235

Political Maps   236

Physical Maps   237

Special Purpose Maps   238

Landforms, Climate Regions,
    and Natural Vegetation Regions   239

Using the Map and Globe Handbook

You may choose to present the Map and Globe Handbook as a special unit of study at the beginning of the year or at another point in the school year. As an alternative, you might prefer to choose among the activities in the Map and Globe Handbook to meet the specific needs of your class or of individual students.

Point out to students that they already know a great deal about maps. Ask them to sketch a quick map of the route from their house to school. Discuss the map elements that students include on their maps.

Read through the page with students.

Lesson Objective

Identify and define the five themes of geography.

Lesson Plan

1 Engage

Warm-Up Activity

Work with students to define the word *theme*. (An underlying idea built into or expanded upon in a work of art or study.)

Activating Prior Knowledge

Have students work in small groups for five minutes to write a definition of *geography*. Discuss their definitions. Then write the five themes on the chalkboard and ask students to break up their definitions, putting phrases under the proper headings. For example, if students wrote "studying where other countries are," that would fall under the theme of location. Add to students' definitions as needed.

2 Explore

Read the first verse of the poem "Midwest Town" by Ruth De Long Peterson to the class:

Farther east it wouldn't be on
  the map—
Too small—but here it rates a
  dot and a name.
In Europe it would wear a
  castle cap
Or have a cathedral rising like
  a flame.

Ask students to identify the geography themes in the verse (location and place).

Five Themes of Geography

Studying the geography of the entire world can be a huge task. You can make that task easier by using the five themes of geography: location, place, human-environment interaction, movement, and regions. The themes are tools you can use to organize information and to answer the where, why, and how of geography.

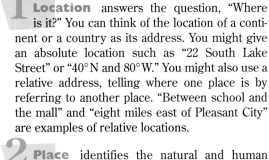

1. Location
Chicago, Illinois, occupies one location on the Earth. No other place has exactly the same absolute location.

1 **Location** answers the question, "Where is it?" You can think of the location of a continent or a country as its address. You might give an absolute location such as "22 South Lake Street" or "40° N and 80° W." You might also use a relative address, telling where one place is by referring to another place. "Between school and the mall" and "eight miles east of Pleasant City" are examples of relative locations.

2 **Place** identifies the natural and human features that make one place different from every other place. You can identify a specific place by its landforms, climate, plants, animals, people, or cultures. You might even think of place as a geographic signature. Use the signature to help you understand the natural and human features that make one place different from every other place.

2. Place
Ancient cultures in Egypt built distinctive pyramids. Use the theme of place to help you remember features that exist only in Egypt.

226

3 Human-Environment Interaction focuses on the relationship between people and the environment. As people live in an area, they often begin to make changes to it, usually to make their lives easier. For example, they might build a dam to control flooding during rainy seasons. Also, the environment can affect how people live, work, dress, travel, and communicate.

4 Movement answers the question "How do people, goods, and ideas move from place to place?" Remember that, often, what happens in one place can affect what happens in another. Use the theme of movement to help you trace the spread of goods, people, and ideas from one location to the next.

5 Regions is the last geographic theme. A region is a group of places that share common features. Geographers divide the world into many types of regions. For example, countries, states, and cities are political regions. The people in these places live under the same type of government. Other features can be used to define regions. Places that have the same climate belong to a particular climate region. Places that share the same culture belong to a cultural region. The same place can be found in more than one region. The state of Hawaii is in the political region of the United States. Because it has a tropical climate, Hawaii is also part of a tropical climate region.

3. Human-Environment Interaction
Peruvians have changed steep mountain slopes into terraces suitable for farming. Think how this environment looked before people made changes.

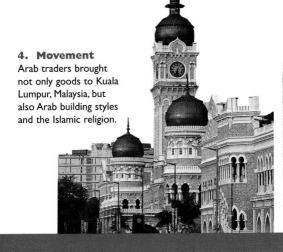

4. Movement
Arab traders brought not only goods to Kuala Lumpur, Malaysia, but also Arab building styles and the Islamic religion.

PRACTICE YOUR WORLD EXPLORER SKILLS

1. What is the absolute location of your school? What is one way to describe its relative location?

2. What might be a "geographic signature" of the town or city you live in?

3. Give an example of human-environment interaction where you live.

4. Name at least one thing that comes into your town or city and one that goes out. How is each moved? Where does it come from? Where does it go?

5. What are several regions you think your town or city belongs in?

5. Regions
Wheat farming is an important activity in Kansas. This means that Kansas is part of a farming region.

3 Teach

After students have read the definitions of the themes of geography, begin discussion. Encourage students to relate the themes to what they already know about the Earth and its people. Invite them to provide additional examples for each theme.

4 Assess

Have students work in pairs to create a geographic description of where they live. Descriptions should include one or more items for each of the five themes of geography. Students may need an atlas to find the absolute location of your community. If your community is not in the atlas, accept the absolute location of the nearest city, or other political landmark.

As an alternative, have students complete the Practice Your World Explorer Skills. Assess students' understanding by the accuracy of their answers.

Answers to . . .

PRACTICE YOUR WORLD EXPLORER SKILLS

Sample answers are given for Chicago, Illinois.

1. 33 North Green street, between Green Park and the highway
2. It's along the shore of Lake Michigan.
3. The city built bridges over the river.
4. Manufactured goods leave the city on railroads to other parts of the country. Fruits and vegetables from nearby farms come into the city on trucks.
5. the Midwest, the Great Lakes region

Lesson Objective

Explain how the movement of the Earth causes night and day, as well as the seasons.

Lesson Plan

1 Engage

Warm-Up Activity

To introduce the skill, remind students that the movement of the Earth accounts for some of the differences between places.

Activating Prior Knowledge

Ask students how we know that the Earth moves.

2 Explore

Read the page with students. Discuss anything they have difficulty understanding.

3 Teach

Darken the room and put a lighted lamp on a table. Hold a globe close enough to the lamp to catch the light. Slowly turn the globe to show the movement from day to night. Hold the globe in the positions shown in the diagram to show the changing seasons. Have students practice manipulating the lamp and the globe.

4 Assess

Ask students to apply the skill by explaining why days are longer in the summer in most places in the world—except around the Equator. (The sun's rays hit the Earth most directly near the Equator year-round.)

You may also assess students' understanding by asking them to complete the Practice Your World Explorer Skills.

1. the Earth's tilt
2. March and September

Planet Earth is part of our solar system. The Earth revolves around the sun in a nearly circular path called an orbit. A revolution, or one complete orbit around the sun, takes 365 1/4 days, or a year. As the Earth revolves around the sun, it is also spinning around in space. This movement is called a rotation. The Earth rotates on its axis—an invisible line through the center of the Earth from the North Pole to the South Pole. The Earth makes one full rotation about every 24 hours. As the Earth rotates, it is daytime on the side facing the sun. It is night on the side away from the sun.

The Earth's axis is tilted at an angle. Because of this tilt, sunlight strikes different parts of the Earth at certain points in the year, creating different seasons.

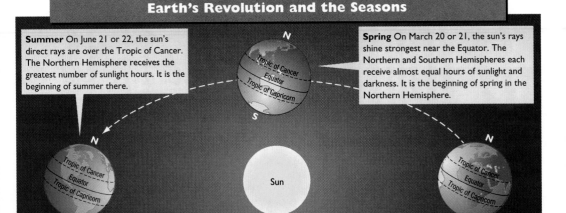

Earth's Revolution and the Seasons

Summer On June 21 or 22, the sun's direct rays are over the Tropic of Cancer. The Northern Hemisphere receives the greatest number of sunlight hours. It is the beginning of summer there.

Spring On March 20 or 21, the sun's rays shine strongest near the Equator. The Northern and Southern Hemispheres each receive almost equal hours of sunlight and darkness. It is the beginning of spring in the Northern Hemisphere.

Autumn On September 22 or 23, the sun's rays shine strongest near the Equator. Again, the Northern and Southern Hemispheres each receive almost equal hours of sunlight and darkness. It is the beginning of fall in the Northern Hemisphere.

Winter Around December 21, the sun is over the Tropic of Capricorn in the Southern Hemisphere. The Northern Hemisphere is tilted away from the sun and it is the beginning of winter there.

▲ **Location** This diagram shows how the Earth's tilt and orbit around the sun combine to create the seasons. Remember, in the Southern Hemisphere the seasons are reversed.

PRACTICE YOUR WORLD EXPLORER SKILLS

1. What causes the seasons in the Northern Hemisphere to be the opposite of those in the Southern Hemisphere?

2. During which two months of the year do the Northern and Southern Hemispheres have about equal hours of daylight and darkness?

Resource Directory

Media and Technology

 Color Transparency 105

Maps and Globes Represent the Earth

Globes

A globe is a scale model of the Earth. It shows the actual shapes, sizes, and locations of all the Earth's landmasses and bodies of water. Features on the surface of the Earth are drawn to scale on a globe. This means a smaller unit of measure on the globe stands for a larger unit of measure on the Earth.

Because a globe is made in the true shape of the Earth, it offers these advantages for studying the Earth.

- The shape of all land and water bodies are accurate.
- Compass directions from one point to any other point are correct.
- The distance from one location to another is always accurately represented.

However, a globe presents some disadvantages for studying the Earth. Because a globe shows the entire Earth, it cannot show small areas in great detail. Also, a globe is not easily folded and carried from one place to another. For these reasons, geographers often use maps to learn about the Earth.

Maps

A map is a drawing or representation, on a flat surface, of a region. A map can show details too small to be seen on a globe. Floor plans, mall directories, and road maps are among the maps we use most often.

While maps solve some of the problems posed by globes, they have some disadvantages of their own. Maps flatten the real round world. Mapmakers cut, stretch, push, and pull some parts of the Earth to get it all flat on paper. As a result, some locations may be distorted. That is, their size, shape, and relative location may not be accurate. For example, on most maps of the entire world, the size and shape of the Antarctic and Arctic regions are not accurate.

PRACTICE YOUR WORLD EXPLORER SKILLS

1. What is the main difference between a globe and a map?

2. What is one advantage of using a globe instead of a map?

Global Gores

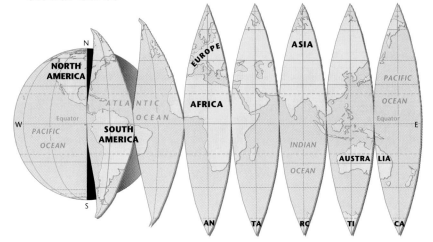

◀ **Location**
When mapmakers flatten the surface of the Earth, curves become straight lines. As a result, size, shape, and distance are distorted.

Teaching Resources

📁 **Comparing Globes and Maps,** in the Social Studies and Geography Skills booklet, p. 12, helps students understand and apply the skill of understanding differences between maps and globes.

Lesson Plan

1 Engage
Warm-Up Activity

Ask students what it might be like to see the Earth from space.

Activating Prior Knowledge

Ask students whether they would use a map or a globe to plan a vacation. Discuss how they might use both.

2 Explore

Have students read the page and study the illustrations. Discuss with them similarities and differences between maps and globes.

3 Teach

Roughly sketch the continents on a large grapefruit with a ballpoint pen. Explain that the grapefruit is like the Earth. Carefully peel the grapefruit and then challenge students to reassemble the continents into a flat map.

4 Assess

Assess students' understanding by asking them to complete the PracticeYour World Explorer Skills.

Answers to . . .

PRACTICE YOUR WORLD EXPLORER SKILLS

1. A globe is a scale model of the Earth; a map is a drawing of the Earth or a region of it.
2. Students should be able to support their choices of either accurate shape, true direction, or accurate distance.

Lesson Objectives

1. Define the hemispheres of the Earth.

2. Locate places on a map using the coordinates of latitude and longitude.

Lesson Plan

1 Engage

Warm-Up Activity

Present this challenge to the class. Tell students that they are sailing alone around the world. They have been in a huge storm and have run out of food. They have not seen land for weeks, but when they radio for extra supplies, they can give their exact location. How? (They know their latitude and longitude.)

Activating Prior Knowledge

Draw an unlabeled grid on the chalkboard. Place a large dot somewhere on the grid. Ask students how they could use the grid to describe where the dot is.

The Hemispheres

Another name for a round ball like a globe is a sphere. The Equator, an imaginary line halfway between the North and South Poles, divides the globe into two hemispheres. (The prefix *hemi* means "half.") Land and water south of the Equator are in the Southern Hemisphere. Land and water north of the Equator are in the Northern Hemisphere.

Mapmakers sometimes divide the globe along an imaginary line that runs from North Pole to South Pole. This line, called the Prime Meridian, divides the globe into the Eastern and Western Hemispheres.

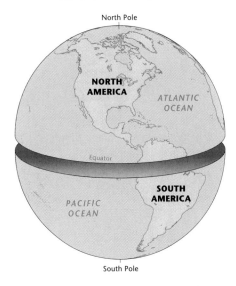

Northern Hemisphere

North Pole

NORTH AMERICA

ATLANTIC OCEAN

Equator

SOUTH AMERICA

PACIFIC OCEAN

South Pole

Southern Hemisphere

▲ The Equator divides the Northern Hemisphere from the Southern Hemisphere.

ATLANTIC OCEAN

EUROPE

Prime Meridian

AFRICA

Western Hemisphere **Eastern Hemisphere**

▲ The Prime Meridian divides the Eastern Hemisphere from the Western Hemisphere.

Resource Directory

Teaching Resources

Understanding Hemispheres, in the Social Studies and Geography Skills booklet, p. 7, helps students understand and apply the skill of identifying hemispheres.

Media and Technology

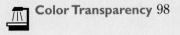 Color Transparency 98

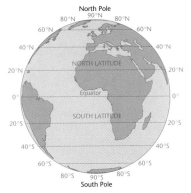

Parallels of Latitude
The Equator, at 0° latitude, is the starting place for measuring latitude or distances north and south. Most globes do not show every parallel of latitude. They may show every 10, 20, or even 30 degrees.

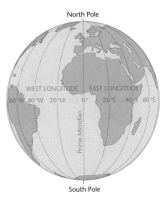

Meridians of Longitude
The Prime Meridian, at 0° longitude, runs from pole to pole through Greenwich, England. It is the starting place for measuring longitude or distances east and west. Each meridian of longitude meets its opposite longitude at the North and South Poles.

The Global Grid

Two sets of lines cover most globes. One set of lines runs parallel to the Equator. These lines, including the Equator, are called *parallels of latitude.* They are measured in degrees (°). One degree of latitude represents a distance of about 70 miles (112 km). The Equator has a location of 0°. The other parallels of latitude tell the direction and distance from the Equator to another location.

The second set of lines runs north and south. These lines are called *meridians of longitude.* Meridians show the degrees of longitude east or west of the Prime Meridian, which is located at 0°. A meridian of longitude tells the direction and distance from the Prime Meridian to another location. Unlike parallels, meridians are not the same distance apart everywhere on the globe.

Together the pattern of parallels of latitude and meridians of longitude is called the global grid. Using the lines of latitude and longitude, you can locate any place on Earth. For example, the location of 30° north latitude and 90° west longitude is usually written as 30°N, 90°W. Only one place on Earth has these coordinates—the city of New Orleans, in the state of Louisiana.

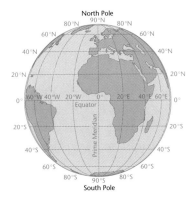

The Global Grid
By using lines of latitude and longitude, you can give the absolute location of any place on the Earth.

1. Which continents lie completely in the Northern Hemisphere? The Western Hemisphere?

2. Is there land or water at 20°S latitude and the Prime Meridian? At the Equator and 60°W longitude?

Read through these two pages with students. Using a large map, have students begin at the Prime Meridian and put their fingers on each of the meridians of longitude as they move east and then west. Do the same with the parallels of latitude, moving from the Equator to the North Pole and then to the South Pole. Some students may need help in understanding the definition of *parallel.* (Parallel lines are lines that never meet.)

3 Teach

Ask a volunteer to work with a large map or globe. Have other students name cities around the world. The volunteer must locate them and state their coordinates.

4 Assess

To assess students' understanding, give students coordinates that you have found in an atlas and ask them to locate the city. Have students discuss the process. Use students' discussion to assess their understanding of how to locate places on maps and globes.

Teaching Resources

 Understanding Latitude and Longitude and **Using Latitude and Longitude,** in the Social Studies and Geography Skills booklet, pp. 10–11, helps students understand and apply the skill of reading latitude and longitude lines.

Media and Technology

Color Transparency 99

Answers to . . .

PRACTICE YOUR WORLD EXPLORER SKILLS

1. Asia, North America, Europe; North America, South America
2. water; land

Lesson Objectives

1. Compare maps of different projections.
2. Describe distortions in map projections.

1 Engage

Warm-Up Activity

Ask students to look at the maps on these two pages. To introduce the skill of understanding map distortions, ask them to find as many differences as they can between the maps.

Activating Prior Knowledge

Ask students whether a person traveling in space could ever see the entire Earth at one time. Ask them why people want or need to use maps that show the entire world.

I magine trying to flatten out a complete orange peel. The peel would split. The shape would change. You would have to cut the peel to get it to lie flat. In much the same way, maps cannot show the correct size and shape of every landmass or body of water on the Earth's curved surface. Maps shrink some places and stretch others. This shrinking and stretching is called distortion—*a change made to a shape.*

To make up for this disadvantage, mapmakers use different map projections. Each map projection is a way of showing the round Earth on flat paper. Each type of projection has some distortion. No one projection can accurately show the correct area, shape, distance, and direction for the Earth's surface. Mapmakers use the projection that has the least distortion for the information they are studying.

Same-Shape Maps

Some map projections can accurately show the shapes of landmasses. However, these projections often greatly distort the size of landmasses as well as the distance between them.

One of the most common same-shape maps is a Mercator projection, named for the mapmaker who invented it. The Mercator projection accurately shows shape and direction, but it distorts distance and size. In this projection, the northern and southern areas of the globe appear stretched more than areas near the Equator. Because the projection shows true directions, ships' navigators use it to chart a straight line course between two ports.

Mercator Projection

Teaching Resources

Understanding Projection, in the Social Studies and Geography Skills booklet, p. 13, helps students understand and apply the concept of map projection. You may also wish to use the following:

Maps With Accurate Shapes:
Conformal Maps on p. 15,
Maps With Accurate Areas:
Equal-Area Maps on p. 16, and
Maps With Accurate Directions:
Azimuthal Maps on p. 18.

Equal-Area Maps

Some map projections can show the correct size of landmasses. Maps that use these projections are called equal-area maps. In order to show the correct size of landmasses, these maps usually distort shapes. The distortion is usually greater at the edges of the map and less at the center.

Robinson Maps

Many of the maps in this book use the Robinson projection. This is a compromise between the Mercator and equal-area projections. It gives a useful overall picture of the world. The Robinson projection keeps the size and shape relationships of most continents and oceans but does distort size of the polar regions.

Azimuthal Maps

Another kind of projection shows true compass direction. Maps that use this projection are called azimuthal maps. Such maps are easy to recognize—they are usually circular. Azimuthal maps are often used to show the areas of the North and South Poles. However, azimuthal maps distort scale, area, and shape.

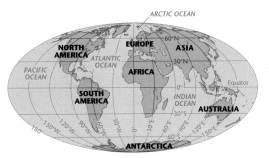

Equal-Area Projection

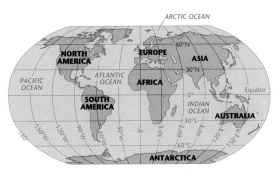

Robinson Projection

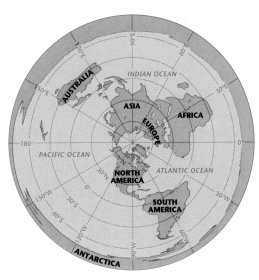

Azimuthal Projection

PRACTICE YOUR WORLD EXPLORER SKILLS

1 What feature is distorted on an equal-area map?

2 Would you use a Mercator projection to find the exact distance between two locations? Tell why or why not.

3 Which would be a better choice for studying the Antarctic—an azimuthal projection or a Robinson projection? Explain.

2 Explore

After students have read the two pages, have them look up the word *distortion* in a dictionary. Ask them why we use maps that we know are distorted. (All maps are somewhat distorted.)

3 Teach

Students can practice the skill by comparing the maps to a globe. Ask them to note especially the sizes and positions of Greenland and Antarctica.

To apply their understanding of the skill, students can suggest reasons why many maps use the Robinson projection. (It shows the sizes and shapes of the continents with the least amount of distortion.)

4 Assess

Assess students' understanding by the accuracy of their answers.

Media and Technology

 Color Transparency 100

Answers to. . .

PRACTICE YOUR WORLD EXPLORER SKILLS

1. shapes
2. No; the Mercator projection distorts distances.
3. An azimuthal projection centered on the South Pole would show all of Antarctica, a Robinson projection would not.

Lesson Objective

Identify and use the parts of a map.

Lesson Plan

1 Engage

Warm-Up Activity

If possible, show students several maps, such as subway or bus route maps and road maps. To introduce the skill, ask students to describe several parts that all of the maps seem to have in common (probably titles, keys, scales, and compasses).

Activating Prior Knowledge

Ask students why they should pay attention to different parts of a map. (They help the user locate places on it.)

2 Explore

Read the page with students. Help them identify the title, compass, scale, and key on several different maps.

3 Teach

Show students several maps, including those in the Atlas of this book. Students can practice and apply using the parts of a map by asking each other questions such as What is this map about? Which city is north of the river? How far apart are these two cities?

4 Assess

Assess students' understanding by the accuracy of their answers.

Answers to ...

PRACTICE YOUR WORLD EXPLORER SKILLS

1. the title
2. key
3. scale

Mapmakers provide several clues to help you understand the information on a map. As an explorer, it is your job to read and interpret these clues.

Compass
Many maps show north at the top of the map. One way to show direction on a map is to use an arrow that points north. There may be an N shown with the arrow. Many maps give more information about direction by displaying a compass showing the directions, north, east, south, and west. The letters N, E, S, and W are placed to indicate these directions.

Title
The title of a map is the most basic clue. It signals what kinds of information you are likely to find on the map. A map titled *West Africa: Population Density* will be most useful for locating information about where people live in West Africa.

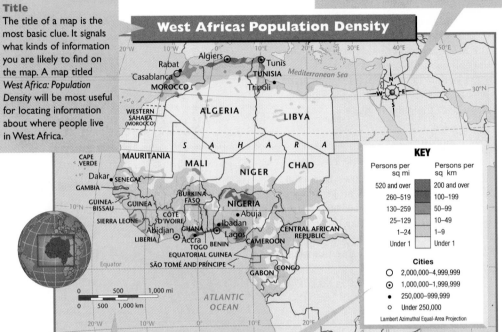

West Africa: Population Density

KEY

Persons per sq mi	Persons per sq km
520 and over	200 and over
260–519	100–199
130–259	50–99
25–129	10–49
1–24	1–9
Under 1	Under 1

Cities
- ◯ 2,000,000–4,999,999
- ◉ 1,000,000–1,999,999
- ● 250,000–999,999
- ○ Under 250,000

Lambert Azimuthal Equal-Area Projection

Scale
A map scale helps you find the actual distances between points shown on the map. You can measure the distance between any two points on the map, compare them to the scale, and find out the actual distance between the points. Most map scales show distances in both miles and kilometers.

Key
Often a map has a key, or legend, that shows the symbols used on the map and what each one means. On some maps, color is used as a symbol. On those maps, the key also tells the meaning of each color.

PRACTICE YOUR WORLD EXPLORER SKILLS

1. What part of a map tells you what the map is about?

2. Where on the map should you look to find out the meaning of this symbol? ●

3. What part of the map can you use to find the distance between two cities?

234 MAP AND GLOBE HANDBOOK

Resource Directory

Teaching Resources

Using the Map Key, in the Social Studies and Geography Skills booklet, p. 3, helps students understand and apply the skill of using parts of a map. You may also wish to use the following:
Using the Compass Rose on p. 4 and
Using the Map Scale on p. 5.

Comparing Maps of Different Scale

ere are three maps drawn to three different scales. The first map shows Moscow's location in the northeastern portion of Russia. This map shows the greatest area—a large section of northern Europe. It has the smallest scale (1 inch = about 900 miles) and shows the fewest details. This map can tell you what direction to travel to reach Moscow from Finland.

Find the red box on Map 1. It shows the whole area covered by Map 2. Study Map 2. It gives a closer look at the city of Moscow. It shows the fea-

tures around the city, the city's boundary, and the general shape of the city. This map can help you find your way from the airport to the center of town.

Now find the red box on Map 2. This box shows the area shown on Map 3. This map moves you closer into the city. Like the zoom on a computer or camera, Map 3 shows the smallest area but has the greatest detail. This map has the largest scale (1 inch = about 0.8 miles). This is the map to use to explore downtown Moscow.

Map 1

KEY

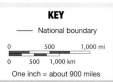

National boundary

0   500   1,000 mi
0 500 1,000 km

One inch = about 900 miles

Map 2

KEY

Built-up area

Road or street

0   5   10 mi
0 5 10 km

One inch = about 12.5 miles

Map 3

KEY

Road or street

■ Point of interest

0   .5   1 mi
0 .5 1 km

One inch = about 0.8 miles

PRACTICE YOUR WORLD EXPLORER SKILLS

1. Which map would be best for finding the location of Red Square? Why?

2. Which map best shows Moscow's location relative to Poland? Explain.

3. Which map best shows the area immediately surrounding the city?

Teaching Resources

Comparing Maps of Different Scale, in the Social Studies and Geography Skills booklet, p. 6, helps students understand and use maps of different scale.

Lesson Objective

Compare maps with different scales.

Lesson Plan

1 Engage
Warm-Up Activity

To introduce the skill, ask students why they cannot find the exact location of their school on a world map. Ask them what kind of map would show the exact location of their school.

Activating Prior Knowledge

Ask students what the zoom on a video camera does. Tell students that changing a map scale can help them "zoom in" on a small area.

2 Explore

Have students read the page and study the maps. How are the maps alike? How are they different?

3 Teach

To practice and apply the skill, work with students to identify the steps in drawing a map of their classroom to the scale of 1 inch = 1 foot. Ask students how the map would be different if the scale were 1 inch = 3 feet.

4 Assess

Have students complete the Practice Your World Explorer Skills. Assess their understanding by the accuracy of their answers.

Answers to...
PRACTICE YOUR WORLD EXPLORER SKILLS

1. map 3 2. map 1 3. map 2

Lesson Objective

Use political maps.

Lesson Plan

1 Engage

Warm-Up Activity

To introduce the skill, tell students that American writer Mark Twain once wrote about people in a hot-air balloon who were confused because the ground below them was not colored like maps.

Activating Prior Knowledge

Point out that the word *political* comes from a Greek word meaning "citizen." A political map is one that emphasizes the boundaries of an area established by its citizens.

2 Explore

Read through the page with students. Make sure they realize that a political map mainly shows how people have divided and named the land.

3 Teach

Ask students to practice using a political map by locating a boundary between countries, the capital of Russia, and a river that is also a boundary.

4 Assess

Have students complete the Practice Your World Explorer Skills. Assess their understanding by the accuracy of their answers.

Answers to ...

PRACTICE YOUR WORLD EXPLORER SKILLS

1. red line
2. star in a circle; solid circle
3. none

Mapmakers create maps to show all kinds of information. The kind of information presented affects the way a map looks. One type of map is called a political map. Its main purpose is to show continents, countries, and divisions within countries such as states or provinces. Usually different colors are used to show different countries or divisions within a country. The colors do not have any special meaning. They are used only to make the map easier to read.

Political maps also show where people have built towns and cities. Symbols can help you tell capital cities from other cities and towns. Even though political maps do not give information that shows what the land looks like, they often include some physical features such as oceans, lakes, and rivers.

Political maps usually have many labels. They give country names, and the names of capital and major cities. Bodies of water such as lakes, rivers, oceans, seas, gulfs, and bays are also labeled.

PRACTICE YOUR WORLD EXPLORER SKILLS

1. What symbol shows the continental boundary?
2. What symbol is used to indicate a capital city? A major city?
3. What kinds of landforms are shown on this map?

▲ The keys of political maps may include symbols. Study the key to learn what the symbols on this map mean.

Resource Directory

Teaching Resources

Reading a Political Map, in the Social Studies and Geography Skills booklet, p. 19, helps students practice using political maps.

Physical Maps

Like political maps, physical maps show country labels and labels for capital cities. However, physical maps also show what the land of a region looks like by showing the major physical features such as plains, hills, plateaus, or mountains. Labels give the names of features such as mountain peaks, mountains, plateaus, and river basins.

In order to tell one landform from another, physical maps often show elevation and relief.

Elevation is the height of the land above sea level. Physical maps in this book use color to show elevation. Browns and oranges show higher lands while blues and greens show lands that are at or below sea level.

Relief shows how quickly the land rises or falls. Hills, mountains, and plateaus are shown on relief maps using shades of gray. Level or nearly level land is shown without shading. Darkly shaded areas indicate steeper lands.

Hawaii: Physical

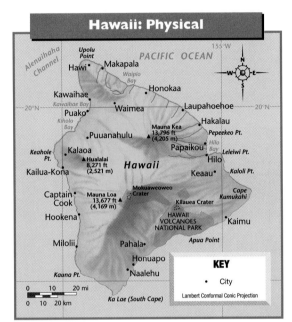

▲ On a physical map, shading is sometimes used to show relief. Use the shading to locate the mountains in Hawaii.

1. How is relief shown on the map to the left?

2. How can you use relief to decide which areas will be the most difficult to climb?

3. What information is given with the name of a mountain peak?

▼ Mauna Kea, an extinct volcano, is the highest peak in the state of Hawaii. Find Mauna Kea on the map.

237

Teaching Resources

📂 **Elevation on a Map,** in the Social Studies and Geography Skills booklet, p. 20, helps students understand and read physical maps that show elevation of land.

Lesson Objective

Use physical maps.

Lesson Plan

1 Engage
Warm-Up Activity

To introduce the skill, tell students that they are going for a hike in the mountains. Encourage them to consider that a map showing the heights of the mountains might be useful.

Activating Prior Knowledge

Remind students that political maps do not necessarily show features of the landscape.

2 Explore

Have students read the page. Point out that a physical map makes the physical features of a place clearer than a political map does.

3 Teach

Students can practice using a physical map by checking this one for the highest mountain it shows. Have students apply the skill by pointing out other physical features on the map.

4 Assess

Have students complete the Practice Your World Explorer Skills. Assess their understanding by the accuracy of their answers.

Answers to ...

PRACTICE YOUR WORLD EXPLORER SKILLS

1. shading
2. Darkly shaded areas are steep and more difficult to climb.
3. its elevation

Lesson Objective

Use special-purpose maps.

Lesson Plan

1 Engage

Warm-Up Activity

Discuss with students the tools they would need during an archaeological dig in the desert of South Asia. Ask what kinds of maps they would need.

Activating Prior Knowledge

Ask students to think of as many meanings for the word *special* as they can. Have them define special-purpose map, and then read the lesson to check their definitions.

2 Explore

When students have read the page, ask them to offer other examples of special-purpose maps.

3 Teach

Review the importance of the map title and the map legend. Discuss the purposes of the map on the page. How is it different from political maps and physical maps?

4 Assess

Have students complete the Practice Your World Explorer Skills. Assess their understanding by the accuracy of their answers.

Answers to ...

PRACTICE YOUR WORLD EXPLORER SKILLS

1. its title
2. the key

As you explore the world, you will encounter many different kinds of special purpose maps. For example, a road map is a special purpose map. The title of each special purpose map tells the purpose and content of the map. Usually a special purpose map highlights only one kind of information. Examples of special purpose maps include land use, population distribution, recreation, transportation, natural resources, or weather.

The key on a special purpose map is very important. Even though a special purpose map shows only one kind of information, it may present many different pieces of data. This data can be shown in symbols, colors, or arrows. In this way, the key acts like a dictionary for the map.

Reading a special purpose map is a skill in itself. Look at the map below. First, try to get an overall sense of what it shows. Then, study the map to identify its main ideas. For example, one main idea of this map is that much of the petroleum production in the region takes place around the Persian Gulf.

PRACTICE YOUR WORLD EXPLORER SKILLS

1 What part of a special purpose map tells what information is contained on the map?

2 What part of a special purpose map acts like a dictionary for the map?

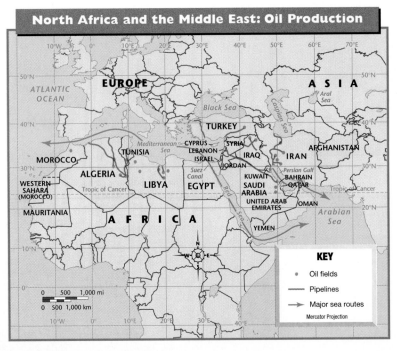

North Africa and the Middle East: Oil Production

KEY
- • Oil fields
- — Pipelines
- → Major sea routes

Mercator Projection

◀ The title on a special purpose map indicates what information can be found on the map. The symbols used on the map are explained in the map's key.

238 MAP AND GLOBE HANDBOOK

Resource Directory

Teaching Resources

Reading a Time Zone Map, in the Social Studies and Geography Skills booklet, p. 24, helps students understand and use this type of special-purpose map. You may also wish to use the activities on pp. 25–39. Each covers a different type of special-purpose map.

Landforms, Climate Regions, and Natural Vegetation Regions

Maps that show landforms, climate, and vegetation regions are special purpose maps. Unlike the boundary lines on a political map, the boundary lines on these maps do not separate the land into exact divisions. A tropical wet climate gradually changes to a tropical wet and dry climate. A tundra gradually changes to an ice cap. Even though the boundaries between regions may not be exact, the information on these maps can help you understand the region and the lives of people in it.

Landforms

Understanding how people use the land requires an understanding of the shape of the land itself. The four most important landforms are mountains, hills, plateaus, and plains. Human activity in every region in the world is influenced by these landforms.

- **Mountains** are high and steep. Most are wide at the bottom and rise to a narrow peak or ridge. Most geographers classify a mountain as land that rises at least 2,000 feet (610 m) above sea level. A series of mountains is called a mountain range.

- **Hills** rise above surrounding land and have rounded tops. Hills are lower and usually less steep than mountains. The elevation of surrounding land determines whether a landform is called a mountain or a hill.

- A **plateau** is a large, mostly flat area of land that rises above the surrounding land. At least one side of a plateau has a steep slope.

- **Plains** are large areas of flat or gently rolling land. Plains have few changes in elevation. Many plains areas are located along coasts. Others are located in the interior regions of some continents.

▶ A satellite view of the Earth showing North and South America. What landforms are visible in the photograph?

239

Teaching Resources

📁 **Four Types of Landforms,** in the Social Studies and Geography Skills booklet, p. 21, helps students understand and read maps that show mountains, hills, plateaus, and plains.

Lesson Objective

① Define landforms, climate regions, and natural vegetation regions.

② Compare climate regions and natural vegetation regions.

Lesson Plan

1 Engage
Warm-Up Activity

Ask students how they would describe their community to someone moving to their area from Australia. What words would they use to describe the land, the general climate, and the kinds of trees and plants?

Activating Prior Knowledge

Invite volunteers who have moved to your area from a different region to explain how the climate and vegetation are different.

2 Explore

Write the terms *landforms, climate regions,* and *natural vegetation regions* on the chalkboard. As students read the material on this page and the following page, have them find examples for each term.

3 Teach

Divide the class into small groups. Ask each group to draw a picture of one of the following landforms: a mountain, a hill, a plateau, a plain. Then ask each group to find the landform on a map in this book or in an atlas.

Direct each student to choose one of the 12 climate types. Ask them to use the maps in this book or in an atlas to find a place in the world with that climate. Then have students use one of the natural vegetation maps in the textbook to figure out which of the 12 natural vegetation regions covers that climate location.

Climate Regions

Another important influence in the ways people live their lives is the climate of their region. Climate is the weather of a given location over a long period of time. Use the descriptions in the table below to help you visualize the climate regions shown on maps.

Climate	Temperatures	Precipitation
Tropical		
Tropical wet	Hot all year round	Heavy all year round
Tropical wet and dry	Hot all year round	Heavy when sun is overhead, dry other times
Dry		
Semiarid	Hot summers, mild to cold winters	Light
Arid	Hot days, cold nights	Very light
Mild		
Mediterranean	Hot summers, cool winters	Dry summers, wet winters
Humid subtropical	Hot summers, cool winters	Year round, heavier in summer than in winter
Marine west coast	Warm summers, cool winters	Year round, heavier in winter than in summer
Continental		
Humid continental	Hot summers, cold winters	Year round, heavier in summer than in winter
Subarctic	Cool summers, cold winters	Light
Polar		
Tundra	Cool summers, very cold winters	Light
Ice Cap	Cold all year round	Light
Highlands	Varies, depending on altitude and direction of prevailing winds	Varies, depending on altitude and direction of prevailing winds

Resource Directory

Teaching Resources

Reading a Climate Map, in the Social Studies and Geography Skills booklet, p. 26, helps students understand and read maps that show different climate regions.

Natural Vegetation Regions

Natural vegetation is the plant life that grows wild without the help of humans. A world vegetation map tells what the vegetation in a place would be if people had not cut down forests or cleared grasslands. The table below provides descriptions of natural vegetation regions shown on maps. Comparing climate and vegetation regions can help you see the close relationship between climate and vegetation.

Vegetation	Description
Tropical rain forest	Tall, close-growing trees forming a canopy over smaller trees, dense growth in general
Deciduous forest	Trees and plants that regularly lose their leaves after each growing season
Mixed forest	Both leaf-losing and cone-bearing trees, no type of tree dominant
Coniferous forest	Cone-bearing trees, evergreen trees and plants
Mediterranean vegetation	Evergreen shrubs and small plants
Tropical savanna	Tall grasses with occasional trees and shrubs
Temperate grassland	Tall grasses with occasional stands of trees
Desert scrub	Low shrubs and bushes, hardy plants
Desert	Little or no vegetation
Tundra	Low shrubs, mosses, lichens; no trees
Ice Cap	No vegetation
Highlands	Varies, depending on altitude and direction of prevailing winds

PRACTICE YOUR WORLD EXPLORER SKILLS

1. How are mountains and hills similar? How are they different?

2. What is the difference between a plateau and a plain?

Teaching Resources

📁 **Reading a Natural Vegetation Map,** in the Social Studies and Geography Skills booklet, p. 25, helps students understand and read maps that show natural vegetation regions.

4 Assess

Ask students to complete the Practice Your World Explorer Skills. Assess their understanding of landforms by the accuracy of their answers.

Assess students' understanding of the effect of climate on vegetation by asking them to share the results of their work in finding places with their assigned landform, climate, and vegetation. Have students check one another's work and match appropriate climate and vegetation regions.

Answers to ...
PRACTICE YOUR WORLD EXPLORER SKILLS

1. Mountains and hills rise above the surrounding land. Hills are usually lower and less steep than mountains.
2. Both plains and plateaus are mostly flat areas. A plateau rises above the surrounding land, and one side may have a steep slope.

Atlas

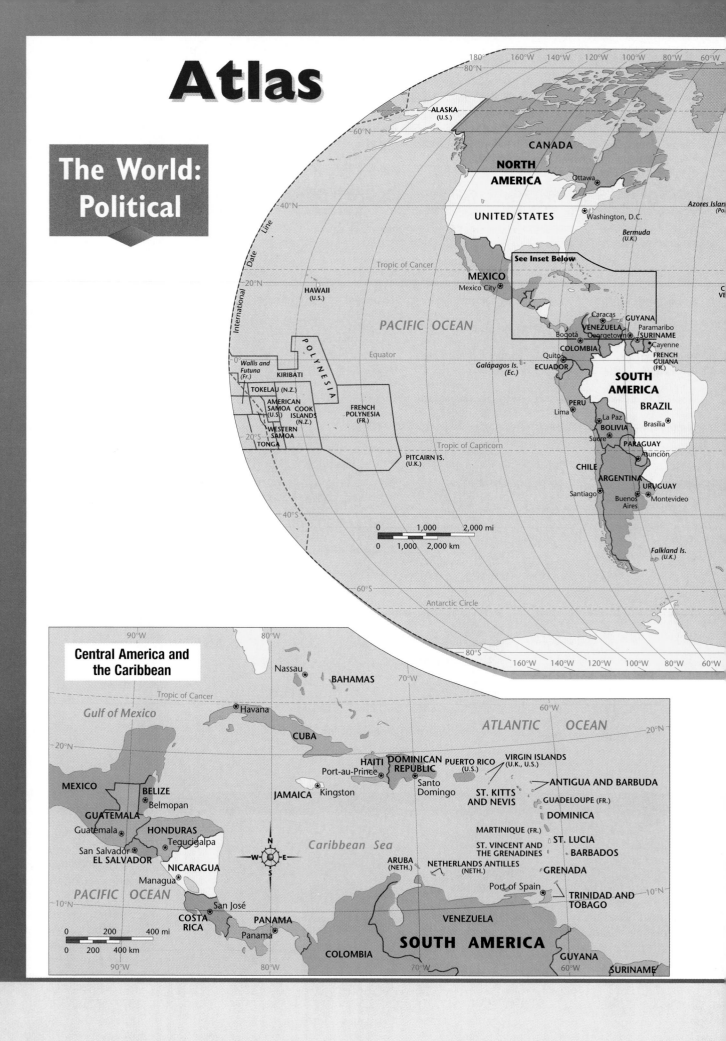

Central America and the Caribbean

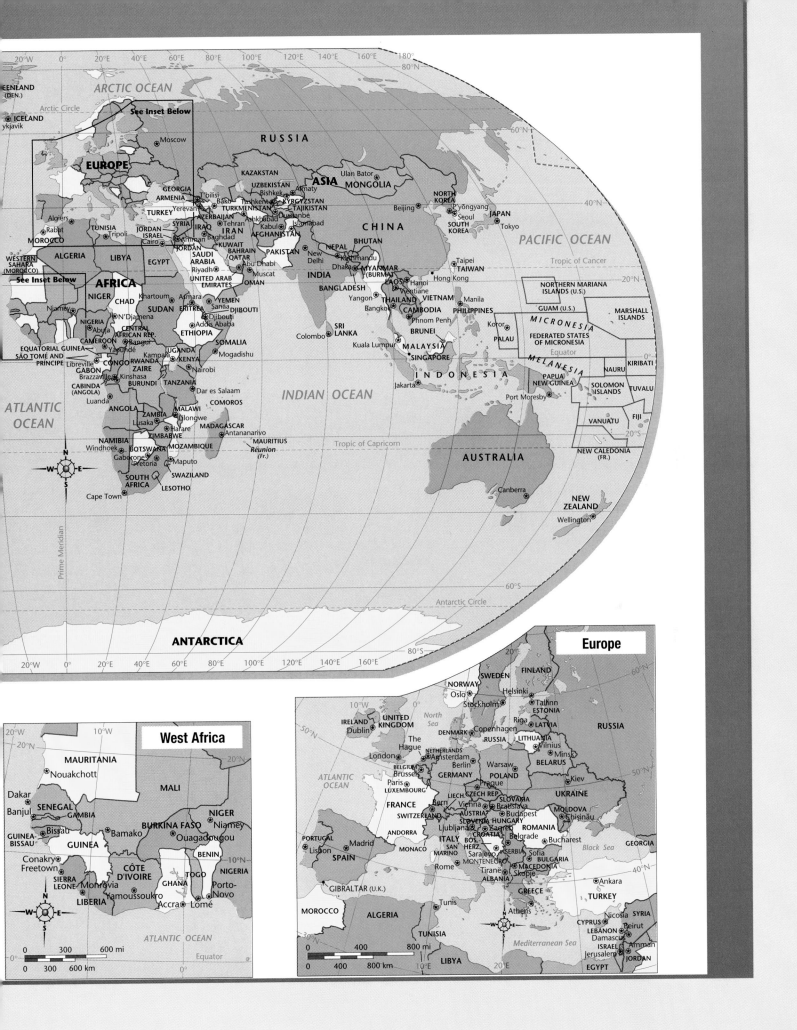

ATLAS 243

The World: Physical

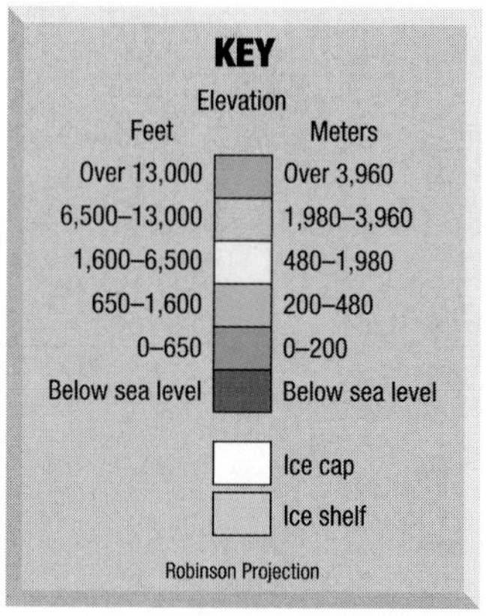

ARCTIC OCEAN

GREENLAND
(DEN.)

80°N

Beaufort
Sea

Bering
Sea

60°N
Sea

Yukon R.

Mackenzie R.

Hudson
Bay

NORTH
AMERICA

CANADIAN SHIELD

Aleutian Islands

ROCKY MOUNTAINS

GREAT PLAINS

Missouri R.

Great
Lakes

St. Lawrence R.

APPALACHIAN MTS.

40°N

ATLANTIC
OCEAN

Colorado R.

Rio
Grande

SIERRA MADRE
OCCIDENTAL

SIERRA MADRE
ORIENTAL

Gulf of
Mexico

Hawaiian Islands

Tropic of Cancer

West Indies

20°N

Caribbean Sea

PACIFIC OCEAN

Orinoco R.

GUIANA
HIGHLANDS

P O L Y N E S I A

0°

Equator

AMAZON
BASIN

Amazon R.

SOUTH
AMERICA

BRAZILIAN
HIGHLANDS

ANDES MOUNTAINS

20°S

Tropic of Capricorn

PAMPAS

Rio de
la Plata

40°S

PATAGONIA

Cape Horn

Drake Passage

60°S

Antarctic Circle

ANTARCTIC
PENINSULA

80°S

160°W   140°W   120°W   100°W   80°W   60°W

180   160°W   140°W   120°W   100°W   80°W   60°

KEY

Elevation

Feet		Meters
Over 13,000		Over 3,960
6,500–13,000		1,980–3,960
1,600–6,500		480–1,980
650–1,600		200–480
0–650		0–200
Below sea level		Below sea level

Ice cap

Ice shelf

Robinson Projection

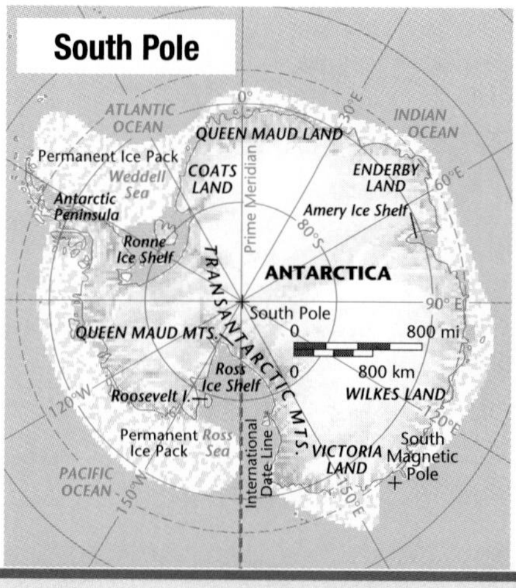

South Pole

ATLANTIC
OCEAN

INDIAN
OCEAN

QUEEN MAUD LAND

Permanent Ice Pack

Weddell
Sea

COATS
LAND

ENDERBY
LAND

Antarctic
Peninsula

Ronne
Ice Shelf

Amery Ice Shelf

Prime Meridian

ANTARCTICA

TRANSANTARCTIC MTS.

South Pole

90° E

QUEEN MAUD MTS.

0   800 mi

0   800 km

Ross
Ice Shelf

WILKES LAND

Roosevelt I.

Permanent Ross
Ice Pack

Ross
Sea

VICTORIA
LAND

South
Magnetic
Pole

International
Date Line

PACIFIC
OCEAN

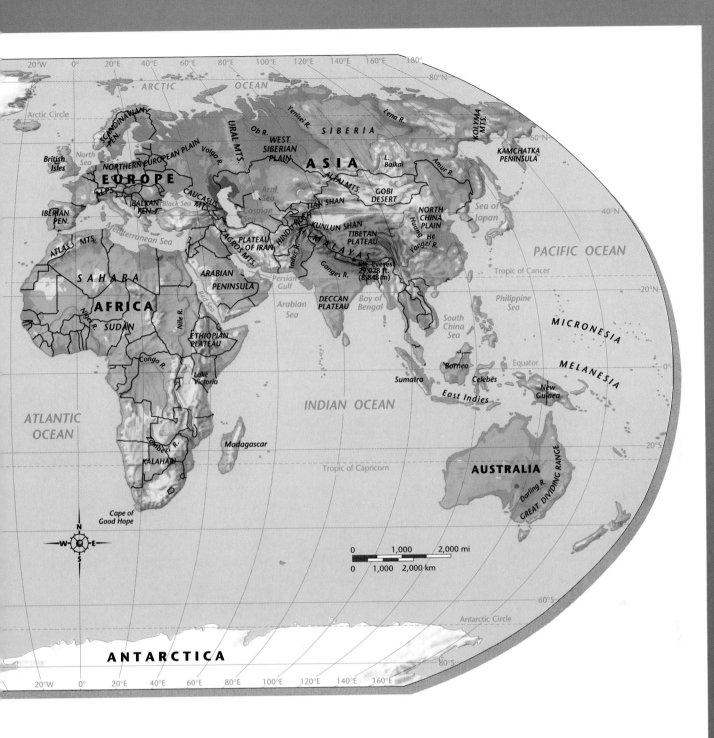

ARCTIC OCEAN

80°N
60°N
40°N

SCANDINAVIAN PEN.
North Sea
British Isles
EUROPE
NORTHERN EUROPEAN PLAIN
ALPS
IBERIAN PEN.
BALKAN PEN.
Black Sea
CAUCASUS MTS.
Mediterranean Sea
ATLAS MTS.

Volga R.
URAL MTS.
Aral Sea
Caspian Sea
ZAGROS MTS.
PLATEAU OF IRAN
HINDU KUSH
Persian Gulf
ARABIAN PENINSULA
Red Sea

Ob R.
WEST SIBERIAN PLAIN
Yenisei R.
SIBERIA
ASIA
ALTAI MTS.
TIAN SHAN
KUNLUN SHAN
HIMALAYAS
Mt. Everest 29,028 ft. (8,848 m)
TIBETAN PLATEAU
Indus R.
Ganges R.
DECCAN PLATEAU
Arabian Sea
Bay of Bengal

Lena R.
L. Baikal
GOBI DESERT
Amur R.
Huang He
Yangzi R.
NORTH CHINA PLAIN

KOLYMA MTS.
KAMCHATKA PENINSULA
Sea of Japan

PACIFIC OCEAN
Tropic of Cancer
20°N
Philippine Sea
South China Sea
MICRONESIA
MELANESIA
Equator
Borneo
Celebes
New Guinea
Sumatra
East Indies

AFRICA
SAHARA
SUDAN
Niger R.
Nile R.
ETHIOPIAN PLATEAU
Congo R.
Lake Victoria

ATLANTIC OCEAN
Zambezi R.
KALAHARI
Madagascar
Cape of Good Hope

INDIAN OCEAN
Tropic of Capricorn
AUSTRALIA
Darling R.
GREAT DIVIDING RANGE
20°S
40°S

N
W E
S

0   1,000   2,000 mi
0   1,000   2,000 km

60°S
Antarctic Circle
80°S
ANTARCTICA

20°W 0° 20°E 40°E 60°E 80°E 100°E 120°E 140°E 160°E

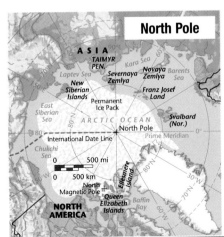

North Pole

ASIA
TAIMYR PEN.
Laptev Sea
New Siberian Islands
East Siberian Sea
Severnaya Zemlya
Kara Sea
Novaya Zemlya
Barents Sea
Franz Josef Land
Svalbard (Nor.)
Permanent Ice Pack
ARCTIC OCEAN
North Pole
International Date Line
Prime Meridian
Chukchi Sea
North Magnetic Pole
Ellesmere Island
Queen Elizabeth Islands
Baffin Bay
NORTH AMERICA

0   500 mi
0   500 km

North and South America: Political

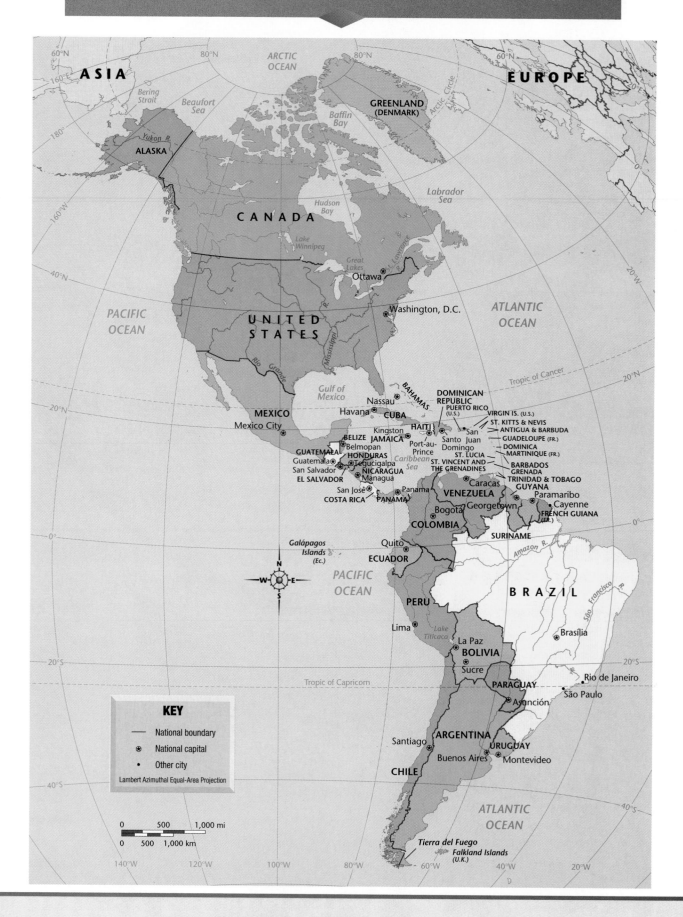

ASIA

EUROPE

ARCTIC OCEAN

Bering Strait

Beaufort Sea

GREENLAND (DENMARK)

Baffin Bay

ALASKA

Yukon R.

Labrador Sea

Hudson Bay

CANADA

Lake Winnipeg

Great Lakes

St. Lawrence R.

⊛ Ottawa

PACIFIC OCEAN

ATLANTIC OCEAN

UNITED STATES

⊛ Washington, D.C.

Rio Grande

Mississippi

Tropic of Cancer

Gulf of Mexico

MEXICO

⊛ Mexico City

Nassau

Havana ⊛

BAHAMAS

CUBA

DOMINICAN REPUBLIC

PUERTO RICO (U.S.)

VIRGIN IS. (U.S.)

Kingston

HAITI

San Juan

ST. KITTS & NEVIS

BELIZE

JAMAICA

Port-au-Prince

Santo Domingo

ANTIGUA & BARBUDA

GUADELOUPE (FR.)

GUATEMALA

Belmopan

HONDURAS

Caribbean Sea

DOMINICA

MARTINIQUE (FR.)

Guatemala

Tegucigalpa

ST. LUCIA

San Salvador

⊛ **NICARAGUA**

ST. VINCENT AND THE GRENADINES

BARBADOS

EL SALVADOR

Managua

GRENADA

TRINIDAD & TOBAGO

San José ⊛

• Panama

Caracas

GUYANA

COSTA RICA

PANAMA

VENEZUELA

Paramaribo

Georgetown

• Cayenne

Bogotá ⊛

FRENCH GUIANA (FR.)

COLOMBIA

SURINAME

Galápagos Islands (Ec.)

Quito ⊛

ECUADOR

Amazon R.

B R A Z I L

São Francisco R.

PERU

Lima ⊛

Lake Titicaca

• Brasília

La Paz ⊛

BOLIVIA

Sucre ⊛

• Rio de Janeiro

Tropic of Capricorn

PARAGUAY

• São Paulo

⊛ Asunción

Santiago ⊛

ARGENTINA

URUGUAY

Buenos Aires ⊛

• Montevideo

CHILE

PACIFIC OCEAN

ATLANTIC OCEAN

Tierra del Fuego

Falkland Islands (U.K.)

KEY

— National boundary

⊛ National capital

• Other city

Lambert Azimuthal Equal-Area Projection

0   500   1,000 mi

0   500   1,000 km

North and South America: Physical

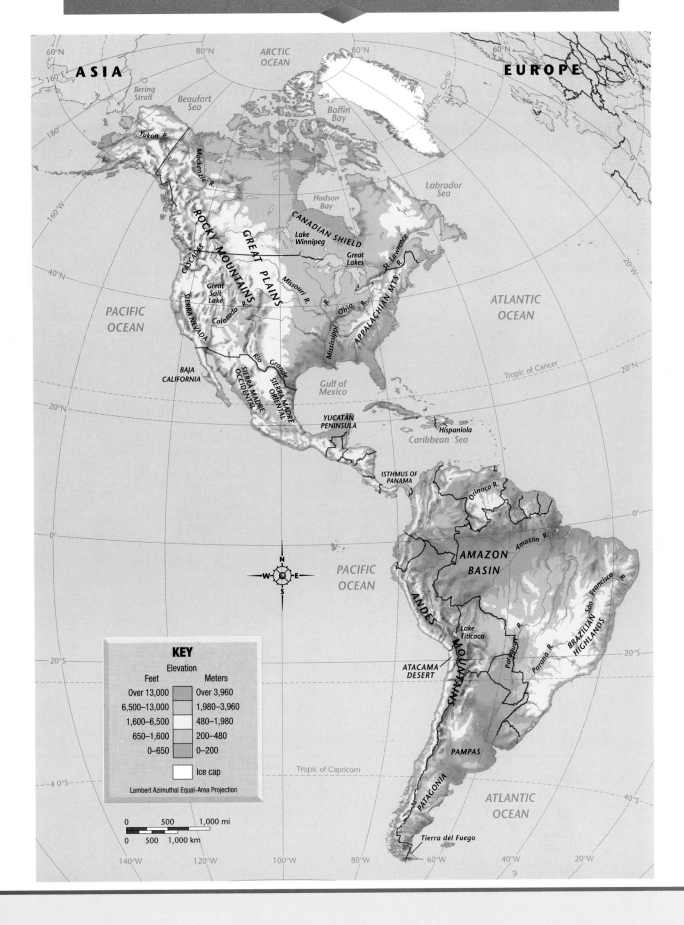

ASIA

EUROPE

ARCTIC OCEAN

60°N 80°N 80°N 60°N
160°E 180°

Bering Strait

Beaufort Sea

Baffin Bay

Labrador Sea

Arctic Circle

Yukon R.

Mackenzie R.

Hudson Bay

CANADIAN SHIELD

Lake Winnipeg

Great Lakes

St. Lawrence R.

ROCKY MOUNTAINS

GREAT PLAINS

CASCADES

Great Salt Lake

Missouri R.

Ohio R.

APPALACHIAN MTS.

SIERRA NEVADA

Colorado R.

Mississippi

40°N

20°W

PACIFIC OCEAN

ATLANTIC OCEAN

BAJA CALIFORNIA

Rio Grande

SIERRA MADRE OCCIDENTAL

SIERRA MADRE ORIENTAL

Gulf of Mexico

Tropic of Cancer

20°N

20°N

YUCATÁN PENINSULA

Hispaniola

Caribbean Sea

0°

ISTHMUS OF PANAMA

Orinoco R.

Amazon R.

AMAZON BASIN

0°

PACIFIC OCEAN

ANDES MOUNTAINS

Lake Titicaca

São Francisco R.

BRAZILIAN HIGHLANDS

ATACAMA DESERT

Pilcomayo R.

Paraguay R.

Paraná R.

20°S

20°S

KEY

Elevation

Feet	Meters
Over 13,000	Over 3,960
6,500–13,000	1,980–3,960
1,600–6,500	480–1,980
650–1,600	200–480
0–650	0–200
Ice cap	

Lambert Azimuthal Equal-Area Projection

PAMPAS

Tropic of Capricorn

40°S

PATAGONIA

ATLANTIC OCEAN

40°S

0   500   1,000 mi
0   500   1,000 km

Tierra del Fuego

140°W 120°W 100°W 80°W 60°W 40°W 20°W

Europe: Political

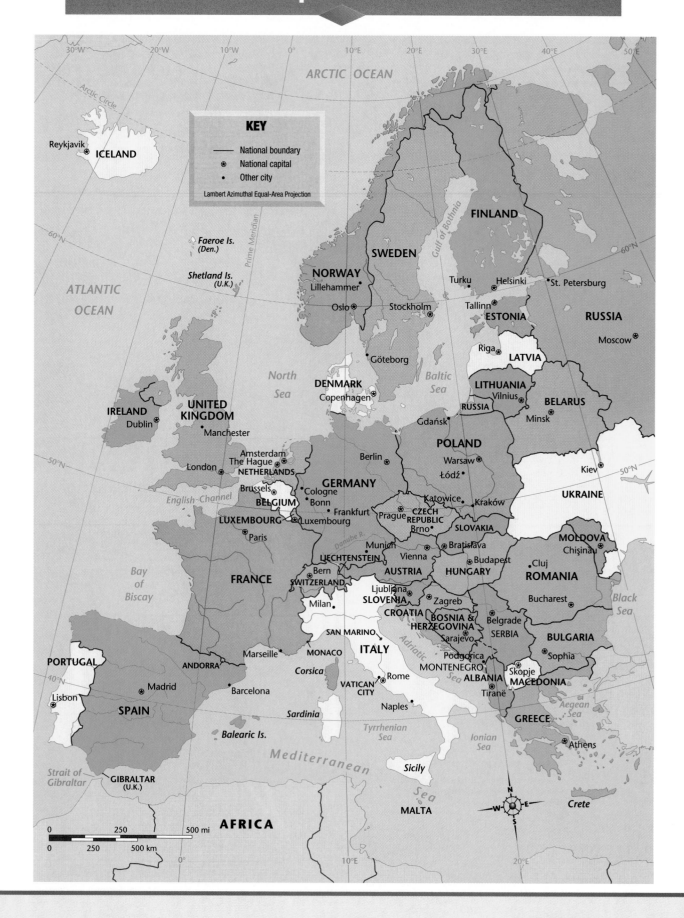

KEY

— National boundary
⊛ National capital
• Other city

Lambert Azimuthal Equal-Area Projection

ARCTIC OCEAN

ICELAND
Reykjavik ⊛

Arctic Circle

Faeroe Is.
(Den.)

Shetland Is.
(U.K.)

ATLANTIC
OCEAN

Prime Meridian

FINLAND

Gulf of Bothnia

SWEDEN

NORWAY
Lillehammer •

Oslo ⊛   Stockholm ⊛

Turku •   Helsinki ⊛   • St. Petersburg

Tallinn ⊛
ESTONIA

RUSSIA

Moscow ⊛

• Göteborg

Riga ⊛
LATVIA

Baltic
Sea

North
Sea

DENMARK
Copenhagen ⊛

LITHUANIA
Vilnius ⊛

BELARUS

RUSSIA

Minsk ⊛

IRELAND
Dublin ⊛

UNITED
KINGDOM

• Manchester

Gdańsk •

POLAND

Warsaw ⊛

Łódź •

Kiev ⊛

London ⊛

Amsterdam ⊛
The Hague ⊛
NETHERLANDS

Berlin ⊛

UKRAINE

Brussels ⊛
BELGIUM

English Channel

LUXEMBOURG

GERMANY

Cologne •
Bonn •

• Frankfurt

Katowice •
• Kraków

Luxembourg ⊛

Prague ⊛
CZECH
REPUBLIC

SLOVAKIA

MOLDOVA
Chişinău •

• Paris

Danube R.

Munich •

Brno •

• Bratislava

LIECHTENSTEIN

Vienna •

• Budapest

• Cluj

Bern ⊛
SWITZERLAND

AUSTRIA

HUNGARY

ROMANIA

FRANCE

Bay
of
Biscay

Ljubljana ⊛
SLOVENIA

Milan •

• Zagreb

CROATIA

Bucharest ⊛

Black
Sea

BOSNIA &
HERZEGOVINA

Belgrade ⊛

SAN MARINO

Marseille •

MONACO

ITALY

ANDORRA

Corsica

Sarajevo ⊛

SERBIA

BULGARIA

Adriatic

Podgorica •

Sophia ⊛

PORTUGAL

Madrid ⊛

• Barcelona

VATICAN
CITY

Rome •

MONTENEGRO
Sea

Skopje ⊛
ALBANIA   MACEDONIA

Lisbon ⊛

SPAIN

Sardinia

Naples •

Tiranë •

Aegean
Sea

Balearic Is.

Tyrrhenian
Sea

Ionian
Sea

GREECE

Mediterranean

Sicily

• Athens

Strait of
Gibraltar

GIBRALTAR
(U.K.)

Sea

Crete

MALTA

AFRICA

0   250   500 mi

0   250   500 km

Europe: Physical

30°W 20°W 10°W 0° 10°E 20°E 30°E 40°E

ARCTIC OCEAN

Arctic Circle

Norwegian Sea

LAPLAND

KJØLEN MTS.

SCANDINAVIAN PENINSULA

Gulf of Bothnia

Faeroe Is.
(Den.)

Glittertind
8,110 ft.
(2,472 m)

Lake
Ladoga

Shetland Is.
(U.K.)

60°N

**ATLANTIC
OCEAN**

Ben Nevis
4,406 ft
(1,343 m)

Lake
Vänern

*North
Sea*

JUTLAND
PENINSULA

*Baltic
Sea*

BRITISH ISLES

Dnieper R.

50°N

NORTHERN EUROPEAN PLAIN

Vistula R.

Thames R.

RUHR
VALLEY

Elbe River

Oder River

English Channel

Seine River

Rhine R.

Danube River

Dniester River

CARPATHIAN MTS.

Loire River

Bay
of
Biscay

Mont Blanc
15,771 ft.
(4,807 m)

A L P S

Rhône River

Po River

TRANSYLVANIAN
ALPS

*Black
Sea*

Garonne R.

MASSIF
CENTRAL

DINARIC ALPS

Danube River

BALKAN MTS.

Bosporus

PYRENEES

Ebro R.

A P E N N I N E S

BALKAN PENINSULA

Douro R.

MESETA

Corsica

*Adriatic
Sea*

40°N

ASIA

Tagus River

ITALIAN PENINSULA

PINDUS MTS.

Dardanelles

**IBERIAN
PENINSULA**

Sardinia

*Tyrrhenian
Sea*

*Ionian
Sea*

*Aegean
Sea*

Strait of
Gibraltar

Balearic Is.

Sicily

PELOPONNESE

Crete

KEY

Elevation

Feet	Meters
Over 13,000	Over 3,960
6,500–13,000	1,980–3,960
1,600–6,500	480–1,980
650–1,600	200–480
0–650	0–200
Below sea level	Below sea level
Ice cap	

Lambert Azimuthal Equal-Area Projection

AFRICA

30°N

0°

20°E

Mediterranean Sea

N
W E
S

Africa: Political

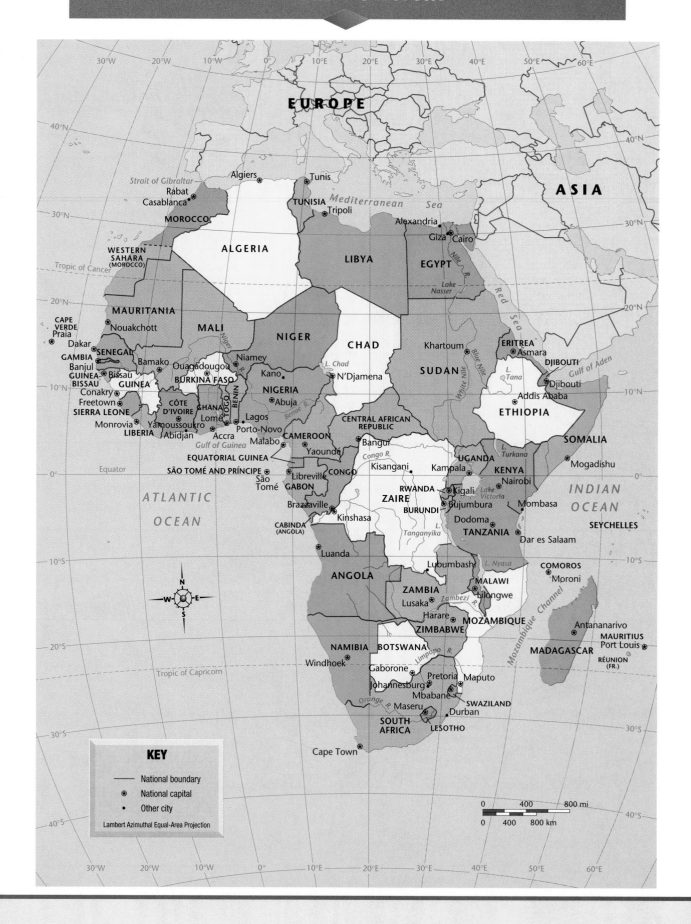

EUROPE

ASIA

Strait of Gibraltar
Algiers ⊛
Tunis ⊛
Rabat ·
Casablanca ·
TUNISIA
Mediterranean Sea
·Tripoli
Alexandria ·
Giza · ⊛ Cairo

MOROCCO

WESTERN
SAHARA
(MOROCCO)

ALGERIA

LIBYA

EGYPT

Nile R.
Lake
Nasser

Tropic of Cancer

MAURITANIA

MALI

NIGER

CHAD

Khartoum ⊛

Blue Nile

ERITREA
⊛ Asmara

DJIBOUTI

Gulf of Aden

CAPE
VERDE
Praia ·
Dakar ·

⊛ Nouakchott

Niger R.

Niamey ⊛

L. Chad

SUDAN

L.
Tana

· Djibouti

White Nile

GAMBIA
Banjul ⊛
GUINEA-
BISSAU ·Bissau
SENEGAL

Bamako ⊛

Ouagadougou ⊛

Kano ·

N'Djamena ·

⊛ Addis Ababa

Conakry ⊛
Freetown ⊛
SIERRA LEONE
Monrovia ⊛
LIBERIA

GUINEA

BURKINA FASO

NIGERIA

⊛ Abuja

ETHIOPIA

CÔTE
D'IVOIRE
Yamoussoukro ⊛
Abidjan ·

GHANA
Lomé ⊛
Accra ⊛

TOGO
BENIN

Lagos ·
Porto-Novo ⊛

Benue R.

CENTRAL AFRICAN
REPUBLIC

SOMALIA

⊛ Mogadishu

Gulf of Guinea
Malabo ⊛

CAMEROON

Bangui ⊛

L.
Turkana

EQUATORIAL GUINEA

Yaoundé ⊛

Congo R.

UGANDA

SÃO TOMÉ AND PRÍNCIPE ⊛
São
Tomé ·

Libreville ⊛
GABON

CONGO

Kisangani ·

Kampala ⊛

KENYA
Nairobi ⊛

INDIAN
OCEAN

Equator

Brazzaville ⊛

ZAIRE

RWANDA
⊛ Kigali

Lake
Victoria

· Mombasa

ATLANTIC
OCEAN

Kinshasa ⊛

BURUNDI
⊛ Bujumbura

Dodoma ⊛

SEYCHELLES

CABINDA
(ANGOLA)

L.
Tanganyika

TANZANIA

· Dar es Salaam

Luanda ⊛

Lubumbashi ·

L. Nyasa

COMOROS
· Moroni

ANGOLA

ZAMBIA

MALAWI
⊛ Lilongwe

Lusaka ⊛

Zambezi R.

Harare ⊛

MOZAMBIQUE

Mozambique Channel

· Antananarivo

NAMIBIA

BOTSWANA

ZIMBABWE

MADAGASCAR

MAURITIUS
Port Louis ·

Tropic of Capricorn

Windhoek ⊛

Limpopo R.

RÉUNION
(FR.)

Gaborone ⊛

Pretoria ⊛
· Maputo

Johannesburg ·

Orange R.

Mbabane ⊛

SWAZILAND

Maseru ⊛

· Durban

SOUTH
AFRICA

LESOTHO

Cape Town ·

KEY

— National boundary

⊛ National capital

· Other city

Lambert Azimuthal Equal-Area Projection

0   400   800 mi
0   400   800 km

Africa: Physical

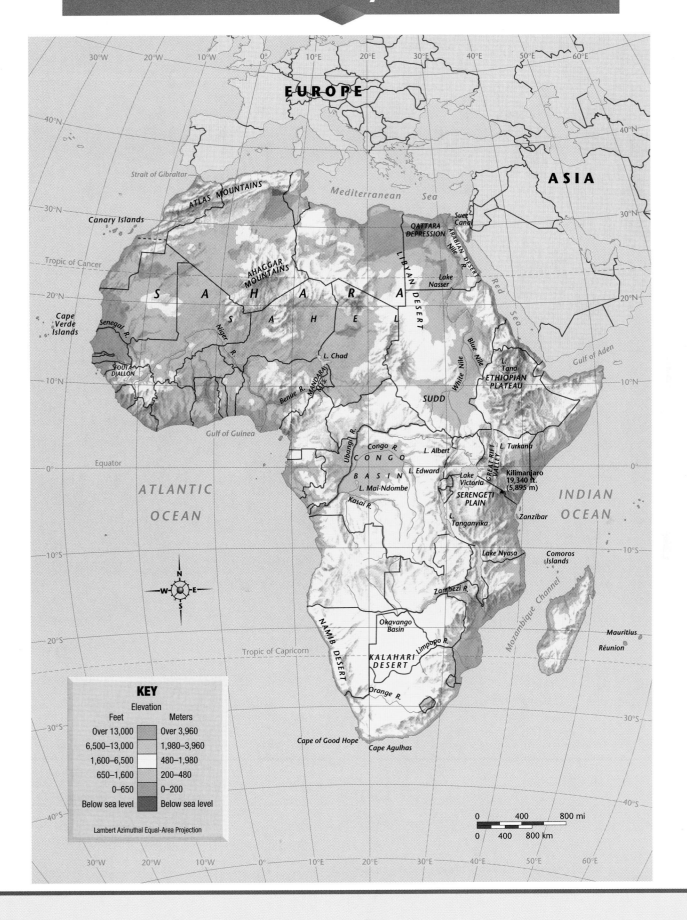

EUROPE

ASIA

Strait of Gibraltar

ATLAS MOUNTAINS

Canary Islands

Mediterranean Sea

Tropic of Cancer

QATTARA DEPRESSION

Suez Canal

ARABIAN DESERT

Nile R.

LIBYAN DESERT

AHAGGAR MOUNTAINS

S A H A R A

S A H E L

Cape Verde Islands

Senegal R.

Niger R.

FOUTA DJALLON

L. Chad

Benue R.

MANDARA MTS

Gulf of Guinea

Lake Nasser

Red Sea

Gulf of Aden

Blue Nile

White Nile

L. Tana

ETHIOPIAN PLATEAU

SUDD

Ubangi R.

Congo R.

C O N G O

B A S I N

L. Mai-Ndombe

Kasai R.

L. Albert

L. Edward

Lake Victoria

GREAT RIFT VALLEY

L. Turkana

Kilimanjaro
19,340 ft.
(5,895 m)

SERENGETI PLAIN

Zanzibar

L. Tanganyika

ATLANTIC OCEAN

Equator

INDIAN OCEAN

Lake Nyasa

Comoros Islands

Zambezi R.

Mozambique Channel

Mauritius

Réunion

NAMIB DESERT

Okavango Basin

Limpopo R.

Tropic of Capricorn

KALAHARI DESERT

Orange R.

Cape of Good Hope

Cape Agulhas

KEY

Elevation

Feet	Meters
Over 13,000	Over 3,960
6,500–13,000	1,980–3,960
1,600–6,500	480–1,980
650–1,600	200–480
0–650	0–200
Below sea level	Below sea level

Lambert Azimuthal Equal-Area Projection

0   400   800 mi

0   400   800 km

Asia: Political

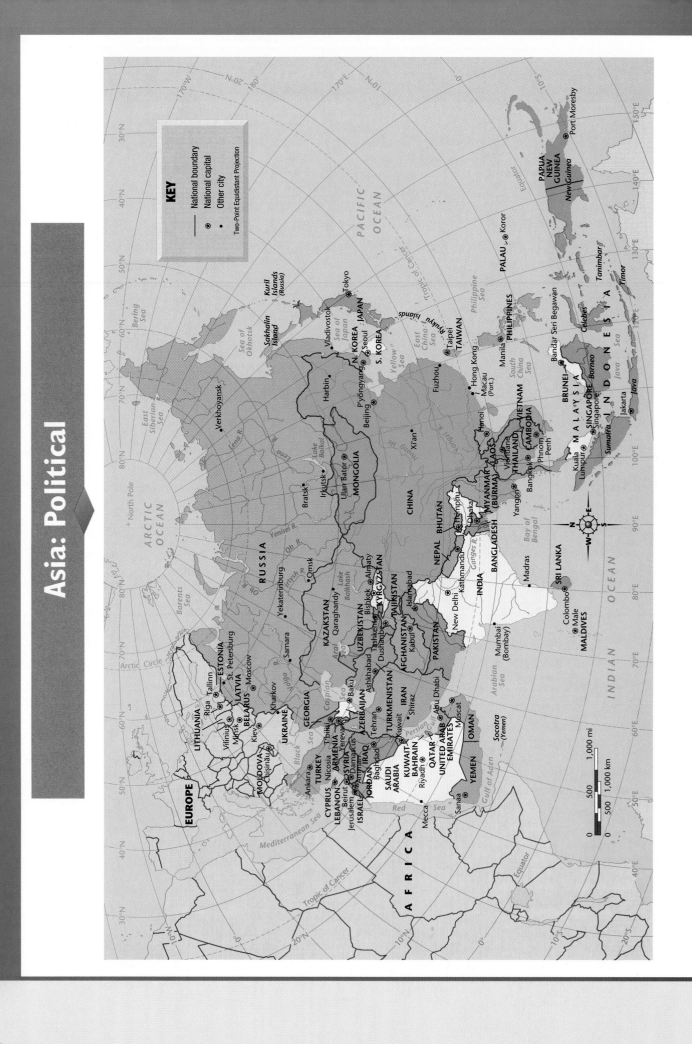

KEY

— National boundary
⊛ National capital
• Other city

Two-Point Equidistant Projection

EUROPE

AFRICA

ARCTIC OCEAN

North Pole

PACIFIC OCEAN

RUSSIA

Verkhoyansk

Bratsk

Irkutsk

Omsk

Yekaterinburg

Samara

St. Petersburg

Moscow

ESTONIA

LATVIA

LITHUANIA

BELARUS

Vilnius

Minsk

Kiev

UKRAINE

Kharkov

MOLDOVA

Chişinău

Riga

Tallinn

GEORGIA

Tbilisi

ARMENIA

Yerevan

AZERBAIJAN

Baku

TURKEY

Ankara

Nicosia

CYPRUS

LEBANON

Beirut

ISRAEL

Jerusalem

JORDAN

Amman

Damascus

SYRIA

IRAQ

Baghdad

SAUDI ARABIA

Riyadh

KUWAIT

Kuwait

BAHRAIN

QATAR

UNITED ARAB EMIRATES

Abu Dhabi

OMAN

Muscat

YEMEN

Sanaa

Mecca

Socotra (Yemen)

IRAN

Tehran

Shiraz

TURKMENISTAN

Ashkhabad

KAZAKSTAN

Qaraghandy

UZBEKISTAN

Tashkent

TAJIKISTAN

Dushanbe

KYRGYZSTAN

Bishkek

Almaty

AFGHANISTAN

Kabul

PAKISTAN

Islamabad

INDIA

New Delhi

NEPAL

Kathmandu

BHUTAN

Thimphu

BANGLADESH

Dhaka

MYANMAR (BURMA)

Yangon

CHINA

Beijing

Xi'an

Harbin

MONGOLIA

Ulan Bator

N. KOREA

Pyŏngyang

S. KOREA

Seoul

JAPAN

Tokyo

Vladivostok

Sakhalin Island

Kuril Islands (Russia)

Fuzhou

Macau (Port.)

Hong Kong

TAIWAN

Taipei

LAOS

Vientiane

THAILAND

Bangkok

VIETNAM

Hanoi

CAMBODIA

Phnom Penh

PHILIPPINES

Manila

MALAYSIA

Kuala Lumpur

SINGAPORE

Singapore

BRUNEI

Bandar Seri Begawan

Borneo

INDONESIA

Sumatra

Jakarta

Java

Celebes

Timor

Tanimbar

PALAU

Koror

PAPUA NEW GUINEA

Port Moresby

New Guinea

SRI LANKA

Colombo

MALDIVES

Male

Madras

Mumbai (Bombay)

Aral Sea

Caspian Sea

Black Sea

Mediterranean Sea

Red Sea

Persian Gulf

Gulf of Oman

Gulf of Aden

Arabian Sea

Bay of Bengal

INDIAN OCEAN

Java Sea

South China Sea

Philippine Sea

East China Sea

Yellow Sea

Sea of Japan

Sea of Okhotsk

Bering Sea

East Siberian Sea

Barents Sea

Lake Baikal

Lake Balkhash

Ganges R.

Lena R.

Yenisei R.

Ob R.

Irtysh R.

Volga R.

Ryukyu Islands

Arctic Circle

Tropic of Cancer

Equator

Ulan Bator

1,000 mi

1,000 km

500

500

0

0

Asia: Physical

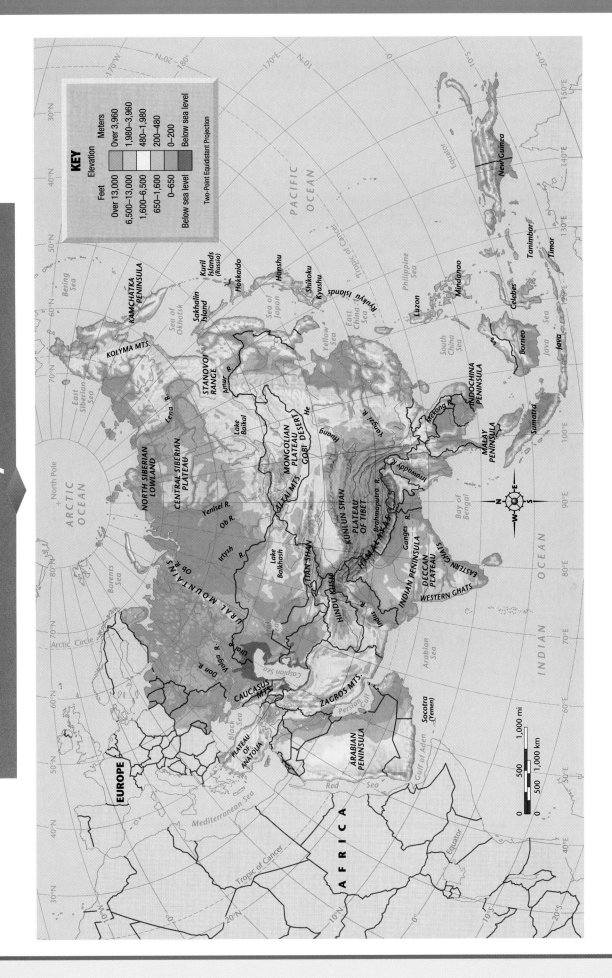

KEY

Elevation

Feet	Meters
Over 13,000	Over 3,960
6,500–13,000	1,980–3,960
1,600–6,500	480–1,980
650–1,600	200–480
0–650	0–200
Below sea level	Below sea level

Two-Point Equidistant Projection

EUROPE

AFRICA

KAMCHATKA PENINSULA
KOLYMA MTS.
STANOVOI RANGE
NORTH SIBERIAN LOWLAND
CENTRAL SIBERIAN PLATEAU
URAL MOUNTAINS
ALTAI MTS.
MONGOLIAN PLATEAU
GOBI DESERT
KUNLUN SHAN
PLATEAU OF TIBET
TIAN SHAN
HINDU KUSH
HIMALAYAS
CAUCASUS MTS.
ZAGROS MTS.
PLATEAU OF ANATOLIA
ARABIAN PENINSULA
INDIAN PENINSULA
DECCAN PLATEAU
WESTERN GHATS
EASTERN GHATS
INDOCHINA PENINSULA
MALAY PENINSULA

Kamchatka Peninsula
Sakhalin Island
Kuril Islands (Russia)
Hokkaido
Honshu
Shikoku
Kyushu
Ryukyu Islands
Luzon
Mindanao
Celebes
Borneo
Sumatra
Java
Timor
Tanimbar
New Guinea

North Pole
Arctic Circle
Tropic of Cancer
Equator

Bering Sea
East Siberian Sea
Barents Sea
Sea of Okhotsk
Sea of Japan
Yellow Sea
East China Sea
Philippine Sea
South China Sea
Java Sea
Bay of Bengal
Arabian Sea
Gulf of Aden
Red Sea
Persian Gulf
Black Sea
Caspian Sea
Mediterranean Sea
Lake Baikal
Lake Balkhash

ARCTIC OCEAN
PACIFIC OCEAN
INDIAN OCEAN

Lena R.
Amur R.
Yenisei R.
Ob R.
Irtysh R.
Ural R.
Volga R.
Don R.
Huang
Yangzi R.
He
Mekong R.
Irrawaddy R.
Brahmaputra R.
Ganges R.
Indus R.

Socotra (Yemen)

0   500   1,000 mi
0   500   1,000 km

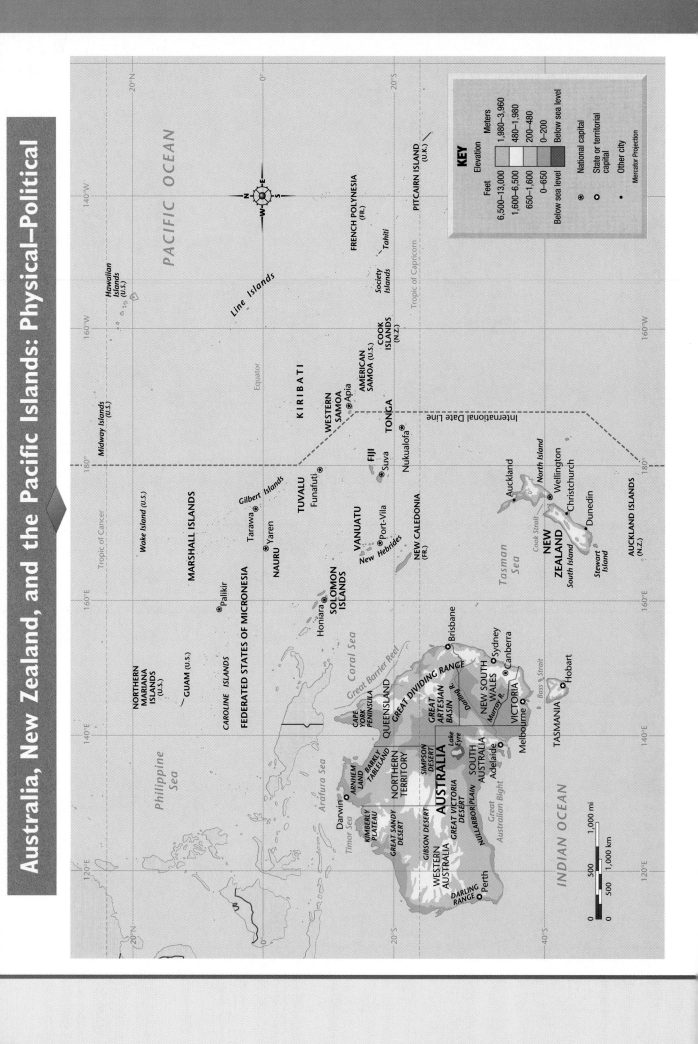

KEY

Elevation

Feet	Meters
6,500–13,000	1,980–3,960
1,600–6,500	480–1,980
650–1,600	200–480
0–650	0–200
Below sea level	Below sea level

⊛ National capital
✪ State or territorial capital
• Other city

Mercator Projection

PACIFIC OCEAN

PACIFIC OCEAN

Hawaiian Islands (U.S.)

Line Islands

FRENCH POLYNESIA (FR.)

Society Islands

Tahiti

PITCAIRN ISLAND (U.K.)

Tropic of Capricorn

Midway Islands (U.S.)

COOK ISLANDS (N.Z.)

AMERICAN SAMOA (U.S.)

Equator

K I R I B A T I

WESTERN SAMOA

Apia

Tropic of Cancer

Wake Island (U.S.)

TONGA

Nukualofa

International Date Line

MARSHALL ISLANDS

Gilbert Islands

Tarawa

FIJI

Suva

TUVALU

Funafuti

NAURU

Yaren

VANUATU

Port-Vila

New Hebrides

NEW CALEDONIA (FR.)

North Island

Auckland

Wellington

Christchurch

Dunedin

NEW ZEALAND

South Island

Cook Strait

Stewart Island

Tasman Sea

AUCKLAND ISLANDS (N.Z.)

NORTHERN MARIANA ISLANDS (U.S.)

GUAM (U.S.)

CAROLINE ISLANDS

FEDERATED STATES OF MICRONESIA

Palikir

SOLOMON ISLANDS

Honiara

Coral Sea

Great Barrier Reef

Brisbane

Sydney

Canberra

NEW SOUTH WALES

Murray R.

Darling R.

VICTORIA

Melbourne

Bass Strait

TASMANIA

Hobart

GREAT DIVIDING RANGE

GREAT ARTESIAN BASIN

QUEENSLAND

CAPE YORK PENINSULA

AUSTRALIA

Lake Eyre

SOUTH AUSTRALIA

Adelaide

Great Australian Bight

NULLARBOR PLAIN

SIMPSON DESERT

BARKLY TABLELAND

NORTHERN TERRITORY

ARNHEM LAND

Darwin

Timor Sea

Arafura Sea

KIMBERLEY PLATEAU

GREAT SANDY DESERT

GIBSON DESERT

GREAT VICTORIA DESERT

WESTERN AUSTRALIA

Perth

DARLING RANGE

Philippine Sea

INDIAN OCEAN

0   500   1,000 mi

0   500   1,000 km

The Arctic

Antarctica

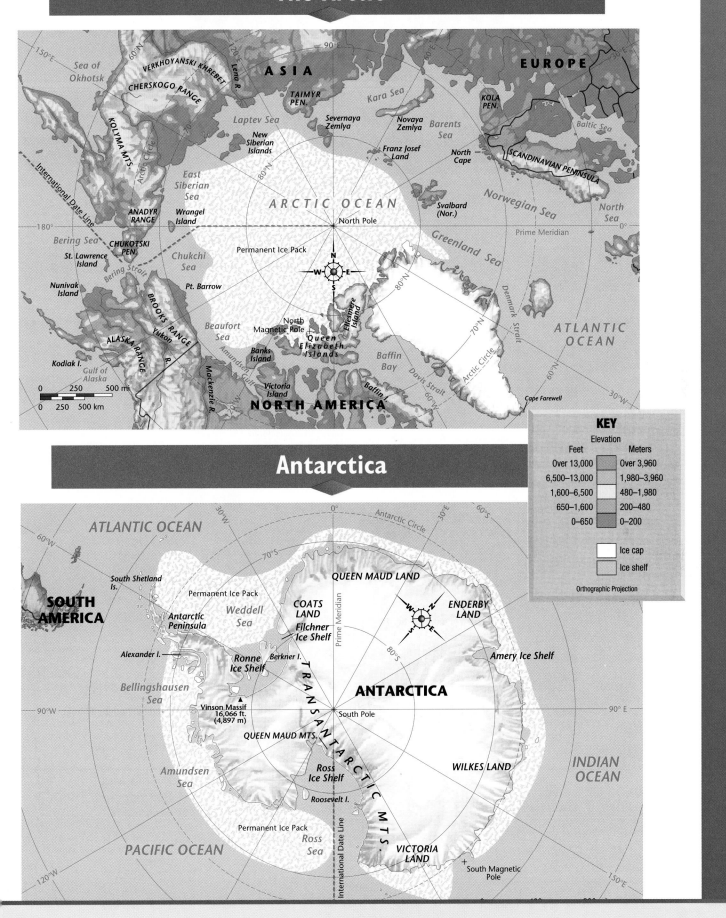

KEY

Elevation

Feet		Meters
Over 13,000		Over 3,960
6,500–13,000		1,980–3,960
1,600–6,500		480–1,980
650–1,600		200–480
0–650		0–200

Ice cap

Ice shelf

Orthographic Projection

World View

Afghanistan
CAPITAL: Kabul
POPULATION: 21,251,821
MAJOR LANGUAGES: Pashtu, Afghan Persian, Turkic, and 30 various languages
AREA: 250,010 sq mi; 647,500 sq km
LEADING EXPORTS: fruits and nuts, handwoven carpets, and wool
CONTINENT: Asia

Albania
CAPITAL: Tiranë
POPULATION: 3,413,904
MAJOR LANGUAGES: Albanian, Tosk dialect, and Greek
AREA: 11,101 sq mi; 28,750 sq km
LEADING EXPORTS: asphalt, metals and metallic ores, and electricity
CONTINENT: Europe

Algeria
CAPITAL: Algiers
POPULATION: 28,539,321
MAJOR LANGUAGES: Arabic (official), French, and Berber dialects
AREA: 919,626 sq mi; 2,381,740 sq km
LEADING EXPORTS: petroleum and natural gas
CONTINENT: Africa

Andorra
CAPITAL: Andorra La Vella
POPULATION: 65,780
MAJOR LANGUAGES: Catalan (official), French, and Castilian
AREA: 174 sq mi; 450 sq km
LEADING EXPORTS: electricity, tobacco products, and furniture
CONTINENT: Europe

Angola
CAPITAL: Luanda
POPULATION: 10,069,501
MAJOR LANGUAGES: Portuguese (official), Bantu, and various languages
AREA: 481,370 sq mi; 1,246,700 sq km
LEADING EXPORTS: oil, diamonds, and refined petroleum products
CONTINENT: Africa

Anguilla
CAPITAL: The Valley
POPULATION: 7,099
MAJOR LANGUAGE: English (official)
AREA: 35 sq mi; 91 sq km
LEADING EXPORTS: lobster and salt
LOCATION: Caribbean Sea

Antigua and Barbuda
CAPITAL: Saint John's
POPULATION: 65,176
MAJOR LANGUAGES: English (official) and various dialects
AREA: 170 sq mi; 440 sq km
LEADING EXPORTS: petroleum products and manufactures
LOCATION: Caribbean Sea

Argentina
CAPITAL: Buenos Aires
POPULATION: 34,292,742
MAJOR LANGUAGES: Spanish (official), English, Italian, German, and French
AREA: 1,068,339 sq mi; 2,766,890 sq km
LEADING EXPORTS: meat, wheat, corn, oilseed, and manufactures
CONTINENT: South America

Armenia
CAPITAL: Yerevan
POPULATION: 3,557,284
MAJOR LANGUAGES: Armenian and Russian
AREA: 11,506 sq mi; 29,800 sq km
LEADING EXPORTS: gold and jewelry, and aluminum
CONTINENT: Asia

Australia
CAPITAL: Canberra
POPULATION: 18,322,231
MAJOR LANGUAGES: English and various languages
AREA: 2,968,010 sq mi; 7,686,850 sq km
LEADING EXPORTS: coal, gold, meat, wool, and alumina
CONTINENT: Australia

Austria
CAPITAL: Vienna
POPULATION: 7,986,664
MAJOR LANGUAGE: German
AREA: 32,376 sq mi; 83,850 sq km
LEADING EXPORTS: machinery and equipment, and iron and steel
CONTINENT: Europe

Azerbaijan
CAPITAL: Baku
POPULATION: 7,789,886
MAJOR LANGUAGES: Azeri, Russian, Armenian, and various languages
AREA: 33,438 sq mi; 86,600 sq km
LEADING EXPORTS: oil and gas, chemicals, and oil field equipment
CONTINENT: Asia

Bahamas
CAPITAL: Nassau
POPULATION: 256,616
MAJOR LANGUAGES: English and Creole
AREA: 5,382 sq mi; 13,940 sq km
LEADING EXPORTS: pharmaceuticals, cement, rum, and crawfish
LOCATION: Caribbean Sea

Bahrain
CAPITAL: Manama
POPULATION: 575,925
MAJOR LANGUAGES: Arabic, English, Farsi, and Urdu
AREA: 239 sq mi; 620 sq km
LEADING EXPORTS: petroleum and petroleum products
CONTINENT: Asia

Bangladesh
CAPITAL: Dhaka
POPULATION: 128,094,948
MAJOR LANGUAGES: Bangla and English
AREA: 55,600 sq mi; 144,000 sq km
LEADING EXPORTS: garments, jute and jute goods, and leather
CONTINENT: Asia

Barbados
CAPITAL: Bridgetown
POPULATION: 256,395
MAJOR LANGUAGE: English
AREA: 166 sq mi; 430 sq km
LEADING EXPORTS: sugar and molasses, and rum
LOCATION: Caribbean Sea

Belarus
CAPITAL: Minsk
POPULATION: 10,437,418
MAJOR LANGUAGES: Byelorussian and Russian
AREA: 79,926 sq mi; 207,600 sq km
LEADING EXPORTS: machinery and transportation equipment
CONTINENT: Europe

Belgium
CAPITAL: Brussels
POPULATION: 10,081,880
MAJOR LANGUAGES: Dutch, French, and German
AREA: 11,780 sq mi; 30,510 sq km
LEADING EXPORTS: iron and steel, and transportation equipment
CONTINENT: Europe

Belize
CAPITAL: Belmopan
POPULATION: 214,061
MAJOR LANGUAGES: English (official), Spanish, Maya, and Garifuna
AREA: 8,865 sq mi; 22,960 sq km
LEADING EXPORTS: sugar, citrus fruits, bananas, and clothing
CONTINENT: North America

Benin
CAPITAL: Porto-Novo
POPULATION: 5,522,677
MAJOR LANGUAGES: Fon, Yoruba, and at least 6 various languages
AREA: 43,484 sq mi; 112,620 sq km
LEADING EXPORTS: cotton, crude oil, palm products, and cocoa
CONTINENT: Africa

Bermuda
CAPITAL: Hamilton
POPULATION: 61,629
MAJOR LANGUAGE: English
AREA: 19.3 sq mi; 50 sq km
LEADING EXPORTS: semitropical produce and light manufactures
LOCATION: Atlantic Ocean

Bhutan
CAPITAL: Thimphu
POPULATION: 1,780,638
MAJOR LANGUAGES: Dzongkha (official), Tibetan dialects, and Nepalese dialects
AREA: 18,147 sq mi; 47,000 sq km
LEADING EXPORTS: cardamon, gypsum, timber, and handicrafts
CONTINENT: Asia

Bolivia
CAPITAL: La Paz
POPULATION: 7,896,254
MAJOR LANGUAGES: Spanish, Quechua, and Aymara
AREA: 424,179 sq mi; 1,098,580 sq km
LEADING EXPORTS: metals, natural gas, soybeans, jewelry, and wood
CONTINENT: South America

Bosnia and Herzegovina
CAPITAL: Sarajevo
POPULATION: 3,201,823
MAJOR LANGUAGE: Serbo-Croatian
AREA: 19,782 sq mi; 51,233 sq km
LEADING EXPORTS: none
CONTINENT: Europe

Botswana

CAPITAL: Gaborone
POPULATION: 1,392,414
MAJOR LANGUAGES: English and Setswana
AREA: 231,812 sq mi; 600,370 sq km
LEADING EXPORTS: diamonds, copper and nickel, and meat
CONTINENT: Africa

Brazil

CAPITAL: Brasília
POPULATION: 160,737,489
MAJOR LANGUAGES: Portuguese, Spanish, English, and French
AREA: 3,286,600 sq mi; 8,511,965 sq km
LEADING EXPORTS: iron ore, soybean, bran, and orange juice
CONTINENT: South America

British Virgin Islands

CAPITAL: Road Town
POPULATION: 13,027
MAJOR LANGUAGE: English
AREA: 58 sq mi; 150 sq km
LEADING EXPORTS: rum, fresh fish, gravel, sand, and fruits
LOCATION: Caribbean Sea

Brunei

CAPITAL: Bandar Seri Begawan
POPULATION: 292,266
MAJOR LANGUAGES: Malay, English, and Chinese
AREA: 2,228 sq mi; 5,770 sq km
LEADING EXPORTS: crude oil and liquefied natural gas
LOCATION: South China Sea

Bulgaria

CAPITAL: Sofia
POPULATION: 8,775,198
MAJOR LANGUAGE: Bulgarian
AREA: 42,824 sq mi; 110,910 sq km
LEADING EXPORTS: machinery and agricultural products
CONTINENT: Europe

Burkina Faso

CAPITAL: Ouagadougou
POPULATION: 10,422,828
MAJOR LANGUAGES: French (official) and Sudanic languages
AREA: 105,873 sq mi; 274,200 sq km
LEADING EXPORTS: cotton, gold, and animal products
CONTINENT: Africa

Burundi

CAPITAL: Bujumbura
POPULATION: 6,262,429
MAJOR LANGUAGES: Kirundi, French, and Swahili
AREA: 10,746 sq mi; 27,830 sq km
LEADING EXPORTS: coffee, tea, cotton, and hides and skins
CONTINENT: Africa

Cambodia

CAPITAL: Phnom Penh
POPULATION: 10,561,373
MAJOR LANGUAGES: Khmer and French
AREA: 69,902 sq mi; 181,040 sq km
LEADING EXPORTS: timber, rubber, soybeans, and sesame
CONTINENT: Asia

Cameroon

CAPITAL: Yaounde
POPULATION: 13,521,000
MAJOR LANGUAGES: 24 various languages, English, and French
AREA: 183,574 sq mi; 475,440 sq km
LEADING EXPORTS: petroleum products and lumber
CONTINENT: Africa

Canada

CAPITAL: Ottawa
POPULATION: 28,434,545
MAJOR LANGUAGES: English and French
AREA: 3,851,940 sq mi; 9,976,140 sq km
LEADING EXPORTS: newsprint, wood pulp, timber, and crude petroleum
CONTINENT: North America

Cape Verde

CAPITAL: Praia
POPULATION: 435,983
MAJOR LANGUAGES: Portuguese and Crioulo
AREA: 1,556 sq mi; 4,030 sq km
LEADING EXPORTS: fish, bananas, and hides and skins
CONTINENT: Africa

Cayman Islands

CAPITAL: George Town
POPULATION: 33,192
MAJOR LANGUAGE: English
AREA: 100 sq mi; 260 sq km
LEADING EXPORTS: turtle products and manufactured goods
LOCATION: Caribbean Sea

Central African Republic

CAPITAL: Bangui
POPULATION: 3,209,759
MAJOR LANGUAGES: French, Sangho, Arabic, Hunsa, and Swahili
AREA: 240,542 sq mi; 622,980 sq km
LEADING EXPORTS: diamonds, timber, cotton, coffee, and tobacco
CONTINENT: Africa

Chad

CAPITAL: N'Djamena
POPULATION: 5,586,505
MAJOR LANGUAGES: French, Arabic, Sara, Songo, and over 100 various languages and dialects
AREA: 495,772 sq mi; 1,284,000 sq km
LEADING EXPORTS: cotton, cattle, textiles, and fish
CONTINENT: Africa

Chile

CAPITAL: Santiago
POPULATION: 14,161,216
MAJOR LANGUAGE: Spanish
AREA: 292,269 sq mi; 756,950 sq km
LEADING EXPORTS: copper and other metals and minerals
CONTINENT: South America

China

CAPITAL: Beijing
POPULATION: 1,203,097,268
MAJOR LANGUAGES: Mandarin, Putonghua, Yue, Wu, Minbei, Minnan, Xiang, and Gan and Hakka dialects
AREA: 3,705,533 sq mi; 9,596,960 sq km
LEADING EXPORTS: textiles, garments, footwear, and toys
CONTINENT: Asia

Colombia

CAPITAL: Bogota
POPULATION: 36,200,251
MAJOR LANGUAGE: Spanish
AREA: 439,751 sq mi; 1,138,910 sq km
LEADING EXPORTS: petroleum, coffee, coal, and bananas
CONTINENT: South America

Comoros

CAPITAL: Moroni
POPULATION: 549,338
MAJOR LANGUAGES: Arabic, French, and Comoran
AREA: 838 sq mi; 2,170 sq km
LEADING EXPORTS: vanilla, ylang-ylang, cloves, and perfume oil
LOCATION: Indian Ocean

Congo

CAPITAL: Brazzaville
POPULATION: 2,504,996
MAJOR LANGUAGES: French, Lingala, Kikongo, and other languages
AREA: 132,051 sq mi; 342,000 sq km
LEADING EXPORTS: crude oil, lumber, plywood, sugar, and cocoa
CONTINENT: Africa

Cook Islands

CAPITAL: Avarua
POPULATION: 19,343
MAJOR LANGUAGES: English and Maori
AREA: 95 sq mi; 240 sq km
LEADING EXPORTS: copra, fresh and canned fruit, and clothing
LOCATION: Pacific Ocean

Costa Rica

CAPITAL: San José
POPULATION: 3,419,114
MAJOR LANGUAGES: Spanish and English
AREA: 19,730 sq mi; 51,100 sq km
LEADING EXPORTS: coffee, bananas, textiles, and sugar
CONTINENT: North America

Côte d'Ivoire

CAPITAL: Yamoussoukro
POPULATION: 14,791,257
MAJOR LANGUAGES: French, Dioula, and 59 other dialects
AREA: 124,507 sq mi; 322,460 sq km
LEADING EXPORTS: cocoa, coffee, tropical woods, and petroleum
CONTINENT: Africa

Croatia

CAPITAL: Zagreb
POPULATION: 4,665,821
MAJOR LANGUAGE: Serbo-Croatian
AREA: 21,830 sq mi; 56,538 sq km
LEADING EXPORTS: machinery and transportation equipment
CONTINENT: Europe

Cuba

CAPITAL: Havana
POPULATION: 10,937,635
MAJOR LANGUAGE: Spanish
AREA: 42,805 sq mi; 110,860 sq km
LEADING EXPORTS: sugar, nickel, shellfish, and tobacco
LOCATION: Caribbean Sea

Cyprus

CAPITAL: Nicosia
POPULATION: 736,636
MAJOR LANGUAGES: Greek, Turkish, and English
AREA: 3,572 sq mi; 9,250 sq km
LEADING EXPORTS: citrus, potatoes, grapes, wines, and cement
LOCATION: Mediterranean Sea

Czech Republic

CAPITAL: Prague
POPULATION: 10,432,774
MAJOR LANGUAGES: Czech and Slovak
AREA: 30,388 sq mi; 78,703 sq km
LEADING EXPORTS: manufactured goods
CONTINENT: Europe

Denmark

CAPITAL: Copenhagen
POPULATION: 5,199,437
MAJOR LANGUAGES: Danish, Faroese, Greenlandic, and German
AREA: 16,630 sq mi; 43,070 sq km
LEADING EXPORTS: meat and meat products, and dairy products
CONTINENT: Europe

Djibouti

CAPITAL: Djibouti
POPULATION: 421,320
MAJOR LANGUAGES: French, Arabic, Somali, and Afar
AREA: 8,495 sq mi; 22,000 sq km
LEADING EXPORTS: hides and skins, and coffee (in transit)
CONTINENT: Africa

Dominica

CAPITAL: Roseau
POPULATION: 82,608
MAJOR LANGUAGES: English and French patois
AREA: 290 sq mi; 750 sq km
LEADING EXPORTS: bananas, soap, bay oil, and vegetables
LOCATION: Caribbean Sea

Dominican Republic

CAPITAL: Santo Domingo
POPULATION: 7,511,263
MAJOR LANGUAGE: Spanish
AREA: 18,815 sq mi; 48,730 sq km
LEADING EXPORTS: ferronickel, sugar, gold, coffee, and cocoa
LOCATION: Caribbean Sea

Ecuador

CAPITAL: Quito
POPULATION: 10,890,950
MAJOR LANGUAGES: Spanish, Quechua, and various languages
AREA: 109,487 sq mi; 283,560 sq km
LEADING EXPORTS: petroleum, bananas, shrimp, and cocoa
CONTINENT: South America

Egypt

CAPITAL: Cairo
POPULATION: 62,359,623
MAJOR LANGUAGES: Arabic, English, and French
AREA: 386,675 sq mi; 1,001,450 sq km
LEADING EXPORTS: crude oil and petroleum products
CONTINENT: Africa

El Salvador

CAPITAL: San Salvador
POPULATION: 5,870,481
MAJOR LANGUAGES: Spanish and Nahua
AREA: 8,124 sq mi; 21,040 sq km
LEADING EXPORTS: coffee, sugar cane, and shrimp
CONTINENT: North America

Equatorial Guinea

CAPITAL: Malabo
POPULATION: 420,293
MAJOR LANGUAGES: Spanish, Pidgin English, Fang, Bubi, and Ibo
AREA: 10,831 sq mi; 28,050 sq km
LEADING EXPORTS: coffee, timber, and cocoa beans
CONTINENT: Africa

Eritrea

CAPITAL: Asmara
POPULATION: 3,578,709
MAJOR LANGUAGES: Tigre, Kunama, Cushitic dialects, Nora Bana, and Arabic
AREA: 46,844 sq mi; 121,320 sq km
LEADING EXPORTS: salt, hides, cement, and gum arabic
CONTINENT: Africa

Estonia

CAPITAL: Tallinn
POPULATION: 1,625,399
MAJOR LANGUAGES: Estonian, Latvian, Lithuanian, and Russian
AREA: 17,414 sq mi; 45,100 sq km
LEADING EXPORTS: textiles, food products, vehicles, and metals
CONTINENT: Europe

Ethiopia

CAPITAL: Addis Ababa
POPULATION: 55,979,018
MAJOR LANGUAGES: Amharic, Tigrinya, Orominga, Guaraginga, Somali, Arabic, English, and various languages
AREA: 435,201 sq mi; 1,127,127 sq km
LEADING EXPORTS: coffee, leather products, and gold
CONTINENT: Africa

Fiji

CAPITAL: Suva
POPULATION: 772,891
MAJOR LANGUAGES: English, Fijian, and Hindustani
AREA: 7,054 sq mi; 18,270 sq km
LEADING EXPORTS: sugar, clothing, gold, processed fish, and lumber
LOCATION: Pacific Ocean

Finland

CAPITAL: Helsinki
POPULATION: 5,085,206
MAJOR LANGUAGES: Finnish, Swedish, Lapp, and Russian
AREA: 130,132 sq mi; 337,030 sq km
LEADING EXPORTS: paper and pulp, machinery, and chemicals
CONTINENT: Europe

France

CAPITAL: Paris
POPULATION: 58,109,160
MAJOR LANGUAGES: French and regional dialects and languages
AREA: 211,217 sq mi; 547,030 sq km
LEADING EXPORTS: machinery and transportation equipment
CONTINENT: Europe

Gabon

CAPITAL: Libreville
POPULATION: 1,185,749
MAJOR LANGUAGES: French, Fang, Myene, Bateke, Bapounou/Eschira, and Bandjabi
AREA: 103,351 sq mi; 267,670 sq km
LEADING EXPORTS: crude oil, timber, manganese, and uranium
CONTINENT: Africa

The Gambia

CAPITAL: Banjul
POPULATION: 989,273
MAJOR LANGUAGES: English, Mandinka, Wolof, Fula, and various languages
AREA: 4,363 sq mi; 11,300 sq km
LEADING EXPORTS: peanuts and peanut products, and fish
CONTINENT: Africa

Georgia

CAPITAL: T'bilisi
POPULATION: 5,725,972
MAJOR LANGUAGES: Armenian, Azeri, Georgian, Russian, and various languages
AREA: 26,912 sq mi; 69,700 sq km
LEADING EXPORTS: citrus fruits, tea, and wine
CONTINENT: Asia

Germany

CAPITAL: Berlin
POPULATION: 81,337,541
MAJOR LANGUAGE: German
AREA: 137,808 sq mi; 356,910 sq km
LEADING EXPORTS: machines and machine tools, and chemicals
CONTINENT: Europe

Ghana

CAPITAL: Accra
POPULATION: 17,763,138
MAJOR LANGUAGES: English, Akan, Moshi-Dagomba, Ewe, Ga, and various languages
AREA: 92,104 sq mi; 238,540 sq km
LEADING EXPORTS: cocoa, gold, timber, tuna, and bauxite
CONTINENT: Africa

Greece

CAPITAL: Athens
POPULATION: 10,647,511
MAJOR LANGUAGES: Greek, English, and French
AREA: 50,944 sq mi; 131,940 sq km
LEADING EXPORTS: manufactured goods, foodstuffs, and fuels
CONTINENT: Europe

Grenada

CAPITAL: Saint George's
POPULATION: 94,486
MAJOR LANGUAGES: English and French patois
AREA: 131 sq mi; 340 sq km
LEADING EXPORTS: bananas, cocoa, nutmeg, and fruits and vegetables
LOCATION: Caribbean Sea

Guatemala

CAPITAL: Guatemala
POPULATION: 10,998,602
MAJOR LANGUAGES: Spanish, Quiche, Cakchiquel, Kekchi, and various languages and dialects
AREA: 42,044 sq mi; 108,890 sq km
LEADING EXPORTS: coffee, sugar, bananas, cardamom, and beef
CONTINENT: North America

Guinea

CAPITAL: Conakry
POPULATION: 6,549,336
MAJOR LANGUAGES: French and various languages
AREA: 94,930 sq mi; 245,860 sq km
LEADING EXPORTS: bauxite, alumina, diamonds, gold, and coffee
CONTINENT: Africa

Guinea Bissau

CAPITAL: Bissau
POPULATION: 1,124,537
MAJOR LANGUAGES: Portuguese, Criolo, and various languages
AREA: 13,946 sq mi; 36,210 sq km
LEADING EXPORTS: cashews, fish, peanuts, and palm kernels
CONTINENT: Africa

Guyana

CAPITAL: Georgetown
POPULATION: 723,774
MAJOR LANGUAGES: English and various dialects
AREA: 83,003 sq mi; 214,970 sq km
LEADING EXPORTS: sugar, bauxite/alumina, rice, and shrimp
CONTINENT: South America

Haiti

CAPITAL: Port-au-Prince
POPULATION: 6,539,983
MAJOR LANGUAGES: French and Creole
AREA: 8,784 sq mi; 22,750 sq km
LEADING EXPORTS: light manufactures and coffee
LOCATION: Caribbean Sea

Holy See (Vatican City)

CAPITAL: Vatican City
POPULATION: 830
MAJOR LANGUAGES: Italian, Latin, and various languages
AREA: 17 sq mi; 44 sq km
LEADING EXPORTS: none
CONTINENT: Europe

Honduras

CAPITAL: Tegucigalpa
POPULATION: 5,549,743
MAJOR LANGUAGES: Spanish and various dialects
AREA: 43,280 sq mi; 112,090 sq km
LEADING EXPORTS: bananas, coffee, shrimp, lobsters, and minerals
CONTINENT: North America

Hungary

CAPITAL: Budapest
POPULATION: 10,318,838
MAJOR LANGUAGES: Hungarian and various languages
AREA: 35,920 sq mi; 93,030 sq km
LEADING EXPORTS: raw materials and semi-finished goods
CONTINENT: Europe

Iceland

CAPITAL: Reykjavik
POPULATION: 265,998
MAJOR LANGUAGE: Icelandic
AREA: 39,770 sq mi; 103,000 sq km
LEADING EXPORTS: fish and fish products, and animal products
LOCATION: Atlantic Ocean

India

CAPITAL: New Delhi
POPULATION: 936,545,814
MAJOR LANGUAGES: English, Hindi, Bengali, Telugu, Marathi, Tamil, Urdu, Gujarati, Malayam, Kannada, Oriya, Punjabi, Assamese, Kashmiri, Sindhi, Sanskrit, and Hindustani (all official)
AREA: 1,269,389 sq mi; 3,287,590 sq km
LEADING EXPORTS: clothing, and gems and jewelry
CONTINENT: Asia

Indonesia

CAPITAL: Jakarta
POPULATION: 203,583,886
MAJOR LANGUAGES: Bahasa Indonesia, English, Dutch, Javanese, and various dialects
AREA: 741,052 sq mi; 1,919,251 sq km
LEADING EXPORTS: manufactures, fuels, and foodstuffs
CONTINENT: Asia

Iran

CAPITAL: Tehran
POPULATION: 64,625,455
MAJOR LANGUAGES: Farsi (official) and Turkic languages
AREA: 634,562 sq mi; 1,643,452 sq km
LEADING EXPORTS: petroleum, carpets, fruit, nuts, and hides
CONTINENT: Asia

Iraq

CAPITAL: Baghdad
POPULATION: 20,643,769
MAJOR LANGUAGES: Arabic, Kurdish, Assyrian, and Armenian
AREA: 168,760 sq mi; 437,072 sq km
LEADING EXPORTS: crude oil and refined products, and fertilizers
CONTINENT: Asia

Ireland

CAPITAL: Dublin
POPULATION: 3,550,448
MAJOR LANGUAGES: Irish Gaelic and English
AREA: 27,136 sq mi; 70,280 sq km
LEADING EXPORTS: chemicals and data processing equipment
CONTINENT: Europe

Israel

CAPITAL: Jerusalem
POPULATION: 7,566,447
MAJOR LANGUAGES: Hebrew, Arabic, and English
AREA: 10,421 sq mi; 26,990 sq km
LEADING EXPORTS: machinery and equipment, and cut diamonds
CONTINENT: Asia

Italy

CAPITAL: Rome
POPULATION: 58,261,971
MAJOR LANGUAGES: Italian, German, French, and Slovene
AREA: 116,310 sq mi; 301,230 sq km
LEADING EXPORTS: metals, and textiles and clothing
CONTINENT: Europe

Jamaica

CAPITAL: Kingston
POPULATION: 2,574,291
MAJOR LANGUAGES: English and Creole
AREA: 4,243 sq mi; 10,990 sq km
LEADING EXPORTS: alumina, bauxite, sugar, bananas, and rum
LOCATION: Caribbean Sea

Japan

CAPITAL: Tokyo
POPULATION: 125,506,492
MAJOR LANGUAGE: Japanese
AREA: 145,888 sq mi; 377,835 sq km
LEADING EXPORTS: machinery, motor vehicles, and electronics
CONTINENT: Asia

Jordan

CAPITAL: Amman
POPULATION: 4,100,709
MAJOR LANGUAGES: Arabic and English
AREA: 34,447 sq mi; 89,213 sq km
LEADING EXPORTS: phosphates, fertilizers, and potash
CONTINENT: Asia

Kazakstan

CAPITAL: Almaty
POPULATION: 17,376,615
MAJOR LANGUAGES: Kazak and Russian
AREA: 1,049,191 sq mi; 2,717,300 sq km
LEADING EXPORTS: oil, and ferrous and nonferrous metals
CONTINENT: Asia

Kenya

CAPITAL: Nairobi
POPULATION: 28,817,227
MAJOR LANGUAGES: English, Swahili, and various languages
AREA: 224,970 sq mi; 582,650 sq km
LEADING EXPORTS: tea, coffee, and petroleum products
CONTINENT: Africa

Kiribati

CAPITAL: Tarawa
POPULATION: 79,386
MAJOR LANGUAGES: English and Gilbertese
AREA: 277 sq mi; 717 sq km
LEADING EXPORTS: copra, seaweed, and fish
LOCATION: Pacific Ocean

Korea, North

CAPITAL: P'yongyang
POPULATION: 23,486,550
MAJOR LANGUAGE: Korean
AREA: 46,542 sq mi; 120,540 sq km
LEADING EXPORTS: minerals and metallurgical products
CONTINENT: Asia

Korea, South

CAPITAL: Seoul
POPULATION: 45,553,882
MAJOR LANGUAGES: Korean and English
AREA: 38,025 sq mi; 98,480 sq km
LEADING EXPORTS: electronic and electrical equipment
CONTINENT: Asia

Kuwait

CAPITAL: Kuwait
POPULATION: 1,817,397
MAJOR LANGUAGES: Arabic and English
AREA: 6,881 sq mi; 17,820 sq km
LEADING EXPORT: oil
CONTINENT: Asia

Kyrgyzstan

CAPITAL: Bishkek
POPULATION: 4,769,877
MAJOR LANGUAGES: Kyrgyz and Russian
AREA: 76,644 sq mi; 198,500 sq km
LEADING EXPORTS: wool, chemicals, cotton, metals, and shoes
CONTINENT: Asia

Laos

CAPITAL: Vientiane
POPULATION: 4,837,237
MAJOR LANGUAGES: Lao, French, English, and various languages
AREA: 91,432 sq mi; 236,800 sq km
LEADING EXPORTS: electricity, wood products, coffee, and tin
CONTINENT: Asia

Latvia

CAPITAL: Riga
POPULATION: 2,762,899
MAJOR LANGUAGES: Lettish, Lithuanian, Russian, and various languages
AREA: 24,750 sq mi; 64,100 sq km
LEADING EXPORTS: oil products, timber, and ferrous metals
CONTINENT: Europe

Lebanon

CAPITAL: Beirut
POPULATION: 3,695,921
MAJOR LANGUAGES: Arabic, French, Armenian, and English
AREA: 4,016 sq mi; 10,400 sq km
LEADING EXPORTS: agricultural products, chemicals, and textiles
CONTINENT: Asia

Lesotho

CAPITAL: Maseru
POPULATION: 1,992,960
MAJOR LANGUAGES: Sesotho, English, Zulu, and Xhosa
AREA: 11,719 sq mi; 30,350 sq km
LEADING EXPORTS: wool, mohair, wheat, cattle, and peas
CONTINENT: Africa

Liberia

CAPITAL: Monrovia
POPULATION: 3,073,245
MAJOR LANGUAGES: English and Niger-Congo
AREA: 43,002 sq mi; 111,370 sq km
LEADING EXPORTS: iron ore, rubber, timber, and coffee
CONTINENT: Africa

Libya
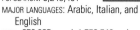
CAPITAL: Tripoli
POPULATION: 5,248,401
MAJOR LANGUAGES: Arabic, Italian, and English
AREA: 679,385 sq mi; 1,759,540 sq km
LEADING EXPORTS: crude oil and refined petroleum products
CONTINENT: Africa

Liechtenstein
CAPITAL: Vaduz
POPULATION: 30,654
MAJOR LANGUAGES: German and Alemannic
AREA: 62 sq mi; 160 sq km
LEADING EXPORTS: small specialty machinery and dental products
CONTINENT: Europe

Lithuania
CAPITAL: Vilnius
POPULATION: 3,876,396
MAJOR LANGUAGES: Lithuanian, Polish, and Russian
AREA: 25,175 sq mi; 65,200 sq km
LEADING EXPORTS: electronics, petroleum products, and food
CONTINENT: Europe

Luxembourg
CAPITAL: Luxembourg
POPULATION: 404,660
MAJOR LANGUAGES: Luxembourgisch, German, French, and English
AREA: 998 sq mi; 2,586 sq km
LEADING EXPORTS: finished steel products and chemicals
CONTINENT: Europe

Macedonia
CAPITAL: Skopje
POPULATION: 2,159,503
MAJOR LANGUAGES: Macedonian, Albanian, Turkish, Serb, Gypsy, and various languages
AREA: 9,781 sq mi; 25,333 sq km
LEADING EXPORTS: manufactured goods and machinery
CONTINENT: Europe

Madagascar
CAPITAL: Antananarivo
POPULATION: 13,862,325
MAJOR LANGUAGES: French and Malagasy
AREA: 226,665 sq mi; 587,040 sq km
LEADING EXPORTS: coffee, vanilla, cloves, shellfish, and sugar
CONTINENT: Africa

Malawi

CAPITAL: Lilongwe
POPULATION: 9,808,384
MAJOR LANGUAGES: English, Chichewa, and various languages
AREA: 45,747 sq mi; 118,480 sq km
LEADING EXPORTS: tobacco, tea, sugar, coffee, and peanuts
CONTINENT: Africa

Malaysia

CAPITAL: Kuala Lumpur
POPULATION: 19,723,587
MAJOR LANGUAGES: Malay, English, Mandarin, Tamil, Chinese dialects, and various languages and dialects
AREA: 127,322 sq mi; 329,750 sq km
LEADING EXPORTS: electronic equipment
CONTINENT: Asia

Maldives
CAPITAL: Male
POPULATION: 261,310
MAJOR LANGUAGES: Divehi dialect and English
AREA: 116 sq mi; 300 sq km
LEADING EXPORTS: fish and clothing
CONTINENT: Asia

Mali
CAPITAL: Bamako
POPULATION: 9,375,132
MAJOR LANGUAGES: French, Bambara, and various languages
AREA: 478,783 sq mi; 1,240,000 sq km
LEADING EXPORTS: cotton, livestock, and gold
CONTINENT: Africa

Malta
CAPITAL: Valletta
POPULATION: 369,609
MAJOR LANGUAGES: Maltese and English
AREA: 124 sq mi; 320 sq km
LEADING EXPORTS: machinery and transportation equipment
LOCATION: Mediterranean Sea

Marshall Islands
CAPITAL: Majuro
POPULATION: 56,157
MAJOR LANGUAGES: English, Marshallese dialects, and Japanese
AREA: 70 sq mi; 181.3 sq km
LEADING EXPORTS: coconut oil, fish, live animals, and trichus shells
LOCATION: Pacific Ocean

Mauritania

CAPITAL: Nouakchott
POPULATION: 2,263,202
MAJOR LANGUAGES: Hasaniya Arabic, Wolof, Pular, and Soninke
AREA: 397,969 sq mi; 1,030,700 sq km
LEADING EXPORTS: iron ore, and fish and fish products
CONTINENT: Africa

Mauritius
CAPITAL: Port Louis
POPULATION: 1,127,068
MAJOR LANGUAGES: English (official), Creole, French, Hindi, Urdu, Hakka, and Bojpoori
AREA: 718 sq mi; 1,860 sq km
LEADING EXPORTS: textiles, sugar, and light manufactures
LOCATION: Indian Ocean

Mayotte
CAPITAL: Mamoutzou
POPULATION: 97,088
MAJOR LANGUAGES: Mahorian and French
AREA: 145 sq mi; 375 sq km
LEADING EXPORTS: ylang-ylang and vanilla
CONTINENT: Africa

Mexico

CAPITAL: Mexico City
POPULATION: 93,985,848
MAJOR LANGUAGES: Spanish and Mayan dialects
AREA: 761,632 sq mi; 1,972,550 sq km
LEADING EXPORTS: crude oil, oil products, coffee, and silver
CONTINENT: North America

Micronesia

CAPITAL: Federated states of Kolonia (on the Island of Pohnpei)
*a new capital is being built about 10 km southwest in the Palikir Valley
POPULATION: 122,950
MAJOR LANGUAGES: English, Turkese, Pohnpeian, Yapese, and Kosrean
AREA: 271 sq mi; 702 sq km
LEADING EXPORTS: fish, copra, bananas, and black pepper
LOCATION: Pacific Ocean

Moldova

CAPITAL: Chisinau
POPULATION: 4,489,657
MAJOR LANGUAGES: Moldovan (official), Russian, and Gagauz dialect
AREA: 13,012 sq mi; 33,700 sq km
LEADING EXPORTS: foodstuffs, wine, and tobacco
CONTINENT: Europe

Monaco

CAPITAL: Monaco
POPULATION: 31,515
MAJOR LANGUAGES: French (official), English, Italian, and Monegasque
AREA: .73 sq mi; 1.9 sq km
LEADING EXPORTS: exports through France
CONTINENT: Europe

Mongolia

CAPITAL: Ulaanbaatar
POPULATION: 2,493,615
MAJOR LANGUAGES: Khalkha Mongol, Turkic, Russian, and Chinese
AREA: 604,270 sq mi; 1,565,000 sq km
LEADING EXPORTS: copper, livestock, animal products, and cashmere
CONTINENT: Asia

Morocco

CAPITAL: Rabat
POPULATION: 29,168,848
MAJOR LANGUAGES: Arabic (official), Berber dialects, and French
AREA: 172,420 sq mi; 446,550 sq km
LEADING EXPORTS: food and beverages
CONTINENT: Africa

Mozambique

CAPITAL: Maputo
POPULATION: 18,115,250
MAJOR LANGUAGES: Portuguese and various dialects
AREA: 309,506 sq mi; 801,590 sq km
LEADING EXPORTS: shrimp, cashews, cotton, sugar, copra, and citrus
CONTINENT: Africa

Myanmar (Burma)

CAPITAL: Rangoon
POPULATION: 45,103,809
MAJOR LANGUAGE: Burmese
AREA: 261,979 sq mi; 678,500 sq km
LEADING EXPORTS: pulses and beans, teak, rice, and hardwood
CONTINENT: Asia

Namibia
CAPITAL: Windhoek
POPULATION: 1,651,545
MAJOR LANGUAGES: English (official), Afrikaans, German, Oshivambo, Herero, Nama, and various languages
AREA: 318,707 sq mi; 825,418 sq km
LEADING EXPORTS: diamonds, copper, gold, zinc, and lead
CONTINENT: Africa

Nauru

CAPITAL: Government offices in Yaren District
POPULATION: 10,149
MAJOR LANGUAGES: Nauruan and English
AREA: 8 sq mi; 21 sq km
LEADING EXPORTS: phosphates
LOCATION: Pacific Ocean

Nepal

CAPITAL: Kathmandu
POPULATION: 21,560,869
MAJOR LANGUAGES: Nepali (official) and 20 various languages divided into numerous dialects
AREA: 54,365 sq mi; 140,800 sq km
LEADING EXPORTS: carpets, clothing, and leather goods
CONTINENT: Asia

Netherlands

CAPITAL: Amsterdam
POPULATION: 15,452,903
MAJOR LANGUAGE: Dutch
AREA: 14,414 sq mi; 37,330 sq km
LEADING EXPORTS: metal products and chemicals
CONTINENT: Europe

New Caledonia

CAPITAL: Noumea
POPULATION: 184,552
MAJOR LANGUAGES: French and 28 Melanesian-Polynesian dialects
AREA: 7,359 sq mi; 19,060 sq km
LEADING EXPORTS: nickel metal and nickel ore
LOCATION: Pacific Ocean

New Zealand

CAPITAL: Wellington
POPULATION: 3,407,277
MAJOR LANGUAGES: English and Maori
AREA: 103,741 sq mi; 268,680 sq km
LEADING EXPORTS: wool, lamb, mutton, beef, fish, and cheese
LOCATION: Pacific Ocean

Nicaragua

CAPITAL: Managua
POPULATION: 4,206,353
MAJOR LANGUAGES: Spanish (official), English, and various languages
AREA: 50,000 sq mi; 129,494 sq km
LEADING EXPORTS: meat, coffee, cotton, sugar, seafood, and gold
CONTINENT: North America

Niger

CAPITAL: Niamey
POPULATION: 9,280,208
MAJOR LANGUAGES: French (official), Hausa, and Djerma
AREA: 489,208 sq mi; 1,267,000 sq km
LEADING EXPORTS: uranium ore and livestock products
CONTINENT: Africa

Nigeria

CAPITAL: Abuja
POPULATION: 101,232,251
MAJOR LANGUAGES: English (official), Hausa, Yoruba, Ibo, and Fulani
AREA: 356,682 sq mi; 923,770 sq km
LEADING EXPORTS: oil, cocoa, and rubber
CONTINENT: Africa

Niue

CAPITAL: (Free association with New Zealand)
POPULATION: 1,837
MAJOR LANGUAGES: Polynesian and English
AREA: 100 sq mi; 260 sq km
LEADING EXPORTS: canned coconut cream, copra, and honey
LOCATION: Pacific Ocean

Norway

CAPITAL: Oslo
POPULATION: 4,330,951
MAJOR LANGUAGES: Norwegian (official), Lapp, and Finnish
AREA: 125,186 sq mi; 324,220 sq km
LEADING EXPORTS: petroleum and petroleum products
CONTINENT: Europe

Oman

CAPITAL: Muscat
POPULATION: 2,125,089
MAJOR LANGUAGES: Arabic (official), English, Baluchi, Urdu, and Indian dialects
AREA: 82,034 sq mi; 212,460 sq km
LEADING EXPORTS: petroleum, re-exports, and fish
CONTINENT: Asia

Pakistan

CAPITAL: Islamabad
POPULATION: 131,541,920
MAJOR LANGUAGES: Urdu (official), English (official), Punjabi, Sindhi, Pashtu, Urdu, Balochi, and other languages
AREA: 310,414 sq mi; 803,940 sq km
LEADING EXPORTS: cotton, textiles, clothing, rice, and leather
CONTINENT: Asia

Palau

CAPITAL: Koror
POPULATION: 16,661
MAJOR LANGUAGES: English (official), Sonsorolese, Angaur, Japanese, Tobi, and Palauan
AREA: 177 sq mi; 458 sq km
LEADING EXPORTS: trochus, tuna, copra, and handicrafts
LOCATION: Pacific Ocean

Panama

CAPITAL: Panama
POPULATION: 2,680,903
MAJOR LANGUAGES: Spanish (official) and English
AREA: 30,194 sq mi; 78,200 sq km
LEADING EXPORTS: bananas, shrimp, sugar, clothing, and coffee
CONTINENT: North America

Papua New Guinea

CAPITAL: Port Moresby
POPULATION: 4,294,750
MAJOR LANGUAGES: English, pidgin English, and Motu
AREA: 178,266 sq mi; 461,690 sq km
LEADING EXPORTS: gold, copper ore, oil, logs, and palm oil
LOCATION: Pacific Ocean

Paraguay

CAPITAL: Asuncion
POPULATION: 5,358,198
MAJOR LANGUAGES: Spanish (official) and Guarani
AREA: 157,052 sq mi; 406,750 sq km
LEADING EXPORTS: cotton, soybeans, timber, and vegetable oils
CONTINENT: South America

Peru

CAPITAL: Lima
POPULATION: 24,087,372
MAJOR LANGUAGES: Spanish (official), Quechua (official), and Aymara
AREA: 496,243 sq mi; 1,285,220 sq km
LEADING EXPORTS: copper, zinc, and fish meal
CONTINENT: South America

Philippines

CAPITAL: Manila
POPULATION: 73,265,584
MAJOR LANGUAGES: Pilipino and English (official)
AREA: 115,834 sq mi; 300,000 sq km
LEADING EXPORTS: electronics, textiles, and coconut products
CONTINENT: Asia

Poland

CAPITAL: Warsaw
POPULATION: 38,792,442
MAJOR LANGUAGE: Polish
AREA: 120,731 sq mi; 312,680 sq km
LEADING EXPORTS: intermediate goods
CONTINENT: Europe

Portugal

CAPITAL: Lisbon
POPULATION: 10,562,388
MAJOR LANGUAGE: Portuguese
AREA: 35,553 sq mi; 92,080 sq km
LEADING EXPORTS: clothing and footwear, and machinery
CONTINENT: Europe

Qatar

CAPITAL: Doha
POPULATION: 533,916
MAJOR LANGUAGES: Arabic (official) and English
AREA: 4,247 sq mi; 11,000 sq km
LEADING EXPORTS: petroleum products, steel, and fertilizers
CONTINENT: Asia

Romania

CAPITAL: Bucharest
POPULATION: 23,198,330
MAJOR LANGUAGES: Romanian, Hungarian, and German
AREA: 91,702 sq mi; 237,500 sq km
LEADING EXPORTS: metals and metal products, and mineral products
CONTINENT: Europe

Russia

CAPITAL: Moscow
POPULATION: 149,909,089
MAJOR LANGUAGES: Russian and various languages
AREA: 6,952,996 sq mi; 17,075,200 sq km
LEADING EXPORTS: petroleum and petroleum products
CONTINENT: Europe and Asia

Rwanda

CAPITAL: Kigali
POPULATION: 8,605,307
MAJOR LANGUAGES: Kinyarwanda (official), French (official), and Kiswahili
AREA: 10,170 sq mi; 26,340 sq km
LEADING EXPORTS: coffee, tea, cassiterite, and wolframite
CONTINENT: Africa

Saint Kitts and Nevis

CAPITAL: Basseterre
POPULATION: 40,992
MAJOR LANGUAGE: English
AREA: 104 sq mi; 269 sq km
LEADING EXPORTS: machinery, food, and electronics
LOCATION: Caribbean Sea

Saint Lucia

CAPITAL: Castries
POPULATION: 156,050
MAJOR LANGUAGES: English and French patois
AREA: 239 sq mi; 620 sq km
LEADING EXPORTS: bananas, clothing, cocoa, and vegetables
LOCATION: Caribbean Sea

Saint Vincent and the Grenadines

CAPITAL: Kingstown
POPULATION: 117,344
MAJOR LANGUAGES: English and French patois
AREA: 131 sq mi; 340 sq km
LEADING EXPORTS: bananas, and eddoes and dasheen (taro)
LOCATION: Caribbean Sea

San Marino

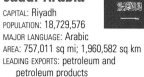

CAPITAL: San Marino
POPULATION: 24,313
MAJOR LANGUAGE: Italian
AREA: 23 sq mi; 60 sq km
LEADING EXPORTS: building stone, lime, wood, and chestnuts
CONTINENT: Europe

Sao Tome and Principe

CAPITAL: Sao Tome
POPULATION: 140,423
MAJOR LANGUAGE: Portuguese (official)
AREA: 371 sq mi; 960 sq km
LEADING EXPORTS: cocoa, copra, coffee, and palm oil
CONTINENT: Africa

Saudi Arabia

CAPITAL: Riyadh
POPULATION: 18,729,576
MAJOR LANGUAGE: Arabic
AREA: 757,011 sq mi; 1,960,582 sq km
LEADING EXPORTS: petroleum and petroleum products
CONTINENT: Asia

Senegal

CAPITAL: Dakar
POPULATION: 9,007,080
MAJOR LANGUAGES: French (official), Wolof, Pulaar, Diola, and Mandingo
AREA: 75,752 sq mi; 196,190 sq km
LEADING EXPORTS: fish, ground nuts, and petroleum products
CONTINENT: Africa

Serbia and Montenegro

CAPITAL: Belgrade
POPULATION: 11,101,833
MAJOR LANGUAGES: Serbo-Croatian and Albanian
AREA: 39,436 sq mi; 102,350 sq km
LEADING EXPORTS: none
CONTINENT: Europe

Seychelles

CAPITAL: Victoria
POPULATION: 72,709
MAJOR LANGUAGES: English (official), French (official), and Creole
AREA: 176 sq mi; 455 sq km
LEADING EXPORTS: fish, cinnamon bark, and copra
CONTINENT: Africa

Sierra Leone

CAPITAL: Freetown
POPULATION: 4,753,120
MAJOR LANGUAGES: English (official), Mende, Temne, and Krio
AREA: 27,700 sq mi; 71,740 sq km
LEADING EXPORTS: rutile, bauxite, diamonds, coffee, and cocoa
CONTINENT: Africa

Singapore

CAPITAL: Singapore
POPULATION: 2,890,468
MAJOR LANGUAGES: Chinese, Malay, Tamil, and English
AREA: 244 sq mi; 633 sq km
LEADING EXPORTS: computer equipment
CONTINENT: Asia

Slovakia

CAPITAL: Bratislava
POPULATION: 5,432,383
MAJOR LANGUAGES: Slovak and Hungarian
AREA: 18,860 sq mi; 48,845 sq km
LEADING EXPORTS: machinery and transportation equipment
CONTINENT: Europe

Slovenia

CAPITAL: Ljubljana
POPULATION: 2,051,522
MAJOR LANGUAGES: Slovenian, Serbo-Croatian, and various languages
AREA: 7,837 sq mi; 20,296 sq km
LEADING EXPORTS: machinery and transportation equipment
CONTINENT: Europe

Solomon Islands

CAPITAL: Honiara
POPULATION: 399,206
MAJOR LANGUAGES: Melanesian pidgin and English
AREA: 10,985 sq mi; 28,450 sq km
LEADING EXPORTS: fish, timber, palm oil, cocoa, and copra
LOCATION: Pacific Ocean

Somalia

CAPITAL: Mogadishu
POPULATION: 7,347,554
MAJOR LANGUAGES: Somali (official), Arabic, Italian, and English
AREA: 246,210 sq mi; 637,660 sq km
LEADING EXPORTS: bananas, live animals, fish, and hides
CONTINENT: Africa

South Africa

CAPITAL: Pretoria (administrative), Cape Town (legislative), Bloemfontein (judicial)
POPULATION: 45,095,459
MAJOR LANGUAGES: Afrikaans, English, Ndebele, Pedi, Sotho, Swazi, Tsonga, Tswana, Venda, Xhosa, and Zulu (all official)
AREA: 471,027 sq mi; 1,219,912 sq km
LEADING EXPORTS: gold, other minerals and metals, and food
CONTINENT: Africa

Spain

CAPITAL: Madrid
POPULATION: 39,404,348
MAJOR LANGUAGES: Spanish, Catalan, Galician, and Basque
AREA: 194,892 sq mi; 504,750 sq km
LEADING EXPORTS: cars and trucks, and semifinished goods
CONTINENT: Europe

Sri Lanka

CAPITAL: Colombo
POPULATION: 18,342,660
MAJOR LANGUAGES: Sinhala (official) and Tamil
AREA: 25,333 sq mi; 65,610 sq km
LEADING EXPORTS: garments and textiles, teas, and diamonds
CONTINENT: Asia

Sudan

CAPITAL: Khartoum
POPULATION: 30,120,420
MAJOR LANGUAGES: Arabic (official), Nubian, Ta Bedawie, Nilotic, Nilo-Hamitic, and Sudanic dialects
AREA: 967,532 sq mi; 2,505,810 sq km
LEADING EXPORTS: gum arabic, livestock/meat, and cotton
CONTINENT: Africa

Suriname

CAPITAL: Paramaribo
POPULATION: 429,544
MAJOR LANGUAGES: Dutch (official), English, Sranang, Tongo, Hindustani, and Japanese
AREA: 63,041 sq mi; 163,270 sq km
LEADING EXPORTS: alumina, aluminum, and shrimp and fish
CONTINENT: South America

Swaziland

CAPITAL: Mbabane
POPULATION: 966,977
MAJOR LANGUAGES: English (official) and SiSwati (official)
AREA: 6,641 sq mi; 17,360 sq km
LEADING EXPORTS: sugar, edible concentrates, and wood pulp
CONTINENT: Africa

Sweden

CAPITAL: Stockholm
POPULATION: 8,821,759
MAJOR LANGUAGES: Swedish, Lapp, and Finnish
AREA: 173,738 sq mi; 449,964 sq km
LEADING EXPORTS: machinery, motor vehicles, and paper products
CONTINENT: Europe

Switzerland

CAPITAL: Bern
POPULATION: 7,084,984
MAJOR LANGUAGES: German, French, Italian, Romansch, and various languages
AREA: 15,943 sq mi; 41,290 sq km
LEADING EXPORTS: machinery and equipment
CONTINENT: Europe

Syria

CAPITAL: Damascus
POPULATION: 15,451,917
MAJOR LANGUAGES: Arabic (official), Kurdish, Armenian, Aramaic, Circassian, and French
AREA: 71,501 sq mi; 185,180 sq km
LEADING EXPORTS: petroleum, textiles, cotton, and fruits
CONTINENT: Asia

Taiwan

CAPITAL: Taipei
POPULATION: 21,500,583
MAJOR LANGUAGES: Mandarin Chinese (official), Taiwanese, and Hakka dialects
AREA: 13,892 sq mi; 35,980 sq km
LEADING EXPORTS: electrical machinery and electronics
CONTINENT: Asia

Tajikistan

CAPITAL: Dushanbe
POPULATION: 6,155,474
MAJOR LANGUAGES: Tajik (official) and
    Russian
AREA: 55,253 sq mi; 143,100 sq km
LEADING EXPORTS: cotton, aluminum, fruits,
    and vegetable oil
CONTINENT: Asia

Tanzania

CAPITAL: Dar Es Salaam
POPULATION: 28,701,077
MAJOR LANGUAGES: Swahili, English, and
    various languages
AREA: 364,914 sq mi; 945,090 sq km
LEADING EXPORTS: coffee, cotton, tobacco,
    tea, and cashew nuts
CONTINENT: Africa

Thailand

CAPITAL: Bangkok
POPULATION: 60,271,300
MAJOR LANGUAGES: Thai and English
AREA: 198,463 sq mi; 511,770 sq km
LEADING EXPORTS: machinery and
    manufactures
CONTINENT: Asia

Togo

CAPITAL: Lome
POPULATION: 4,410,370
MAJOR LANGUAGES: French, Ewe and Mina,
    Dagomba, and Kabye
AREA: 21,927 sq mi; 56,790 sq km
LEADING EXPORTS: phosphates, cotton,
    cocoa, and coffee
CONTINENT: Africa

Tonga

CAPITAL: Nukualofa
POPULATION: 105,600
MAJOR LANGUAGES: Tongan and English
AREA: 289 sq mi; 748 sq km
LEADING EXPORTS: squash, vanilla, fish, root
    crops, and coconut oil
LOCATION: Pacific Ocean

Trinidad and Tobago

CAPITAL: Port-of-Spain
POPULATION: 1,271,159
MAJOR LANGUAGES: English, Hindu, French,
    and Spanish
AREA: 1,981 sq mi; 5,130 sq km
LEADING EXPORTS: petroleum and
    petroleum products
LOCATION: Caribbean Sea

Tunisia

CAPITAL: Tunis
POPULATION: 8,879,845
MAJOR LANGUAGES: Arabic and French
AREA: 63,172 sq mi; 163,610 sq km
LEADING EXPORTS: hydrocarbons and
    agricultural products
CONTINENT: Africa

Turkey

CAPITAL: Ankara
POPULATION: 63,405,526
MAJOR LANGUAGES: Turkish, Kurdish, and
    Arabic
AREA: 301,394 sq mi; 780,580 sq km
LEADING EXPORTS: manufactured products,
    and foodstuffs
CONTINENT: Europe and Asia

Turkmenistan

CAPITAL: Ashgabat
POPULATION: 4,075,316
MAJOR LANGUAGES: Turkmen, Russian,
    Uzbek, and various languages
AREA: 188,463 sq mi; 488,100 sq km
LEADING EXPORTS: natural gas, cotton, and
    petroleum products
CONTINENT: Asia

Tuvalu

CAPITAL: Fongafale,
    on Funafuti atoll
POPULATION: 9,991
MAJOR LANGUAGES: Tuvaluan and English
AREA: 10 sq mi; 26 sq km
LEADING EXPORT: copra
LOCATION: Pacific Ocean

Uganda

CAPITAL: Kampala
POPULATION: 19,573,262
MAJOR LANGUAGES: English, Luganda,
    Swahili, Bantu languages, and
    Nilotic languages
AREA: 91,139 sq mi; 236,040 sq km
LEADING EXPORTS: coffee, cotton, and tea
CONTINENT: Africa

Ukraine

CAPITAL: Kiev
POPULATION: 51,867,828
MAJOR LANGUAGES: Ukranian, Russian,
    Romanian, Polish, and Hungarian
AREA: 233,098 sq mi; 603,700 sq km
LEADING EXPORTS: coal, electric power, and
    metals
CONTINENT: Europe

United Arab Emirates

CAPITAL: Abu Dhabi
POPULATION: 2,924,594
MAJOR LANGUAGES: Arabic, Persian,
    English, Hindi, and Urdu
AREA: 29,183 sq mi; 75,581 sq km
LEADING EXPORTS: crude oil, natural gas,
    re-exports, and dried fish
CONTINENT: Asia

United Kingdom

CAPITAL: London
POPULATION: 58,295,119
MAJOR LANGUAGES: English, Welsh, and
    Scottish Gaelic
AREA: 94,529 sq mi; 244,820 sq km
LEADING EXPORTS: manufactured goods,
    machinery, and fuels
CONTINENT: Europe

United States

CAPITAL: Washington, D.C.
POPULATION: 263,814,032
MAJOR LANGUAGES: English and Spanish
AREA: 3,618,908 sq mi; 9,372,610 sq km
LEADING EXPORTS: capital goods and
    automobiles
CONTINENT: North America

Uruguay

CAPITAL: Montevideo
POPULATION: 3,222,716
MAJOR LANGUAGES: Spanish and Brazilero
AREA: 68,041 sq mi; 176,220 sq km
LEADING EXPORTS: wool and textile
    manufactures
CONTINENT: South America

Uzbekistan

CAPITAL: Tashkent
POPULATION: 23,089,261
MAJOR LANGUAGES: Uzbek, Russian, Tajik,
    various languages
AREA: 172,748 sq mi; 447,400 sq km
LEADING EXPORTS: cotton, gold, natural gas,
    and minerals
CONTINENT: Asia

Vanuatu

CAPITAL: Port-Vila
POPULATION: 173,648
MAJOR LANGUAGES: English, French, pidgin,
    and Bislama
AREA: 5,699 sq mi; 14,760 sq km
LEADING EXPORTS: copra, beef, cocoa,
    timber, and coffee
LOCATION: Pacific Ocean

Venezuela

CAPITAL: Caracas
POPULATION: 21,004,773
MAJOR LANGUAGES: Spanish and various
    languages
AREA: 352,156 sq mi; 912,050 sq km
LEADING EXPORTS: petroleum, bauxite and
    aluminum, and steel
CONTINENT: South America

Vietnam

CAPITAL: Hanoi
POPULATION: 74,393,324
MAJOR LANGUAGES: Vietnamese, French,
    Chinese, English, Khmer, and various
    languages
AREA: 127,248 sq mi; 329,560 sq km
LEADING EXPORTS: petroleum, rice, and
    agricultural products
CONTINENT: Asia

Western Samoa

CAPITAL: Apia
POPULATION: 209,360
MAJOR LANGUAGES: Samoan and English
AREA: 1,104 sq mi; 2,860 sq km
LEADING EXPORTS: coconut oil and cream,
    taro, copra, and cocoa
LOCATION: Pacific Ocean

Yemen

CAPITAL: Sanaa
POPULATION: 14,728,474
MAJOR LANGUAGE: Arabic
AREA: 203,857 sq mi; 527,970 sq km
LEADING EXPORTS: crude oil, cotton, coffee,
    hides, and vegetables
CONTINENT: Asia

Zaire (Democratic Republic of Congo)

CAPITAL: Kinshasa
POPULATION: 44,060,636
MAJOR LANGUAGES: French, Lingala,
    Swahili, Kingwana, Kikongo, and
    Tshiluba
AREA: 905,599 sq mi; 2,345,410 sq km
LEADING EXPORTS: copper, coffee,
    diamonds, cobalt, and crude oil
CONTINENT: Africa

Zambia

CAPITAL: Lusaka
POPULATION: 9,445,723
MAJOR LANGUAGES: English (official) and
    about 70 various languages
AREA: 290,594 sq mi; 752,610 sq km
LEADING EXPORTS: copper, zinc, cobalt, lead,
    and tobacco
CONTINENT: Africa

Zimbabwe

CAPITAL: Harare
POPULATION: 11,139,961
MAJOR LANGUAGES: English, Shona, and
    Sindebele
area: 150,809 sq mi; 390,580 sq km
LEADING EXPORTS: agricultural products and
    manufactures
CONTINENT: Africa

Glossary of Geographic Terms

basin
a depression in the surface of the land; some basins are filled with water

bay
a part of a sea or lake that extends into the land

butte
a small raised area of land with steep sides

▲ butte

canyon
a deep, narrow valley with steep sides; often has a stream flowing through it

cataract
a large waterfall; any strong flood or rush of water

◄ cataract

delta
a triangular-shaped plain at the mouth of a river, formed when sediment is deposited by flowing water

flood plain
a broad plain on either side of a river, formed when sediment settles on the riverbanks

glacier
a huge, slow-moving mass of snow and ice

hill
an area that rises above surrounding land and has a rounded top; lower and usually less steep than a mountain

island
an area of land completely surrounded by water

isthmus
a narrow strip of land that connects two larger areas of land

mesa
a high, flat-topped landform with cliff-like sides; larger than a butte

mountain
an area that rises steeply at least 2,000 feet (300 m) above surrounding land; usually wide at the bottom and rising to a narrow peak or ridge

► glacier

◀ delta

mountain pass
a gap between mountains

peninsula
an area of land almost completely surrounded by water and connected to the mainland by an isthmus

plain
a large area of flat or gently rolling land

plateau
a large, flat area that rises above the surrounding land; at least one side has a steep slope

river mouth
the point where a river enters a lake or sea

strait
a narrow stretch of water that connects two larger bodies of water

tributary
a river or stream that flows into a larger river

volcano
an opening in the Earth's surface through which molten rock, ashes, and gasses from the Earth's interior escape

▶ volcano

Gazetteer

A

Aksum an ancient town in northern Ethiopia; a powerful kingdom and trade center about A.D. 200–600, p. 49

Algeria (28°N, 1°E) a country in North Africa; officially known as the Democratic and Popular Republic of Algeria, p. 205

B

Baghdad (33°N, 44°E) capital city of present-day Iraq; capital of the Muslim empire during Islam's golden age, p. 29

C

Cahokia (38°N, 11°W) a village in what is now the state of Illinois; formerly a large, prehistoric city known for its Native American mounds, p. 73

Cape Bojador (26°N, 14°W) an extension of the western Sahara coast into the Atlantic Ocean, p. 145

Constantinople (41°N, 29°E) a city located on both the European and Asian sides of the Bosporus; known as Istanbul in present-day Turkey; also known as Byzantium in the medieval Byzantine empire, p. 9

Cuzco (13°S, 71°W) a city in Peru; the capital city of the ancient Incan empire, p. 65

D

Delhi (28°N, 77°E) the third-largest city in India, popularly known as Old Delhi, p. 94

E

Ethiopia (7°N, 37°E) a country in East Africa, officially the People's Republic of Ethiopia, pp. 49, 51

F

Florence (43°N, 11°E) a city in the Tuscany region of central Italy, p. 139

G

Gaul a region of France, Belgium, and parts of Germany and northern Italy occupied by the ancient Gauls, p. 107

Ghana (8°N, 2°W) a country in West Africa; officially known as the Republic of Ghana, p. 45

Grand Canal the 1,085-mile (1,747-km) channel connecting the Huang He and Chang Jiang rivers in China; the longest artificially made waterway in the world, p. 87

Great Zimbabwe former kingdom in the highlands of Southern Africa, located between the Zambezi and Limpopo rivers; founded in A.D. 1100 by the Shona people, p. 53

H

Hiroshima (34°N, 132°E) a city in southwestern Honshu, Japan; the first city in the world to be hit by an atomic bomb, dropped by the United States during World War II, p. 203

Holy Land (31°N, 35°E) a small region at the eastern edge of the Mediterranean Sea, also known as Palestine, which includes parts of modern Israel and Jordan; considered holy by Jews, Christians, and Muslims, p. 117

J

Jerusalem (31°N, 35°E) the capital city of modern Israel; a holy city for Jews, Christians, and Muslims, p. 118

K

Kilwa a medieval Islamic city-state on an island near present-day Tanzania, p. 51

L

Lake Texcoco a lake, now drained, in central Mexico, where Mexico City now stands; formerly the site of the ancient Aztec capital of Tenochtitlán, p. 59

M

Mali (15°N, 0.15°W) a country in West Africa, officially the Republic of Mali; powerful West African trading kingdom from about 1240 to 1500, p. 43

Mecca (31°N, 35°E) a city in western Saudi Arabia; birthplace of the prophet Muhammad; the holiest Muslim city, p. 15

Medina (24°N, 39°E) a city in western Saudi Arabia; one of the two holiest cities of Islam (the other being Mecca), p. 19

Moscow (55°N, 37°E) the capital city of modern Russia and the third-largest city in the world; home of the czars, p. 9

N

Nagasaki (32°N, 129°E) a city in Kyushu, Japan; the site of the second atomic bomb dropped by the United States during World War II, p. 203

O

Orléans (47°N, 1°E) a city in north-central France; the site of the Hundred Years' War and the defeat of the English by the French under the leadership of Joan of Arc, p. 128

P

Paris (48°N, 2°E) capital of France, p. 116

R

Rome (41°N, 12°E) the capital city of modern Italy; capital of the ancient Roman empire (753 B.C.–A.D. 476), pp. 10, 11, 12

Runnymede (51°N, 34°W) a meadow along the Thames River in England, p. 126

S

Sahara the world's largest desert, covering almost all of North Africa, p. 37

Silk Road a 4,000-mile-long (6,400-km) series of ancient trade routes linking China to the Mediterranean Sea, p. 86

Songhai an ancient empire and trading state in West Africa that reached its peak in the 1400s, p. 48

South Africa (28°S, 24°E) the southernmost country in Africa, officially known as the Republic of South Africa, p. 209

Strait of Magellan (52°S, 64°W) the channel linking the Atlantic and Pacific oceans between the mainland tip of South America and the island of Tierra del Fuego; discovered by Ferdinand Magellan, p. 148

T

Taj Mahal a spectacular tomb near Agra, India, built by the Mughal emperor Shah Jahan in memory of his wife, Mumtaz Mahal, p. 98

Tenochtitlán (approximately 19°N, 99°W) the capital city of the ancient Aztec empire, located on islands in Lake Texcoco, now the site of Mexico City, p. 59

Tombouctou (16°N, 3°W) a city in Mali near the Niger River; in the past an important center of Islamic education and a trans-Saharan caravan stop (also spelled Timbuktu), p. 47

V

Venice (45°N, 12°E) a city and major seaport in northern Italy, known for its canals, p. 13

Versailles (48°N, 2°E) a city in France; site of the Palace of Versailles built by Louis XIV, p. 152

W

Waterloo (50°N, 4°E) village south of Brussels, Belgium, where Napoleon was defeated, p. 192

Biographical Dictionary

A

Akbar (AK bar) (A.D. 1542–1605) greatest of the Mughal emperors and reformers of India, p. 97

B

Babur (BAH boor) (A.D. 1483–1530) descendant of Genghis Khan and Tamerlane; founder of the Mughal dynasty and emperor from 1526 to 1530, p. 96

C

Charlemagne (SHAR luh mayn) (A.D. 742–814) king of the Franks who conquered much of Western Europe, p. 107

Confucius (kuhn FYOO shuhs) (551 B.C.–479 B.C.) Chinese philosopher and teacher; his beliefs, known as Confucianism, greatly influenced Chinese life, p. 83

Cortés, Hernan (kor TEZ hur NAN) (A.D. 1485–1547) Spanish explorer who reached Mexico in 1519, conquered the Aztecs, and won Mexico for Spain, p. 157

E

Elizabeth I (A.D. 1533–1603) Queen of England from A.D. 1558 to 1603; restored England to Protestantism; admired for her courage and intelligence, p. 169

G

Galileo Galilei (gal uh LAY oh gal uh LAY ee) (A.D. 1564–1642) Italian mathematician, astronomer, and physicist; his claim that the Earth revolves around the sun and is not the center of the universe caused the Catholic Church to arrest him, p. 174

Gandhi, Mohandas K. (GAHN dee) (A.D. 1869–1948) known as Mahatma ("great soul") Gandhi, he led Indian nationalists to use nonviolent methods to win freedom from British rule; assassinated in 1948, p. 207

Gregory VII, (C. A.D. 1020–1085) pope who reigned from A.D. 1073 to 1085; considered one of the great papal reformers of the Middle Ages, p. 124

H

Harun ar-Rashid (hah ROO nar ash EED) (A.D. 766–806) fifth caliph of the Abbassid dynasty who ruled Baghdad at the height of its empire, p. 30

Henry IV (A.D. 1050–1106) king of Germany and the Holy Roman Empire; argued with Pope Gregory VII and was banned from the Church, p. 124

Henry VIII (A.D. 1491–1547) king of England from 1509 to 1547; had 6 wives; separated the English Church from Catholicism to begin the English Reformation, p. 169

Hitler, Adolf (A.D. 1889–1945) dictator of Nazi Germany; led military invasions that began World War II; led a campaign of genocide against European Jews and others, p. 200

I

Ieyasu, Tokugawa (eye yaw soo toh kug oh wah) (A.D. 1543–1616) founder of the last shogunate in Japan; closed his country off from the rest of the world, p. 93

J

Joan of Arc (C. A.D. 1412–1431) peasant girl who led the French army to victory over the English in the Hundred Years' War, p. 128

John I (A.D. 1167–1216) king of England who was forced to sign the Magna Carta in 1215 under threat of civil war, p. 126

Justinian (A.D. 483–565) Byzantine emperor who reorganized government, sponsored a code of laws, p. 11

K

Khadijah (kha DEE jah) (died A.D. 619) first wife of the Prophet Muhammad, the founder of Islam, p. 18

Khayyám, Omar (OH mahr ky YAHM) (A.D. 1048–1131) Persian poet, mathematician, and astronomer, p. 28

L

Lenin, Vladimir (A.D. 1870–1924) founder of the Russian Communist party; leader of the Russian Revolution of 1917 and of the Soviet state, p. 198

Leonardo da Vinci (lee uh NAR doh duh VIN chee) (A.D. 1452–1519) the most famous artist of the Renaissance, painter of the *Mona Lisa* and *The Last Supper;* also a talented sculptor, scientist, architect, and engineer, p. 137

Locke, John (A.D. 1632–1704) English philosopher whose writings helped start the Enlightenment, p. 177

Louis XIV (A.D. 1638–1715) king of France from 1643 to 1715 and the symbol of absolute monarchy; expanded France's borders in a series of wars, p. 150

Luther, Martin (A.D. 1483–1546) German teacher who founded the Protestant Reformation of the 1500s in revolt against the Roman Catholic Church, p. 140

Magellan, Ferdinand (muh JEL un FUR din and) (c. A.D. 1480–1521) Portuguese explorer whose crew was the first to sail around the world, p. 147

Maimonides (my MAHN uh deez) (A.D. 1134–1204) a Spanish-born Medieval Jewish philosopher and teacher, p. 31

Malinche (mah LIHN chay) (c. A.D. 1501–1550) Native American princess who became the companion, guide, and interpreter for conquistador Hernan Cortés, p. 157

Mandela, Nelson (man DEL uh) (A.D. 1918–   ) South African lawyer and nationalist; imprisoned for 28 years; in 1994 elected as South Africa's first black President, p. 209

Mansa Musa (MAHN sah moo SAH) (died c. A.D. 1332) Muslim emperor of Mali known for his pilgrimage to Mecca in 1324; encouraged the arts and learning, p. 43

Mary (A.D. 1662-1694) queen of England who ruled with her husband, William of Orange; William and Mary accepted the English Bill of Rights during the Glorious Revolution, p. 173

Michelangelo (my kul AN juh loh) (A.D. 1475–1564) Renaissance painter, sculptor, and architect; known for his painting of the ceiling of Rome's Sistine Chapel, p. 139

Moctezuma (mahk the ZOOM uh) (A.D. 1466–1520) last emperor of the Aztec empire; his empire was destroyed by Spanish conquerors in 1521, p. 156

Muhammad (c. A.D. 570–632) prophet of Islam who proclaimed the message of God; considered by Muslims to be the last of the prophets, p. 15

Napoleon Bonaparte (A.D. 1769–1821) general, consul, and emperor of France; fought to extend France's rule, but was defeated and exiled, p. 190

Peter the Great (A.D. 1672–1725) emperor of Russia from 1682 to 1725; one of Russia's greatest statesmen, organizers, and innovators, p. 154

Pizarro, Francisco (c. A.D. 1475–1541) Spanish explorer who conquered the Incas in South America and founded the city of Lima, Peru, p. 159

Richelieu (RISH loo) (A.D. 1585–1642) cardinal and chief minister to King Louis XIII of France and supporter of royal absolute power, p. 152

Robespierre, Maximilien (rohbz PYAIR) (A.D. 1758–1794) radical Jacobin leader; figure in the French Revolution; led the Committee of Public Safety in the Reign of Terror, p. 190

Shah Jahan (shah juh HAHN) (A.D. 1592–1666) Mughal emperor of India and builder of the Taj Mahal, p. 98

Sundiata (sun JAHT ah) (died A.D. 1255) West African king who founded the Kingdom of Mali, p. 46

Tamerlane (TAM ur layn) (A.D. 1336–1405) Turkish conqueror active in India, Russia, and the Mediterranean, known for his brutality, p. 94

Tang Taizong (tung ty zung) (A.D. 600–649) second emperor of the Tang dynasty, p. 83

Urban II (c. A.D. 1035–1099) pope who developed reforms begun by Pope Gregory VII, began the Crusades, and built political power for the papacy, p. 117

William of Orange (A.D. 1650–1702) king of England who ruled with his wife, Mary; William and Mary accepted the English Bill of Rights during the Glorious Revolution, p. 173

Yoritomo, Minamoto (yor ee toh moh mee nah moh toh) (A.D. 1147–1199) founder of the shogunate, a Japanese feudal system that lasted for 700 years, p. 92

Glossary

A

absolute monarch a king or leader who has complete power over every part of life in a kingdom, for example, Louis XIV of France, p. 151

alliance an agreement between nations to support each other in case of attack by another nation; nations who have such an alliance are called allies, p. 199

apprentice an unpaid worker who is being trained in a craft; in medieval Europe, boys became apprentices at the age of 12 and trained for seven years, p. 115

aqueduct a system of pipes or channels to carry water from distant sources; used by the Aztecs to bring fresh spring water to Tenochtitlán, p. 62

armistice a cease-fire or end to fighting in a war; World War I ended with an armistice in 1918, p. 200

arms race the attempt by the former Soviet Union and the United States to each build nuclear weapons so as to have the largest arsenal in the world, p. 212

artisan a skilled worker who practices a trade, such as jewelry making, ceramics, or sculpture; in Aztec society, artisans were the third most important class, under the royal or religious leaders and warriors, p. 64

astrolabe a device used by sailors to measure latitude, or distance north or south of the Equator, p. 144

atomic bomb a powerful nuclear weapon developed in the United States during World War II and used on the Japanese cities of Hiroshima and Nagasaki, p. 203

B

bill of rights a summary of all the rights held by the people under their government; in England, a statement that William and Mary had to accept when offered the throne after the Glorious Revolution, p. 173

bushido a Japanese samurai warrior's set of rules that stressed honor, discipline, bravery, and simple living, p. 91

C

caliph an Islamic ruler between the 600s and 1200s, p. 29

capitalist country a country that allows people to own property and businesses and compete for profit in a free market, p. 211

caravel a sailing vessel designed by Prince Henry's shipbuilders that was larger, stronger, faster, and easier to steer than other ships of the day, p. 144

caste system a Hindu social class system that controlled every part of daily life; the four castes were made up of: (1) priests, teachers, and judges; (2) warriors; (3) farmers and merchants; (4) craftworkers and laborers; casteless poor people were "Untouchables," p. 95

causeway a raised street made of hard earth, used for travel over wetland or lakes; causeways connected the Aztec city of Tenochtitlán to the mainland, p. 62

chivalry the noble qualities that knights were to have: bravery, loyalty, and doing heroic deeds to win the love of a worthy woman, p. 116

circumnavigate to travel completely around the Earth, p. 149

city-state a city that has its own independent government and often controls much of the surrounding land; Aksum was one of East Africa's ancient city-states, p. 51

civil disobedience the deliberate breaking of a law to protest it; practiced by Mohandas K. Gandhi in India to free his country from British rule, p. 207

civil war a war for power among groups within a single country, p. 172

clan a group of families who trace their roots to the same ancestor, p. 40

clergy persons ordained to perform certain religious duties, p. 111

Cold War the period from 1945 until 1991, during which there was great international tension and risk of war between the capitalist countries led by the United States and the communist countries led by the former Soviet Union, p. 212

colony a territory ruled by another nation, often one that is far away, p. 178

communism a kind of government where all people together own the farms and factories, share work equally, and earn rewards equally; revolutionaries who took over Russia under Lenin wanted a communist government, p. 198

conquistador a conqueror; the Spanish soldiers who traveled in the Americas and claimed the land and people for Spain and the Roman Catholic Church, p. 159

constitutional monarchy a type of government in which a monarch has only the powers granted by a constitution and the laws of the nation, p. 173

Crusades several military expeditions between A.D. 1095 and 1272, supported by the Catholic Church, to win the Holy Land back from the Seljuk Turks; the Holy Land included Jerusalem and parts of present-day Israel and Jordan, p. 117

czar a Russian emperor; Nicholas, the last czar, was forced to give up the throne in A.D. 1917, p. 197

D

daimyo the powerful estate owners in Japan who hired their own samurai warriors to protect them, and peasants to farm their lands, p. 91

democracy a system in which the people are governed by elected representatives, p. 151

developed nation a nation that has many industries; many former colonies are developed nations, p. 209

developing nation a nation that has few industries; some former colonies are among the world's developing nations, p. 209

divine right a belief that the right to rule comes directly from God; a belief held by many European kings during the 1600s, p. 151

dynasty a series of rulers from one family; periods of Chinese history are referred to by dynasty, for example, Tang or Song, p. 84

E

encomienda an economic system introduced by the Spanish in Mexico, in which settlers received the land and the forced labor of Native Americans, p. 158

Enlightenment a time in Europe when people emphasized reason and rational thinking; sometimes called the Age of Reason, p. 174

excommunicate to expel or prevent someone from taking part in church life; in the Middle Ages, Catholic Church leaders threatened to excommunicate a lord who rebelled against Church power, p. 112

F

feudalism a system of power in Europe during the Middle Ages, in which kings and queens had the most power, followed by nobles, knights, and peasants, p. 108

feudal system a system of government in which less powerful people promise loyalty to more powerful ones; in Japan, the powerful person was the shogun, p. 91

G

genocide the systematic killing of an entire group of people; in Nazi Germany during World War II, members of different ethnic groups, especially Jews, were murdered, p. 202

guild an association of all the people in a town or village who practiced a certain trade; weavers, grocers, masons, and others in the Middle Ages formed guilds and set standards for quality and prices, p. 114

H

hajj for Muslims, a pilgrimage or sacred journey to Mecca; Muslims throughout the world who can afford to do so try to make the hajj once in their lives, p. 23

hieroglyphs a kind of picture writing in which some pictures stand for ideas or things and others stand for sounds; in this text, the written signs and symbols used by the Mayan people; Egyptians and other groups also developed hieroglyphic writing systems, p. 61

hijra the migration in A.D. 622 of Muslims from Mecca to Yathrib (now called Medina), p. 19

Hinduism a religion developed in India, introduced by the Aryans, and based on sacred books called the Vedas; Hindus accept many gods as different aspects of one supreme being, p. 94

Holocaust the slaughter of six million Jews and millions of other Europeans by Nazi Germany during World War II, p. 202

I

icon a painting or an image of a holy person or saint, often painted on wood; icons are seen as sacred by some Christians, p. 12

imperialism a country's policy of extending its rule over other countries, or colonizing; during the 1800s, Europeans obtained raw materials and created markets for their goods using such a policy, p. 193

indulgence an official pardon given by the pope in return for money in the Middle Ages; people could pay the Catholic Church to be forgiven for their sins, a practice opposed by Martin Luther, p. 141

Industrial Revolution a period beginning in the late 1700s, when goods that had been produced by hand began to be made by machines in factories, p. 182

interdependent depending upon one another, p. 213

L

labor union an organization to help workers improve their pay and working conditions, p. 187

M

Magna Carta the "Great Charter"; an agreement between King John of England and his nobles and clergy in which the king's power over his nobles was limited, p. 127

maize corn; the most important crop of Mayan farmers and other ancient Native American groups, p. 60

manor a large estate, often including a village and farmlands, ruled by a lord in medieval Europe, p. 108

medieval of the Middle Ages, p. 106

merit system a system introduced in China to hire government officials for their ability, which was proved by taking tests, rather than for their family connections, p. 84

Middle Ages the years between ancient and modern times; from about A.D. 500 until 1500, p. 106

migration the movement of people from one place to another, p. 39

mosque an Islamic house of worship, p. 21

movable type a kind of printing first used in China and fully developed in Korea; each character is a separate piece of type, which can be moved and reused, p. 87

muezzin a man who calls all Muslims to prayer by chanting; in Islamic cities today, the call is broadcast over loudspeakers, p. 21

N

Napoleonic Code a reform of the laws of France; Napoleon Bonaparte had all the laws rewritten so that they were clear and easily understood, p. 191

nation a community that shares a government and sometimes a common language and culture; in medieval Europe, kingdoms became nations as the kings gained power and unified their lands, p. 126

nationalism great pride in one's country, p. 193

natural law pattern in the behavior of the universe, including laws of motion and gravity; observed during the European Enlightenment by thinkers such as Isaac Newton, p. 176

navigator a expert sailor who guides a ship across the ocean, p. 144

nomad a person who moves from one area to another and does not have a permanent home, p. 16

O

oasis an area of vegetation fed by underground springs and surrounded by desert, p. 38

P

Parliament a council that advised the English king or queen in government matters; today, a group of elected officials who make up the legislative branch of the British government, p. 127

patriarch the founder of a tribe or family; in this text, the leader of the Byzantine Christian Church in Constantinople during medieval times, p. 12

patron someone who supports others or the arts; Caliph Harun ar-Rashid of Baghdad was a great patron of artists, p. 30

perspective a technique in drawing and painting that shows objects as they appear to the eye, for example, making distant objects smaller in relation to closer objects, p. 139

porcelain a strong, beautiful kind of ceramic first made in China; porcelain vases, plates, cups, bowls, and figurines are often called "china," p. 85

prophet a religious leader or other person who claims to carry the message of God, p. 19

Protestants Christians who are not members of the Catholic or Orthodox churches; in this text, the people who shared the religious views of Martin Luther and others who protested against the Roman Catholic Church, p. 142

province a smaller region within a country or an empire, p. 47

pueblo a village built into the sides of steep cliffs or on top of tall mesas; the Pueblo and Anasazi people both adopted this style of building, p. 74

Q

quipu a sequence of knotted strings used by Incan government officials to count and record information about births, deaths, taxes, and harvests, p. 67

Quran the holy book of Islam containing what God revealed to Muhammad: the rules of Islam, stories, promises, warnings, and instructions, p. 23

R

racism the prejudiced belief that one race is better than another, still a serious problem in many parts of the world, p. 209

Ramadan a month in the Islamic calendar during which all Muslims fast from sunrise to sunset, p. 22

Reformation the change or reform of the Catholic Church begun by Martin Luther that led to the establishment of Protestant churches, p. 140

Reign of Terror a period after the French Revolution when Maximilien Robespierre had 70 to 80 people executed each day; the Reign of Terror ended when Robespierre himself was executed, p. 190

Renaissance a rebirth of learning in Europe between about A.D. 1300 and 1600, p. 137

reunification the rejoining of two or more things that had been separated; in this text, the rejoining in 1989 of East and West Germany into one nation, p. 210

revolution a complete overthrow of an established government; a sudden change in the way people think, p. 172

S

samurai the warriors in Japan who swore to serve their leaders and obeyed a strict code of rules without question, p. 89

savanna an area of gently rolling land covered by grasses, occasional trees, and thorny bushes, p. 38

schism a split, often in a church or religion, over different points of view; during the 1000s, a schism in the Christian Church split it into Byzantine and Roman Catholic sections, p. 13

scientific method a method of performing experiments under controlled conditions, recording the findings, and drawing conclusions; begun during the Enlightenment, p. 176

self-sufficient able to supply one's own needs; the residents of a medieval manor were self-sufficient, p. 109

serf a peasant in medieval Europe considered to be part of the land; a noble's manor included serfs, pp. 110, 197

shogun the most powerful lord in feudal Japan; the first shogun took power in A.D. 1192, p. 91

silent barter trading without speaking; used by gold miners and salt traders in West Africa, p. 44

slash-and-burn agriculture a type of farming in which farmers cleared forests, burned tree stumps, and used the ash for fertilizer; when soil was depleted, they moved to a new area; the Mayan farmers used this type of agriculture, p. 60

strait a narrow passage or channel linking two larger bodies of water, p. 10

sultan a Muslim king; between A.D. 1206 and 1526, a sultan ruled the Muslim empire, including what is now India, Bangladesh, and Pakistan, p. 95

Swahili the culture and language of the people of Kilwa and other East African city-states; today, Tanzania and Kenya use Swahili as their official language, p. 52

T

terrace a steplike ledge cut into a steep mountainside, used to grow crops and stop erosion; terraces were used by the ancient Incas of South America, p. 70

textile cloth; the textile industry was one of the first to move into factories during the Industrial Revolution, p. 183

tolerance the acceptance of differences; Muslims were tolerant of Jews and Christians who accepted Muslim rule during the golden age (about A.D. 800 to 1100), p. 30

troubadour a traveling performer who wandered from place to place in France, Italy, and Spain, singing songs and reciting poems about the chivalrous deeds of knights, p. 116

V

vassal in medieval Europe, a man who promised to be loyal to a landowner, who in return gave him a share of the land, called a fief, p. 108

The *italicized* page numbers refer to illustrations. The *m, c, p, t,* or *g* preceding the number refers to maps *(m)*, charts *(c)*, pictures *(p)*, tables *(t)*, or graphs *(g)*.

Index

A

Abraham, 20, 23
absolute monarchy, 189–190
absolute rule, 152
Activity Atlas, 2–7
Africa, *m 245, m 252, m 253;* Bantu migrations in, 39–42, *m 39;* farming in, 38, 39; independent nations of, 206; physical geography of, 38–39
Africanus, Leo, 47
Age of Reason. *See* Enlightenment
Akbar, 97–98, *p 98*
Aksum, 49; trade and, 50
Aladdin. *See Thousand and One Nights, The*
Alcazar Castle, *p 154*
algebra, *p 32*
Algeria, 205, *p 205*
Allied Powers, 201
American colonies: independence of, 178–179
American Revolution, 179
Anasazi, 74
Andes Mountains, *p 60,* 65–67, 69
Angkor Wat, 114
Antarctica, *m 245*
apprentice. *See* guilds
aqueducts, 62
Arabian Peninsula, 8; geography of, 15–17
armistice, 200
art: Aztec, *p 63, p 64;* Chinese, 86; in Elizabethan England, 171; Mayan, *p 61;* in the Mughal empire, 98; Renaissance, 139–140
artisans: in Aztec culture, 64
Asia, *m 245, m 254, m 255*
astrolabe, 144, *p 144*
atomic bomb, 203
Aurangzeb, 99
Australia, *m 245, m 256*
Axis Powers, 201
Azimuthal projection, 232
Aztecs, 59, *p 59,* 62–64; conquest of, by Spain, 157–159; floating gardens of, *p 62;* role of women in culture of, *p 64;* warlike way of life of, 63–64, *p 63*

B

Babur, 96, 97. *See also* Mughal empire
Baghdad: bazaar in, *p 30*
Bangladesh, *p 208*
banking, beginnings of, *p 121*
Bantu languages, 42
Bantu migrations, 39–42, *m 40, p 41;* physical barriers to, *p 39*
baptism, *p 112*
Baryshnikov, Mikhail, 199
Battle of Orléans, 129
Battle of Yorktown, *p 179*
Bedouins, 16–17
Bell, Alexander Graham, 184
Berlin Wall, 196
Bi Sheng, 87

Bible. *See* Christianity
bill of rights, 173
Black Death. *See* bubonic plague
Black Sea, 9
Black Stone, 17, *p 17*
block printing. *See* China: invention of printing in
Bonaparte, Napoleon: accomplishments of, 190–191, *p 190, m 191;* downfall of, 191–192
Bosporus strait, 10
Brunei, *p 25*
bubonic plague, 116, *p 116*
bushido, 91
Byzantine empire, 8, 118; building of, 10–11; cultural contributions of, 14; fall of, 12–13; holy painting of, *p 12;* trade routes of, 9
Byzantium, 10–11

C

Cahokia, Illinois: mounds at, *p 71,* 72, 73
Cairo, Egypt, *p 32,* 43
calendar: Mayan, 61
caliph, 29–30
calligraphy, *p 22*
camels: in Arab trading caravans, *p 44*
Canon of Medicine, *p 32*
Cape Bojador, 145
Cardinal Richelieu. *See* Richelieu, Cardinal
caste system, 95
cathedral, *p 111*
Catherine of Aragon, 169
causeways, 62
census: in the Incan empire, 66
Chang Jiang River, 87
Charlemagne, 107, *p 107*
Charles I, 155, 172, *p 172*
China: invention of compass in, *c 88;* invention of gunpowder in, *c 88;* invention of printing in, 87–88, *c 88;* invention of smallpox vaccine in, *c 88*
Chinese dynasties. *See* Tang dynasty; Song dynasty
chivalry, 116
Christianity, 20; and the Crusades, 117–121; and the Sistine Chapel, 140; and the Reformation, 140–142; arrival of missionaries in Japan, 93; in Europe in the Middle Ages, 111–112; king of Aksum and, 50; Muslim relationship to, 23–24
Church of England, 169. *See also* Protestantism
Church of St. George, *p 51*
Cipango, 147
circumnavigation, 149
city-states: defined, 51; East African, 52–53; Kilwa, 51–52
civil disobedience, 207
clans: Bantu, 40
climate regions, 240
coat of arms, *p 108*
Cold War, 211–213, *p 212*

colony: defined, 178. *See also* American colonies
Colorado Plateau, 74
Columbian exchange, 6–7, *p 6, m 7*
Columbus, Christopher, 136, 146
communism, 198–199; and the Cold War, 211–213; in East Germany, 210
Confucius, 83
conquistadors, 159
Constantinople, 8, 11, 119; geography of, 10, *p 10;* invasion of, by Igor of Moscow, 9
constitutional monarchy, 173
Copernicus, Nicolaus, 174, 175
Cortés, Hernan, 157–159, *p 158*
Cromwell, Oliver, *p 173*
Crusades, 117–121, 125, 126, *p 118, m 119;* growth of trade during, 121
Cuzco, 68, *p 68*

D

daimyo, 91, *p 91,* 93
Day of Atonement. *See* Yom Kippur
Declaration of Independence, *p 178*
Delhi Sultanate, 95–96
democracy: in West Germany, 210
developed nations, 214
developing nations, 208–209, 214
Diamond Sutra, 87
Diaz, Bernal, 158
divine right of kings, 151
Drake, Sir Francis, 171, *p 171*
Dresden, Germany, *p 210*

E

Eanes, Gil, 145
Earth Day: celebration of, *p 215*
Eastern Woodlands, 73
Edison, Thomas, 184, *p 184*
Edward III, 128
Electronic Numerical Integrator and Calculator (ENIAC), *p 211*
Elizabeth I, 169–172, *p 170*
Elizabethan England. *See* Elizabeth I
encomienda, 158
Enlightenment, 174–179
equal-area projection, 232
Equator, 230, 231, 232
ethnic groups: slaughter of, by Nazis, 202
Europe, *m 245, m 250, m 251;* coffeehouse speeches in, *p 177;* department stores in, *p 185;* feudalism in, 107–110, 125–126; major religions of, *m 141;* trade in, during the Middle Ages, 113–116; overcrowded cities in, 115–116; unification of, 126–127; voyages of exploration, *m 146–147*
excommunication, 112, 127

F

false gods. *See* idols
farming: in Africa, 38, 39; effects of Industrial Revolution on, 185; in Incan culture, 70; in Mayan culture, 60;

Roman Catholic Church and, 112; slash-and-burn, 60; terrace, 70, *p 70*
Ferdinand, Franz, 200
Ferdinand II, 146, 154, *p 154*
feudalism: in Japan, 90–92; in Europe, 107–110, 125–126
fief. *See* feudalism: in Europe
Five Pillars of Islam, 21, 22–23
floating gardens, *p 62*
Florence, Italy, *p 138*
Franklin, Benjamin, 178
French Revolution, 188–189, *p 188*

G

Galilei, Galileo, 174, *p 174,* 175, 176
Gallup, New Mexico, *p 74*
Gandhi, Mohandas K.: assassination of, 208; beliefs of, 207–208
genocide: Armenian, 200; Germans and, 202
Ghana, 45–46, 204, *p 204*
Globe Theater, 171, *p 171*
Gobi Desert, 86
gold: as symbol of wealth, *p 45*
Gold Coast, 204
Grand Canal, 87
Great Enclosure. *See* Great Zimbabwe
Great Serpent Mound, *p 72,* 73. *See also* Mound Builders
Great Zimbabwe, 53, *p 53*
"Greek fire," 8–9, *p 9,* 11
Greek Orthodox, 20
Greenland, 107
Gregory VII, 124–125, *p 124*
griot, *p 37*
Guide for the Perplexed, 31
guilds, 114–115, *p 115*
Gupta dynasty, 94, 95

H

Hagia Sophia, *p 14*
hajj, 23; Mansa Musa and, 46. *See also* Five Pillars of Islam
Harun ar-Rashid, 30
Henry the Navigator, 144
Henry IV, *p 124,* 124–125
Henry VII, 155, 169
Henry VIII, *p 169*
herders: Bantu, 40
hieroglyph, 61
Hijra, 19
Hinduism, 94–95
Hiroshima, 203, *p 203*
Hitler, Adolf, 200–201
Holocaust, 202, *p 202*
Hopi corn dancers, *p 75*
Huang He River, 87
Huitzilopochtli, 59
human sacrifice: in Aztec culture, 63
Hundred Years' War, 128–129, *p 128*

I

Ibn Battuta, *p 52*
Ibn Sina, *p 32*
icons, 12, *p 12*
idols, 18
imperialism, 193, *p 193*
Incas, 65–70; conquest of, by the Spanish,

159; cultural achievements of, 68–70; farming and, 70, *p 70;* language of, 66; roads and bridges of, 67, *p 67;* rule of, 66–67; use of gold by, *p 66*
India: Muslim invasion of, 94–96; Gupta dynasty of, 94; *p 96*
indulgences, 141
industrialization: and cities, 186
Industrial Revolution, 182–187; factory workers and, 186–187; growth of, 184–185; importance of textile production in, 183–184, textile factory, *p 183;* modern steel furnace, *p 182;* problems of, 185–187, *p 186*
interdependence: among nations, 213–215
Iron Age, 39; tools of, *p 42*
irrigation system: Pueblo development of, 74
Isabella I, 146, 154, *p 154*
Islam, 18; expansion of, 19–20; Five Pillars of, 21, 22–23; golden age of 28–33; intellectual achievements of, 31–33, *p 32;* role of women in, 24. *See also* Muhammad

J

Jalal ad-Din ar-Rumi, 33
James I, 172
Japan: *m 90;* feudalism in 89–90; isolation of, 92–93; rule of the shogun in, 92
Jefferson, Thomas, 178, *p 178,* 179
Jerusalem, 49; Shrine of the Rock and, *p 18; m 120*
Jesuits, 142
Joan of Arc, 128–129, *p 129*
journeyman. *See* guilds
Judaism, 20, 23; Yom Kippur and, 22
Justinian, 11–12; Code of, 13–14

K

Kabah, 17, *p 17*
kachina, 75
Khadijah, 18
Khan, Kublai. *See* Kublai Khan
Khayyám, Omar, 28–29, 32
Khmer empire, 114
Kilwa, 51, *p 52*
King John, 126, *p 126,* 127
Kirov Ballet, 199
kiva, 75
Kublai Khan, 92, *p 92*
Kumbi Saleh, 46
Kyoto, Japan, 90

L

lateen sails, *p 144*
L'Ouverture, Toussaint, 190
labor unions: and the Industrial Revolution, 187, *p 187*
Lake Texcoco, 59, 62
Lalibela, *p 51*
landforms, 239
latitude, 231
Lenin, Vladimir, 198, *p 198*
Leonardo da Vinci, 137,138; flying machine by, *p 137*
Li Bo, 84

light bulb: invention of, 184
Limpopo River, 53
Locke, John, 177–179
longitude, 231
Lorenzo de Medici, 139
Louis IX, *p 118*
Louis XIV, 150–153, *p 151,* 152, 154
Louis XVI, 188–189
Loyola, Ignatius, 142, *p 142*
Luther, Martin, 140–141, *p 140*

M

Maasai, *p 41*
Machu Pichu, 69, *p 69*
Magellan, Ferdinand, 147–149, *p 148*
Magna Carta, 127, *p 127,* 171
Mahal, Mamtaz, 98–99
Maimonides, 31, *p 31*
Mali, 43, 46–47
Malinche, 157
Mandela, Nelson, 209, *p 209*
manor. *See* feudalism: in Europe
Mansa Musa, 43, *p 43,* 46–47
maps: of the Columbian exchange, 7; of Copernican view of universe, 175; of European colonies in Africa, 192; of European exploration voyages, 146–147; of human settlement, A.D. 500, 3; of independence since 1945, 206–207; of major religions in Europe, 141; of Napoleon's power in Europe, 191; of Spanish and Portuguese empires in the Americas, 159; of oil production in North Africa and the Middle East, 238; of Tamerlane's empire, 95, of Tang and Song empires, 84; of the Crusades, 119; of the Mughal empire, 97; of trade centers of Europe, 113; of West African trade routes, 44; of world as viewed by the Christians in the 1200s, 120; of world from 1470s, 143; of world's leading exporters, 213; physical, of Africa, 253; physical, of Asia, 254; physical, of Europe, 251; physical, of Hawaii, 237; physical, of Africa, 39; physical of Japan, 90; physical, of North and South America, 249; physical, of the world, 2, 244–245; political, of Africa, 252; political, of Asia, 254; political, of Europe, 250; political, of North and South America, 248; political-physical, of Australia and the Pacific Islands 256; political-physical, of world about 1500, 4–5; political, of Russia, 236; political, of the United States, 246–247; political, of the world, 242–243; of West African population density, 234; of the world about 1500, 4–5
mathematics, 31, *p 32*
Mayas, 60–61; cultural achievements of, 61; farming and, 60; religion of, 61; wall paintings of, *p 61*
Mazarin, Cardinal. *See* Cardinal Mazarin
measles, 159
Mecca, 15–16; Islamic practice of facing, 21
Medina, 19
Mercator projection, 232

Merchant's Handbook, 121
merit system, 84
Mesa Verde, Colorado, *p 74*
metalworking: Bantu, 42
Mexico City, 158
Michelangelo, 139–140; works of art by, *p 139*
Middle Ages: defined, 106
middle class: rise of, during the Middle Ages, 113
migration. *See* Bantu migrations
Minamoto family, 92
Mishneh Torah. *See* Torah
Moctezuma, 156. *See also* Aztecs
Mongols: invasion of India and, 94
Monk's Mound, *p 71. See also* Mound Builders
Moses, 10, 23
mosque, 21, *p 25;* at Kilwa, *p 52*
Mound Builders, 72–73
Mount Kilimanjaro, *p 39*
movable type. See China: invention of printing in
muezzin, 21, *p 21,* 22
Mughal empire, 96–99, *m 99*
Muhammad, 15, 16, 17–19, *p 18,* 20, 120. *See also* Islam
murals. *See* art: Mayan
Murasaki Shikibu, 92
Muslim empire, 8
Muslims. *See* Islam

Nagasaki, 203
Napoleon. *See* Bonaparte, Napoleon
Napoleonic Code, 191
nation: defined, 126
nationalism, 193, 199
Native Americans: Anasazi, 74; Cortés and, 157–159; immunity to disease of, 159, 160; Mound Builders, 72–73; Pueblos, 74–75, *p 75*
natural laws: Isaac Newton's realization of, 176
navigators, 144. *See also* Columbus, Christopher; Magellan, Ferdinand
Nazis. *See* Hitler, Adolf
New Spain, 158
Newton, Isaac, 176
Nicholas II, 197, *p 197*
Nkrumah, Kwame, 204
no: form of theater, *p 93*
nobles, *p 125;* dress of, 152
nomads, 16
North America, *m 244, m 248, m 249;* cultures of, 71–78
nuclear war: the Cold War and, 211
Nureyev, Rudolf, 199
Nzingha, 164

oasis, 38
Ottoman empire, 200

P

Palace of Versailles, *p 153*
Palestine. *See* Crusades
Parcheesi, 97

Parliament, 127; American colonists' demands on British, 178; conflict between Elizabeth I and, 171–172
patron of the arts, 30
Pegolottia, Francesco, 121
"people of the Book," 23
pesticides: dangers of, 214
Peter the Great, 154
Peter the Hermit, 119
Philippines: Ferdinand Magellan and, 149
phonograph: invention of, 184
Pizarro, Francisco, 159
Poland: invasion of, by Germany, 201
pollution, 214, *p 214*
Popes. *See* Gregory VII; Urban II
porcelain, 85, *p 85*
Portugal: world exploration and, 144–145; empire in the Americas, *m 159*
Prester John, 51
Prime Meridian, 230–231
Prince Igor of Moscow, 9, *p 9*
printing: Chinese invention of, 87–88, *c 88*
prophet, 19. *See also* Abraham; Muhammad; Moses
Protestantism, 142; King Henry VII and, 169; in Elizabethan England, 170–171
provinces, 47
pueblo: defined, 74
Pueblos, 74–75

Q

Quechua language, 66
Quetzalcoatl, 156; mask of, *p 156*
quipus, 67
Quran, 23, *p 23,* 24, 25. *See also* Islam

R

racism: defined, 208
radiation poisoning. *See* atomic bomb
Raleigh, Sir Walter, 171
Ramadan, 22, *p 22. See also* Five Pillars of Islam
recycling, 215
Red Sea, 15
Reformation, 140–142; Catholic, 142; Protestant, 141
Reign of Terror, 190
religions: Christianity, 20; Greek Orthodox, 13; Hinduism, 94–95; Islam, 18, 19–20; Judaism, 20; Lutheranism, 141; Roman Catholicism, 13, 111–112, 140–141, 142; Protestantism, 142, 169, 170–171
religious disputes: in the Byzantine empire, 12–13, 24; and the Crusades, 117–121; within Islamic religion, 24–25
Renaissance, 137–139
reunification: of Germany, 210
revolution: defined, 172
Richard I, 120
Richelieu, Cardinal, 152, *p 152*
Robespierre, Maximilien, 190
Robinson projection, 232
Roman Catholicism, 13; in Europe in the Middle Ages, 111–112; and the Reformation, 140–141, 142
Roman Empire, 10, 11, *m 106*
Runnymede, 126
Russian Revolution, 197–199, *p 199*

S

Sahara Desert, 37
"Sailing to Byzantium," 11
St. Vincent de Paul, 142
Saladin, 120
salt: importance of to West African trade, 44, 45
samurai, 89, *p 89;* rise of the, 90–91
Sanskrit, 95
São Paulo, Brazil: population of, 186
savanna, 38
schism. *See* religious disputes
Scientific Revolution, 175–176; achievements of, *c 176*
scientific method, 176
Sea of Marmara, 9
Seljuks, 117, 118
Shah Jahan, 98–99
Shakespeare, William, 171, *p 171*
Sheba: queen of, 49, *p 49*
Shiite. *See* religious disputes: within Islamic faith
shogun, 91: rule of Japan, 92
Shona, 53
Shrine of the Rock, *p 18*
silent barter, 44
silk: importance of, to Chinese trade, 85, *p 85. See also* Silk Road
Silk Road, 86–87; goods carried along, *p 86;* travelers on, *p 86*
Sistine Chapel, 139–140, *p 139*
slash-and-burn agriculture, 60
slavery: in Aztec culture, 64; effects of, 161; and slave ships, 160, *p 160,* 161
smallpox, 159. *See also* China.
"Smoke That Thunders." *See* Victoria Falls
Social Studies Skills Activities: assessing your understanding, 100–101; recognizing cause and effect, 20–21; using route maps, 122–123
Society of Jesus. *See* Jesuits
Solomon, 49, *p 49*
Song dynasty, 84–85, *m 84;* inventions of, *c 88*
Songhai, 48
South Africa: Nelson Mandela and, 209, *p 209*
South America, 65–66, *m 244, m 248, m 249*
Southwest (U.S.): early peoples of, 73–74
Soviet Union, 199; collapse of, 213
spindle, 183
Spain: empire in the Americas, *m 159*
spinning jenny, 183
squire, 105, *p 105*
Strait of Magellan, 148
Stuart, James. *See* James I
Sufi, 32, 33, *p 33*
sultan, 95
sun god: in Incan religion, 66, *p 66*
Sundiata, 46
"Sun King." *See* Louis XVI
Sunni. *See* religious disputes: within Islamic religion
Swahili language, 52

T

Taira family, 92
Taj Mahal, 98–99, *p 99*
Tales of the Greenlanders, The, 108
Tamerlane, 94, *p 94,* 96; empire of, *m 95*
Tang dynasty, 82, 84–85, *m 84;* inventions of, *c 88*
Tang Taizong, 83–84, *p 83*
telephone: invention of, 184
telescope, 175
Tenochtitlán, 59, 62, *p 62;* Spanish conquest of, 157–158, *p 157*
"Tennis Court Oath," *p 189*
terrace farming, 70, *p 70*
textile industry: and the Industrial Revolution, 183–184
Thames River, 126
Theodora, 11, *p 11. See also* Justinian
Thousand and One Nights, The, 31–32
Tierra del Fuego, p 149
tolerance: religious, 30
Torah, 23, *p 31. See also* Judaism
Toyotomi Hideyoshi, 91
troubadors, 117
Truman, Harry S., 203
Turks: rise of, 118

U

unions. *See* labor unions
"Untouchables." *See* caste system
Upper Niger Valley, 46
Urban II, 117, 118–119, *p 117*
Uthman, 25

V

Valley of Mexico, 62
Vasco da Gama, 145
vassal. *See* feudalism: in Europe
Vatican, 140
Versailles. *See* Palace of Versailles
vegetation regions, 241
vessel, *p 85*
Victoria Falls, *p 39*
Vikings, 107–108
Vietnam War, 212; protests against, *p 212*

W

Wangara, West Africa, 44
Washington, George, *p 179*
Waterloo, Belgium. *See* Bonaparte, Napoleon: downfall of

Western Sahara, 206
Whirling Dervishes, 33
William of Orange, 173
Winter Palace, *p 155*
Wittenberg, Germany, 140
women's roles: in Islamic cultures, 24; in Aztec culture, *p 64*
World Wars and Revolutions: time line of, 198–199
World War I, 199–200, *p 200*
World War II, 200–203, 205, *p 201*

Y

Yathrib. *See* Medina
Yeats, William Butler, 11
Yom Kippur, 22

Z

Zambezi River, 39, 53
zero: invention of, in mathematics, 31
Zimbabwe. *See* Great Zimbabwe

Acknowledgments

Program Development, Design, Illustration, and Production

Proof Positive/Farrowlyne Associates, Inc.

Cover Design

Olena Serbyn and Bruce Bond

Cover Photo

Jon Chomitz

Maps

GeoSystems Global Corp.

Text

28, from *The Concise History of Islam and the Origin of Its Empires* by Gregory C. Kozlowski. Copyright © 1991 by The Copley Publishing Group. Reprinted with permission from the Copley Publishing Group. 33, from *Love's Fire: Re-Creations of Rumi* by Andrew Harvey. Copyright © 1988 by Andrew Harvey, published by Mother Meera Publications. 80, from *The World in 1492* by Jean Fritz et al. Excerpt copyright © 1992 by The Native Land Foundation. Reprinted by permission of Henry Holt & Co., Inc. 88, from *China's Examination Hell* by Ichisada Miyazaki. Copyright © 1981 by Yale University Press. Reprinted by permission of Weatherhill Inc. 89, from *Legends of the Samurai* by Hiroake Sato. Copyright © 1995 by Hiroake Sato. Published by The Overlook Press, Woodstock, NY 12498. Used by permission. 132, Reprinted with the permission of Atheneum Books for Young Readers, an imprint of Simon & Schuster Children's Publishing Division, from *Of Swords and Sorcerers: The Adventures of King Arthur and His Knights* by Margaret Hodges and Margery Evernden. Text copyright © 1993 by Margaret Hodges and Margery Evernden.

Photo Research

Feldman & Associates, Inc.

Photos

1 T, BL, © Robert Frerck/Odyssey Productions, 1 BR, © Hugh Sitton/Tony Stone Images, 3, © Michael Kirtley/National Geographic Society Image Collection, 5, © Mark Thayer, Boston, 6 BL, Phil Schermeister/© Corbis, 6 BR, 7, © Felicia Martinez/PhotoEdit, 9, © The Granger Collection, 10, © Robert Frerck/Woodfin Camp & Associates, 11, © North Wind Picture Archives, 12, © Kammerhofmuseum, Gmunden, Austria/A. K. G., Berlin/SuperStock, 13, © Bibliotheque Nationale, Paris Ms Fr. 9087, fol 207 v./Laurie Platt Winfrey Inc. 14, © Robert Frerck/Tony Stone Images, 15, © Robert Azzi/Woodfin Camp & Associates, 17, © Nabeel Turner/Tony Stone Images, 18 BL, © Sarah Stone/Tony Stone Images, 18 BR, © Sylvain Grandadam/Tony Stone Images, 19, © Bridgeman/Art Resource, 21, © SuperStock International, 22, © Reuters/Corbis-Bettmann, 23 TL, © R. & S. Michaud/Woodfin Camp & Associates, 23 TR, © SEF/Art Resource, 24, © Tchehel Stun, Ispahan/Giraudon, Paris/SuperStock International, 25, © Paul Chesley/Tony Stone Images, 26, © Michael Newman/PhotoEdit, 28, © Scala/Art Resource, 29, © Nik Wheeler/Nik Wheeler, 30, © The Granger Collection, 31, © Bibliotheque Nationale, Jerusalem/SuperStock International, 32 TL, © Private Collection/Bridgeman Art Library, London/The Granger Collection, 32 TR, © Topkapi Serail-Museum, Istanbul, Turkey/Giraudon, Paris/SuperStock International, 32 BL, © The Granger Collection, 32 BR, © Roland & Sabrina Michaud/Woodfin Camp & Associates, 33, © Oxford, U.K./Bodleian Library, 37, © Jason Laure'/Laure' Communications, 39 TL, © Daryl Balfour/Tony Stone Images, 39 TR, © Ian Murphy/Tony Stone Images, 41, © Renee Lynn/Tony Stone Images, 42, © Boyd Norton/Boyd Norton, 43, © L. Platt Winfrey/Woodfin Camp & Associates, 44, © Explorer, Paris/SuperStock International, 45 BL, BR, © Lee Boltin/Boltin Picture Library, 46, © James Alan Brown/Visuals Unlimited, 47, © Betty Press/Woodfin Camp & Associates, 48, © Lee Boltin/Boltin Picture Library, 49, © Getachew G. Hiwot, 50 BL, BR, © Kjell B. Sandved/Visuals Unlimited, 51, © Lawrence Manning/Tony Stone Images, 52, © Marc & Evelyne Bernheim/Woodfin Camp & Associates, 53, © Jason Laure'/Woodfin Camp & Associates, 54, 55, © David Young-Wolff/PhotoEdit, 59, © Robert Frerck/Woodfin Camp & Associates, 60 TL, © North Wind Picture Archive, 60 TR, © Tony Morrison/South American Pictures, 61, © Kal Muller/Woodfin Camp & Associates, 63, © ET Archive, London/SuperStock International, 64 TL, © The Granger Collection, 64 TR, © Mireille Vautier/Woodfin Camp & Associates, 65, © Gianni Dagli Orti/Corbis, 66 TL, TM, TR, © Lee Boltin/Boltin Picture Library, 67, © Loren McIntyre/Woodfin Camp & Associates, 68, © Douglas Mason/Woodfin Camp & Associates, 69 T, © Jeremy Horner/Tony Stone Images, 69 B, © Ed Simpson/Tony Stone Images, 70, © Mireille Vautier/Woodfin Camp & Associates, 71, © Kevin O'Mooney/Odyssey Productions, 72, © SuperStock International, 73, © John D. Cunningham/Visuals Unlimited, 74, © North Wind Picture Archives, 75 T, © Lee Boltin/Boltin Picture Library, 75 M, © Greg Probst/Tony Stone Images, 76, © Steven W. Jones/FPG International, 77, © Robert Frerck/Odyssey Productions, 81, © North Wind Picture Archives, 83, © Giraudon/Art Resource, 85 BL, © SuperStock International, 85 BM, BR, 86 BL, © Lee Boltin/Boltin Picture Library, 86 BM, BR, © Viktor Ivanovich Sarianidi/National Geographic Society Image Collection, 87, © Werner Forman Archive/British Library, London/Art Resource, 88, © Tony Wiles/Tony Stone Images, 89, 91, © Lee Boltin/Boltin Picture Library, 92, © North Wind Picture Archives, 93, © The Lowe Art Museum, The University of Miami/SuperStock International, 94, © Giraudon/Art Resource, 96, My Village, by Paramita Hazra, age 11, India. Courtesy of the International Children's Art Museum, 98, © The Granger Collection, 99, © David Sutherland/Tony Stone Images, 100, © Michael Newman/PhotoEdit, 105, © The Granger Collection, 107 T, © Scala/Art Resource, 107 B, © SuperStock International, 108, © Biblioteca Civica, Padua, Italy/SuperStock International, 110, © The Granger Collection, 111, © Charles Harris Phelps/National Geographic Society Image Collection, 112, © The Granger Collection, 114, © SuperStock International, 115, © Castle at Issogne, Valle d'Aosta, Italy/ET Archive, London, SuperStock International, 116, © The Granger Collection, 117, © North Wind Picture Archives, 118 T, © North Wind Picture Archives, 118 B, © Castle of Castelnaus, Prudhommat. (Dorka)/Laurie Platt Winfrey Inc., 120, © The Granger Collection, 121, © British Library, London/Bridgeman Art Library, London, SuperStock International, 122, © The Granger Collection, 124, © SuperStock International, 125, © North Wind Picture Archives, 126, © Hulton Getty/Tony Stone Images, 127 TL, © Bridgeman/Art Resource, 127 TR, © Brown Brothers, 128, © The Granger Collection, 129, © The Granger Collection, 133, © North Wind Picture Archives, 134, © Bob Krist/Corbis, 136, © AP/World Wide Photos, 137 T, B, © Archivo GBB/G. Neri/Woodfin Camp & Associates, 138, 139 BL, © Scala/Art Resource, 139 BR, © Ed Simpson/Tony Stone Images, 140, © SuperStock International, 142, © North Wind Picture Archives, 143, © National Geographic Society Image Collection, 144 TL, © Roland Et Sabrina Michaud/Woodfin Camp & Associates, 144 TR, © North Wind Picture Archives, 145 BL, © Metropolitan Museum of Art, New York City/SuperStock International, 145 BR, © Brown Brothers, 148, 149, © North Wind Picture Archives, 150, © Gianni Dagli Orti/Corbis, 151 TL, © North Wind Picture Archives, 151 TR, © Giraudon/Art Resource, 152, © North Wind Picture Archives, 153 T, © Adam Woolfitt/Woodfin Camp & Associates, 153 B, © Chad Ehlers/Tony Stone Images, 154 BL, © Antochiw Collection, Mexico/ET Archive, London/SuperStock International, 154 BR, © Robert Frerck/Woodfin Camp & Associates, 155, © John Lamb/Tony Stone Images, 156, © Lee Boltin/Boltin Picture Library, 157, © South American Pictures, 158, © North Wind Picture Archives, 160, © The Granger Collection, 161, © SuperStock International, 166, © Kathleen Campbell/Tony Stone Images, 167 T, B, © Robin L. Sachs/PhotoEdit, 168, © Giraudon/Art Resource, 169, © Galleria Nazionale d'Arte Antica, Rome, Italy/Canali Photo Bank, Milan/SuperStock International, 170, © The Granger Collection, 171 TL, © Adrian Arbib/Corbis, 171 TR, © National Portrait Gallery, London/SuperStock International, 172 BL, © Stock Montage, 172 BR, © North Wind Picture Archives, 173, © National Portrait Gallery, London/SuperStock International, 174, © The Granger Collection, 175, © The Granger Collection, 177, © North Wind Picture Archives, 178 T, © L. Platt Winfrey/Woodfin Camp & Associates, 178 B, © The Granger Collection, 179, © SuperStock International, 181 T, © North Wind Picture Archives, 181 B, © SuperStock International, 182, Estate of Margaret Bourke-White/© Time Inc./Time Life Syndication, 183, 184 BL, © The Granger Collection, 184 BR, © John D. Cunningham/Visuals Unlimited, 185, © Hulton Getty/Tony Stone Images, 186, 187, 188, © The Granger Collection, 189, © Giraudon/Art Resource, 190, © Chateau de Malmaison, Paris, France/ET Archive, London, SuperStock International, 193, © The Granger Collection, 196, © Tom Stoddart/Woodfin Camp & Associates, 197, © Corbis-Bettmann, 198 BL, BR, © SuperStock International, 199, © Corbis-Bettmann, 200, © Hulton Getty/Tony Stone Images, 201 M, B, © UPI/Corbis-Bettmann, 202 M, Estate of Margaret Bourke-White/© Time Inc./Time Life Syndication, 202 B, © Hulton Getty Collection/Tony Stone Images, 203 TL, © The Granger Collection, 203 TR, © SuperStock International, 204, © Victor Englebert/Victor Englebert Photography, 205 BL, © AP/Wide World Photos, 205 BR, © AFP/Archive Photos, 208, Zoo, by Nayeem Hassein, age 11, Bangladesh. Courtesy of the International Children's Art Museum, 209 TL, © AP/Wide World Photos, 209 TR, © Reuters/Corbis-Bettmann, 210, © Richard Elliott/Tony Stone Images, 211 TL, © UPI/Corbis-Bettmann, 211 TM, © Corbis-Bettmann, 211 TR, 212 T, © SuperStock International, 212 B, © Bernard Gotfryd/Woodfin Camp & Associates, 214, © James Wilson/Woodfin Camp & Associates, 215, © Barbara Filet/Tony Stone Images, 217, © Sue Cunningham/Tony Stone Images, 220, © Robin L. Sachs/PhotoEdit, 222, © Mark Thayer, Boston, 223, © Cheryl McNee/Tony Stone Images, 225, © Mark Thayer, Boston, 226 T, © Steve Leonard/Tony Stone Images, 226 B, © Robert Frerck/Odyssey Productions, 227 T, © Wolfgang Kaehler/Wolfgang Kaehler Photography, 227 BL, © John Elk/Tony Stone Images, 227 BR, © Will & Deni McIntyre/Tony Stone Images, 237, © G. Brad Lewis/Tony Stone Images, 239, © Nigel Press/Tony Stone Images, 264 T, © A. L. Sinibaldi/Tony Stone Images, 264 B, © John Beatty/Tony Stone Images, 265 T, © Hans Strand/Tony Stone Images, 265 BL, © Spencer Swanger/Tom Stack & Associates, 265 BR, © Paul Chesley/Tony Stone Images.

Teacher's Notes

Teacher's Notes

Teacher's Notes

Teacher's Notes

Teacher's Notes